Sport in a Changing World

Howard L. Nixon II

Paradigm Publishers
Boulder • London

181368766

green
press
INITIATIVE

Paradigm Publishers is committed to preserving ancient forests and natural resources. We elected to print *Sport In A Changing World* on 30% post consumer recycled paper, processed chlorine free. As a result, for this printing, we have saved:

14   Trees (40' tall and 6-8" diameter)
6,053 Gallons of Wastewater
2,434 Kilowatt Hours of Electricity
667 Pounds of Solid Waste
1311 Pounds of Greenhouse Gases

Paradigm Publishers made this paper choice because our printer, Thomson-Shore, Inc., is a member of Green Press Initiative, a nonprofit program dedicated to supporting authors, publishers, and suppliers in their efforts to reduce their use of fiber obtained from endangered forests.

For more information, visit www.greenpressinitiative.org

Copyright © 2008 Paradigm Publishers

Published in the United States by Paradigm Publishers, 3360 Mitchell Lane Suite E, Boulder, CO 80301 USA.

Paradigm Publishers is the trade name of Birkenkamp & Company, LLC,
Dean Birkenkamp, President and Publisher.

Library of Congress Cataloging-in-Publication Data
Nixon, Howard L., 1944–
  Sport in a changing world / by Howard L. Nixon II.
      p. cm.
  Includes bibliographical references and index.
  ISBN 978-1-59451-442-5 (hardcover : alk. paper)
  ISBN 978-1-59451-443-2 (paperback)
  1. Sports—Sociological aspects. 2. Sports—Social aspects. I. Title.
  GV706.5.N593 2008
  306.4'83—dc22

                                    2007045857

Printed and bound in the United States of America on acid free paper that meets the standards of the American National Standard for Permanence of Paper for Printed Library Materials.

Designed and Typeset by Mulberry Tree Enterprises.

12   11   10   09   08   1   2   3   4   5

To Sara

Contents in Brief

Contents

Special Features

Acknowledgments

I would like first to thank Dean Birkenkamp and his outstanding editorial, production, marketing, and support staff at Paradigm, especially Melanie Stafford, Sharon Daugherty, Beth Davis, Jessica Priest, and Pete Hammond. All of you have consistently displayed professionalism, dedication, responsiveness, and a commitment to quality that I have very much appreciated. Forgive me if I have forgotten anyone. I would also like to thank the copy editor, Anna Kaltenbach, and the manuscript reviewers for their valuable contributions to this project. I am fortunate to be married to the most resourceful, knowledgeable, and helpful reference librarian anywhere, Sara Nixon. The extent of my scholarship for this book would have been substantially diminished without her help. In addition, her questions and suggestions clarified my thinking and pointed me in more fruitful directions, and her support was an important source of encouragement. My son Dan also deserves thanks for his design suggestions for the cover. Finally, I would like to acknowledge my colleagues at Towson University who regularly offer good ideas and support, my colleagues in sport sociology who have made the knowledge in our still relatively young field much richer, deeper, and wider over the years, and of course, my students, who are the main reason I wrote this book.

1

Sport, the Body, and Forces of Change: An Introduction to Sport Sociology

When the news seems to contain too many stories of war, terrorist threats, environmental dangers, risks to our health and well-being, and a multitude of social problems from family violence and divorce to a variety of crimes on the street and in the corporate suite, we can easily understand why people may seek refuge or escape in the world of play and games. Philosopher Michael Novak (1976) wrote about the special joy that could be found in sport as a diversion from everyday stresses and concerns. Some have even attributed a religious meaning to sport. For example, Novak and others have written about the religious qualities of sport as a source of inspiration and fulfillment, capable of inspiring devotion and dedication that more traditional religion often seems incapable of inspiring in contemporary society. Still others have written about sport as a symbolic refuge, offering a safe haven of fantasy in a world often filled with too many real-world stresses, strains, frustrations, disappointments, and problems (e.g., see Nixon 1984:207–211; Nixon and Frey 1996:55–56).

Of course, sport is real and is part of the same society that we may sometimes try to escape. Athletes are real people, as are the coaches, managers, owners, investors, officials, commentators, reporters, and spectators who watch them, depend on them, or influence or control their lives. The games athletes play are real, too. They incite real passions, even violent ones at times. People spend large sums of money on them. Newspaper publishers and radio and television producers created sports sections and sports programming because they realized that a lot of people follow sports and many do so faithfully and passionately. Politicians and world leaders sometimes use sports to further their careers or their political or national interests. Major corporations use athletes and the games they play to increase their market and their bottom line.

The purpose of sport sociology is to provide perspectives and facts to make sense of the social and cultural realities and complexities in the world of sport. Sport sociologists, as sociologists, focus on sport and society—how people interact with each other in relation to sport, how we organize our actions in various types of social networks in sport from teams to leagues to national and international sports bodies, and how sport is connected to the various institutions that make up society, from the economy, politics, and the mass media to the family. Sport sociologists are also interested in culture, or the things we value or believe in, and how they shape our lives. In addition, sport sociologists are interested in social and cultural change.

A dominant theme of this book is how society and culture are changing today and how major forces of social and cultural change are leaving their imprint on sport. Thus, we will focus on the dynamic forces of social demographic, organizational, economic, political, and technological change as well as changes in social institutions and in the patterns of social interaction and social relationships linking people, groups, and organizations to each other. We are ultimately interested in how these various kinds of social factors influence sport and cause it to change. We will also see how various inequalities weave their way through sport in different contexts and at different levels of sport. Sport itself will be understood in terms of a dominant network of powerful and intertwined people and organizations in highly commercialized sports, the media, and the corporate world, which we will call the Golden Triangle. Since we cannot understand change today without seeing it in global perspective, we will look at sport in a changing world and try to understand how the most visible and commercially successful sports are being shaped by forces and patterns of change occurring in a global context.

The ensuing chapters will build on the foundation constructed in this chapter around three general sets of questions: (1) What is sociology, what is the sociological imagination, and what is the sociology of sport? (2) What is sport, and what are its major aspects and forms? (3) What are the primary social and cultural forces driving change in contemporary society and sport?

Sociology

Sociology is the study of how people typically behave in social interaction, social relationships, and social networks. A focus on social structure in sociology emphasizes recurrent or enduring characteristics of social interaction, relationships, and networks rather than the qualities of individual persons involved in these social relations. Patterns of social interaction, social relationships, and social networks are built on a foundation of social expectations incorporated in social norms or rules, social roles, and the social ties that link people together. Social interaction, relationships, and networks represent how human beings take each other into account, become involved with each other, influence each other, and organize our relations or connections to each other. We interact with various types of people in many different ways in our everyday lives. We become involved in more enduring relationships with some of these people. We also relate to other people in social networks of varying size and complexity, which could range from small groups such as sports teams to large and complex global organizations such as the Olympics. Sociologists try to identify and understand the underlying structure of society; its basic patterns of social relations found in social interaction, relationships, and networks; and how structures change over time. Sociologists are also interested in the meanings we associate with our social relations; the shared values, understandings, and material things that make up our culture or way of life; and how these social meanings and cultural factors influence our behavior in society. In this book, we will use sport as a means of showing how sociologists study and try to understand the complexity of society, social relations, and culture and how they are changing.

In the next chapter, we will examine some prominent theoretical perspectives that sport sociologists use to try to interpret or understand sport and society. We will also consider a number of social research methods that sport sociologists use to collect and analyze data from the real world—called "empirical" data. These data enable sport sociologists to test and validate their theoretical ideas. Sport sociologists with a more scientific orientation believe that there is a degree of order in the social world that can be discovered with careful measurements and predicted with some degree of accuracy. Others in sport sociology are less concerned about discovering order, measuring things, or making predictions and focus more on what the human experience and human interaction mean to people involved in sport. The richness and diversity of sociology will be conveyed in this book, reflecting my assumption that insightful ideas and empirically grounded knowledge about sport and society can be derived from a variety of perspectives and methods used by sport sociologists.

When people think about sport sociology, they may focus primarily on its theories *or* its research findings, but understanding sport sociologically depends on both theory and research. Theory and research have a symbiotic relationship in sport sociology, meaning that both are necessary and contribute to each other. We see things in society and sport because we have concepts, assumptions, and theories about what they are, what they mean, and how they affect or are affected by other things. These concepts, assumptions, and theories are ultimately useful for understanding the world only after they have been validated and refined by research. So, theories provide us with glasses to see the world in particular ways, and research provides us with the assurance that our glasses are properly focused so that we can see the world accurately.

Sociological Imagination

The "sociological imagination," a term coined by C. Wright Mills (1959, 2000), refers to a perspective focused on understanding the patterns of human behavior in larger social, cultural, and historical contexts. The sociological imagination pushes our perspective beyond seeing the uniqueness of each individual's behavior to seeing human behavior in a broader social, cultural, and historical context, where the behavior of people in one context can be compared and contrasted with the behavior of people in other contexts. Thus, the serious injury you sustained when you were training for a marathon becomes a number in a statistical pattern of training injuries sustained by runners or recreational athletes. By looking at statistics about rates of training injuries over time for different types of athletes in different types of sports, we begin to see that human behavior is not merely a collection of unique random events or experiences that happen only to particular individuals. We also see that certain kinds of behavior form patterns where the same kinds of things happen repeatedly to the same kinds of people under the same social or cultural circumstances or conditions.

With sociological imagination, we can understand that many types of behavior have causes that are embedded in our social interactions, relationships, and networks and in our culture. In addition, we can see that our behavior is

Professor of sociology C. Wright Mills at Columbia University, January 1954. Mills wrote about the "sociological imagination." (Photo by Fritz Goro/Time Life Pictures/ Getty Images)

like the behavior of particular types of other people in some cases and unlike their behavior in other cases, and that there are reasons for these similarities and differences. The sociological imagination enables us to see beyond the things that make us unique to patterns of social behavior that tend to characterize groups or categories of people and tend to recur when the same causal factors are present in the contexts of our experience. Thus, we may find, for example, that in contact sports that are played at high levels of competitive intensity by big, strong, and well-conditioned athletes, we can expect fairly predictable rates of certain types of injuries over time. The sociological imagination implies this type of clear and precise thinking and generalizing about the social world, which is often different than the ways we think and talk about our experiences in our everyday lives. I should add, however, that what people think and say about sport in their everyday interactions are important to sport sociologists as data that inform their own sociological imaginations and help them make sense of sport and society. One of the most basic purposes of this book is to use sport sociology to convey an understanding of sport and society that enriches and broadens your sociological imagination and helps you see the social world of sport with new eyes and new insights.

Critical Thinking and Objectivity in Sociology

Undergraduate catalogs for colleges and universities in the United States frequently say that one of the important objectives in their general education is to develop critical thinking. In sociology, critical thinking involves raising questions about the beliefs that people take for granted about the social world and looking for systematic empirical evidence to support what people say is true about the world. More specifically, in sociology, we ask: Is it true? Under what conditions is it true? How do you know that it is true? Why is it true? What are the causes of the patterns we observe in the social world, and what are their implications for other aspects of society or social life? In his *Invitation to Sociology*, which sits alongside *The Sociological Imagination* as a sociological classic, Peter Berger (1963) wrote about a "debunking motif" that captures the essence of the critical perspective. This motif is defined by an unwillingness to accept without question what we see on the surface or are told about society. It pushes us to look beneath the surface, behind closed doors, beyond the obvious.

Sociology as a social science also requires scientific detachment or objectivity. That is, we must be willing to step back from our personal opinions, values, biases, and interests to see the social world in factual terms. We begin with a critical perspective, raising questions, even about the things we ourselves think we know. We formulate theoretical ideas based on the most accurate possible assessment and interpretation of the relevant research literature about our subject. We also accept the idea of falsifiability, which is the idea that what we hypothesize or think is true about the social world may not be supported by new research evidence. We collect and analyze evidence according to the established rules of sociological inquiry and interpret what we have found in the context of a community of sociological colleagues with similar kinds of expertise. Thus, objectivity, which involves trying to be as accurate as possible in interpreting and representing what we know or have learned in the research process, is not just a personal or individual matter. It is a matter involving a community of scholars. When we disseminate what we find in research and tell others how we collected and analyzed our evidence, we give others the chance to question and try to validate or falsify our findings.

Sociological knowledge results from a cumulative process of posing theoretical ideas based on what we already know and what we do not yet know, testing these ideas, rejecting or refining them, adding what we have learned to the body of knowledge, and then starting the process all over again by posing new ideas. Sociological knowledge represents our current understanding of what existing theories and facts tell us about reality. Future theories and research will build on current knowledge, refine it, or even challenge and replace it with new knowledge.

Sport Sociology

Sport sociology is the application of sociology to the study of sport. Its purpose is to produce knowledge to help us interpret, understand, and predict patterns of social interaction and organization in sport. For sociologists, sport is a useful lens for understanding social patterns, problems, and issues that are found in other parts of society, but sport itself is important to study because it is part of the established institutional structure of society and because many people take it very seriously, invest a great deal of their identity and resources in it, and organize much of their lives and the structures of society around it. Thus, the sociological study of sport helps us understand an important part of society, and the sociology of sport enables us to see significant and recurring patterns, problems, and issues of social life and societies. Sport sociology also can have useful applications in helping sports policymakers, sports officials, and others with responsibility for making decisions about sport and sports participants to be more informed in their policies, plans, and actions.

Sport sociology, like the systematic study of sport in general, has a relatively short history, with most of the scholarly work in the field produced over the past thirty-five to forty years. It may be an indication of the significance we attribute to sport in society and in our individual lives and of the complexity of sport that it is now studied from many different disciplinary perspectives. Scholars now study sport from psychological, anthropological, political and policy science, business, economic and financial, management, legal, biomedical and human performance, nutritional, cultural studies, literary, aesthetic, media, geographic, and philosophical perspectives as well as from sociological perspectives. Sport sociology is the broadest of the social and behavioral science perspectives.

In the United States and other societies with capitalist economies, there are strong beliefs in the power of individualism and the ability of individuals to shape their own destinies. These beliefs make people more inclined to explain their own sports experiences and the things they observe or think they know about sport in terms of individualistic perspectives, which is why sports teams are more likely to hire sport psychologists than sport sociologists to deal with team problems and improve team performance. There are limits, however, to what personality profiles or psychological assessments can tell us about the dynamics of team relationships or team performance. We sometimes fail to grasp that acknowledged influences such as peer pressure or team cohesion are social forces and not qualities of individuals. Smart coaches understand that players who work effectively together are likely to be more successful than are players who seek individual success. Consider, for example, the success of the Detroit Pistons over the star-studded Los Angeles Lakers in the 2004 NBA Finals and the struggles of NBA "dream teams" of U.S. professional basketball superstars in the Olympics and other international competitions in recent years.

Thus, sport sociologists have important insights to teach us, insights that complement the insights derived from psychological and other perspectives of sport. In a society emphasizing individual more than social influences, sport sociology can lead us to insights and knowledge that may surprise us and challenge our more casual everyday ways of understanding sport and society. The critical perspective that is a central element of sociological thinking should make us question the things we are sure we know about sport because we assume they are "common sense." We have already considered how teams with more physical talent or superstars than their opponent may lose to their less-talented foes. This may seem counterintuitive, but sport sociology focuses our attention on the influence on team performance of social forces, which could minimize the influence of factors such as individual talent. Sport sociology also compels us to look at theoretical ideas and concrete research evidence before we draw conclusions or make predictions about matters such as the types of teams that are most likely to win. Being pushed to look at the realities of sport may be uncomfortable. If we are passionate about sport; have committed a great deal of our lives to playing, coaching, administering, or following sport; have depended on sport for a major part of our identity or our livelihood; and have been taught that sport is inherently virtuous and beneficial, we are unlikely to accept or want to see that sport has the same kinds of warts or problems we find elsewhere in society. For those who are devoted to sport and who seek in sport a refuge from the problems and pressures of everyday life, sport sociology can represent a very unappealing way of looking at sport. It is difficult for us to acknowledge that the assumptions we take for granted may not be true, especially if they cast sport in a less positive light than we want to see or accept.

In challenging or invalidating assumptions we have taken for granted, sport sociology can open windows on sport and society through which we may have never looked or that we have purposely ignored or avoided. In fact, along with the heroic and glamorous side of sport many media present to us, there are contexts of sport where we find sexism, racism, exploitation, homophobia, abuse of the body, and various forms of social deviance, from drug use to violence and other crimes. It is not the purpose of this book to emphasize the ugly and unattractive qualities of sport to make it less appealing and seem less worthy of commitment, investment, or interest. In trying to reveal and understand the realities of sport, we will see a realm of society that has the complexities, diversity, richness, excitement, and challenges that we find in society's other realms. We will also see how sport is related to these other realms of society. In providing this kind of picture of sport and society, sport sociology should be as exciting and interesting as sport itself. Looking at sport through the eyes of a sociologist, with an open and objective mind, sociological imagination, and a critical perspective will lead to discoveries about sport that are exciting and interesting. Thus, I hope to make the study of sport as exciting and interesting as the realities of sport are.

The Concept of Sport

Most of us have informal or intuitive conceptions of what sport is and are not particularly concerned about being precise or consistent in talking about sport. As I suggested earlier, sociologists try to be careful, precise, and systematic in defining and using concepts. To be sure that we are talking about or studying the same thing, we need to agree on or at least be explicit about the terms we use. In the sociology of sport, the most important concept is sport itself. Although there are various possible definitions, *sport* will be defined here as *institutionalized physical competition occurring in formally organized or corporate structures* (Nixon and Frey 1996:3–4). The most basic component of the definition of sport is that it is physical competition. That is, sport is about individuals and groups using their physical skills to try to defeat their opponents in interaction that has winners and losers. In sport sociology, however, we are interested not only in the social aspects of the competition itself, but also in the broader organizational context in which the competition is embedded. Thus, sport is defined here in terms of both the physical competition and its larger organizational context.

The organizational context of sport is formally structured, which means that it has official rules, official enforcement of the rules by regulatory bodies, a hierarchical arrangement of positions or statuses, and, usually, a bureaucratic form. *Bureaucracy* is a type of administrative organization based on rational-legal authority in which people are supposed to interact with each other in terms of their competence, their productivity, the rules and goals of the organization, and the positions they hold rather than in terms of their personalities and how much they like each other. The idea of bureaucracy today generally implies hierarchical organizations run by "officials," "executives," or "management." Getting things done efficiently and effectively is more important in bureaucracies than is making sure everyone feels good or is personally happy. Presumably, organizational success or profitability makes people feel happy in a bureaucracy.

The formal organization of sport is corporate as well as bureaucratic. The *corporate* organization of sport implies that it is a legally defined entity that has a formal legal existence that is distinct from the legal status of its individual members. As such, sports organizations can enter into formal legal agreements with individuals or other organizations; can make their own rules and policies; can have boards, officials, and employees who run them and do their work; can sell tickets, merchandise, and media broadcast rights; and can make money that can be used to pay employees, make investments, build and maintain facilities, and market their business. If they are for-profit corporations, they pay taxes and earn profits for their private owners or dividends for stockholders. The corporate organization of many sports clubs, leagues, and governing bodies involves business operations that are intended to generate revenue or financial profits. The business-like corporate organization of contemporary sport is one of its most distinctive characteristics, which means that it often is difficult to separate what happens on the field from the influence of money or the behavior of people trying to make money from sport.

Sport is *institutionalized* in the sense that it is structured with an established and relatively stable pattern of social rules or norms, statuses, roles, and relationships. Institutionalized structures are familiar to us because they have a very predictable and recognizable form, with people repeatedly doing the same kinds of things and interacting with others in the same kinds of statuses, roles, and relationships in the same kinds of settings over time. These structures tend to be relatively stable over time because they exist in formal or corporate organizations or networks that have officials, executives, or managers responsible for making and articulating rules and policies and for making sure that people follow the rules and conform to formal expectations for their roles and relationships.

It should be evident that whether an activity is or is not a sport may not be immediately obvious. For example, people competing against each other in volleyball may look like they are playing a sport, but we need to look more closely to determine whether their activity is actually sport. Are the players representatives of formal teams? Do they have a formal coach? Is their competition part of a formal schedule devised and monitored by the officials in a formal league? Are the length of the game, who plays, how many play at one time, how points are scored, and how games and matches are won determined by formal rules? Is the game formally refereed? Is this match part of a championship or does it have a bearing on whether the teams are eligible for a championship with trophies and other formal rewards? Do the players receive some type of subsidy or compensation or special privileges for competing? Does the game receive media attention? Are there spectators and do they pay to watch? These questions suggest the kinds of activities we are interested in studying as sport. If we do not carefully distinguish between casual pickup games of volleyball and volleyball played as part of interscholastic or intercollegiate athletics or professional leagues, we might make incorrect generalizations about the players, how they interact, and what happens to them as a result of their participation in this game.

Impromptu or informal games of volleyball are also sociologically interesting, but they are different from the institutionalized and formally organized corporate behavior we are defining here as sport, and they have different social implications. What is especially interesting from a sociological perspective about the conception of sport we have presented here is that by virtue of its type of organization, it is connected to many aspects of the major institutional structures of society as well as to significant contemporary global social patterns and forces of social change. We should recognize, though, that sport is complex, is played in many different venues, has many different forms, and exists at different levels, from local sports leagues and tournaments for very young children to professional and Olympic competition at the global level. We know, too, that even for young children, sport can be organized at an international level, as in the case of Little League Baseball, Inc.

Although the corporate character of sport generally implies that it is commercialized and may involve paid professionals, sport may not be commercial or professional. A number of activities that begin as informally organized recreational physical activities evolve into formally organized sports and ultimately become commercialized and professionalized. In the discussion of alternative sports subcultures or "extreme sports" in chapter six, for example, we will consider how sports such as snowboarding have been transformed from leisure activities into "big-time" sports on a global scale. Thus, it is important to view the definition of sport presented here as a sociological model of the kinds of social structural characteristics that are generally associated with the idea of modern sport. We will be interested in how sport contrasts with more informally organized recreation, play, and games; how certain kinds of activities evolve into sports; and the different implications of sport and more informal physical activities.

I assume that sport is *serious* competition, which means that the results are not known or fixed in advance. This assumption is important because people who watch and play sport expect it to have integrity. The appeal of sport depends in part on the assumption that "anything is possible" when even badly mismatched individuals or teams take the floor, court, or field. Sport would lose its integrity and appeal if the results were fixed in advance. This fact is what distinguishes professional wrestling as a theatrical performance from the sports of high school, college, and Olympic wrestling. The underdog winner often captures the imagination of fans in the United States because many Americans believe in the American Dream, which assumes that all things are possible for those who try hard enough. I have to add that sport sociologists examine this kind of belief critically, but this does not mean that dreams of success are any less inspiring in sport. In general, sport would lose its character and appeal if the results were not from honest competition. This is why it is so important to try to prevent or control the influence of cheaters, fixers and gamblers, and performance-enhancing drugs in sport.

The evolution and complexity of sport are seen in the historical development of track-and-field events that originated in ancient Greek and Roman times and in sports today that use modern technology, such as automobiles, snowboards, and skateboards. As suggested earlier, there are sports that have evolved as informal "extreme sports" and ultimately became part of the established order of corporate sport. Sports events have been very exclusive, limited only to the elite members of society, but democratization has made more sports accessible to more people. Indeed, we have seen sports evolve to accommodate societal outsiders or special interests, including sports for people with disabilities, such as the Special Olympics and Paralympics, and sports for people who are gay, such as the Gay Games.

The Contemporary Social Organization of Sport

We were reminded when the Summer Olympic Games took place in Athens, Greece, in 2004 that sports have evolved over many centuries from the time of the ancient Olympics. I have noted elsewhere (Nixon and Frey 1996:19) that permanent facilities and playing fields were built for the Olympics in 550 B.C.E., reflecting the rising popularity and increasing political significance of games and early versions of sport in Greece at that time. Male Olympians competed in sports such as chariot racing, wrestling, boxing, jumping, javelin, discus, running, and archery. Although women's participation in sport was limited, girls and women in ancient Greece participated in contests such as footraces in events such as the Heraean Games and earned crowns of olive for winning, just as the male Olympic victors did.

Although the early forms of sport in ancient Greece had a number of the characteristics we associate with modern sport, they differed in significant ways as well. In particular, games and sport in Greece before 100 B.C.E. were rooted in mythology and religion, lacked complex administrative or bureaucratic structures, and did not pay attention to measurement and records as we now do (Nixon and Frey 1996:19). Historian Allen Guttmann (1978) has identified a number of characteristics of the social organization of modern sport that distinguish it from forms in earlier eras.[1] We will summarize his characterization, and add some features that have been especially significant in recent years.

According to Guttmann, modern sport is organized as a *secular* rather than a sacred activity. That is, even though a number of athletes, especially winners, say that they are dedicating their performance to the glory of their god or that they are thankful to God for enabling them to win, the *purpose* of sport today is not religious or sacred. Sport is not organized to satisfy, appease, or glorify deities. It is a form of secular entertainment, and it is played by people who are very much interested in rewards such as trophies, money, fame, or influence that they can enjoy or use in this world. In fact, devout athletes, coaches, and fans often experience conflicts between sport and religion today because so many sports events are scheduled on holy days when believers are not supposed to be focused on secular or worldly activities.

Guttmann has also proposed that modern sport is organized with an emphasis on equality of opportunity, quantification or counting, and records and is bureaucratic, rational, and specialized. These characteristics are generally consistent with the definition of sport we presented earlier. For example, we considered that the organization of modern sport tends to be *bureaucratic*, which implies that it is *rational*, *specialized*, and focused on the *measurement* of performance and formal *record keeping*. The *rationality* of modern sport is related to its planned, intentional, purposeful, and formal mission and goal-seeking behavior and to its corporate legal and commercial structure. Sport has become increasingly *specialized* in the modern era as sports officials, coaches, and athletes have performed more and more narrowly defined roles. For example, in U.S. football, players rarely play both offensive and defensive positions, and some who play a defensive position such as linebacker may enter the game only for anticipated passing or running plays. There are also different people who punt, kick extra points and ordinary-length field goals, and kick off and attempt long field goals. In the earlier, less-specialized years of the sport, the same player may have been the quarterback, played safety on defense, punted, kicked off, kicked extra points, and kicked field goals. In the modern period, the computer and similar devices have made it much easier to *measure* and *record performances*, and with more precise measuring instruments records have become more precise. For example, the world track record for the 100 meters is measured in hundredths of a second, with two runners tied at 9.77 seconds in June 2006. Swimming and other sports that time their competitors rank them by hundredths of a second. Our increased capacity and desire to measure things have produced a plethora of categories of records. For example, the *Baseball Almanac* website (2006) listed information about three types of base-running records, twenty-eight types of hitting records, seventeen types of pitching records, and six types of fielding records for seven different positions or position clusters (e.g., outfield).

Bureaucracies are hierarchical, with people in higher positions having more authority than people in lower positions do. This kind of inequality in the organized world of modern sport is accompanied by inequalities that are created by the outcomes of competition. That is, we generally give winners more rewards than losers, from publicity and fame to cash prizes and salaries. In earlier historical periods, sport was also unequal in another way. Access to sport or at least certain kinds of sport favored by the elite was limited to people in the higher social classes or in dominant ethnic or racial groups. Democratization, which is the opening of sports to people from more diverse social class or status backgrounds, is a characteristic of the modern era of sports, and it has meant that more people from middle and working classes, more racial and ethnic minorities, more people with disabilities, and more women have been able to participate in a wide range of sports in a variety of roles, from athlete to spectator. Democratization implies equality of opportunity, which means that even though competitors are unequal—as winners and losers—at the end of the competition, those who want to and are able to compete are all supposed to have a chance to be at the starting line at the beginning of the competition, regardless of their social background. A number of modern sports have some degree of stratification or inequality in their opportunity structures, but even the formerly elite sports such as golf and tennis espouse the *principle of equality of opportunity* and talk about trying to attract minority and less-advantaged people. Thus, when we refer to equality of opportunity as a characteristic of the organization of modern sport, we would be more precise in referring to the *principle or goal* of equality of opportunity. In some sports, the cost of training, access to facilities, travel, clothing, and equipment is so high that the idea of equal access is more myth than reality.

Following Guttmann's lead, then, we would characterize the major characteristics of the modern social organization of sport in terms of (1) secularism, (2) bureaucracy, (3) rationality, (4) specialization, (5) quantification, (6) records, and (7) the principle or goal of equality of opportunity. Much of contemporary sport is also mediated, especially by television. Castells (1996) observed that television has a major influence on how prominent events and activities are communicated to the public in society today. It also has a lot to do with making particular events, activities, and people highly prominent. Later in the book, we will discuss the role of television and other mass media in creating contemporary sports celebrities.

A major reason for the power of television and, more recently, the Internet and other electronic media is their capacity to convey sharp, intense, and compelling images to people around the world in real time (Smart 2005:8). It is difficult to think of contemporary sport without thinking of mass-mediated images of it, and it is difficult to understand the organization of contemporary sport without recognizing the powerful influence of the mass media on it. Sport would not have developed as a corporate and commercial enterprise in the modern era or have become as globally popular as it is today without the publicity and financial investment of the mass media, beginning with books and the newspapers in the nineteenth century.

The rise of industrial capitalism in the nineteenth and twentieth centuries also contributed to the growth of modern sport. That is, sport has been developed by owners and entrepreneurs as a form of capitalist production in which events, teams, athletes, and some coaches have become commodities to be manufactured, marketed, and sold to make money or earn a profit. Furthermore, sport has become a major vehicle for the global expansion of capitalism today. In his study of "Michael Jordan and the New Global Capitalism," LaFeber (2002) has argued that the construction and selling of Michael Jordan as a global sports icon illustrate how transnational capitalist corporations have used sport and high-tech telecommunications technology to sell their products around the world. Thus, *contemporary sport* has largely become a *mediated capitalist enterprise with defining elements of modern rational bureaucratic and corporate commercial organization.* It seems relevant to conclude this section by noting Guttmann's (2000:258) observation that modern sports are least popular in the Islamic world, where religious fundamentalism prevails and an aversion to the products of modern scientific rationality and consumer capitalism is strongest—that is, where powerful and pervasive traditional cultural elements contrast sharply with the dominant characteristics of the modern social organization of sport.

Sport, the Body, and Contested Terrain

Sport sociology incorporates a broad range of insights from a variety of perspectives beyond the discipline of sociology, such as cultural studies, popular culture, media studies, and sports management. The sociology of sport has also stretched its boundaries to focus on the body as a social and cultural phenomenon. Many scholars and scientists now recognize that the body is more fully understood if we extend traditional perspectives and include social and cultural ones. For example, Atkinson and Wilson (2002) have noted that bodies and body images are now viewed as commodities that are advertised, bought, and sold. Bodies are also viewed as "mortal engines" that are refined and manipulated with the latest scientific advances and technologies to produce the best possible performances (Hoberman 1992). Furthermore, Cole (2000) showed the wide range of sport sociology approaches to the body in her review of relevant literature in the sociology of sport field. For example, she looked at studies concerning the relationship of the body to contemporary athletes' roles and identities and the organization of modern sport; to science; to social deviance, including violence; to homosexual identities; to HIV-infected and drugged identities; to bodybuilding; to celebrity; to consumer culture and the fitness industry; and, ultimately, to the complex network of power in society.

Coakley (2007:21) has suggested that in contemporary sport, pain is culturally defined as a more appropriate experience for the bodies of serious athletes than pleasure is. A body that can endure pain and injury is a good body, and this belief encourages athletes to take significant risks with their bodies. Similarly, in some sports, coaches expect their athletes to be very thin, whatever their level of athletic proficiency, and this expectation may result in serious eating disorders in sports ranging from distance running to gymnastics. Coakley pointed to a number of types of questions that sport sociologists and others who study culture and society are now addressing about the body. Combined with Cole's overview of topics concerning the body in the sociology of sport, Coakley's questions indicate how prominent the study of the body has become in sport sociology and how important it is to understand the body as a social and cultural phenomenon if we are to understand the contemporary social organization of sport. His questions also reveal more specifically how the body can be seen as a social and cultural phenomenon. Coakley asked, for example, about how sporting bodies are represented in the mass media. This is an important issue for athletes in disability sport, who want to be viewed as athletes and do not want people paying disproportional attention to what the media define as "deviant," "inferior," or "flawed" bodies. For many years, women athletes who engaged in strength training were thought to be risking developing masculine bodies, because muscles were associated with male and not female bodies. The body has become an increasingly popular focus of sport sociologists, and Atkinson and Wilson have proposed integrating the study of the body with the study of subcultures in the sociology of sport. One interesting point of departure for such work, they suggest, is the study of how liberating body movements in new or alternative sports subcultures, such as skateboarding or snowboarding, create bonds or ties among the members of these subcultures or social networks and at least symbolically subvert outside control of their sports. Thus, distinctive and creative bodily movements have special meaning for members of these distinctive subcultures that link them together and also differentiate them from outsiders, including those who would control their sport from the outside.

For those approaching sport and the body from more critical perspectives, which challenge the established structures of status and power relations in sport, the concept of *contested terrain* is especially relevant. The body could be seen as a site where different groups in society and sport struggle for status, power, and control. For example, do the mass media and fans prefer to portray or watch black bodies, brown bodies, or white bodies? Male bodies or female bodies? Massive bodies or lithe and finely muscled bodies? Perfect bodies or disabled bodies with "flaws"? We can also see a clash of interests and values between the NBA management and players regarding the NBA dress code, created in 2005, that required players to shed the casual attire many favored and instead clothe their bodies in conservative "business casual" attire for official league functions or when they were out of uniform and seated on the bench during games. These various struggles over the body clearly illustrate the relevance of the idea of contested terrain in identifying and analyzing areas of disagreement or conflict between groups with differing status and power in sport.

Contemporary Forces of Change in Society and Sport

Modern sport is different than sport in earlier historic eras. Sport has changed for various reasons. For example, change has resulted from rational planning on the one hand and social conflicts on the other hand. In addition, sport has changed because it has been influenced by major forces of social change in the larger society and culture. In recent years, a number of powerful *social demographic, organizational, economic, political,* and *technological forces* have been reshaping societies and cultures, and sport has felt their imprint. We have seen the imprint of these kinds of forces in our discussion of the social organization of contemporary sport.

Introductory textbooks in sociology and sport sociology often focus on social change at the end of the book as part of a discussion of future trends. We are considering the forces of social change at the beginning and throughout this book because as a social institution, sport reflects the dominant social forces at work in the society and culture in which it is embedded. To understand sport sociologically, we must focus on how major social forces in society are shaping the contemporary character of sport. Thus, we will be considering the scope and rate of change in the contemporary landscape of society and sport and how the major forces of change are shaping contemporary sport. In this section, we will identify major types of change processes and consider examples of how sport is being influenced by each of these processes. This discussion will introduce major topics and issues to be examined in the ensuing chapters.

Social demographic forces are transforming the characteristics of populations, and include powerful trends in global migration. In the United States, Americans are increasingly addressing matters concerning immigration and increasing ethnic and racial diversity, which are changing the face of many cities and other communities and raising issues about how much to respect, tolerate, or accept social and cultural differences in the population. Arguments about "guest workers" from other nations tend to focus on legal and illegal immigrants crossing the border to fill jobs generally unwanted by U.S. citizens, but we are also seeing increasing numbers of foreign-born athletes in high school, college, and professional sports. In many of these venues, athletes occupy an elite status, and at the professional level, they may earn large salaries. In the current climate of disagreement about immigration laws and the status of immigrants, questions may be raised about how much Americans embrace or respect these foreign-born athletes. Similar questions may be asked about Americans and other foreign-born athletes participating in sports in other countries. Demographic changes are influencing sport in other ways as well, as we observe the increasing number of women who have entered sport in the United States and other nations over the past thirty-five years, and consider the extent to which the dominance of African Americans in certain U.S. sports will persist as the ethnic diversity of U.S. society increases. The pattern of the graying of the U.S. population also may be relevant to sport, as we consider the rising or falling popularity of sports favored by different age groups, and the extent to which mass media coverage of sports is influenced by the tastes of the demographic groups with the most appeal to commercial advertisers.

A major force of *organizational* change in contemporary society is *McDonaldization*, which refers to the application of the principles of rational organization used by McDonald's restaurants to many other types of organization in societies around the world. McDonaldization is based more specifically on principles of *efficiency* to produce the best products with the fewest resources; *calculation* and *counting* to make it easier to evaluate resource expenditures, outcomes, and success; *standardization* to make services and products more efficient to produce in large quantities and more predictable for customers; and *control*, which is achieved by substituting nonhuman technology for people whenever possible. This type of organization incorporates elements of the scientific management approach made popular by Frederick Taylor in the early part of the twentieth century and of Henry Ford's assembly line.

Ritzer (1993) worried that McDonaldization stifled individual freedom, creativity, and flexibility, but the global diffusion of its basic principles of organization is evident. We can see a version of them in sport in Billy Beane's rational approach to managing the Oakland Athletics Major League Baseball team "by the numbers" (Lewis 2003), and his approach seems to have influenced a few of the younger or less traditional general managers in his sport, such as Theo Epstein of the Boston Red Sox. Ritzer (2004b:76–79) wrote more generally about an emphasis on calculation or counting that was spreading through sport in various ways as sports organizations have increasingly set numerical standards for production or results. For example, television producers know that they must include a predetermined number of commercial advertisements in game telecasts to meet the requirements of their contracts with their advertisers, and as a result, we now see "TV time-outs" at regular intervals, even though the flow of the game may be altered at times by these interruptions. Fans, management, players, players' agents, and the mass media are often consumed by an interest in the players' statistical performance, even when individual players improve their "numbers" at the expense of team success or when the outcome of the game has long been decided. We have seen coaches run up large margins of victory over much weaker teams to impress bowl or championship selection committees. In individual sports such as tennis, athletes are ranked according to numbers; in judged sports, such as gymnastics and figure skating, the numbers represent the quality of performance, even when our own eyes might reach a different conclusion. As we observed earlier, more precise measuring instruments have made it possible to establish new records by hundredths of a second in sports such as swimming and track and field. Officials in sports such as basketball have decided that fans want to see a faster pace, and as a result, teams are required to hit the rim with a shot within a prescribed time limit or lose possession of the ball. In U.S. baseball and football, rules committees routinely try to figure out ways to increase scoring, assuming that only "purists" would want to watch great pitching performances or defensive battles.

Ritzer has suggested that a concentration on numbers reflects a conception that quantity equals quality. In fact, an emphasis on numbers is a defining characteristic of modern sport. In sport, this emphasis reflects a particular value judgment that more spectators in the stadium or arena, higher game scores, more points, faster speeds, a faster pace of the game, and, ultimately, bigger purses or prizes, bigger contracts for players and coaches, bigger television contracts, and more revenue are better than their alternatives. This value judgment is based on what sports and media executives believe the sports public wants, since ultimately the concerns about calculation, McDonaldization, and rationality in general are focused on how to make sports more appealing and profitable.

The emphasis on profitability is an example of another important force of change in contemporary society. That is, *economic* processes, such as the growth of consumption-oriented capitalism and the related focus on profits, are influencing societies and cultures on a global scale. Economics is an important part of the contemporary social organization of sport. We have noted the centrality of corporate commercial and capitalist elements in our definition of contemporary sport. A basic thrust of capitalism is growth, in new products,

Barry Bonds's record-tying 755th home run at Petco Park, San Diego, 2007. Extensive media attention to his quest for the record illustrates the fascination with numbers in modern sports, which Ritzer identified as a major element of McDonaldization. (Karl Drilling 2007/Shutterpoint Photography)

in new markets, in new consumers, and in additional profits. The growth of capitalism on a global scale creates the conditions for the ongoing worldwide expansion of sports as corporate commercial and capitalist enterprises.

The marketplace has become a metaphor that has been increasingly embraced by institutional leaders across modern societies with capitalist economies, from traditional businesses to the mass media, higher education, the arts, and sport. In higher education, for example, students are viewed as consumers or customers, as administrators try to generate higher enrollments and more tuition revenue (Bok 2003). In the corporate business of contemporary sport, dominant patterns of McDonaldized organization are combined with a strong capitalist market orientation. For example, in the commercialized realms of college and high school athletics and professional and Olympic sports, the focus on consumers or customers and generating revenue or profits is obvious. Ritzer (2004b:7) wrote about Kowinski's (1985) idea that indoor shopping malls had become modern "cathedrals of consumption" where consumers go to practice their "consumer religion." In an effort to generate increased revenue, new stadiums often seem to resemble shopping malls with a playing field in the middle. They are designed to maximize profit by embedding consumption opportunities wherever possible, reflecting the strong consumption orientation of advanced capitalist societies.

Processes of commercialization and professionalization are pervasive in sport today. Commercialization has made sports organizations increasingly concerned with making and spending money and expanding their reach to new and more lucrative markets, and professionalization has made athletes and coaches increasingly concerned about their sports jobs and incomes and created a new class of professional sports managers. We have seen the influence of these economic processes at all levels of sport, and we have seen the crucial role of the corporate mass media in the economic expansion of contemporary sport. We also have seen that as public subsidies of high school athletics decline and the "arms race" of escalating expenditures in college and high school athletics continues to intensify, high schools and colleges are increasingly turning to private donors and boosters and commercial investors to pay for new facilities, bigger contracts for coaches, and better competitive opportunities for athletes. In this climate, many high-level high school and college athletes in the United States, like their more professionalized counterparts in professional and Olympic sports, have become "commodified," or turned into commodities whose associated images and competitions are marketed and sold to generate revenue for sports organizers, promoters, and investors, including high schools and colleges.

Contemporary *political* forces range from nationalism, protest, and terrorism on the world stage to domestic patterns in the United States of increasing political partisanship, political conservatism, legal intervention and litigiousness, legislative scrutiny of various realms of public life, and a general decline in what political scientist Robert Putnam (2000) called "social capital" or civic engagement in the life of the community. Political influences operate on many levels of society and sport. Many of these political forces have been influencing society and sport for several decades or more, but a number have intensified in recent years. For example, we have seen ongoing patterns in sport involving the creation and promotion of sports cultures and sports heroes to boost the popularity, ideology, or electoral success of national or local political leaders. Politicians and political leaders like to associate themselves with sport because they know that many people are passionate about sport, and they want to bask in the glow of those positive feelings. We have also seen the continuing use of sports for other political purposes, such as advancing a nation's visibility or stature on the world stage or among its own citizens or subjects, with one of the most prominent examples being Hitler's use of the 1936 Berlin "Nazi Olympics" to further his domestic and international political agendas.

In more recent times, U.S. athletes at the 1968 and 1972 Olympic Games engaged in politics, protesting against racism in their nation with demonstrations on the victory stand. At the 1972 Munich Olympics, we also saw terrorists attack and kill Israeli athletes in the Olympic Village, and during the Atlanta Olympics in 1992, a politically motivated bomber set off a series of blasts that killed 2 people and injured 129 others in the city's Centennial Olympic Park. U.S. president Jimmy Carter used the threat of a boycott of the 1980 Moscow Olympics to try to influence the Soviet Union to suspend its military action in Afghanistan. The Soviet leaders retaliated with a boycott of the 1984 Los Angeles Olympics, ostensibly to protest the excessive capitalist influence over the organization of the Games, which were organized by a private corporation rather than a city for the first time (Nixon 1988a). Athletes and sports events have been used as tacit or explicit forms of political endorsement of a war or some other foreign intervention, a particular public policy, or even the legitimacy of elected officials.

The playing of the national anthem, flyovers by military jets, the display of the flag, phone calls from the president or governor or mayor to victorious teams and their visits to the White House or the Governor's Mansion, and other patriotic demonstrations have long been part of the U.S. sports scene. On the world stage, despite the discouragement of political displays in the Olympics by Olympic officials, we continue to see athletes march into the opening and closing ceremonies as representatives of their nations carrying their national flags, and we watch national flags raised and national anthems played as athletes receive their medals on the victory podium. Furthermore, just as President Nixon used ping-pong to launch diplomatic contact with China in the early 1970s, Baltimore Orioles owner Peter Angelos tried to facilitate rapprochement with Cuba with a series of exhibition baseball games between his team and the Cuban national team.

On the national level in the United States, legislators have created an Amateur Sports Act to provide more resources for Olympic sports training, among other purposes. In contrast, a 1972 state referendum to use public funds to build Olympic facilities in the Denver area was rejected by Colorado voters because they feared adverse environmental effects and rising costs, and as a result, Denver became the first city to turn down an invitation to host an Olympics. Prior to the 1984 Los Angeles Olympics, Los Angeles citizens voted against using public funds for the Olympics, causing the International Olympic Committee to permit a private corporation to host an Olympics for the first time. As we noted, this decision ultimately was used as a rationale by the Soviet Union to boycott the "Capitalist Games." The public and city council members have also been drawn into matters of politics and economics by the issue of public support for professional sports stadiums. For example, city council members in the U.S. capital city debated about whether to spend substantial tax dollars on the construction of a stadium for a Major League Baseball team in Washington, D.C., which was a requirement for Major League Baseball's approval of a new team in the area. This case is part of a pattern of continuing efforts by professional sports franchise owners and leagues to obtain public subsidies to build new sports facilities for franchises that are typically privately owned.

Political concerns about money have been raised about the National Collegiate Athletic Association (NCAA), but in this case the concerns were not prompted by fears of deficits, cost overruns, or inappropriate or dubious public subsidies. Instead, Congress has cast a suspicious and critical eye on the NCAA and the large amount of money it earns from its television contract for the men's basketball "Final Four." Congress has raised questions about the nonprofit status of the NCAA and whether it should have some tax liability for the money it earns. Congress has also debated possible new laws to restrict monopolistic practices in professional and college sports, since the courts have failed to enforce existing antitrust laws against sports.

A primary function of the NCAA has been governance, which has involved creating and enforcing rules to regulate the activities of member institutions and their athletes, coaches, and boosters. Despite the NCAA's regulatory efforts, there has been a long and continuing history of questionable and deviant practices in college athletics, which have prompted periodic calls for reform. For example, as a result of recent reformist political pressures, higher education institutions now publish the graduation rates of athletes (and other students) each year, and athletic programs are penalized by the NCAA when their athletes make insufficient progress toward graduation.

In interscholastic athletics, legislative bodies have passed laws requiring athletes to achieve a minimum grade point average to be eligible for high school sports participation, and state and local high school sports bodies have tried to regulate athletic eligibility of students who try to transfer between districts or schools. We have seen cases of athletes with disabilities who have sought court injunctions to prevent local school boards from blocking their participation in mainstream sports events alongside able-bodied opponents. In youth sports, parents have increasingly relied on formally and professionally organized sports programs with paid coaches for their children. This pattern parallels a pattern documented by Robert Putnam (2000) in his widely read book *Bowling Alone*. Putnam found declining voluntary participation of U.S. citizens over the past thirty-five years in a range of civic activities that are increasingly staffed and run by professionals, from political campaigns to lobbying and fund-raising by local community organizations.

The law has been used for and against sports organizations for various political and economic purposes. For example, athletes have gone to court to sue agents, teams have gone to court to sue for the right to move their franchise to another city, leagues have gone to court to prevent teams from relocating, injured athletes have taken worker's compensation claims to court, women have sued for gender equity under Title IX, and athletes with disabilities have sued for the right to compete with special accommodations under the Americans with Disabilities Act.

A number of other instances of politics, the law, and sport have occurred in the current era of sports. For example, professional athletes have organized strikes against the owners in their sport, and owners in turn have locked out players in labor disputes. Athletes have used arbitration to resolve contract and salary disputes. Athletes have also been involved with the criminal justice system as a result of their sports-related actions, such as when hockey players have been arrested, tried, and convicted for assaulting other players during the course of a game. In addition, professional, college, and Olympic athletes have gotten involved with the criminal justice system when they have been arrested and convicted for crimes outside the sports arena, including use of illegal drugs, homicide, spousal abuse, rape, and other forms of criminal assault. Athletes have also been victims of crimes or drawn into criminal behavior, at times because of their public prominence as athletes. Gambling is an example of an illegal activity that has attracted some coaches, athletes, and referees, at times to their significant detriment—as in the notorious case of baseball star Pete Rose, who has been blocked from participation in the sport and induction into the Baseball Hall of Fame as a result of his gambling activities. Some athletes have also found it easier to obtain illegal goods and services because of their fame or money. For example, two days after star University of Maryland basketball player Len Bias was selected first in the National Basketball Association draft by the Boston Celtics, he was offered cocaine during a celebratory party. This celebration ended in Bias's death from a drug overdose. Thus, the relationships of sport to the law and crime, as well as to politics, have been complex and extensive.

In its most general sense, *technology* refers to the application of knowledge or ways we do things to solve problems or adjust to life in a society. Technological forces shape the basic structures of societies, their cultures, and their productive capacities. In moving to a postindustrial era in which electronic and information technologies are replacing older industrial manufacturing technologies, the computer has replaced the factory smokestack as the symbol of the dominant technology of our time. Rapid changes in the technologies of computers, telecommunications, and the Internet have been transforming how and how much we know about the world; how we work, communicate and develop relationships with each other, engage in politics, raise our children, and entertain ourselves; how we deliver medical care and take care of our bodies; and how we access and compete in sports. In the history of sport, new technologies have been used to push the limits of performance to higher levels to achieve greater success. In contemporary sports, new capabilities in biotechnology and genetic engineering raise bioethical issues. These new "technologies of the body" raise issues about athletes as robotic or bionic "mortal engines." Indeed, efforts to alter the body and even change human genetic makeup, creating "designer athletes," conjure up images of the *Brave New World* of Huxley. At the same time, mechanical body parts may replace injured limbs, restore athletic capabilities, and improve performance, which could reduce concern about injuries if science is able to repair the damage and provide stronger artificial body parts in place of the damaged human ones.

New technologies raise questions about what constitutes fair competition. We can ask whether the athlete or the technology or the athlete's ability to master the technology is the primary cause of an athlete's performance. Such questions arise when we consider the latest advances in equipment or clothing, ranging from baseball bats to shoes or boots, apparel, golf clubs, tennis rackets, skis, bicycles, and race cars that are made with new materials that can help athletes be stronger, faster, more durable, or more aerodynamic or fleet in the water than their opponents. These questions are already raised about the use of performance-enhancing drugs. Related to the fairness issue is the issue of access to sport if it requires a reliance on increasingly expensive performance or training technologies to be successful. Athletes and teams with access to superior and more sophisticated training facilities start the competition with an advantage. We also know that teams utilize different types of artificial or natural outdoor playing surfaces or facilities in their capacity to control the weather—such as stadiums with retractable roofs—to maximize their chances of competitive success and gain an advantage over opponents less experienced with their playing surface or climate.

We have already considered the profound effects of the mass media on the contemporary social organization of sport. Computers, telecommunications media, and the new electronic media based on satellite and digital technologies have created new ways of accessing and experiencing sport and sports-related activities. Sports fans now can obtain up-to-date or real-time results of sports contests or even watch streaming video displays of specific contests on their computer or cell phone. They can participate as coaches, owners, or general managers in virtual competition in sports such as auto racing, football, basketball, hockey, baseball, or golf fantasy leagues that offer championships and cash prizes. Fans can also play video games modeled on actual sports or learn how to play a sport by watching a demonstration online or on their DVD player. Podcasts, which are a way of distributing multimedia files based on Apple's iPod technology, allow users or subscribers to access interviews with prominent sports figures or broadcasts of games automatically on their computers. The primary use so far has been to share audio files, and it generally has been offered at no cost. These new technologies provide future opportunities for wider distribution of sports media and the possibility of generating new revenue, from advertisers and from consumers, just as commercial online general and sports news services require subscriptions to access special areas of their websites.

Rapid technological change or new scientific discoveries can lead to new practices in a sport that challenge prevailing values or are not governed by the existing rules or policies in that sport. This form of cultural or structural "lag," where certain elements of culture or social structure are slow to respond to new technologies and the cultural or social practices they make possible, has occurred in the realm of performance-enhancing drugs. Drug laboratories have created new performance-enhancing substances that have been adopted by athletes before these substances have been tested by sports officials, methods for detecting them in athletes' bodies have been discovered, or rules governing their use have been established. Another example of the cultural or structural contradictions or inconsistencies that can occur after technological innovations is when a new type of equipment or clothing is invented or a new type of training technique is discovered, and coaches or athletes are slow to accept or adopt these innovations due to entrenched traditional values, unwillingness to risk change, or insufficient resources to afford the innovation. Sports officials also may be unwilling to accept change because they fear its effects on the quality of play in their sport or its traditions. In Major League Baseball, for example, one league has adopted the designated hitter rule, but the other has not. Unwillingness to change in sport often evaporates in the face of evidence that innovations lead to greater success, since sport is so focused on winning.

The forces of change in society and sport may have a broad influence, which could have implications for sport that reach beyond the local, regional, and national levels to the global level. For example, imagine that an increasing number of high school budget makers across the country restrict public funds for interscholastic athletics. This action pushes high schools to seek private funding from businesses and donors and look for other ways to generate revenue to support athletics. They try to find money to recruit better coaches for the most popular sports teams, which typically are football and boys' basketball. These ambitious coaches try to improve the quality of their athletic teams by recruiting better athletes, not only from neighboring school districts but also from other countries, knowing that commercial sponsors and the mass media have become more interested in organizing and covering regional and national competition between top high school teams. As a result of entrepreneurial promoters, coaches, and school officials, a number of top high school basketball teams play against opponents who are also highly ranked in national rankings of high school basketball teams, and they play in front of large live and television audiences in high-stakes games that generate revenue for the schools and national exposure for the players and coaches, who ultimately aspire to compete on bigger and more lucrative stages at the college and professional levels.

This imagined example illustrates the actual direction of development and change in "big-time" high school athletics today. It also illustrates the influence of organizational, economic, and media factors that have made the structure of popular high school sports and other sports realms more complex, commercialized, publicized, and seriously competitive. In high school and youth sports, teenagers are pressured to mature quickly as they face reporters, cameras, and recruiters on a national rather than a local stage. Of course, in some sports, such as soccer, young athletes compete on a world stage in youth development programs or they compete as individuals in national or world competitions for their age groups in sports such as tennis, golf, gymnastics, and figure skating. These young athletes quickly learn that they are valuable commercial commodities whose names can be used to sell news stories, media broadcasts, and game tickets. They also may be invited to participate in special competitions or camps sponsored by McDonald's or Nike, which create a link between their names and their sponsors. This world of sport is not your grandparents' or parents' sports world. It exists today, and sport is changing rapidly and substantially in many ways. Indeed, this is a book about *sport in a changing world* seen through the eyes of a sociologist. In the chapters that follow, we will focus on contemporary social and cultural patterns of sport, see how they have been influenced by the dominant forces of change in society and culture, and see how sport has left its own imprint on society and culture.

Plan for the Book

The specific plan for this book is to follow this chapter with a chapter summarizing the major social theories and research methods used in sport sociology. I will use these theories and refer to these methods throughout the book in trying to clarify what sport sociologists know about sport. We will also consider social network analysis in chapter two because it is a valuable tool that provides a way of seeing the basic contours of social structure, which is a central concept in sociology. More specifically, the concept of social network describes basic structural patterns of social, economic, and political relations among the sports, media, and corporate business "actors" in the "Golden Triangle" that dominates sports around the world.

After chapter two, we will move on to four chapters that examine major aspects of the social structure and culture of sport. Structured social inequalities, called "social stratification" by sociologists, are an enduring part of social structure in all societies and in sport. Chapter three introduces social stratification, presents major concepts and theories of stratification and their relevance to sport, and focuses on elements of class stratification in sport and on global sports stratification. Chapter four continues the discussion of stratification by considering major dimensions of social inequality beyond social class:

dimensions of gender, sexual orientation, race and ethnicity, and physical disability. Social inequality themes will be interwoven throughout the text of the ensuing chapters as a major focus of this book.

Chapter three introduces the important concept of the "Golden Triangle." This term was proposed by Smart (2005) in his book *The Sport Star* and was inspired by Aris's (1990) conception of the "Sportsbiz." According to Aris, the "twin props" of the business of sports were television and sponsors (xi). In my conception of the Golden Triangle, I am emphasizing links among commercialized sports, television and other major sports media, and corporate sponsors as the dominant network of power in sport, which shapes the global sports culture and makes prominent athletes global sports stars. The concept of the Golden Triangle is defined essentially the same way that Messner, Dunbar, and Hunt (2000) defined the "Sports/Media/Commercial Complex" and is similar to Maguire's (1999) conception of the "Global Media-Sport Complex." The Golden Triangle will be considered in relation to global stratification in chapter three and will be applied throughout the remaining chapters as a major integrating theme and as an important part of the explanation for many of the dominant patterns in sport today. The Golden Triangle is a product of global capitalism and is oriented primarily to expanding commercial markets and generating profits.

"The" Golden Triangle is actually many different Golden Triangles associated with different sports in different local, regional, or national domains, and these different Golden Triangles may be loosely or tightly linked to one another and may cooperate or compete, depending on the social, economic, political, or sports circumstances. I will use "the Golden Triangle" many times in a generic sense to refer generally to patterns or influences associated with the dominant network of power in sport, and other times I will refer to a particular Golden Triangle associated with a specific sport or sports context. In the broadest sense, the (generic) Golden Triangle refers to the high-level or macro-level networks of power in sport that operate on a global scale, such as in the Olympics. At the local level, Golden Triangles may involve local television and radio stations that have agreements with local commercial sponsors to broadcast games of local teams. Thus, the Golden Triangle term may be used in various ways, but in all cases, the term refers to a dominant power structure within the global cultural economy of capitalism operating in some commercialized domain of sport. The term may seem to be an abstraction when it is applied to vast global networks of power, but there should be no mistaking the fact that there are macro-level networks of power in sport that exert substantial influence over sport at all levels.

Smaller and more localized or regionalized Golden Triangles may compete economically with other Golden Triangles that are operating in their markets and perhaps on a larger scale as well, and they are often formally affiliated with larger corporate organizations that are part of larger-scale Golden Triangles. Whatever the connections or competition between different Golden Triangles, they are all likely to be controlled by the same kinds of people and organizations, which embrace the same kinds of cultural values and general economic interests. Thus, despite their differences, they will typically have the same kind of influence on sport, on people in the sports world, and on sports consumers. For these reasons, we can assume there is one loosely integrated Golden Triangle network that includes an array of commercial sports, media operations, and corporate sponsors and has common values and interests, which is why I will frequently refer to "the" Golden Triangle. At the end of the third chapter, we will examine one type of influence of an important component of Golden Triangles, the mass media. We will look at how the media construct images and stories about inequality themes. The power of the mass media as part of a Golden Triangle makes the nature of these media constructions especially important, since it implies that they can influence how the public thinks about and treats people of lower status in society as well as sport.

The main focus of chapter five is globalization, global sports culture, and the Golden Triangle, and the various forms of globalization and the tensions and resistance provoked by globalization are major themes of this book. It is a major aspect of the "world" part of the "sport in a changing *world*" focus of the book. Special attention is given in chapter five to how various globalization concepts and perspectives and the idea of the Golden Triangle apply to sport and the global sports culture. The role of television and corporate sponsors in the contemporary globalization of sport is also an important theme in this chapter. The idea of U.S. "exceptionalism" (from Markovits and Hellerman's 2001 book about soccer and American exceptionalism) is a prominent focus in this chapter as well.

Chapter six focuses on how the Golden Triangle uses the mass media and corporate advertising to spread their global sports culture and turn star athletes into celebrities and cultural icons who can be powerful vehicles in the selling of the cultural values and products of the Golden Triangle, from TV spectacles to running shoes and the myriad of other products these athlete-salespeople endorse. It also considers the centrality of individualism in U.S. culture and the culture of capitalism and how the dominant cultural belief systems in the United States and U.S. sport function as ideologies to support each other and dominant institutional structures of U.S. society and sport. In addition, it looks at sport as a form of secular religion that provides its most devoted fans with a form of sacred escape at the same time that it is a very worldly commodity in the contemporary cultural economy. Finally, this chapter considers the nature of alternative sports subcultures and how they resist and accommodate themselves to the hegemonic sports culture.

Chapter seven begins with a consideration of theoretical ideas about socialization and its social or societal implications, and the ideas of socialization into and through sport are discussed. The primary emphasis of the chapter will be socialization into and through youth sports and high school athletics. After examining the different types of contexts in which children and adolescents participate in sport, the chapter examines the various types of lessons youths may derive from sport—about status and the self, about character and what adults expect, and about citizenship and nationalism. Infused throughout the discussion of socialization, status, and the self are the recurring themes of gender, race, ethnicity, social class, sexual orientation, and disability. Turning to high school athletes, the chapter considers the relationship between academics and athletics and other aspects of the experiences of high school student-athletes. The increasing imprint of the Golden Triangle on youth sports and the related development of big-time youth sports will be discussed, along with parental influence, dropout and access issues, and how youth sports is changing in the context of the forces of social change in the world. The chapter concludes with a special feature about how athletes and the "jock culture" of the high school may play a role in explosive situations such as the violence at Columbine High School in Colorado. Another special feature in this chapter focuses on an examination of what youth sports in different countries reveal about patterns of globalization at the local level.

Chapter eight will consider the nature of theories and concepts of social deviance that apply to sport and then give special attention to the idea of social deviance and social problems in sport as social constructions, influenced by powerful interests in sport connected to the Golden Triangle. The chapter will mainly focus on social deviance and contemporary social issues and problems of sport. It will examine in some detail a variety of major social problems that have attracted substantial public attention and press scrutiny in recent years. Some have had a long history in sport. These problems of sport include violence in the sports arena, crime, sexual violence and abuse, doping, gambling and fixing, and hazing. Special interest will be paid to how and why these issues and problems arise in sport or for sports participants; how they affect perceptions of sports, athletes, and coaches; and how sports officials, the media, and corporate sponsors manage these issues and problems.

Chapter nine will consider sport and higher education. After a brief discussion of the historical roots of "big-time" commercialized college athletics, the chapter will assess the justifications for big-time college sports. The highly bureaucratized and commercialized development of big-time college athletics in the United States distinguishes it from sport in college in the rest of the world. The chapter will examine the organization and stratification of big-time U.S. college sports, especially in terms of the growth of women's college sport in relation to the NCAA. Gender equity, the financial arms race, and the business of college athletics will be major themes of the chapter, along with the relationship between athletics and education for student-athletes. Throughout this chapter, we will see the imprint of the Golden Triangle on college athletics in the United States. Commercialism and the role of the Golden Triangle help explain the recent reform efforts in U.S. college sports, and these reform efforts will be examined in the context of a history of attempted reforms in this sports realm.

Chapter ten will examine the professional sports industry and sports careers. This chapter will develop a fuller conception of the structure of the Golden Triangle and how it has shaped the nature of the highly commercialized and global professional sports industry. It will examine monopoly capitalism and the economics of professional sports leagues and look at the numbers that describe the financial structure of professional sports and sports careers today. It will also focus on the effects of sports monopolies on players, fans, and communities and consider the global expansion of professional sports as an expression of the capitalist imperative to expand markets. The discussion of professional sports careers as "life on the run" will contrast the careers of athletes in different kinds of sports and in sports in the major and minor leagues. A major focus of this part of the chapter will be how athletes deal with the risk, pain, and injuries that constantly threaten their careers and can affect their lives many years after their sports careers have ended. The chapter will conclude with a discussion of professional athletes and professional sports in a changing global cultural economy.

The eleventh and final chapter will consider sport, politics, and the future. The chapter will begin with discussions of concepts of power and theoretical perspectives for understanding the politics of sport. It will focus on government power and the political uses of sport, sport and international relations, the politics of the Olympics, and sport as contested terrain in which individuals, organized activists, and nongovernmental organizations challenge the power structure of sport and the Golden Triangle. Examining sport and Green politics will help us see how powerful elements in the natural and political environment of sport may shape its future and the future role of the Golden Triangle in sport. The book will conclude with a discussion of contemporary forces of change and the future of sport. At the end, we will have come full circle as we return, once again, to the themes and forces of social change introduced in this first chapter and reconsider the themes of inequality, power, globalization, and the dominance of the Golden Triangle in the global cultural economy of sport that were major integrating threads of the book.

Jas Saiz of Madison, Wisconsin, and Hugh Danforth of Oneida, Wisconsin, protest the use of Indian mascots, including Illinois' mascot, Chief Illiniwek, outside the Kohl Center on Friday, March 22, 2002, in Madison, Wisconsin. This protest illustrates the concept of sport as "contested terrain." (AP Photo/Morry Gash)

Beginning with the third chapter, each chapter will include special features, including "Sport in the News," about items from the mass media concerning recent issues and debates, and "Focus on Research," which presents recent research about an important topic in the sport sociology or social science literature that has contemporary social relevance. Global themes will be infused in many of these features, and many of the sports trends and issues examined in the book will be considered from a global, international, or cross-national comparative perspective. Discussions of theory and research methods throughout the book will show the various ways that sport sociologists use their distinctive analytical tools to illuminate the nature of contemporary "big-time" sports, the connections between sport and society, and how sport is changing in the context of society. From various sociological perspectives, we will see sport and the influence of the Golden Triangle through social, cultural, economic, political, and global lenses.

Since the world and sport are continually changing, there will be sports innovations; new approaches to playing, coaching, organizing, communicating, and consuming sport; and new sports issues and problems that did not exist and I did not anticipate in writing this book. However, with its sweep across the global terrain of contemporary sports and with its focus on fundamental social structures and processes of sport and society, this book will help you understand these changes and their implications as well as current realities. My aim is not to take away the thrill or excitement from playing or watching the games of sport, but instead to make the basic social and cultural patterns in which they are embedded more understandable and predictable. In doing so, I should help you develop your sociological imagination. Seeing the world through the lens of sport sociology and with sociological imagination should bring into focus things you never saw before and make a number of those things that were familiar and you assumed you understood appear in a new, clearer, and sharper light.

Note

1. Coakley (2007:60–61) provides a concise summary of Guttmann's conception of the major characteristics of what Coakley calls "dominant sports forms" in contemporary society.

2

Social Theories and Research Methods in Sport Sociology

Major Theoretical Perspectives in Sport Sociology

We have already considered a general definition of theory. In the broadest terms, theories in sociology are disciplined, organized, or systematic means of making sense of the social world through the use of logically connected concepts, assumptions, and conclusions about society, how it works, and what causes things to happen. For sport sociologists, theories describe, explain, and predict social and cultural patterns in sport and society. They represent our knowledge about the sociological aspects of sport and society and are substantiated by research. Theoretical ideas and knowledge are important and useful because they can guide policymaking, decisions, and actions. Theoretical thinking about cause and effect may lead us to predict particular outcomes of particular factors or conditions, such as the expansion or contraction of athletic programs or new rules to make certain types of sports less dangerous. Theoretical predictions might cause us to act in ways that are meant to create the conditions we think will lead to predicted desired outcomes. In the simplest sense, we cannot understand society sociologically without applying the coherent framework embedded in a theory.

Sociology does not have a single theoretical perspective that explains everything sociologists study or that enables us to predict all types of social behavior, nor does it have a single research method that all sociologists use to collect social data. In this chapter, we will consider major theoretical perspectives in sociology, which provide different sets of glasses for seeing various aspects of society and sport. They are distinguished by different general conceptions of society, and they tend to pose different kinds of assumptions and raise different kinds of questions about how society works. While these perspectives may be seen as competing or conflicting at times, they also could be viewed as complementary in providing insights into different aspects of society and sport.

Introductory sociology texts usually present three general theoretical perspectives to represent the major types of theoretical thinking in the field. They are structural functionalism, social conflict theory, and symbolic interactionism. In recent years, increasing attention has been given to a variety of alternative perspectives, including feminist, rational choice, and postmodern approaches.[1] In addition, more sociologists have utilized the techniques of social network analysis to identify the various ways that people, positions, or social organizations, from groups to entire nation-states, have been directly and indirectly linked to each other through social relations ranging from authority, influence, and power to economic or financial transactions and sentiments of friendship, cooperation, and respect. My aim here is not to provide a detailed summary of each of these theoretical perspectives or analytical approaches. It is, instead, to show how different prominent theoretical perspectives in sociology enable us to see different aspects of the social structure and dynamics of society and sport.

While its roots can be traced to many centuries before then, sociologists generally say that their discipline was founded in the mid-nineteenth century by the French author and observer of society August Comte, who first used the label *sociology* to refer to a new discipline established to produce scientific knowledge about society. Sociology emerged amidst the turmoil of momentous social changes brought about by the confluence of the powerful social processes of industrialization, democratization, bureaucratization, and the rise of cities. Traditional ways of working and living were being threatened and replaced by new forms of social organization. New ideas about the value of the individual vis-à-vis the traditional community emerged. Early structural functionalist and conflict theory ideas were formulated in this context to try to understand the major social changes that were happening at the time.[2]

Structural functionalism, which we will also refer to as "functionalism," derives from the classic work of Comte and another, even more prominent nineteenth-century sociologist, Emile Durkheim. To understand this perspective, one must understand the ideas of "structure" and "function." We considered the concept of social structure earlier. Building on that prior consideration, *social structure* is defined here as an enduring pattern of social arrangements of social rules or norms, related social roles that people fill to meet their social obligations or others' expectations, and social relationships that develop from social interactions between and among individuals, groups, and organizations in social networks. Social structure is the underlying framework of society that is unseen but gives society its form or shape. If we think of a body, its structure is its anatomy, organs, and tissues. They are the components of the body that persist over time, and give the body its basic definition, identity, or order. As in the social structure of society, these components of the body are unseen by ordinary eyes, hold the body together, and have enduring connections to each other as well as a life of their own.

Although we cannot see the components of social structures, we can see their sometimes very powerful effects. For example, we cannot

Emile Durkheim (Bettmann/Corbis)

see or touch a norm of team loyalty or a role of a team member, but we know that for teams with high degrees of team loyalty, athletes may be willing to make great sacrifices of their bodies and perhaps their careers to help the team achieve success. They make these sacrifices because they have learned during their socialization into their role as a member of their team and as a result of interaction with their teammates and coach that the team comes first and that full membership on the team depends on accepting and conforming to such shared norms. When athletes are perceived as not being "team players" on teams that value the norm of team loyalty and sacrifice, they are likely to face pressures and other repercussions that reflect the disapproval of their coach and teammates and are meant to bring their behavior into line with the team norms.

Thus, social structures do not merely exist. They have *functions* or purposes and consequences. Returning to our metaphor of the body, each structure in the body as well as the overall body structure contributes to the life, vitality, and orderly organization of the body as a source of human life. Similarly, in society, social structures, such as social institutions of the family, government, the economy, and religion, contribute to the life, vitality, and orderly organization of the society. With the image of a healthy body in mind, we can imagine society to be a social system with a stable set of interrelated parts or structural components that work together to ensure the health and well-being of the entire system. In fact, one of the most prominent structural functional theorists of the twentieth century, Talcott Parsons (1951), wrote about society as a social system. The basic structural functional assumptions and questions are about how various parts of society become structured and contribute to social stability, social order, cultural consensus about core values and beliefs, and the survival of the society as a whole or specific social systems in society, such as groups and organizations.

Loy and Booth (2000) provided an overview of the various types of structural functionalism, considered contributions of functionalism to sport sociology, challenged the assertions that sport sociology has been dominated by a functionalist perspective and that the concept of a function is inherently or necessarily conservative, and briefly discussed new forms of structural functionalism and how they have been applied to the study of sport (see also Loy and Booth 2002). Sport sociologists might use a structural functional perspective to study how sports participation socializes us by teaching us how to conform to established social norms or expectations for our behavior, such as team or group loyalty, or how to act in socially acceptable ways in social roles in society. Another example of a structural functional analysis of sport might be an explanation of the contribution to society and social stability that comes from excluding girls from more aggressive forms of team sports. This practice teaches a socialization lesson about appropriate gender roles, which reinforces traditional ideas about gender and gender roles and helps maintain established gender-differentiated structures in society. Loy and Booth also pointed to a more radical use of structural functional analysis by Harry Edwards (1969), who used this analytical framework as the basis for advocating a radical restructuring of the basic social patterns and practices in U.S. sport, especially as they contributed to racial discrimination against black athletes.

Although structural functionalism could be used to understand even radical social change, the kind of more typical structural functional perspective we have outlined here tends to assume that societal stability, order, consensus, and the survival of the existing structures of society are normal, expected, and necessary and beneficial for society. The idea of conflict as a typical part of society tends to be relatively absent from more classic forms of structural functionalism derived from Durkheim (Loy and Booth 2002:56). The thrust of this kind of perspective is quite different from the basic thrust of social conflict theory. Whereas structural functionalism might be understood in terms of the metaphor of a healthy body with all the organs working in harmony, social conflict theory could be understood in terms of the metaphor of a body of water that is periodically or routinely roiled or disturbed by a riptide, heavy winds, a storm, or some other source of turbulence. With the metaphor of the body of water, we get the sense that a period of calm is likely to be temporary, always subject to possible disruption.

Social conflict theorists tend to assume that consensus does not or should not exist in society and that stability, order, and the survival of dominant societal structures are precarious. Based on the ideas of Karl Marx (see Marx and Engels 1978), social conflict theory assumes that the normal state of affairs in society is tension between major economic interests or classes. In capitalist societies, these major classes are the dominant capitalist class of owners of the resources used in industrial production and the subordinate class of industrial workers, who are exploited by the capitalist owners and are paid less than their work is worth and as little as possible so that the capitalists can earn as much profit as possible. According to Marx, this fundamental clash of class interests will ultimately result in a revolutionary conflict by workers to overthrow the capitalist class when workers develop a collective consciousness of their true class interest of revolution and subsequently organize to engage in this revolution. This revolution was seen as a means of establishing a classless society with no fundamental economic differences among people and where technology and the productive process would be harnessed to meet the basic needs of all people.

Karl Marx (Library of Congress)

This is an oversimplification of Marx's theory of class conflict, but it is useful in conveying the different image of society typically advanced by conflict theorists in contrast to structural functionalists. Both are *macro* perspectives in that they focus on whole societies on a broad scale. However, unlike structural functionalists, conflict theorists focus on basic differences in interests and values as well as the ever-present possibility and eventual likelihood of instability and disorder brought about by revolution, which is assumed to lead to a totally transformed structure of society. Thus, instead of posing assumptions and questions about what brings people together or integrates them and makes society work effectively for people in general, as structural functionalists do, social conflict theorists pose assumptions and questions about what divides people and how dominant groups exploit or oppress less economically advantaged and less powerful segments of society to further their own interests. The case of salary caps, or limits on players' salaries in professional sports leagues, further demonstrates the differences between structural functional and social conflict perspectives. While structural functionalists might view salary caps as necessary for maintaining the financial viability of a sports league, conflict theorists are more likely to see them as a tool serving the class interests of owners who want to limit player salaries so that they can maximize their own profits.

A variety of Marxist, neo-Marxist, feminist, and other critical perspectives have been applied to the study of sport (e.g., Andrews 2000; Beamish 2002; Birrell 2000; Rigauer 2000; Thompson 2002). While not necessarily explicitly rooted in classic Marxism, contemporary critical and feminist theories incorporate elements of Marxist conflict theory in their emphases on conflicts or struggles over ideology, status, power, or economic advantage involving minorities and women. Unlike structural functionalists, who see existing social and cultural patterns in terms of their functional value to an entire group, organization, society, or other social system, social conflict, critical, and feminist theorists tend to see these patterns in terms of how they are related to the particular interests of different social classes or strata or how they reinforce the dominance of the dominant class or social stratum. Thus, sport sociologists influenced by structural functionalism focus on the things that bring people together in society and serve society's interests, while social conflict theorists focus on the things that divide people and serve the particular economic, social, or political interests of different social classes. Social conflict, critical, and feminist theorists tend to make assumptions and ask questions about how and why existing structures in society advantage certain social classes, races, or ethnic groups over others or advantage men over women. They also focus on the conditions under which the disadvantages, exploitation, or oppression associated with economic, political, and social inequalities can be challenged and changed and society can be made more fair or just.

Contemporary Marxist critiques of sport and the critical analyses of sport based on neo-Marxist ideas generally share Marx's critique of capitalist society and its processes of domination and exploitation of workers and his idea that political structures are intimately intertwined with economic structures in patterns of political economy. They also reflect Marx's influence in their belief that the subordination of working people in society and in sport needed to be eliminated by a transformation of the inequalities embedded in capitalist structures. However, as Beamish (2002:28) observed, *neo-Marxist critical theorists* have tended to drift from Marx's basic focus on how capitalism and the pursuit of profit lead to worker dehumanization and exploitation. Instead, they have emphasized other forms and sources of dehumanization and exploitation, as in Rigauer's (1981) analysis of how processes of scientific rationality to improve efficiency and performance exploit workers and athletes in modern society and sport. Other critiques of sport have taken off from this point of departure, as in Hoberman's (1992) analysis linking the evolution of "scientific sport" to the values of industrial technology, which has led to the dehumanizing treatment of athletes as "mortal engines." Thus, an appropriate metaphor for neo-Marxist critical theory might be of robots and particularly of athletes as robots.

Feminist critiques of sport have also departed from classic Marxist assumptions in centrally focusing on the structures and ideologies of subordination, exploitation, and oppression of women rooted in patriarchy or male dominance and on the implications of these structures for women in sport. A relevant metaphor for this perspective is the 1970s television situation comedy *All in the Family*. It marked a sharp break from earlier programming about families, such as the classic 1950s program *Father Knows Best*, which portrayed a very traditional midwestern family with the traditional roles of the father as breadwinner and the mother as housewife. *All in the Family* challenged the view that families had to be patriarchal, with the husband and father clearly the dominant figure in the household—that is, the view that "father knows best." Feminists typically assume that this kind of patriarchal family structure represents and reinforces the gender inequalities that they criticize. *All in the Family* could be seen as a metaphor for the feminist critique of patriarchy because Archie Bunker, the would-be patriarch in the Bunker family, was treated as an object of humor and even ridicule for his sexist (and racist) views. His somewhat goofy wife, whom Archie called "Dingbat," strikes us as calmer and wiser than her outspoken, bigoted, and misinformed or uninformed husband. Archie also has to face a steady stream of questions and criticisms from his very liberal daughter and son-in-law. This is a family obviously caught up in the massive societal and cultural changes of the 1970s, and its experiences represent the challenge of feminists and other critical theorists to the established structures of gender inequality and other types of inequality in society.

Major feminist theorists in sport sociology (e.g., Birrell 1988) have generally agreed that Ann Hall's monograph on sport and gender in 1978 was the first major attempt to apply modern feminist ideas to the study of sport (Hall 1978). Since then, we have seen a continuing series of feminist publications about sport (see Birrell 2000). As Shona Thompson (2002) observed, feminists shifted the way questions were being posed about gender, women, and sport. For example, the more traditional question "Why do women display limited interest in sports?" might be reframed by feminists as "How and why have women been prevented from participating in various kinds of sports?" Or, feminists might shift the focus from "How has Title IX threatened the existence of men's non-revenue intercollegiate sports?" to "What are the sources of continuing resistance to the full implementation of Title IX and gender equity in high school and college athletics?" In addition, feminists direct our attention to other questions about a variety of gender-related social issues in sport, such as ongoing sexism, gender discrimination, and male dominance in sport; sexist media images and discourses about female athletes and their bodies; homophobia and lesbian athletes; and sexual exploitation and abuse of women by male athletes. Feminist critiques generally state or imply the need for restructuring sport to reduce or eliminate gender inequalities and sexist beliefs and treatment of women in sport, and many suggest or advocate an agenda for change.

Symbolic interactionists present a third, and significantly different, type of theoretical perspective for understanding social behavior. Unlike structural functionalism and various social conflict and critical theories, it focuses on the *micro* level of society, where individuals and groups directly interact with one another. Symbolic interactionists tend to be less concerned with uncovering the causes that predict patterns of large-scale social behavior than they are with providing rich and detailed descriptions of the patterns of everyday social life. Symbolic interaction refers to the construction and exchange of meanings in social interaction through which we define ourselves, our roles, and our experiences in society. This emphasis on symbolic interaction derives from the work of Charles Horton Cooley at the turn of the twentieth century and the work of George Herbert Mead a few decades later. This perspective focuses on how we form ideas about ourselves, understand others' expectations for us that are embedded in social roles, and perceive the expectations of society that are incorporated in social norms, ranging from informal everyday rules for interaction to highly formalized regulations and laws.

We are able to think about ourselves, others, and the larger society in terms of the symbols represented in language, and we use talk and other forms of communication to develop or negotiate mutually acceptable ways of referring to each other and interacting with each other. Of course, people with higher status and more power can exert more influence on how they and other people are labeled and treated in society. Higher-status and more powerful people may react to others they like or respect with recognition, admiration, affection, or other positive forms of attention, sentiment, or status, which can help these others become more accepted or successful in established social circles. For example, consider the value to a high school soccer player of being blessed as a "future star" by a prominent college or professional coach. On the other hand, people with high status and considerable power also can impose negative or deviant labels on those they do not like or respect, who threaten them, or who disagree with them. Imagine being a college football star who is criticized as having a "bad attitude" or being lazy by a major scouting service or by prominent sports columnists prior to the draft by the National Football League. Negative or deviant labels can be difficult to shed when those who are labeled have less status and power than those imposing the label, and like positive labels they can have significant effects on how we are treated, the opportunities we have in society, and even how we think of ourselves.

Cooley (1961) discussed the formation and development of the self—or the sense of who we are—as a social process in which we use others as a mirror and try to see who they think we are. Mead (1934) developed the idea of self-consciousness, and proposed a dynamic process of internal or symbolic conversation between our acting selves and our reflective selves, in which we are capable of looking at ourselves and our actions objectively, or in a detached manner, from the perspective of others. Contemporary symbolic interactionists study various forms and aspects of social behavior in great detail to understand more about how we "construct" reality and give meaning to it through our symbolic interaction.

A prominent example of a contemporary interactionist perspective is Erving Goffman's (1959, 1967) *dramaturgical* approach to the study of everyday life, which conceptualizes social life as theater. On the stage of this theater of life, we perform as if we were actors playing roles. Goffman assumed that we actively and intentionally create and negotiate "scripts" for our interactions that are meant to make positive impressions on others and make social relations go as smoothly as possible, as in a well-scripted and well-performed play. An important conceptual distinction in Goffman's perspective is the difference between "front stage" and "back stage" behavior. For example, professional athletes perform on the front stage of athletic fields and sports arenas, where they are observed in action by spectators, television viewers, sports reporters, and many others who form impressions of these athletes as competitors. These athletes also interact with boosters, fans, and the press in assorted other public venues off the field. What makes these settings front stage settings is the wide visibility of the athletes' performances and the careful construction and management of impressions by the athletes, who play their roles as sports stars and role models. We expect these athletes to conform to our expectations of what professional athletes are, and these athletes often try to follow this script. Their behavior is not restricted to the front stage, however. They also act more informally, and sometimes "out of character," on the back stages of the closed locker room, their homes, and other private venues where they do not expect the public to see them. At times, we learn things about athletes that reveal substantial discrepancies between their public selves, seen only in front stage areas, and their private selves, played out on the back stages of these athletes' lives. For example, those who saw O.J. Simpson as a sport hero and embodiment of the American Dream who entertained us after his football career was over by running through airports in televised ads for a car rental company were shocked and dismayed to learn that he had allegedly been engaged in violent or murderous behavior in his personal life. We can understand in this context why professional athletes might be wary of the close scrutiny of the public and especially probing sports reporters, who are interested in learning more about the back stage of athletes' lives.

We can use Cooley's metaphor of the mirror and Goffman's metaphor of the theatrical stage to represent major forms of symbolic interactionism. They contrast with the metaphorical references to the human body (structural functionalism), a turbulent body of water (social conflict theory), a robot (neo-Marxist critical theory), or "All in the Family" (feminism). They should help us see more clearly the differences between symbolic interactionism and each of the other types of perspectives. The mirror suggests a certain amount of detachment as we step back to observe how others might see us and how we should look at ourselves. From Mead's perspective, the mirror shows us an image of ourselves that we can modify to create an impression on others we want them to see. In the various symbolic interactionist approaches, we see a common emphasis on how the self and patterns of social interaction are constructed, negotiated, and reconstructed and renegotiated in everyday life. Indeed, these perspectives assume that everyday life is largely about finding or establishing meanings of the self and social interaction that either are mutually acceptable or are imposed by more powerful people and groups on those who are less powerful.

Sport sociologists have used a symbolic interactionist approach to study many aspects of sport. For example, in a classic study of failure in sport, Donald Ball (1976) observed how athletes interpret and cope with being cut in different professional sports and how the person who delivers the news (called the "grim reaper" on some teams) interacts with the person targeted to be cut. He found that in sports such as baseball, in which players cut from Major League rosters are "sent down" to a minor league team, players were likely to experience this failure as a form of degradation or embarrassment as a "deadman" or "nonperson." Teammates, especially those who felt insecure about their own status and wanted to maintain their confidence, often avoided them as if they were social outcasts or lepers. In contrast, players who were cut in sports without a lower tier or minor league to which cut players are sent, such as professional football, did not experience as much humiliation or embarrassment as players in two-tiered sports because they typically were out of the public eye after being cut. They tended to be treated with relatively more sympathy by teammates than their counterparts in baseball were. Ball's study is distinctive in its focus on the micro level of social interaction and on how social or cultural contexts shape people's experiences and how they think about, evaluate, and label them. In general, symbolic interactionists share the basic approach of all interpretive sociologists in their primary focus on "human agency," or how we actively construct and reconstruct social reality in an ongoing process of social negotiation (Donnelly 2002). This perspective contrasts with more structural approaches, such as structural functionalism and some forms of conflict theory, which place more emphasis on how established social structures of social norms, roles, relationships, and networks constrain or limit our perceived choices for action in society.

The classical and contemporary theoretical perspectives we have considered so far convey a sense of the richness of sociological theory and the variety of ways of looking at and understanding society and sport. In fact, books of sociological theory are filled with many other distinctive ways of theorizing about society. They include theories that concentrate on the micro level of everyday social relations and those that take a sweeping view of whole societies and their global relations. There are also frameworks that try to integrate different theoretical perspectives and ideas. We will conclude this overview of sociological theory with brief summaries of theories that have emphasized rationality in modern society or have looked at the problematic nature of rationality in postmodern societies. We will also briefly consider how social network analysis enables us to understand what social structures are and to see how social relations are structured in sport and society. A fuller understanding of social structures is very important in trying to grasp how many social theorists have looked at the social world.

Sociologists have been interested in rationality in modern societies since Max Weber drew attention to rational-legal authority and its role in bureaucracies (see Ritzer 2003:26–34). The rationalization of society includes emphases on scientific or technical calculation, efficiency, impersonality and formal structure, standardization, planning, and prediction. *Rational choice* and *social exchange theorists* focus on how people make choices in their relationships with others on the basis of their self-interest. They assume that we are calculating actors in our social relations, who try to get the best "deal" for ourselves, ranging from an employment contract or salary to a marital arrangement.

An emphasis on rationality characterized Max Weber's classic conception of modern society and the dominant form of organization in modern

Max Weber (Photo by Hulton Archive/Getty Images)

society, bureaucracy. Rational ideas about social organization were applied in management by advocates of Frederick Taylor's "scientific management" approach in the early twentieth century (called Taylorism) and of Henry Ford's use of the assembly line in his automobile factories (called Fordism). In the first chapter, we considered how George Ritzer (1993) applied Weberian ideas of rational organization to conceptualize a dominant form of organization in the late twentieth century, *McDonaldization*, which has been spreading its influence around the world through the globalization of culture and the economy. Oriard (1993:43) drew an interesting parallel between Frederick Taylor's scientific management approach to industrial production and Walter Camp's approach to U.S. football. Walter Camp was responsible for the initial development and popularization of the modern game of football in the United States. His annual college football "All America" lists during the first quarter of the twentieth century became part of the official lore of the sport, and such lists are now a source of great prestige for players. Oriard pointed out that in developing football, Camp emphasized the importance of scientific planning in various aspects of the game, such as creating plays, training regimens, and methods of coordinating team play on the field. Camp's scientific management approach contrasted with more aristocratic approaches to sport at the time that emphasized the "amateur spirit," sportsmanship, recreation, and informality (Smart 2005:32). Echoing Weber's concerns about the possible dehumanizing effects of rational organizations, Ritzer (1993:145) has expressed concern that McDonaldization could stifle individual freedom, creativity, and flexibility as people rigidly conform to the systems and strategies they have created to make their organizations more efficient and productive. A simple example is the established pattern in football today of sending plays to the quarterback instead of permitting him to call plays on his own. Ritzer called this loss of human control over their organizations the "irrationality of rationality."

While a number of sport sociologists have expressed concerns about various excesses of scientific or bureaucratic rationality in modern sport, as it increasingly relies on new rational strategies and technologies to increase human performance, some observers of contemporary sport have pointed to the reluctance of management in some sports to rely on a rational approach in making key decisions, such as the recruitment, hiring, trading, and firing of players. Michael Lewis's (2003) book *Moneyball* is about how the maverick general manager of the Oakland Athletics, Billy Beane, achieved success on the field despite a relatively small budget by defying tradition and basing his personnel decisions on the rational use of statistics rather than the intuitive judgment of experienced scouts, managers, and other "baseball people" in Major League Baseball.

While Billy Beane's highly rational actions could be seen as a kind of McDonaldization, they are probably more precisely characterized as a rational choice approach to his sport. James Coleman is largely responsible for the popularization of the rational choice model of human behavior in social science and sociology (Ritzer 2003:166–169). Coleman established the scholarly journal *Rationality and Society* in 1989 and wrote a book titled *Foundations of Social Theory* (1990), which presents his conception of rational choice theory. He has assumed that people are rational actors who intentionally try to achieve goals that are consistent with their preferences or values, and he emphasized the important role of objective constraints on our efforts to achieve our goals. Two major sources of constraint in his theory are the resources that are accessible to us and that we can control and the limitations on our actions posed by the rules, regulations, laws, or other norms of the various social institutions and organizations that affect us. Since this perspective assumes that rational actors try to make choices that are most likely to lead to their most preferred outcomes or goals, it should be apparent that having good information about available options and where they will lead is crucial to making rational choices. In Billy Beane's case, he was especially interested in using the best available baseball statistics as a basis for his decisions. Athletes and coaches who rely on the latest advances in exercise science, nutrition, sports medicine, and performance products and technologies reflect a rational approach to sports performance—and perhaps are intentionally or unintentionally creating the mortal engines that Hoberman (1992) analyzed.

In this age of proliferating information, however, we can imagine how easy it is to be overwhelmed by information or how difficult it could be to gain access to all of the information that might be relevant to our choices. None of us is likely to have perfect information for making rational choices. Coleman realized that people do not always act rationally (Ritzer 2003:169), but his perspective enables us to understand how, or the extent to which, rational ideas, resources, and structural constraints may affect the actions of the various "social actors" and decision makers in sport and elsewhere in society. His perspective also gives us insights into the behavior of various social actors in sport, from general managers such as Billy Beane to the multitude of coaches, trainers, athletes, and other social actors in the many realms of high-performance sport, and this perspective helps us understand the rationale and implications of their actions and decisions. Of course, choices and actions that might seem rational in the short term to athletes and other social actors in sport, such as trading for an aging star, engaging in risky training regimens, using dubious or illegal performance-enhancing substances, or placing bets, may have adverse consequences and be viewed as unwise or irrational in the longer term.

Rational choice theory in sociology bears the imprint of economic models of rational actors and is related to social exchange theories derived from "rat psychology" and social behaviorism that emphasize the pursuit of rewards and the avoidance of punishments or costs in human interaction. In one prominent version of social exchange theory, formulated by George Homans (1961, 1974), human behavior is explained in terms of a series of assumptions or "propositions" about how people intentionally and rationally seek to profit—that is, derive more rewards than costs—from their interactions with others. Rational choice and exchange theories provide ways of thinking about how our everyday interactions and decisions are constructed and become patterned. These theories direct our attention to questions about our efforts to act rationally or negotiate rational exchanges in our relations with other social actors. However, they also raise questions—which these theorists may or may not address—about how our efforts to act rationally are blocked, constrained, or facilitated by large-scale cultural forces such as religious or economic beliefs or large-scale social structural factors such as the cumbersome procedures or inefficiencies of big bureaucracies. Although actual efforts to be rational can be sidetracked in various ways, it still may be useful to think of rational choice theories in terms of the metaphor of a computer or a calculator, which operates according to precisely defined rules and has access to all the information it needs to produce precisely predictable results.

While rationality and rationalization are the focus of a number of contemporary critical analyses of sport, there is little or no evidence of the specific influence of rational choice or exchange theories on recent theoretical thinking in sport sociology (e.g., see Maguire and Young 2002). However, money, commercialism, and other economic factors seem to motivate much of the behavior in high-level sports today, and sports management programs seem to be proliferating in universities in the United States and other countries today. For these reasons, rational choice and exchange theories could be useful lenses for trying to understand how and why decisions are made in sport by the new sports managers, such as Billy Beane, who will increase their influence as sport becomes more rationalized. Rational choice models may be especially useful in drawing attention to the intentions, preferences, or values of social actors in sport, as well as to the social structural and cultural factors that prevent or distract some people from achieving what they want and enable others to get what they want. In Beane's case, he eventually realized that his small-budget approach had its rational limitations and that instead of letting his star players go when they became a lot more expensive, he had to respond to the marketplace and sign these players to multiyear, multi-million-dollar contracts to remain competitive. He realized that it was more rational to retain players who had established their value to the team than to let them go and take a chance on developing promising and less expensive, but unproven, talent.

While social theorists may argue about the direction of modern society or modern sport, for example, about whether society and sport are becoming too rational or are not rational enough, some social critics have argued that we have moved beyond the structures and culture of modern society created by rationalization, industrialization, bureaucratization, and related social processes. That is, they have argued that we have moved to a post-structural or postmodern era of great skepticism among intellectuals and others about the social processes that created modern society. The growth of contemporary corporate sport has been linked to these processes of modernization, and hence, sport has faced the same kind of skepticism and criticism launched by post-structuralists and postmodernists toward modern society in general (Andrews 2000). This kind of critical theory points to problems of modern societies and sport associated with structural and cultural emphases on order, individualism, rationality, objectivity, scientific progress, democracy, meritocracy, and violence. Focusing on the failure of modernism to create a more understandable and just world in which people live more meaningful and fulfilling lives, post-structural and postmodern analyses have constructed very different lenses for seeing society and sport than previously established social theories have offered. Although there are numerous variants of post-structural and postmodern thinking and there is some danger in wedding post-structural and postmodern analyses, we will label these various critiques of modern society as forms of *postmodernism*. An appropriate metaphor for postmodernism, which represents the presumed elusiveness of meaning in post-structural or postmodern society, might be a murky pond where we cannot see our own image or what lies beneath the surface.

According to Andrews (2000), who favored the language of "post-structuralism," these critical perspectives represent a new way of thinking about sport and doing sport sociology. He suggested that these perspectives shift our attention away from the structural analyses of both functionalism and Marxism and away from neo-Marxist and other structural critiques of modern society that focus on the intertwining of the political and the economic in political economy, the dominance of large-scale rational organizations of the modern state and economy, the influence of modern culture, and the various political, economic, and social inequalities of the postmodern era. Instead, our attention shifts to issues of the body, sexuality, identity, consumerism, and humanistic concerns in medicine, science, and technology in a world in which meaning is often ambiguous and little is certain. Furthermore, postmodern perspectives in the sociology of sport would draw our attention to the declining influence of history as we are bombarded with a steady stream of new images and stories produced by the mass media, which sometimes create confusion about what is real and what is fantasy. In this context, subjectivity has a powerful influence over language and social relations in society and sport.

The lens of postmodernism presents us with a picture of a highly diverse and complex world where there seems to be little agreement about the direction we are heading. This is a picture of a world where we engage in ongoing and intense cultural debates or struggles over whose values or interests should prevail, and it is a picture of a world where the meanings we construct come from a continuing stream of ideas and images manufactured by mass media interested primarily in their own profits. Thus, contrary to the materialist thrust of Marxist theory and other structural critiques of modern (capitalist) society and their assumed centrality of the economic conditions of society, postmodernists tend to focus more on the importance of ideas and images in the modern world. Where this mediated world has become dominated by the new technologies of the Internet, we seem to respond more to fantasy or "virtual" constructions than to concrete things and real people. In sports, for example, there has been an increasing interest in fantasy leagues, and sometimes it is difficult to separate the fantastic from the real.

Table 2.1 shows the metaphorical images, key ideas, and key questions about sport that distinguish the major theoretical perspectives we have considered in this chapter. Each provides a distinctive way of understanding society and sport. These perspectives do not entirely represent the rich theoretical diversity of sociology or sport sociology, but they underscore the importance of avoiding a single interpretation of what we think we see in sport or what researchers have learned about sport. Sometimes these perspectives offer contradictory or very different lenses for seeing society and sport, but rather than confuse us, they should help us recognize the complexity of human behavior as we try to make sense of what we see, hear, or read about society and sport. The challenge is to construct descriptions and explanations of sport that are consistent with systematically produced research findings and with established facts.

Despite the criticisms of modernism and structural thinking advanced by postmodernism, we will focus on the structural patterns and social and cultural meanings and practices associated with contemporary modern sport. We will rely on a mix of structural functional, conflict, critical, symbolic interactionist, and rational choice perspectives that help us see and understand these aspects of sport. We will not ignore the postmodernist criticisms, however.

42

Table 2.1 Theoretical Perspectives in Sociology and Sport Sociology

Theory	Metaphor	Key Ideas	Major Sports Questions
Structural Functionalism	Healthy human body	Structure * Functions * Purposes * Social stability * Social order * Societal integration * Cultural consensus * Societal or social system survival	How is the institution of sport integrated into society? How do the structure and culture of sport contribute to the structural and cultural stability of society? How does socialization into sport help participants learn traditional gender roles? How do player strikes disrupt the stability of a sport?
Social Conflict Theory	Stormy or turbulent body of water	Structures of inequality * Dominant and subordinate social classes * Societal tensions * Social instability * Social conflict * Social change	How do owners and coaches exploit athletes in a sport or on a team? How does a salary cap reflect the interests of owners in a sports league? How do players' strikes represent battles between the interests of owners and the interests of players?
Neo-Marxist Critical Theory	Athlete as robot	Domination * Inequalities * Worker dehumanization * Worker exploitation * Scientific rationality	How are athletes exploited and dehumanized by processes of scientific rationality in modern sport? What are the major forms of domination and inequality in modern sport?
Feminism	*All in the Family*	Patriarchy and male privilege * Gender inequality * Sexist gender ideology	How and why have women been prevented from participating in various kinds of sports? How and why are resources allocated unequally for men and women in sport? How does sexist ideology contribute to patterns of prejudice and discrimination against women in sport? What are the sources of continued resistance to gender equity in sport?
Symbolic Interactionism	Mirror and theatrical stage	Self and social interaction as social constructions * Impression management * Everyday life as social performance * Negotiating meanings of self and social relations * Social labeling	How are athletes labeled by the mass media, the public, their coaches, and others, and how do these labels affect their sense of self and how they perform their roles? What are the most powerful symbols in culture and social relations in sport that shape the meaning of sport, sports roles, and sports experiences?

continues

Theory	Metaphor	Key Ideas	Major Sports Questions
			Who are the significant others who are most influential in shaping the self and social experiences of athletes and other social actors in sport? How do the mass media create and destroy heroes? How do social actors in sport construct and renegotiate norms, roles, and relationships and make their sports experiences meaningful through everyday interactions? What does it mean to be an athlete, and how do athletes reconstruct their identity when they leave their athlete role?
Rational Choice	Computer or calculator	Self-interest * Rationality or reason * Social exchange * Science * Calculation * Efficiency * Predictability * Planning * Using information effectively * Scientific management * McDonaldization	What are the "best deals" that athletes can negotiate with management and their coaches? What are the most rational choices for social actors in sport? How can sports be rationally organized and controlled to make them more efficient, productive, and profitable? How can technology contribute to greater success in sport for athletes, teams, and organizations? How can we make the outcomes of sports contests more predictable?
Postmodernism	The murky pond	The failures of modernity * Limits of scientific progress * Ambiguity of issues of the body, sexuality, identity, and consumerism * Declining influence of history * Subjectivity * Contested terrain * Diversity * Social and cultural complexity * Uncertainty about the future * Virtual realities	What are the limitations and problems of scientific rationality and progress in sport today? What are the major cultural debates, battles, and lines of division in sport today? What major ideas and images shape contemporary sports experiences, and what is the role of the mass media in shaping these ideas and images? How are the new media, from real-time streaming video to interactive Internet experiences to fantasy leagues, reshaping traditional conceptions of sports participation? What is the relationship between reality and fantasy in the mediated world of contemporary sport?

These perspectives will be especially useful in helping us to see and understand the major forces of change that are shaping and reshaping sport and society. In combination, they will enable us to focus on sport and society from the micro level of social relationships to the macro levels of interactions between and among leagues, sports, and even nations on the athletic field. We will view sport as a global corporate structure dominated by the Golden Triangle, whose primary social actors compete on a variety of "stages," from the local level to international venues such as the Olympics and the World Cup of soccer. A critical factor we will examine in the "big-time" contexts of contemporary sport is the mass media, which both shapes and uses sport, and is a major "player" in the Golden Triangle. Sociological imagination will enable us to see how the mass media and the Golden Triangle operate in sport and influence it in the various historical, social, and cultural contexts in which sport is embedded.

Social Network Analysis

An interest in social structure directs our attention to enduring social arrangements that link people, the positions they occupy, and the groups, organizations, and larger social bodies to which we belong. Through *social network analysis* (Nixon 2002), we can see the basic structural "skeleton" of sport and society. We can also trace the influence of various kinds of resources and social processes that link us in social networks. For example, we can trace the flow of sentiments, resources, and influence through social networks. Major sentiments include love, friendship, deference, and respect, along with enmity, envy, and debasement. Major resources may vary from abstract symbols, such as shared values, to material things, such as money and property, to physical force or its threatened use. Influence processes include persuasion, inducement, and authority and power. Sentiments, resources, and influence flow through our social relations, define their content or character, and affect how they change.

If we wanted to find out the friendship networks of athletes at a particular college or university, we could ask the athletes who their closest friends are and then diagram the friendship links or ties of these athletes on the basis of the sentiments they express about close friends. On a number of campuses, we are likely to find that athletes are most likely to choose other athletes on their campus, which suggests that athletes may not be well integrated into the general student subculture on their campus. The links in their friendship networks are likely to be limited to contacts with others in the athletic subculture or their specific sport. For their book *The Game of Life: College Sports and Educational Values*, Shulman and Bowen (2001) studied students recruited as athletes at public and private Division I universities, Division IAA Ivy League institutions, and Division III colleges and universities. They found in essentially all sports and at all competitive levels, including Division III coed liberal arts colleges, that these athletes tended to segregate themselves into networks of athletes, which constituted an "athletic subculture" on campus. These networks tended to place more emphasis on athletics than on academics and other values and not to be strongly linked to faculty members. The combination of limited contacts with the general student body and subcultural values that did not emphasize academic performance helps explain why these athletes did not perform as well academically as their high school grades and standardized test scores predicted they would. Since Shulman and Bowen's sample was skewed toward athletes at elite institutions, it is not surprising that these athletes tended to graduate, but their concern was about how the values emphasized in their segregated social networks and the narrowness of their social contacts limited their academic opportunities and diversity of experiences or chances to learn how to interact with people having different backgrounds, interests, values, and attitudes than themselves.

The social networks that interest sport sociologists link athletes, other social actors in sport, and their organizations to each other and to the larger society. At this stage of history, many people who study sport are especially interested in how sport and society are linked through the mass media (Raney and Bryant 2006). We have seen the growing influence of the new media such as the Internet, as well as "older" mass media and other global communication systems, on people and organizations in sport. These media provide valuable resources such as visibility, information, and money to support the popular and commercial growth of modern sports. They facilitate the growth of many sports as global enterprises, as people are able to follow athletes and teams competing many thousands of miles away.

Network analysis enables us to trace global linkages and influences and the flows of resources through sports networks. For example, young men who play basketball in African villages may become connected through local coaches or teachers to recruiters for college teams in the United States and as a result may move to the United States to become part of the social world of NCAA college basketball. This process of global migration, which connects the United States and U.S. basketball to other countries through processes of cultural diffusion and competitive or commercial growth, indicates how extensive networks can be in sport and society. We will be especially interested in considering how powerful social forces such as globalization in contemporary societies are creating, sustaining, expanding, and otherwise changing the major sports networks of our time and how people interact with each other in these sports networks. The social network of primary interest throughout this book is the Golden Triangle, which consists of social, economic, and political relations linking powerful individuals and organizations in corporate commercialized sport to the sports media and the corporate sponsors that invest in sport. The nature of the major actors and their relations in the Golden Triangle will be discussed in the most detail in chapter ten, about the professional sports industry, but we will see that the Golden Triangle also shapes sports in many other realms, including youth, high school, college, and Olympic sports.

Social Research Methods

We observed earlier that social research methods exist alongside social theories as core elements of sociology. In the early years of sport sociology in the 1960s, what we knew and taught about sport and society tended to rely on the work of anthropologists, historians, and journalists. Sociologists who studied sport generally did not identify themselves as sport sociologists in the early years of the

Renel Brooks-Moon was the first woman to announce a World Series game when she covered the 2002 game between the San Francisco Giants and Anaheim Angels at Pacific Bell Park in San Francisco. As a media representative, she was part of the Golden Triangle, which also included Pacific Bell as a corporate-sponsor partner of the Giants. (AP Photo/ Kevork Djansezian)

emerging sport sociology discipline. Systematic research about sport and society in those early years tended to be limited and scattered in focus. In one of the early anthologies of work in sport sociology (Loy and Kenyon 1969), we find a diverse array of studies, including ones about the culture of physical activities and games, witchcraft in Pueblo baseball, the popularity of various types of sports and physical recreation in different nations, social inequality and social mobility of participants in different types of sports, the importance of sport in the status systems of U.S. adolescents, the relationship between the characteristics of British coaches and when they adopted new training methods, the occupational culture of boxing, the relative likelihood of competitive success—or winning—of sports teams with different group characteristics, and the relationship of the positions baseball players played and their amount of on-field interaction with other players to their chances of becoming field managers.

A fairly substantial body of research literature has been produced by self-identified sport sociologists since the early years of the discipline in the 1960s. In some areas, there have been numerous studies, which make sport sociologists more confident about what they can say about the social world of sport. There remain many gaps in the literature about important social aspects and issues of sport, however, and we will point to those areas as well, indicating what remains to be done to make fairly confident generalizations about these aspects and issues. The theoretical perspectives we considered earlier will enable us to make sense of the meaning of the social patterns that researchers have uncovered.

Sport sociologists often face the challenge of convincing students and the public that what they know about sport from their personal experiences may not be true or at least may need some qualification. At the same time, sport sociologists must acknowledge that there is much we do not know about sport and there is much more to learn. Students of sport sociology often seem more skeptical of what sport sociologists have learned than of what they have been taught about sport by coaches, teammates, or sports announcers, especially when their entrenched beliefs are challenged. People with a lot of experience in sport or a lot of information about the facts and trivia of sport often have difficulty thinking objectively about sport because they are so passionate about it and find it easier or more comfortable to accept myths, opinions, or unsubstantiated assertions rather than the careful systematic research of sport sociologists, who may challenge these myths, opinions, and assertions. Thus, sport sociologists must convince students and the broader public in sport and society that carefully formulated theories are a more systematic way of trying to understand and explain the realities of sport and society and that these realities are best understood on the basis of systematic social research.

We have considered a variety of major theoretical perspectives in sociology for understanding sport. In this section, we will consider an overview of various types of social research methods for collecting facts about the realities of sport and society. This overview is intended to raise questions and point to limitations about our ordinary ways of knowing and to show that the gathering of facts about social patterns in sport requires careful procedures that conform to well-defined rules that sport sociologists generally understand and follow. Sport sociologists can be fairly confident that we know the things we say we know when a number of different studies find similar results. Some research methods allow us to talk about cause and effect, which means that differences or changes in one factor, the cause, such as the type of reward structure of sports teams, lead to differences or changes in another factor, the effect, such as the amount of interpersonal attraction or friendship among team members or the level of competitive success of the team. Other research methods are less oriented to cause and effect and focus more on describing what social experiences or interactions mean to people. In this section, we will consider four of the major types of research methods that sport sociologists have used to collect data about the social world of sport: (1) experiments, (2) social surveys, (3) field studies, and (4) secondary data analysis (see Babbie 2007; Nixon and Frey 1996:297–305).

Experiments are a type of controlled observation in which hypotheses about cause-and-effect relationships are tested. Causal factors, called "independent variables," are factors assumed to produce changes in other factors, called "effects" or "dependent variables." In the example about sports teams, "type of reward structure of a sports team," which could be defined in terms of teams' having more or less unequal or hierarchical distributions of rewards, is the independent variable. As in our example, we could hypothesize that differences in this factor have effects on two dependent variables, amount of interpersonal attraction among teammates and level of competitive success. More specifically, on the basis of the best knowledge available, we might hypothesize—or make an "educated guess"—that professional teams with smaller differences between the top- and lowest-paid players have higher levels of interpersonal attraction and higher levels of competitive success than teams that have larger differences in their salary structure. We also could hypothesize that professional sports teams with less inequality in salaries will be more successful than teams with more salary inequality, if we assume that these teams are alike in other key respects, such as the average ability of players and the quality of coaching.

In experiments, researchers try to create conditions where groups are generally alike in all major respects except in terms of the independent variable, which the researcher manipulates. Imagine that we have created an experimental basketball league. The players are randomly assigned to different teams, which means that players on one team should generally be similar to players on other teams. Then, imagine that we pay the players after their first game. Half the teams have an equal distribution of pay, while the other half have an unequal distribution, with the top scorer in the game given more than the other players. In our imaginary experiment, the only major difference among teams in the league should be their reward structure. After teams play a second game, we can measure how much players say they like or dislike their teammates. We can also observe how well teams perform in their second game, that is, whether they win or lose and by how many points. If teams differ in their amount of interpersonal attraction and level of success in the direction predicted by the hypothesis—that is, teams with equal rewards like each other more and do better competitively than teams with unequal rewards, we can conclude that our hypothesis about the effects of type of reward structure on amount of interpersonal attraction and level of competitive success has been supported by the evidence.

If the results do not support our hypothesis, we must think about whether our experiment had flaws, such as a poor measure of one or more variables or failure to control other possible causal factors, including the ability or experience of players, which might have influenced the results. Or, if there were no major flaws in the design of the experiment, its execution, or our measures, we would interpret the results as casting doubt on our hypothesis. We would consider revising it and doing additional research to refine our understanding of how or whether the reward structure of teams influences interpersonal attraction among team members and the competitive success of the team. This imaginary experiment has some relationship to reality, since I constructed an experimental basketball league in my own research, but in this research I made team success the independent variable. This research was not a classic experiment, since I manipulated some of the conditions to which the subjects were exposed, but I did not manipulate the independent variable. I created a competition with winners and losers, so that teams that were more successful could be compared with teams that were less successful in relation to a number of specific dependent variables, including players' perceptions of the importance of friendly relations among team members, their perceptions of the actual level of friendliness among teammates, the importance of team membership (or cohesiveness), and the players' willingness at the end of the season to share a Most Valuable Player (MVP) monetary prize equally with teammates or give it to an individual, including themselves. Other aspects of this research were controlled, such as the random assignment of volunteer players to teams, having players fill out questionnaires at prescribed times during the season, and asking them to choose how to award a monetary prize at the end of the season. This research showed that more successful teams tended to value friendliness more, see themselves as more friendly, value team membership more, and be more willing to share rewards (Nixon 1976, 1977).

Classic experiments and even "quasi-experiments" such as my own have the advantage of controlling possible alternative causal factors, which makes interpreting the causal impact of the independent variable easier and gives us more confidence in drawing conclusions about our cause-and-effect hypothesis. It is also relatively easy for other researchers to try to replicate the results, since the procedures are very clearly and precisely spelled out. My own research and studies of the effects of team cohesiveness on team success (Martens and Peterson 1971) and of the effects of viewing aggressive sports on the hostility level of spectators (Arms, Russell, and Sandilands 1987) are among the relatively few examples of experimental research in sport sociology. Sport sociologists seldom do laboratory or natural experiments because it is difficult to simulate the full complexity of the social settings that interest them theoretically, especially when they are studying large social networks. It also is difficult or unethical to manipulate hypothetical causal factors in many cases. For example, one could not and would not want to create experimental conditions that tempt players to cheat to see whether they actually cheat, that encourage racism to see whether players or coaches display racism, or that promote violence to see whether athletes or fans act violently. Sport sociologists are much more likely to rely on other social research methods to collect data. One of these other methods is the social survey.

Social surveys enable researchers to make generalizations about large populations of people, organizations, or other social networks on the basis of information collected from only a portion of those people, organizations, or networks. According to probability theory, as long as researchers rely on *random samples* of members of the population of interest to them, which give all the members of these populations an equal chance of being included in the sample, they can expect that the major characteristics of the population of interest will be represented in their sample. Thus, randomly drawn representative samples of three thousand members of the U.S. population allow us to make generalizations about the entire population of nearly three hundred million people or major segments of it. Survey researchers use interviews or mailed questionnaires to collect standardized information about the social characteristics, attitudes, beliefs, or behavior of various types of people or about the characteristics of social relations in groups, organizations, or other social networks.

We are generally familiar with the methodology of survey research because so many organizations, including news departments of newspapers and television networks, political campaign organizations, and marketing departments of businesses, conduct surveys or polls of our attitudes, opinions, tastes, buying habits, and a variety of other things. When a Major League Baseball player or world champion bicycle racer is accused of using illegal, performance-enhancing drugs, public attitudes are surveyed by news organizations. Online technology makes possible instant surveys of our opinions, even about the outcome of a sports contest that is in progress.

While serious news organizations tend to be careful about relying on *scientific* surveys, which use random sampling methods, so that they can make accurate generalizations about what we think, feel, or do, organizations interested more in using surveys for entertainment purposes or to attract viewers or customers pay less attention to generating representative samples. We should be wary of generalizations based on nonrepresentative samples because the results may not accurately represent what all women or all men or all sports fans or all athletes or all sports executives or all members of a particular racial or ethnic group in a particular population think, feel, or do. For example, imagine that the website of a sports-oriented cable television network posts a question at two o'clock in the morning about whether there is too much, about enough, or too little coverage of women's sports on television. The next morning, it reports results indicating that "the American public" believes there is "about enough" television coverage of women's sports. These results would not be a systematic basis for drawing conclusions about what the U.S. public actually thinks or for making decisions about how much to cover women's sports on television. They could be *biased* in a number of ways, reflecting only the views of the visitors to the website at the time of night the question was posted. Thus, instead of representing the U.S. public or even the U.S. sports public in general, the results actually might disproportionately represent the views of college-age males awake late at night who have access to computers, are computer savvy, can afford an online connection, and are interested enough in sports to visit this website and answer the question. We may learn very little about the views of older sports fans; sports officials; women, including female athletes; people not affluent enough to own a computer or have a connection to the Internet; or other significant segments of the general public. We can judge the scientific value of a survey with certain crucial facts, such as how the sample was generated, how many people were sampled, and how representative of the population of interest the sample is.

A survey questionnaire with carefully constructed questions that is systematically administered to a sample of a targeted population can produce useful information about the population of interest and enable us to address significant research questions and social issues. For example, in the late 1970s, gender equity and female sports participation were significant issues. Traditionally, U.S. females had been excluded from most realms of sport as active participants, but Title IX of the Higher Education Act of 1972 had opened the door to girls and women in high school and college sports. Thus, it was an opportune time in the late 1970s to conduct a survey about public attitudes about females in sport.

In this context, two undergraduate students and I conducted a survey at two colleges to learn whether male and female students differed in their attitudes about the female opportunity structure in sport, females in traditionally male sports, and sports-related sex role socialization (Nixon, Maresca, and Silverman 1979). Perhaps not surprisingly, we found that female acceptance of females in sport tended to be substantially greater than male acceptance on most of the eleven attitude items, but it was noteworthy that a majority of males disagreed with the statements that females did not play sports well enough to justify equal facilities and equipment to males in high school and college, that participation opportunities in organized sport should be restricted mostly or entirely to males, that high school and college women should concentrate more on cheerleading and similar types of activities rather than on being athletes, and that girls and women should try extra hard to display their femininity if they participated in sports. No effort was made in this study to determine how strong the effect of sex or gender differences was on the attitudes that were surveyed. More elaborate survey designs and more sophisticated statistical procedures than we used in this attitudinal study can show the relative causal influence of particular variables on dependent variables. For example, in a study of a sample of college athletes (from a different institution than the ones previously studied), I was able to show how much impact each of a set of independent variables had on dependent variables concerning help seeking by athletes about pain and injuries (Nixon 1994b). More specifically, I found that among the various independent or predictor variables I studied, the most powerful predictor of the willingness of athletes to talk to or seek help from significant others in their athletic networks, such as coaches, teammates, and trainers, regarding their pain and injuries was the extent to which these significant others were perceived as sympathetic and caring.

In survey research, statistical analysis, rather than manipulation of the research setting, is the basis for drawing conclusions about cause and effect. Survey researchers may administer their questionnaires in a variety of ways, including mail, telephone, in-person interviews, and the Internet. They also sample in particular ways to ensure that they get sufficient representation of minority groups and other categories of people or organizations that are relatively less numerous. In addition, it is standard procedure in surveys to ask for background information about factors such as gender, age, race, ethnicity, education, type of job, income, and where the respondent lives because these kinds of factors could influence the dependent variables more than the hypothesized independent variables.

Surveys may be designed with great care and survey researchers may use highly sophisticated statistics, but survey research, like experiments, may have limitations or flaws. For example, respondents may not answer questions openly or accurately. They may not understand or be informed about the questions, care about them, or want to respond in the terms of the standardized fixed-choice questions presented by the researcher. Or respondents may not answer at all. Scientifically designed procedures meant to produce representative samples lose their value when large numbers of people or organizations do not respond. If only first-year students respond to a survey sent to all classes of college students, for example, the extent of generalization of the results will be substantially limited. Furthermore, preparing, administering, and analyzing the results of surveys, as well as identifying the sample and following up to increase the response rate, can be expensive. Despite these possible problems and the basic theoretical problem that the researcher has failed to anticipate and measure factors that could have significant effects on the dependent variables of interest, survey research is an efficient way to gather large amounts of data about large populations.

It is important to keep in mind that even the most quantitatively sophisticated survey researchers, who impress us with their manipulation of numbers, think in terms of statistical probabilities rather than causal certainties. That is, they can tell us with varying degrees of probability or likelihood whether a particular type of social behavior, event, or condition will result from the presence of particular hypothesized causal factors. In sport, we are accustomed to dealing with probabilities or possibilities rather than certainties, despite the most sophisticated, diligent, and rational efforts to control events and outcomes. This uncertainty is, of course, part of the appeal of sport.

Researchers who wish to collect rich and detailed information about how people interact and construct meaning in their interactions or organize themselves in groups or organizations are likely to rely on nonexperimental observational approaches or *field studies.* In some of the studies, the researcher is a participant in the setting she or he is studying, and in others, the researcher is a detached observer. While experimenters and survey researchers typically are interested in testing hypotheses, finding causes and effects, and predicting social behavior, researchers conducting field studies generally are more interested in the description of major patterns of social interaction or organization. The *case study* is a major type of observational or field research. It describes prominent and recurring social patterns and processes in groups, organizations, or wider social networks. The scope of the description and analysis tends to be limited to what the researcher can directly observe or learn from those she or he directly observes. Since researchers are able to use this method to uncover the complex and subtle meanings of social interaction in everyday life, we can understand why symbolic interactionists are especially inclined to rely on field studies or observational research to collect data.

My participant observation of faculty and staff recreational swimmers at a university pool over a ten-year period illustrates the field study method (Nixon 1986). As a recreational swimmer for many years, I was impressed by how regular swimmers in settings such as the university pool where I did most of my observations organized their behavior through informal and often nonverbal interaction. My initial casual observations led to a more systematic approach as a "participant observer," in which I began to record notes about the patterns of behavior in and around the pool.

There was a lifeguard and a list of "pool rules" that was posted on the wall, but the "regular" swimmers were much more influential in organizing social relations during the noon swim hour. Indeed, I quickly learned about how the swimmers maintained "social order in the water" on my first day at the pool. I unknowingly wandered into the "Fast Lane" that first day and my transgression—as only a moderately fast swimmer—prompted a rare verbal reaction, suggesting it would be more appropriate for me to swim in the "Medium" or "Slow" section of the pool. With a few additional pieces of advice and some observation, I learned that the swimmers had a code of appropriate behavior, and they had a variety of ways, which were informal and mostly nonverbal, of maintaining conformity to the code.

The code was the basis for a social structure, which included established patterns in the direction and pace of movement of swimmers in each lane, the discouragement of staring at other swimmers, when and how to yield to faster swimmers in your lane, and how much and what kind of poolside conversation was acceptable in each lane. There were subtle and not-so-subtle ways in which the code was enforced, including light touches of swimmers who tried to pass others at inappropriate times or, as in my case, a few words to new swimmers who were in the wrong lane. In some cases, transgressions prompted more severe reactions, such as kicking the transgressor on a flip turn at the end of the lane. The pool also had a status hierarchy, with regulars having higher status than nonregulars and, among regulars, faster swimmers having higher status than slower swimmers. Behavior in the pool reflected an organizing principle found in informal settings involving strangers, which Karp and Yoels (1979:104) called the "mini-max principle." That is, strangers, even "familiar strangers" who see each other relatively frequently, try to minimize their personal involvement with each other while trying to maximize order in their social relations. In the pool, this principle meant that regular swimmers tried to minimize interference and contact with each other, while also maximizing orderly patterns of interaction, sociability, and their own sense of privacy. The swimmers were in the pool to get exercise and not to socialize and make friends, and their informal code of the pool reflected these purposes and the mini-max principle.

While field studies can provide insights about important principles underlying social interaction and rich details about patterns of social interaction and what they mean to social actors, they also have limitations as a method of collecting data. First, the quality of the research is substantially related to the observational skills of the researcher and his or her subjective interpretation. Second, with research typically requiring informed consent of participants or subjects in most settings, it can be awkward or difficult to get prospective participants to agree to be studied. Third, researchers who observe the same people for extended periods of time could become close to their subjects and lose their objectivity. Fourth, the advantage of obtaining a great depth of knowledge from concentrating on a single case, social setting, or set of social actors may be offset by the disadvantages of potentially limited generalizability and difficulties in replication of the results. Despite these limitations, the accumulation of systematically conducted field studies contributes substantially to what we know about social life.

Along with experiments, social surveys, and field studies, sport sociologists may use *secondary data analysis* to collect data. This method involves the analysis of data collected by someone else for purposes other than those of the researcher's own study. It could involve data collected by another individual researcher or data collected by an organization, such as survey data produced by a large research organization or institute, demographic data collected by the Census Bureau, crime data collected by a law enforcement organization, or graduation data provided by colleges and universities to the National Collegiate Athletic Association (NCAA). It also could rely on existing documents or texts produced by historians, journalists, authors, and others who create mass media content or culture. Thus, secondary data could be shared between researchers, or it could be official records, historical documents, or the content of mass media, such as books, newspapers, magazines, and websites. Studies of the mass media and sport might involve a *content analysis* of the nature or meaning of ideas, images, or words in media texts. Secondary analysis can be used to identify social trends, correlations, or even causes, depending on the nature of the data available to the researcher. Sport sociologists also may use historical documents or studies to do comparative analyses of social history to reveal similarities and differences in social patterns of sport in different cultures or nations. An example is Knoppers and Anthonissen's (2003) study of women's soccer in the United States and the Netherlands, which we will examine more closely as a "Focus on Research" feature in chapter four.

In my own work, I used content analysis to identify the nature and implications of messages about risk, pain, and injury in sport found in a popular U.S. sports magazine, *Sports Illustrated*, over a period of twenty-two years (Nixon 1993). I discovered a set of cultural beliefs that the media and sports officials promoted, which encouraged athletes to accept risk, pain, and injury as a normal, if not heroic, aspect of sport. The major themes of this culture of risk, pain, and injury subsequently became a focus of a social survey I conducted in which athletes and coaches were asked the extent to which they accepted various aspects of risk, pain, and injury in sport (e.g., Nixon 1994a, 1996). This was the same survey cited earlier, which also generated data about predictors of help-seeking behavior by college athletes regarding their pain and injuries (Nixon 1994b). The belief identified in the content analysis that was most widely accepted by athletes was "Being an athlete means that you have to accept risks." Overall, the survey found that a majority of the athletes at the sampled university agreed with twenty of the thirty-one items conveying a willingness to play hurt. In a parallel survey of coaches at this university (Nixon 1994a), I found that coaches' beliefs tended to be similar to those of their athletes. A majority of the coaches agreed with almost two-thirds of the items reflecting the culture of risk, pain, and injury I had identified in my content analysis.

Content analysis and other types of secondary data analysis benefit from the time, effort, and money invested by others in collecting or publishing data or possible research content, but this method also has limitations related to the fact that as secondary data, they were not collected by the researcher for his or her research purposes. For this reason, these data may not directly or fully address important research questions. They also may have problems of *validity* in not accurately representing the concepts or variables of interest to the researcher or of *reliability* in not being easily reproducible in the same form by other researchers. In content analysis, for example, different researchers may disagree about whether a particular statement or set of statements by a coach or athlete about playing with injuries reflects a valid measure of acceptance of playing hurt. Or, in regard to reliability, one researcher may identify a number of statements as important data about the culture of risk, pain, and injury in sport, while another researcher reading the same text may completely overlook or disregard those statements. Thus, it may be difficult in this type of research to produce measures of key concepts or variables that are accepted by all researchers as having the meaning associated with these concepts or variables (the validity issue) or to have measures that repeatedly produce the same results (the reliability issue). Despite their shortcomings, content analysis and other forms of secondary data analysis can be very valuable in providing evidence revealing important social patterns or bearing upon important theoretical questions or social issues.

All four major types of social research methods are summarized in Table 2.2. More specifically, it summarizes whether each method produces quantitative data (represented in numbers) or qualitative data (represented in words) and the major advantages and possible disadvantages of each method. It also cites the examples of the application of each method in sport sociology research that

Table 2.2   Research Methods in Sociology and Sport Sociology

Research Method	Qualitative/ Quantitative	Advantages	Disadvantages	Sport Sociology Example
Experiment	Quantitative	Control over variables and research setting * Tests causal hypotheses * Can show cause and effect with some precision	Questions about possible artificiality and limited generalizability * Practical and ethical constraints simulating real-life conditions of theoretical interest	Study of the effects of team reward structures on interpersonal relations and team success
Social Survey	Qualitative or quantitative	Efficient way to collect large amounts of data * Random representative samples permit generalizations about large populations * Can collect standardized data for quantitative analysis or detailed descriptive interview data for qualitative analysis * Statistical procedures permit inferences about cause and effect	Possibility of untrue responses, inappropriate responses (with fixed-choice questions), unmotivated or uninformed responses * Low response rates restrict accuracy of generalizations * Limited depth of response to standardized fixed-choice questions * Can be expensive to administer and analyze	Survey of male and female college students' attitudes toward women in sport * Survey of college athletes' and coaches' attitudes and social behavior concerning risk, pain, and injury in sport
Field Study	Qualitative	Means of obtaining rich and detailed descriptive data about social actors, social patterns, and the meanings of social interaction and social experiences	Quality of research highly dependent on skills and knowledge of researcher * Possible subjectivity of researcher * Potentially limited generalizability * Difficulties replicating study and results * Not usually intended to test hypotheses	Participant observational study of informal social structure of recreational swimmers in a university pool
Secondary Analysis	Qualitative or quantitative	Efficient and economical way to use previously collected data or existing documents or texts to address research hypotheses, questions, or issues * Provides a range of possible data sources	No control over original data sources * Possible questions about validity, reliability, relevance, or completeness of data	Content analysis of sports magazine stories to identify the content or dominant beliefs of a culture of risk, pain, and injury in sport

was presented in the previous discussion. Over time, many of the shortcomings of individual research projects are offset by the critical scrutiny of the community of sociological researchers and scholars, refinement of past studies by new research, and the accumulation of similar research results from different studies. The accumulation of sociological evidence about sport and society, in combination with theoretical analysis of its meaning, represents the body of knowledge in sport sociology. This research and theory are the focus of this book.

Looking Ahead

Armed with a general understanding of sociology, the sociological imagination, the concepts of sport and the Golden Triangle, sport sociology, important social forces that have been transforming contemporary sport, and major social theories and research methods used by sport sociologists, we are now ready to explore sport and society in more depth. In the next chapter, we will consider social stratification and social class inequalities and how they relate to sport. In chapter four, we will examine major dimensions of social inequality in sport beyond class inequalities. In subsequent chapters our attention will turn to globalization, global sports culture, and the cultures of U.S. sport, youth and high school sports, social deviance and social problems, higher education, economics, business, sports careers, politics, and the future of sport. Our overview of theory and methods in this chapter should have emphasized the value of trying to be objective, critical, systematic, and sociological in thinking about sport and society throughout the remainder of this book and in our everyday lives.

Notes

1. Ritzer (2003) provides a broad and readable overview of major classical and contemporary theoretical perspectives in sociology.

2. See Giddens, Duneier, and Appelbaum (2007) for brief, clear, introductory-level summaries of most of the major theoretical perspectives discussed in this section.

3

Stratification and Social Class in Sport

One of the basic truths that people everywhere realize fairly early in life is that things are not equal. Some people make more money and are wealthier than others; some people are respected a lot more than others; and some people have more authority and power than others. These are basic facts of social life, and they apply to groups, organizations, towns and cities, and whole nations as well as to individual people in sport as in other areas of society. For example, when the USA Basketball "Dream Team" (USA Basketball 2004) played in the first open Olympic competition, including National Basketball Association (NBA) and other professional players, in 1992, it showed how far the United States was above the rest of the teams in the global basketball hierarchy at that time. With a collection of legendary players such as Michael Jordan, Larry Bird, Magic Johnson, Charles Barkley, and David Robinson, who were in or just beyond their prime, they began their quest for gold with a 116–48 victory over Angola and won the gold by defeating Croatia 117–85. In their eight games, they scored an average of over 117 points to less than 76 points per game for their opponents, which was an average margin of victory of over 40 points per game. The U.S. team had the best, best paid, and most respected players in the world. The distance between them and their opponents was a measure of the amount of global inequality in basketball in the summer of 1992.

A fundamental aspect of social organization is that people and organizations occupy different positions or statuses, which give them a particular location in the social structure in relation to other positions or statuses. In the world of basketball in 1992, the United States occupied the position of the top team. We expect different things of people and organizations in different statuses and we reward people and organizations differently according to their status. For example, Team USA was expected to win the Olympic competition in 1992, and its rewards for its Olympic championship were gold medals for the players as well as further enhancement of their reputations and endorsement value. In addition, the U.S. team solidified its position as the best basketball team in the world.

All societies are structured in terms of status differences. Sport is often organized in terms of differences in competitive performances and outcomes among individual athletes and among teams. However, we do not merely make distinctions among or between people and organizations in terms of their statuses. As the example of the Team USA basketball team suggests, we evaluate and rank according to these differences. Saying that the U.S. team was the top team implies a hierarchy of teams of different ranks and different perceived value or worth. People construct hierarchies, or structures of inequality, based on status differences.

Societies are structured in various ways that reflect, reinforce, and reproduce inequalities. For example, people and organizations of higher statuses are materially better off, more respected, or more influential than others of lower statuses. In sport, the most fundamental status distinction arguably is between winners and losers, but other status distinctions such as social class, gender, sexual orientation, race and ethnicity, and ability/disability influence the chances that people or organizations have to win, or even play the game, and be rewarded by it. Social inequalities based on these kinds of status distinctions are major structural aspects of sport and society. Social class inequalities will be a major focus of this chapter, and other major types of social inequalities will be the focus of the next chapter. All of these inequalities will be prominent themes in subsequent chapters because they are basic dimensions of the social structure of sport in all its forms and in all its social and cultural settings.

Social Stratification and Mobility

In sport, the specific individuals, teams, and sports programs or organizations that are the best and the worst, the richest and the poorest, and the most and least respected or admired may change over time. For example, established stars age and are replaced by younger players who are better, get paid more, and attract more attention. The same can be said for sports teams, clubs, leagues, and organizations. Yet, as in musical chairs, some individuals may change positions with each other, move from one step to another, and displace others on higher steps on the hierarchy or ladder of inequality, but the *structure* of the ladder remains pretty much the same over time, with the same number of steps in the same positions in relation to each other. The ladder is the hierarchical structure, and the pattern of the relatively stable organization of society into unequal steps or levels is called *social stratification*.

Social stratification involves persisting patterns of inequality in which certain categories or strata of people repeatedly get more or less of the valued resources in society. According to Marx, the most consequential kind of stratification involves *class*, which refers to the economic position of people in society. In his theory, the most important classes in capitalist societies were capitalists, who owned the means of production, and proletarians or workers in the urban workforce, who were employed by capitalists in their factories (Marx and Engels 1978). A revolutionary struggle between them was predicted to lead to a fundamental restructuring of society that would result in a "classless society" with virtually no stratification.

In Weber's conception of stratification, along with the economic classes, social and political dimensions of stratification also could be consequential. His perspective included a broader conception of *economic or class inequalities* than in Marx's theory. Weber's conception of class referred to the relative amount of marketable skills, qualifications, and property that people possessed, along with their material wealth, and he assumed that class differences were associated with different *life chances* of people. Weber also focused on *social inequalities* of prestige, deference, social worth, or social honor associated with different positions or occupations and *political inequalities* of access to authority and the opportunities or resources for exercising power (Weber 1978). Weber's multidimensional perspective enables us to see stratification in broader and more complex terms than Marx's perspective allows, but we do not want to dismiss Marx as too narrow because, as we will see throughout this book, economic class inequalities have powerful effects on people's lives in sport and in the larger society. Both Marx and Weber inform us about important ways that people of different strata are unequal, that is, in terms of valued economic, social, and/or political resources. In this book, we will be interested in both (1) the nature and implications of *social class* differences in sport and (2) the nature and implications of men and women (*gender*), heterosexuals and homosexuals (*sexual orientation*), whites and nonwhites (*race*), ethnic majority and minority groups (*ethnicity*), and able-bodied people and persons with disabilities (*physical disability*) being organized into economic, social, and political hierarchies in sport.

People or organizations of different statuses may move up or down the stratification hierarchy in sport or society. For example, young players develop over time into highly paid and admired superstars, established stars lose their star power as they age, struggling teams develop into dynasties, and top teams fall from the top over time. Their movement up or down the stratification hierarchy is called upward or downward *social mobility*. Although individuals or teams may move up or down the stratification hierarchy of their sport, the sport remains stratified as long as the athletes and teams who are most successful in competition generally earn the most money, get the most publicity, are the most famous, and exert the most influence in their sport. That is, even when the faces change, the basic way of differentially ranking winners and losers above and below each other and of differentially rewarding them according to their rank remains the same.

In sport and society, people often strive to move up the stratification hierarchy, whether it is from substitute to regular to star; from being paid less to being paid more or the most; from being a relative unknown to being famous; from being a subordinate to being the captain, the leader, or the boss; or from being in the working class to being in a more affluent class. Sociologists refer to societies, such as the United States, that have some degree of movement, including some big leaps upward and some downward plunges, as *class-stratified societies*, which are relatively open to mobility. That is, people are not necessarily fated to remain in basically the same location in the stratification system for their entire lifetime, as they are in societies with *caste systems*, such as traditional India with its well-defined castes. In the United States, people have some chance, even though it may be limited for most, to move up—or down. The American Dream is an ideology of upward mobility, which encourages people to aspire to move up the ladder of success and conveys the idea that it is possible for those who work and compete hard enough to achieve such mobility. Its influence is not confined to the United States. Wherever it has influence, belief in this ideology is reinforced by the fact that some, including well-publicized cases of sports stars or miracle teams, actually achieve upward mobility, sometimes quite spectacularly rising from "rags to riches" over their careers or in their lifetimes. Of course, many also fail in their quest for success, in part because preexisting status inequalities make the competition for success unfair from the beginning. Not everyone begins the competition at the same starting line.

Serious sports fans and even casual observers usually can point to individual women, blacks, members of ethnic minority groups, or individuals from poor or working-class backgrounds who have achieved national or global prominence in sport. Although we do not see many cases of self-acknowledged gay men in mainstream sports, we have seen some lesbian women become very successful in sport. In recent years, a number of athletes with disabilities have gained fame as wheelchair athletes in marathons with able-bodied runners, and others have received international publicity for their achievements in the Paralympics, the Olympic Games of disability sports. We have even seen the image of a wheelchair racer on a Wheaties cereal box (see Nixon and Frey 1996: 223). Wheaties has advertised itself as "the breakfast of champions."

In view of these facts about sport, we might ask why sport sociologists focus a significant amount of attention on structured social inequalities in sport and talk about the myth of the American Dream (e.g., Eitzen 2003:ch. 9; Nixon 1984:chs. 1, 7). Critical sport sociologists are especially interested in the contested terrain in sport where inequality issues are at the center of struggles between the more and less powerful and the more and less privileged. How much do status differences and inequalities actually matter? Is the sports opportunity structure really restricted? Is the American Dream of social mobility a myth or a reality for those who try to move up and do better? Chapters three and four will address these questions, but the short answer is that sociologists pay a lot of attention to stratification because, despite ideologies to the contrary, stratification is a basic and very consequential fact of social life. Societies are structured to be unequal in various ways, which affect how people live, what they can do, and how much of the valued things in their society they are likely to attain. An important structural feature of stratification hierarchies in society and sport is that they generally have relatively few places at the top. In a number of cases, the hierarchies in sport resemble pyramids, with a tiny top and a wide base, and the climb to the top is along a slippery slope. That is, many try, but few make it up to the top, or even very far from where they started.

Existing patterns of inequality and the related ideologies that justify them, such as elitism, sexism, and racism, can create major obstacles to the achievement of success and the American Dream in the larger society and in sport. Sport sociologists are interested in social inequalities for these reasons, and also because inequalities have turned many venues of sport into contested terrain where people of lower status have struggled for more access, opportunities, rights, and rewards. When it is widely perceived in sport or in the larger society that persisting inequalities of certain categories of people, such as women, ethnic minorities, blacks, gays or lesbians, or people with physical disabilities, are unfairly derived from *prejudicial attitudes* and *discriminatory treatment*, stratification can lead to discontent, turbulence, and efforts to change society. We will discuss the relationship of inequality to perceptions of unfairness, injustice, or inequity in the next section. For now, it is important to recognize that it takes sociological imagination to understand that social stratification is not something that occasionally happens to a single person or to some unrelated people in society. Through sociological eyes, we can see stratification as a *general* pattern of *recurring* inequalities of *categories* of similar types of people that exist in the broader contexts of sport and society, despite some individual cases that are exceptions. The sociological imagination enables us to distinguish general structural patterns from specific individual cases that may or may not be consistent with the general pattern.

Even the most rigidly stratified societies and sports have cases of low-status people or organizations that overcome all kinds of obstacles to become successful. We know that underdogs occasionally win. However, the charm of the underdog's victory derives from the fact that it is so infrequent. In sport sociology, a structural orientation implies a focus on pervasive and enduring general patterns of social behavior and organization that characterize sport and society. Social stratification historically has been one of the most pervasive and enduring structural features of all societies. Its specific form varies from society to society and sport to sport, and its form changes over time. However, despite these variations and changes, we have not yet seen an established society or popular sport without the imprint of enduring patterns of inequality in social class, gender, sexual orientation, race, ethnicity, and/or disability. Furthermore, we will discuss later in this chapter how a globally powerful Golden Triangle, which combines the influence of major sports, media, and transnational corporations, contributes to the global stratification of sport. An indication of this stratifying influence of the Golden Triangle is that some sports, sports organizations, and athletes receive much more global media attention than others, attract much more global interest from spectators than others, generate much more revenue than others from global sales of sports commodities, and have more global influence over the direction of sports policy and investment than others. Thus, stratification is an important fact of social life in sport, and it has global implications. In the next section, we will consider concepts and theoretical perspectives that have been used by sociologists and sport sociologists to understand the various meanings, possible causes, and social implications of structures of inequality, and we will tie these ideas to sport.

Social Theory and Inequality in Sport

I have found that my students and others sometimes assume that inequality and injustice or inequity are the same thing or that a policy meant to ensure equity or justice necessarily implies or requires equality. Distinguishing conceptually between inequality and inequity is important because inequality could be disruptive when it is perceived as inequitable or unjust, but it is likely to be accepted when it is seen as equitable or just and "fair." Inequality is a structural condition of society, and perceptions of justice or injustice, equity or inequity, and fairness or unfairness relate to judgments of whether people have gotten what they deserve. People with low status are most likely to become unhappy, angry, resentful, or even rebellious and violent when they see their low status as undeserved and inequality as unfair.

In Homans's (1974) social exchange theory, the concept of "distributive justice" refers to conditions of interaction or social exchange in which social actors believe that the rewards they derive from their relations with others are proportional to their investments or contributions and performance. Investments might include such things as time, effort, skill, status, and personal reputation. This conception of distributive justice implies that people may accept inequality if they believe it is justified by their levels of investment and performance. Assessments of relative investments or contributions may be influenced by our personal biases and self-interest. For example, white males may think that being a male or white should "count" as a significant "investment" in social exchanges with women or racial minorities and entitle them to relatively more rewards. According to Homans, people do not necessarily react negatively to inequality if they believe their opportunities, rewards, or status correspond to their investments and performance. Negative reactions and protests are more likely when people believe they are getting less than they deserve.

When inequality in sport is believed to result from prejudice or discrimination and is perceived as unjust, inequitable, or unfair, sports settings could become contested terrain. The persisting issue of gender inequity demonstrates how complicated conflicts about inequality and inequity in sport can be. In the battle over gender equity, both women and men in some lower-profile non-revenue sports have seen themselves as unfairly treated, and they have made competing claims for limited resources. Advocates for women in sport believe that gender discrimination has resulted in allocations of sports opportunities and rewards that unfairly favor males over females. That is, being a male in sport has traditionally been a "positive investment," while being a female has not counted at all or has been viewed as "negative investment" unworthy of opportunity or reward. These advocates believe that the opportunity and reward structure should not be based on a biased view of the "investment" of gender but should reflect such things as the relative number of males and females at schools and colleges and their relative levels of sports interest. They also believe that males and females in the same sports should be treated in the same way. Advocates for sports such as college wrestling believe that decisions based on Title IX to redress gender inequities in sport have diverted resources away from their programs and caused the elimination of many of these programs. They believe that women's efforts to get what they think they deserve have resulted in males in lower-profile sports being treated unfairly and getting less than they deserve. Thus, struggles over inequality and inequity may pit different aggrieved parties against each other instead of against the people with power to influence how opportunities and rewards are distributed. We will have more to say about gender equity in subsequent chapters.

People are overrewarded as well as underrewarded, and overrewarded people tend to feel guilty about getting too much or try to rationalize their good fortune. For example, athletes or teams that win as a result of a widely acknowledged bad call may attribute it to the "breaks of the game" and argue that such things balance out over time. We tend to be more concerned about underreward because of the kind of unfairness and unjustified deprivations it represents and the frustrations and hostility it may provoke. Underrewarded people may turn their anger or resentment into action and may contest the structure or people perceived to be responsible for their unfair treatment, especially if they find some support for their perception of injustice and desire for corrective action. Underreward may not be unexpected if it has occurred in the past.

A structural consequence of prejudice and discrimination is that there are people in low-status categories who repeatedly are excluded from prestigious organizations and activities and get less pay, less respect, and fewer chances for positions of authority, despite their talents and potential for strong performances or outstanding achievements, because they have devalued statuses. Prejudice and discrimination are unfair in ignoring contrary facts and in automatically perceiving and treating people as inferior or incapable merely because they are in a low-status category. Situations where justice is widely perceived to prevail are assumed to be balanced and relatively stable, while situations where a significant number of people perceive injustice are assumed to be imbalanced and unstable. Such imbalanced situations are likely to become contested terrain when aggrieved people or groups who believe they are underrewarded challenge injustice and press those in authority or power to minimize or eliminate prejudice and discrimination (Nixon 1979:268–276).

A number of significant types of structured inequality or stratification and perceived inequity or injustice have been part of the history of sport. We have suggested the prevalence and significance of inequalities related to social class, gender, sexual orientation, race, ethnicity, and physical disability. Although these types of inequality can be found in sport to varying extents in different societies in all historical eras, we have relatively seldom seen open contesting of injustices related to them. The logical question is why these inequalities have not prompted more open expressions of injustice and more public anger, resentment, rebellion, or violence in the history of sport, as distributive justice theory—and Marx—would seem to predict. There are several possible answers, and they suggest the complexities of connecting structural conditions, culture, perceptions, and social action.

First, people may not feel aggrieved because both they and their culture devalue their statuses, which lowers their expectations of what they deserve. For example, women may grow up believing that sport is an activity "for the boys," and that it is unfeminine to play sports. Thus, even athletic females learn to accept as proper, appropriate, or right that they are generally excluded from sport and receive little support when they participate. Lower-class and black athletes may accept their segregation and discrimination in sport because they know it is not their "place" to play in the more lavish and visible realms of sport where whites play or to expect the amount of attention and respect that higher-class and white athletes receive for their sports achievements. Many sports realms have become contested terrain over the past few decades in societies such as the United States because the cultural devaluation of women and minorities has been challenged and because people desiring change in sport have joined with broader civil rights movements in society to try to reduce various status inequalities and eliminate the cultural values that have reinforced them. We suggested earlier that critical theorists have focused special attention on these areas of contested terrain in sport, arguing for the need for change and the conditions needed to facilitate it.

A *second* possible answer is that people may not feel aggrieved because they believe that inequality is a result of a fair contest, which they have lost due to their own deficiencies or the superiority of others. On the one hand, sport is recognized as a competition that inevitably produces winners and losers. This kind of inequality and the differential rewards of fame, money, and influence it can produce are typically accepted in sport, although there are "sore losers" among athletes, coaches, team officials, and fans who never accept losing. The cultural value of sportsmanship encourages competitors in sport to be gracious in victory and defeat and to recognize that in a fair contest, our opponent deserved to win. In general, sport, like democratic politics, could not survive if losers were unwilling to accept or at least walk away from defeat and prepare to compete again on another day.

There is another context for understanding the acceptance of defeat in sport, however. For people of lower status, defeat might result from playing against opponents who are better coached, have more time to train, train and play in better facilities, have better equipment, receive more support from sponsors, and have more high-level experiences in the sport. Or, people of lower status might have fewer chances to compete for more prestigious and better-compensated positions and teams, to play in more "elite" sports, or to receive publicity and commercial support or rewards. Disadvantaged athletes and coaches may not see the inherent inequalities and unfairness in these situations if they believe that sport is structured to be fair, everyone who plays has a chance to succeed, and those who start with some disadvantages will win if they work hard enough and compete aggressively enough. The ideology of the American Dream encourages acceptance of this kind of view of sport. Thus, it can be an effective instrument for getting minority athletes, for example, to accept their unequal treatment and view it as a result of their own personal deficiencies.

The American Dream teaches us that we succeed or fail as a result of our own effort, and losing is our own fault. We need to try harder next time. The American Dream may distract us from seeing that losing or lack of access to sport may be related to the social backgrounds of people and not their lack of effort or talent. The relatively few cases of athletes from less-advantaged backgrounds—the exceptions—who "make it" contradict the criticisms of the American Dream and sustain the myth. Even when lower-status sports participants realize that they are not at fault, they do not get much sympathy from those of higher status in society, who are likely to embrace the American Dream and question their complaints as "excuses." The American Dream is not an ideology of excuses. It is a justification for the structures of entrenched inequality in society and it encourages us to believe that people with higher status have it because they deserve it. It is meant to distract us from seeing inequalities as undeserved, resulting from things beyond the control of perpetually lower-status people. For example, it diverts our attention from structural obstacles of discrimination built into the ways society typically does things, such as how it allocates resources for school sports or how it chooses people for coaching and administrative positions in sport, and it distracts us from noticing pervasive attitudes of prejudice among higher-status and powerful people and others in society that lead to people from lower-status backgrounds being ignored, disliked, degraded, or underrewarded.

A *third* possible reason why inequality may not lead to open challenges or protests in sport is that people may feel aggrieved but fail to act because they believe they lack the resources to mount an effective challenge to those in power. For example, they may feel aggrieved but see relatively few others, even others like themselves, who agree with their perception of injustice; they may not see enough support from others to engage in more than symbolic individual or collective action to try to bring about social change; and they may lack access to the resources of power needed to challenge those in power with some effectiveness. Festering resentment and discontent may build up in these situations, which ultimately could lead the aggrieved persons to become less committed and cooperative and either to quit or to organize resistance to those in power. In professional team sports in the United States, such as Major League Baseball (MLB), the National Football League (NFL), the NBA, and the National Hockey League (NHL), athletes accepted for many years their lack of freedom to move between teams and their limited pay because they feared the power of owners or did not want to be branded as a "militant" or "troublemaker" for challenging owners, for example by failing to sign their contract or by actively participating in the players' association in their sport.

We will see in the chapter on the professional sports industry that the combination of factors such as effective union leadership, favorable court decisions, the use of agents, and a lot of television money transformed the relationship between players and owners in the major U.S. team sports, significantly reducing the structured inequalities in this relationship. That is, the players acted on their perceptions of unfairness and effectively challenged the social structure of their sport that disadvantaged them. As suggested earlier, we will also see later in this chapter and throughout the rest of this book how the sports arena generally has become a more volatile and contested terrain because women, blacks, ethnic minorities, homosexuals, and people with disabilities have perceived inequalities as forms of injustice and have acted individually and collectively to resist and change these inequalities or at least to voice their concerns.

Homans's social exchange theory and conception of distributive justice were focused on the micro level of interactions between individuals and members of groups, but the ideas of distributive justice and injustice can be applied to macro-level analyses of the implications of inequalities in sport, as when players in a sport organize collectively to challenge the power structure of their sport. The most prominent theories of inequality in sport sociology have generally been macro-level perspectives, and they have derived from the work of social theorists such as Marx and Weber, structural functionalists, and more contemporary critical theorists and feminists (Sugden and Tomlinson 2000). Marx did not consider the relationship between sport and class, but neo-Marxists, such as Hoch (1972), have taken off from Marx to focus on how the power structure in society uses sport to diminish the threat from exploited classes. Just as Marx argued that religion was the "opiate of the masses" in diverting them from their real-world exploitation to hopes for salvation in the afterlife, Hoch argued that lower-class and working-class sports fans were distracted from their exploited status and failed to develop a radical class consciousness as a result of their consuming passion for sports. In this vein, research by Martin and Berry (1987) showed that involvement of working-class men in motocross racing distracted them from the alienating routine, boredom, and powerlessness they experienced in their work environment. They were able to achieve a sense of rugged individualism, competition, achievement, and success that was absent in their jobs.

Sport sociologists have used a Marxist perspective to analyze relations between owners or management and players, as in the example given earlier. Tensions in these relations are predictable if one assumes, as Marxists would, that owners exploit and oppress players by paying them as little as possible and maintaining as much control as possible over them so that owners can maximize their profits and power, and that players collectively resist their exploitation and oppression, for example, by organizing and supporting unions, once they develop a "class consciousness" of their common exploitation and oppression. In this model, owners are the capitalist class and players are the working class. This model may not seem very credible or valid when we think of how much money professional athletes earn today or earned even thirty years ago when they began to become more organized and militant. However, the huge leap in salaries and the increased freedom to choose their employer, which occurred after players began to organize and resist owners effectively in the 1970s, indicates, first, how much players' salaries and movement to other teams had been suppressed by owners and, second, the effects of organized resistance by "the workers" after they developed a shared "class consciousness" of their exploitation and oppression.

Marx's argument was that capitalists tried to pay their workers as little as they could get away with and to invest as little as possible in their working conditions to maximize their profits and that they used institutionalized devices such as the law to maximize their control over workers. An example of this kind of use of a legal device in sport is the "reserve clause," which legally bound a player to a team until the player was traded, sold, or released by the team owner. Thus, players had no choice about the team for which they played, which severely limited their bargaining power in salary negotiations with owners. In this context of sport, the "workers' revolution" came in the form of court challenges, the use of agents to represent player interests, the formation of effective labor unions, and the use of traditional labor tactics such as strikes to achieve more favorable collective bargaining agreements with owners. Although the capitalists of sport were not removed, the workers were successful in improving their bargaining position and thereby substantially increased their salaries and freedom of movement. Changes in relations between owners and players are somewhat more complex than this example shows, and we will explore these relations more fully in the chapter about the sports industry. At this point, though, this example is useful in showing how Marx's conflict perspective can help us understand these changes in social relations in professional sports.

More recent critical analyses of sport have also drawn from Marx's emphasis on the exploitative and oppressive influence of dominant capitalist classes. However, they have focused more broadly on the "hegemonic" or dominant groups in the various institutional sectors of society and how their domination has served to maintain their status and reinforce existing patterns of inequality in society. Sage's (1998) critical analysis of "power and ideology in American sport" is an example of this perspective. Sage was interested in the power of the dominant classes who controlled major societal institutions such as government, the economy, the mass media, and education as well as sport and how they maintained patterns of stratification in the United States. More specifically, he focused on how structures of inequality of social class, gender, and race in sport and society were reinforced by the ideologies and actions of the hegemonic groups in sport and society. His critical analysis also considered how various forms of resistance to the current hegemonic structures dominating sport could transform it.

Sage's conception of the hegemonic or dominant groups in society is similar to the view of the U.S. power structure proposed by Mills (1959), which he called the "power elite." Mills characterized this elite as a network of the wealthiest and most powerful people in the major institutional sectors of society, who were predominantly white Anglo-Saxon Protestants (WASPs) and were tied together by their common affiliations with the most prestigious universities and the most exclusive social clubs, memberships on major corporate boards, and associations with powerful government committees. An important insight from Mills is that powerful people and organizations in sport and society tend to be linked by contacts in networks of political power, money and property, and social life. Although it may lack the social ties of Mills's power elite, the coalescence of powerful forces in the Golden Triangle helps us understand why these kinds of networks are so powerful and achieve a position of hegemony in sport and society. In this book, we will consider what it looks like for dominant networks such as the Golden Triangle to pursue their own, usually capitalist, interests and also how these hegemonic structures or networks influence the dominant structures and cultures of sport within nations and on a global scale.

Although sport sociologists now seem primarily interested in an array of neo-Marxist, critical, and feminist perspectives for analyzing contemporary social stratification, we cannot ignore structural functional perspectives because they were very influential in earlier stages of sociology and sport sociology (Sugden and Tomlinson 2000). In addition, from a practical standpoint, they help us understand a theoretical rationale for some currently dominant ideologies, such as the American Dream, that justify existing structures of society, including stratification. Instead of focusing on the possible exploitative or oppressive consequences of stratification, Davis and Moore (1945) considered the benefits to society of inequality in their classic structural functional analysis of stratification. They emphasized the motivational value of unequal rewards in the productive process, which critics of Marx said he failed to recognize or accept. The Davis-Moore thesis is that society needs people to do the functionally important jobs. Some jobs are easy and can be done by almost anyone. Others are demanding or difficult and require people with unusual talents or extensive training. Thus, social stratification, especially in occupational prestige and income, is a motivational device that society uses to ensure that the right people, with appropriate talents, skills, and training, are in the functionally important and demanding jobs and are productive in them.

From a structural functional perspective, we could argue, for example, that sport needs inequalities in pay and in recognition between winners and losers and between more- and less-successful athletes and coaches to be able to attract talented people to play, coach, and invest in sport and to encourage athletes and coaches to make the sacrifices needed to create the exciting competitions that draw fans and allow sports as we know them today to flourish. One could fault structural functionalists for seeming to ignore the dysfunctional consequences of excessive inequalities in sport and society and question whether the amounts earned by the best-paid athletes and coaches in sport today are excessive and necessary for motivational purposes, especially when we consider them in the context of the larger society. However, structural functionalists are likely to counter that societies having relatively small differences or lacking sufficient differences in rewards between more- and less-productive members will be much less productive than societies that offer the chance for some to do much better than others. As I previously noted, the American Dream legitimates this kind of perspective, in promising big rewards and a better life to those willing to make the effort.

A logical extension of the structural functional perspective could be that sport *needs* losers, minor leaguers, and benchwarmers to reinforce a belief in the importance of sacrificing and winning by showing the adverse consequences to reputation, economic status, and influence of not trying hard enough to win. This view of the functions of having a "lower class" of losers and also-rans in sport is similar to Gans's analysis of the functions of the "undeserving poor" for U.S. society, particularly those who are more advantaged. In his creative use of the functionalist perspective, Gans (1972) suggested that more advantaged people want and need us to believe that poor people deserve their poverty. They hold an enduring stereotype of poor people as undeserving of help and a better life because, among other things, they are perceived as irresponsible and lazy. This kind of stereotype of the undeserving poor allows advantaged members of society to blame the poor as scapegoats for the ills of society, stigmatize them as perpetual losers, and ignore or dismiss them. This stereotype also reinforces the idea that failure to be serious about the pursuit of the American Dream can have very negative consequences, and it obscures the facts that many disadvantaged people actually share the same aspirations and work just as hard as those who are more advantaged.

In sport, as in the larger society in the United States, widespread recognition of the *myth* of the American Dream is not functional, though, because the power elite needs the American Dream to legitimize its hegemony. It *is* functional for people to believe that failure happens when the American Dream is not embraced sufficiently. This belief contributes to the perception that advantaged people deserve their prominence, privilege, and power, just as losers and other disadvantaged people deserve theirs. When people generally believe that prominence, privilege, and power are deserved and especially when disadvantaged people believe they deserve to be disadvantaged, the existing hegemonic structures in society and sport are likely to remain relatively stable.

Social Inequalities, Access, and Opportunity: Sport and the American Dream

The American Dream is about the chance for upward mobility, and it implies that inequality of status, outcomes, and rewards is acceptable as long as the chance to move up is available to everyone who wants to be successful and works hard to achieve it. It implies that stratification systems are very flexible and that people will not be stuck in their status if they make enough effort to move up. While inspiring, the American Dream is not true as a generalization, since many who strive for upward mobility face significant structural obstacles such as discrimination or limited opportunities and those who achieve mobility often achieve less than they desire, despite their hard work. In sport as in the rest of society in the United States and other countries, having lower status has historically restricted opportunities for upward mobility and access to valued activities and the roles and rewards associated with them.

The history of sport is marked by various types of discrimination that have prevented lower- and working-class people, members of racial or ethnic minority groups, females, homosexuals, and persons with physical disabilities from participating in various types of established sports. Many sports were initially reserved for the privileged, and some remain that way today. For example, athletes who participated in sports in ancient Greece were originally from wealthy families. Access to sport in ancient Greece opened up to less-advantaged athletes who were sponsored and paid by wealthy patrons and city-states as sport became more popular and politically significant. There were professional athletes in the second century B.C.E. who organized early versions of player unions as guilds to give them more bargaining power in decisions about their sports and compensation. With the notable exception of the Heraean Games, women did not participate in sports in ancient Greece. The Olympics were for males, who competed in activities such as chariot racing, boxing, wrestling, archery, and foot races (Nixon and Frey 1996:18–21).

We noted in the first chapter that the development of modern sport has been characterized by an increasing commitment to the kind of principle or goal of equality of opportunity that we have associated with the American Dream. Nevertheless, the history of sport has been characterized by substantial class, gender, and other types of inequality in access. Although wealthy patrons sponsored and paid athletes in ancient Greece, the upper classes have generally favored amateur sports because the lack of commercial sponsorship and pay generally restricted sports to wealthier members of society. In effect, the ethos of pure amateurism is an ethos of class exclusivity.

Smart observed that social class differences were associated with the distinction between amateur and professional sport during the development of modern sport in England and to a great extent in the United States, and that the rise of amateur sports at the end of the nineteenth century in the United States reflected the influence of the English (Smart 2005:42–43). Many sports in England, the United States, and other countries have become more *democratized* over the past two centuries. That is, they have become more accessible to people from various social class and status backgrounds. This increased democratization has been associated with the increased influence of professionalism. Even the bastion of amateurism in modern sport, the Olympics, finally relented and gave in to open professionalism over two decades ago, allowing the international governing body in each sport to decide who could participate. The victory of the 1992 U.S. basketball Dream Team may be the most prominent example of this break in tradition in the Modern Games. Of course, professionalism was not really new in the Olympics, since professionals had competed in the Games in ancient Greece and athletes received money "under the table"—as "shamateurs"—in the Modern Games in the era before open competition was permitted.

Access is still affected by social class and other kinds of status differences, despite democratization trends in a number of sports. In the United States, there were periods of widespread racial, ethnic, and gender exclusion; discrimination; and segregation in major sports throughout most of the twentieth century. Accessibility problems for homosexuals and people with disabilities were not even noticed by most people until the later decades of the twentieth century. Today, poor people, blacks, ethnic minorities, women, homosexuals, and people with disabilities still find it difficult or impossible to compete without sponsors in a number of sports requiring expensive training, equipment, coaching, and travel, beginning with the individual and club sports of childhood and adolescence. Even for an urban playground game such as basketball, top high school and club team players need subsidies from sponsors such as Nike to compete at a high level. Since the Heraean Games of ancient Greece, women have found that they either competed in less visible venues than the men or did not compete at all. One of the most dramatic changes in sport over the past several decades has been the burst in sports access by girls and women.

Some traditionally exclusive or elite sports are not likely to become highly democratized, and that may be part of their appeal to participants in them. Participants are able to maintain their status distinction from the rest of society by their involvement in activities accessible to only the richest and most prominent members as a result of restrictive rules or the sheer cost of competing. Yet even some traditionally very exclusive elite sports are being affected by global influences that are opening them up beyond their traditional social circles. An example of an exclusive sport undergoing this kind of change is America's Cup yachting (Phillips 2006), and it is the focus of the "Sport in the News" feature on "Elite Sport in the Contemporary Global Sports Culture." This feature also considers the applicability of Veblen's (1899) classic ideas of *conspicuous leisure* and *conspicuous consumption* to elite sports such as the America's Cup. These ideas assume that the upper classes try to gain recognition of their status through public displays of their wealth.

We may wonder why the American Dream continues to inspire people in the United States and other countries. After all, in sport, for example, access is not really open to everyone in every sport, and many try to succeed but relatively few actually climb very far up the ladder of success. As Eitzen (2003:chs. 7, 9) has argued, sport has continued to be unfair for racial minorities and women; athletic programs with less financial support have continued to be at a disadvantage in competing against wealthy programs; and sport does not provide a significant way out of poverty or a viable career option for the vast majority of those seeking mobility and a road to success through sport. Furthermore, as Coakley (2007:343–345) has pointed out, the evidence shows that sports career opportunities are limited; the length of professional athletes' careers tends to be relatively short; and career opportunities for women and racial and ethnic minorities in sport remain relatively limited, despite major advances in participation for women over the past few decades and a significant amount of success for minorities in a few major sports. He cites odds estimates from 2004 statistics about advancing from high school sports to the National Collegiate Athletic Association (NCAA) and from the NCAA to a professional career in a number of U.S. sports to show how difficult it is to "make it" in sport. For example, the percentages of athletes moving from high school sport to the college

☐ **Sport in the News Feature 3.1:**
Elite Sport in the Contemporary Global Sports Culture

Beginning in 1851, the elite America's Cup yachting competition rotated among England; New York; Newport, Rhode Island; Australia; San Diego; and Auckland, New Zealand (Mellgren 2006; Phillips 2006). In 2007, the America's Cup competition took place for the first time in a non-English-speaking location, Valencia, Spain, and one that was not the home waters of the club defending the trophy. The location became a dilemma because the victor in the 2003 race was from a landlocked nation, Switzerland. The event was named for the first winner, the U.S. yacht *America*. Mellgren (2006) pointed out that from the beginning, the America's Cup trophy has officially represented "a perpetual challenge cup for friendly competition between nations." Mellgren (2006) also observed that the America's Cup has evolved from this competition between gentlemen into "a lesson in team diversity." The team diversity reflected two developments in the Cup competition: the variety of nations represented by boats in the race and the eligibility of sailors from other countries to be part of a team's crew. The twelve competitors were from ten different nations. Entrants reflected the globalization of this elite sport, as Germany, China, and South Africa were entering boats for the first time in 2007. In addition, residency requirements for crews were dropped for the 2007 race. A national restriction still in effect is that the hulls of the boats must be from the nation each represents, but parts, like crews, could come from anywhere else in the world.

Although the America's Cup has traditionally been viewed as a competition among nations or wealthy yacht owners representing nations, it actually has been a race among exclusive yacht clubs. For example, the defending Cup holder, *Alinghi*, is often characterized as a Swiss boat, but it actually represents Geneva Yacht, just as the U.S. entrant, the BMW *Oracle*, represents the San Francisco Golden Gate Yacht Club. In fact, the race has become more than a contest among nations or yacht clubs. According to Mellgren, the America's Cup has become a "high-tech battle among wealthy global syndicates." In addition, the 2007 race was the first time it was administered by professional managers rather than yacht club members. America's Cup teams now are large and well-financed networks of professional sailors, boat architects and builders, and sail makers (Mellgren 2006). These syndicates are corporate and international. For example, the U.S. boat is partially sponsored by German automaker BMW and has a New Zealand skipper. The Swiss *Alinghi* is skippered by an American, and the sponsors of the New Zealand entrant are a United Arab Emirates airline and a Japanese car manufacturer. The Chinese boat is sponsored by a Swiss watchmaker and led by a French skipper.

Because the Cup is a highly commercialized event involving very substantial investments by racing teams, the host city and nation, and professional crews, it is not surprising that winning, more than national or club honor, is the primary motivation of competitors and their fans. Reflecting both the competitive and the global perspective of contemporary Cup competitors, the head of the New Zealand team said that the nationality of crew members no longer mattered if a team won (Mellgren 2006). As in commercialized sports in general, winning has significant financial implications. Hoping to generate a billion dollars in revenue and economic development benefits, the host city and nation in 2007 invested an estimated $600 million to $1.2 billion to upgrade port facilities (Phillips 2006). Perhaps surprisingly, though, despite investing tens of millions of dollars in campaigns to win the Cup, the winner will not receive a monetary prize along with the "Auld Mug" trophy.

Ordinary people cannot afford to spend large sums of money and years of effort without expecting some monetary return. In the elite circles of sport, however, the prestige of winning is a powerful motivator, and this kind of motivation is consistent with Thorstein Veblen's (1899) classic notions of "conspicuous consumption" and "conspicuous leisure." He theorized that the wealthiest classes in capitalist societies were driven by a deeply rooted need for approval, respect, or status envy. Since capitalist societies value money and possessions, being able to show

continues

off one's financial worth can convey one's status. Thus, we can assume from Veblen's perspective that the wealthy engage in conspicuous displays of their wealth by pursuing expensive leisure and spending extravagantly on sporting events. Critics have faulted Veblen for overestimating interest in such conspicuous displays among the upper classes and underestimating its importance among those trying to climb the socioeconomic ladder and make a name for themselves. His perspective also fails to account adequately for the seriousness of the wealthy competitor in elite activities such as the America's Cup (Nixon and Frey 1996:211). Notwithstanding these criticisms, spending $50 million to $100 million on a very exclusive race that involves only twelve competitors from around the world and offers no monetary prize is the kind of status display that conforms to Veblen's ideas of conspicuous leisure and consumption. Of course, the America's Cup is also an opportunity for major or upwardly mobile transnational corporations to advertise themselves among the wealthiest segments of competing nations. For them, commercial considerations are definitely important.

Although the professional sailors who crewed the boats may come from a variety of nations and social backgrounds, the syndicates that own or sponsor the boats generally are individual billionaires and wealthy corporations from the upper echelons of the global corporate stratification hierarchy. The BMW *Oracle*, for example, was owned by the U.S. billionaire CEO of the software company Oracle, and along with BMW, the team was sponsored by a global financial services provider, a Swiss manufacturer of precision timepieces, and other corporate partners. This syndicate invested $100 million in two new boats and their campaign to win the trophy. Other teams were owned or sponsored by other wealthy individuals, including the king of Spain, and by transnational corporations in the fashion, ferryboat, pharmaceutical, energy, and media industries. While we may stereotypically associate elite sports with the amateur ideals of the joy of competing and sportsmanship and think of the America's Cup primarily as a chance for status display by wealthy individuals, this elite sport is very much like other global sports. For the competitors, the only acceptable outcome is victory, or, as those involved said to a reporter, "there is no second" (Phillips 2006). Thus, we can see that contemporary elite sports have retained their exclusivity in many respects, but also reflect major aspects of change from the globalization of the economy and sport. Sports such as the America's Cup mix traditional elements of amateur sports, such as exclusivity and the quest for the Auld Mug, with very modern elements of professionalism, commercial investment, and an intense commitment to winning, which reflect the imprint of the Golden Triangle.

level and from college to professional sport (or at least of being drafted by the professional league) were 2.9 percent and 1.3 percent in men's basketball, 3.1 percent and 1 percent in women's basketball, 5.8 percent and 2 percent in football, 5.6 percent and 10.5 percent in baseball, 12.9 percent and 4.1 percent in men's ice hockey, and 5.7 percent and 1.9 percent in men's soccer. The percentages are even smaller when we consider the likelihood of high school athletes becoming professional athletes, which was 0.03 percent for men's basketball, 0.02 percent for women's basketball, 0.09 percent for football, 0.5 percent for baseball, 0.4 percent for men's ice hockey, and 0.08 percent for soccer.[1] Coakley suggested that these numbers were rough estimates and probably overestimated the chances of moving up to the next levels of sport. His point is clear, though. The opportunity structure is a funnel with a wide opening at the base but a narrow tube that leads to a very small opening at the top or, to use a different image, a very slippery pyramid with a wide base and very little room at the top.

Neither image of the realities of the opportunity structure in U.S. sport, the funnel nor the slippery pyramid, is consistent with the American Dream.

(Keystone/Laurent Gillieron)

The America's Cup, with its expensive yachts, is a striking contrast to the poverty seen in youth soccer in the Brazilian favelas or slums. This chapter is about the inequalities of social stratification in sport and society. (AP Photo/Silvia Izquierdo)

However, the American Dream does not have to be true for people to believe it and for it to affect their behavior. In fact, it functions as a *cultural ideology*, which is an argument or set of claims about society that is accepted as true because powerful people assert its validity and because it is learned as an indisputable truth during socialization. Even though it is more of an ideology than a scientifically valid set of factual statements, the inspirational quality of the American Dream makes it difficult to refute, even with systematic evidence, because many less-advantaged people *want* it to be true and because it serves the interests of advantaged and powerful people in implying that they deserve to be where they are and deserve the rewards and power of their status. This ideology is consistent with the currently ascendant *neoliberal economic policies* that encourage capitalistic enterprise and individual risk-taking and investment without government interference and put responsibility on individuals for their own welfare. Belief in it helps us understand how elites in society justify structures of inequality that allow them to enjoy more economic advantages, respect, and influence than others and how those in power are able to obscure the structural obstacles that prevent or discourage people from challenging their hegemony.

Global Sports, Sports Hierarchies, and the Golden Triangle

Just as nations are stratified into structures of rich and poor, more and less respected, and more and less powerful, sports are stratified into a global hierarchy. The sports that are centrally situated in the Golden Triangle and receive the most media attention and the most investment from corporate sponsors are at the top of this hierarchy. The richest and most powerful media and transnational corporate sponsors make certain sports richer, more popular, and more powerful than the others, and they choose certain athletes to be part of their Golden Triangle. In making selected athletes celebrities and endorsers of the products of major corporate sponsors, they make these athletes famous and rich, but the athletes themselves reinforce the popularity and prominence of the sports they play. They draw audiences to the media that construct their images and give them visibility, and they bring attention to the corporate sponsors who pay them and sell their images. That is, star athletes who are part of the web of the Golden Triangle benefit from its wealth and power and also help reinforce it by playing its sports, appearing on its broadcasts, and endorsing its products.

While no one would dispute the global preeminence of soccer, or "football" as it is known outside North America, it actually poses a dilemma for the Golden Triangle. Its global popularity across national boundaries and class differences makes it difficult or impossible to ignore, but the continuous flow of uninterrupted action makes it difficult to fit commercial advertising into broadcasts. In contrast, U.S. football is ideally suited for television and corporate sponsors because it has so many breaks in the action in the course of a game. Nevertheless, the World Cup and European Soccer Championships outrank all other sports events in the world in the size of their television audiences (National Geographic 2006). Furthermore, four of the five richest sports teams in the world generating the most revenue in 2004–2005 were soccer clubs, with only the Washington Redskins football club squeezing into third place among Real Madrid (Spain), Manchester United (England), AC Milan (Italy), and Juventus (Italy) (National Geographic 2006). In the soccer stratification system, outstanding players often emerge in poor nations in South America and Africa, for example, or in nations with weaker soccer infrastructures, such as the United States, and then move up to more prestigious and richer leagues and teams in Europe. The United States is moving up the global soccer hierarchy, with high rates of participation in youth clubs and on high school and college teams and with the rise of its most prominent professional league, Major League Soccer. Nevertheless, it is unlikely to challenge the hegemony of more established sports in the United States, such as football, baseball, basketball, and ice hockey.

We will discuss this U.S. "exceptionalism" in the global sports culture in chapter five, but for now, we should note that the lesser popularity of soccer in relation to other, more prominent sports in the United States demonstrates that sports stratification systems within nations may be inconsistent with the global stratification structure of sport. As in the United States, soccer has had to compete with more popular sports in other countries. In Australia, for example, cricket, rugby, and Australian Rules football overshadow soccer, and India and Pakistan prefer cricket. However, in the United States, Australia, and a number of Asian countries, soccer is growing in popularity, and may eventually challenge more popular sports. In China, soccer and basketball have become more popular than the traditionally most popular Chinese sport of table tennis (National Geographic 2006).

Thus, just as individuals and teams may move up and down hierarchies of popularity, wealth, and influence, sports also may achieve upward or downward mobility. For example, in the United States, professional football replaced professional baseball as the most popular and commercially successful sport. In general, the successful promotion and development of sports in and through the Golden Triangle are major factors in their increased status. Sports such as soccer have become popular among youths in poorer countries because only a ball of some sort and some open space are required to play the game. When sports become popular and especially when they are adopted or supported by a fairly large number of relatively affluent people, they become more organized and begin to attract the interest and investment of the commercial media and corporate sponsors. That is, they begin to attract the attention of the Golden Triangle. Once the Golden Triangle develops, publicizes, endorses, and invests in a sport and its top players, they move up the sports stratification hierarchy at a local, national, and, eventually, global level, and they continue to move up as long as their popularity and the revenue they produce increase.

The lofty position of soccer in the global stratification hierarchy suggests that other sports that are played by a lot of people should also rank high in global or national sports hierarchies and receive a lot of attention from the commercial media and corporate sponsors. However, the rank of a sport in these sports hierarchies is affected by the interest of the Golden Triangle and reflects more than popularity alone. For example, in the United States, many more people bowl and play soccer than play golf and tennis, but golf and tennis receive more television coverage and attract more commercial sponsorship money. The answer to this apparent paradox lies in the influence of social class. The Golden Triangle is generally more strongly influenced by the tastes and purchasing power of more-affluent members of society than by those of less-affluent ones. More affluent people can buy more, and more expensive, consumer goods. Golf is played and watched by more affluent audiences than bowling is, which makes golf more attractive to television executives and corporate sponsors. In the case of soccer in the United States, the audience seems to be growing, but it cannot yet compete with the more established sports for coverage. Thus, it is a combination of the size and the social class composition of the audience, called "demographics," that shapes the relative interest and investment of the Golden Triangle in sports. What puts soccer at the top of the global sports hierarchy—beyond North America—and makes it so appealing to corporate investors and the Golden Triangle is the combination of the ethnic diversity of its huge global audience and its appeal to affluent consumers as well as poor people.

Media Constructions of Inequalities in Sport

We have seen that the mass media, and particularly television, are a major component of the Golden Triangle. Especially when they coordinate their influence with major sports and corporate sponsors, they can have a powerful influence on public perceptions and can be a significant socializing agent in shaping values, attitudes, and role conceptions. To the extent that the media are commercialized and linked to corporate sport and sponsors in a Golden Triangle, they are likely to have a conservative influence, reinforcing dominant patterns of culture and social structure in a society.

In regard to inequalities of class, gender, sexual orientation, race and ethnicity, and disability, the media have communicated words and images that have tacitly or explicitly justified or approved existing patterns of prejudice, discrimination, and inequality in sport. For example, they present stories, individual profiles, and images of athletes and coaches who achieve success in sport by working hard, taking advantage of opportunities, persevering, and overcoming obstacles. The series of *Rocky* films represents this kind of media construction, telling the inspiring story of a working-class Italian American who overcame seemingly insurmountable odds to become a world champion. However, it also tells us what happens when you lose your edge, become cocky, and indulge in extravagance. You can lose your title, and then have to return to the hard work and sacrifice that originally made you a champion. These are stories that reinforce traditional conceptions of the American Dream and established ideas about who deserves to be successful and who does not. *Rocky* was fiction, but the commercial media in the Golden Triangle also present these kinds of stories about real sports figures, and the effect is the same. They reinforce the interests of the dominant culture and structures of power in society by conveying the idea that high-status people in sport and society deserve their dominant status because they have earned it.

Thus, the powerful commercial media of the Golden Triangle deal with inequalities as obstacles to be overcome by worthy competitors rather than as enduring and deeply entrenched structural obstacles that unfairly restrict access and success opportunities for people of lower status in society and need to be contested. They typically prefer heroic stories of determined striving to stories of talented people who cannot achieve success or even play the game despite their best efforts. In the dominant cultural ideologies interwoven with the media constructions of success and failure in sport, both higher and lower status are supposed to be deserved, depending on the amount of effort attributed to the winners and losers. The media have the power to transform elitist, sexist, homophobic, racist, and ableist ideas and related practices in society that devalue and disadvantage people of the lower classes, women, homosexuals, racial and ethnic minorities, and people with disabilities, respectively. However, since the commercial media are tied to the dominant network of power in sport and the corporate world in Golden Triangles, they tend to reinforce hegemonic conceptions of these types of people that reinforce their unequal status in society.

The research literature shows that the dominant media often shortchange women and minorities in sport (Whannel 2000). They give them less airtime or print coverage than their higher-status counterparts, and when they cover women and minorities, they generally portray them with less respect and may even demean them in various obvious or not-so-obvious ways. African-American superstars such as Michael Jordan and Tiger Woods are portrayed in more positive ways, in part because their images are carefully constructed by the Golden Triangle to take advantage of their superstar status and maximize their potential as commercial commodities. In general, researchers have found limited evidence of negative or biased media coverage of black male athletes in recent years, but Asian and Latino or Hispanic[2] athletes have been portrayed in stereotypical terms (Whannel 2000:299). Douglas and Jamieson's (2006) study of Latina golfer Nancy Lopez's "farewell tour" in 2002 suggests that the media can be flexible in their interpretation of the ethnicity of minority athletes when they are light-skinned, especially if they are upwardly mobile, heterosexual, and married, and embody dominant ideologies such as the American Dream. In addition, Nancy Lopez was appealing to the media and the public because she avoided controversy and presented herself as both likeable and vulnerable. She sidestepped the debate in U.S. society about multiculturalism and bilingualism because she projected an image of someone who only spoke English and was fully assimilated into U.S. society. For these reasons, it is easy for the media to "whiten" her image, according to Douglas and Jamieson. We will discuss a similar "color-blind" approach to the construction of Michael Jordan's image in our analysis of the globalization of Michael Jordan in chapter six.

A subtle form of racial stereotyping was found in Woodward's study of the sports guides used by NFL scouts to critique college football players eligible for the draft. This study showed that African-American players were relatively more likely than their white counterparts who played the same position to be described in physical terms rather than in terms of mental abilities, which conforms to racial stereotypes of black athletes as physically gifted but having some intellectual deficiencies. This kind of racial stereotyping may be diminishing somewhat in other settings, though. A study of sports commentary on black and white players in the 2000 NCAA men's and women's basketball "Final Four" showed that black athletes were praised for their athleticism and physicality, but they also received some praise for their intelligence and leadership ability (Denham, Billings, and Halone 2002). The researchers found support for their hypothesis that athleticism descriptors would be applied more often to black players than to white players, but contrary to their prediction, intelligence descriptors were also applied more frequently to black players. Among both races, male players received substantially more commentary than females about both their athleticism and intelligence. Comments about appearance were made twelve times more often about female than male players. The researchers suggested that the announcers may have been coached by television executives to avoid racial biases in their comments, at least in regard to black male players, which could have accounted for the greater number of comments about the intelligence of black than white male players. It was not evident that they were made sensitive to gender biases in appearance-related comments.

Other kinds of race-related stereotypes, of "good guys" and "bad guys," have been used to distinguish black athletes more or less worthy of praise. That is, "good guy" black athletes, such as Michael Jordan and Tiger Woods, have been used as a counterpoint to "bad guy" black athletes, such as boxer Mike Tyson, who bring up stereotypical images of black men as overly aggressive, irresponsible, and, in Tyson's case, rapists (Whannel 2000:300). The "good guy" minority sports heroes cooperate with the Golden Triangle and enhance their images by trying to remain apolitical and avoid controversy, similar to the case of Nancy Lopez.

Recent developments, such as the rise of black quarterbacks in the NFL, give the dominant media and the Golden Triangle a chance to show that race now has little or no influence on sports opportunities and decisions in U.S. sports and perhaps that U.S. society is indeed becoming more color-blind, as the cases of Nancy Lopez and Michael Jordan might suggest. However, Buffington's (2005) content analysis of newspaper and magazine articles between 1999 and 2003 regarding the rise of black quarterbacks indicates that the current state of race relations and racial inequality needs to be interpreted carefully. The press overwhelmingly applauded the increased opportunities for black quarterbacks, many suggested that the old stereotypes that held them back in the past were largely gone or are rapidly disappearing, and some hinted at the declining significance of race in the larger society. Yet a number of the black quarterbacks in the stories were quoted as saying they believed that they were held to a different standard than their white counterparts and that they were being stereotyped, for example, for their running ability, rather than as complete quarterbacks in the classic NFL mold traditionally favored by coaches. In fact, in an interview early in the 2007 NFL season, African-American quarterback Donovan McNabb of the Philadelphia Eagles said that black quarterbacks had to deal with more pressure and more criticism than white quarterbacks faced (ESPN 2007). The mixing of critical comments and concerns by some of the players with more positive comments by players and journalists suggests that the NFL and sport remain contested terrain regarding race.

In some cases, even media that are oriented to minority audiences present athletes in terms that do not challenge the dominant conceptions of them in society. Hardin and Hardin (2004) found, for example, that *Sports n Spokes*, a disability sport publication, published stories from the mainstream media that reflected mainstream values and images of athletes with disabilities. The mainstream has tended to be patronizing and sometimes stigmatizing in their (limited) coverage of disability sports and athletes with disabilities, portraying "supercrips" who are considered superhuman because they are able to play sports well or even just play. We will have more to say in the coming chapters about the coverage of black superstars and athletes with disabilities. However, we should note here that athletes with disabilities and disability sports have been relatively invisible in the major media. Schantz and Gilbert (2001) showed that when disability sports are covered by the media, they tend to construct their coverage in familiar terms rather than in terms of distinct characteristics of these sports that challenge the mainstream. They also tend to be dismissive or less serious and pay less attention to them than to mainstream sports.

The Paralympics are the Olympic Games of disability sports, but they have a somewhat different focus than the mainstream Olympics. Paralympic athletes are serious, but the Paralympics were initially organized to promote a philosophy of empowerment for people with disabilities and of nondiscrimination, fair play, mutual respect, and world peace. In a number of basic respects, this philosophy is similar to the noble principles of the official Olympic charter emphasizing the pure joy of sports, ethics, education, human dignity, nondiscrimination, friendship, international solidarity, and peace. The difference between the Olympics and the Paralympics today is that the Olympics seem to have fallen further away from their ideals than the Paralympics have, as the Olympics are now dominated by nationalism and the "commercial logic" of the Golden Triangle. However, I do not want to suggest an overidealized conception of the contemporary Paralympics. We will see in the last chapter that the Paralympics have also seemed to move away from their founding philosophy. Paralympics organizers today seem to want to emulate big-time mainstream sports events, as they have been increasingly influenced by the commercialism of the Golden Triangle. The problem for Paralympics organizers is that they do not receive nearly as much attention from the media and corporate sponsors as mainstream sports receive.

Schantz and Gilbert did a content analysis of the coverage of the 1996 Paralympics in Atlanta in over one hundred articles in French and German newspapers with national circulation. They found that these major newspapers chose largely to ignore the distinctive focus of the Paralympics as disability sport and the challenge it represented to hegemonic values and popular stereotypes of people with disabilities. They instead covered the event from the same frame of reference used to cover the Olympics and other major international sports events. They focused on national medal winners and their own medal rankings. Schantz and Gilbert's conclusion paralleled the conclusion of Schell and Duncan's (1999) study of CBS coverage of this event, that is, that the event was treated as less important and a less serious form of sport than the Olympic Games. Schell and Duncan found that coverage was brief, production quality was poor, and commentary about the rules, strategies, and physical demands of the sports was very limited. They also found that some portraits of athletes treated them in the same way able-bodied athletes are treated, but other coverage was patronizing or demeaning, portraying the athletes as "victims of misfortune." Minimal and degrading media coverage explains why the International Paralympic Committee has sought closer ties with the International Olympic Committee and the Golden Triangle. We will discuss these trends in the last chapter.

Like athletes with disabilities, gay and lesbian athletes have received very little coverage by the mainstream media, except to point out the stigma associated with being openly homosexual in sport or society. As one media studies scholar stated, "Homosexuality doesn't sell" (quoted in Coakley 2007:431), which implies that the Golden Triangle is likely to try to avoid openly gay or lesbian athletes. Since some people have associated women's sports with lesbianism, promoters of women's sports have often emphasized sexy heterosexual images of women or focused on them as wives and mothers to allay possible public suspicions.

Women in more masculine sports, such as bodybuilding, have sometimes been very sensitive to lesbian labels and have reacted with exaggerated expressions of femininity. Black women have had the challenge of dealing with a possible combination of biases related to race, gender, and suspicions of lesbianism. They could be perceived as threatening if they were seen as "too black" (Daniels 2000). In its initial marketing campaign, the WNBA, the women's professional basketball league in the United States, softened and "feminized" the image of black players by focusing on players with modeling contracts and young children (Coakley 2007:297). The coverage of openly gay male athletes is a minor or nonexistent issue for the media because male athletes in major sports rarely acknowledge their sexual orientation while they are active in sports.

Media constructions of gender, masculinity, and femininity in sport have been frequent subjects of analysis in sport sociology and media studies research. The most consistent finding is that women receive much less media coverage than men. For example, in a study of gender differences in televised coverage of men and women in sport on news and highlight shows in Los Angeles, which was the fourth in a series begun in 1989, Duncan and Messner (2005) found that local coverage of women was nearly as low in 2004 as it was in 1989. In 2004, women received 6.3 percent of the airtime, compared with 5 percent in 1989. Coverage of women on ESPN's "Sports Center" (2.1 percent) and the Fox network's "Southern California Sports Report" (3 percent) was even less than local coverage in 2004. Although still very limited, the coverage of women tended to include fewer examples of humorous sexualization, nonserious gag features, and trivialization of women athletes than in the past. While the men's sports coverage included a variety of major sports, women's coverage was less varied, with over 42 percent devoted to women's tennis. This research was sponsored by the Amateur Athletic Foundation of Los Angeles (AAF). In her introduction to Duncan and Messner's report, Anita de Frantz, president of the AAF, applauded the improved quality of coverage but criticized its quantity as inequitable, unfair, and wrong. Thus, despite receiving more respectful coverage, it appears that women athletes and their sports had not yet penetrated the dominant sports culture in the United States in the early part of the twenty-first century, which includes the sports that attract the most attention of the Golden Triangle.

In this context, it should not be surprising that the ESPN list of the "Top 100 North American Athletes of the 20th Century" (in U.S. sports) included only eight women: #10 multi-sport star Babe Didrikson, #19 tennis star Martina Navratilova, #23 track star Jackie Joyner-Kersee, #41 track star Wilma Rudolph, #50 tennis star Chris Evert, #59 tennis star Billie Jean King, #65 tennis star Althea Gibson, and #69 speed skating star Bonnie Blair (Billings 2000). The eight women participated in four different sports, although Babe Didrikson could be counted in several sports categories, including golf and track. The men represented thirteen different sports, and there were three horses on the list. About the same percentage, 38 percent, of the men and women on the list were African American, including three of the top five men—#1 basketball star Michael Jordan, #3 star boxer Muhammad Ali, and #4 football star Jim Brown—and five of the top ten men were African American. In addition, the six foreigners on the list were NHL players from Canada, and they outnumbered the two athletes who had non-European ethnic backgrounds, American Indian multi-sport star Jim Thorpe and Latino baseball star Roberto Clemente. Thus, black men were overrepresented on the list, especially in the highest ranks, while women and ethnic minorities were underrepresented.

Some traditions in the sports media that feminists and others have interpreted as highly sexist have had strong staying power. One of those traditions is the annual swimsuit issue of *Sports Illustrated* magazine. The magazine is generally respected for the quality of its sports reporting and serious sports journalism. However, it has had a male bias. For example, according to Messner (2005), women were on less than 5 percent (six) of the covers of the magazine between 1998 and June 2000: legendary University of Tennessee coach Pat Summitt, figure skater Michelle Kwan, tennis player Serena Williams, soccer player Brandi Chastain (in the famous picture in her sports bra after winning the 1999 World Cup), the U.S. women's World Cup team, and Anna Kournikova. The content of the magazine's stories was similarly skewed toward men. This bias upsets advocates for women in sport, but the swimsuit issue makes many of them angry because it portrays women as sex objects, distracts attention from the accomplishments of women as serious athletes, and reinforces hegemonic ideas about masculinity and femininity as well as existing patterns of gender inequality in sport and society.

In the conclusion of her book about the swimsuit issue and sport, Davis (1997) suggested that the swimsuit issue and its narrow scope of coverage of sport showed that *Sports Illustrated* was more about hegemonic masculinity than about sport. In a world in which traditional masculinity has been so much under attack, the magazine provided reassurance and escape for men committed to the traditional gender order. Since the swimsuit issue, in particular, provoked various reactions, Davis perceived it as a "catalyst for a national debate about hegemonic masculinity and hegemonic femininity" (p. 118). This debate apparently has not adversely affected magazine subscriptions, since circulation statistics showed that it ranked #16 among U.S. magazines in 2004, with over 3.3 million subscriptions and a 2.5 percent increase in subscriptions between 2000 and 2003 (Media Info Center 2004).

Messner, Dunbar, and Hunt (2000) used AAF data to draw conclusions about the images of masculinity that were conveyed to U.S. boys by the sports programs they watched the most on television. These programs included ESPN's "Sports Center" and broadcasts of extreme sports, NBA basketball, NFL football, MLB baseball, and the "pseudosport" of professional wrestling. The researchers looked at event coverage, commercials, and pregame, halftime, and postgame shows. They concluded from their content analysis that this programming conveyed a "televised sports manhood formula" that showed their young male audience how to be a man, how to think about females, and what kinds of things they should buy. The dominant themes were: (1) white males are the dominant authority figures; (2) sport is a male realm; (3) men dominate commercials and women only appear with men; (4) women are sex objects, props for men, or

U.S. player Brandi Chastain celebrates after kicking the game-winning overtime penalty shootout goal against China during the Women's World Cup final at the Rose Bowl in Pasadena, California, Saturday, July 10, 1999. The United States beat China five to four on penalty kicks after a zero to zero tie. This widely seen photo illustrates the media tendency to focus on sexualized images of women rather than on women in action in sport. (AP Photo/*San Francisco Examiner,* Lacy Atkins)

prizes for successful men; (5) whites are in the foreground in commercials, while African Americans, Latinos, and Asian Americans are in the background, if they appear at all; (6) you win by being highly aggressive and lose if you are a nice guy; (7) fighting is to be expected for males; (8) athletes need to sacrifice their bodies and endure pain and injuries; (9) sport is combat or war; and (10) winning requires displays of "guts" or courage in the face of physical risks and confrontations. Although it is not clear how all young men—or young women or adults—interpret these themes, it is evident that the media messages in a range of popular televised sports programming in the United States convey stereotypical hypermasculine, sexist, and racist messages.

It may seem surprising that even broadcasts of extreme or action sports, which are often characterized as alternative, countercultural, and new millennium, convey similar messages to those of more traditional sports, such as pro basketball, football, and baseball. Rinehart (2005) found, however, that advertising in a national skating magazine used images we would expect to find in magazines catering to a more traditional male audience. Although the advertisers tried to represent themselves as "outlaws" challenging the mainstream sports culture, the advertisements tended to reflect themes such as the natural "maleness" of North American sports and the sexy and alluring nature of women. Thus, even though there is some inconsistency between the apparently intended messages and the actual messages of this kind of advertising, it seems that the basic thrust of this advertising has a number of the same elements as the "televised sports manhood formula" found by Messner, Dunbar, and Hunt. Like mainstream sports, commercial media influences in "new millennium" sports tend to reinforce rather than challenge hegemonic conceptions of masculinity and established forms of inequality. What is especially significant about the advertising in the skateboarding and in-line skating publications is that they are oriented to adolescents. Therefore, young people appear to be exposed to media constructions of sports of various kinds that encourage the reproduction of existing patterns of inequality and their supporting ideologies. The co-optation of these sports for commercial purposes by Golden Triangles is likely to reinforce this conclusion. We will discuss the transformation of sports countercultures by the Golden Triangle in chapter six.

Conclusion: Sport, Stratification, and Contested Terrain

Sociological theories enable us to understand what social stratification is and why it has significant effects on how people see and experience their world and how they perceive and interact with others. We know that when people perceive that they are different from other types of people, they make judgments about those differences and create hierarchies that reflect these judgments. In these hierarchies, the people who are at the top get more of the things we value in society, such as attention, respect, fame, property, money, and access to prestigious and influential positions. In this chapter, we focused on stratification-related concepts and theories, social class inequalities, and the global hierarchy of sports, and we saw the dominant role of the Golden Triangle, and especially the mass media, in maintaining existing patterns of inequality in sport and society.

Theories of distributive justice or equity enable us to understand why some people may accept their disadvantaged or subordinate status and why others react with resentment and anger and make sport contested terrain about issues of inequality and unfairness. Although many of Marx's central predictions about capitalism and inequality have not yet occurred, it is important to understand Marx's analysis of stratification under capitalism because we will pay considerable attention in future chapters to the influence of global capitalism and the capitalistic pursuit of profit in sport. Structural functional analyses enable us to see the persistence of certain kinds of inequalities as functional, which is a very different perspective than conflict theory. This kind of theoretical thinking is consistent with the ideological justifications for inequalities advanced by those in the top echelons of the hierarchies of power and privilege in sport and society. Weber's multidimensional perspective highlights the basic types of structured inequality of economic class, social status, and political power. In the discussion of media constructions of inequality, we have begun to see how inequalities of class, status, and power are associated with status differences based on social class, gender, sexual orientation, race and ethnicity, and physical disability. We have also begun to see how people in the dominant networks of power in the Golden Triangle of sport construct and perpetuate stories, images, and ideologies that reflect and reinforce their dominant position.

One of the most basic messages that these dominant networks convey in sport and in the larger society is that winners are better than losers, winners deserve to win, and losers deserve to lose. They also convey subtle and not-so-subtle ideas about who deserves to be a winner and get most of the rewards in sport and society. They tell us that the most committed and hardest workers win and deserve to be successful and get the spoils of victory. They also construct images of the types of people we should expect to find on the victory stand or on the field. These are people who embody the dominant cultural values, but conceptions of who they are and should be are often influenced by elements of elitism, sexism, homophobia, racism, and ableism. In modern sport, as in most modern societies, the hegemonic ideologies advanced by those with the most power contain messages that the types of competitors who belong in sport and deserve the most attention and the most success represent the values of the more affluent classes. These messages also tell us that it is fair and appropriate that relatively more competitive opportunities, attention, and chances for success are given to men than to women; heterosexuals than homosexuals, bisexuals, and transsexuals; whites than blacks; ethnic majority group members than ethnic minorities; and able-bodied people than people with disabilities.

Of course, there are exceptions to the general patterns of inequality in sport. There are "rags to riches" stories; black athletes have dominated a few sports; a number of ethnic-minority athletes and coaches have become prominent; and a few women and even a few homosexuals and athletes with disabilities have achieved some success in sport. However, in treating them as exceptional and by emphasizing how they tend to embody dominant ideologies of success, such as the American Dream, the Golden Triangle is able to turn their success into a validation of its dominant ideologies. When successful women and minorities in sport shy away from challenging these ideologies and the structures of inequality they support, they further reinforce these ideologies and structures. We know, however, that in recent decades, many advocates for women and minorities have challenged the power structures, and have made sport contested terrain in a number of different ways. Sometimes symbols have been at the heart of conflicts in sport. For example, the racist and sexist implications of team mascots, names, and rituals (Eitzen 2003:ch. 3) have become highly contentious issues. Many sports realms remain contested terrain in regard to various issues of inequality because these issues have not been resolved in the larger society. Even where sport seems to be making more progress than the surrounding society, for example, regarding opportunities for black male athletes, issues of inequality of opportunity still exist. After all, the much-ballyhooed "black dominance" in sport only applies to black males in a few sports. In the next chapter, we will examine inequalities of race and ethnicity, gender, sexual orientation, and physical disability in more depth and consider the extent to which those who are contesting enduring patterns of inequality are changing sport and society.

Notes

1. These estimated probabilities can be found on the NCAA website (www.ncaa.org) in Appendix C of the document *Pro Sports: A Career in Professional Athletics: A Guide to Making the Transition.*

2. U.S. Census Bureau reports use the terms "Latino" and "Hispanic" interchangeably, referring to people whose heritage, stated ethnic identity, or country of origin is a Spanish-speaking country, usually in Central or South America, in the Caribbean, or Spain. I will generally use "Latino" (male or generic) or "Latina" (female) to refer to this category of people.

4

Dimensions of Social Inequality in Sport

What should success look like in sport? In the last chapter, we considered how the mass media in the Golden Triangle construct stories and images and convey messages about the characteristics of the people who are and should be successful in sport. They tell us who belongs and who does not, sometimes through the subtle means of ignoring certain types of athletes and sports, and other times by demeaning them. Continuing the theme of social inequality introduced in chapter three, we will focus in more detail in this chapter on some of the most fundamental dimensions of social inequality in society and sport, beyond class inequalities.

This chapter will examine how social inequalities related to gender, sexual orientation, race and ethnicity, and physical disability affect social identities, opportunities, interactions, and rewards in sport. Introductory texts in sociology and sport sociology devote separate chapters to gender, race and ethnicity, and perhaps sexual orientation or "sexuality." They typically give very little attention to issues of disability. I would argue that all of these dimensions of inequality are important because all have profound effects on the lives of many people. We will address all of these dimensions of social structure in an integrated fashion in this chapter, as we began to do in the media discussion at the end of the last chapter. Through this integrated approach in these two chapters, it should become evident that these various dimensions of social inequality can be difficult to disentangle from each other when we try to understand how inequality appears in sport and affects its participants. This insight will be helpful in trying to understand the various influences of inequality on sport in future chapters. We will see in these future chapters that inequality in its various forms is pervasive and very consequential in sport in its different forms at different levels. In the next section, we will turn our attention to the relationship of gender to sport.

Gender and Sport

Just as *ideologies of class, race, ethnicity, sexual orientation, and ability/disability* justify the superiority of some classes or categories of people over others, *gender ideologies* justify gender inequalities as necessary, moral, natural, and deserved (Coakley 2007:20–23). Structured inequalities of gender have been as entrenched and consequential as any status inequalities in sport. There may be no more fundamental and pervasive status distinction in society than the distinction between males and females, and in nearly all societies and sports throughout history, men have had a higher status than women. Because we are born with certain biological or *sex* differences as males and females, people have often assumed that differences in *gender* identities and roles traditionally associated with sex differences are natural. In fact, while sex differences are natural, gender differences are socially and culturally constructed. This construction of gender has traditionally made females feel inferior to males and relegated females to subordinate and less-valued and less-rewarded roles than males. In addition, cultural ideologies of gender have typically justified other *sexist* beliefs and the *sexist* treatment of women. These ideologies have shaped personal and societal conceptions of masculinity and femininity and reinforced structures of gender inequality. They have conveyed a broad justification for male privilege in relations with women and encouraged men to think of women as sexual objects rather than in terms of what women are capable of doing with their bodies and minds.

Sport, like the rest of most societies, has historically been *patriarchal*, which broadly refers to male dominance. We noted that in ancient Greece, women participated in the Heraean Games, while men participated in the Olympics, but they were obligated to adhere to a dual ideal of "fertility and femininity" (Nixon and Frey 1996:18–19). This ideal implied that women could participate in athletic activities to help them prepare for the rigors of childbirth and defense of the state in case of war, but they also had to display culturally defined qualities such as dependence and passivity in relations with men. The general historical pattern was for women to be excluded or segregated or to receive little recognition or support for their sports participation. On the brink of Title IX in 1972, when the law redefined the opportunity structure for females in U.S. high school and college sports, sport was viewed as a "male preserve" where males participated to establish their masculinity and women sat on the sidelines to ensure their femininity (Nixon and Frey 1996:252–254). We will have more to say about Title IX and the push for gender equity later, especially in the chapter on college athletics. At this point, it is important to recognize that the law and pressure from a global women's movement in the 1970s began a fundamental restructuring of the opportunity structure of sport in the United States and other countries.

Pressures from earlier women's rights movements in the twentieth century had increased opportunities for women to participate in global competitions, such as the Olympics, with the percentages increasing from 0 percent women in 1896 to over 40 percent in the 2004 Summer Games (Coakley 2007:252). Furthermore, women could be found throughout the century in more "feminine sports," such as tennis, swimming, golf, figure skating, and gymnastics, which seemed more graceful and less reliant on physical strength, aggression, or physical contact. However, support for women's team sports was minimal, and girls and women generally had few chances to participate compared with boys and men. The door opened wide for all kinds of sports participation by women in the United States in the 1970s following the passage of Title IX of the Higher

Education Act, which outlawed sex discrimination in all educational programs and activities receiving federal financial assistance.

Statistics cited by Coakley (2007:238, 241) show how much has changed for girls and women since the early 1970s in the United States. For example, in 1971, 295,000 girls and 3.7 million boys competed for their high schools at the varsity level, and girls' high school teams received 1 percent of the funding for interscholastic sports. In 1971, there were 32,000 female athletes and 180,000 male athletes in college sports, and 1 percent of college athletic budgets went to females. In 2004, participation rates for females increased 1000 percent at the high school level to 2.95 million and increased 500 percent at the college level to 160,000. Among males, participation increased to 4 million at the high school level and 240,000 at the college level. These gains for females are impressive, but they suggest that participation is still unequal, with approximately 42:58 and 40:60 ratios of females to males in high school and college sports, respectively, despite the fact that females outnumber males in the student body, especially at the college level, where the ratio is over 55:45 female to male at many institutions (Cheslock 2007). The perception that these differences in participation and inequalities in scholarship money, recruiting money, operating budgets, coaches' salaries, and access to administrative and coaching positions have resulted from biases has led to accusations of gender inequity or unfairness (Eitzen 2003:ch. 7). These accusations could have been predicted from the discussion of gender inequity in the last chapter. In fact, for the past forty years, there has been a continuing feminist challenge to male dominance of sport and ongoing social pressure and legal action to reduce the persisting gender inequalities in U.S. college sports, in particular.

Some men have seen the growing female majority on college campuses as a crisis for men. With interesting logic, one *New York Times* Op-Ed column, titled "Let the Guys Win One," argued that since women had deservedly become the majority among college students as a result of greater motivation, self-control, and academic preparation, college men ought to be allowed to remain dominant in at least one area, athletics (Tierney 2006). Hence, the columnist argued, Title IX no longer was needed in college sports. The issue of the growing gender gap has generated considerable discussion and disagreement about its causes and implications (Lederman 2006; Lewin 2006), but this *New York Times* column illustrates the implicit message that sport remains a special preserve for males. The acceptance of this kind of belief among powerful people in sport, the media, and other parts of society explains why sport continues to be highly contested terrain among feminists and advocates of women's sport in the United States, despite their gains over the past few decades.

Theberge (2000a) pointed out that the feminist challenge to sport has focused on the underlying gender ideology that has justified traditional gender roles and inequalities. Feminists have made sport contested ideological terrain, as they pointed to the persisting cultural and social constraints that have limited or demeaned women's opportunities, rewards, and experiences. The struggle has been about hegemonic conceptions of masculinity associated with sports participation. Even in new and emerging sports that would seem to reflect new ideas about gender, the assertion of masculinity has been important for males, and the status of women in these sports has been somewhat problematic.

In their ethnographic study of windsurfers in England and other countries, Wheaton and Tomlinson (1998) found that males dominated the sport, but there was a willingness to respect females as windsurfers if they were good enough and serious enough. Approximately 30 percent of windsurfers in the United Kingdom were females and less than 20 percent were females in this study. In general, females were not as adept at the sport as males were, and some women were viewed stereotypically as more concerned about their appearance and avoiding cold water than about getting on the water and sailing. Yet if women could meet the male standards of proficiency and commitment, they earned the respect of the men. One of the male windsurfers commented that windsurfing was not like rugby, where the men "despised women's rugby," and he readily expressed his respect for two women in his sport who were faster than he was. The most talented and committed "core women" in the sport recognized this respect and did not see windsurfing as a masculine realm where women were excluded. They saw it as a setting where women could pursue a very physically demanding activity and retain their femininity. They also distinguished themselves from the "windsurfing widows," who were the wives and girlfriends of the male windsurfers and were spectators rather than active participants. Thus, skilled and committed women could earn respect in the windsurfing subculture and put themselves above the less-active women who stayed on the shore. Yet, as Wheaton and Tomlinson observed, they had earned respect by meeting male physical and competitive standards in the sport. On the one hand, then, core women could be accepted by men for their talent and commitment, but on the other hand, the acceptance of talented and committed women by male windsurfers represented an accommodation to dominant masculine values rather than a challenge to them.

Anderson's (1999) study of the construction of gender in snowboarding similarly showed that male hegemony has an impact, but also may be contested, in other recently emerging sports. Anderson observed that snowboarding emerged from a relatively unorganized subculture as an individual sport with extensive female participation. It did not have the sex-segregated teams, highly organized corporate structure, or exclusive eligibility rules that characterized the most established domains of sport, where hegemonic masculinity prevailed. Males could not automatically assume that competing on a snowboard would define them as masculine, and as a result, male snowboarders engaged in exaggerated behaviors that were meant to define their masculinity. In particular, they created a "street punk" style of masculine impression management that involved an attitude of aggressiveness, stoicism, and superiority and of distinctive "gangsta" dress of baggy jeans and wallet chains. This style also stressed the violent and dangerous nature of their sport and emphasized the men's heterosexuality. The snowboarding media picked up this idea of "street punk masculinity" and portrayed the sport primarily in masculine terms.

In the snowboarding subculture, "girl-boarders" were portrayed as sex objects with more emphasis on their bodies and clothes than on their ability on their boards. If these women were not viewed as mainly drawn to the sport by their interest in men, they were perceived as wanting to be like men and thus were seen as unfeminine or lesbian. Their skills were also devalued, and while the generic term "snowboarder" implied a male, women were referred to as "girl-snowboarders." An irony of this effort to construct a "gangsta" or street punk version of masculinity is that snowboarders tended to be white and privileged. Not surprisingly, this kind of construction of masculinity was not readily embraced by ski-area owners or by more traditional skiers, who were predominantly affluent and had more conventional values and very different ideas than the younger male snowboarders about proper behavior and dress on the ski slopes. This version of hegemonic masculinity and the sexualized and devalued treatment of women associated with it were also resisted by female snowboarders. Thus, the particular manifestations of gender issues can look different in different sports settings, but even in newer forms of sport, women still are likely to have to approach the sport as contested terrain if they want their participation and ideas about their gender defined in their own terms instead of in terms of some version of masculinity.

Hegemonic conceptions of masculinity have typically emphasized force and physical toughness, which is why team sports involving physical contact or confrontation have typically been defined as masculine. Women have challenged the idea that team sports are for men, and over the past several decades, female participation in team sports has gradually increased, with the Olympics adding women's volleyball in 1964, basketball in 1976, and field hockey in 1980. The timing of the addition of field hockey is interesting because it had been the rare example of a female team sport since the 1930s, and girls and women had competed in it from the high school to the international level since that time. The first women's team sport to be added to the Winter Olympics was ice hockey in 1998, and Theberge focused special attention on it as a challenge to hegemonic masculinity.

With aggressive body checking, the men's game embodied the force, power, and aggression associated with dominant ideas about masculinity. In her research, Theberge (2000b) found that elite women ice hockey players in Canada faced ambivalence or resistance to their playing the game, but they developed a sense of community as a team and demonstrated skill, commitment, and love for hockey. They played the same game as the men, except for one noteworthy difference. The women's rules prohibited intentional body checking, but they did not eliminate the extensive body contact that is necessitated by efforts to gain control of the puck and the game. This difference in rules resulted in a different type of game, as the women tended to emphasize speed, strategy, and skill, while the men placed more emphasis on power and aggression. The fact that the women's rules were more likely than the men's rules to limit injuries did not increase appreciation of their game, since the elements of physical aggression and risk probably were part of the reason the men's game was considered more legitimate. The "real game" was one that demonstrated hegemonic masculinity, and women gained less respect for playing a different kind of game that was "less masculine."

Theberge (2000a) also observed that individual sports could impose cultural and social constraints on women and create frustrations for them. For example, she analyzed Crosset's (1995) study of women professional golfers on the Ladies Professional Golf Association (LPGA) Tour. Although the status system within this sport was based on evaluations of players' performances on the golf course, the golfers had to deal with public and media judgments that focused more on their appearance and sexuality. This is similar to the conceptions of less-serious female windsurfers, "windsurfing widows," and "girl-boarders" we previously discussed, and to conceptions of women in a variety of other sports subcultures dominated by masculine values and norms. The golfers realized that the LPGA Tour needed media and corporate support and had to present the sport and the players in appealing ways. This meant that the women had to pay special attention to their appearance and dress, try to look sexy, and convey traditional images of heterosexual femininity and motherhood to try to make a positive impression. They also had to deal with sexist and homophobic comments by a male television golf commentator in a newspaper interview, which asserted that the women players could not be as good as the men and that the sport had a harmful lesbian image. Although his employer, the CBS network, ultimately suspended him—after some hesitation—CBS and LPGA officials generally tried to minimize the incident and avoid offending their audience. According to Theberge, they were less concerned about the sexism and homophobia than about losing audience share, hurting the image of the sport, and reducing the payoff from their investment.

Although male windsurfers respected women who met their standards of prowess and commitment, men typically have had difficulty accepting women in their sports or have been unwilling to accord them respect for playing a sport their own way, as in the case of playing ice hockey without body checking. Even in sports such as golf that have required less physicality, force, and aggression than others, men have reacted quite negatively to women, as the example of the CBS commentator showed. Research about women's soccer in the United States and the Netherlands by Knoppers and Anthonissen (2003) revealed that class, gender, and ideas about masculinity and femininity may intersect differently in different nations and lead to different degrees of acceptance of women in sport. The "Focus on Research" feature about "Cross-National Differences in Inequality in Women's Soccer" examines their study.

Some men have difficulty accepting women in any sport, while others are especially opposed to women competing in sports events with men. Competitions between men and women have happened in a number of sports over time. Perhaps the most famous competition of this sort was the media-manufactured "Battle of the Sexes" in 1973 between the aging onetime tennis champion Bobby Riggs and his female opponent, Billie Jean King. Riggs had prompted the match by making very sexist comments to the press about women's tennis. As a star in women's tennis and a strong advocate for women in sport, King accepted his challenge and made her strongest argument on the tennis court by beating Riggs. In golf, Babe Didrikson once competed against men, and more recently, we have seen Annika Sorenstam and teenager Michelle Wie compete in men's PGA events. In auto racing, there have been Janet Guthrie and Danica Patrick; Ann Meyers had a tryout with the Indiana Pacers of the National Basketball Association (NBA) in 1979; females have been placekickers in men's football; and of course, mixed-doubles have long been part of tennis. There are many other examples that could be cited, but a common element in these types of cases is that they have not only created resistance and resentment among some men; they have also made some male competitors nervous.

If males are supposed to be dominant in sport—and society—the possibility of getting beaten by a girl or woman could be very damaging to the traditional self-concept of the defeated males, and it could be confusing to those who

Focus on Research Feature 4.1:
Cross-National Differences in Inequality in Women's Soccer

The 1994 Women's World Cup final, won by the United States over China in a dramatic penalty kick shootout, was the biggest event in the modern history of women's sports. It attracted over ninety thousand spectators and an estimated eighteen million U.S. television viewers. Although the women were not able to sustain this level of interest with their professional league in the United States, it is clear that U.S. women have been very successful in soccer and have attracted a large number of fans. We also know that women in other nations have become more proficient at soccer and have challenged the dominance of the U.S. women in the sport. Through 2007, the United States had won two of the Women's Cups, which began in 1991, and Norway and Germany won the others. Sweden, Brazil, and China are among the other nations that have been global powers in women's soccer.

While women's soccer is becoming popular in a number of nations around the world, we would expect women's opportunities to be more limited in more traditional societies with more rigid patterns of gender stratification. From a sociological perspective, possible cross-national and cross-cultural variations in the popularity of women's soccer raise questions about the types of social and cultural conditions that contribute to the development of women's soccer in different nations. Knoppers and Anthonissen (2003) did a comparative analysis of the social history of women's involvement in soccer in the United States and the Netherlands to provide some answers to these kinds of questions. They focused on the differing consequences of the struggle for the acceptance of women in soccer in the United States and the Netherlands, and the influence of hegemonic masculinity and social class in shaping soccer development in these two countries. We will see that even nations that we may not view as very traditional, such as the Netherlands, may pose significant obstacles to the participation of women in sport.

Class, ethnicity, and gender influenced the development of soccer in the Netherlands. Initially, soccer clubs were restricted to upper-class men, and as a result, socialist working-class men, members of religious groups, and Jews established their own clubs. As it developed into a national sport, men's soccer drew its players mainly from the working and middle classes. It became a marker of masculinity, and for this reason, the national men's soccer federation (KNVB) opposed the participation of women in the sport. It was thought not only that it was a man's game, but also that it was inappropriate for women to play. The KNVB decided in 1896 that women could not play, and women challenged this ruling for the next seventy years. However, women's soccer advocates received no support from early feminists, who were opposed to the sport for everyone because it emphasized masculine values of roughness and virility. Ironically, though, feminist efforts to change sexist public stereotypes about women made sports, such as soccer, more appealing to women. Women who tried to play and join men's soccer clubs were often labeled as "feminists," but they denied a connection to the women's movement. Parenthetically, this happened later in the century in the United States, as many groundbreaking female athletes also disavowed feminist labels.

Throughout the twentieth century in the Netherlands, there were cycles of women's teams forming (always coached by men), teams dying due to inadequate facilities and objections from husbands and other men, and then new ones forming and dying. In 1955, the General Women's Soccer Association was formed, but the KNVB made access to playing fields very inconvenient for women. Despite continuing efforts by the men to keep them out of the sport, women persisted and by the 1970s, the KNVB finally ended its official ban of women. However, the sport grew slowly because the KNVB dragged its feet in its promotional and organizational efforts. By the end of the twentieth century, the KNVB was promoting soccer as a youth sport for boys and girls and permitted girls as young as six to play. Yet by 2000, girls were 3 percent and women were another 3 percent of the one million soccer players in the Netherlands. To provide playing opportunities for girls in age brackets without enough girls to make teams, a number of clubs permitted mixed teams, and these teams attracted the more talented female players, who saw better opportunities to advance playing with males than with females. In general, though, males have continued to dominate Dutch soccer, and the widespread acceptance of this male dominance in Dutch society has limited the growth of women's soccer and the amount of resources and media attention it gets, making it relatively invisible in the society.

The Dutch situation is a striking contrast to women's soccer in the United States. Soccer started in the same way in the United States as it did in the Netherlands. Upper-class English males brought the game to the United States in the 1860s, but it quickly lost its appeal, first to rugby, and then to the new game of football Americans invented. In comparison with football, soccer was not seen as very rough, which meant that it was appropriate for women. It became a part of physical education and intramural programs for women at elite women's colleges in the early twentieth century. As a team game that was safe and healthy, it was seen as a transitional activity to field hockey. However, it remained essentially outside the competitive arena of more organized intercollegiate sports for women until Brown University fielded the first women's varsity soccer team in 1971. The sport got a boost from Title IX, and the first national collegiate championship game was played in 1981. Since then, soccer has become the fastest-growing sport for girls and women. At the end of the twentieth century, about half of the four million soccer players between the ages of four and eighteen were girls, and nearly 90 percent of colleges and universities had women's soccer teams. As we noted earlier, U.S. women have enjoyed great success at the international level as one of the elite teams, which is a status the men have been unable to achieve.

Knoppers and Anthonissen observed that Dutch women have waged a long and still-frustrating struggle to develop women's soccer, while U.S. women have fought for greater legitimacy, access, and support for women across a wide band of sports, which included soccer. They argued that in both nations, the development of women's soccer has been influenced by the relative popularity of men's soccer and of other men's and women's sports, by dominant conceptions of gender, and, in particular, by the perceived appropriateness of sport and physical activity for women. These factors produced different results in the Netherlands and the United States. The Dutch constructed soccer as a sport for men and it has remained a predominantly male sport. In the United States, soccer evolved into an activity and then a sport that was acceptable for women as well as for men. Hegemonic conceptions of masculinity posed an obstacle to women's soccer advocates in the Netherlands, but have had a less constraining influence on the development of women's soccer in the United States, in part because men had a variety of other sports options, including very aggressive and "manly" sports such as football.

I have noted the influence of social class in the early development period of soccer in both the Netherlands and the United States. Knoppers and Anthonissen found that social class as well as race and ethnicity has played a role in the rise of soccer in both countries. Like gender, though, class, race, and ethnicity have influenced the sport differently in the two countries. In the Netherlands, soccer was played by men from various social backgrounds after its initial development among upper-class males. Clubs tended to represent specific classes, ethnic groups, religious groups, and political beliefs. The men's national team is socially diverse. Among Dutch girls and women, however, soccer is played by middle-class whites, and this pattern is similar to the one in the United States.

An important reason why interest in soccer in the United States among both boys and girls grew mostly in the white, middle-class suburbs between the late 1960s and the middle of the 1980s was that the professional North American Soccer League (NASL) started youth programs in the suburbs to promote the sport during this period. The NASL went out of business in 1984, but its promotional efforts had a lasting imprint on soccer in the United States. References to "soccer moms" by politicians were to white, middle-class mothers, and playing soccer became part of the experience of growing up in suburbia for many girls as well as boys. In this way, soccer became a marker of white middle-class experience in the same way that basketball, football,

continues

wrestling, and other sports were markers of being black or working-class in the United States. The researchers argued that this connection of soccer to the middle class was important for women in the United States because when women are encouraged or permitted to play sports, those sports tend to be connected to the white middle and upper classes. Examples include tennis and golf, the first two professional sports for women, and swimming, one of the earliest women's Olympic sports. They were appropriate for upper-status women because they were associated with feminine grace and did not require the muscles or aggression of more "masculine" sports. They were also viewed as appropriate for women because higher-status women played them. Soccer may have been legitimated for women in the United States precisely because white middle-class women played it in a society dominated by white middle-class values. In the Netherlands, the extensive involvement of working-class, as well as middle-class, men in soccer defined it as a more physical and masculine sport, which may have inhibited women's involvement. Therefore, in both the United States and the Netherlands, social class filtered ideas about the appropriateness of female involvement in soccer—and other sports.

The lack of professional soccer for women in the Netherlands is another basis for gender inequality in soccer there. It has resulted in less media coverage and less support from the KNVB, which has paid more attention to professionalized than to amateur forms of the sport. The absence of women's professional soccer has also restricted high-level coaching opportunities for women. In the United States, male and female national team members are paid, but despite their record of more competitive success at the international level, it took a strike by the women and media publicity to achieve pay parity with the men in their contract with the United States Soccer Federation (USSF). The women had been battling with the USSF for over a decade, but were inspired to continue their fight by the example of Billie Jean King and women tennis players. Thus, the higher relative status of women in soccer in the United States than in the Netherlands has been achieved on contested terrain, where the Dutch women continue their struggle. Furthermore, despite social class, ethnic, and gender differences among soccer players in the United States and the Netherlands, overall control of the sport in both countries is mainly held by white middle-class and upper-class white men, who dominate coaching, ownership, and management. The superiority of U.S. women to the U.S. men in the competitive arena obviously has not translated into female control of the sport. The primary difference between U.S. and Dutch women's soccer is that the U.S. women have gained more competitive opportunities and success due to differences in the relationship of soccer to social class, hegemonic masculinity, and the range of available and acceptable sports options for men and women in the two countries.

learned hegemonic ideas of masculinity. Even more confusing is the case of women in highly masculine sports where they display a high level of aggression, strength, and muscularity. It can also be challenging for women to construct conceptions of their femininity in these types of sports. In a participant-observation and interview study of women boxers and their coaches, Mennesson (2000) found that the women had to navigate the territory between challenging the gender order and showing that they could also display traditional femininity. Thus, they were "women [but] unlike other women" (p. 29). They rejected fragile or passive stereotypes of womanhood and were appropriately combative in the ring, but they also wore sexy attire for matches and miniskirts afterward. The women who had participated in the sport since adolescence were more likely to say they were "tomboys" and tended to be drawn to clubs that emphasized more combative forms of fighting such as kickboxing. They became "hard" boxers. The women who had started boxing later in life tended to be less interested in using their fists in more combative styles and were drawn to clubs that allowed them to learn more aesthetic and technical aspects of the sport. They became "soft" boxers. These softer boxers took a much longer time than harder boxers to learn to use physical force against an opponent. The presence of either type of boxer in the gym was a challenge to traditionalists in the sport and in the larger society, and the hegemony of traditional masculinity in the sport made identity formation challenging for both hard and soft women boxers. The film *Million Dollar Baby* dramatized the challenges a woman faced in the very masculine world of the boxing gym.

Lowe's (1998) interview study of women bodybuilders showed that the women in this sport also had to face sexist stereotypes in forming their identity. Whereas the women boxers had to deal with identity issues in a highly combative sport, the women bodybuilders had to face questions about the appearance of their bodies. Boxing has been a stereotypically masculine activity because it involves physical combat, and women boxers have represented a serious challenge to the idea that men are naturally the physically aggressive sex. Bodybuilding has been a stereotypically masculine activity because it involves big muscles, and female bodybuilders have challenged the ideas that men are the strong sex and women do not have muscles. Thus, both boxing and bodybuilding represent substantially different conceptions of what women can be than are conveyed by hegemonic conceptions of masculinity. Women in these sports may continue to struggle in varying degrees with their identities as they try to assert both their athletic prowess and their femininity. However, the degrees of interest and acceptance of women in these sports are measures of the erosion of the most traditional stereotypes that are part of hegemonic conceptions of masculinity and sport. It is evident that interest and acceptance are increasing and sport and society are changing, even if only in small steps (e.g., Patton 2001).

Although the damaging consequences of hegemonic masculinity and male dominance for women who like sport and want to participate in it seem fairly obvious, their damaging consequences for men may be less apparent. Much research and writing in sport sociology have examined how sport socializes men to be masculine, and how males often struggle with the masculine expectations imposed on them by sport. Messner (e.g., 1990b, 1992) has done extensive research about sport and the "problem of masculinity" for males, and he has shown how social class affects the dependence of males on sport for their masculine identity and self-respect. Poorer boys and young men have fewer options for defining themselves as successful, which is especially important to males in a culture where males are supposed to be dominant and successful. Thus, the importance of success in sport is inversely related to a male's social class: the lower the class, the more important is sports success.

In the locker room, males of various classes learn to prove their masculinity by degrading women and other males who are not stereotypically masculine. In his research about fraternal bonding in a locker room of a men's college sports team, Curry (1991) found a culture of hypermasculinity that encouraged degrading sexist views and treatment of women. Locker room talk tended to focus on aggression and sex. The men he studied seemed to try to reassure themselves and others of their masculinity by demeaning women, talking about them as sex objects, and, in some cases, suggesting sexual conquests. More respectful talk about women as real persons and not as objects or abstractions

Laila Ali, left, tries to avoid a punch from Jacqui Frazier-Lyde during their match Friday, June 8, 2001, in Verona, New York. Ali, daughter of the legendary boxer Muhammad Ali, won the bout. These women represent counterstereotypical examples of females in a highly aggressive and dangerous "masculine" sport. (AP Photo/Beth A. Keiser)

tended to be in hushed tones, for fear of damaging a man's reputation. In this hypermasculine culture, homosexuals were also degraded to affirm masculinity. These kinds of patterns are not restricted to locker rooms.

Hughson (2000) did an ethnography of young, male Australian-Croatian soccer fans in suburban Sydney, Australia, and found that the identities of these young men were constructed from ideas of exaggerated masculinity or "machismo," male chauvinism, hatred of women or misogyny, and homophobia. These young men often felt compelled to prove their heterosexuality, and a major means of doing so was through claiming sexual conquests of women. They also engaged in fighting, heavy drinking, and attempts to demean opposing players by calling them "fags" or "faggots." While their efforts to assert their masculinity may seem to be "uncivilized" or outside the mainstream, Hughson suggested that their particular expressions of masculinity derived from their marginalized status in Australian society. Although more "civilized" men of higher status may express revulsion at their behavior, Hughson proposed that their expressions of masculinity ultimately were related to the same general ideas of hegemonic masculinity more gracefully or subtly expressed by more "respectable" men.

Misogyny was mainly expressed by the young men in Hughson's study in various forms of verbal abuse. These abusive comments about women were linked to their homophobic comments. It is not unusual for misogyny to be connected to homophobia in subcultures of hypermasculinity, as we saw in Curry's study of the locker room. We turn our attention next to homophobia and the related inequalities of sexual orientation in sport for men and women who are not heterosexual.

Sexual Orientation and Sport

The homophobic remarks by the CBS golf commentator and the efforts by his employer and LPGA officials to play down their significance reflect the continuing problems sport and society have with people who do not conform to dominant heterosexual norms. In fact, there probably was an element of truth in the commentator's remark that lesbians in women's professional golf could hurt the appeal of their sport to corporate sponsors. The corporate world of the Golden Triangle has generally seemed reluctant to embrace openly lesbian or gay athletes. One of the most powerful lessons of sport socialization in a culture of hegemonic masculinity is that sport makes men, and in the most patriarchal contexts of sport, males learn that real men are aggressive, dominate females, and are heterosexual. Women learn in this type of culture that real women do not play sports, or at least they do not play "masculine" sports.

In an age of ostensibly increasing tolerance of homosexuals, it seems anachronistic today for people to believe that homosexual men and feminine or "real" women do not play or do not belong in sport, or that men who do not like sports and women who do must be homosexual. A survey of nearly one thousand Americans about their attitudes toward homosexuals in sport was conducted for NBC/USA Network in 2005 (SI.com 2005; Wertheim 2005). It found that 86 percent of those surveyed thought it was acceptable for male homosexual[1] athletes to play sports, even if they were open about their homosexuality, and that 78 percent expressed the same attitude about female homosexual athletes. In addition, 79 percent thought that homosexuals in sport were more accepted in the United States today than they were twenty years ago; 61 percent believed that homosexuality was a way of life that should be accepted by society; 67 percent said that the private life of athletes was their own business; 66 percent thought that homosexual athletes were treated unfairly in their private and professional lives; and 48 percent said they admired athletes who were openly homosexual. These and other findings suggested fairly widespread acceptance or at least tolerance of homosexuals in sport and society, and indicated a substantial amount of sympathy for obstacles and inequities faced by homosexual athletes.

Other responses seemed to qualify or contradict these generalizations. For example, 68 percent said it would hurt an athlete's career to be openly homosexual; 44 percent thought it was a sin to be homosexual; 40 percent said it was OK for homosexuals to be in sports as long as they were *not* open about their sexual orientation; 52 percent thought the public would react negatively to more emphasis on homosexual athletes in *Sports Illustrated*; 42 percent thought viewers would be "enraged" if ESPN did a special on the achievements of homosexual athletes; 24 percent said an openly homosexual player hurt the whole team; and 24 percent said that they would be less of a fan of an athlete if he or she was known to be homosexual. The respondents seemed more accepting of homosexuals in positions of authority in adult sports than in sports for children and young adults. While between 51 percent and 62 percent had no reservations in saying it was "appropriate" for homosexuals to be in the position of professional sports club owner or manager, referee or umpire, coach or trainer, or college sports referee or umpire, 46 percent said it was appropriate for homosexuals to be college sports coaches or trainers and about one-third thought it was appropriate to have homosexual Little League coaches, referees, or umpires. Thus, respondents may have been especially concerned about the possible negative influence of homosexuals on children and youths in the formative years.

The findings of this survey suggest a number of apparent contradictions and splits in societal attitudes as well as some possible inconsistencies in individual attitudes about homosexuals in sport and society. It is difficult to assess the validity of survey responses to questions about sensitive issues, and people often are able to rationalize inconsistent attitudes. It may be that many respondents in this survey did not see themselves as homophobic but still believed that a number of other people were homophobic, despite the expressed perception by many of increasing tolerance in society. Whether subtle or overt, homophobia is damaging to people who are not heterosexual, just as sexism is damaging to women, racism is damaging to racial and ethnic minorities, and ableism is damaging to people with disabilities. *Homophobia* refers to a pattern of irrational hostile or negative feelings toward people with a nonheterosexual orientation[2] and a fear of homosexuality, and often results in discriminatory or unfair treatment of homosexuals.

Although attitudes may be complex and difficult to interpret, the reality is that being openly homosexual in sport poses problems for gay men and lesbian women athletes. Despite the apparently greater tolerance for openly gay men than openly lesbian women in sports—86 percent versus 78 percent approval—gay athletes are very reluctant to acknowledge their homosexuality publicly, especially if they play team sports. In his article accompanying the publication of the survey, Wertheim (2005) observed that of the 3,500 men who were playing professional basketball, baseball, football, and hockey in North America at that time, none admitted to being gay. Gay athletes who have acknowledged their sexual orientation have been retired from sport or played minor or individual sports (Associated Press 2004; Baltimore Sun 2007b; Steele 2007).

When retired NBA player John Amaechi revealed that he was gay at the time of the publication of a book about his life and career, a former NBA star, Tim Hardaway, said that he "hated gay people," he did not like being around them, and gay players should not be in the same locker room as heterosexual players (MSNBC 2007). Although Hardaway's comments drew widespread public criticism and he later said he regretted using the word "hate," his reaction helps explain the reluctance of gay athletes to reveal their sexual orientation. The men's locker room does not appear to be a place where new or changing attitudes are easily nurtured. As we have seen (Curry 1991), male bonding in the men's locker room of team sports may be dominated by a form of hegemonic masculinity that is very hostile toward gays. Thus, we can readily understand the preference of gay athletes for individual sports (Pronger 2005). It should be added, though, that when he spoke to a gay organization associated with the Republican Party, Amaechi said that he "underestimated America," noting that contrary to his expectations, 95 percent of the correspondence he received following his public disclosure was overwhelmingly "supportive and positive" (Baltimore Sun 2007c). It appears that there is a gap between attitudes among athletes in certain sports and the expressed attitudes of the general population in the United States about homosexuality in sport and society.

While lesbian athletes have also been reluctant to acknowledge their sexual orientation while they were still active, there have been some notable cases of openly lesbian athletes who were still playing their sport, such as tennis player Martina Navratilova. The difficulty in acknowledging a homosexual orientation in both men's and women's sports reflects the perception among athletes that their relationships, image, or endorsement potential will be hurt by this acknowledgment. That is, both male and female athletes generally seem to believe that there is more homophobia in society than the public is willing to admit. However, male athletes may be especially afraid of this public acknowledgment as a result of the influence of hegemonic conceptions of masculinity.

In his study of young Australian males, Plummer (2006) found that as boys, they learned that becoming a man meant *not* being homosexual and that being physical in aggressive team sports was a way to demonstrate masculinity. Gay participants in his study had problems with sport during childhood and adolescence, and as a result developed a strong aversion toward sport as adults. These results imply that whatever the public says it believes about homosexuals, gay males who perceive the prevalence of hegemonic heterosexist conceptions of masculinity in sport are likely to find participation in mainstream sports, and especially aggressive team sports, quite problematic. Male athletes who subscribe to dominant ideas about masculinity as an exaggerated or stereotypical form of heterosexuality are likely to believe that homosexuals are not "real men" and do not belong in the masculine realm of sport. Interaction with these kinds of athletes will make gay men who want to play sports feel very uncomfortable and unwilling to acknowledge their sexual orientation.

On the other hand, the implication of the dominance of hegemonic beliefs about masculinity and sexual orientation in sport for female athletes is that they will be negatively labeled as lesbians for pursuing a masculine activity (Griffin 1992). Twenty percent of the survey respondents said they believed that many female professional athletes were lesbians. In her questionnaire and interview study of women in regional soccer leagues in the United Kingdom, Caudwell (2003) found that many believed that there was a prevailing stereotype of the women soccer players as lesbians, especially if their body size was big. Most of the players tried to assert their heterosexual femininity by denying any connection to the big "butch" or lesbian stereotype. Thus, gay athletes may fear they will face hostility and rejection because athletes are supposed to be demonstrably heterosexual men, while lesbian athletes may expect some general hostility and rejection, but perhaps less than their male counterparts, because a significant number of people automatically assume they are lesbian because they are athletes. For some women athletes who are big and play sports perceived as "manly," it is likely to be much more difficult to fend off labels of "butch" and "lesbian" than it was to discard the "tomboy" label when they were younger. For male athletes who are gay and female athletes who are lesbian, acknowledging their sexual orientation, whether presumed or not by the public, has negative implications wherever hegemonic ideas of masculinity and homophobia prevail.

The case of women's golf indicates that even in sports realms thought to be more appropriate for women and where women have competed for a relatively long time, female athletes have faced accusations of lesbianism. This suggests two types of prejudice: first, that being a lesbian is a bad thing and, second, that women's sport must be a bad thing for women because it is dominated by lesbians. For men, the prejudice is parallel but a little different. Male sports dominated by hegemonic masculinity are likely to foster beliefs that being gay is a bad thing, and that playing sports is a good thing for men because only "real men"—that is, heterosexual males—play sports. These kinds of beliefs are more likely in team sports and sports that emphasize stereotypical masculine qualities of strength, force, and aggression.

We can understand the general reluctance of gay and lesbian athletes to acknowledge their sexual orientation where traditional ideas about sexual orientation and sport prevail, but there is evidence of open resistance to homophobic conceptions of homosexual men and women in sport. For example, the Gay Games were organized in 1982 by Dr. Tom Waddell, a 1968 Olympic decathlete who was gay, to give gay, lesbian, bisexual, and transsexual athletes a chance to enjoy sport and openly display their talents. It was an opportunity to educate the public as well. The 2006 Gay Games Sports and Cultural Festival in Chicago was expected to attract twelve thousand athletes, artists, and musi-

Athletes perform a production number during the figure skating competition for Gay Games VII in Chicago, July 19, 2006. These games represent a celebration of gay pride and also remind us of the relative invisibility and inequalities experienced by gay athletes in mainstream sport. (Reuters/John Gress)

cians from seventy countries, and include thirty sports (Chicago Sun-Times 2004). It appears that enough interest in international sports events for homosexual athletes had developed by 2006 among athletes and government and corporate funders to support a second major international sports event in Montreal, the World Outgames, just one week after the Gay Games.

These types of events demonstrate that while sport has typically made it difficult to be homosexual and an athlete, sport also has been a site for homosexuals to contest hegemonic conceptions of gender and sexual orientation. Sport sociology research has shown that the ways homosexuals deal with their participation in sport can be varied and complex. I will use two ethnographic studies to illustrate this point. Broad (2001) used participant observation, semistructured interviews, and surveys to study a women's rugby club in the western United States. Price and Parker (2003) used similar methods, along with an analysis of relevant documents, to study an amateur rugby union club in the United Kingdom that advertised itself as "the world's first gay rugby union team."

Broad's research addressed questions about how the women rugby players responded to perceptions of their sport as manly and to related concerns and labels regarding their dubious femininity and sexual orientation. She contrasted the strategy of "apologetics" with an assertively "unapologetic" one. The female apologetic involved women trying to assimilate or fit into a sport by conforming to stereotypical conceptions of femininity and heterosexuality. For example, to resolve possible tensions from being women in a men's realm, female athletes might dress and use cosmetics to emphasize their femininity, talk about their desire to get married and raise a family, and disavow any connection to feminist and other "radical" ideas about women's roles and rights. Broad found that other women athletes in her study assertively engaged in an "unapologetic" response that rejected assimilation and represented a form of "queer resistance" to hegemonic ideas of gender and sexual orientation. They did not try to compensate for their "outsider status" as women in a men's sport or rebel against it. They instead delighted in it. They intentionally challenged conventional ideas about passivity associated with white, middle-class, heterosexual versions of femininity. They played their sport aggressively and with toughness and with little concern about scrapes or injuries that could mar their appearance. They were proud to be rugby players and openly displayed this pride with an assortment of impression management techniques ranging from provocative bumper stickers on their cars to clothing and even tattoos that proclaimed their love of their sport, sometimes in outrageous ways.

Broad proposed that these women presented a kind of "female masculinity" that called into question traditional ideas about gender and sexual orientation. As we have seen, this does not mean that the women tried to be like the men. Although they were similar to men in their rough-and-tough style of play and in their after-game partying, drinking, and rugby songs, they did not replicate the men's traditions of misogyny and homophobia. By playing the sport, the women directly challenged hegemonic conceptions of masculinity associated with the men's culture, and their songs and rituals encouraged open-mindedness about sexual orientations and practices. Women rugby players may be different than most women in sport. An assimilationist apologetic type of response by women to hypermasculine and homophobic tendencies in sport seems to make a lot of sense because it enables women to minimize the costs of playing sports by assuring people that they really are feminine and heterosexual after all. However, for some women in "manly" sports such as rugby, accommodating seems to be unsatisfying or inappropriate. As a result, they engage in an unapologetic strategy to assert their pride and joy in playing their sport as "masculine women" unconstrained by any conventional conceptions of gender or sexual orientation.

Price and Parker found that there was tension in the gay rugby club between those who wanted to show that they could compete effectively in mainstream sports and those who saw the team as a symbolic challenge to heterosexist conceptions of sport that would exclude gay men. Those with a more inclusive view of the team were willing to accept bisexual and heterosexual players if they could make the team more competitive. Those who were primarily interested in playing for a team where they were safe from homophobic slurs and treatment had difficulty accepting bisexuals and heterosexuals on the team. These latter team members sought an escape from mainstream sports teams where they either had to "fake straightness" to avoid prejudice, discrimination, and even physical violence or face likely ostracism. On a gay sports team, the gay players could feel a sense of community that mainstream heterosexual clubs could not offer. Thus, the club itself was contested terrain, reflecting different ways of dealing with homophobia in the mainstream sports culture and society.

The mission of the club was to advance the ideal of inclusiveness to be a "role model to the gay community" and "a successful example of friendly cohabitation between people of different sexual orientations." However, among those who were involved in forming the club to contradict stereotypes about gay men being effeminate and incompetent at sport, having bisexual and heterosexual men in the club undermined their original purpose. For these men, the officially apolitical, accommodating, and assimilationist position of the club was problematic because they believed the club simply reinforced heterosexist definitions of sport. First, the club's desire to recruit bisexual and heterosexual players to make the club more competitive was consistent with the dominant mainstream conception of sport as mainly about winning rather than serving social functions. Second, by being more inclusive in their recruitment, the club implied that it could not be competitive enough if it relied only on gay players. Thus, the club's stated mission of trying to win as a means of gaining more acceptance in the mainstream sports culture as a "serious" club was at odds with the ideological aim of a number of club members to have the club be a form of resistance to heterosexist ideas of sport and a safe haven for gay men who wanted to play rugby. Furthermore, the club contradicted its own mission by recruiting bisexuals and heterosexuals to help the team become more competitive.

The studies by Broad and by Parker and Price show the complex nature of the contested terrain in sport and within sports teams around issues of gender and sexual orientation for women and men. The terrain is contested because hegemonic conceptions of what sport is and who should compete privilege some groups over others. The struggle for groups that have experienced prejudice and discrimination has been about whether or how much to accommodate to the mainstream culture to gain access to sport. Some have sought to redefine sport in entirely new ways that go beyond tolerance of women and minorities and avoidance of prejudice or discrimination to a conception of sport that values both men and women equally and both heterosexuals and homosexuals without distinction. The women rugby players Broad studied defiantly asserted very different ideas of gender and sexuality than were dominant in sport and society. We might wonder why those with power in sport, who represented and sustained values that these women challenged, did not try to co-opt or suppress these "unapologetic" women. The answer may be that their influence was not visible enough in the mainstream to be a threat. However, we would expect a reaction if they began to attract more attention and support in the mainstream. As I suggested, society changes, but entrenched structures of inequality change slowly and often as a result of major confrontations. At this point, relatively more progress has been made in struggles to reduce inequalities of social class, gender, race, and ethnicity than in efforts to reduce inequalities of sexual orientation and disability in sport because society in general has lagged in the latter types of efforts. In the next two sections, we will look at patterns and implications of inequalities of race and ethnicity and of physical disability in sport.

Race, Ethnicity, and Sport

Like women, but unlike homosexuals, people in racial minority groups and some ethnic minority groups generally cannot pretend to be members of the dominant status group. Racial identity and some types of ethnic identity are visible or obvious. Like other types of status, race and ethnicity have mattered both because societies have expected different things of different races and ethnic groups and because they have rewarded people differently according to their race and ethnicity. Sport has been stratified by race and ethnicity in nations around the world, reflecting often highly divisive unequal relations of race and ethnicity in the larger society. Sometimes these relations can seem odd, as in South African society under the racial caste system of apartheid, where whites were the numerical minority but dominated the structures of power and privilege. A similar case exists in the NBA, where in the 2005–2006 season, 73 percent of players were black, while the majority owners were 98 percent white, the CEOs and presidents were 88 percent white, the general managers and directors of player personnel were 77 percent white, the coaches were 63 percent white, the radio and television announcers were 74 percent white (Lapchick, Martin, Kushner, and Brenden 2006), and the fans were about 90 percent white (Coakley 2007:224).

These statistics suggest a complex picture of majority-minority relations in sport, and show that numbers alone do not tell us what sociologically defined minority groups are. A *racial or ethnic minority* in sociological terms is a category of people who: (1) are perceived as physically or culturally distinct, (2) experience prejudice and discrimination as a result of their race or ethnicity, and (3) are aware that their race or ethnicity devalues their identity and puts them in an inferior status. Thus, being a member of a minority group means having a devalued identity, disadvantaged status, and limited access to positions of authority and the resources of power. *Racial minority groups* are defined by perceived genetic differences in physical characteristics such as skin color. *Ethnic minority groups* are defined by perceived differences in cultural identity and cultural heritage (Nixon and Frey 1996). Racial minorities also may be ethnic minorities if they share common cultural experiences and practices, but ethnic minorities are not necessarily racial minorities. Although an increasing number of Latino and Asian athletes are playing Major League Baseball (MLB) today and foreign athletes are increasingly competing for teams in other countries, most of the sport sociology literature about race and ethnicity in sport has been about race. Thus, we will first focus on race in this section and then turn our attention to issues of ethnicity in sport.

Racism refers to the ideas and practices that are used by dominant groups in society to devalue and disadvantage minorities. Racism may be so integrated into the structure of everyday life that we take it for granted as normal and do not notice it. This *institutional racism* was found in sport in the patterns of bias and discrimination that kept blacks out of many major U.S. sports for many years, denied them opportunities to play certain prestigious and central positions in certain sports such as quarterback in football, denied them chances to coach or manage, gave them less respect and pay than their white teammates for comparable or better performances, and gave them less access to commercial endorsement opportunities than their white teammates. During the long period of *racial segregation* that lasted without many exceptions until around the middle of the twentieth century in many major U.S. sports, black athletes in these sports competed in segregated sports leagues or at historically black colleges and universities. When they broke the color barrier in the 1940s and 1950s in Major League Baseball, the NBA, and the National Football League (NFL), black players had to stay in segregated hotels and eat at segregated restaurants apart from their white teammates when they traveled to southern cities where these practices were still in place.

Many of the historical patterns of racial exclusion and segregation; "stacking," or racial segregation into more- and less-central positions; and discrimination in hiring, pay, and commercial opportunities diminished over the last few decades of the twentieth century. However, even with the great strides made in sports such as basketball; the global iconic status of boxer Muhammad Ali, basketball player Michael Jordan, and golfer Tiger Woods; the 2007 NFL Super Bowl pitting two African-American head coaches against each other; and the fame and big salaries earned by many star African-American athletes, we need to remember the recent statistics cited earlier about the discrepancies between the percentage of black players in the NBA and the percentages of blacks in other positions of authority and power in the league. In his controversial book *Forty Million Dollar Slaves*, *New York Times* columnist William Rhoden (2006) argued that black athletes still typically remained outsiders looking into the circles of power in the multi-billion-dollar sports industries that their athletic talents created. He provocatively proposed that although blacks no longer literally lived on plantations, they continued to be subject to white domination in sport, despite their outstanding accomplishments on the field. He criticized Branch Rickey, the general manager of the Brooklyn Dodgers who broke the color barrier when he brought Jackie Robinson into the Major Leagues in 1947, and he also criticized Jackie Robinson. Often viewed as courageous pioneers, Rickey and Robinson were faulted by Rhoden for creating a mass migration of African-American stars from the Negro Leagues, which destroyed them, and for failing to push for opportunities for black ownership and control in the Major Leagues. Thus, racial integration was restricted to the playing field, and this pattern has persisted in the more recent history of MLB and other major sports.

Although the success of black athletes in several sports might distract us from Rhoden's main point about limited black power in these sports, it is important to keep in mind that many sports remain largely or entirely racially segregated and that black women have not had the same chances for fame and financial success in commercialized sports as their male counterparts have had. We are reminded of research considered in the last chapter (Buffington 2005) showing that positive developments such as the rise of black quarterbacks have not been without lingering concerns about stereotyping and unfair standards among some of those who have experienced this success. Furthermore, race relations in integrated sports have depended on factors such as the amount of representation of blacks on the team and in the surrounding community. The status of minorities on sports teams may range from being a "token" or tiny minority as in the case of blacks in ice hockey to being the numerically dominant race as in the case of blacks in the NBA and on many men's and women's college basketball teams. Thus, the experiences of blacks may range from social isolation to social integration or segregation. Depending on the climate for racial integration on the campus, in the community, or on the team, blacks may feel comfortable interacting with both black and white teammates or more comfortable in segregated relationships, especially outside the sport (Nixon and Frey 1996:234–235). Difficulties achieving extensive racial integration in sport, which goes beyond relationships on the field to relationships in the locker room and friendships outside sport, are understandable when one considers the persistence of patterns of racial tension and segregation on the campuses and in the cities where sports teams compete.

Perhaps surprisingly, the great success achieved by black male athletes in boxing, basketball, football, baseball, and track in the United States caused concern among some advocates of racial progress. They pointed to the disproportionate media and community attention to black success in sport in comparison with success in other types of occupations, and they feared that young black males would see sport as their only route to success and focus on sport to the detriment of their studies and preparation for other, more realistic careers or jobs. In fact, based on 2004 U.S. Labor Department statistics cited by Coakley (2007:348), African Americans were about nine times more likely to be doctors, lawyers, or college professors than to make a living in a sports-related occupation such as athlete, coach, or umpire. Furthermore, according to Coakley (348), African Americans who become doctors, lawyers, or college professors will earn median incomes between approximately 150 percent and 250 percent higher than the median income in sports-related occupations in general. Another noteworthy fact is that careers of professional athletes in the team sports most often played by African Americans typically have been quite brief, spanning less than seven years on average (Coakley 2007:344). Thus, except for the African-American males who possess the talent and opportunities to become successful professional athletes, coaches, or umpires, these young men would be better advised to concentrate on their studies and pursue careers that utilize their education. They are likely to make more money and have more job security and a much longer career.

Black activist and sport sociologist Harry Edwards was once among those voicing concerns about the unrealistic preoccupation with sport among young black males dreaming of professional sports careers. However, in recent years, his message has changed somewhat as his concerns have become more complex in the context of increasing black urban poverty and the intensifying social problems of young black males (Anderson 1999; Eckholm 2006; Wilson 1996). These problems include high dropout rates from school and high rates of unemployment, gang violence, crime, incarceration, and early death. While these problems have increased, sports interest and participation in school and community sports and recreation programs have declined for these young men, as public funding and facilities also declined. Thus, the reality and the dream of mobility through sport both seem to be eroding in African-American families.

In this context, Edwards (1998) welcomed any legitimate road out of the life of despair in the urban ghetto for young black men. He proposed that deepening problems of the black urban poor required the reinvigoration of black communities with stronger institutions and more opportunities for young black men in the larger society. Wilson (1996) argued that the institutional revitalization of black families, schools, and other institutions needed to begin with better employment opportunities. Edwards agreed, but proposed that building more and better community and school sports programs could be part of the solution. He thought that black youths who had turned away from legitimate institutions or who were at risk of doing so could be brought back to the mainstream and more promising paths to the future by getting involved in respectable activities such as sports, which involved community leaders and represented alternative values and roles to those learned on the streets or in gangs. Thus, he argued that black youths and their parents should dream about sport as a means to stay in school, go to college, or even earn a living because, for some, sport was a realistic vehicle of mobility.

Being realistic also meant "dreaming with their eyes open," recognizing that books and school were ultimately the most likely route to success for most. The rise or fall of the symbolic and practical significance of sport that has existed among African Americans will be a useful lens for interpreting the future of race in U.S. society. Hartmann (2000) suggested that it was important to try to understand the relationship of sport to race, culture, and society precisely because of this cultural significance and also because sport is a source of positive racial images and identities. He also believed that the failure of blacks to achieve a full realization of the American Dream through sport highlights the disappointing realities of the pursuit of the American Dream for many people and implies that change is still needed in society to remove barriers to success for people such as African Americans. In Hartmann's view, sport may be an effective lever for change because blacks may be able to translate their success in sport into effective resistance to the power structure. It is instructive, however, to remember Rhoden's argument about the relative inability of black athletes to gain control in sport so far. Past history suggests that the best opportunity for blacks to improve their life chances through sport is learning to play by the rules of the dominant white power structure and making gradual advances in access to positions of authority and power. Thus, attracting young black males to sport implies challenging the countercultural values and roles of the culture of the streets and the gangs with the more conventional values and roles of the dominant sports culture.

Blacks have generally been attracted to sports that have had lower entry barriers for minorities and lower classes; that depend less on expensive equipment, facilities, and coaching; and that resonate with their everyday life experiences. For example, the blatant aggression of boxing has made it a sport of the underclasses, and the fact that basketball has become a game of the urban playground and only requires a ball, sneakers, and a hoop explains its special appeal for inner-city blacks. In addition, for various reasons, football, track, and baseball have provided significant opportunities for black athletes. In recent years, however, black participation in baseball has declined, and this decline has raised some questions. Klis (2003) cited statistics showing that between 1989–1990 and 2002–2003, the percentage of black players increased in the NBA from 75 percent to 78 percent and in the NFL from 60 percent to 66 percent, while decreasing in MLB from 17 percent to 10 percent. The percentage in MLB had peaked in the late 1970s at 27 percent and in 2002–2003 was at the same level as it had been in 1960. Among his explanations are the increase in Latino players, up from 13 percent to 28 percent between 1989–1990 and 2002–2003, which has edged out black players; the example of the attention paid to LeBron James, who went directly from high school to the NBA; poor facilities in inner cities; perceptions of racism in MLB management and among owners; and the expense of playing youth baseball. The decline is important because there remain relatively few avenues to professional sport for blacks, and lost opportunities affect the overall number of blacks in sports careers.

I have hardly mentioned female black athletes in this section, and this is not an accident. Much less has been written about black women than about black men in sport, in part reflecting the relatively fewer opportunities for success in professional sport for black women and the relatively limited emphasis in the women and sport literature on black women. Black women are especially interesting, though, because they face a potential dual disadvantage as women in addition to being black. We can use statistics from the 2003–2004 NCAA Student-Athlete Ethnicity Report (cited in McKindra 2006) and from Richard Lapchick and his colleagues' (Lapchick, Martin, Kushner, and Brenden 2006) 2005 Racial and Gender Report Card on College Sports (which includes some data for 2005–2006) to compare the recent opportunity structures in college sports for male and female African Americans. According to the NCAA Report, 18.1 percent of male student-athletes were African American, while 10.6 percent of female student-athletes were African American.

According to data a year later from Lapchick and his associates, African-American athletes were concentrated in a few sports at the top, or Division I, level. In Division I men's sports, 24.8 percent of the athletes were African American, and in Division I women's sports, 15.4 percent were African American. African-American athletes tended to be concentrated in basketball, track and field, and, for men, football as well. Lapchick's data showed that in the two major sports for African-American males, 57.8 percent of the players on men's NCAA Division I basketball teams were African American and 45.4 percent of Division I football players were African American. Among the females, 43.7 percent of Division I basketball players and 26 percent of the members of Division I women's college cross-country and track teams were African Americans, while only 4.6 percent of the members of other women's sports teams were

African American. To provide a frame of reference, 10.4 percent of college undergraduates were black males and 13.9 percent were black females in 2002 (NCES 2004). Thus, the opportunity structures for male and female African-American athletes are highly skewed. These athletes are significantly overrepresented in their top two sports and underrepresented in the others, but in general, black females have fewer opportunities to compete in college sports than their black male counterparts have. The sports in which the males are dominant are highly commercialized and provide lucrative professional opportunities for the best players. Women's college basketball has become increasingly popular, but it pales in comparison with the men's game in popularity, commercialization, and professional opportunities.

Racial inequalities in college coaching and administration are greater than the racial inequalities in opportunities for athletes, especially for women. According to Lapchick and his colleagues' report, in 2005–2006, 87.8 percent of the head coaches in Division I men's sports were white men, 6.7 percent were black men, 2.8 percent were white women, and 0.6 percent were black women. In Division I women's sports, 54.3 percent of the head coaches were white men, 35.3 percent were white women, 3.6 percent were black men, and 3.7 percent were black women. Among Division I athletic directors, 85.8 percent were white men, 7.3 percent were white women, 5 percent were black men, and 0.5 percent were black women. In football, only 6 of the 119 coaches at the top (IA) level were African American at the end of 2006, but this doubled the number from 2005. Even in basketball, the sport in which African Americans have been most successful as athletes, coaching is dominated by whites. In Division I men's basketball in 2005–2006, 73.9 percent of the head coaches were white men and 25.2 percent were black men. In Division I women's basketball that year, 54 percent of the head coaches were white women and 9.3 percent were black women. Thus, the overall power structure in big-time college sports is white and male, and white males and white females dominate head coaching positions in men's and women's basketball, the sport in which African-American athletes are most highly concentrated. Although both black men and black women are underrepresented among Division I basketball coaches, black women are especially underrepresented. There are relatively few female and few black Division I athletic directors, and even fewer black women among these athletic directors. Thus, black men experience a limited band of opportunities in college sports—and other sports realms—but women experience these restricted opportunities even more intensely than their male counterparts do.

The gender gap favoring African-American males over females in college sports contrasts with the gender gap in their academic achievement. For example, black women currently earn almost two-thirds of all bachelor's degrees earned by African Americans, and they earn 70 percent of all African-American master's degrees and 60 percent of all African-American doctorates. In addition, they are the majority of African Americans in law, medical, and dental schools (JBHE 2006). In general, it appears that relatively more black females than black males pursue higher education, and black females are more academically successful than their male counterparts. Thus, we can see why sport may be more meaningful as an area of potential accomplishment for black male than for black female college students.

Class-related, as well as racial and cultural, factors restrict the range of sports opportunities and interests of black males and females. Sport has had special symbolic meaning as a source of male identity and hope for young black males, which explains why so many of these young black men who attend college get there because they are athletes and are primarily interested in sports as college students. The lower percentages of black males than females attending and succeeding academically at college reflect both the problems in black communities for young black males that have concerned Edwards and others and the higher value these young men and a number of their families have placed on sports than on academics. African-American females have been relatively less influenced by the destructive forces in black inner-city communities, have felt less pressured to play sports to define themselves as women, and have felt freer to pursue academics seriously. Although they still experience prejudice and discrimination and have fewer and less-rewarding opportunities in sports, especially in positions of authority, than their male counterparts, black females have had relatively more success in other areas than black males have had in recent years. The challenge for black females who want to become successful athletes is that they face sexist as well as racist barriers.

Although we are much more accustomed to talking about black success in sports in male terms, a few black women have become very successful in sports on a global level. For example, Althea Gibson became a great tennis champion a half century ago, and more recently, the Williams sisters, Serena and Venus, became dominant players on the international tennis circuit. The sisters found, however, that despite their success on the tennis court and their lucrative endorsement contracts, they still faced criticism from the press and other players and hostility from spectators for their supreme confidence, which was perceived as arrogance, their coolness and detachment, their very aggressive style of play, and their assorted interests outside the sport (Smart 2005: 184–189). Douglas (2005) proposed that their race played a significant role, along with other factors, in ambivalent assessments of their accomplishments and hostility toward them.

Douglas studied how race influenced the experiences of the sisters and their family at two major tournaments, one in Indian Wells, an affluent community in California, and the other at the French Open in Paris. The two sisters had attained the number one and two rankings in women's tennis, and had faced each other in the finals or semifinals of a number of tournaments. They tended to play worse than usual in these matches against each other, and some in the tennis community and press hinted at "match fixing" by their father, who allegedly decided who was to win these matches. In fact, at Indian Wells, Venus abruptly retired from her semifinal match with her sister due to injury, but some in the press were skeptical. Douglas suggested that the focus on match fixing rather than other explanations of her departure, such as an actual injury or the stresses the sisters experienced in playing each other as siblings, reflected racist reactions to strong and confident black women dominating a white sport in a very affluent white setting. The accusations were pervasive enough to cause the head of the Women's Tennis Association to make a public statement defending the sisters—and the credibility of the sport.

Douglas suggested that the negative public and media reactions reflected a racial filter, which assumed that blacks were more likely than whites to engage in dubious acts. The negative perception of Serena was evident in the final match, which she won. She faced consistent and intense boos and taunts, and her father alleged that racial slurs were directed toward him in the stands. Serena experienced similar crowd hostility in Paris, and negative reactions to her were intensified by feelings of anti-Americanism related to the Iraq War and the preference of the predominantly white fans for a "married, white, blonde, and petite" champion. These were the qualities of her Belgian opponent, who won the final. Serena faced such harsh crowd reactions during the final match that she was brought to tears during the postmatch press conference. Although the fans, media, and her opponents who had expressed antagonism toward her would not acknowledge racist reasons for it, the Williams family clearly perceived racism.

An important insight from this study is the very different ways race filters perceptions and experiences of majority and minority group members. Racist ideologies are about racial superiority and inferiority, identify which race deserves to have dominant status in society, and provide negative stereotypes for majority-group members to interpret the actions of minority-group members. These ideological assumptions may be so deeply embedded that their influence is not perceived or questioned by the dominant group. These assumptions support the dominant social order by diminishing the accomplishments of minority-group members and reinforcing dominant cultural beliefs and practices. Unlike majority-group members, who do not see or acknowledge their own racism, minority-group members are acutely aware of the role of racism in hostile, demeaning, and discriminatory treatment of them as a minority. A fact of life for people in minority groups, even when they are as accomplished as the Williams sisters have been, is that they must conform or overconform to dominant cultural norms or face antagonism. The intensity of negative reactions to the Williams sisters may be at least partially attributed to their being both successful and not sufficiently deferential or stereotypically female in an overwhelmingly white setting.

Like race, ethnicity is a matter of social construction. That is, people with power put labels on people with less power. Waters (2006) suggested that people in dominant groups can decide whether or not they wish to be characterized by ethnic or racial labels, but people in minority groups do not have that option. For example, white Americans can invoke or celebrate their ethnic heritage as Irish or Swedish or Italian when it is convenient to do so. African Americans and Latinos, on the other hand, find that these labels are imposed on them as a result of their minority status. They also find that the labels are difficult or impossible to discard, except perhaps in the case of being light-skinned and highly assimilated into the dominant culture, as the case of Latina golfer Nancy Lopez illustrated in the last chapter. At times, athletes with ambiguous or mixed racial or ethnic backgrounds may try to define themselves for the public and the press. Tiger Woods illustrates this process. He rejected references to him as a black golfer, preferring instead a more complex label of "Cablinasian," reflecting his mixed **Ca**ucasian, **Bl**ack, **In**dian, and **Asian** heritage. Although he was very prominent in his sport and was not threatening to the dominant classes, his efforts to redefine himself had limited success, since the media, other golfers, and fans still generally have referred to him as "black" (Denham, Billings, and Halone 2002:330). It is usually more difficult for minority group members to escape racial than ethnic labels because skin color is generally easier to interpret than ethnic heritage is.

Despite the well-documented history of racial and ethnic discrimination in sport, it has sometimes been heralded as a great social experiment in integration or as a means of uniting people of different racial and ethnic backgrounds who have difficulty interacting with each other elsewhere in society. Waves of new immigrants and blacks found opportunities in certain less-reputable or "lower-class" sports, such as boxing, throughout the nineteenth and twentieth centuries. When Jesse Owens triumphed in track-and-field events at the 1936 "Nażi" Olympics, and the "Brown Bomber" Joe Louis won the heavyweight championship of the world over German Max Schmeling just before World War II, their nationality became more important than their race for some Americans. When Jackie Robinson broke the color barrier in Major League Baseball, sport very visibly stood as a counterexample to lingering patterns of racial segregation and discrimination in the larger U.S. society. Some saw Robinson's entry into the previously segregated world of Major League Baseball as an example for the rest of society, potentially leading the way toward change. At least in sport, Jackie Robinson opened the door in MLB to other black players, just as black athletes opened the door to racial integration in other professional, college, and Olympic sports before and after him. The racially and ethnically diverse French national soccer team, led by superstar Zinedine Zidane, who was of Algerian descent, was considered a unifying force in a French society with significant racial and ethnic tensions. This is why Zidane's infamous head-butting incident at the 2006 World Cup provoked complicated reactions among his fans and the French public. We will focus on this incident and its social implications in a special feature in chapter six.

The picture of sport, race, and ethnicity is more complicated than images of unity amidst diversity, as we have seen. For example, the proud and controversial black boxing champion in the early part of the twentieth century, Jack Johnson, provoked so much antagonism by his defiance of racial conventions, such as dating white women, that he inspired a search for a "Great White Hope" to challenge him as heavyweight champion. The search for other Great White Hopes in boxing and other sports endured long after his career ended in exile. Jackie Robinson faced racist reactions from his own teammates as well as from fans around the league, and his status as an MLB star did little to change the racial segregation in society when he played the game; nor did it prevent the racial tensions that turned into riots in the late 1960s or the more recent patterns of intensifying racial segregation of U.S. cities. Putting aside his head-butting incident, Zidane was a cultural hero, but he and his teammates did not eradicate racial and ethnic tensions in France. Even popular Latino, Asian, and other foreign players in Major League Baseball and the NBA today have not eliminated strong anti-immigrant feelings directed toward illegal, and legal, foreign workers in the United States.

Klein's (2000b) study of fans of and media covering the Boston Red Sox Major League Baseball team showed that the positive media portrayal of Latino fans who attended Red Sox games to watch Dominican Pedro Martinez pitch was misleading. Martinez was one of the best pitchers in the MLB. This was the first time that a large number of people of color had attended Fenway Park, and the media suggested that Martinez was widely accepted among Boston fans

Melissa Perez, a twenty-year-old college student and self-described "Sox junkie," wears a Chicago White Sox jersey and hat in the dressing room adorned with other Sox memorabilia at her home Monday, October 24, 2005, in Chicago. Perez and her mother were just two of the many Latino fans who visited U.S. Cellular Field this season to root for their beloved White Sox or "Las Medias Blancas," who won the pennant for the first time in forty-six years with a roster filled with Spanish-speaking stars. Over the years, the White Sox have built up a healthy Latino fan base, at least partly because of the team's proximity to one of the largest Mexican-American communities in the country. (AP Photo/Nam Y. Huh)

and the city in general. This was significant because Boston had a history of racial tensions, which were especially prominent during the days of desegregation and busing, and NBA star Bill Russell of the Boston Celtics dynasty teams in the 1960s had talked about how difficult it was to play in Boston as a black man. Klein interviewed Anglo and Latino spectators at Fenway Park. He found that Anglo fans held very positive perceptions of Martinez as a Dominican, but were evenly divided in their views of Dominicans in general. The Dominican fans did not care what the Anglos thought and attended the game only to show support for Martinez and enjoy the reflected glory of his stardom. Klein's research revealed that sport may not lead to as much racial or ethnic harmony as the media sometimes report, but he also made the important methodological point that investigators of media content need to be wary of using media content alone to represent reality. I would add, though, that we should expect the commercial media of the Golden Triangle to emphasize positive images of sport because it is in their interest to promote the sports that the Golden Triangle covers and sponsors and to extend its reach to as many sports fans and potential consumers as possible.

We considered earlier that an important by-product of the "Latinizing" of MLB has been the replacement of African-American with Latino ball players, with the percentage of Latinos increasing from 13 percent to 28 percent between 1989–1990 and 2002–2003 and the percentage of African Americans in MLB dropping from 17 percent to 10 percent during that period. White Major Leaguers also declined over that time period, with the percentage of whites dropping from 70 percent to 60 percent (Klis 2003). However, adverse public reaction may have been muted by a relative lack of concern among the predominantly white MLB fans about the decline in black players and by their limited awareness of the decline of whites, first because whites are still in the majority, and second because many Latino ball players are fairly light-skinned. Despite the growing Latino presence, the league is still dominated by whites.

The racial and ethnic mix of many professional sports teams today, including whites from a variety of ethnic backgrounds, blacks, and foreign athletes, suggests that sport has become the social experiment in integration once thought to characterize the Jackie Robinson era in MLB. However, now as then, appearance and reality are not quite in sync with each other. Racial and ethnic tensions exist on some teams, and, as Klein's research suggests, fans may embrace certain foreign stars but that embrace may not be very wide, as other research has indicated. For example, Mayeda (1999) showed that the road to acceptance was initially bumpy for Asian MLB players. We will discuss his research and research about the social experiences and cultural influences of other Asian stars in U.S. sports today, such as Yao Ming, in a special research feature in chapter six.

Racism and ethnic discrimination are not restricted to sport in the United States. For example, Carrington (1998) studied a black men's soccer club in England that was formed as a result of the racism in that sport and in English society. Their club gave these men a chance to define their masculinity apart from the influence of white racism. In ethnically and racially homogeneous societies, such as Japan, being ethnically different seems especially problematic. Foreign athletes there have faced quotas, and ethnic minorities, such as Korean Japanese, have experienced discrimination in sport (Nogawa 2003). In Japan, the process of diminishing ethnic inequalities and discrimination has been slow but significant, perhaps spurred somewhat by the country's being a cohost of the 2002 World Cup. Participation in high school sports for ethnic minorities still seems to be a privilege rather than a right, however.

In recent years, soccer has been a site of significant and growing racial and ethnic tensions, and these tensions have crossed a number of national borders in Europe. Soccer has seen a recent rise in racial slurs and racially motivated incidents among "hooligan" fans in Europe, as formerly all-white teams have become more diverse, more immigrants from African and Arab countries have been recruited to play in Europe, and racial conflicts have received more attention from the media. Unemployment among whites in some regions of Europe also may be spawning racist behavior. Resistance to immigration and immigrants among European soccer fans has led to their unhappiness with the globalization of soccer that has made their favorite teams more diverse. These sentiments seem to have contributed to a series of racist incidents involving soccer fans. Minority players have also experienced racist slurs from coaches and other players (Whiteside 2006). In this context, soccer's global governing body, FIFA, formed an alliance with the Football Against Racism in Europe (FARE) network and the Local Organizing Committee (LOC) in Germany prior to the 2006 World Cup to create an initiative, "Football unites," to try to encourage racial and ethnic harmony during the competition. "Fan embassies" were set up in the World Cup host cities in Germany to encourage positive relations between people from different nations and ethnic and racial backgrounds.

The FIFA president expressed his concerns and hopes in a public statement prior to the competition that emphasized his organization's great respect for ethnic differences. He also said that as the most popular sport, soccer had a major opportunity to fight racism and that FIFA was "totally committed to taking steps to eradicate pernicious trends in society and [soccer]" (FARE 2006). These efforts did not prevent racial incidents in Italy after its World Cup victory over France in 2006, however. These incidents reflected long-standing tensions between Italy and France. In one case, swastikas were spray-painted in the ancient Jewish ghetto in Rome. In another, the former minister of reform, who was a member of a right-wing political party in Italy, said that the Italian team had defeated a French team made up of "Negroes, communists and Moslems." These kinds of racist comments were not unusual in Italian soccer venues (Kiefer 2006).

The experiences of American Indians in sport are distinctive because they have been relatively absent from the racial and ethnic mix of major sports in the United States (Coakley 2007:299–301), reflecting the highly disadvantaged status of American Indians in general in U.S. society (Coakley 2007:299–301). While Jim Thorpe has been recognized as one of the greatest athletes of the past century, most Americans would have difficulty naming other outstanding American Indian athletes. As in the poor black urban ghetto, the poverty and poor equipment and facilities of the typical Indian reservation have made it difficult for Indian youths with athletic talent to participate seriously, become stars in sport, and attract recognition in the larger society and sports culture.

In addition, as Simpson (1987) pointed out a number of years ago, American Indian athletes who have attracted the attention of college athletic recruiters have often been pushed or pulled back to the reservation. They have been *pushed* by social isolation on campus, discrimination, inadequate academic preparation for college, and the perception that their efforts would not pay off in significant returns after college. They have been *pulled* back to the reservation by the distinctive and familiar culture of the reservation and strong family ties. The adjustment difficulties of American Indian recruits in the past have made recruiters more hesitant to spend more time on the reservation looking for new recruits. Thus, according to Simpson, recruiters have tended to be scared away from Native American prospects, despite their athletic talent and financial support from their tribe and the Bureau of Indian Affairs. A number of American Indians who have grown up on reservations have also feared losing their Indian identity from integrating too much into white society. In addition, they have often internalized from their culture a different approach to physical activities and sports than the highly serious and aggressive approach generally expected by coaches in mainstream sports. For this reason, too, Indians have had problems assimilating into the dominant U.S. sports structure. In chapter nine on sport and higher education, we will consider how the issue of the often-condescending use of Indian mascots and team names has become a contested matter in U.S. sport and society. We will also consider in chapter nine a special feature about Jim Thorpe and his Carlisle Indian School teammates, which reveals their little-known contributions to college football in the United States.

Disabilities, Disability Sport, and the Mainstream

Like American Indians, people with physical disabilities have been relatively invisible in mainstream sports in the United States. Unlike other minority groups, people with physical disabilities have faced the formidable barrier of being perceived as incapable of playing serious sports (Nixon 2000). In fact, the term *disabled* is typically used in sport to refer to athletes who are out of action, sidelined by an injury. Obviously, we have to distinguish between *temporary disabilities* that keep athletes out of action for a few games or even for a season or more and can be healed with surgery, rehabilitation, and rest, and *permanent disabilities* that result from a disease, accident, or genetic condition and cannot be reversed. People are *disabled* when an impairment restricts their ability to use certain skills, engage in particular tasks, or perform certain activities or roles. Although there are various types of *impairments*, we are interested in ones such as sensory, motor, mental, organic, or emotional conditions that can be a basis of physical disabilities and make it difficult for people to engage in sport without accommodations.

Disability is not a condition of a person, but is a relationship between what a person is able or unable to do and the specific demands or expectations in a situation. Even though people may be impaired and be unable to do certain kinds of things, the demands or expectations of a situation could be modified, other capabilities could be used, or aids could be used to enable a person to engage in an activity that could not be pursued without such accommodations. What this means in sport is that a person who is blind, for example, could wrestle if the rules required constant contact between opponents. Or, a person who is an amputee or paraplegic and uses a wheelchair for mobility could engage in various types of sports if a wheelchair could be used and the rules were slightly modified. Of course, these are more than possibilities, since people who are blind wrestle, and people in wheelchairs compete in various sports. In some cases, an impairment, such as deafness, which makes ordinary verbal communication difficult with other people unable to sign or use visual aids, may pose minimal barriers to participation in mainstream sports. Gallaudet University, the only university in the United States for people with hearing impairments, fields teams in baseball, men's and women's basketball, football, indoor and outdoor track, men's and women's soccer, softball, swimming, men's tennis, and volleyball. Furthermore, people with one functional arm or hand such as pitcher Jim Abbott have played Major League Baseball. Abbott also led his high school football team to the finals of the Michigan state championships as its quarterback and was named the outstanding college player of the year as a pitcher at the University of Michigan. When he made the unusual move of going directly into Major League Baseball without playing in the minor leagues, it was thought to be a publicity stunt, but he had a successful rookie year and a ten-year MLB career.

Although people with many types and degrees of disability have been capable of participating in sport, sometimes at a very high level, people with disabilities have experienced various forms of prejudice and discrimination that have restricted their opportunities or completely excluded them. *Ableism* is an ideology that has paralleled class elitism, sexism, homophobia, and racism in viewing people with disabilities as inherently *un*able and physically, socially, and morally inferior to those perceived as able-bodied in society. Ableism *handicaps* people with disabilities. By "handicap," I mean that people stigmatized or discredited by their perceived impairment or disability are also socially devalued and relegated to inferior or minority status. Being "handicapped" in this sense also means that the capabilities of people with disabilities are not recognized, their opportunities are restricted, and their accomplishments are not adequately rewarded. In other cases, people may be so surprised that people with disabilities can do ordinary things that they "valorize" them or treat them as exceptional for these achievements when other people with similar disabilities have the same capabilities or are capable of doing much more. Sometimes, athletes with disabilities have been characterized in the media and by the public as "supercrips" because their sports accomplishments have been perceived as superhuman. Perhaps surprisingly, this image has been offensive to a number of athletes with disabilities because it makes them seem different, and less human, than other athletes without their disability.

Hardin and Hardin (2004) pointed out that the supercrip image was like the "helpless victim" stereotype, which is also applied to people with disabilities, because both reinforce the idea that not much should be expected from most people with disabilities because they cannot help themselves (helpless victim), with a few heroic exceptions (supercrips). The supercrip concept further reinforces the idea that other people with disabilities would be able to accomplish what disabled heroes can, if they tried. This is a variation of the American Dream, which holds people personally responsible, as a moral matter, for their level of accomplishment or failure and overlooks the structural barriers faced by minorities. Thus, the supercrip idea reinforces ableism, according to Hardin and Hardin, and could be both stigmatizing and patronizing. They conducted ten in-depth interviews with competitive wheelchair athletes about their reactions to the supercrip model in the mainstream media, and their findings revealed that even among just ten interviewees, reactions were varied and complex. Most were not aware of the *supercrip* term, but they understood the heroic stereotype it represented and the possible negative implications of it. Some feared that it would both raise and lower societal expectations for people with disabilities, but even those wary of it tended to acknowledge that it could have positive role-modeling benefits for other people with disabilities. They preferred more empowering models, which held society more accountable for restrictions in their opportunities, but generally believed that they probably would be rejected in an ableist culture. Hardin and Hardin observed that as serious sports fans, the athletes they interviewed accepted hegemonic media conceptions of sports heroes and were likely to accept the supercrip idea because even the disability sports media that they read, such as *Sports n Spokes*, presented supercrip stories.

The documentary film *Murderball* focuses on athletes with disabilities who represented a major contradiction to the idea that people with disabilities were incapable of playing demanding sports. The documentary is the story of quadriplegic indoor full-contact wheelchair rugby players and their rough and very demanding sport. The film portrayed these athletes as both highly competitive and skillful athletes and normal human beings, with the same range of qualities and emotions characterizing their able-bodied counterparts in sport and society. That is, the film humanized or normalized them, and the athletes preferred this portrayal to the supercrip image.

Perhaps the biggest obstacle for athletes with physical disabilities in mainstream society and sport is the idealization of the body, which is why *Murderball* is so counterstereotypical. Able-bodied people typically have preconceptions about what normal bodies and normal athletic bodies should look like, and when people depart from these expectations or stereotypes, people often have difficulty accepting physically disabled people as like them. Able-bodied people either *stigmatize* them (assuming their identity has been spoiled), view them as supercrips who are so unusual that they are not really like other people with disabilities because of their exceptional talents, or simply underestimate or ignore them. Ableist beliefs have distorted perceptions of the capabilities and achievements of people with disabilities, and handicapist practices have reflected and reinforced deeply entrenched patterns of inequality regarding ability and disability in sport and society. These practices have begun to change over the past few decades.

Legal changes and civil rights activism have created new rights, resources, and opportunities for people with disabilities in the United States and other countries. In sport, initiatives such as the Disability and Sport Program, led by Eli Wolff and located in the Sport in Society Center at Northeastern University in Boston, have tried to increase sports opportunities for people with disabilities by making mainstream sports more inclusive and by increasing support for disability sports. This program has also encouraged scholars to pursue more research and scholarship about social issues concerning sport and people with disabilities. In doing these things, advocates and activists have at least indirectly made sport contested terrain regarding ability and disability.

One of the issues I have addressed in my own research in this area has been the types of sports structures that could most appropriately accommodate the range of abilities and interests of people with disabilities (e.g., Nixon 2007a). This has been a contested issue among disability scholars and activists and athletes with disabilities. I have argued that models of sports opportunity for people with disabilities should reflect considerations of choice, fairness, and structure. *Choice* implies having a range of sports options in the mainstream and in segregated disability sport settings, from more casual and less competitive recreational sports to more organized and intensely competitive sports. *Fairness* implies that people can choose the sports that they wish to pursue. The *structure* issue is a matter of organizing sports so that they match sports roles and interaction requirements with the capabilities and interests of participants. This is a general principle that applies both to able-bodied people and to people with disabilities.

My model, in Table 4.1, of diverse opportunities for people with disabilities distinguishes seven types of opportunities in terms of five organizing principles or structural features. These types are "ideal types" in the sense that they are not meant to be perfect representations of actual sports, but instead they are intended to serve as useful models for comparing and contrasting the elements of different possible types of sports settings that could accommodate the range of sports abilities and interests of people with disabilities. They are meant to

Table 4.1 Models of Sports Opportunity for People with Disabilities (Nixon 2007a)

Model	Type of Disability-Related Sport Classification	Segregated or Integrated Access and Selectivity	Amount of Disability Adaptation or Accommodation	Level of Competitive Intensity	Direct Competition between Disabled and Able-Bodied
Special Olympics	Generally single disability classified by functional ability	Segregated disability sport; open to selective	As needed	Controlled to high	None
Paralympics	Disability-specific events classified by functional ability within larger event with different disabilities	Segregated disability sport; highly selective or elite	As needed	High	None
Mixed Paralympics	Mixing of multiple disabilities by functional or performance ability in same competitions	Segregated disability sport; elite	As needed	High	None
Reverse Integration	Mixing of able-bodied people with a single or multiple disabilities classified according to functional ability	Integrated disability sport; open	Artificial accommodations for able-bodied participants	Low to high	Direct
Marathon	Single or multi-disability classified by functional or performance ability or special disability divisions	Integrated mainstream; open to selective	As needed for disability	Moderate to high	Direct or in special divisions
Minimally Adapted Mainstream	No disability classification but usually higher-functioning participants with disabilities	Integrated mainstream; moderately selective to elite	Minor accommodations for disability	Moderate to high, with tendency toward higher levels	Direct
Mainstream	No disability classification but generally higher-functioning people with disabilities	Integrated mainstream; open to elite	No accommodations for disability	Low to high	Direct

This table appears in my copyrighted article in the *Journal of Sport & Social Issues*, and it appears here with permission from the publisher, Sage Publications.

stimulate thinking about the organization of sport to make it more inclusive, so that people with or without disabilities can participate in appropriate settings that are stimulating and enjoyable and where they do not have to fear being stigmatized or resented because they are perceived as out of place.

The five basic structural elements in these models are: (1) type of classification, which specifies who is eligible to participate in terms of their type or degree of disability, (2) segregated or integrated access and the amount of selectivity based on athletic skill, (3) amount of adaptation or accommodation for disability, (4) level of competitive intensity or seriousness, and (5) amount of direct competitive interaction between able-bodied athletes and athletes with disabilities. The seven models are called: (1) Special Olympics, (2) Paralympics, (3) Mixed Paralympics, (4) Reverse Integration, (5) Marathon, (6) Minimally Adapted Mainstream, and (7) Mainstream. Terms such as "Special Olympics" and "Paralympics" are meant to suggest certain characteristics of the actual events that bear these names, but in using them as labels for ideal types, they are intended only to be suggestive and not to represent these types of sports settings in precise detail. These models represent a range of choices for the diverse range of abilities and interests of people with disabilities. Since my argument is that sports experiences are most stimulating, enjoyable, and productive when sport and the athlete are appropriately matched, some models are more appropriate for certain people than others are and none of these models is an appropriate match for everyone. Thus, I am reframing the debate about which type of sports setting, for example mainstream or segregated, is most desirable. I have tried to move the debate from either-or to a continuum of possible choices.

The *Special Olympics* model refers to settings where people with a single type of disability participate in segregated disability sports with people having a range of abilities, where disability adaptations or accommodations are provided as necessary, the competitive intensity may vary, and there is no competition with able-bodied people. Although we tend to think of the actual Special Olympics as involving low-keyed local events where "everyone is a winner," more serious athletes in this competition have progressed up to the international level. The *Paralympics* model also involves segregated disability sports settings, but they are more selective than Special Olympics settings. Disability-specific events are classified by functional ability within a larger event with different disabilities represented; adaptations and accommodations are provided as needed; competitive intensity is high; and no able-bodied athletes are involved. As I noted in the last chapter, the actual Paralympics have become the Olympic Games for athletes with disabilities. They usually follow the Olympics on the same site, but with much less commercial sponsorship and media coverage, reflecting the relative status of disability sport in the global sports hierarchy at this time. The *Mixed Paralympics* model is selective, like the Paralympics model, but it mixes athletes with different types of disabilities in the same competitions according to the level of athletic ability in the sport. It tends to be more intensely competitive than the Paralympics model because it is likely to select out lower-functioning athletes in favor of more elite ones. Since it combines athletes with different disabilities, it has fewer types or categories of events than the Paralympics model has. In general, it is based on a multiple-disability principle and strongly emphasizes athletic ability and competitiveness.

These participants in elite international-level wheelchair rugby defy popular ableist stereo-types of people with disabilities as incapable of playing highly competitive and aggressive sports (from the documentary *Murderball*). Seen from left to right are Rob Tarr, Gerry Tinker, Troye Collins, Curtis Palmer, and Tony Stackhouse. (AP Photo/Petros Giannakouris)

The Mixed Paralympics model integrates people with different types of disabilities, but it is still a disability sport model because it does not include able-bodied athletes. The remaining four models involve integration of able-bodied athletes and athletes with disabilities in various formats. The *Reverse Integration* model involves adaptations and accommodations for both able-bodied competitors and competitors with disabilities. For example, able-bodied people compete in wheelchair sports as "walkies" with the artificial accommodation of a wheelchair. Or, normally sighted people could compete in sports for people who are blind by wearing a covering over their eyes. These kinds of integrated sports settings could involve able-bodied people competing with or against people with a single type or various types of disabilities; eligibility is open; and the competitive intensity could vary. The National Wheelchair Basketball Association opposed this kind of model for their sport because they perceived it as a reflection of an outdated view of their sport as rehabilitation rather than as serious sport (Thiboutot, Smith, and Labanowich 1992).

Each of these models could provoke controversy, and the *Marathon* model is another example of an integrated model that has caused opposition or resistance, this time from mainstream sports organizers who have resisted the inclusion of people with disabilities in their events. Brandmeyer and McBee (1986) suggested that resistance to wheelchair racers in marathon road races was based on claims that it would be unsafe, make the event too much of a spectacle, or threaten the perceived seriousness of the event. Wheelchair racers have overcome these obstacles and competed in some of the most prestigious mainstream races, such as the Boston Marathon. The Marathon model I am proposing includes athletes with a specific disability or different types of disability who compete directly against able-bodied athletes or in special divisions in the same integrated mainstream event. Eligibility may be open or selective; appropriate adaptations or accommodations are allowed for competitors with disabilities; and the intensity of competition may vary from moderate to high.

The last two models are *Minimally Adapted Mainstream* and *Mainstream* models. The two models have no formal disability classification. They are most likely to include higher-functioning athletes with disabilities, and as integrated mainstream models, they involve direct competition between able-bodied athletes and athletes with disabilities. The Minimally Adapted Mainstream model is illustrated by high school or college wrestling employing the "constant contact rule" when wrestlers who are visually impaired compete. Another example is professional golfer Casey Martin, who was permitted by a Supreme Court ruling to compete on the PGA Tour using a golf cart to accommodate for his difficulty walking, despite resistance from the PGA and a number of fellow golfers. These kinds of settings tend to be selective or elite, allow minor accommodations to disability, and tend to be more competitive. The Mainstream model could have varying levels of selectivity from open to elite, makes no accommodations for disability, and could vary from low to high in competitive intensity. Thus, we could imagine people with disabilities competing with or against able-bodied athletes in mainstream recreational settings or in elite professional sports or the Olympics, as illustrated by the case of pitcher Jim Abbott and runner Marla Runyon. Runyon was a five-time Paralympic gold medalist, but she also finished in eighth place in the 1500-meter race at the 2000 Olympics, after becoming the first runner who was legally blind to qualify for the U.S. Olympic team.

Some advocates of sport for people with disabilities have argued for "sport without disability" (Wolff and Hums 2003). This idea does not mean denying the existence of real impairments or disabilities. However, it implies structuring sports settings that make disability irrelevant to the competition through appropriate adaptations and accommodations, which would shift the focus from disability to sport. This is similar to the desire of athletes with disabilities to reject "supercrip" labels and focus attention on their abilities and performances as athletes rather than as athletes with disabilities.

Conclusion: Sport and Inequality in a Changing World

Despite the persuasive power of the American Dream and similar kinds of ideologies and media constructions of sport that reinforce these types of ideas, sport is and has been stratified in a number of ways that have made access to sport and movement up the sports hierarchy very unequal. Heterosexual able-bodied white men in the ethnic majority have had an advantage just because of who they are. That is, the hegemonic structures and culture of sport represented by the Golden Triangle have been dominated by people like them, with their values, and those who control these networks of power have tended to make decisions, provide opportunities, and give rewards in ways that favor other people like themselves. Despite pervasive ideologies that convey sexist, homophobic, racist, and ableist ideas and reinforce patterns of inequality through subtle or more overt prejudice and discrimination, women and minorities have made sport contested terrain in regard to these various dimensions of inequality.

The forces of change in the larger society, along with intentional efforts to bring about change, have contributed to the gradual erosion of entrenched forms of inequality in sport. Sport has been affected by the increasing sociodemographic diversity of society; the increasing number of women who are graduating from college, earning professional degrees, and attaining influential positions in business and politics; the social and economic decline of black urban communities; and increasing political pressure to make sport more accessible to women and minorities. The organizational expansion of certain sports, such as soccer in the United States, has provided women and ethnic minorities with new avenues of sports opportunity and enjoyment as athletes and fans. In addition, new technologies have enabled the Golden Triangle to reach more people around the world, which has increased the diversity of the sports market and exposed more young people from diverse racial and ethnic backgrounds with athletic talent to the possibilities of sports careers. Technological advances have also increased the sophistication and effectiveness of assistance devices, such as wheelchairs and artificial limbs, used by athletes with disabilities. Advocates of change have also been able to use the media to promote new conceptions of sport, such as sport for gay and lesbian people and sport for people with disabilities, but they have had to confront media images that have often reinforced damaging or demeaning stereotypes.

In these various ways, established patterns of inequality in sport have been eroded or challenged in recent decades, but patterns of inequality have been among the most intractable aspects of social structure in society and sport. It is evident that change can be slow, high-status people do not readily yield power or privilege, and sport will remain contested terrain. The Golden Triangle is well entrenched as the dominant power structure in sport, and we will look more closely at its cultural, as well as economic, power in the next two chapters.

Notes

1. The survey used the term "gay" where I am using "homosexual." I will generally follow a convention of using "gay" to refer to homosexual males, "lesbian" to refer to homosexual women, and "homosexual" to refer to both gays and lesbians.

2. Homophobia may be directed at homosexuals, bisexuals, or transsexuals because they do not conform to the heterosexual norm of sexual orientation. The use of the term *homosexuality* in this book often implies the inclusion of bisexuals and transsexuals as well, although it is recognized that elements of their experiences can be quite different.

5

Globalization, Global Sports Culture, and the Golden Triangle

Social Theory, Culture, and Sport

We will begin thinking about globalization, the global sports culture, and the Golden Triangle in this chapter by focusing on a number of theoretical perspectives concerning culture and globalization. Our initial focus will be on *cultural studies*, which has been a major development in scholarly work prompted in part by the growth of the mass media and popular culture. It is an interdisciplinary area, drawing largely from the humanities and media studies but also including contributions from anthropologists and sociologists, and it offers some valuable insights about sport, culture, and society (e.g., see Hargreaves and McDonald 2000; Howell, Andrews, and Jackson 2002). We generally think of the concept of culture as the special province of anthropology, but many contemporary sociologists, scholars in cultural studies, and other scholars now study culture as well. An interest in globalization has broadened the study of culture across a variety of disciplines.

Klein (2000a:129–130) observed that anthropology and cultural studies approach culture in quite different ways. First, scholars in cultural studies typically do not use ethnographic field studies or similar social science methods of data collection conventionally used in anthropology. Second, scholars in cultural studies usually are not trained in the kind of cross-cultural analysis that is common in anthropology. Klein suggested that lack of interest in cross-cultural analysis in cultural studies may be a result of the influence of *postmodernism*, which has led cultural studies scholars to place more emphasis on the standardization of culture through processes such as globalization and McDonaldization than on cultural differences. The work of cultural studies scholars is relevant to sport sociology because it draws attention to the forces of globalization and the development of a *global cultural economy*. In the global cultural economy, cultural products such as sports events and sports-related merchandise are manufactured, marketed, sold, and consumed. The growth of this global cultural economy has been closely associated with the growth and increasing influence of the Golden Triangle.

In sociology, structural functionalism and neo-Marxist and critical theories are among the major types of theoretical perspectives that can be used to understand culture and sport. They provide very different ways of analyzing culture in relation to society, sport, and social change. On the one hand, *structural functionalists* are likely to emphasize the patterns and importance of cultural homogeneity, uniformity, and consensus within and across societies. For example, within societies, structural functionalists might analyze how the dominant values of sport are aligned with the dominant values of the larger society and other institutional realms in that society or focus on how sports involvement contributes to societal consensus about dominant cultural values. In the global context, modernization theories have reflected a structural functional view in assuming that the replacement of traditional values with modern ones in lower-income nations will make society "better" by contributing to economic development and greater prosperity (Giddens, Duneier, and Appelbaum 2007:273). They have argued that people in these nations are held back by their traditional religious values, their belief in fatalism, and their commitment to outdated technologies and ways of life and that they need to adopt a modern culture emphasizing industrialization and the values of capitalist enterprise, progress, and modernity to push their society forward and improve their own lives (see Rostow 1960; Berger 1986). Thus, the basic argument of modernization theories from a cultural standpoint is that if people embrace the values of industrialization, capitalism, and modernity, they will become more like Western capitalist nations, alleviate their problems of "underdevelopment," and become more successful as they join the global capitalist system. The Golden Triangle is part of this global capitalist system.

Neo-Marxist and critical theories, such as Wallerstein's (1974) world systems theory and Frank's (1979) dependency theory, have questioned structural functional assumptions about the economic and cultural benefits of modernization for people in lower-income nations. They have argued instead that industrial capitalism as a global economic system has exploited the people and resources of these countries and made their economies and cultures dependent on the powerful advanced industrial nations and transnational corporations that have used them for their own growth and profit. Critics have further argued that the globalization of culture that accompanies modernization processes is moving in the direction of a single global culture reflecting Western cultural values. This perceived globalization process provokes concerns and fears about the possible contamination or corruption of traditional culture and the loss of cultural autonomy as a result of the global spread of Western values, technology, media, consumer goods, popular culture, and lifestyles. For example, some fear that the spread of McDonald's and its fast food culture to other nations could replace the cuisines of these nations that help make their cultures distinctive. These fears are deeper and broader for many who see their traditions severely threatened by the global spread of Western "McDonaldized" culture, economics, and politics. We are familiar with the militant resistance of many fundamentalist Muslims to such globalization (Giddens, Duneier, and Appelbaum 2007:566–571). We sometimes see this cultural clash played out in sport when the culture of globalized popular sports conflicts with conservative cultural beliefs in nations where modern sports are played, as the "Sport in the News" feature on "Iranian Women at the Soccer Stadium" shows.

Sport in the News Feature 5.1:
Iranian Women at the Soccer Stadium

It can be difficult to protect cultural traditions against globalization, even in culturally conservative nations such as Iran, where a fundamentalist Islamic political regime is committed to the preservation of traditional culture. Dilemmas arise when globalization and the spread of popular culture, such as music and sports, expose people to values and experiences that conflict with traditional beliefs. Esposito (1986, 1992) called Islamic fundamentalism "Islamic revitalism," and he characterized it as a reaction to the shortcomings of modern Muslim nations.

A prominent cultural element of this revitalization movement included a rejection of Western secular and materialistic values. Part of the traditional belief system or ideology advanced by the post-1979 revolutionary Iranian regime was a set of beliefs about the status of women that have been viewed as very conservative or even oppressive in the West. These Western views may be stereotypical or oversimplified and fail to account for the appeal of the conservative Islamic ideology to both women and men who saw material excess in Western lifestyles and were opposed to the previous regime of the Western-oriented Shah, which they perceived as unjust and politically oppressive (Bahramitash 2004). It nevertheless has been true that in Iran and under other conservative Islamic regimes, women have experienced limited rights and autonomy, have had to display modesty in public settings, especially where men have been present, and have been segregated in a variety of settings from education and employment to sport. The culture has been patriarchal and, in a number of respects, protective of women. Concern about exposing women to male athletes in soccer shorts or to the foul language or aggressive behavior of men on the field or in the stands may have contributed to a ban on women's attendance at soccer matches in public stadiums, imposed by the revolutionary Iranian regime in 1979. In general, it was thought to be "un-Islamic" for women to attend men's sports events (Radio Free Europe 2006).

This ruling was consistent with Iran's Islamic law, which included a number of restrictions on women regarding work, travel, education, and public behavior. In general, women have needed male permission to engage in a number of activities. The popularity of soccer among many women as well as men in Iran created cultural tension in this nation, and in 2005, one hundred Iranian women defied the ban and attended a World Cup qualifier for the national team in Azadi Stadium in Tehran, along with eighty thousand male fans (Hughes 2006). They faced resistance from the militia in their efforts to push inside the stadium, and some women were injured. They had occasionally been allowed to attend public sports events, such as basketball and volleyball, which were played in smaller arenas, and some women had tried to enter stadiums disguised as men or with foreign spectators (Whitaker 2006).

Responding to international pressure related to the upcoming World Cup and to domestic pressure from some women's groups in Iran, President Mahmoud Ahmadinejad announced on state television in April 2006, only about forty days before the 2006 World Cup in which Iran was competing, that he had instructed the Ministry for Sports to permit women to attend soccer games. He also ruled that force should not be used to enforce the strict Islamic dress codes for women that required that they cover their heads and bodies. In making his announcement, the president reportedly said that for national and other significant games, the best seating in the stadium should be reserved for women and families, whose presence, he expected, would help bring "morality and chastity" to these settings. Despite his generally strong endorsement of conservative Islamic ideology and the support for his election that had come from powerful conservative Islamic clerics and hard-line religious militias in his country, his order was opposed by conservative clerics because he did not consult with them before making his decision and because they believed it violated Islamic law.

continues

The regime initially retreated somewhat from the decision by stating that the ban still applied to single women and that only women who attended with their families would be permitted in the stadium. His justification—to improve behavior in the stadium—and his concession were not enough to appease opponents, though. Two weeks after the president's announcement, he was forced to reverse his decision because Iran's Supreme Leader, Ayatollah Ali Khomeini, opposed it. According to the national constitution, the Ayatollah's word was final (Associated Press 2006).

Beyond any kind of religious or moral interpretation, this rejection of women's attendance at men's sports events by the most powerful conservative elements in Iran represented a strong rebuff of the perceived intrusion of corrupt Western values into their society through popular culture. The disagreement between the president and the Ayatollah and the willingness of some women to oppose the ban openly by speaking out against it and to try to use a form of subterfuge or a ruse to get into the stadium reflect the cultural tensions within Iran. It is not coincidental that sport was at the center of this conflict. Soccer has become a major global cultural phenomenon and a source of national pride in many nations. Thus, it is understandable why the soccer stadium became contested terrain as the site for gender-related globalization issues and cultural tensions between tradition and modernity to be played out on a national stage in Iran.

Iranian women watch a friendly soccer game between their women's national football team and German team Al-Dersimspor at Tehran's Ararat stadium April 28, 2006. Hardline President Mahmoud Ahmadinejad announced that Iranian women can now go to stadiums to watch sporting events, putting an end to a ban imposed after the 1979 Islamic revolution. This is the first female soccer match held in Iran since the revolution. (STR/AFP/Getty Images)

Globalization Theories and Sport

Ritzer (2003:143) has suggested that a major contemporary issue dividing *globalization theorists* concerns the extent to which globalization represents movement toward a single homogeneous global culture. While many see this kind of general trend, there are others who see interesting new hybrid forms of culture or cultural practices, such as fusion music and cuisine and alternative cultures of sport and leisure, developing today at the local level of societies. Donnelly (1996) discussed different ways sport sociologists have interpreted globalizing trends in sport. For example, some have seen these globalizing trends as a form of ongoing modernization, which made sports around the world generally more secular, highly organized, and rational. Others have viewed global trends in the development of sport as a reflection of Americanization or American influences, which some called American "cultural imperialism." Still others have seen broader forces of globalization at work, which bore the imprint of increasingly wealthy and powerful transnational corporations that reached beyond U.S. borders and had their own interests. Whatever the interpretation of globalization in sport and other realms of society, it seems apparent that a unidirectional model of influences oversimplifies the cultural changes that are happening on the international level.

Donnelly (1996:241) pointed out that trying to separate cultural from economic and political forces of globalization is artificial. The interweaving of these forces in the Golden Triangle illustrates the difficulty of trying to separate their influences. Donnelly proposed analyses of globalization and Americanization in sport sociology that capture the variety and complexity of relations among the global, external, and local in cultural and other forms of development.

Robertson and Ritzer have presented concepts and perspectives that enable us to understand the varied and complex forms of globalization. Robertson (2001), a leading expert on globalization theory, has suggested that we focus on whether global change is more likely to involve increased homogeneity of culture, increased local heterogeneity of culture, or some combination of these forces and, also, how global cultural change is related to local cultural change (462). Ritzer (2004a:73) used Robertson's homogeneity-heterogeneity and global-local distinctions in his formulation of the concept of "*glocalization*"— which combines the words *global* and *local*—to emphasize heterogeneity in the interplay and integration of global and local cultural influences.

Ritzer (2004a:73) added his own concept of "*grobalization*," which emphasizes "growth," to sit alongside glocalization and to expand our conceptual grasp of global processes of change. According to Ritzer, grobalization is fueled by the related processes of the spread of profit-driven capitalist development, Americanization or the diffusion of U.S. culture, and McDonaldization. Unlike glocalization, which involves cultural creativity, adaptation, and innovation at the local level, grobalization involves efforts to make local cultures around the world conform to the cultural directives of powerful global forces, such as capitalism, Americanization, and McDonaldization. In sports, we can see grobalization in efforts to replace indigenous sports with modern corporate and commercialized sports. The imprint of the Golden Triangle is apparent in this process when we see sports developed and played at the local level, perhaps as recreational pursuits, become popular, get co-opted by the media and corporate sponsors, and become highly organized corporate and commercial enterprises that are produced and marketed for national and global audiences. These sports and their stars are turned into vehicles for the global expansion of the commercial mass media and corporate sponsors in the Golden Triangle. In the next chapter, we will consider how this kind of grobalization process has characterized the development of initially alternative sports subcultures of extreme or action sports. Grobalization also characterizes efforts by North American professional sports leagues to Americanize sports in foreign nations that are inexpensive sources of new talent.

In looking at the globalization literature, Harvey, Rail, and Thibault (1996) found "conceptual clutter," which produced "theoretical confusion" (258). Terms such as *internationalization* and *Americanization* were sometimes used interchangeably with *globalization* without clarifying their common, or distinct, meanings. Acknowledging the work of Robertson (1992) as well as Giddens (1990), they defined globalization in terms of the processes that made the world seem smaller, increased awareness of the world as a whole, intensified social relations at the global level, and connected distant locations so that local events were shaped by influences from other parts of the world. In their reading of the globalization literature, they concluded that the most important factor contributing to contemporary trends in globalization was the combination of neoliberal forces that arose during the early 1980s, including transnational corporations, international capital, and neoliberal economics. These forces led to the dismantling of the welfare state in many nations, deregulation of financial markets, and freer movement of capital around the world. New forms of communication technology resulted in the instant movement of capital through world financial networks, which created the conditions for a global economy. In this new global context, the flow of cultural and political as well as economic influences intensified. Things were happening in this new world order that were beyond the influence of individual nations. This is the kind of environment that has been conducive to the growth of the Golden Triangle.

Harvey, Rail, and Thibault proposed a theoretical model to guide research about the effects of globalization on national sports organizations and policies. They were especially interested in guiding research about how sport was affecting and being affected by globalization and, more specifically, how national-level sports were being affected by the globalization of sport. Their theoretical model for studying globalization in sport adds a social dimension to the cultural, economic, and political dimensions we have been considering, and all four dimensions are identified at the global and national levels. The *social* dimension concerns issues of how social policy and new social movements, for example to increase public access to sports participation opportunities, guide or change the organization of sport and the actions of sports actors in nations.

The *cultural* dimension concerns issues of how national culture and identity and global culture are related to sport. For example, it raises questions about the capacity of sport to foster nationalism in the context of substantial social and cultural diversity and tensions within a nation and about whether citizens in a nation identify more with the sports and sports stars of other nations than with those of their own. In the latter regard, globalization may be considered as a form of cultural imperialism in which powerful nations or transnational corporations try to impose their sports cultures or push their sports products on the people of less-powerful nations, often in the pursuit of profit.

The *economic* dimension concerns issues about the relationship of global and national economic processes to the development of sport. In this context, we would also consider how the development of sport has been related to commercialization, corporate sponsorship, and the growing influence of transnational corporations in the Golden Triangle. We will examine later in this chapter how these kinds of factors have combined with television in the Golden Triangle to extend the reach of sport and make sport and sports stars more prominent around the world.

The *political* dimension in Harvey, Rail, and Thibault's model concerns issues about how the global growth of sport is related to national sovereignty or the regulation of sports played within a nation's borders. It also concerns efforts to resolve control issues between national and international governing bodies in sport. Political forces will be the specific focus of chapter eleven.

As Donnelly observed, we may be able to separate these dimensions of globalization processes on paper, but they tend to be intertwined in reality. For example, cultural issues of nationalism, cultural imperialism, and sport have political implications; attempts to create policies to regulate or deregulate economic activities in sport raise social and political as well as economic issues; and efforts to control the migration patterns of athletes across national borders have possible social, cultural, political, and economic implications. Furthermore, the globalization of consumer culture through sport by the Golden Triangle has both economic and cultural dimensions. Harvey, Rail, and Thibault provide a useful conceptual framework for seeing the complexity of globalization and the issues it raises for sport as it moves through the twenty-first century.

Grobalization reflects the powerful globalizing influence of the Golden Triangle in sport, but, as I suggested earlier, glocalization also may play a role in national and international sports contexts. In his study of the Americanization of baseball in the Dominican Republic, Klein (1991a, 1991b) showed that the people of the Dominican Republic exhibited some resistance to the North American cultural influence of Major League Baseball, which we have called "glocalization." He found that Major League Baseball (MLB) clubs were actively developing and recruiting young players and importing the best ones to play in their leagues in the United States and Canada. Klein also found that the Dominican people were not completely happy with this foreign involvement in baseball in their country, which was a source of great national pride for them. They were proud of the accomplishments of their homegrown stars in the North American Major League, but Dominican sportswriters were critical of the efforts by MLB clubs to influence winter baseball in the Dominican Republic to serve their own interests. The Dominican people expressed their national cultural pride by wearing hats of Dominican rather than Major League teams. In these and other modest ways, they expressed their resistance to complete domination by North American culture, showing that baseball was "contested cultural terrain" in their society. Klein observed, however, that while they resisted Americanization to some extent in baseball, the Dominican people willingly consumed many other elements of North American popular culture, from fashion to movies and music (Nixon and Frey 1996:53).

In looking north, it is understandable that a small Caribbean nation might not distinguish between the cultural influences of the United States and Canada, seeing them collectively as "North American." After all, although Major League Baseball is predominantly located in the United States, it has included Canadian teams. The same can be said for the National Hockey League (NHL) and the National Basketball Association (NBA), and the Canadians play the same kind of football as the National Football League (NFL) in their Canadian Football League (CFL). Some Canadians, however, seeing their nation in the economic, political, and cultural shadow of the United States, have perceived Americanization as a distinctively U.S.-driven phenomenon. For example, at the time of the emergence of the "New World Order" following the collapse of the "Soviet Empire" in the early 1990s, when nations were seeking their national identity and place in this world order, Canadian sport sociologist Bruce Kidd (1991) pointed to the strong imprint of U.S. commercial interests on Canadian sport. He called this influence "Americanization." He argued that *Americanization* was a more relevant term than *globalization* in explaining the development of Canadian sport and popular culture, and that one could see this influence in the prevalence of U.S.-oriented events, images, and souvenirs in Canada (Nixon and Frey 1996:52).

Globalization, individual foreign nations, transnational corporations, and international organizations all could play significant roles in building economic, political, social, and cultural institutions in both less- and more-industrialized nations. In less-powerful nations, though, which are more vulnerable to external influences, externally driven grobalization may overwhelm glocalization processes. Even in more industrialized but smaller nations such as Canada, it may be difficult to resist powerful external influences on their culture, including their sports values and practices, for example, from bigger and more powerful nations such as the United States. In yielding to these external influences and allowing others to shape the form of their culture, they demonstrate a kind of *cultural dependency*. This condition can lead to resentment and cultural resistance among those who seek control over the cultural values, traditions, and practices in their own nations. Dominicans demonstrated this in small ways, such as wearing hats of their national baseball teams, and the Iranian revolutionary regime has demonstrated this more extensively in banning practices associated with Western societies, including the mixing of the sexes in public venues, such as sports stadiums.

At times, we may be too hasty in drawing conclusions about foreign or global cultural domination when we see evidence of the influence of an outside culture in a country. For example, in their study of the influence of the NBA in New Zealand, Jackson and Andrews (1999) showed that acceptance of foreign culture may be complex and selective. First, they pointed out that as a result of the influence of television, the NBA had been transformed from a U.S. cultural product and economic commodity to a global one that was transmitted and sold around the world. They also argued that wearing Nike shoes endorsed by NBA stars, collecting NBA player cards, or treating African-American NBA stars as heroes did not necessarily imply that New Zealand culture had been Americanized.

For young New Zealanders, the attraction of the NBA may not be that it is from the United States, but instead that it is not part of New Zealand culture.

Lealand's (1994) study of U.S. popular culture and emerging nationalism in New Zealand suggests that these young people were looking for a more exciting world that could help them escape the constraints of their youth, family, and where they lived, at least in their imaginations. Thus, the NBA and the United States may have been less important to them than the idea that they represented an alternative culture, which was different than the culture of their own country.

We could conclude from Jackson and Andrews and others who have studied globalization that even North American sports such as the NBA that have been spread around the world by television and the Golden Triangle are not necessarily making the world more American. In addition, increasing global popularity of sports such as NBA basketball does not necessarily mean that local sports interests and identities are being obliterated by a homogeneous or universal global sports culture. In some cases, such as the young New Zealanders in Lealand's study, people attach their own distinctive local meanings to imported cultural practices and products of the Golden Triangle. However, this is not a matter of pure glocalization, since these cultural products are imports from a global cultural economy of sport constructed by major global actors in the Golden Triangle such as the NBA and its commercial partners. Following the NBA in New Zealand may make young people there feel like they are asserting their autonomy from the cultural and social constraints on them in their society, but they are still engaging in the cultural practices that make them similar to other young people elsewhere in the world. In watching the NBA and buying its merchandise, they are actually yielding to another powerful force in their lives, the Golden Triangle, but unlike parents, teachers, and conventional expectations and practices in their local community and society, the influence of the Golden Triangle in shaping their interests and tastes may be less evident to them.

Thus, even sports-related cultural practices, such as those displayed by young New Zealanders, that have locally defined meanings still may reflect the imprint of the more global culture of the Golden Triangle. Television has had much to do with which sports have become major sports in the Golden Triangle and with how major sports are perceived and experienced around the world today. Although its effects on local sports cultures, perceptions, and experiences may vary, television helps embed the consumer culture of the global Golden Triangle in local cultures by using sports and sports stars to carry the powerful commercial messages of its corporate sponsors. Thus, television has connected local cultures to the global cultural economy of sport.

Television and the Mediated Construction of Global Sport

We previously considered how television and the other mass media often play a powerful role in shaping our perceptions of various forms of inequality and our acceptance of ideologies related to these inequalities. In this chapter, we will be primarily interested in the role of the mass media, and especially television in recent decades, in increasing the global exposure and cultural significance of sport and sports stars. *Symbolic interactionism* enables us to see this role more clearly. Symbolic interactionism emphasizes the social construction of reality, and in relation to the mass media it draws special attention to the processes through which the mass media construct or "mediate" reality for us with images, words, and stories meant to represent reality. Since we cannot directly experience most of what we know about the world, we often rely on television and the other mass media for our understanding of the world. Thus, the media shape how we experience sport and its cultural significance and meanings within and across nations. The concept of "*sportainment*"—a term coined by Lipsyte (1996)—clarifies how our experiences as sports viewers are mediated by television.

Smart proposed that the symbiotic relationship among television and the other components of the Golden Triangle has catapulted sport into a position of unprecedented global cultural significance, surpassing even the popularity of music and other forms of popular culture. The excitement and glamour of sport have enabled it to extend its appeal across national and cultural borders, as sports events, images, and stars have generated worldwide interest. Television has had so much influence on our sports perceptions and experiences because we rely so much on it to experience the sports world. However, television does not and cannot show us or talk about everything that happens on the field or in the larger environment surrounding and influencing the game we are watching. The sportainment idea suggests in part that the television production of sport is mediated by television producers who try to entertain us and keep our attention and do not inform us as serious journalists would. Thus, the mediated construction of sport is meant to serve the interests of television and its

Pelé, on the left, and David Beckham, on the right, are iconic stars of different eras in the world's most popular sport of soccer. The fame and fortune of both are products of the Golden Triangle. (AP Photo/File)

Mitsu Makamura, a television cameraman for Fuji television in Japan, looks out over Roger Dean Stadium before the Boston Red Sox spring training game in Jupiter, Florida, Tuesday, March 6, 2007, against the Florida Marlins. Japanese and American media are in town to report on the Red Sox starting pitcher Daisuke Matsuzaka, also of Japan. On the chair is a script for the reporter to read written in Japanese. This photo illustrates the global imprint of the Golden Triangle on sport. (AP Photo/James A. Finley)

corporate sport and business partners in the Golden Triangle. Sport becomes for us, as viewers, what television and the mass media show us and tell us.

Television transmits words and images of sports and athletes and associated messages about their commercial sponsors and their products around the world. Its role has gone beyond showing us sports events and athletes. Television broadcasts construct events and provide us with interpretations of their meaning that

reflect television production values (Silk 1999). Television executives and producers make choices about the events they cover, how and when they cover them, to
whom they choose to give special attention, and the story lines they incorporate
into their commentaries about events and profiles of athletes in an effort to attract more viewers and sell more and more expensive advertising minutes. Television sports broadcasts emphasize particular cultural values, such as talent,
achievement, courage, sacrifice, overcoming odds, and the American Dream, that
reflect the values and interests of sport and its corporate sponsors. Furthermore,
their commercial advertisements do more than expose their audiences to the
products their sponsors sell. They also convey the message that we should value
consumerism, which reinforces the values of consumer capitalism. Thus, watching television sports broadcasts subtly but powerfully influences the tastes, interests, values, and identities of viewers, who learn to "be like Mike"—that is,
Michael Jordan. They are encouraged by these broadcasts, and particularly by
the advertisements on them, to buy the various products and live the lifestyles
that sports stars and cultural icons such as basketball player Michael Jordan,
soccer player David Beckham, and golfer Tiger Woods endorse or display. We also
learn from watching sports on television—and the accompanying commercial
advertisements—that the products of companies such as Nike, adidas, McDonald's, Coca-Cola, Pepsi, Anheuser-Busch, and General Motors have special value
because they are endorsed by star athletes.

Television also can turn attractive but moderately successful athletes, such
as tennis player Anna Kournikova, into media stars and cultural icons through
skillful manipulation and exposure of their images (Smart 2005). For women
athletes, such as Anna Kournikova, physical attractiveness or "sex appeal" is
an especially important part of their constructed image in a context dominated
by the stereotypical conceptions of femininity we considered in previous chapters. The mass media have played a significant role in perpetuating these
stereotypes. The role of the mass media, and especially television, in creating
a global sports culture and making sports stars global celebrities and cultural
icons will be discussed at greater length in this chapter and the next one, and
we will see in more detail how the global Golden Triangle functions in this
process.

The Golden Triangle and the
Global Diffusion of Sports Culture

The growth of sport from the end of the nineteenth century into the twentieth
century in countries such as England and the United States is closely associated with the rise of mass-circulation daily newspapers and competition for
readership in these countries during this period (McChesney 1989; Smart
2005:ch. 4). The relationship of sport and the mass media in general has attracted extensive scholarly attention (e.g., Raney and Bryant 2006). Media
studies of the more recent history of sport have focused on television (e.g.,
Brown and Bryant 2006; Sullivan 2006; Wood and Benigni 2006; Whannel
2000). Two important reasons why sports are attractive to television are their
entertainment value and their revenue-generating potential. Smart (2005:194)
has argued that sport is particularly appealing today because it has a quality

of *authenticity* not found in many other realms of contemporary culture. The idea of authenticity implies that the sports performance can be trusted. Unlike film, music, and even religion, which manipulate words and images to produce desired effects, the sports competition itself essentially involves something that is difficult and often illegal to manipulate. That is, sport is a competition in which the outcome remains uncertain until the game has been played, and the outcome may defy the most confident predictions because on a particular day, some athletes exceed expectations and others fall short. This description may seem to fit politics, too, but the public often is suspicious of the role of "consultants" and "spin doctors" in politics and wonders what to believe about political candidates and elected officials. If we put aside recent evidence and allegations about drug use and gambling, the public and especially devoted sports fans typically have not had the same kinds or degree of suspicion about misrepresentations, fraud, or deceit in regard to sport.

One possible qualification of the appeal of sport to television and corporate sponsors is the local sports newscast, since there is evidence that interest in sports news on local news broadcasts may be declining. According to Schulz and Sheffer (2004), viewers have been tuning out the sports news for a while, and they cited statistics showing that more than twice as many viewers were interested in the weather than in the sports news on local broadcasts and that women had much less interest in watching the sports news than men did. As a result of this declining interest, a number of stations have either reduced minutes allotted for the sports segment or even eliminated it completely. Others have focused on sport in new ways, with more emphasis on news stories than on scores and on features that focus on local sports events and figures that appeal to general news viewers more than to diehard sports fans. This pattern of declining local sports viewers may seem puzzling in view of the extensive interest in sports events and athletes, but it is understandable if we consider a number of factors: for example, competition for sports news viewers from all-sports networks; real-time access to sports events and scores on the Internet; a wide variety of taped and live televised sports programming choices on network, cable, and home satellite television; and scrolling news crawl across the bottom of television screens showing live sports, sports talk, and sports news programs. If serious sports fans are interested in the scores, they do not need to wait for the local news to learn what they can find out immediately or much more quickly from the Internet or other sources. For the broader and more casual sports audience, watching sports events and following their favorite sports stars are more entertaining than watching a local newscaster report scores.

The decline of the local TV sports newscast, at least in some U.S. markets, suggests that the use of sport by television and corporate sponsors has limitations. Television and corporate sponsors, along with the corporate world of sport itself, are interested in what is profitable. The big corporations that have bought local television stations have put pressure on the local stations to increase viewers by broadening the appeal of their newscasts (Schulz and Sheffer 2004), for example, with breaking news, special profiles or interviews of athletes, or, in some cases, "behind the scenes" stories of new developments or problems in sport. "Big media" and big corporations realize that their sports "product" must be broadly appealing. If their local stations cannot develop interesting and appealing ways to include sports in their newscasts, then the sports news segment is likely to dwindle or disappear. In general, people in the sports audience seem more interested in the "real thing" than in straightforward sports news reports from their local TV newscast, which tend to attract more serious sports fans. Thus, television, the other media, and corporate sponsors construct sports events as spectacles that are made to seem special by emphasizing their authenticity as well as their broad entertainment value.

Although the contest on the field is inherently authentic, Lipsyte's concept of sportainment reminds us that we should not mistake what we see on television for "the real thing." He characterized televised sportainment as like a docudrama, or a fictionalized version of a real story that has been constructed to be entertaining. For example, producers choose to focus on specific aspects of the action on the field from particular camera angles and give more attention to certain athletes or types of play than others, and announcers and commentators use story lines to emphasize the dramatic, heroic, or exciting elements of the game and sport. Thus, watching sports on television is not the same experience as being in the stadium or arena.

The mediated construction of televised sports exposes us to a number of ideological themes that reflect and reinforce the values and interests of those in the Golden Triangle who present and sponsor sports. Coakley (2007:428–440) suggested that the types of themes that are frequently overtly or subtly conveyed by mediated sports today are that: (1) competitive success is worth working for; (2) men's sports are more important than women's sports; (3) race and ethnicity do not matter in sports and minority athletes have as much chance of succeeding in sport as anyone else; (4) teamwork and doing what the coach says are important but individual performance and success are important, too; (5) nationalism is important; (6) it is necessary to be aggressive and even violent sometimes to succeed; and (7) buying the kinds of things that sponsors advertise makes you a better person; makes your life easier, happier, or more successful; or enhances your status. Thus, as sport culture is dispersed locally, nationally, and around the globe, broader values and beliefs associated with established structures of corporate and consumer capitalism are also being disseminated. In the remainder of this chapter, we will focus on the themes of the capitalist imperative and consumerism in the global sports culture and U.S. exceptionalism in the global sports culture. We will also continue examining how the Golden Triangle shapes the global sports culture and mediates our sports experiences.

Global Sports Culture, the Capitalist Imperative, and Consumerism

Part of the global sports culture is an ideological belief in the special quality of sport as authentic culture. We recall from previous chapters that *ideologies* are sets of beliefs that we accept without question and that influence how we look at the world and act. Even though mediated sport may be sportainment, viewers often believe it is real, and this perceived authenticity is, as Smart argued, an appealing quality of sport today. Television and transnational corporations have invested in sport because they have recognized the global appeal of the perceived authenticity of professional sports, their capacity to captivate and entertain, and their ability to generate revenue from their popularity. Thus, the global sports culture is a significant segment of the economy of global capitalism, and in this global cultural economy, the games, merchandise, and images of the stars of sport are commodities that are marketed and sold. We might ask who benefits most from this partnership of professional sport (and other corporate and commercialized forms of sport), television, and corporate sponsors in the global cultural economy of sport and how much sport has had to compromise its integrity to be the popular entertainment commodity that television and sponsors want. There is little doubt, however, that all three parties willingly participate in this relationship and have gained large sums of money and much exposure and prominence from it. The mutually beneficial nature of these relationships explains why Golden Triangles exist.

Driven by the *capitalist imperative* of expanding markets to increase profits, corporations try to reach as many potential customers as possible with their advertising. Commercial television executives and producers seek sponsors for their programming and try to maximize the number of viewers of their programs who are targeted by their advertisers so that they can maximize their advertising revenue. Television sets advertising rates for programming based on the size of the audience. Sports try to increase their exposure to get as many people as possible into the stadium or arena, but in the modern era of television, they also want to attract as many viewers as possible so that they can earn as much television revenue as possible. Sports organizations, including individual clubs, conferences, leagues, and national and international governing bodies, sell broadcast rights to television, and these rights fees have been escalating rapidly over the past few decades. For example, according to Coakley (2007:414–415), annual broadcast rights fees increased between 1986 and 2006 from $400 million to $3.7 billion for the NFL, from $183 million to $560 million for MLB, from $30 million to $767 million for the NBA, from $22 million to $70 million for the NHL (after a big drop the year before due to a season-long suspension of play), from $3 million to $560 million for NASCAR, from $31 million to $550 million for the NCAA Men's Basketball Tournament, and from zero dollars to $18.5 million for all women's NCAA championships. He also cited figures indicating that U.S. broadcast rights fees for the Summer Olympics increased from $400,000 in 1960 for the Rome Games, to $225 million in 1984 for the Los Angeles Games, to $456 million in 1996 for the Atlanta Games, to $894 million for the 2008 Olympics in Beijing. Winter Olympics rights fees increased from $50,000 for the 1960 Games in Squaw Valley, California, to $613 million for the 2006 Games in Torino, Italy.

Smart (2005:93) noted that in partnership with the British Broadcasting Corporation (BBC), Rupert Murdoch's BSkyB global television network won the rights to televise live English Premiership soccer matches, and the amount of money significantly changed both the financial status and the scheduling of professional soccer in England. The contract began with the 1992–1993 season and paid the sports league £304 million for five years, which was six times more than the previous contract with a much more limited broadcast area. Murdoch paid the league £670 million to renew the contract in 1996. The escalating rights fees were based in large part on the expanded reach of new broadcast technologies, including cable and satellite, and this change brought profound changes in the effects of the Golden Triangle on the exposure of sports and sports stars and the growth of markets for television and transnational corporate sponsors.

Sport is obviously more than play, that is, boys, girls, men, or women competing against each other to win a game, and television and corporate sponsors have played an important role in making sport a cultural element and commodity that is bigger than informal play and games. The idea of sport as a commodity that can be manufactured, marketed, bought, and sold as entertainment reflects the contemporary corporate commercial character of the dominant forms of modern sport. In a prescient article in 1955, Stone anticipated the powerful influence of television on sport, arguing that it had begun to transform sport from pure play into an entertainment spectacle. The spectacle has evolved into displays involving bobblehead dolls of star players, balls, shirts, and other giveaways as spectators enter the stadium; cheap beer; fireworks; contests and other entertainment during timeouts; professional cheerleaders; huge overhead screens with a constant stream of images; exploding scoreboards; famous names in halftime shows to keep spectators in the stadium; and interviews with players and coaches before, during, and after games to build up and retain interest in current and future games and focus attention on associated commercial advertising.

Television has heightened the spectacular display aspects of sport and enabled sport to grow and prosper. It has been the vehicle through which modern sport has both spread its own influence and helped convey the values and ideologies of its corporate sponsors around the world. By telecasting sports events all over the world, television has helped to construct a global sports culture featuring a number of different sports and sports spectacles, such as soccer and the World Cup. The corporate sponsors of global sports and global sports stars, such as English soccer player David Beckham, U.S. NBA player Michael Jordan, Chinese NBA player Yao Ming, and U.S. golfer Tiger Woods, have used their televised—and print—ads associating themselves with these popular athletes and their sports to sell their products. In doing so, they have spread the values of the consumer culture to help them achieve the capitalist imperative of expanding markets and increasing profits.

In making sports more important in more places around the world, television has given its transnational corporate sponsors the chance to use sports to build their brand recognition and make their products more familiar and more appealing. Especially where there have been disposable income, some leisure time, and the desire and opportunity to consume the products of popular culture, sport has become a popular product of consumption as both a form of entertainment and a source of meaning for people who are drawn in by the perceived authenticity of the competition, their favorite teams and athletes, and their stories. Buying things that are endorsed by their favorite teams and athletes gives these sports fans a chance to identify with something bigger than themselves, with broad cultural significance. By watching sports, they are reflecting and reinforcing the power of television. By ardently following sports and sports stars and buying the merchandise endorsed by sports and athletes and advertised on television and in other mass media, they are demonstrating the cultural significance and power of sport and contributing to the legitimacy and profitability of consumer capitalism. Thus, we can see how corporate sports, corporate media, and corporate sponsors mutually reinforce the status, success, and influence of each other as the dominant network of power in the Golden Triangle. Their combined influence has constructed a global sports culture and also contributed to the global cultural diffusion of the values of consumer capitalism. In the next section, we will examine the peculiar place of the United States in the global sports culture.

A visitor takes a swing at QMotions-Baseball video game at the Electronic Entertainment Expo in Los Angeles. Clicking a computer mouse is hardly the most authentic way to play a baseball video game. Why not swing a real bat? The QMotions-Baseball system replaces the game pad, letting players use a bat of their choosing. The setup includes a special bat collar, seen here as a yellow streak on the bat, that wirelessly sends swing movement to a home plate receiver plugged into an Xbox or PC. The device works with Big League Baseball games, including "EA Sports MVP Baseball" and "ESPN Baseball." These innovations of new media in the technologically expanding Golden Triangle challenge or reinterpret ideas about the importance of authenticity in the appeal of sport. (AP Photo/Reed Saxon)

Global Sports Culture and U.S. Exceptionalism: U.S. Sports versus the World

By global standards, U.S. sports fans have been peculiar. Two of the most popular U.S. sports, NFL football and Major League Baseball, and their premier events, the Super Bowl and the World Series, attract large domestic television audiences and extensive coverage by the U.S. press, but they have not been nearly as popular in global terms. Smart (2005:100) argued that efforts to increase the popularity of these and other U.S. sports outside North America with broadcasts of regular-season games and international competitions have had limited success in building television and live audiences in other countries. For example, although the NFL Super Bowl is televised in 225 countries with an estimated potential audience of one billion people, it actually appears to attract between ninety and one hundred million television viewers, with about 97 percent of the North American viewers in the United States and 2 percent or two million outside North America (Rushin 2006).

Major League Baseball has tried to increase its worldwide popularity beyond North America by creating a global competition, the World Baseball Classic (Sheringham 2006). Only 5 percent of MLB's $5 billion in annual revenue was from outside North America. The inaugural three-week event took place in the spring of 2006. Teams from sixteen nations competed, including teams from South Africa, the Netherlands, and China, and in the final, played in San Diego, California, Japan defeated Cuba. Despite a roster of MLB all-stars, the U.S. team was eliminated in the second round. The event was popular in Latin America and in a number of Asian countries, where baseball already was well established, but it attracted much less attention in Europe, where soccer reigned. MLB officials did not claim to be trying to rival soccer, but instead wanted to use the Classic as a major step toward internationalizing their sport. In the same vein, MLB had opened four of the previous seven seasons in foreign cities, in Japan, Mexico, and Puerto Rico. The games of the Classic were televised in all of the competing nations, but the ratings in the United States were lower than in other nations with a baseball tradition. A major target of this baseball marketing effort was China, with its huge population and growing economy. Yao Ming, the Houston Rockets NBA star from China, was a model for MLB, which wanted to create a Chinese baseball player of comparable ability and appeal to help generate interest in MLB in China. Hoping to facilitate the development of baseball at the grass roots in the nations participating in the Classic, MLB planned to give half of the profits from the Classic to the baseball federations in these countries. MLB officials realized that they still had an uphill climb to build the global appeal of their sport and the MLB brand. For example, after being introduced into the Olympics in 1992, baseball was to be dropped after the 2008 Beijing Summer Games.

Although U.S. sports have fallen short of their goals in creating an international following so far, two of the most popular sports for international audiences in the global sports hierarchy, soccer and rugby, are not nearly as popular in the United States as they are elsewhere. The cumulative live television audience for the 2006 World Cup of soccer was estimated to be over 30 billion people, with estimates of the TV audience for the final game between Italy and France ranging widely from 300 million to nearly 1 billion, which was the largest TV audience to date for a single sports contest. These figures are much larger than the estimated 127 million who watched the 2004 Summer Olympics and the estimated 95 million who watched the 2004 Super Bowl (cited in Infante 2006). FIFA also estimated that over 120 million people in the world played the sport that the great star Pelé called "the beautiful game," and the only relatively large countries where soccer was not the most popular sport were the United States, China, Pakistan,

India, Australia, and Canada (Infante 2006). Even though Americans are more inclined to watch homegrown sports, and people in other countries tend to be more interested in watching their own teams play (Dawley 2006), soccer's appeal goes beyond national loyalties. TV audience rankings showed that in 2002, half of the top sixteen viewing countries ranked by audience size did not have national teams in the competition, and for the first round in 2006, seven of the top twenty nations by audience size did not have qualifying teams (Reuters 2006).

FIFA estimated that over 29 million people play soccer in the United States (cited in Infante 2006). The U.S. television audience for the World Cup has been much smaller than this, but the U.S. television audience for the 2006 World Cup final—including 11.9 million on ABC and 5 million on Univision—was bigger than expected. It was 4 million more than the average audience for the 2006 NBA finals between Miami and Dallas, a little less than the audience for the 2006 NCAA men's basketball final between Florida and UCLA, the average audience size for the 2005 World Series between the Chicago White Sox and Houston Astros, and about 1 million less than the 1994 Women's Soccer World Cup final in 1994, which was won by the United States over China on penalty kicks (Sandomir 2006).

However, U.S. audiences do not rival soccer audiences in other countries, and it is a small fraction of the typical NFL Super Bowl audience of over 90 million. Two World Cup games prior to the final drew U.S. audiences of nearly 10 million, United States versus Italy and Argentina versus Mexico. For both games, however, especially the one involving Mexico, a large part of the audience watched on the Spanish-speaking Univision. Nearly 63 million Chinese people watched England play Paraguay and over 60 million Brazilians watched their national team play Croatia (Fatsis 2006). Although China has a population nearly four and one-half times bigger than that of the United States, it did not have a team in the 2006 World Cup. The Brazilian viewers represented nearly one-third of the country's entire population. Furthermore, one media analyst estimated that 84 percent of televisions in use in Italy and 80 percent in France were tuned in to the 2006 World Cup final between the two nations (Sandomir 2006). The main points to be drawn from all these numbers are that: (1) U.S. interest in soccer is growing; (2) the World Cup final has become almost as popular among U.S. viewers as some other major U.S. sports events; (3) the popularity of soccer in the United States is heavily dependent on an ethnic audience; (4) U.S. interest in soccer does not rival soccer interest in other countries; and (5) U.S. interest in soccer is a small fraction of its interest in NFL football. Furthermore, the typical ESPN2 cable audience for Major League Soccer games in the United States was a little over 200,000 households in 2005 (Eichelberger 2006), suggesting that U.S. sports fans were not routinely interested in soccer yet, even with a temporary bump from the World Cup.

These patterns are interesting because we tend to think of globalization as a U.S.-driven process, but they show that the United States is following behind the rest of the world in regard to soccer. In addition, the United States is having difficulty gaining a foothold in other nations for its sports and leagues. U.S.-based transnational corporations, such as Coca-Cola and Nike, have recognized the global appeal of soccer and are among its major corporate sponsors. In contrast, while the 2006 World Cup drew fifteen major corporate sponsors or "partners," the World Baseball Classic had only two global sponsors, MasterCard and

Konami, a Tokyo-based video game maker, among its twenty-six sponsors. The remaining twenty-four Classic sponsors were at the local level (Sheringham 2006).

In their book *Offside: Soccer and American Exceptionalism*, Markovits and Hellerman (2001) analyzed the peculiar relationship between U.S. and global sports cultures. They argued that during the development of U.S. sports at the end of the nineteenth century and the beginning of the twentieth century, U.S. nativism and nationalism, which involved unfavorable attitudes toward foreigners, put a distinctively U.S. mark on its sports, and this type of attitude conflicted with the non-U.S. sport of soccer. Instead of adopting the foreign games of rugby and soccer, Americans created their unique hybrid form of football in the nineteenth century, and instead of playing rounders or cricket, Americans developed baseball. Americans' desire to carve out a distinctive cultural identity in the world of nations and achieve a kind of exceptionalism applied to its sports (Smart 2005:28). Soccer had few advocates or promoters in the United States during the growth of U.S. sports, and by the time soccer had become very popular on a global scale, baseball, football, basketball, and ice hockey had established themselves on U.S. soil, leaving little room for soccer as well (Markovits and Hellerman 2001; Szymanski and Zimbalist 2005).

From Markovits and Hellerman's perspective, baseball, football, basketball, and to some extent ice hockey became part of the "hegemonic sports culture" of the United States, while soccer did not. This concept implies cultural dominance and, in particular, that: (1) a large number of Americans feel a strong emotional attachment to the sport; (2) major events in the sport generate considerable interest and have substantial cultural significance; (3) players of the sport have elevated status as heroes, celebrities, or stars; and (4) the sport is a frequent topic in the everyday conversation of the U.S. public. In contrast, soccer has generally had a marginal status in the United States, even though the first football game in the United States between Rutgers and Princeton in 1869 was more similar to soccer than to modern U.S. football and even though the second organized soccer league in the world developed in the United States (Markovits and Hellerman 2001). In fact, researchers found that even hosting the World Cup in 1994 did not seem to change the position of soccer in relation to the hegemonic sports culture of the United States (Sugden and Tomlinson 1996).

Nevertheless, despite the traditionally marginalized status of soccer in the United States, Americans have shown increasing interest in the sport in recent years. Furthermore, the U.S. women's soccer team has long been a world leader in the sport, and the U.S. men entered the 2006 World Cup ranked fifth in the world. Their ranking proved unjustified, since they failed to get beyond the first round of the competition, as they had in 2002, but the ranking reflected recognition by the world soccer body that soccer was improving in the United States. In addition, live attendance for U.S. soccer's Major League Soccer (MLS) games was showing an upward trend during the 2006 season (Penner 2006).

One of the interesting dynamics of the potential growth of soccer and other globally popular sports in the United States is the increasing size of the Latino and other ethnic and immigrant populations within the United States. There is very visible evidence of the interest of these ethnic fans in the stands at MLS games, and the Latino fans watch the World Cup and other soccer competitions in relatively large numbers on Univision, the Spanish-language network that has become the fifth-largest TV network in the United States. In addition, two soccer-specific TV channels, the Fox Soccer Channel and Gol TV, have emerged in the United States, and along with covering MLS games, ESPN covers the European Champions League (Penner 2006). We should also observe here that the increasing ethnic diversity of U.S. society, which may drive increasing interest in soccer in the United States in the future, also may contribute to a wider interest in U.S. sports in the United States and abroad as teams in these sports become more ethnically diverse. In the major U.S. sports of baseball, basketball, and ice hockey, for example, the locker room has become a mix of multiple nationalities (see Myers 2006).

The preeminence of soccer in the global sports culture, the failure of popular U.S. sports to achieve a comparable status to soccer in the global sports hierarchy, and growing interest in soccer in the United States—at least among the children, adolescents, and college athletes who play it in large numbers and the recent immigrants who watch it—show that the globalization of sport is not exclusively a process of Americanization or U.S. cultural hegemony. Furthermore, FoxSoccer.com's Nick Webster (2006) suggested that the character and appeal of soccer for its worldwide audience differ from the appeal of U.S. sports spectacles. He proposed that the appeal of the World Cup to its fans has to do with their desire to see exciting competition on the field, and he noted that the fans generate their own enthusiasm and excitement while watching the action. In contrast, in the United States, popular sports often rely on clever marketing and promotions, new technologies, engaging and informative announcers and expert commentators, and cheerleaders to get large numbers of people to watch and to keep them entertained.

The movement or lack of movement of sports across national borders reflects the *cross-national cultural diffusion patterns* of these sports. Kaufman and Patterson (2005) have studied how the cross-national cultural diffusion of sport occurs and why certain sports are adopted by some nations and not by others. They focused on the sport of cricket, and a "Focus on Research" feature examines their research. According to Kaufman and Patterson, cricket first became popular in England in the seventeenth and eighteenth centuries, and it is most popular today in countries that were exposed to the sport under the colonial administration of the British Empire. Guttmann (1993) examined the relationship between the diffusion of sports and cultural imperialism. While Kaufman and Patterson's analysis emphasized the influence of social structural factors, such as the class structure and social mobility patterns, in the cross-national cultural diffusion of sport, Guttmann placed more emphasis on cultural factors and how indigenous cultures may put their imprint on imported cultural practices of sport. In fact, we have seen in this chapter that less-powerful countries may display cultural resistance in response to efforts to impose foreign cultural practices in their societies and that the globalization of sport does not always have a "Made in the U.S.A." stamp on it. It is difficult, however, for poorer and less-powerful countries to resist the influence of the powerful forces of the modern Western institutions of television and the transnational corporation, which frequently reflect the influence of U.S. popular culture and economic interests. The Golden Triangle concept implies that the global diffusion of sport will be significantly influenced by the combined forces of professional sport, television, and corporate sponsors. In envisioning the de-

Focus on Research Feature 5.2:
Cross-National Cultural Diffusion of Cricket

Kaufman and Patterson (2005) used the case of the traditional English sport of cricket to study how a symbolically important cultural practice is effectively spread to most but not all nations in the exporting nation's global cultural network. They found no support for a number of explanations of the amount of success in the cross-national diffusion of cricket to other nations with which England had close cultural ties. They rejected explanations from the sociological literature about cultural diffusion that focused on the existence of network ties between change agents and potential change-adopters with similar cultural and social backgrounds, the degree of consistency between the sport and national values, and favorable climatic conditions. Their explanation focused on two other kinds of factors: (1) the extent to which elites either appropriated the game for themselves as an exclusive pursuit and kept the masses from participating in it or promoted widespread participation to reinforce their own elite status and cultural dominance, and (2) the degree to which cultural entrepreneurs popularized the game. Both factors related to the nature and influence of status hierarchies within different societies and the role of elites and entrepreneurs in shaping the significance of cultural practices such as sport in the society.

Cricket was created as an informal activity in rural parts of England, but rapidly developed as a competitive sport. It eventually took its place alongside soccer, rugby, and horse racing as a popular English sport. Cricket was spread to other countries when British soldiers and settlers played it in the colonies of the British Empire, and most, but not all, countries with close historical and cultural ties to England actively support cricket culture today. Kaufman and Patterson were interested in what explained the difference in cultural significance of the sport in the countries in England's sphere of cultural contacts. They observed, for example, that cricket was very popular in Canada and the United States in the middle of the nineteenth century and that the first official international cricket match was between these two countries in 1844. Cricket was as popular as baseball in North America until the end of the nineteenth century, when interest substantially declined. A recent upsurge of interest has occurred with the influx of large numbers of Caribbean and South Asian immigrants into the United States and Canada, but the researchers focused on the earlier period of adoption and then rejection. This pattern of adoption followed by rejection of this imported cultural practice provided Kaufman and Patterson with an opportunity to test various theories about the major factors influencing cross-national diffusion processes.

The researchers used historical data to test their ideas about the cultural diffusion of cricket. They focused on the population of nations that were potential long-term adopters of cricket and on the degree of cricket acculturation, which was a mark of the success of cricket adoption, within each of these nations, including cases where cricket was initially adopted and then rejected later on. They paid special attention to the period of the nineteenth and early twentieth centuries when the game was first institutionalized in England and diffused through its colonies. Cricket had particular sociological interest to the researchers because it was exported as part of British colonial policy, and according to cricket historian Brian Stoddart (1988), it was viewed as a primary means of socializing colonial populations to British moral values and norms.

The cultural diffusion of cricket has been controlled by England, and it has not spread around the entire world. Its diffusion has been an extension of British cultural hegemony as a former colonial power. The sport has never been diffused enough to warrant inclusion in the Olympics, and its main international governing body, the International Cricket Council (ICC), was created by the British Empire. Until 1965, the ICC, which certified official test matches, only included Commonwealth countries as members. The top cricket countries today, such as India and the West Indies, are former British colonies.

Kaufman and Patterson studied twelve countries: Australia, British West Indies, Canada, England, India (including Bangladesh and Pakistan), New Zealand, South Africa, Sri Lanka, the United States, and Zimbabwe. They identified the key period of the popularization of cricket in each of these countries. The sport first became popular in England in the seventeenth and eighteenth centuries, and in the 1830s, the English began to expose their colonies to it, beginning with the British West Indies. Their efforts to spread the sport within their empire continued into the early twentieth century in Zimbabwe. The United States and Canada were the only "failed adopters." The researchers presented data about the average percentage of sports stories about cricket in selected online national newspapers on four different days in 2003 and 2004 in the twelve nations in their study to demonstrate the extent to which cricket was part of the current hegemonic sports culture of each country. Interestingly, among the "cricket nations," England had the lowest percentage, which could be partially explained by factors such as competition from other newsworthy events in England and the other countries. Coverage was highest in Pakistan, Sri Lanka, Bangladesh, and India on the four days that were studied, and, not surprisingly, it was nonexistent in the United States and extremely low in Canada. These data suggested that despite some interest in cricket in the United States and Canada, Americans and Canadians typically had little exposure to the sport.

Kaufman and Patterson also compared newspaper coverage of cricket in the United States and Canada with coverage of baseball in these two countries between the mid-nineteenth and mid-twentieth centuries. Baseball was used as a comparative standard because it has been a popular sport in both countries since the nineteenth century. The researchers used electronic indices to count references to the key words *cricket* and *baseball* in two major U.S. and Canadian newspapers, the *New York Times* (between 1850 and 1950) and the *Globe and Mail* (between 1870 and 2000). According to this measure, coverage of the two sports in the United States was almost equal until 1880, when baseball coverage began to increase while cricket coverage remained relatively the same for the next seventy years. By 1910, a very large discrepancy in coverage had developed, which persisted until 1950. A similar general pattern of coverage of the two sports has existed in Canada, except that coverage was equivalent until 1935, when it began to diverge. Although the disparity in coverage became quite large by 1975, it did not equal the size of the disparity in U.S. coverage. In both cases, then, there was cricket interest or adoption, which then dissipated, unlike in the other nations in this study that adopted cricket and where it has remained part of their hegemonic sports cultures. Kaufman and Patterson provided an explanation of the differences in these interesting patterns of cross-national cultural diffusion. Their analysis helps us understand another case of U.S. exceptionalism, beyond soccer, as well as a form of Canadian exceptionalism in relation to a specific segment of the global sports culture.

Cricket acculturation, the final phase of cultural diffusion in which cricket becomes part of the hegemonic sports culture, did not happen in the United States or Canada to the extent that it happened in other former colonies of England, and none of these other countries went through a period of rejection after adopting the sport. The idea of U.S. and Canadian rejection of cricket as a form of cultural resistance to English influence due to the colonized history of these countries does not make sense because cricket was initially adopted by these two countries and because countries that were colonized by England in more oppressive ways now are major cricket-playing nations. Although competition with the popularity of baseball may partially explain the decline of cricket in the United States and Canada, it does not explain why both sports drew equivalent amounts of attention for many years and then baseball became much more popular than cricket. Kaufman and Patterson turned instead to the role of elites and entrepreneurs to explain the rise of cricket in cricket-playing nations and its limited diffusion in the United States and Canada after initial adoption.

In the United States, cricket initially became popular because working-class immigrants from British nations played it, but more elite members of society eventually squeezed these people

continues

out. U.S. cricket players gravitated to small, elite clubs and the circles of competition became very restricted to other such clubs. Elites sought to encourage a refined image of the sport to separate cricket playing from the cultural practices of the U.S. masses. According to Kaufman and Patterson, a democratic ethos prevailed in the United States and this ethos threatened the status of the more established elites. Status anxiety made U.S. elites more concerned about separating themselves from the nouveaux riches and upwardly mobile who might challenge their dominant place in culture and society. Making cricket an elite sport and unavailable to the masses and others who might threaten their status was a reaction to status anxiety in a society where class distinctions were more murky or flexible. The intentional stratification of cricket to try to reinforce class differences ultimately led to a general decline in the number of people who played the sport, except in a few places such as Philadelphia, which have retained a relatively dense network of cricket-playing teams. In general, though, cricket has suffered from an exclusionary elitism that blocked the wider diffusion of the sport. It also suffered from not having the kinds of entrepreneurs, such as baseball entrepreneur A.G. Spalding, who tirelessly and effectively spread the sport through the United States.

Kaufman and Patterson found that the rise and decline of cricket in Canada was related to the place of cricket in elite universities and secondary schools. While elite universities and boarding schools in England used cricket to perpetuate elitism, Canadian universities tended to reject elite cultural practices, which included playing cricket. At the end of the nineteenth century, only the most elite boarding schools in Canada played cricket, and they began to turn their attention to more indigenous sports such as ice hockey and lacrosse as well as football. Furthermore, because the country had a similar kind of dynamic class structure to that in the United States, members of the upper classes in Canada feared the implications of losing to their social inferiors in sport. Thus, elite sports teams became less willing to compete against non-elite teams. As the number of players and teams and the quality of play diminished, cricket was pushed to the margins of the Canadian sports culture.

Kaufman and Patterson concluded that the lack of rigid social class structure in the United States and Canada fostered elitist attitudes about cricket and helped make cricket an indicator of high social status in these countries. Members of the upper classes, anxious about retaining their status in societies where upward mobility was emphasized, tried to maintain cricket as a mark of class distinction and keep people of lower status from playing it. As a result, cricket was not widely diffused through the U.S. and Canadian populations. In contrast, in the other nations in this study, in which cricket was part of their hegemonic sports cultures, rigid social structures that made the upper classes secure in their status contributed to a wider diffusion of cricket through the population.

As the researchers observed, because the colonial elites in these other countries were secure in their status, they were comfortable with their social inferiors playing a game that represented the traditional cultural and political dominance of the English over their colonies. It helped socialize them to colonial values, while also providing the lower classes with a means of demonstrating their skills against the upper classes in a competition not otherwise provided to them in their societies. That is, they could beat the British or the upper classes at their own game, which had great symbolic significance. An important sociological insight from Kaufman and Patterson's work is that cultural diffusion can be successfully facilitated in a "top-down" manner—rather than in networks of social and cultural equals—as elites share their cultural practices with the masses, and that this pattern of diffusion is more likely to occur in societies with more rigid than flexible social structures. In nations with relatively more social mobility, such as the United States and Canada in Kaufman and Patterson's study, elites were more insecure about their status and were less willing to share with their social inferiors cultural practices, such as cricket, that marked their elite status. Thus, the cross-national cultural diffusion of a sport can be a complex process, influenced by the broader social structure of a society.

velopment of the Golden Triangle, we can imagine, for example, that television will be joined by other mass communication technologies, such as the Internet, as powerful influences in spreading sport in the future.

U.S. exceptionalism shows the power of the United States to make the sports it imports and invents distinctively American as well as the capacity of the U.S. sports establishment and its hegemonic sports culture to place U.S.-manufactured sports such as football, baseball, and basketball above sports such as soccer, rugby, and cricket that excite widespread interest and deep passion elsewhere in the world. Major U.S. sports leagues may not yet be successful in getting the rest of the world to be as passionate about their sports as Americans are, but the globalization of sport nevertheless tends to reflect cultural values and practices that are embedded in U.S. society and the Western-oriented global Golden Triangle.

Conclusion: Sport in a Changing Cultural World

U.S. exceptionalism suggests both the desire for cultural distinctiveness in U.S. sport and the U.S. nation and the fact that despite or because of its cultural, economic, and political power, the United States is somewhat peculiar in the global sports culture. We have seen that globalization is a complicated process, with components of homogenization or standardization and cultural differentiation and patterns of grobalization and glocalization. We have also seen that globalization does not necessarily mean Americanization. Furthermore, cultural conflicts can be played out in sport when traditional nations compete in the world of modern global sports, as the case of Iranian women in the stands—or not in the stands—illustrated.

Structural functional theorists might argue that the development of sport in poorer and less-powerful countries as a result of globalization processes is functional because it makes their sports look more like the sports of richer and more powerful nations. Globalization is functional in this sense because it spreads the cultural values and practices of modern corporate and consumer capitalism that are assumed to contribute to cultural progress, economic growth, and societal development. This is essentially the same type of argument advanced by modernization theorists about how poorer, "less-developed" nations can stimulate progress, growth, and development by adopting the cultural values and practices, technologies, and economic structures of modern capitalism. Adopting modern sports can be part of this development equation.

Globalization as grobalization, which emphasizes Western-style growth, is not viewed so positively by all theorists of globalization. Those who view globalization from a conflict or critical perspective may see this process as a form of cultural imperialism, imposing outside cultural influences of transnational corporations and other nations on less-powerful nations and local cultures to serve their own interests. In this type of perspective, those with more power, such as the British colonizers who spread cricket to the people of their colonies, try to "civilize the natives" by teaching them "more advanced" forms of sport to make them more like their colonizers. In this way, they suppress local cultural expression and autonomy and reduce subcultural differences within and among nations. Thus we see that cultures in sport and society can change when powerful people use their superior resources to persuade, induce, or coerce less-powerful people to do and be what they think is right or better. This exercise of power is meant to reinforce or expand the power and wealth of those in dominant positions. It certainly was easier for the British Empire to deal with their colonies if the colonial populations learned to think and act like the British. As Kaufman and Patterson's research showed, teaching them cricket was one way to try to achieve this end.

Globalization is not restricted to one-way causal processes that impose the cultures of powerful outsiders on less-powerful people and nations. We have seen that in sport, in small and big ways, external cultural influences may be contested through glocalization. As in the Dominican Republic, local people may find ways of protesting or rejecting the influence of outsiders such as Major League Baseball. In addition, the relative lack of success of Major League Baseball, the National Hockey League, and, especially, the National Football League in spreading their sports to other nations shows the limits to the globalization of North American sports. People throughout the world continue to display their passion for soccer, a sport that traditionally has had only a lukewarm reception in the United States. Glocalization and U.S. cultural exceptionalism reflect the complexity in processes of cultural diffusion of sport and other cultural products through global networks. We will examine the tensions between globalization and antiglobalization influences in a context of global economics and politics in chapter eleven.

In the next chapter, we will focus on how the Golden Triangle uses the mass media and corporate advertising to spread their global sports culture and to turn star athletes into celebrities and cultural icons. These sports stars can be powerful vehicles in selling cultural values and products of the Golden Triangle, from TV spectacles to running shoes and the myriad of other products these athlete-salespeople endorse. We will also consider how the dominant cultural belief systems in the United States and U.S. sport function as ideologies to support each other and to reinforce dominant institutional structures of U.S. society and sport. In addition, we will look at sport as a form of secular religion that provides its most devoted fans with a form of sacred escape at the same time that it is a very worldly commodity in the contemporary cultural economy. Finally, we will consider the nature of alternative sports subcultures and how they resist and accommodate themselves to the hegemonic sports culture.

6

From the Global Cultural Economy to U.S. Sports Cultures and Subcultures

Golden Triangles of corporate sports, the mass media, and corporate sponsors create and use images of modern sports stars, and these images of top stars may make them heroes, cultural icons, or more transient celebrities in the global sports culture and cultural economy. We will begin this chapter by examining this role of the global Golden Triangle, and especially the mass media. We will pay special attention to the "globalization of Michael Jordan," which is a prominent and frequently studied example of a cultural icon constructed by the global Golden Triangle of his sport for the global sports culture and the cultural economy of global capitalism. Then we will shift our focus from the global sports culture to the United States, and look at the culture of individualism in which images of sports stars are created in the United States. We will examine how individualism is related to dominant cultural beliefs in the United States embodied in the American Dream, and we will consider the relationship of the American Dream to two prominent sets of cultural beliefs about sport in the United States, the "Dominant American Sports Creed" and the "Sport Ethic." The American Dream, the Dominant American Sports Creed, and the Sport Ethic are all cultural ideologies in the sense that they make claims that are supposed to be accepted without question. These claims are about such things as what it takes to succeed in society and sport and how society, sport, and sports participants benefit from involvement in sport. We will see how they reflect the values and interests of the dominant power structures in U.S. society and sport and how they have shaped the way sports are perceived, played, and experienced.

For devoted sports fans, sport can serve as a "sacred escape," and we will look at its paradoxical role as both sacred escape and cultural commodity in the contemporary cultural economy. Alternative sports subcultures have arisen in the United States and other countries, often among young people, in reaction or opposition to dominant patterns in the corporate world of sport. However, when they become popular, they attract the interest of the Golden Triangle, and we will see what happens when these nascent sports are captured or co-opted by the sports establishment and the Golden Triangle and become full-blown and commercialized global sports.

Television and the Construction of
Global Sports Heroes and Celebrities

A number of legendary names quickly come to the minds of sports fans when they think of the historical traditions of their favorite sports. These legendary fig- ures arise or are created to give cultural legitimacy and stature to individual sports or sports in general in a nation. Sports also create their own Halls of Fame as repositories of memorabilia to retain the memories of their great stars and make them an enduring part of the culture of the sport and of the society. For example, in the United States, the lore of National Football League (NFL) football includes the names of Chicago Bears player, owner, and coach George Halas, who was a driving force in the development of the league; Green Bay Packers coach Vince Lombardi; and Cleveland Browns quarterback Otto Graham and running back Jim Brown. The names of Celtics coach Red Auerbach and super- star players such as George Mikan, Bill Russell, Wilt Chamberlain, and Kareem Abdul-Jabbar are part of the lore of the National Basketball Association (NBA). In Major League Baseball (MLB), the names of New York Yankees manager Casey Stengel and Yankee stars Babe Ruth, Lou Gehrig, and Joe DiMaggio and Brook- lyn Dodger Jackie Robinson occupy places of special prominence in its Hall of Fame. English soccer fans have the names of the stars of their 1966 World Cup champion team, Bobby Moore, Geoff Hurst, and the Charlton brothers, Bobby and Jack, indelibly imprinted on their memories, and even those with a casual acquaintance with soccer, or "football" as it is known outside the United States, know the name of Brazilian star Pelé, who went to the United States in the lat- ter part of his career to promote his sport. Canadians have had special reverence for the stars of its national sport, ice hockey, and names such as Gordie Howe and Wayne Gretzky have shone especially brightly among these stars. U.S. sports fans have not been as enamored with hockey as their northern neighbors have been, but even Americans who were not fans of the sport were captivated by the heroic "miracle on ice" achieved by the U.S. Olympic hockey team in 1980, when they defeated a powerful and more highly regarded Soviet team. The legends of the modern history of golf have come from different continents, ranging from South African Gary Player to the U.S. players Arnold Palmer and Jack Nicklaus. In Australia, star batsman Sir Donald Bradman is a cricket and national legend in a nation that has long been passionate about this sport.

While discrimination and prejudice made it more difficult in the past for racial and ethnic minorities and women to achieve a place in the hegemonic sports culture of nations or the popular lore of individual sports, some achieved this distinction. For example, world champion heavyweight boxer Joe Louis and Olympic track star Jesse Owens received acclaim as U.S. sports stars on a world stage, even though racial segregation, prejudice, and discrim- ination were deeply entrenched in many parts of U.S. society during their ca- reers. Their stardom reflected both racial pride among African Americans and the willingness of whites to put nationalism above racism in their response to these sports stars, as long as they did not pose a threat to the existing social order (Nixon and Frey 1996:231–232). Their sports historically left the door open for lower-class and minority athletes, but many other sports did not, until the middle of the twentieth century and afterward. When the door to integra- tion opened in these other sports, minority athletes began to make their mark on the sports landscape and some became stars, including Jackie Robinson and Hank Aaron in baseball, Jim Brown in football, and Bill Russell and Wilt Chamberlain in basketball.

Until recently, women have had relatively few opportunities in sport, and relatively few women have achieved respect for their athletic accomplishments. Exceptions include the multitalented Babe Didrikson, who was named by the Associated Press in 1950 as the greatest female athlete of the twentieth century. Even rarer was the African-American female sports champion. In 1957, tennis player Althea Gibson was the first African American to earn the distinction of Associated Press Female Athlete of the Year. Of course, all devoted sports fans could name sports legends in their favorite sports whom they revere the most, and these choices are likely to reflect differences in sports preferences and in the nationality, race, age, and gender of the fan.

Sports legends are often celebrated as heroes. Heroes embody dominant and enduring social myths and cultural values of a society or a subcultural segment of society (Nixon 1984:172–175). They are idealizations of the qualities that people think are important or revere in a society, and in this sense, heroes are not real people. They are names and faces we associate with our values. Heroes are constructed by the mass media, and with the dynamic nature of today's societies and the constant mass media scrutiny of public figures, it is difficult for the mass media to sustain their heroic conceptions of certain people. With the dynamic nature of contemporary popular culture, which makes people famous one day and then turns to someone else the next, it is difficult to find traditional heroes of culture in sport or anywhere else in society. As new lifestyles, cultural values, and cultural practices replace existing ones, the mass media look for new names and faces to thrust before their audiences and help them keep the attention of their viewers, readers, or listeners. In fact, there seems to be a pattern where the mass media create new "heroes" and then deflate them by showing us that they are human after all.

Wieting (2000) showed the tenuous status of contemporary sports heroes in his analysis of the Tour de France bicycle race. He looked at eighty-six races, from the inaugural race in 1903 won by Maurice Garin to the 1999 race won by Lance Armstrong. Scandals were part of the second race and the 1998 race, and in a number of other races, some riders gained notoriety for their alleged or actual improprieties or outright violations of the rules, even as winners were praised and honored. Wieting found that the riders were judged in two different cultural and normative contexts, one the subculture of the racers themselves and the other the larger society, which initially was France as the site of the race and then became a more global context. He discovered tensions between these cultural contexts.

In 1998, two teams were expelled for using banned drugs, five others withdrew in protest, and fewer than half of the 198 riders who started the race completed it. During the race, police searched athletes' rooms and there were numerous allegations of illegal drug use or doping, and the 1998 winner, an Italian, Marco Pantini, was ineligible for the 1999 race because he had used EPO, a banned substance, during the 1999 Giro d'Italia race. This news and the turbulence during the 1998 Tour created an atmosphere of suspicion for the 1999 Tour de France, which ultimately affected winner Lance Armstrong during his record seven consecutive Tour victories.

Although he was a certified hero for the U.S. public, which was not as knowledgeable or passionate about bicycle racing or the Tour de France as its European counterparts, he had to fend off a barrage of criticisms and accusations of doping from the French press during his reign and even afterward. Americans admired him both because he was a sports star and because he had overcome cancer and then had translated his sports fame into efforts to fight cancer through his Lance Armstrong Foundation (LAF). The LAF is a joint venture with Nike, which has an endorsement contract with Lance Armstrong and produces a line of clothing and the yellow "livestrong" wrist bands associated with LAF. Thus, while Americans applauded Armstrong for his accomplishments, the French and others in the international cycling community saw his 1999 victory as unlikely after recovering from cancer. For the French, there was also the cynicism related to the fact that none of the stages of the Tour in 1999 were won by a French rider, which had not occurred since 1926.

According to Wieting, this cultural context was made more complex by inducements and temptations to break the rules within the subculture of the riders and teams. They were competing for lucrative race prize money, commercial endorsements, and team commercial sponsorships as well as for Tour de France stage and overall victories and awards and prizes for special team and individual designations such as best team, best sprinter, and best climber. Wieting concluded that the Tour de France had developed into an event that was affected by a combination of global and local, external and internal cultural, political, and market factors, along with new performance-enhancing technological innovations. This combination of factors now conspires against the creation of completely unblemished and globally accepted heroes in this event and perhaps other similar international sports competitions. The tainted reputation of the Tour de France has seemed to become even more tarnished in recent years with additional cases of doping by race leaders, teams, and even an apparent champion, Floyd Landis, in 2006.

In this context, it is possible that Lance Armstrong will never completely escape the allegations that challenge and stain his legend, as long as he denies them and members of the press and cycling community still suspect him and seek to resolve the issue. In addition to the foreign press, some segments of the U.S. press continued to cover the story of his illicit drug use many years after it allegedly happened. Journalists generally feel compelled, as journalists, to uncover myths or fabrications to get to the truth whenever there seems to be any reason for doubt. The mass media are likely to continue to cover the story as long as it is news, attracts public attention, and gets people to buy their newspapers, books, or magazines or watch their broadcasts. This case illustrates how the mass media serve as vehicles both for creating sports celebrities, heroes, and legends as cultural icons and for exposing those legends as frauds when it seems difficult to sustain the legends or more sensational to deflate them.

In these processes of media construction and deconstruction or destruction, it should be evident that the person is not the same as the image. On his Saturday *Weekend Edition* program on (U.S.) National Public Radio (June 24, 2006), host Scott Simon hoped that the controversy about Armstrong the man would not tarnish the powerful and uplifting symbolic value of his livestrong wristbands for cancer victims. He added that these wristbands and the hope they symbolized had become bigger than Armstrong himself. His commentary

Floyd Landis of the U.S., right, holds the winner's trophy, and Oscar Pereiro of Spain, left, holds the trophy for second place, on the podium after the final stage of the 93rd Tour de France cycling race in July 2006. Landis never received the winner's yellow jersey because he was disqualified for a doping violation. His rapid rise as a hero during this race and his even more sudden fall from grace reflect the precarious status of the celebrity as a media-constructed star in the Golden Triangle. (AP Photo/Bernard Papon, Pool)

followed a story on the NPR broadcast, the veracity of which Armstrong denied, about his alleged hospital-room disclosure ten years earlier during his recovery from cancer surgery that he had taken a number of performance-enhancing drugs such as EPO and steroids. Whatever the facts, which may never be definitively proven, Armstrong had a vested interest in fending off challenges to his legend, while the press found value in publicizing these challenges for journalistic, or other, purposes. We see in this story the complexities in the making and possible unmaking of heroes by the media and the distinction between heroes as constructed "hyperreal" images and real people who are likely to be revealed under the continuous probing of the media as having unheroic human imperfections.

Who, indeed, can remain a hero for long with cameras and microphones following every move and recording every word and action on and off the field and with probing or cynical reporters trying to find the hidden warts that heroes must be trying to cover up? For these reasons, we are more likely to talk today about media celebrities of the moment rather than more traditional heroes. Heroes grow bigger in our imaginations with the passage of time, but celebrities arise in the glare of constant media attention and then lose their hold on the public as they eventually become overexposed or are revealed as less heroic or inspiring than we thought they were. The "Sport in the News" feature about French soccer star Zinedine Zidane illustrates how precarious the status of hero can be under the unblinking eyes of television cameras.

Boorstin (1962, 1964) proposed that heroes were made by folklore and history books, while celebrities were images made by gossip, public opinion, and the fleeting tastes of the mass media. Rather than representing enduring cultural values, celebrities are public figures who are "known for being known" and are especially likely to achieve attention or notoriety in societies where the individual and a cult of personality predominate (Henderson 1999; Smart 2005:11). One of the accomplishments of the mass media and corporate sponsors of modern sport has been to elevate the status of the individual athlete above the team in team sports and to make individual sports stars celebrities and, in some cases, widely admired as cultural idols or icons, at least for a while.

Boorstin (1962, 1964) wrote about "pseudo-events" and the importance of images and celebrity in modern culture and society, which provided a point of departure for later postmodern cultural analyses. Depending on how skillful television sports producers and directors are at manipulating images, sportainment may have elements of pseudo-events. Baudrillard's postmodern concepts of "hyperreality" and "simulacra" draw attention to the simulation of reality and the blurring of differences between reality and illusion, imagination, or fiction (Andrews 2000:126–131). The implication of his and Boorstin's analyses is that in the "Hollywood" or "Disneyland" of contemporary sports spectacles, we cannot distinguish image from reality. For example, in a world influenced by movies, amusement parks, video games, and other constructed elements of popular culture, we might begin to wonder if the movie *Rocky* depicts the story of a real boxer or is a fictional creation or even whether the actor who plays Rocky, Sylvester Stallone, is like Rocky in real life. We also might wonder how real fantasy leagues are to those who play these games.

In the contemporary world of sport created by the Golden Triangle, sports celebrities are often created for purposes that are largely rooted in commercial motives. Smart (2005:9–12) proposed that the sports celebrities of today are "idols of mass consumption" whose image and name help sell the products of contemporary capitalist society. Thus, as contemporary celebrities, their public images are closely associated with the contemporary culture of commodity consumption, and they become commodities themselves consumed by their fans. The media, public relations consultants, and advertisers create these celebrities, and encourage the public to believe what is written and said about them. They want us to identify with these celebrities, their public images, and their lifestyles, and to buy the products they endorse.

Furthermore, television, newspapers, magazines, Internet websites, and their corporate sponsors use images and stories about celebrities to attract customers to themselves and their products. These images and stories cater to dreams and fantasies about lives and lifestyles we might want for ourselves. The images and stories of celebrities may be media or public relations fabrications to some extent, and they may be embellished to increase their appeal and

Sport in the News Feature 6.1:
From Hero to Villain—The Precarious Status of Sports Heroes

The case of the great French soccer player Zinedine Zidane, affectionately called "Zizou" by his many fans around the world, shows how quickly a superstar's own public actions can unmake the heroic image constructed of him by the media. In an instant during the 2006 World Cup, Zidane went from hero to villain. Football stars O.J. Simpson and Michael Vick and numerous other athletes have unmade their heroic images with their questionable or criminal off-field behavior in their private lives, and stars such as Pete Rose, Barry Bonds, and Marion Jones have unmade their images with a series of accusations of sports-related deviance such as gambling and drug use. Zidane unmade his image with a single action in the heat of competition on the field and in front of approximately 70,000 spectators and hundreds of millions of television viewers in nearly 190 countries.

Prior to the World Cup, Zidane was already a legendary player. He was considered one of the most gifted players in soccer history. He had been three-time FIFA World Player of the Year, and he had led his national team to its only World Cup in 1998. He had come out of retirement to lead his national team in the 2006 Cup and compete for the final time. As the games progressed, his play got stronger and stronger, until France became an unlikely finalist against the talented Italian team. Zidane had added to his legend by scoring the winning goal on a penalty kick in the semifinal game and then started the scoring in the final with another successful penalty kick. The Italians tied the game, and it went into overtime tied 1–1, with Zidane playing a key role in keeping pressure on the Italian defense. In the second overtime, he barely missed scoring a goal, when his header was tipped by the goalie. Then it happened. In an instant of a pique of temper, he head-butted an Italian opponent, received a red card and was sent off the field, and ultimately had to deal with his team's losing the game in a penalty kick shootout.

The announcers and commentators had extolled his virtues for several games, portrayed him as a national hero as well as a sports hero, and seemed to wish that he could end his career on a positive note with a victory. Then in an instant of infamy, they quickly shifted focus to references about how he had disgraced himself and let down his team and country. The sympathetic aging superstar seeking his last hurrah had become an object of scorn. Since his actions were shown on a screen in the stadium as well as on television across the world, they were not easily glossed over or ignored. The television announcers and commentators expressed some sadness about this incident, but they did what they needed to do in this situation, that is, disavow their previous story line and find another one. Zidane was quickly transformed from a hero into a villain with very human frailties, and the new story became his fall from grace and the difficulties his action had created for his team. The journalists similarly condemned Zidane and added to his remade image of human imperfections. Virtually within minutes of the end of the game, they posted stories on the Internet that focused on Zidane's red card. They also suggested that his action might not have been so out of character as the heroic image TV had created and then discarded seemed to imply. The Internet news reports noted earlier notorious instances when the great star had lost his temper and received red cards for head butting and stomping on opponents, and they reminded their audience that he had been suspended for a game in the 2006 World Cup after receiving two yellow cards in the previous game (e.g., Pugmire 2006).

The status of superstar, hero, and cultural icon provides some degree of protection of an athlete's image after less-than-heroic behavior. Zidane's outstanding performance up to the point of the incident could not be overlooked, and he was voted the winner of the Golden Ball as the best player of the tournament by an international panel of journalists. In addition, some early news reports seemed to try to explain or justify his action by suggesting that Zidane might have been provoked by an insult to his mother or a racial slur linking his Algerian background with terrorism (Moore 2006a). After several days without comment, Zidane himself apologized in an interview on a French television network (Moore 2006b). He was especially concerned about the millions of children who saw his act. He admitted that it was wrong and said he should have been

continues

punished, but he explained that he was provoked by repeated insults from Italian defender Marco Materazzi about his mother and sister. "As a man," he said, he had no choice but to retaliate. Although he did not admit to saying anything about Zidane's mother, the victim of his assault acknowledged making an insult. Neither he nor Zidane was explicit about what the insult was and both said it had nothing to do with terrorists. Over a year later, Materazzi said he had called Zidane's sister a whore (Baltimore Sun 2007d).

The combination of Zidane's superior talent and outstanding accomplishments for his national team with his Algerian ethnicity had been important in France in the context of substantial racial and ethnic tensions in the society. The French national team was one of the few organizations in French society that reflected the nation's ethnic and racial diversity. Seventeen of the twenty-three members of the team were ethnic or racial minorities (Moore 2006b). Since heroes represent important cultural values, Zidane's head butt represented more than the fall from grace of a sports star. It had significant cultural implications for French society, where he was so widely admired. Zidane understood the implications of what he did, and had difficulty looking directly at his fans as they cheered him on his arrival home. French fans reacted with disbelief, disappointment, and sadness, and looked for ways to reconcile his heroic image with the ugly incident (Moore 2006a). A newspaper poll by *Le Parisien* newspaper, conducted shortly after the incident, showed that Zidane was forgiven by 61 percent of those surveyed and that 52 percent said they understood his reaction to the insults (Moore 2006b). French president Jacques Chirac undoubtedly spoke for many French people when he welcomed Zidane home after the World Cup with the words, "You are a virtuoso, a genius of world football. You are also a man of the heart, of commitment, of conviction, and that's why France admires and loves you" (News24 2006).

While it upset fans, the soccer establishment, and corporate sponsors and made television coverage more awkward, the revised story line about Zidane may have served the unsentimental purposes of the news media. The story was mined in various ways by news reporters, sports talk shows, and columnists trying to explain or moralize about the incident, and one story in the *Baltimore Sun* examined the anthropological and cultural origins of the head butt and looked at its meaning and at other head-butting incidents in sports and society (Hiaasen 2006). The story of Zidane's fall from glory almost seemed to overshadow the story of Italy's victory. Of course, the Italians had their own notorious story line, since a number of top clubs in the Italian soccer league's first division were accused of match-fixing and faced demotion to a lower division.

News operations may have felt compelled by their journalistic mission to uncover Zidane's "real character" and to reveal the facts about the brewing Italian soccer scandal, and television producers of the World Cup were unable to ignore the news. It was likely, however, that FIFA, the television producers, and corporate sponsors wished for a different ending to Zidane's story and wished that the Italian scandal would go away. In fact, the FIFA executive board was investigating the incident to determine whether Zidane's Golden Ball award should be revoked because they had a "right and duty" to "intervene when faced with behavior contrary to the ethics of the sport" (Berlin 2006). Along with ethics, they were very likely concerned about the image of the sport in the press and with corporate sponsors.

The FIFA investigation resulted in a $6,000 fine and a three-game suspension for Zidane, but also a $4,000 fine and a two-game suspension for Materazzi for provoking Zidane. The suspension was more meaningful for Materazzi, since Zidane retired after the World Cup final. However, perhaps because he was contrite or because he wanted to clean up his image, Zidane volunteered to do three days of community service with children in a FIFA humanitarian program. An unblemished, and victorious, hero and a winning team untouched by scandal would have made promotion of the sport easier and would have made it easier to sell the winners as heroes in a new post–World Cup ad campaign. A tainted but contrite hero very likely minimized the public relations damage to the sport and to Zidane's own image. Whatever the specific outcomes of this case, it illustrates how challenging it can be at times for the Golden Triangle to create or sustain heroic images or even celebrity status in the context of very visible human frailties in their would-be heroes and celebrities.

our curiosity about them. In sport, however, even constructed images of celebrity athletes may have a special appeal today because the dramatic and outstanding accomplishments of athletes in the heat of competition are real. That is, the images of star athletes seem to incorporate elements of undisputed authenticity, which make the sports they play so appealing in a culture where it is often difficult to distinguish the real from the fabricated, fictionalized, and virtual online forms of constructed reality. Their images may be carefully crafted, just as the images of celebrities from film, music, art, literature, politics, and other public spheres are, but the performances of athletes that we find so compelling have an element of spontaneity that we do not often find in contemporary culture and society—what Boorstin (1962, 1964) called "uncorrupted authenticity."

Smart (2005:17) pointed out that the mass media made sports figures into public figures and then, with more repeated attention, turned some of the most prominent public figures in sport into celebrities and stars. Cinema newsreels and then television and now the Internet have been especially effective in making sports stars part of the popular imagination because they have been able to give us more striking, intense, dramatic, and dynamic images of athletes in action than most newspaper and magazine photos and stories could. The mass media of the past created heroes with their uncritical, sometimes fawning, and idealized coverage, which overlooked the flaws and foibles of heroes such as Babe Ruth, but today they are much more likely to create celebrities of the moment who help the media, as businesses, satisfy their advertisers by attracting readers and viewers to sports broadcasts and stories and sports-related ads. By using images of sports stars for their corporate and commercial purposes and turning them into commodities, like the products these stars endorse, the mass media and their corporate sponsors may saturate the public with these images and make them less interesting and appealing after a while. Certainly, they make them less heroic.

The contemporary era of the Golden Triangle has created its own sports superstars and cultural icons, and they reflect different values than what made sports figures heroic or iconic in the past. There may be some athletes today who are exceptions, such as the rodeo cowboy, who conjures up memories of the heroic past. Pearson and Haney (1999) concluded from their ethnographic study that the rodeo cowboy was a throwback to an earlier era of the frontier and the American West, while also being a risk taker as an athlete in a dangerous sport and as an entrepreneur willing to rely entirely on his competitive sports success for his economic livelihood. Thus, the rodeo cowboy is iconic because he is a successful athlete who takes the kinds of risks we traditionally associate with success in the United States. The rodeo cowboy is distinctive because he is not associated with the large-scale corporate culture that has been driving most of the development of contemporary sport.

Even with the possible exception of rodeo cowboys and athletes in a few other sports, traditional sports heroes are rarer today than in the past. Yet there are still some contemporary sports figures who achieve a special status above even their celebrity peers because they have combined a series of spectacular achievements in major competitions with admirable or alluring personal qualities such as outstanding athletic talent, a charismatic or compelling personality, physical attractiveness, and an exciting or exemplary lifestyle. In contemporary sports, MLB Hall of Famer and "Iron Man" Cal Ripken, Jr., golfer Tiger Woods, soccer player David Beckham, and tennis player Anna Kournikova have been raised to this lofty status, along with the most iconic figure in contemporary sport, Michael Jordan. In the next section, we will consider the globalization of Michael Jordan and other major sports stars.

The Globalization of Michael Jordan . . . and Other Sports Stars

As a cultural icon of contemporary sport, Michael Jordan has attracted a great deal of scholarly attention. For example, an entire issue of the *Sociology of Sport Journal* has focused on "deconstructing Michael Jordan" (in an academic sense); a popular book by Walter LaFeber (2002) focused on "Michael Jordan and the new global capitalism"; and Smart's (2005) book about "modern sport and the cultural economy of sporting celebrity" made Michael Jordan one of its featured "sports stars." Even though he retired from the NBA in 2003, Michael Jordan remained the most popular U.S. athlete in a nationwide Harris poll for the next two years, until he was pushed to second place in 2006 by Tiger Woods (Tucker 2006). Of course, Michael Jordan is and has been more than a popular U.S. sports star. *USA Today* referred to him as "bigger than basketball" and a "pop icon" (Snider 1996:3D). He is a global star, recognized by billions of people around the world, and the operation of the Golden Triangle explains how he was elevated to this status.

Michael Jordan has been called "the best who will ever play (basketball)" by such astute and critical students of the game as coach Bobby Knight (LaFeber 2002:28). Although he was cut from his high school varsity basketball team as a sophomore, within two years he became good enough to earn a scholarship to play for one of the top college basketball teams in the country at the University of North Carolina under renowned coach Dean Smith. He started his own legend in his freshman year when he played with a painful throat infection and helped his team win the Atlantic Coast Conference championship and then sank the winning shot to beat Georgetown in the national championship game. He established his reputation for hitting clutch shots, which became part of his legend, and after another year at North Carolina, he entered the NBA to build his legend further. However, as talented as he was, Jordan's place in the global culture depended on more than his basketball talents.

Michael Jordan's reputation and cultural significance grew exponentially as a result of his association with Nike founder Phil Knight, who made him Nike's lead athlete in their marketing, and as a result of the combined influence of media moguls Ted Turner and Rupert Murdoch and transnationals such as Disney, Viacom, and Time-Warner, which spurred the growth of global media. According to LaFeber (2002:156–157) the linkages tying Michael Jordan to Knight, Turner, and Murdoch represented two major themes of the new information age and post-Soviet period. *First* was what we have called the "capitalist imperative," which is to expand markets, create new ones, and increase profits. *Second* was the accumulation of massive amounts of capital by transnational corporations and elite individuals and their development of markets that were receptive to U.S. popular culture presented by the mass media. The Jordan-Knight/Nike-

Chicago Bulls guard Michael Jordan flies to the hoop over the Indiana Pacers' Reggie Miller and Mark Jackson (13), March 19, 1995, in Indianapolis, Indiana. Nicknamed "Air Jordan" for his superb athleticism, he was named the National Basketball Association's Most Valuable Player in 1988, 1991, 1992, 1996, and 1997. Jordan led his Chicago Bulls team to six NBA championships. He retired from basketball on January 13, 1999, as perhaps the best-known and most iconic hero created by the global Golden Triangle of his era. (AP Photo/Michael Conroy)

Turner-Murdoch connections are a configuration of the Golden Triangle that elevated Jordan's status by exposing his superb accomplishments to a global audience, associating his name with multiple versions of a top-selling Nike shoe,
the "Air Jordan," using him in a major Nike advertising campaign that made the
Nike swoosh known around the globe, and associating his name or brand with
numerous other products he endorsed. In the contemporary stage of capitalism
involving a global cultural economy, which Nike helped to usher in, economic
growth is associated with creating marketing brands that have powerful symbolic appeal and become part of global advertising campaigns.

In this cultural economy, the competition is among brands, for example, Nike
versus adidas versus Reebok versus Converse, although Nike now owns Converse. Nike looked for athletes who could transform their sports with their attitude or style and bring to life their "Just Do It" tagline, that is, athletes such as
antiestablishment working-class track star Steve Prefontaine at first (Walton
2004), then the irreverent John McEnroe in tennis, and, after him, Michael Jordan in basketball (Smart 2005). Through clever advertising, Michael Jordan,
Nike, and the swoosh became linked as a brand in the public mind, and this
linkage made the athlete better known and his commercial sponsor richer. Television contributed to this relationship by increasing the global visibility of Jordan's athletic performances, the advertisements that featured him and the
products he endorsed, and his image. In this Golden Triangle, Michael Jordan
became a member of "Team Nike," and demonstrated his brand loyalty on a
number of occasions, for example, resisting efforts to wear official Olympic
sponsor Reebok's team jacket as a member of the 1992 U.S. Olympic "Dream
Team" and avoiding criticism or comment when Nike was under fire for using
sweatshops in poor countries to manufacture its goods. Nike's initial investment
in Jordan when he was a promising NBA rookie turned out to be justified, as
his combination of exceptional ability, dramatic performances, and personal
charisma increased Nike's global marketing success and transformed Jordan
into a global cultural icon (Smart 2005:108–120). Furthermore, he became, in
the words of writer David Halberstam (1991:76), "the first great athlete of the
wired world." The new global media significantly contributed to the globalization
of Michael Jordan—and Nike.

One of the interesting aspects of the construction and selling of the Jordan
image was the extent to which his "blackness" was downplayed or ignored. He
was marketed to white and black communities as a "crossover hero," and for
many whites at least, he was without color (Smart 2005: 123). According to Andrews (1996), there were four major elements in the treatment of Jordan's race.
First was the idea that he was like many other African-American athletes, in
being perceived as a "natural athlete" with a number of natural physical gifts.
Second was the careful cultural construction of him by the mass media as having "all-American" qualities of motivation, integrity, responsibility, and success
that exemplified virtue across a broad cross section of the United States. Furthermore, his success demonstrated that the American Dream was achievable
to all, whether black or white. Thus, he was easy to accept and admire across
the racial divide in the United States. *Third* was a period when Jordan's all-
American (white) image was somewhat tarnished by stories in the early 1990s
about his alleged arrogance, selfishness, obsession with personal statistics,
lack of respect for teammates, excessive competitiveness, preoccupation with

his image, and gambling. Jordan himself was quoted as saying during this period that the media seemed to be increasingly portraying him as "Michael Jordan the black guy" (Andrews 1996:147). This kind of coverage seemed to recede after the tragic murder of his father, as his all-American image began to resurface and become more prominent once again. The *final element* of the media construction of his race related to his return to the NBA after retiring and playing minor-league baseball. Without Jordan and with a new generation of young black stars who were portrayed as arrogant, irresponsible, and self-centered, the NBA's image had suffered. His return enabled the NBA and the media to refocus on Jordan's all-American qualities that had appealed across racial lines and to defuse some of the negative conceptions of race that were associated with the younger black players.

The portrayal of Michael Jordan's race and his image in general demonstrates the power of the media to shape public perceptions of sports figures. Although Jordan the man may not have changed, media coverage of him did at various stages of his career. His enduring worldwide popularity clearly shows that media and corporate constructions of his image have typically been positive and effective across class, racial and ethnic groups, and national borders. While white Americans may not have seen his color, young African Americans and black youths in other countries such as Great Britain may have identified with him and bought the products he endorsed because he was black (Andrews, Carrington, Jackson, and Mazur 1996). In fact, it may be that white youths bought Air Jordans and other Jordan-branded merchandise because he was a star basketball player, while black youths bought these things because he was a *black* basketball star. Ethnographic research in Canada by Wilson and Sparks (1996) that relied on focus groups of black and nonblack adolescents provided support for this interpretation and also demonstrated the cultural power of commercial advertising using prominent sports figures.

The global Golden Triangle of professional sport, the media, and corporate sponsors has used other sports stars, along with Michael Jordan, to advance their commercial interests in the modern global cultural economy. Global interest in soccer, tennis, and golf has made stars of prominent athletes in these sports, such as David Beckham (soccer); John McEnroe, Andre Agassi, and Roger Federer (tennis); and Tiger Woods (golf). Relatively few women have achieved the status of global sports star, but tennis player Anna Kournikova became a global media and cultural star on the basis of her early athletic promise (which was not fully realized) and her physical and sexual attractiveness. The media have generally accorded women's sports limited attention, reflecting the dismissive or ambivalent attitudes the sports public has traditionally felt about women in sport. Although women in sport have attracted more media attention and corporate sponsors over the past two or three decades, the attention and sponsorship have tended to be selective. Female tennis players have attracted this interest in part because tennis has traditionally been seen as a more "feminine" sport, in contrast to the more aggressive team sports or more "physical" and masculine sports such as bodybuilding. Perhaps because they did not trust the public's willingness to accept female athletes merely as athletes, the media and corporate sponsors have chosen to highlight attractive female athletes in feminine sports, that is, athletes such as tennis player Anna Kournikova and, more recently, another attractive tennis player, Maria Sharapova.

We have seen that even being a star in tennis has not assured women extensive media coverage and lucrative commercial endorsements. For example, while all-American-looking Chris Evert became a media favorite, her rival, who was her superior on the tennis court, Martina Navratilova, earned some respect but relatively few endorsements because she openly acknowledged her lesbian sexual orientation. Although Nike was somewhat willing to take risks with countercultural stars, such as Steve Prefontaine, John McEnroe, and skier Bode Miller, most commercial sponsors tend to try to avoid controversial figures who might offend the public and potential consumers. Commercial sponsors and sports promoters use the sex appeal of male athletes to promote the athletes and their sports, but their primary focus is their athletic talent. For women, though, athletic talent or promise is significant, but sex appeal often seems to be more important (Hargreaves 1994:206). Although she showed exceptional promise at a young age, turning pro a week before turning sixteen, golfer Michelle Wie demonstrated the willingness of the press to focus on attractive and promising female athletes, while generally ignoring or paying much less attention to more-accomplished athletes in her sport. When the U.S. women won the Women's World Cup in 1999, more media attention seemed to focus on Brandi Chastain's victory demonstration in her sports bra than on the skills of her teammates or her own feat of striking the winning kick in the penalty kick shootout.

Different cultural filters seem to be applied to male and female athletes, teams, and sports in the world of the Golden Triangle. In her content analysis of a series of three Nike advertisements for women, Lucas (2000) critically assessed whether these ads empowered the girls and young women whom they targeted. The three commercials had the themes of "If you let me play," "There's a girl being born in America," and "The Fun Police." Her conclusion was that, despite Nike's expressed intent to convey empowering messages for young females, their "cause-related marketing" or "ads with conscience" tended to imply that females could not make decisions or take action on their own. Nike hoped to gain favor with female consumers with messages that they were helping girls get a chance to participate in sports, contributing to their health and happiness, teaching them the rules of the game, and giving them a chance to have fun by encouraging their sports involvement (in Nike apparel). Lucas argued that instead of empowering girls and young women, these ads took away their sense of agency or control by implying that they had to rely on someone else to grant them access to sport, teach them how to take care of their bodies, play, and have fun. That is, Nike was more interested in having viewers remember its brand than in empowering females. In fact, according to Lucas, their messages were that females needed permission to play sports, that some types of girls were better than others at sport, and that the male model of sport, and basketball in particular, was the most fun for players and spectators, especially when it incorporated the bravado and confrontational style of NBA players.

The increasing ethnic diversity of the United States and other nations and the global spread of sport suggest opportunities to market new kinds of images of athletes that reflect multicultural identities or the ethnicity of people in new and potentially lucrative markets such as China and other parts of Asia. The multicultural Tiger Woods and Asian-American Michelle Wie represent this new image, along with popular Chinese NBA star Yao Ming. The cases of Yao Ming and Japanese players in Major League Baseball show the complexities of

NBA Houston Rockets star Yao Ming speaks during a news conference at an event sponsored by Reebok in Beijing, China, Tuesday, September 25, 2007. Reebok and Yao teamed up in Beijing for the unveiling of the brand's newest marketing and advertising campaign, "Fuel Yao's Unlimited Power," celebrating the prospect of Yao's participation in the 2008 Olympic Games in his homeland. Yao, as the "China Global," represents the latest era of the globalization of sport by the Golden Triangle. (AP Photo/Andy Wong)

the contemporary patterns of globalization of Asian sports stars and indicate the apparently increasing willingness of U.S. sports fans to embrace foreign players on their soil. A "Focus on Research" feature examines research that addresses the experiences and global implications of Asian sports stars in the United States.

The globalization of Michael Jordan, Yao Ming, and other star athletes; the complex media and corporate constructions of star athletes as global cultural icons; and the navigation of star athletes through global sports networks reveal the varied and complicated relationships between sport and media, economic, and cultural forces in the modern global cultural economy. To add another level of complexity, Silk and Andrews (2001) suggested that some transnational corporations, such as Nike, were beginning to target their advertising to local cultures within nations by using a variety of emerging sports stars from different nations in sports such as soccer to appeal to specific local and national loyalties. Thus, just as cable TV fragmented the sports-watching public by televising a wide range of sports to satisfy audiences with different interests and tastes, these kinds of more "localized"—rather than global—advertising campaigns may be splitting the global cultural economy. These various approaches to marketing or advertising, buying goods, and selling goods in the global marketplace through sport tend to be similar, though, in their shared emphasis on

**Focus on Research Feature 6.2:
Globalization from Asia—Asian Stars in U.S. Sports**

Wang's (2004) analysis of "Yao Ming, Asian America, and the China Global" is an example of how scholarship from cultural studies can provide valuable insights for the sociological analysis of sport. Based on his reading of a variety of relevant texts written by academic scholars and journalists, Wang argued that Yao represented a new phenomenon of Chinese transnationality in the modern cultural economy and global sports culture, which he called "the China Global." As a Chinese sports celebrity, he was a vehicle for moving capital through global economic networks. At 7'6", he was the tallest player in the NBA, but as the China Global he represented "bigness" in other ways, for example in terms of the demands of a growing global capitalism and the expansionist aspirations of China in the global marketplace. Wang proposed that Yao provided a lens for seeing how ethnicity, nationalism, and the marketplace came together in a "spectacle of bigness." That is, he symbolized an American Dream of a capitalist and nationalist aspiration of "bigness." Let us consider what these rather abstract ideas mean.

Yao represents a complex cultural icon with an identity that could be associated with Asian, Chinese, and Asian-American cultures. In fact, it seems noteworthy that Yao's first U.S. television commercial placed him in an ad for Macintosh's then-new line of PowerBook laptop computers. This type of ad is noteworthy because it made what could be viewed as a stereotypical connection between an Asian and new technology. However, Yao's identity is more complex and broad than one based only on a particular ethnicity, region, or nationality. He represents China and the Chinese market in the global cultural economy, and he has also increased ticket sales among a growing number of Asian-American NBA and Houston Rockets fans in the United States. Just as Michael Jordan represented the realization of the American Dream for African Americans and blacks elsewhere in the world, Yao Ming represented the realization of the American Dream for those with Asian, Chinese, or Asian-American backgrounds. Wang proposed that in Jordan's case, his global appeal was based on an all-American image that transcended race, but that in Yao's case, his appeal was based on his transnational ethnic identity as the China Global, which crossed national and cultural borders. Wang observed, however, that while the China Global idea affirmed the American Dream, this affirmation was paradoxical because it represented two images. First was the idea of China's cultural resistance to U.S. hegemony or dominance in globalization, and second was the idea of individuals who achieve cultural and economic success in the West serving as symbols of China's progress. That is, the United States was both a competitor in the international cultural and economic marketplace and a place where individuals from China could become successful. Yao embodied these paradoxical elements. Yet, as the China Global, he has fostered a process of globalization in which the forces of global capitalism embodied in transnational corporations blur national distinctions of geography, culture, economics, and politics, even for nations as powerful as the United States or ones as potentially powerful as China is likely to be. The question is whether the United States, China, and other nations will be able to retain their national identities and influence in the context of this globalization. This is, of course, the question raised in a different context in the discussion of globalization, grobalization, and glocalization in this book.

Real-time global telecasts of Yao's NBA games in Asian global cities such as Shanghai, Tokyo, Taipei, and Seoul as well as in Houston and across the United States gave the media an important role in the globalization of Yao Ming as a modern multicultural sports icon. His popularity in the United States suggests a degree of acceptance by Americans of Asian athletes playing U.S. sports in the United States, but other research from a slightly earlier period in the 1990s indicated that this public acceptance of Asian athletes in the United States may be a recent phenomenon or apply only to certain athletes. We can assume that the construction of media images of these athletes has contributed to their degree of acceptance. Yao is distinctive in the amount and type of attention he has received from the Golden Triangle.

Mayeda (1999) did a content analysis of articles about Major League Baseball (MLB) pitchers Hideo Nomo and Hideki Irabu in the sports sections of the *Los Angeles Times* and the *New York Times* newspapers from 1995 to 1997, which he supplemented with an analysis of the relatively few articles about these pitchers in *Sports Illustrated* during this period. Both pitchers were Japanese, and Mayeda found that the media coverage tended to reinforce negative stereotypes of Asian Americans and Asian nationals as model minorities and economic threats. The model minority stereotype appears to be very positive because it suggests that Asian Americans embrace core U.S. values by being law-abiding, hardworking, and self-sufficient citizens, who do well in school and their careers. Mayeda noted that this seemingly positive conception could have negative implications by engendering resentment from other minority groups and the majority culture similar to the resentment about the disproportionate success of Asian Americans in gaining admission to the top universities and colleges in the United States. This stereotype is based on an oversimplified conception of the diversity among Asians and Asian Americans in the United States. The second stereotype, of Asians as economic threats, has a long history but most recently has been related to the global economic success of Japan and could be applied to the emergence of China as a rising global economic power.

It is doubtful that Yao's popularity has eradicated all of these stereotypes. Yet, like Yao, Japanese and other foreign athletes have become more popular in the United States as U.S. professional baseball, basketball, and hockey continue to recruit overseas. In fact, in view of the Asian stereotypes, it is ironic that Major League Baseball has depleted the talent in Japanese professional baseball by recruiting Japanese superstars and cultural icons such as Ichiro Suzuki (Seattle Mariners), Hideki Matsui (New York Yankees), and Daisuke Matsuzaka (Boston Red Sox), who have become popular MLB stars. These athletes may not have achieved the global "star power" of Yao Ming as the China Global, but collectively they represent the changing complexion and greater diversity of stars in the global sports culture and cultural economy. Their rise indicates that even in U.S. sports, Americans must share the pedestal with athletes from Asia and other parts of the world as the global sports culture and cultural economy continue to expand. Athletes with transnational identities may be especially effective in the future in helping the Golden Triangle realize its capitalist imperative in a diverse global context. David Beckham and Michael Jordan may have been the face of the Golden Triangle for the past two decades, but Yao Ming, Tiger Woods, and other "multicultural" stars appear to be its future face.

the values of capitalism and the American Dream of materially improving one's life. These localized ad campaigns suggest a degree of glocalization when, in fact, they represent the powerful influence of the global Golden Triangle.

Even apparently anticorporate icons such as Steve Prefontaine ultimately represent capitalist values in their individualism. It was, after all, Prefontaine's relationship with Phil Knight that helped Nike grow in its early years, as Prefontaine himself became a hero of the antiestablishment culture (Walton 2004). Steve Prefontaine was one of the great hopes for U.S. track and field in the 1970s. In her study of various media texts about Prefontaine, Walton (2004) used his case to show how corporate-created images of sports stars have shifted in the context of changing cultural values since the 1970s. Prefontaine was a rebel, and the main target of his rebellion was the Amateur Athletic Union (AAU), which controlled amateur sports and athletes when Prefontaine was competing in the 1970s. He was opposed to AAU restrictions on his opportunities to compete against the top runners in the world, and he was unhappy with their unwillingness to provide financial support for his training and running. He claimed that the AAU exploited athletes, and he became a prominent spokesperson for the rights of amateur athletes. He became involved in promoting a tour of the United States by the Finnish national team in 1975 so that he could run against the legendary Finnish distance runner Lasse Viren.

Prefontaine's attitude was what made him appealing to Nike, which had developed a corporate marketing strategy emphasizing an "anticorporate style" and the idea of breaking new ground (Smart 2005:109). On the other hand, the Nike brand was clearly corporate and Nike was a business focused on making money. Thus, we can see some irony in Walton's (2004) characterization of Prefontaine's career as evolving "from rebel with a cause to hero with a swoosh." When Prefontaine first became involved with Nike, however, it was a fledgling and struggling shoe company started with the help of his college and Olympic coach, the legendary Bill Bowerman. In the 1970s, AAU rules forbade professionalism and open endorsement arrangements, giving athletes very modest stipends—such as the $3 per day Prefontaine received—while the AAU appropriated the fees athletes earned from their appearance at track meets (Walton 2004). Nike found ways of circumventing AAU amateurism rules, for example by sponsoring a major track club and giving club members its shoes and apparel and employing star athletes such as Prefontaine in its store, using them as company representatives, and having them run clinics for aspiring runners. Prefontaine, in turn, got the support he needed for his training. He was drawn to Nike through his ties to Bill Bowerman, who was involved with Phil Knight in creating Nike as a shoe manufacturer.

Prefontaine died in 1975 at the age of twenty-four in an auto accident, in which alcohol may have been a contributing factor. Walton (2004:72) observed that in the 1970s, Prefontaine's drinking was portrayed as a part of his "love of life." His image was of a tough, outspoken, charismatic rebel from a working-class background who worked hard and sacrificed to defy the odds and become successful. This was the kind of image Nike promoted at the time. As the cultures of the United States and sport changed, however, Nike's constructed image of Prefontaine changed, too. In the 1970s, the connection between Prefontaine's drinking and his death was acknowledged. By the 1990s, though, in a moral culture thought to be less forgiving of such behavior than in the 1970s, Nike funded a documentary and two films about Prefontaine that ignored this part of Prefontaine's life and death. In the 1990s, through these media portrayals, Prefontaine became a nostalgic reminder of Nike's beginnings in track and field and of a time when white, working-class, male, and American runners could become stars. Thus, Nike was able to present itself as true to its roots and "authentic" in the new global sports culture and subtly connect itself to the white male sports market in addition to the black sports market that responded to Nike's prominent black athlete endorsers.

According to Walton (2004:61), Prefontaine became a "commodified maverick celebrity" or hero who represented the shifting values of white and classless masculine culture, and his Nike-promoted image in the 1990s reinforced the ideology of individualism in the contemporary culture of consumer capitalism. The "Sport in the News" feature focusing on U.S. skier Bode Miller shows how complicated the image making and sponsorship of more recent maverick celebrities or "antiheroes" can be. Like Prefontaine, Miller has been noted for his individuality and independence, but the media have sometimes been extremely harsh in their criticism of him, branding him more as a hypocrite than

Sport in the News Feature 6.3:
Bode Miller and the Slippery and Bumpy Slope of Celebrity

Leading up to the 2006 Winter Olympics in Torino, Italy, U.S. alpine skier Bode Miller was touted by the major corporate media as one of the great U.S. hopes at the Olympics, with a chance to win five gold medals. He was on the covers of major U.S. newsmagazines, the focus of innumerable news stories in the print and online media, and the subject of an interview on the popular CBS TV newsmagazine *60 Minutes*. He also had lucrative sponsorship deals with over ten corporations, including major ones with the Italian pasta maker Barilla, the ski manufacturer Atomic, Visa, and Nike. His performance on the ski slopes seemed to warrant celebrity. He had proven himself to be a great skier, winning the Alpine Skiing World Cup overall championship in 2005, over ten individual World Cup and U.S. championships, and two silver medals at the 2002 Olympics. He was the first American in 22 years to be men's overall World Cup champion. He was also very durable, establishing a streak of 136 straight World Cup races before breaking the streak by resting before the Olympics in 2006.

What made Bode Miller an unusual celebrity, in the vein of Steve Prefontaine, was his independent, antiestablishment, wild, and even hedonistic approach to life and his daring approach to skiing. He skied on the edge and was nearly as likely to fall as to win. He once finished a race on one ski after losing the other in the midst of a run. His case illustrates the different and complex ways that antiestablishment sports celebrities are constructed, marketed, and evaluated by their sport, the mass media, and the corporate world in contemporary global sports culture.

Bode Miller's story begins with his upbringing. His parents were hippies who dropped out of conventional society to live self-sufficiently and modestly on a mountain in New Hampshire, where they raised their four children without electricity, a telephone, or indoor plumbing. He was home-schooled until third grade, spending a lot of time in the woods around his home. He also skied a lot, and after high school, his talent earned him a spot on the U.S. Ski Team. He developed into an outstanding skier in all five disciplines of his sport, combining risk taking with speed and balance. While ski team officials appreciated his skills and success, which attracted the attention of corporate sponsors and the media, officials and coaches were not happy with his approach to the sport or what he said to the public. Miller said he wanted to do things his own way, and asserted that he was not concerned about other people's expectations or perceptions of him. While his head coach was concerned about dangerous actions such as finishing a race on one ski at eighty miles per hour, other ski team coaches believed his independent, daring, and unorthodox style made him a great skier. He trained hard, but in his own way, for example using a machine he invented himself to build his strength and endurance, walking a tightrope, riding a unicycle, and pushing a friend in a wheelchair.

Bode Miller's unusual approach to training and racing made him stand out in skiing, but his outspoken and controversial statements about his sport and his lifestyle made him a thorn in the side of the skiing establishment, even as he attracted extensive media attention and fan adoration, especially in Europe. Because the company was seeking "athletes with attitude," Miller fit the Nike mold, and they built an ad campaign around him, capitalizing on his antiestablishment and unconventional image. He made a lot of money, but said he feared its corrupting influence, since his primary goal was to have fun rather than simply to win. His coaches said he had too much fun, and they worried about the effects of Miller's comments during his *60 Minutes* interview about skiing when he was under the influence of alcohol. He apologized, but Nike felt compelled to make a statement that it did not condone drinking and skiing and appreciated Miller's explanation of his comment and his apology. Miller also caused controversy when he questioned the banning of certain performance-enhancing drugs, said that drug tests were demeaning, complained that he had been targeted too many times for drug testing by his sport (which he had never failed), and mentioned in his autobiography that he had used recreational drugs. He also criticized the governing bodies of his sport.

continues

The combination of Miller's style on the slopes and his success, along with his tendency to push himself to the point of crashing or missing slalom gates, has made it difficult for the media, corporate sponsors, the skiing establishment, and fans to ignore him. What is most interesting about his celebrity status, however, is the lack of media consensus about how to cover him. Unlike other celebrities who go through periods of widespread media and popular adulation and almost heroic status, Miller has provoked both positive and negative reactions from the beginning of his rise to celebrity status, and his negative publicity has seemed to contribute as much to this status as positive images of him have. For a number of his corporate sponsors, the "bad boy" reputation that was conveyed in a number of critical media reports was reconstructed as a renegade image of an athlete who pushed the boundaries, revolutionized his sport, and brought excitement to the 2006 Olympics. The online report of the CBS *60 Minutes* interview was titled "Golden Boy Bode Miller," and major newsmagazines, such as *Newsweek* and *Time*, put him on their covers with headlines such as "American Rebel" and "Miller Time" (a play on the tagline of the Miller Brewing Company). He appeared on the cover of *Sports Illustrated*'s Olympic preview issue, which referred to "Bode Miller's Bumpy Ride."

While a number of these reports simultaneously had elements of fascination, anticipation, caution, and at least mild criticisms in their coverage, the major news media, including television, seemed to treat him as a failure after he didn't win any Olympic medals in Torino. On the other hand, with the exception of his first million-dollar sponsor, Italian pasta maker Barilla, corporate sponsors generally did not terminate their relationship with Miller after his controversial comments and lack of Olympic success, since they focused more on the market within skiing and the skiing nations of Europe. They realized that he was still a big star on the ski circuit who continued to attract public attention in skiing circles.

Some media commentaries focused on lost opportunities, the overhyping of his chances for gold, and Miller's own misgivings and defense of his approach and choices. For example, *MSNBC/Newsweek* commentator Devin Gordon (2006a) wrote prior to the Olympics about Miller's Olympic promise. After Miller's disappointing performance, Gordon (2006b) wrote about "why Bode's been a nobody," criticizing his partying during the Olympics, his disrespectful attitude toward the press, his poor skiing, and his recent poor training and race preparation. The media also questioned Miller's own stated desire to restore a sense of thrill, joy, and sportsmanship to the Olympic Games and noted how he wrestled with a conflict between not liking the emphasis on money and medals at the Olympics and the fact that his own lucrative sponsorship deals contractually obligated him to compete. Gordon (2006b) concluded that Miller had lost his chance to advance his noble platform by failing to win and focusing more attention on his controversial statements and misdeeds than on his stated philosophy. In an interview, Miller talked about the burden that his past success and celebrity had placed on him as the "favorite," preferring instead his role of underdog in the 2002 Olympics, when he won two silver medals (Litke 2006). He defended his choice of endorsement opportunities, saying he only accepted money from companies that allowed him to say what he wanted without being censored or filtered by the media or his sponsors. He also defended his approach to the social experience of the Olympics, saying that he had a chance "to party and socialize at an Olympic level" (Litke 2006). Thus, he did things "his way," which he professed was most important to him. His philosophy was expressed on Nike's "Join Bode" website, where he expressed his boredom with the mass media and his search for truth and happiness and encouraged others to post their views.

A number of blogs and newspaper columns found Miller and his website arrogant, hypocritical, and pretentious. They harshly criticized him for his attitude and his approach to sport and life. For example, a *Seattle Times* columnist wrote an "Ode to Bode" that exhorted him to "join the team or get off it" (Judd 2006), rebuked him for being self-absorbed, or not a "team player," and called him hypocritical for condemning the commercial influence in sport while willingly accepting money from a number of commercial sponsors. In fact, after the 2006 Olympics, Miller switched from Atomic to Head skis, the fifth time he had switched skis in his career, and his switch to Head clearly implied a commercial motivation, since the deal would make him the best-paid ski racer in the world. A *USA Today* columnist explicitly expressed his "antipathy" toward Miller (Saraceno 2006). He was upset because, in his view, Miller was apathetic toward the Olympic ideals of competition and trying to be the best, conveyed the wrong message to young people with his public statements about his love of partying and skiing "wasted" while competing, and showed disrespect toward his fellow athletes in saying he did not care about winning. Perhaps worst, according to this columnist, he squandered his talent. Another column, in the *Washington Post*, was titled "Only Medal for Bode Is Fool's Gold" and called Miller "the biggest disappointment in the Winter Olympics" (Jenkins 2006).

Many more columns, stories, and opinions could be cited, reflecting Bode Miller's celebrity status. However, certain elements of his story reveal important insights about the making, remaking, and unmaking of celebrities who do not conform to conventional values and expectations that are held and advanced by mainstream sports officials, media, and corporations. His case helps us see more clearly how mainstream media coverage of celebrities can build up unrealistic expectations to create popular interest—for example, winning five gold medals in Bode Miller's case—deflate them to generate more publicity, and then move on to the next promotional vehicle for their programming and advertisers. Media coverage of celebrities is also dynamic and varied, changing over time and differing for media sources inside and outside a sport. In addition, we can see in this case how challenging it can be to construct a credible, compelling, consistent, and marketable image of a celebrity with a "bad boy" or "antiestablishment" reputation. We also see how athletes contribute to their own image in making comments and acting in ways that can be used in media and corporate sponsors' constructions. In Bode Miller's case, his antiestablishment persona was criticized by the mainstream media and sports officials, but it was also used by these media to hype their coverage and by corporate sponsors such as Nike to reinforce their self-promoted image as a company that was "different" and should be supported by their target market of young people. Even Nike, though, found it challenging at times to be associated with a rebel with an ostensibly countercultural attitude.

The case of Bode Miller as antihero shows that falling or fallen maverick celebrities can be useful to the mass media, until the public loses interest in them. They are also useful to corporate sponsors as long as they continue to embody dominant corporate values such as independence and individualism and as long as they help their sponsors sell products. The media criticism of Bode Miller's unwillingness to be a team player and keep his controversial attitudes to himself misses the point that in the contemporary global cultural economy and sports culture advanced by the Golden Triangle, individualism, contrary attitudes, and even hedonism are valued more than being a quiet straight arrow with a modest lifestyle and a willingness to sacrifice for the team. As a footnote, Miller continued to win major World Cup races and national titles and annoy his coaches after his Olympic experience. However, even achieving the status of one of the greatest World Cup skiers of all time is not likely to erase Miller's media-constructed reputation as the "great hope" of the 2006 Winter Olympics who squandered his big chance for attaining multiple-gold-medal fame in the larger sports world beyond skiing enthusiasts. Perhaps the final postscript to the story of Bode Miller "the antihero" is that he left the U.S. Ski Team after the 2007 season in the midst of continuing differences with team officials. Although he was still the top skier on the team, he continued to rankle ski team officials and coaches with his free-spirited personal life and provocative public comments.

[Note: Some additional sources were used to prepare this feature in addition to those cited (i.e., Gordon 2006a, 2006b; Jenkins 2006; Judd 2006; Litke 2006; Saraceno 2006). They are Isidore 2006; Olian 2006; Pennington 2006; Vinton 2006.]

as a hero for allegedly failing to live up to his own radical values and standards for his sport and his life. Thus, even though some media, his corporate sponsors, and skiing fans have seen Bode Miller as a brightly shining star, despite the controversies he has provoked by his outspoken public statements and his lapses on the ski slopes, others have seen a disappointment, failure, or fallen star. Thus, Bode Miller illustrates the slippery and bumpy slope of being a contemporary sports celebrity.

The Culture of Individualism and the American Dream

For a number of critics, Bode Miller is an example of the excesses of the contemporary culture of individualism. Although Americans value the spirit of independence associated with the idea of individualism, critics of the contemporary culture of individualism in the United States view it much more unfavorably when it is expressed in asocial or hedonistic ways. Sociological theorists have recognized individualism as a central element of modern societies, and they have long debated its societal implications. Kivisto (2004) identified individualism as one of the four "key ideas" in the history of sociological thought, and he pointed out that some theorists emphasized its positive implications related to freedom from social constraints and oppression, while others focused on its more destructive tendencies to separate us from others and to undermine our commitment to reciprocity and the welfare of others in social relations (Kivisto 2004:83). Durkheim recognized that excessive individualism could lead to suicide when individuals become socially isolated, but he also pointed to the benefits of individualism in modern societies, where free and autonomous individuals could be linked together in structures of interdependency by their shared individual interests. For example, in sport, I may be most interested in pursuing my own career goals of money and fame and may not be very concerned about the personal welfare of any of my teammates. I realize, however, that I have to work together with my teammates, who have their own personal interests, if any of us is going to be recognized as an individual success. In a culture that values winning, individuals in team sports tend to achieve the most prominence when their team wins.

The form of socially destructive individualism that Frenchman Alexis de Tocqueville (1853) called "egoism" in his observations about U.S. democracy over 150 years ago helps explain the decline of marriage, community, social capital, and civil society in contemporary U.S. society. Individualism becomes destructive when individuals put themselves above or outside the group, have little commitment to the group, and only care about the group and other people to the extent that they can advance their individual interests. In these cases, individualism is out of balance with the societal need for strong group and community ties. Late-twentieth-century analyses of the decline of social commitment and community in the United States and the need for renewed civic engagement, such as Bellah and colleagues (1985) and Putnam's (2000) *Bowling Alone*, have reflected concerns about excessive and destructive individualism.

In sport, excessive individualism may take a number of forms. Individuals may realize that their own success will be based on the success of their team, but they may not be willing to sacrifice their own chances to be the star or care enough about their team to give up the ball or the puck to a teammate in a better position to score, and they may not be willing to give credit to teammates for their outstanding performance, to try their hardest in relay events or doubles matches when they could interfere with their preparations for their individual competition, to play a supportive rather than a dominant role when the team needs it, to compete for their national team when it does not advance their personal career or pay them much money, or to stay with a team as a coach when a better offer comes along, even though commitments have been made to new recruits and a contract will be violated by a move. As a result, individuals may score more points or goals, have a higher batting average, hit more home runs, throw more pass completions, win more individual races or matches, and go to more prestigious or better-paying positions, but they may leave their team at a disadvantage and contribute to their losing. Thus, in the contemporary culture of individualism in sport, there may arise contradictions between individual motivations and team commitments.

Clearly, then, individualism can have positive or negative consequences, depending on how, how much, and where it is expressed. Whether its consequences are positive or negative, however, it is embedded in modern societies and sport. Individualism and the individual entrepreneur are at the heart of traditional conceptions of capitalism; individual rights are a central element of modern democracies; the new economy of the neoliberal state focuses on the economic interests of individuals and corporations; and the pursuit of self-interest and doing what is best for oneself—even to the detriment of others or our relationships with them—define the contemporary culture of individualism. A culture of individualism and a related cult of personality promoted by the Golden Triangle also might help us understand part of the reason why we have elevated individual athletes above the team in team sports (Smart 2005:11).

In some sports cultures, such as Japanese baseball, where the team traditionally has been valued more than the individual and individuals have been expected to sacrifice for the team and suppress their individual interests and desires, it has been difficult for athletes from societies with more individualistic values, such as the United States, to adjust to the lack of attention to them as individuals (Smart 2005:41, footnote 6). For athletes and others in the United States, the importance of the individual is learned during socialization, which is why it is disorienting to be in a society where the culture places the interests and achievements of the group or team above the interests and achievements of the individual. In the United States, individualism occupies a central place in the dominant ideology of the American Dream. A universally accepted set of cultural beliefs is not likely to be found in a country with the diverse population of the United States, but the American Dream is widely accepted in the United States and may be the closest thing to a U.S. culture that Americans have (Nixon 1984; Nixon and Frey 1996:ch. 3).

We know from past discussion about the American Dream in this book that it highlights the opportunities available in U.S. society for individuals from even the most modest backgrounds to achieve upward mobility and material and occupational success. Success is believed to come to those who are ambitious, work hard, and outcompete others in an ongoing process of competitive striving. The American Dream is a vision of material comfort and success available to anyone who makes the effort and believes in the possibility of "making it" in U.S. society. It is an inspiring vision of opportunity, which gives hope to those born poor in the United States and to those from other countries who seek a better life in the United States. The American Dream emphasizes individualism because it implies that success and failure in U.S. society are individual matters, that is, that individuals become successful because they work harder than other people, and individuals fail because they do not work hard enough. Thus, individuals deserve their success and failure.

Individualism is a core aspect of the American Dream, and it has become a central tenet of the global sports culture shaped and promoted by the Golden Triangle. As noted earlier, the individual star is elevated above the team in contemporary culture, and the ascendance of the individual sports star is associated with the prominence of capitalist values. Thus, even though we can point to great teams in the history of sport, we are likely today to single out particular individual stars as the reason for the success of these teams. In the contemporary cultural economy promoted by the Golden Triangle, those who watch sports and follow popular sports figures are encouraged to emulate individual sports stars as "idols of consumption," reflecting the cultural emphasis on consumerism in modern societies. This contrasts with an emphasis on productivity in earlier stages of capitalism (Smart 2005:11–12). Even as idols of consumption, however, as celebrities in the global sports culture, modern sports stars typically embody values we associate with the achievement of the American Dream—that is, effort, ambition, toughness, strength, and, of course, winning. This should not be surprising, since the values of the American Dream are closely associated with the emphasis on individual self-interest and materialism that surfaced during the growth of entrepreneurial, industrial, and consumer capitalism in the United States and the world.

It also should not be surprising that the dominant values of U.S. society conveyed by the American Dream are closely intertwined with the dominant values in the hegemonic sports culture of the United States and other countries in the global sports culture shaped by the Golden Triangle. In this context, images of individual sports stars have been manufactured to show what success means in modern society, and it generally means being a winner on the field and having an appealing personality and an attractive lifestyle. Both the winning and the lifestyle are associated with the products that modern sports stars endorse.

Consistent with other critical and postmodern analyses of contemporary culture, Lasch (1979:96) proposed that success had become an image with no actual content. That is, success had become an image or, in regard to sport, a *winning image* created by professional image makers. The implication of his analysis is that actual hard work and achievement in the pursuit of upward mobility are less important than appearing to be successful, as defined by the contemporary values of consumer culture and the images constructed by the image makers in the Golden Triangle. In fact, though, we still expect the images of sports celebrities and heroes to be associated with some evidence of real sports success and the kinds of values we associate with success in sport and society. We will examine the nature of these values in the United States in terms of the Dominant American Sports Creed and the Sport Ethic.

From the Dominant American Sports Creed to the Sport Ethic and Other Cultural Values

The ideology of the American Dream is closely related to a set of popular cultural beliefs about U.S. sport that sport sociologist Harry Edwards (1973) called the *Dominant American Sports Creed*. Edwards (1973) formulated his conception of the most prominent beliefs about sport in the United States on the basis of his content analysis of statements about U.S. sport and its effects found in newspapers, magazines, and a leading journal in athletics over several decades of the twentieth century up to the 1960s. He viewed the central or most common beliefs as ideological statements about the virtues of sport, which were meant to persuade people to participate in sport and support it. We will see that the dominant values and beliefs in the sport culture reflect the dominant cultural values and beliefs in the larger society, and this is because sport is part of the institutional structure of the society. Just as belief in the American Dream has reinforced acceptance of the dominant structure of the larger society in the United States and the institutional structure of sport, belief in the Dominant American Sports Creed may have reinforced acceptance of the dominant institutional structure of modern U.S. sport and society in the past.

According to Edwards, the central themes of the Dominant American Sports Creed assert that: (1) sport builds character by emphasizing such things as clean living, loyalty, and altruism; (2) sport teaches discipline by encouraging both self-control and obedience to authority; (3) sport encourages competitiveness, which results from courage, perseverance, and aggressiveness and which helps people meet the challenges of life and get ahead in society; (4) sport makes people more physically fit; (5) sport contributes to mental fitness by making people more mentally sharp and encouraging them to value education; (6) sport contributes to religiosity by encouraging acceptance of traditional Christian beliefs; and (7) sport makes people more patriotic (Nixon 1984:19–22). Like the American Dream, this set of beliefs was a persuasive argument, in this case for the cultural legitimacy and significance of sport, despite lacking a basis in systematic research. People who were involved in sport believed the Dominant American Sports Creed because sport was important to them and the creed was an inspiring vision of sport.

The Dominant American Sports Creed may have been part of the dominant culture of U.S. sport through most of the twentieth century, but U.S. society has changed, mediated images have become more pervasive and influential, consumption now may be more important than productivity or achievement, and the egoism described by Tocqueville—called "narcissism" by recent cultural critics (e.g., Lasch 1979)—seems to have become a preoccupation in the United States and other contemporary Western capitalist societies. Indeed, to some extent, the American Dream now may be more about mediated images or the appearance of success than about actual achievement. Therefore, in the contemporary hegemonic sports culture shaped by the Golden Triangle, a somewhat different and more focused set of values and normative beliefs may dominate sports.

The dominant belief system in U.S. sport today may be more about what it takes to be a serious athlete than about the effects of participating in sport. Hughes and Coakley (Coakley 2007:161–164) proposed that the dominant cultural standards that defined what it meant to be a serious athlete in big-time sport in the late part of the twentieth century were part of a belief system they called the *Sport Ethic*. Its four major values emphasized: (1) dedication to "the game" above everything else; (2) striving for distinction by constantly striving to be the best, achieve perfection, and win; (3) accepting risks and playing with pain; and (4) believing that all things are possible and nothing can or will get in the way of success. These values push athletes to their limits, make sports and athletic performances exciting and entertaining for spectators, and make sport profitable for its major corporate investors in the Golden Triangle. Thus, the Sport Ethic presumes an acceptance of the value of sport and defines how you become a serious athlete, and this kind of belief system serves the interests of the Golden Triangle.

Coakley (2007:161) argued that Nike and other corporations benefit from images in their advertising of extreme adherence to the Sport Ethic. For example, in addition to their "Just Do It" ad campaign, Nike presented an ad in *Sports Illustrated* magazine during the 1996 Atlanta Summer Olympics that asked: "Who the Hell Do You Think You Are? Are You an Athlete?" Coakley observed that Nike's answer conveyed major themes of the Sport Ethic, including doing whatever it takes to be the best. He also pointed out that in other ads, Nike has used images of bodies that have been pushed to their physical limits, glorifying the idea of physical sacrifice. Thus, in these ways, the Sport Ethic becomes intertwined with commercial interests of corporate sponsors and the Golden Triangle in general, making sports seem more exciting and turning star athletes into celebrities by featuring their bodies on commercials as well as in sports performances. Some athletes and coaches may become overzealous in their pursuit or advocacy of the Sport Ethic, however. Extreme adherence to the Sport Ethic may become a form of social deviance, which is destructive to the athlete and ultimately may threaten the integrity of the game, when taken beyond the boundaries of acceptable or legal behavior. This initially "well-intentioned deviance" will be part of the discussion of social deviance and social problems in sport in chapter eight. What is most relevant to keep in mind here is that such behavior may be spawned by an acceptance of dominant cultural ideas in society and sport about individualism, competitive striving, self-improvement, and success.

Sport as a Sacred Escape

The major sports produced and promoted by the Golden Triangle are interesting combinations of contradictions. They are highly organized, commercialized, and McDonaldized forms of entertainment. They are appealing to spectators and viewers in part because the producers of sportainment in the Golden Triangle make them seem dramatic, exciting, and real through the skillful manipulation of images. At the same time that sport is all of these things, it is also a kind of religious experience for those most passionate about it. Indeed, some have said that sport is appealing to fans as an escape from the pressures and problems of everyday life (Segrave 2000), while others have called sport a "secular religion" (Nixon and Frey 1996:63–66). That is, it has a special meaning and, for some, it provides a kind of sacred escape from the mundane problems of everyday life. It appears that at least televised sport is more likely to be an escape for males than for females and for fans of team versus individual sports (Raney 2006:320).

Of course, sport is not really a religion. It cannot solve the ultimate questions of human existence about life, death, and apparently needless suffering, and it has no supernatural deities. Yet for the most passionate sports "believers" or "followers," sport provides a sense of stability and authentic meaning that is not easily found in a world that often seems turbulent, chaotic, superficial, or contrived. It can be inspiring and absorbing, qualities often missing in people's highly organized or otherwise dull lives. Rojek (2001:53) suggested that sports celebrities can become objects of cult worship in a culture of celebrity, and, like the gods of ancient religion, they can serve as exemplars or role models in modern society. As Smart (2005:9) noted, however, they show us how important it is today to be consumers of quite material rather than sacred things. Nevertheless, sports celebrities' iconic status, similar to that of religious icons, gives them great power over those who idolize them. The spiritual qualities associated with images of "magical" performances and "supernatural" talent enable the Golden Triangle to promote them more effectively as representatives of their worldly material interests. While these connections may seem quite abstract most of the time, sometimes they are made very concrete. Smart (2005:158) cites the example of a one-foot-high statue of David Beckham in his Manchester United uniform that was placed next to other statues at the foot of the image of Buddha in a Bangkok temple where minor deities normally were located. Local religious leaders commented that soccer could be viewed as a type of religion with millions of followers and the statue reflected the high regard in which many held Beckham. There have been other similar types of images of Beckham, which reinforce the connection between sport and religion, even though his global image is a construction of very secular interests.

We know that commercialism, image making, and sportainment characterize modern mediated sports and that sports heroes typically are much less heroic than they are portrayed as being. For devoted sports fans, however, these facts of sport tend to be minimized, denied, or ignored. Seen through the filters constructed by the Golden Triangle, sport is perceived as awesome, thrilling, compelling, real, and meaningful. This perceived version of sport can make it a "symbolic refuge" imbued with values, images, and meaning that transport serious fans into a world of fantasy, dreams, and pure enjoyment (Nixon and Frey 1996:55–56). Even when their favorite teams and players do not live up to expectations, the sports faithful often remain faithful. They are buoyed by examples that fuel their hope that their faith will be rewarded—eventually. After all, the loyalty of the long-suffering Boston Red Sox baseball fans was finally rewarded with a World Series victory in 2004 after eighty-six years (and then another in 2007), and the Chicago White Sox baseball team overcame eighty-eight years of frustration for their loyal fans with a World Series victory in 2005, giving hope to Chicago Cubs fans, who had not seen a World Series championship since 1908. Similarly, in the birthplace of soccer, English soccer fans remain rabid, even though in 2007 their national team had won only one World Cup and that was in 1966. The appeal or love of sport is regularly stoked by beliefs that underdogs sometimes win, all things are possible, and loyalty will eventually be rewarded. When these things happen, even for rival teams or in other sports, these core beliefs and the attachment to sport are reinforced among the faithful. For the most dedicated sports fans, hope is more important than statistical tendencies, and fantasies are more compelling than studies and analyses of sport that probe beneath the sports veneer and reveal contrary or ugly facts.

From a sociological perspective, we can point to the paradox of sport as both a sacred escape and a manufactured commodity for sale. It is an object of love and devotion for many millions of fans around the world, and it is also a cultural product produced and sold by sports, media, and corporate investors to make money. For both fans and investors, it has considerable cultural meaning and significance, and both derive something of value from this meaning and significance. This paradox is sustainable because Golden Triangles create images and encourage beliefs that make sport and its stars seem special and different from the other celebrities of contemporary popular culture, perhaps even as sacred cultural icons. As we have already noted in regard to ideologies, reality may be less compelling than images or perceptions that capture our imagination or fulfill our desires or interests. Thus, the values and structures of the contemporary cultural economy and global capitalism are reinforced and spread by the ways the global Golden Triangle produces and disseminates sport and sports stars as culturally significant experiences *and* alluring commodities on a global scale.

Alternative Sports Subcultures

Although there are global sports such as soccer that appeal to huge numbers of people around the world, there are also many other sports that appeal to people in particular regions or countries of the world or to local or regional populations within countries. This variation in sports interests should not be surprising in the context of the rich cultural diversity of nationalities, social classes, races, and gender around the world and in many nations. This cultural diversity may be the basis for the formation of subcultures in sport and other areas of society. For example, there are subcultures of classical music, reggae, punk, rock, and many other types of musical tastes that are very different from each other, except that those who are within each of these subcultures share a passion for a particular type of music. A subculture of "Trekkies" arose around the *Star Trek* television series and films, and members of this subculture have conventions, wear costumes to look like the futuristic characters in these shows, maintain websites, and engage in many different activities that link them together through their common passion. There are also videos, games, books, mugs, T-shirts, posters, and assorted other merchandise that are sold to *Star Trek* devotees. Subcultures revolve around a variety of interests, such as politics, social causes, and different dimensions of popular culture, including sport as well as music, TV series, and films.

There are many ways to define and use the concept of a subculture, and some of these uses may overlap with related terms, such as *subworld* (Crosset and Beal 1997). We will sidestep the conceptual differences and disagreements and conceptualize *subcultures* as social networks in which people are linked by shared values, attitudes, interests, tastes, and activities that make them different from people in general in a society. People in a subculture may look different, talk differently, and act differently than most people in a society, and they are likely to identify themselves as different to some extent. When the values, norms, and actions of a subculture challenge established values, norms, and behavior in the larger society by their contrast to them, the subculture is an *alternative subculture* or a *counterculture*. When the values, norms, and actions of a subculture threaten or violate the values and norms of the larger society, the subculture may be viewed as a *deviant subculture* if its threat is perceived as serious enough by the dominant power structure. The relationships between subcultures and the dominant cultural patterns in mainstream society and between different types of subcultures can be dynamic. For example, alternative subcultures can emerge as a reaction to mainstream culture and may evolve into deviant subcultures or, if they become popular enough, may be co-opted by the mainstream and become part of the mainstream. We also see in the case of the *Star Trek* phenomenon that a variety of commercial products may be sold by mainstream companies to members of popular subcultures.

Deviant subcultures, such as subcultures of violent soccer hooligans in England, may arise in sport (Maguire, Jarvie, Mansfield, and Bradley 2002: 166–168), but we are more likely to see alternative subcultures in sport. They exist outside the mainstream and may be a reaction to the mainstream, but they are not seen as deviant. Alternative sports subcultures are not likely to pose a serious threat to the hegemonic sports culture, which is where most of the power and money in sport reside. A number of "sports" subcultures may develop as recreational activities among thrill seekers, people who make creative uses of new technologies, or people who want an alternative to the highly organized and controlled forms of established sport. These activities may not develop into full-blown sport in the sense we have defined the term. However, when alternative sports subcultures seem to be gaining popularity, members of the sports establishment and businesses may try to co-opt them and profit from their popularity. Activities that have attracted people interested in alternatives to mainstream sports have included BMX freestyle racing, skateboarding, acrobatic freestyle or big-air motocross competitions, wakeboarding (on water), snowboarding, windsurfing, automobile rally racing, bungee jumping, rock climbing, in-line skating, and deep-sea diving.

Some "extreme sports" or "action sports" illustrate the process of transforming the activities of alternative recreational subcultures into organized and commercialized sports with professional athletes (Heath 2006b; Ruibal 2001; Wile and Amato 2006). ABC and its cable affiliate ESPN covered a number of these kinds of activities and then created a competition called the "X Games" to institutionalize the most popular ones as sport. They sponsor annual Winter X Games and X Games in the summer as well as international X Games and the X Fest, which includes highly competitive action sports, a mini skate park, live music, and opportunities to get autographs from stars in the extreme sports subculture. The NBC television network entered the action games arena by creating the Dew Action Sports Tour, a league intended to attract the valued but hard-to-attract "demographic," or audience, of twelve- to thirty-four-year-olds. These activities originally attracted participants because they offered chances for creativity and individual expression that were often hard to find in the mainstream. They were initially countercultural. The involvement of television and corporate sponsors has transformed these activities into sports and made their competitors into stars within the subcultures of each of these individual sports. Spencer (1997) used the case of the evolution of women's professional tennis from its status as a subculture during the era of open tennis in the early 1970s to illustrate how sports subcultures that initially represent resistance to the dominant sports culture and have some capacity to change it lose their potency as an agent of change—and their status as a subculture—when they become accepted in the mainstream. However, if formerly countercultural activities such as action sports become popular and commercially successful enough within the mainstream, they may be vehicles for changing the composition of the hegemonic sports culture as the population ages and its tastes change. In retaining some of their subcultural characteristics as alternative sports, they have the capacity to change conceptions of what sport is like and what its stars are like.

Coverage of alternative action sports by the major sports networks; the creation of a special section in the *Washington Post* devoted to action sports; the inclusion of some of these sports, such as snowboarding, freestyle skiing, tae kwon do, and triathlon, in the Olympic Games as official Olympic sports; magazine covers and billboards in New York City featuring snowboarders; and the growing interest of suburban youths and commercial sponsors in these sports all reflect the transformation of the status of these alternative subcultures from countercultural activities to mainstream sports. Borrowing from Nike, we may want to call this "mainstream with an attitude or style." We are not accustomed to referring to the stars of mainstream sports as "The Flying Tomato," the name given to Shaun White, the red-haired teenage Olympic snowboarding champion in 2006, who used words such as "rad" and was mainly interested in "doing his own thing." Doing his own thing included competing in skateboarding on the Dew Action Sports Tour and at the X Games as well as in snowboarding. Like more mainstream sports stars, though, he was developing a video game, working on his own clothing line, appearing on talk shows and television ads, and trying to take maximum advantage of the fame his sports success had brought, realizing that as a star in a lower-profile sport his commercial opportunities could fade quickly.

In her analysis of the life cycle of snowboarding, Heino (2000) argued that snowboarding initially contested the traditional meaning of sport through its subversive style. It was oriented more to the self-expression and fun of athletes than to the performance for others, which tends to be the focus of the sports spectacles of the hegemonic sports culture. It was more playlike than sportlike. It represented an alternative to the more established sport of skiing and its more conventional sports values. However, as snowboarding has become more mainstream, the media and advertisers have appropriated its rebellious image and commodified it. This process of assimilation into the sports mainstream has lessened its contentiousness with more traditional skiing. For example, ski resorts, which initially resisted snowboards on their slopes, generally allow them now, and some have snowboard parks as they try to adjust to the decline in the number of skiers. In fact, Heino pointed out that the fastest-growing category of new snowboarders is adults.

Donnelly (2006) has raised the question of whether snowboarding ever was an alternative sporting subculture. Although its youthful participants may be seen as rebellious against their parents and their more conventional sports preferences, its cost has limited it to the middle class and upper-middle class.

These affluent young people pursued snowboarding at the same resorts where their parents skied, and some of these parents may have turned to snowboarding themselves, albeit without the same style and clothing as their children. However one characterizes snowboarding, it is evident that it has been "mainstreamed," and this change has provoked some discussion in the snowboarding subculture about its "lost authenticity" in the context of the commercial influence of the mass media and corporate sponsors, and the transformation of its star performers into media celebrities and commodities. While it may have retained the individualism associated with its beginnings as a subculture, it seems to have lost its original countercultural anticompetitive and anticapitalist values, at least among its core participants. These changes reflect the power of the hegemonic sports culture and the Golden Triangle to resist change and to control and transform the subcultures that challenge it.

Those alternative sport subcultures that fail to attract a wide following or fail to adapt to the pressures of co-optation and the mainstream are likely to remain on the margins of sport or outside it entirely, perhaps where many of those engaged in these subcultural practices want them to remain. Skateboarding, for example, may not yet have achieved the mainstream status of snowboarding because many of its participants are black males who represent a challenge or threat to middle-class white culture and white corporate culture. Brayton (2005) studied the skateboarding media and found that skateboarding attracted white as well as black males, but for the whites, who often tried to adopt black "gangsta" personas and clothing, the focus shifted from the cultural resistance of blacks to the symbolic quest to be a "white male antihero." This kind of contested terrain in alternative sports subcultures is interesting in what it tells us about important cultural and identity conflicts in some segments of society, but the hegemonic sports culture is not likely to show much interest in these subcultures if they cannot attract the number of viewers and customers they need to make a profit and if they cannot be profitably commodified. The alternative sports cultures most likely to interest the Golden Triangle and penetrate the hegemonic sports culture are those with the authentic and dramatic qualities that the Golden Triangle can effectively promote and sell and whose core participants are willing to accept the values and practices of the dominant culture.

Conclusion: Shaping Culture and Making Change in Global and U.S. Sports Cultures

The accommodation of alternative sports subcultures to the dominant cultures of sport and society helps explain why hegemonic sports cultures remain relatively stable over time. Structural functional theorists might argue that society and sport function better when they avoid culture-based conflicts and have cultural consensus and social stability. They might add that powerful people in sport contribute to this consensus and stability when they influence core participants in alternative subcultures to accommodate to dominant cultural values and practices in sport and society. Social conflict or critical theorists are more likely to emphasize how the Golden Triangle serves its own interests by co-opting, controlling, or suppressing possible challenges to its dominance. It also serves its interests by exercising its power to maintain its profitability and the dominance of the existing hegemonic sports culture, which reflects its capitalistic cultural values and practices.

Although the power of dominant nations, corporate investors in sport, media corporations, and other transnational corporations that sponsor sport has limits, it seems evident that the Golden Triangle of sport, global media, and transnational corporate sponsors has had a great deal of influence in shaping the contemporary global sports culture. This partnership has exposed people around the world to a variety of sports and sports stars. Extensive media coverage has made sport culturally significant in many nations, and carefully constructed images of sports stars have made these athletes global celebrities and even heroes and cultural icons in some cases, such as Michael Jordan and Yao Ming. These stars are not only stars of sport, however. They are also "idols of consumption" that serve as vehicles for socializing sports fans around the world to consume the products of the global sports culture and the corporate sponsors of sport. Thus, they are representatives of global capitalism as well as of sport.

The American Dream of individual success and the "good life" for those who work and dream hard enough is a major U.S. export. The promoters of U.S. sport and leaders in other realms of U.S. society often point to successful athletes who have "made it" despite modest beginnings to validate the American Dream and the related cultural values of capitalism. Prominent among these values is individualism, which makes individuals celebrities and heroes and puts the accomplishments of individuals above those of the team. We have considered how the culture of the American Dream and belief systems such as the Dominant American Sports Creed have functioned as ideologies to reinforce each other and the dominant cultural practices and structures of power in U.S. society and sport. We have also seen how the Sport Ethic has shifted the focus from the benefits of sport for participants to the socialization of athletes to values and roles that serve the interests of the contemporary hegemonic sports culture, the Golden Triangle, and the cultural economy of capitalism in the United States and around the world. However, although its specific values may be associated with an earlier era, the Dominant American Sports Creed is not very different from the Sport Ethic in its functioning as an ideology that reinforces the prevailing dominant cultural beliefs and power structure of the larger society as well as of sport.

Sport and its stars have become commodities in modern sports, but, paradoxically, sport also represents a form of "sacred escape" for the most devoted fans. It transports them to a world of thrills and excitement away from the cares and problems of their everyday lives. Sport has been able to function in this way at least partially because the Golden Triangle has been successful in elevating sport to a level of major cultural significance and convincing many people that it has a quality of authenticity not found elsewhere in popular culture today. Despite the paradox of sport as both escape and commodity, the Golden Triangle has skillfully created images of sports and sports stars that make fans think that sport is different from the ordinary realms of life. Thus, they have made certain sports stars cultural icons in the emerging global cultural economy of capitalism. We can put the implications of this kind of globalization in perspective when we realize that sports stars such as Michael Jordan, David Beckham, and Yao Ming are bigger global celebrities and better known in many parts of the world than are the leaders who are making the major political and economic decisions shaping our future. In sport, they are the faces of the Golden Triangle that is shaping the future of global sport, but we must remember that their images and their influence are not completely in their control. They are employed, managed, or manipulated by more powerful people who run sports, control the media, and are in charge of the major transnational corporate sponsors of sport and make up the power structure of the Golden Triangle.

Although the cases of alternative sports subcultures that we examined suggest that it is very difficult to change established cultural values and practices in sport, we know that sport has changed over history and that it continues to change. Alternative sports subcultures, such as snowboarding, may seem to accommodate themselves to the hegemonic sports culture more than to affect it, but when big media corporations and corporate sponsors decide to invest in "extreme sports" such as snowboarding and Olympic officials begin to incorporate these sports into their list of official sports, they are doing more than expanding their corporate portfolios or sports options. They are acknowledging the forces of change in society and sport and modifying their business plans to respond to new cultural directions.

In the case of extreme or action sports, for example, we can see the influence of sociodemographic, organizational, economic, political, and technological forces of change in sport. Young people uninterested in or rejecting the sports of their parents' generation or the control over their leisure by their parents and other adults in organized youth sports turned to other kinds of athletic pursuits. These activities were daring and fun, and they gave their young participants chances for self-expression and control. Business entrepreneurs noticed these trends and began making new types of equipment and clothing for a variety of these activities, from snowboarding to skateboarding, dirt biking, hang gliding, rock climbing, and windsurfing. The Golden Triangle noticed, too, and they created competitions to attract spectators and viewers and focused attention on the young stars of these "countercultural" sports to help them sell their events and products. Despite the reluctance of a number of participants, who feared losing their autonomy, losing their authenticity, and "selling out," core participants in a number of these new sports willingly competed and took advantage of the commercial opportunities their new celebrity status brought them.

Some of these originally alternative sports subcultures exerted enough power to edge them closer to the hegemonic sports culture they had initially resisted or opposed. As these sports and their stars changed to accommodate the expectations of the dominant sports culture, the sports culture and its power structure made their own accommodations to include some of these sports in the "big-time" realm. These changes reflect the adaptability of the hegemonic sports culture and the Golden Triangle that is its center of power. Sports are shaped and reshaped by the owners and officials who run sport, the corporate media, and transnational corporate sponsors in the Golden Triangle, but these people and organizations are responsive to changes in their environment and marketplace. They reshape their own cultural values and practices to retain their dominant position and profitability. Thus, we can see that the dominant culture and cultural economy of sport are dynamic as well as complex. Those who shape this culture may influence the forces of change, but they themselves also change in response to dynamic sociodemographic, organizational, economic, political, and technological forces in their environment. Power, we must remember, is a *social* process, and it can move in different directions through the social networks of sport. Even the most powerful can be influenced, and as we saw in the last chapter, large-scale macro processes such as globalization incorporate elements of local influence through glocalization along with imprints of the cultures of powerful nations, multinational corporations, and dominant sports through grobalization.

We have examined how powerful people in the Golden Triangle and dominant sports cultures can shape our values, experiences, and consumer choices by making sports and sports stars culturally and personally significant in our lives. In the next chapter, we will consider in more depth the influence of sport as a socializer on the values, attitudes, identities, roles, and development of youths. It will focus on the socialization effects of sport on children and adolescents in youth and high school sports.

7

Socialization in Youth Sports and High School Athletics

We use the terms *socialization* and *socializing* in various ways. For example, we sometimes refer to socialization or socializing with people as meaning we are interacting with them. *Socialization* as sociologists use the term involves interaction, but it has a more specific meaning than simply talking to one another. It refers to processes of social interaction and social influence that shape: (1) how we think of ourselves in terms of our self-concept, identity, and self-esteem and (2) how we become part of society by learning cultural values and attitudes and how to interact with each other in terms of social norms and roles. This definition may not convey the profound nature of this process, but consider what it would be like if you had no answer to the question "Who are you?" or if you had no idea what other people expected of you when you got together with them. Socialization is a social learning process that contributes to social order in society by enabling us to develop relatively stable or reliable ideas about who we are, who other people are, how we should interact with others, and how others are likely to interact with us in the various social settings, roles, and relationships of society. We may develop flawed self-concepts or be confused or annoyed by what others expect of us, but socialization still enables us to be part of society, and it is a process that continues throughout our lives.

We have already had much to say about socialization in previous chapters. For example, we have considered how televised sports may convey a "manhood formula" that shows boys how to become "real men," and we have considered how ad campaigns by corporations such as Nike have tried to convince young women that sport can empower them and be fun—if they embrace the male competitive model (and use Nike equipment). We have also considered how popular media images of athletes with disabilities can influence public perceptions of disability and the perceptions of people with disabilities about their own capabilities in sport and in society in general. In addition, we have considered the important role sport can play in shaping the identities and perceived life opportunities of young black men in the United States and in making homosexual men and women feel uncomfortable about their sexual orientation.

In all these cases, sport is assumed to be a potentially powerful socializing influence. It is assumed that sport can have a significant influence on how we see ourselves and how we interact with others. Among the major socialization questions in sport sociology are questions about how and how much sport shapes our character. As we noted in an earlier chapter, a basic tenet of the Dominant American Sports Creed proposed by Harry Edwards (1973) is that sport builds character by emphasizing clean living, loyalty, and altruism. That is, sport is supposed to make you a better person, at least in terms of the general social and moral values and expectations of society. This kind of belief has been used as a traditional justification for sport by schools in England and the United States and by community organizations such as the YMCA that teach sports and run sports programs (Nixon and Frey 1996:68–69, 125).

Although socialization is a lifelong process, this chapter will focus on socialization into and through youth sports, since youth is generally considered an especially formative period in our lives. I will stretch the definition of "youth" here to include a focus on childhood as well as adolescence, and I will focus on sport both outside schools and in schools, in particular in high schools. Socialization *into* sport is the social learning process by which we learn identities, values, norms, roles, and relationships that enable us to participate in sport. A community recreation program that teaches young children the fundamental rules and skills of a particular sport, such as tennis or basketball, illustrates this process. Socialization *through* sport is the social learning process by which sports experiences shape broader identities, values, norms, roles, and relationships. The case of a sports program at a community youth center that turns a delinquent boy into a "good boy" who stays out of trouble and becomes a model student and citizen is an example of socialization through sport. Another example of socialization through sport is a woman who is able to achieve success and become a top executive in a business world dominated by men because she learned to compete and succeed in sport.

In this chapter, we will consider a number of aspects of socialization in various youth sports contexts, from recreation programs to big-time corporate sports. We will examine types of socialization that may occur in youth sports, the athlete as student in high school athletics, big-time youth sports and the Golden Triangle, parental influence, dropout and access issues in youth sport, and the relationship of youth sports to major forces of change in contemporary society. It should be evident throughout this chapter that youth sports experiences and their influence on the young people who play them are being shaped by the same types of social change processes that are shaping sport more generally today. We will once again see the imprint of the major themes in this book concerning inequality, globalization, and the influence of the Golden Triangle. Our examination of socialization in youth sports in nonschool and school contexts will begin with a general discussion of theoretical ideas about the dynamics of socialization and its social implications.

Theoretical Ideas about Socialization and Its Social Implications

Traditional structural functional social learning approaches to socialization have emphasized how we try to model or imitate others' behavior. This type of perspective focuses on socialization as a process through which we become what society wants us to become. In addition, it helps us see how society and social order depend on people's learning to behave according to prevailing norms and to do what society expects of us. The concept of *internalization* implies that people learn norms and roles so well that they consistently and unreflectively conform to societal expectations because they believe that what society expects of them is what they want and because they think that any normal or successful person in their situation would not consider being or acting differently. For example, banged-up athletes who have internalized the Sport Ethic may continue to play hurt because they believe their coaches want them to play and because they think it is what all serious athletes must do.

Socialization involves the construction, and reconstruction, of our sense of *self*, or who we think we are; our sense of *identity*, or where we think we fit in society; and our conception of relevant *norms* and *roles*. Most of us generally have a fairly stable sense of self and identity, and we internalize to some extent many or most of the relevant social norms and roles in the settings where we interact. Despite such internalization, though, we always have the capacity for personal reflection and change regarding our self and roles and for putting our personal stamp on the roles we play. Thus, a high school coach may have grown up wanting to be a coach and teacher, may have defined herself in these terms for many years, and may have interacted with players and students in fairly similar ways for a long time. While this person acts like other high school coaches and teachers in many ways, she also acts in certain distinctive ways, for example as a disciplinarian with a set of values that reflect her conservative religious beliefs. She has given very little thought for many years to the way she coaches or teaches, her training methods, her classroom behavior, or what she expects of her players or students. She has seemed to settle into her identity and roles. However, this person could become more flexible and sympathetic as a coach, teacher, and parent after one of her players suffers a seriously disabling injury as a result of the coach's urging her to play hurt, when one of her students quits school because she repeatedly told the student how "dumb" she was for failing to meet her expectations, or after her daughter runs away from home because she cannot handle the excessively strict discipline and restrictive rules at home.

Socialization is not a passive or mechanical process, since people do not always embrace or conform to established role models and conventional expectations (see Nixon 1990). Although we may often internalize norms and role expectations and may not even think about trying to be a different kind of person or acting differently, there are times when we may think about changing who we are or the things we do. The concept of *resocialization* means that self-concepts, identities, and role behavior change over time. Thus, we need to avoid assuming, as we might from a structural functional perspective, that people always try to see themselves as society wants them to see themselves or that they always do what is expected of them. Resocialization implies a more dynamic conception of socialization. It implies that change is a normal part of our social experience.

A symbolic interactionist perspective of socialization implies that we are active agents in our own socialization, constantly negotiating with others how we should think about who we are, where we fit in society, and how we should play our roles. Thus, we need to understand that people may not routinely, automatically, or passively accept or yield to the forces of socialization, which might include parental influence, the influence of other authority figures such as teachers and coaches, pressure from peers, and the images and messages in popular culture and the mass media. Especially as we get older, we are likely to think about what is expected of us and at times subtly or obviously question, challenge, and even resist cultural and structural pressures or constraints on us.

Sometimes it is difficult to resist becoming or doing what powerful others expect of us. For example, if our basketball coach tells us that our role is to pass and defend and not to score and we consistently shoot the ball (and miss), we might find ourselves on the bench or off the team. To avoid the coach's wrath, we learn to become "team players" and accept that we are not destined to become stars, at least with this coach. Or, we may find that it is very difficult to ignore a league's drug policy when getting caught for using banned substances could result in fines, suspensions, or being banned for life from playing in the league. Thus, despite our past use of performance-enhancing drugs and our desire or perceived need to continue using them to elevate our performance or save our career, we decide to conform to the league's expectations because it is too risky not to do so. Our behavior has been resocialized by the league's drug policy and the fear of its enforcement. That is, we learn to do things differently. Socialization and resocialization change us, but with sufficient resources and power, we have the capacity to create, modify, or transform cultural values, norms, roles, and relationships. How sport socializes young participants depends on the sports contexts in which they participate. In the next section, we will turn our attention to major differences in youth sports contexts.

Contexts of Socialization: Types of Youth Sports

Even among unathletic children and adolescents, some type of involvement in sport is often part of the process of growing up in the United States and a number of other countries. For boys, sport has been a way of establishing their emerging masculine identity, and over the past several decades, sport has become a popular activity for girls as well. According to one estimate, about 40 million boys and girls between the ages of five and eighteen participate in sport in the United States (Fullinwider 2006:6). Most youths are involved in sports with a national sponsor, such as Little League Baseball. It has been estimated that approximately 22 million children and adolescents play these kinds of sports. In addition, an estimated 2.4 million participate in club sports; 14.5 million play "recreational" sports organized by city and county recreation departments or nonprofit organizations; and 7.4 million participate in interscholastic athletics (Fullinwider 2006:37, footnote 65).[1]

We can think of several reasons why boys and girls get involved in sports, such as parental pressure, peer influence, media sports coverage, urging from teachers or coaches, curiosity, and genuine interest. The outcomes of their sports experiences and the kinds of lessons they learn from sport about such things as sportsmanship, fair play, and competition tend to reflect the influence of the attitudes and actions of their parents and other adults (Fullinwider 2006:7). These experiences are also likely to be significantly shaped by the contexts of the cultural values and of the social organization of the sports they play. Children or teenagers may be involved in the same sport, such as baseball, basketball, or softball, but have very different sport and socialization experiences if the context of their involvement differs. The concepts of globalization and Americanization, which we discussed in chapter five, suggest that the sports contexts and experiences of U.S. youths are increasingly similar to the sports contexts and experiences of youths elsewhere in the world. Rees, Brettschneider, and Brandl-Bredenbeck (1998) compared the sports interests and orientations of suburban New York youths and German youths in Berlin to test globalization and Americanization hypotheses regarding youth sports. They were interested in whether the youths in the United States and Germany liked the same sports and shared the same degree of interest in achievement or winning in their physical activities. Their findings are presented in the "Focus on Research" feature concerning "Globalization of Youth Sports."

In this section, we will consider important differences in the various contexts of youth sports. The broadest distinction in youth sports in the United States is between *nonschool* and *school* sports. The *nonschool sports* include sports existing under the auspices of private nonprofit membership organizations such as Little League, Inc. These *corporate youth sports* may sponsor competitions at the local, state, regional, national, and international levels. The biggest of these kinds of organizations are highly bureaucratic and complex, with numerous formal policies, rules, and regulations that are applied to various levels of competition. The central corporate body may provide resources as well as a regulatory framework for its sponsored programs, leagues, and competitions, and it is likely to receive financial support from its members and outside corporate sponsors. Along with Little League Baseball, Pop Warner Football, the Amateur Athletic Union youth sports programs, and Junior Olympics are other examples of major corporate youth sports programs in the United States. Other examples are programs sponsored by the official international or national regulatory body of a sport, such as FIFA, U.S. Youth Soccer, USA Swimming, and USA Gymnastics.

Club sports involve locally organized teams or sports programs that often have the goal of providing high-level developmental and competitive opportunities for serious and talented young athletes. Clubs may be affiliated with state, regional, and national corporate sports organizations, including the national governing bodies of specific sports, such as swimming, figure skating, gymnastics, golf, basketball, and soccer, and private sponsors, such as local businesses and wealthy individuals, subsidize them. Some clubs achieve elite status through their competitive success at progressively higher levels of competition. The larger corporate bodies with which clubs are affiliated may sponsor leagues, competitions, and developmental and training programs for athletes and coaches.

Although a majority of the boys and girls who are involved in sports may be involved in programs with a corporate structure, relatively few ascend to the elite level of big-time corporate sports. In addition, many other youths participate in *recreational sports programs*, sponsored by city and county recreational departments or nonprofit organizations, that are primarily intended to help children learn a sport or to promote fun. There tend to be major *structural differences* between these kinds of youth sports programs and corporate programs.

⚲ Focus on Research Feature 7.1: Globalization of Youth Sports

Rees, Brettschneider, and Brandl-Bredenbeck (1998) were interested in learning whether the assumed globalization and Americanization trends that had been much discussed and debated regarding big-time sports in the world of the Golden Triangle could be found in youth sports. Their research was part of a large-scale cross-cultural project that compared the significance of sport and the body for German and U.S. teenagers. For this study, they administered a questionnaire to white seventh-, ninth-, and twelfth-grade students in suburban Nassau County in New York and their German counterparts in Berlin. They excluded nonwhite students in the United States and non-German students in Berlin who were in the larger sample to avoid the confounding effects of ethnicity on their data. In particular, they looked at the specific sports and physical activities in which these male and female teenagers in these two countries participated and the ways they thought about the concept of sport.

When asked in what physical activities they had participated in the last year, swimming, biking, and jogging were found to be the most popular among the German girls, followed by basketball, dancing, gymnastics, and horseback riding. Among the German boys, biking, basketball, soccer, swimming, table tennis, and jogging were the six most popular. Among the New York girls, jogging, basketball, swimming, soccer, tennis, and walking were the six most popular physical activities, while among the New York boys, basketball, football, baseball, jogging, soccer, and swimming were the six most popular. We can make some interesting observations about these findings. First, we see that swimming, jogging, and basketball are on all four lists. Second, biking was popular among Germans but not Americans. Third, only German girls mentioned dancing and gymnastics, only German boys mentioned table tennis, only U.S. girls mentioned tennis and walking, and only U.S. boys cited football and baseball among the top six physical activities. Fourth, all except the German girls listed soccer.

What do these results mean? Although there was a common interest in the "American" sport of basketball, which supports the Americanization theory, there were also sports interests that were unique to each nationality. Biking was among the most popular physical activities for German boys and the second most popular for German girls, but was not in the top six for either U.S. girls or boys. The "European" sport of soccer was popular among U.S. girls and boys and among German boys, but not among German girls, perhaps reflecting different organized sports opportunities for girls and boys in Germany or in Berlin. U.S. boys' top three choices of basketball, football, and baseball were distinctive in reflecting the kinds of sports promoted heavily by the Golden Triangle in their country. In Europe, bicycle racing is much more emphasized by the Golden Triangle than it is in the United States. Among German boys, biking was the most popular physical activity, and among German girls, it was second most popular. Overall, then, there is as much evidence for local or national influences as there is for global influences in the physical activity choices of the youths in this study. In addition, it appears that the imprint of the Golden Triangle could be inferred from male and female choices in both countries, although the boys in both countries seemed to be more influenced by the "Golden Triangle sports" than the girls were. In thinking about these results and the findings concerning conceptions of sport, it is important to keep in mind that nearly all students in U.S. public schools are exposed to a heavy emphasis on organized and team sports, especially at the high school level, whereas in Germany, students have relatively little experience with interscholastic sports, and physical education classes may be their only exposure to organized physical activity.

Just as sports choices were both similar and different, conceptions of sports revealed similarities and differences. When asked what they thought of when they thought of "sport," the U.S. respondents were more likely to identify team sports and less likely to identify individual sports and leisure or recreational activities than were the German respondents. The Americans were less likely than the Germans to associate images of health and fitness and physical effort with sport but more likely to associate the ideas of victory or winning with sport than the Germans were. Respondents in both countries were similarly much more likely to think of sport in positive than in negative terms. There were significant gender effects that cut across cultures. Girls in Germany and in the United States rated the importance of fun higher than their male counterparts did, while the boys in these two countries rated the importance of competition higher than their female counterparts did. Competition was an especially important aspect of physical activity for the U.S. boys. Regular practice was an important element of sport for both males and females in New York, but this part of sport was more important for males than for females in Berlin. In general, it appears that although there are some overlapping conceptions of sport among teenagers in the United States and Germany, U.S. boys may be most influenced by highly institutionalized and narrower conceptions of competitive team sports, promoted by the Golden Triangle and reinforced by the distinctive level of organization and culture of interscholastic sports in the United States. For U.S. boys, in particular, organized team sports in the school have been a primary source of identity and status for many years, and this kind of school-related socialization experience may be distinctive for U.S. males in the global context.

For example, the organization of corporate youth sports tends to place more emphasis than that of recreational sports on: (1) paid professional coaches; (2) selectivity mechanisms such as competitive tryouts; (3) fees for membership and access to facilities; (4) expensive clothing, equipment, coaching, training, and travel; (5) competitive intensity and the significance and rewards of winning; (6) sport specialization with mandatory year-round participation in practice, training, and competition; (7) spectators; and (8) commercial sponsorship. In addition, the organization of corporate youth sports is more likely to involve larger, more complex, and more bureaucratic structures and more external or nonlocal regulation and control. We will consider the structure and implications of "big-time" corporate youth sports programs in more detail later in the chapter when we examine the relationship of these sports programs to the forces of the Golden Triangle.

Some young people opt out of traditional forms of sport to pursue *alternative* or *extreme sports*. In the last chapter, we considered how some extreme sports were transformed from alternative recreational subcultures into highly organized and commercialized sports with professional athletes (Heath 2006a; Ruibal 2001; Wile and Amato 2006). An ethnographic study of youth participation in a BMX bikers subculture showed that participation in this activity is quite different for those who pursue it in different contexts or "spaces" (Rinehart and Grenfell 2002). The researchers studied a group of young people who participated in BMX riding in two different types of settings: a grassroots context where the more experienced riders set up the ramps, courses, and jumps themselves and a BMX indoor/outdoor riding circuit at a skate park that was organized as a corporate commercial venture by adults to make money by providing a safe place for youths to practice BMX riding skills. In contrast to the commercial site, the grassroots site did not cost money to use and was free from adult supervision, organization, and interference. In addition, the riders could take risks and ride as they wished at the grassroots site. Because they were freer from external adult intervention, their own site was more playlike and relaxed, and the riders were more spontaneous and more cooperative and helpful toward each other.

The more recreational youth-driven site coexisted with the corporate commercial site, and the BMX riders moved in and out of both types of venues. It might seem surprising that young BMXers who had a chance to ride at their own site would be attracted to the commercial site. It was expensive for many of them, it had formal rules, and riding there was more intense as riders tried to "get their money's worth." However, as we noted in our earlier discussion in this book about the Golden Triangle in sport, commercially organized sports and facilities construct powerful marketing messages to attract customers. The skate park studied by Rinehart and Grenfell advertised itself as "cutting edge" and "rider friendly" and promoted the kinds of clothing, equipment, and other products that appealed to many young people. Thus, we can see that trying to understand how alternative or extreme sports socialize young people is complicated by their participation in both countercultural and mainstream contexts, which are organized in very different ways.

The participation statistics cited earlier showed that although many young people participate in recreational and alternative sports and physical activities, many also participate in highly organized and "serious" corporate sports. As Rinehart and Grenfell's research suggests, some participate in both kinds of contexts. In addition to those who play club sports, over seven million boys and girls participate in high school sports, and a number of these young people have to deal with the competing demands of both club and high school sports. There is some evidence that the pull of elite club programs, such as AAU basketball, is stronger and more compelling than that of high school sports for an increasing number of outstanding young athletes (e.g., Prisbell 2006). However, we are also seeing a number of high school sports programs becoming elite or "big-time," too.

The structure of interscholastic athletics or *school sports* at the high school level may vary a great deal across schools and even within schools. The structure of the most organized and lavishly supported varsity programs tends to be more like nonschool corporate sports than recreational sports programs. In fact, certain trends in high school athletics that have made them more like big-time college athletic programs have prompted serious concerns among educational leaders. For example, a study commissioned by the National Association of State Boards of Education (NASBE 2004) pointed to concerns about the exploitation of high school athletes and the distortion of academic and moral values. Commission members were worried about the influence of shoe manufacturers, ambitious and self-serving coaches, questionable recruiting practices, steroids and other performance-enhancing drugs, lavish gifts to athletes, and increasing specialization encouraged by club sports. They urged state boards to play an active role in making sure that academics remained the top priority in public education, that the integrity of competition was protected, that access was available to all students who wished to participate in high school sports, and that schools were acting responsibly in raising and spending money for athletics. The report suggests an underlying concern among commission members that high school athletics was straying from the ideals that originally justified sports in the schools. Commission members recognized the need for research to clarify how high school athletic participation actually affects students. In the next section, we will begin to consider in more detail the current state of knowledge in sport sociology about how youths are affected, or socialized, by their involvement in various contexts of sport in and out of the schools.

Learning about Status and the Self in Youth Sports

The major types of socialization we will examine in this section involve lessons participants may learn about status and the self, character building and conformity, and citizenship and nationalism. We will see that socialization is a complex process that may involve a variety of overlapping lessons of social learning. This complexity will first become evident in our discussion of various types of learning about status and the self that may occur in youth sports.

Gender and Social Class

One might see little similarity between a YMCA tee ball program for young children in a small southeastern U.S. town and an inner-city recreation and drop-in center for "at-risk" low-income youths in southern Ontario, Canada. However, the results of the studies of five- and six-year-old boys and girls in the tee ball program (Landers and Fine 1996) and of teenage girls at the recreation and drop-in center (Wilson, White, and Fisher 2001) reveal a common lesson, that is, sport favors the more talented and, especially, males. The girls in tee ball tended to react to their experience by losing interest over the season, and the teenage girls at the Ontario center tended to accept the gender hierarchy and their marginal status in sport as normal, as "the way it's always been here" (Wilson, White, and Fisher 2001:315). Thus, sport may provide early lessons about the gender hierarchy in society for both girls and boys. The lessons seem to be basically the same across different sports contexts, even in upper-middle-class settings in the United States where both boys and girls have extensive sports opportunities. Adler and Adler (1998) found in their research in an upper-middle-class community that girls were less likely than boys to participate in informal or alternative sports because they received less encouragement and rewards for their participation, and that by the time they reached adolescence, the girls were more likely than the boys to drop out of mainstream sports. The girls who were the best athletes were most likely to continue. Not surprisingly, unlike their male counterparts, girls did not rely much on their sports participation or prowess for social acceptance or status.

Although sport favors males over females, Fine's (1987) study of preadolescent boys in Little League Baseball showed that boys with certain types of "masculine" qualities were more favored than others. The boys in this study were socialized in a culture that emphasized displays of toughness, dominance, and risk taking and expressions of condescension or contempt for girls and for boys who did not conform to these stereotypical conceptions of masculinity. As Coakley (2007:108) suggested, Little League was not the source of these kinds of ideas about gender, masculinity, and sexual orientation. These ideas were rooted in the culture of the larger society. However, Little League, like the tee ball program and the recreation center, was a context where these ideas could be conveyed and reinforced by coaches, parents, and other adults, and further reinforced by peers. Not surprisingly, studies of other children's sports settings, such as peewee ice hockey (Ingham and Dewar 1999), have produced similar findings about the gender lessons of youth sports.

In his interview study of thirty male former athletes, Messner (1990a) asked them about their boyhood sports experiences. Messner observed that sport was both a gendered institution and a gendering institution for these men when they were boys. That is, sport was *gendered* in the sense that dominant cultural conceptions of masculinity and femininity prevailed, and it had a *gendering* function in the sense that it taught boys about masculinity in ways that reproduced traditional dominant stereotypes about masculinity and femininity. They learned that the rules were important in sport, that you had to be very competitive to succeed in sport, and that you had to accept the hierarchy of sport. In this context, boys learn that acceptance as men depends on being a winner and that one has to be wary of getting too close to other people in this competitive and hierarchical world. These youthful lessons of masculinity seemed to be especially compelling for the men he interviewed who were from lower- and working-class backgrounds because they had fewer social choices in their lives and thus depended more on athletics to define their identity. Thus, it seems that youth sports are likely to be most influential in socialization for the young athletes who have the fewest alternative role options.

The increasing participation of girls and young women in sport in the United States and a number of other countries over the past few decades suggests that females have overcome the obstacles of discouragement and challenges to their femininity and sexual orientation. Black females also have had to overcome the additional obstacle of racism. However, increasing female participation has not necessarily meant that this discouragement has turned to encouragement or that the self-concept of female athletes has been totally secure. We have examined too much research and analysis in this chapter and earlier ones that are consistent with Messner's conclusion about sport as a gendered and gendering institution that emphasizes traditional conceptions of masculinity and femininity. This aspect of the context of many youth sports implies that learning about gender in sport can be problematic for both boys and girls, especially if the boys are unathletic or unaggressive and the girls are the opposite in the team sports typically associated with males. We know from this and previous chapters how sport has traditionally socialized males and females to accept ideas about sport as a male preserve, about male privilege in sport, and about how females may have to compromise their femininity to play sports.

Gender and Race

Like social class, race filters gender socialization experiences in youth sports. This is especially evident for black males because sport has been so closely associated with black male identity. Because they are poor and black, young black males in the inner city who have a chance to play sports are likely to rely heavily on sports for their masculine identity and status. Although he recognized the problems for these young black males of being consumed by sport, Edwards (1998) believed that pursuing a sports dream—with eyes wide open— was preferable to the high dropout rates from school and the high rates of unemployment, gang violence, crime, incarceration, and early death that were increasingly characterizing the lives of black teenagers in the inner city. His concern was that there were fewer sports facilities and programs in these neighborhoods than in the past. However, even with few legitimate alternatives, sports participation could be a mixed blessing for young black males. On the one hand, it provides them with a chance to achieve legitimate success.

On the other hand, by concentrating on sport, young black sports participants may be confirming a racist ideology held by at least some in the dominant class that black males are good at sports but not other things that are important in society.

In the fourth chapter, we considered the case of the tennis-playing Williams sisters as an example of the problems of being a black female athlete. Douglas (2005) proposed that their race played a significant role, along with other factors, in ambivalent assessments of their accomplishments and hostility toward them. Daniels (2000) observed that black females have had the challenge of dealing with a possible combination of biases related to race, gender, and suspicions of lesbianism. As we noted in chapter three, the WNBA was careful in its initial marketing campaign to present soft and highly feminized images of these players that focused on modeling contracts and motherhood. Like the challenge faced by the NBA in marketing a league of mostly black players to a mostly white public, the WNBA did not want to encourage stereotypes of these black female athletes that might seem threatening to the mostly white and heterosexual fans (Daniels 2000).

Class, Race, and Ethnicity in High School Athletics

The story about the Permian High School Panthers football team in Odessa, Texas, has been made famous by H.G. Bissinger's (1990) popular book *Friday Night Lights* and by a film and television series based on the book. Bissinger showed what it was like to grow up and play football in a depressed west Texas oil town that was passionate about high school football and dreamed about championships. Along with Bissinger's journalistic account, ethnographic studies by social scientists (e.g., Foley 1990; Grey 1992) have generally found that social patterns in U.S. public high school athletics tend to mirror the social patterns of their communities. While high school sports may integrate or unify some members of a community around a common passion, the socialization of high school athletes generally seems to reflect and reinforce existing patterns of class, race, ethnic, and gender inequalities in the community. They learn "how things are," who is privileged, who has power, and how to treat minorities and females. For example, Foley's study of a football season in a south Texas town showed how racial and ethnic stereotypes could bias decisions about whether the "strong-armed Mexican boy" should start at quarterback over the "all-around-smart Anglo boy."

High school sports are unlikely to be a social integrator when they exist in a community beset by racial divisions and distrust (Miracle and Rees 1994: 170). Sometimes, minority group members in sport find themselves in a position of potential change agent, for example as a coach or team leader, and they learn how difficult it can be to bring about change. For example, a Mexican American had been chosen as the head football coach for the first time in the town Foley studied. He wanted to bring about racial and ethnic harmony, but instead he found that he was caught between the dominant Anglo and minority Latino cultures. He faced hostility from racist whites who were unhappy that a conservative white coach was not chosen for his position, and he faced hostility from Latino activists who believed that he had compromised his ethnic pride and integrity by trying to accommodate himself to the dominant

This scene is from the film *Friday Night Lights*. The film was based on Bissinger's popular book, and it spawned a television show. *Friday Night Lights* reminds us of the culture of big-time high school football in towns where high school football players are heroes and experience the highs and lows of this status. (Universal/The Kobal Collection/Ralph Nelson)

Anglo power structure. Although he had a 7–4 record and his team was second in its conference, he resigned and left his hometown in reaction to the pressure, limited acceptance, lost friends, and ulcer he experienced (Nixon and Frey 1996:137).

While it is difficult for people in sport to bring about major changes in entrenched patterns of racism, sexism, and class bias in their sport or in their community, Foley's research also showed that there were people who try to resist racist, sexist, and elitist rituals and practices in sport. In addition, some research has shown that under certain conditions, youth sports could contribute to racial and ethnic integration in a community. For example, Grasmuck (2003) studied a youth baseball league in a socially diverse gentrifying neighborhood with a history of racial and ethnic tensions. She found that the experience of having parents from different racial and ethnic backgrounds sit together each season to watch their children play in a neighborhood baseball league expanded the network of interracial social ties in the community and helped develop a sense of community that bridged racial and ethnic differences in a neighborhood in transition. As a result, youth baseball may have had a role in defusing possible racial and ethnic tensions in the community.

It appears that even though football and some other high school sports may be a means to achieve upward mobility and social acceptance for white working-class boys in predominantly white high schools, social status and social acceptance are often problematic for boys with ethnic minority backgrounds in these types of settings. Grey's (1992) ethnography of sport at a Kansas high school showed that recent Latino and Southeast Asian immigrants faced special problems of integration through sport when they had little or no experience with the dominant sports, such as football, and did not make the team or failed to try out. Their lack of participation in the mainstream sports in the school and their preference for less-valued sports, such as soccer, were perceived as evidence of their lack of acceptance of the mainstream culture and made their social integration in the school and community more difficult. In this context, the mainstream or more popular school sports served a cultural and social gatekeeping function, since they were more likely to be accessible to members of the dominant group than to members of more socially marginal minority groups (Nixon and Frey 1996:140).

Although they may face obstacles to sports participation in predominantly white high schools, members of ethnic and racial minority groups, and especially African Americans, have participated and excelled in mainstream sports such as football and girls' and boys' basketball. Basketball may have the most meaning among black teenagers in schools where racial biases in the general student culture of the school are strongest. Goldsmith (2003) found that dominance in basketball was a way for black students to resist or oppose the dominant white culture of the school and demonstrate black equality or superiority. Playing and succeeding at basketball has been especially meaningful for blacks because it has symbolically represented black success in the popular culture in the United States.

In one of the few studies about ethnic minority females in sport, Hanson (2005) found that Asian-American females were not as involved in high school sports as their Asian-American male counterparts. However, they were overall just as likely, if not more likely, to participate in high school sports than their female white, black, and Latina peers. The facts that they tend to live in urban areas, to be from families of higher socioeconomic status, and to have mothers in higher-status occupations probably contributed to the higher sports participation rates among Asian-American females.

Sexual Orientation

A powerful message conveyed by the hegemonic ideas about sport and gender in the mainstream culture of sport is that sport is for males, and part of this message is that sport is for *heterosexual* males. We have seen that the narrow conception of masculinity learned in sport can be problematic for heterosexual males in their roles outside sport, but the emphasis on heterosexual masculinity in sport is especially problematic for boys who are developing an awareness of their homosexuality. Pronger (2005) found that some of the thirty-two gay men he interviewed saw both the informal sports of their peers and the more formally organized school sports of their boyhood as hostile worlds that emphasized traditional ideas of masculinity and made homosexuals feel unwelcome. For them, this was a world they should avoid. Only one of his interviewees enjoyed playing aggressive team sports. Those who were interested in sports tended to be most comfortable in the least-aggressive sports because they were the least stereotypically masculine.

Pronger found that even those gay men who were good at individual sports such as swimming or gymnastics found that they were last picked for team games when they were boys because they were perceived as "sissies" or effeminate because they were not interested enough in stereotypical displays of aggressive masculinity. Discomfort with team sports was often intensified in the locker room, when talk turned to dating or sexual exploits with females. Pronger concluded from his interviews that gay men involved in mainstream sports organizations felt uncomfortable talking about their "sissy sensibilities." Their perception of likely homophobic reactions helps explain why we hear or read so little about gay men in sport. Although being a lesbian is more expected than being gay in sports, we have seen that lesbians also face homophobic reactions, which discourage them from public expressions of their sexual orientation. Thus, we can conclude that most traditional youth sports contexts are likely to be problematic environments for boys and girls trying to understand and adjust to an emerging sense of their homosexual identity.

Disability

As in the case of sexual orientation, mainstream sports generally do not encourage or welcome people with disabilities or help them develop stable or secure positive identities that acknowledge their disability. An important difference between the experiences of children and adolescents with physical disabilities and gay and lesbian youths is that physical disabilities tend to be visible while sexual orientation can be hidden. Thus, disability is more likely to be a public matter. For children and adolescents with physical disabilities, the visible nature of their disability is typically used as a reason to exclude them from sports. Gay and lesbian youths can gain access to sport more easily than their counterparts with disabilities, as long as they hide their sexual orientation. However, as we have seen, having to hide a part of their identity can make sports quite uncomfortable or aversive for gay and lesbian youths.

Boys and girls with disabilities are typically excluded from more formally organized and competitive sports programs with able-bodied peers. However, there is some research (Taub and Greer 2000) that suggests that participation in physical activities with their peers can help these young people develop a sense of physical competence, become more socially accepted, and increase their social ties to able-bodied peers. That is, physical activity can help youths with disabilities to overcome negative stereotypes to some extent and to achieve more "normalized" identities and peer relations. Thus, giving children and adolescents broader access to integrated and more competitive sports in high school and the community could significantly broaden the normalization opportunities for these children and adolescents. This normalization process is a learning process for both youths with disabilities and their able-bodied peers, since both have a chance to learn about the ways they are similar. Perceptions of similarities are often the basis for developing mutual respect and friendships (Nixon 1979:86–92).

Since young people with disabilities frequently are more dependent on their parents than their able-bodied peers are, parents of children with disabilities can have a significant influence on how and how much their children participate in sports and on their socialization experiences in sport (Nixon 1988b). However, athletes competing in elite national or international disability sports events have said that their parents were not the major source of inspiration or support for their high-level sports involvement (Sherrill 1986). Their involvement in sport was more likely to be encouraged by rehabilitation professionals and coaches and athletes in disability sports (Williams and Kolkka 1998). My research (Nixon 1988b) showed that professionals and volunteers who worked with young people with disabilities tended to favor mainstream experiences for them, but they often had difficulty locating appropriate integration opportunities.

Parents of children with disabilities may tend to be most comfortable with sports that are structured to be unthreatening and over which they have some control (Castañeda and Sherrill 1999). However, as children with disabilities become adolescents and get older, they may find that their own empowerment is more important than their parents' comfort with controlled and "safe"—and unchallenging—sports. The case of a young Paralympian in Maryland who wanted to compete with her high school classmates in the mainstream illustrates the challenges faced by athletes with disabilities, even when they are very good athletes and have strong parental support, if they want to compete with and against able-bodied peers (Chadiha 2007; Olson and Seidel 2006). After a judge granted her the right to compete in her wheelchair on the same track with her able-bodied peers, sixteen-year-old Tatyana McFadden and her teammate were disqualified from a state championship race because Tatyana was accused of racing just ahead of her teammate to "pace" her. After additional pressure, the Maryland Public Secondary Schools Athletic Association's executive council agreed to allow wheelchair participants to compete alongside able-bodied runners in six different race categories, from 100 meters to 3200 meters, but wheelchair competitors were not permitted to score points for their teams (Seidel 2007). Tatyana continued her legal battle for equality through the courts by seeking a change in the Maryland Public Secondary Schools Athletic Association rules so that athletes with disabilities would be able to have their performances count in their team's score (Dolan 2007). This case illustrates the complexities of creating viable models of integration in the mainstream for athletes with disabilities. Access to *appropriate* sports opportunities in integrated or segregated settings for children and adolescents with disabilities along the continuum I proposed in chapter four ultimately depends on acceptance in the communities where these young people live that they deserve the same chance to participate in sports that their able-bodied counterparts have.

Character and What Adults Expect

The most frequent claims about the socializing effects of sport on young people have to do with character building. They have included historical justifications linking sport to moral virtue and religiosity in terms of ideas such as "muscular Christianity." Along with coaches and sports officials, religious and educational leaders have been among those who have promoted sport as a character builder. Although *character* could be interpreted in various ways, *good character* has generally meant conforming to parental and other adult expectations and being perceived as displaying the personal qualities and behaviors, such as cooperation, courage, honesty, hard work, and sportsmanship, that are considered desirable and are widely valued in society. *Bad character*, on the other

A young athlete is consoled by a coach, suggesting the intense pressures young people may experience in sport. (iStockphoto)

hand, has typically referred to the tendency to get into trouble by not following the rules, not accepting authority, or being "too independent."

The presumed character-building function of sport has been a tenet of the Dominant American Sports Creed, despite the fact that sport sociology researchers have been unable to find a consistent pattern of effects of sports participation on character. Furthermore, some research has found that former athletes may display both "good character" and "bad character." For example, a study using the National Education Longitudinal Study (NELS) database showed that eight years after their senior year in high school, former elite high school athletes who were team captains and voted most valuable team members were less likely to smoke tobacco but more likely to engage in binge drinking than their nonathlete classmates were (Carlson, Scott, Planty, and Thompson 2005). It is not clear how or whether sports participation *directly* contributed to these kinds of behavior.

Youths may be exposed to a variety of lessons about character in their sports experiences. They may learn to value fair play, sportsmanship, and other moral values if coaches and other adults in their sports programs explicitly teach and model these values. Success in getting young sports participants to accept these values and the norms for "good behavior" that adults espouse may depend on how adults handle competition. The challenge is to make sport fun but also serious enough to satisfy those who enjoy competing. Coaches in different types of sports contexts are likely to handle competition and winning in different ways. Coaches in recreational programs may be unsure how much to emphasize competition and winning as children get older because participants in their programs—and their parents—may develop a range of attitudes toward competition and winning as they become more experienced in sport. Coaches in intensely competitive corporate programs often believe that they have to make winning most important because their status as coach is tied to winning. Reactions to coaches' comments about making sports fun, giving everyone a chance to play, playing by the rules, being good sports, and accepting losing with grace are likely to vary among children and adolescents—and their parents—who have different sports motivations and goals.

Participants in youth sports may learn that adults condone or encourage doing "whatever it takes" to win, even when it involves bending or breaking the rules or degrading their opponent, and they may see adults reward "poor sports" and their deviant behavior. A study of a boys' basketball team in a predominantly black high school (May 2001) revealed situations where young athletes had to reconcile ideas about sportsmanship with their coach's strong emphasis on winning, for example, when referees sometimes seemed to allow "hard fouls" or even "cheap shots." When these young athletes perceive contradictions between talk about sportsmanship and the need to win, they are likely to conclude that adult rhetoric about sportsmanship and character is not always consistent with how adults act, that winning is paramount, and that it can make up for or excuse "bad behavior." Fine's (1987) study of Little Leaguers revealed that children become cynical about adult values and expectations if adults fail to act in the ways they tell the young people to act. He found that the players did not necessarily internalize the values they were taught by adults in Little League, but they learned how to manipulate coaches and enhance their status in the eyes of coaches by saying the kinds of things coaches wanted to hear. Thus, youth sports might teach participants about the character traits and behaviors that adults say they want to see. However, the lessons about character and conformity that youths internalize from their sports experiences are likely to depend on how much respect they have for adults who do what they espouse.

We will conclude this section with a combined "Sport in the News" and "Focus on Research" feature that reveals the serious consequence of clashes between athletes and nonathletes in networks of social relations in high school, where being an athlete is highly valued and being "different" is not. The news portion of this feature is about the case of violence at Columbine High School in Colorado, where male athletes had an inflated sense of their importance in the jock-oriented culture of their school and displayed "bad character" by belittling and abusing classmates who were "outsiders" not accepted in their social circle. The resentment and anger produced by these divisive and abusive

---

☐ **Sport in the News and Focus on Research Feature 7.2:** 🜍
High School Violence and "Jock Culture"

Two seniors at Columbine High School in suburban Littleton, Colorado, near Denver went to school on April 20, 1999, with guns and bombs, killed twelve students and a teacher, and wounded twenty-three other students before committing suicide. This school shooting provoked outrage and much media attention around the world (e.g., Glick et al. 1999; Harris 1999). It was one of the deadliest incidents in U.S. school history, and it was one of a dozen school shootings in the United States during a period of eighteen months. The Columbine incident has been dissected in many different ways by the news media, but we will focus here on elements related to "jock culture" and peer relations between athletes and nonathletes at the school. In particular, we will apply the insights of Brian Wilson (2002) about an anti-jock movement among "marginalized youths" that has connections to violent video game culture and the Internet and also has global implications.

Among the factors that may explain this incident are the tension and hostility between the two shooters, Dylan Klebold and Eric Harris, and a number of the athletes at their high school. According to one news story (Harris 1999), Klebold and Harris had both played Little League Baseball and were in a fantasy baseball league, were bright and quiet, and enjoyed computer games. By the time they were in middle school, playing violent computer games consumed their time after school. When they entered high school, they had some friends, but they saw themselves as outsiders, not fitting into the mainstream social groups or cliques in the school. To gain some acceptance, they became friendly with members of the "Trenchcoat Mafia," a group that wore all-black clothes or military fatigues and at times long coats reminiscent of the Gestapo. The two shooters also became very interested in Hitler, reflecting their deepening racist and anti-Semitic attitudes. They got into trouble with the law in their junior year, breaking into a car and being sentenced to a year of community service.

continues

Some of the football players viewed the Trenchcoat Mafia as "losers," and a number of the jocks made fun of the way this group dressed, while others pushed them against the lockers and called them "fags." Although the shooters may not have been fully integrated into the Mafia, they seem to have identified with this group of outsiders and their antagonism toward athletes. They created a tape for a video-production class in which they cast students as gunmen in long coats who shot athletes in the hallway of the school. Furthermore, Harris's website and emails hinted at violence on April 20, Hitler's birthday, indicating it was a day for "something big." "Kill 'em AALLL!!!" it said. During their killing siege, Klebold and Harris said they were looking for anyone wearing a white ball cap, which was an identifying marker of the Columbine athletes, and one of the shooters screamed, "All jocks are dead. All jocks stand up. Any jock wearing a white baseball cap stand up!" (Wilson 2002:216) before he began shooting.

It is not unusual for male athletes to play a dominant role in high school social circles (Nixon and Frey 1996:127), for them to pick on nonathletes, or for athletes in contact sports to look down on athletes in other sports. The violence at Columbine High School is relatively unusual, but it reflects serious tensions in social relations between male jocks and nonathletes outside their subculture, and it shows how these tensions may escalate for the "losers" (that is, "non-jocks" or "nerds") when they are socially rejected, are unable to fit into the mainstream of the high school culture, have no constructive outlets for their frustrations and resentment, and are involved in activities such as video games and Internet communication that exacerbate these feelings and encourage violence. Wilson's (2002) analysis helps us see these connections more clearly.

He examined the online "anti-jock" movement, which consisted of self-described outsiders who used anti-jock websites and emails to express their hostility toward people and institutions in society that inflated the importance of hypermasculine contact sports and the athletes who played them. Since the Internet links members of this movement, it has the potential to be global, and Wilson found that these anti-jock sentiments crossed national borders. This movement included youths who targeted the athletes who were members of these hypermasculine sports subcultures, whom they called "jocks." Wilson portrayed the rampage at Columbine High School as at least partially an act of vengeance against jock "bullies" who harassed social outsiders, which made it a violent manifestation of the movement he was studying. His analysis pointed to the bullying by the athletes as well as the increasing social marginalization and related hostile attitudes of the shooters as precipitating factors in the Columbine incident. That is, there may have been a social dynamic in which the privileged status of male athletes in popular sports made some of those outside this jock culture resent them and feel some degree of alienation as students at this school. In fact, some parents and students reportedly perceived certain jocks as being indulged by school officials and many other students, who overlooked their criminal convictions, abusive behavior toward some of their classmates, and racial and homophobic bullying (Wilson 2002:208). For example, the homecoming king was a football player who was on probation for burglary. Permissiveness toward this kind of behavior by star athletes could have fueled the anger, resentment, and, ultimately, the violence by less-privileged members of the student body, such as Klebold and Harris.

Wilson reminds us that most young people who exist on the margins of the social cliques in high schools find nonviolent ways to deal with harassment by jock bullies and with the general lack of recognition of their nonsports talents and achievements. For example, he cited Walker's (1988) study of an Australian inner-city boys' school in which three of the nonathletes reacted to their school's strong emphasis on sports by taking over the school newspaper. He also cited Foley's (1990) research about ethnic and racial tensions in school sports. Foley found that football players often made fun of male members of the school band as "band fags" and questioned their manhood. Taunting their weaker classmates reinforced the status of the more "macho" athletes in the jock-dominated social hierarchy of the school. However, Foley also observed that the jocks sometimes displayed their dominant position by showing restraint in relations with less-athletic and "less-masculine" classmates. Furthermore, a number of unathletic males avoided bullying and being relegated to outsider status by playing less-aggressive sports, by hanging around with jocks and helping them with their homework, or by being in rock-and-roll bands and doing drugs. Others, however, were loners and were labeled as "nerds" or "weirdos." There were also working-class Latino rebels at the school he studied who were overtly "anti-jock." They preferred being "hip" and using drugs and frequently intimidated spectators at football games and tried to "hit on" females from other towns. Thus, Foley's research suggests that not all jocks are bullies and that bullies may not be jocks. At Columbine High School in 1999, however, it appears that jock culture was more dominant than at the schools that Walker and Foley studied. One former Columbine student referred to "jock elitism" at his high school and to substantial hostility between cliques there as more present than at other schools in the area. He believed that athletes thought they could do or say whatever they wanted (Wilson 2002:216).

Wilson's article was about one type of response to the dominance of jock culture—that is, the production and consumption of anti-jock websites and web magazines, or "webzines." The more thoughtful and constructive webzines tended to focus on creating a community to oppose jock culture, but a number of personal websites focused on negative experiences with jocks and expressions of anger toward them, even identifying with the rage of the Columbine shooters in some cases. In combination, though, the social movement represented by these anti-jock Internet networks was generally interpreted by Wilson as an attempt to challenge and change the dominance of a hypermasculine sports culture and of "jocks" in many realms of society, including high school. Wilson suggested that, despite the U.S. stamp on the Columbine tragedy, the elements of this story could have international relevance to those trying to understand and deal with adolescent bullying behavior and other excesses of the jock culture. If the violence at Columbine can be explained by a lack of constructive outlets for frustration and anger with the dominant culture of the high school, including the jock culture, then access to Internet sites that provide constructive nonviolent ways of challenging and changing bullying behavior and other excesses of the jock culture might channel frustrations, anger, and resentment toward jocks and other dominant youth cliques or subcultures into more socially constructive actions.

social relations may have played a significant role in triggering the violence at Columbine. The research portion of this feature shows that although the reactions are rarely as violent as Columbine, hostility toward the "jock culture" among adolescents is not uncommon, which implies that the existence of sports subcultures in broader adolescent subcultural contexts can have complex socialization consequences for nonathletes as well as athletes.

Citizenship and Nationalism

From 1960 to 1964, George Davis coached the St. Helena High School football team to a then California state record of forty-five consecutive wins (Amdur 1971; Nixon and Frey 1996:131–133). Although Davis cared about winning, he was also committed to teaching his players lessons about being a citizen in a democracy. Believing that an important part of his role as a high school coach was to be an educator, he wanted his players to understand that citizenship involved active participation in decision making and both individual and shared responsibility for getting things done. His lessons about democracy involved having his players vote for the starting lineup and allowing them to decide what positions they should play and to provide input about their roles during competition.

Since George Davis's players had little or no prior experience with this kind of responsibility beyond their informal games on the playground, we can understand why they initially reacted with some reluctance and uncertainty. However, opposition from parents and fans to this experiment in democracy seems more surprising. It appears that those who opposed this experiment perceived it more as a coach abandoning his responsibility than as an educator teaching about democracy. Even winning was not enough to offset expectations that sport should teach boys about accepting adult authority rather than about learning how to exercise authority responsibly themselves. The backlash faced by George Davis raises questions about the extent to which adults cared about having high school athletics serve educational purposes during the 1960s when he was coaching. Limited evidence of similar experiments since the 1960s indicates that adult expectations about the lessons learned about democracy and authority from high school team sports have not changed much since then.

Even though it seems that parents, fans, and high school coaches generally have not embraced George Davis–like experiments in democracy, his players ultimately learned how important it was for them to trust in each other, accept peer leadership, and share responsibility for the team's success. George Davis believed that his players would become better citizens if they learned about the importance of these aspects of shared decision making on the football field. Recent research has suggested that simply being a participant in high school sports may have a moderate positive effect on a number of aspects of civic engagement. Even though high school sports participation rarely involves the kinds of responsibilities George Davis expected of his players, students' being involved in a school activity such as sports is potentially important for democracy in the United States because it counteracts a well-documented general decline in political and community involvement since the 1960s (Putnam 2000). Democracy depends on civic participation, and high school sports may provide a kind of lesson in civic participation that promotes or encourages other kinds of extracurricular civic engagement for at least some students.

The extensive involvement of children, adolescents, and adults in youth sports programs could be viewed as a significant countertrend to the pattern of declining involvement in community groups and organizations in the United States in recent decades. We have already noted the estimated 40 million children and adolescents in youth sports, and many of these children have parents who are also involved in these programs, as administrators, coaches, team managers, and regular spectators and in other leadership and support roles. Furthermore, there has been a pattern of seventeen consecutive *increases* in annual participation rates from 5.3 million to over 7 million participants in high school athletics between 1990 and 2005–2006 (Lopez and Moore 2006; NFHS 2006). This increase admittedly reflects demographic changes such as the echo baby boom, and many of the younger participants and even a number of older ones may participate because of parental pressure. Nevertheless, whatever its extent, sports participation itself should be seen as a kind of community participation where social ties in the community are built and extended.

Carlson, Scott, Planty, and Thompson (2005) found a relationship between participation in high school athletics and that in other extracurricular activities, especially for the elite athletes who were team captains and Most Valuable Players on their teams. There is further evidence that high school athletic participation has civic engagement effects beyond the high school years. For example, Lopez and Moore (2006) analyzed data about high school sports participation and civic engagement from the 2002 National Youth Survey of Civic Engagement. They found that eighteen- to twenty-five-year-olds who had participated in sports while in high school were more likely than nonparticipants to have volunteered, registered to vote, voted in 2000, and said they followed the news closely (especially sports news). Thus, although other studies failed to show a relationship between interscholastic athletic participation and adult political participation (e.g., Glanville 1999; Verba, Scholzman, and Brady 1995:424), it appears from Lopez and Moore's analysis that there may at least be some short-term civic benefits from participation in high school athletics.

We have seen that the possible lessons learned from youth sports participation are many and varied. Some affect how children and youths approach sports, while others may influence the kinds of people young athletes become, the self-concepts and values they develop, and the roles they play and aspire to play both inside and outside sport. Along with these socializing effects of youth sports participation we have already considered, the relationship of high school sports participation to academics has been a prominent focus of educational policymakers and researchers. It will be the primary focus of the next section, about the high school student-athlete in the United States.

The High School Student-Athlete in the United States

Recent research reviews and reports (e.g., Carlson, Scott, Planty, and Thompson 2005; Fullinwider 2006; NASBE 2004) have suggested a number of positive academic outcomes of interscholastic athletic participation, including higher grades, a better academic self-concept, fewer disciplinary problems in school, fewer missed days of school, lower dropout rates, higher tenth-grade standardized test scores, better preparation for college, higher high school graduation rates, higher college attendance and graduation rates, and higher educational aspirations two years after high school for athletes than for their nonathlete counterparts. These outcomes may be related to the level of athletic commitment in an interesting way. For example, athletes who identify themselves as "jocks" and see themselves as *more committed* to sports *may not do as well academically* as other athletes who do not identify themselves as jocks (Miller, Melnick, Barnes, Farrell, and Sabo 2005).

Despite the qualification concerning the possibly negative academic effects of being too serious about sports, existing data show that high school athletes *generally* seem to be better students than their nonathlete counterparts on various measures. Since there apparently are qualifications, though, we must ask *why* and *for whom* sports participation has positive academic or educational benefits. Fullinwider (2006:16) cited possible answers to the "why" question, which were suggested by other researchers. One possible explanation is the idea that being on a high school team increases students' respect for their school and its academic values. Another is that being on the team links students to important social networks, enhances their status, and encourages character traits that collectively contribute to more academic commitment and success.

A fairly straightforward explanation of differences in grades, school attendance, graduation rates, and postsecondary educational aspirations is that unlike their nonathlete counterparts, athletes are motivated to meet certain academic standards to remain athletically eligible. The concern raised in the past by some critics that black high school athletes from the inner city were forsaking academics to pursue athletics is somewhat allayed by the facts that athletes must have passing grades in all or most of their academic courses to be able to play high school sports in many public school districts and that they must meet increasingly tougher initial academic eligibility standards to qualify for college athletics. Athletics may be especially important for students from less socially and economically advantaged backgrounds who lack academic motivation from other sources, such as the family and peers in their community. We are reminded of Edwards's appeal to young black athletes in poor communities to continue to nurture their athletic dreams, but to do so with their eyes open about what it takes academically to play college sports or succeed in life in general.

Research by Eitle and Eitle (2002) suggests that to be able to benefit from their high school experience, high school students from less-advantaged backgrounds need to keep their eyes focused on activities that give them an opportunity to develop *cultural capital*. Athletics may not be one of these activities. The Eitles defined "cultural capital" in the high school context as elements of the middle-class lifestyle that were distinct from elements of the lifestyles of the lower and working classes. Cultural capital such as cultural trips to museums and art galleries and classes such as art, dance, and music enabled students to do better in middle-class institutions such as the school, which place special value on these kinds of practices. Middle-class students have more cultural capital of other types as well, such as more educational resources at home.

The Eitles found that being more culturally disadvantaged and being less involved in activities such as classes that increased cultural capital were associated with relatively higher rates of participation in football and basketball for the males they studied. It appears that male students from disadvantaged backgrounds and with less cultural capital in school may become more dependent than their more-advantaged classmates on sports such as basketball and football for their opportunities and status, even though such participation may not enhance their academic achievement. It may be that for high school boys from disadvantaged backgrounds, accumulating cultural capital from school-sponsored cultural trips and cultural classes may have more of an educational payoff than the social connections or social capital and status gained from playing prominent sports such as football and basketball. To the extent that students from less-advantaged backgrounds trade opportunities to accumulate cultural capital for participation in certain sports, they may pay the price of not building the kind of educational motivation and background needed for better academic achievement.

The commission cited earlier in this chapter that was established by the National Association of State Boards of Education (NASBE) to study high school athletics proposed that state boards of education needed to consider policies and programs that made students, especially those from minority backgrounds, aware of the limitations of concentrating exclusively on sports and neglecting their studies (NASBE 2004). The commission proposed a reform agenda with sixteen recommendations to try to strengthen the connection between high school athletics and educational purposes. The recommendations encouraged broadening the number and range of sports opportunities for high school students and including students with different levels of athletic talent and commitment.

Even if we acknowledge that high school athletic participation has several benefits for student-athletes, we still might ask whether public investment in athletics in the school is justified. The United States is unusual in its emphasis on athletics in the school. Although athletics is only 1 percent to 3 percent of public education spending in the United States, as some have estimated (see NASBE 2004), this spending has an *opportunity cost*. That is, money spent on athletics is money not spent elsewhere. A study of athletic budgets and academic performance in Texas showed that where school districts spend relatively more on athletics, overall student academic performance is lower (Meier, Eller, Marchbanks, Robinson, Polinard, and Wrinkle 2004). Thus, athletic participation may have positive educational benefits for some students in some sports, but nonathletes seemed to suffer in school districts that spent relatively more on athletics. Furthermore, since school budgets differ a great deal across districts and states, poorer districts and schools are likely to provide fewer and poorer-quality sports opportunities for their students. If poorer school districts try to keep up with more affluent districts in sports funding, other areas of the school budget more central to the academic mission of the school are likely to suffer. While many high schools struggle to find enough money to fund high school athletics sufficiently in the context of declining public investment in schools, some schools with big-time teams engage in financial "arms races," trying to outspend their competitors with money raised from generous individual and corporate investors. Eichelberger (2005) wrote about high school fundraising campaigns that generated $2.7 million to give a high school football team new artificial turf and a scoreboard with video replays.

Possible inequities in sports access and opportunities raise a number of public policy questions about youth sports investment. For example, we may ask whether the educational and socialization benefits from high school athletic participation are extensive and important enough to justify public investment in school sports and whether the public interest might be more broadly and better served by investing tax money in public recreation programs outside the school. These kinds of questions are made more salient where high school athletic programs are becoming highly commercialized and increasingly influenced by private interests. We will see in the next section that youth sports policies, programs, and commitments are being shaped in a number of cases by powerful external forces associated with the Golden Triangle.

The Golden Triangle and Making Youth Sports Big-Time

The case of U.S. Youth Soccer enables us to see the organizational structure of a big-time corporate youth sport and how it is connected to the Golden Triangle. U.S. Youth Soccer is a complex bureaucracy, which is ultimately linked to FIFA, the premier governing body in the soccer world. U.S. Youth Soccer is the umbrella organization for a vast network of state and local soccer associations

Crane Technical Prep's Sherron Collins winds up for a dunk during the first round of the McDonald's All American Slam Dunk Contest Monday, March 27, 2006, in San Diego. The McDonald's All American High School Basketball Game illustrates how the Golden Triangle has made high school sports "big time." (AP Photo/Chris Park)

and individual soccer clubs across the nation. The organization sponsors elite age-group competition at the regional, national, and international levels; elite Olympic Development Programs; and major championships in individual states.

Like other big-time youth sports, U.S. Youth Soccer is tied to elements of the Golden Triangle. Its elite international championship is the adidas Cup, which is sponsored by the shoe and apparel manufacturer. Its website provides a link to a media kit for administrators to help them promote their organizations, and it also includes links that provide information about how to become a sponsor and about its current sponsors and strategic partners. The website also has sponsor and strategic partner Internet links. The primary official national sponsors of U.S. Youth Soccer include corporate enterprises such as Burger King, the Fox Soccer Channel, and Kohl's department stores, along with adidas. Its strategic partner links connect the organization to its national commercial sponsors; an official supplier, Kwik Goal, which sponsors major youth soccer workshops and publications; websites for professional soccer leagues and clubs and for referees; national soccer institutions, such as the National Soccer Hall of Fame and the U.S. Soccer Foundation; and the soccer media, such as Fox, *Sports Illustrated*, and other publications.

Parents of children and adolescents with soccer aspirations are exposed to the corporate and commercial structure of the sport as soon as they enroll their child in an officially sanctioned club, program, or workshop sponsored by U.S. Youth Soccer. They quickly learn that success in the sport requires a serious year-round commitment beginning at an early age, and they learn about the many ways they can invest their money and their own time to improve their child's chances for success. Children as young as six or seven play on "travel" clubs, compete in indoor and outdoor leagues and tournaments throughout the year, and have paid coaches, and their parents may make substantial financial investments in coaches, trainers, referees, registration, team and tournament fees, summer camps, rental of facilities, equipment, clothing, and travel. Referees and even volunteer coaches are required or expected to attend certification workshops and clinics, and local associations and clubs often have elected officers and a board responsible for enforcement and administration of league and club policies; managers who handle finances, logistics, and paperwork; and support from local sponsors as well as coaches and referees.

In many youth sports, such as tennis, golf, gymnastics, swimming, figure skating, and ice hockey as well as soccer, mobility up to the elite levels often requires participation in clubs and competition outside the school. In sports such as basketball, football, and baseball in the United States, high school sports participation typically has been viewed as a valuable and necessary step to becoming a college and professional athlete. Popular high school sports programs are increasingly developing the characteristics of big-time sports, including the early professionalization of their athletes, private funding, and national-level competition, which attract major commercial sponsors and media. This type of structure of nonschool and school sports has enabled talented young athletes to develop into stars and move up through the ranks into major college, Olympic, and professional sports.

Competition between serious club sports programs and high school sports programs to gain the commitment of talented young athletes seems to be increasing, and the "eroding" relationship between community-based club sports programs and high school athletics was one of the significant issues raised by the NASBE (2004) commission. While commission members appreciated the possibility of experiencing fair competition and teamwork and developing achievement motivation in organized youth sports programs, they worried about the pressure toward specialization created by community-based club sports programs, such as Amateur Athletic Union (AAU)–sponsored programs. They realized that with 500,000 participants in 34 sports and with 250 national championships and over 10,000 local events, these programs had become a formidable force in youth sports. While the AAU's philosophy of "Sports for All, Forever" is supposedly shared by all of its participants and its 50,000 volunteers, its elite programs with major corporate sponsors tend to encourage only the best to play and to concentrate on a single sport throughout the year.

The influence of big-time, community-based club sports programs is illustrated by the case of a 16-year-old, 6-foot-10-inch, 245-pound rising star, Renardo Sidney (Prisbell 2006). He was unable to play for his high school team after transferring to a private school because he could not satisfy state eligibility standards. However, as a star in a highly competitive AAU summer league, he was still able to gain national attention. His success attracted the interest of college recruiters who wanted to offer him an athletic scholarship, sports agents who hoped to sign him in the future, shoe companies that sponsored touring teams and tournaments and had endorsement contracts waiting for him if he continued to excel, and AAU coaches who wanted him on their team. As a result of his AAU success, he focused his attention on the AAU competition rather than on high school basketball, and his father believed he had "outgrown" high school athletics. His family had moved to Los Angeles, where he could play for the top-ranked high school team in California, but he was more focused on playing for the Southern California All-Stars, an AAU team sponsored by Reebok. He was working out with NBA players and former college stars at a local athletic club. His father, a onetime financially struggling school security guard, became a much better-paid "consultant" for Reebok. He was also offered a fee by a number of colleges to run basketball camps at their school. In writing about this case, journalist Eric Prisbell (2006) observed that Renardo Sidney was caught between the worlds of a teenager and a quasi-professional.

Although Renardo Sidney's case may be exceptional, it illustrates a number of key elements of elite youth sports, which are increasingly characterizing high school athletics as well as big-time club sports. They been described by a number of journalists (e.g., Bresnahan 2005; Ryan 2005; Tye 2005; Wolff 2002) and include: (1) professionalization of athletes involving sport specialization, year-round training and competition, living and training at sports academies among the most promising athletes, and pursuit of competition at increasingly higher levels of intensity; (2) overuse injuries related to specialization and intense training while young bodies are still developing; (3) paid coaches who place a very strong emphasis on winning and expect a single-minded commitment to their team, even among young children; (4) elite high school teams with players recruited from other communities, including, in some cases, players recruited illegally across school districts; (5) extensive travel; (6) eating disorders among female athletes; (7) corporate sponsorship of a selected elite of high school sports teams by companies such as Nike; and (8) parents who embrace the "brass ring theory," which is that their child's intense devotion to sport will result in a college athletic scholarship and/or, ultimately, a lucrative professional sports career.

We can see much evidence of the imprint of the Golden Triangle on this big-time youth sports world. For example, top high school sports programs in boys' basketball participate in nationally televised games; receive fees plus expense money to play in these games; and generate equipment contracts for themselves, broadcast rights fees for ESPN and regional sports networks, and investment from corporate sponsors (Wertheim and Dohrmann 2006). In addition, *Sports Illustrated* ranks the top high school athletic programs in the United States and *USA Today* ranks the "Super 25" U.S. high school basketball teams, just as *U.S. News & World Report* ranks top colleges. In addition, young athletes have been drawn into "sneaker wars," in which recruiters representing sneaker manufacturers such as Nike, adidas, and Reebok have competed for talented young athletes to play for the amateur teams they represent (Boston Globe 2006; Hohler 2006a, 2006b, 2006c). This commercial competition has exposed young athletes to significant pressures and dubious practices, with recruiters focusing on increasingly younger players and criticizing coaches for putting more emphasis on studying than on sports. Some of the coaches and promoters involved with travel teams acknowledged paying young basketball players for expenses that were not related to their sport, which could later jeopardize their National Collegiate Athletic Association (NCAA) eligibility.

One of the socialization lessons for talented young athletes and their families is that boys and girls with athletic talent in certain sports are valuable commodities for corporate sponsors, appealing subjects for the mass media, a source of revenue for sports academies and camps, and a vehicle for professional coaches and trainers and elite sports programs to enhance their status and careers. Even talented athletes in elementary school may draw the interest of the Golden Triangle, as the case of a ten-year-old basketball prospect in the Baltimore area showed (Saslow 2006d). Such players could look forward to being ranked by college recruiting websites as fifth graders. Thus, the social world of this boy involved the possibility of national attention in elementary school, special coaches to hone his skills, and overtures from a number of AAU coaches and local private school recruiters. The young prospect's father wanted him to be "comfortable and carefree" and "a little kid at home," but he also told his son he had to be serious, "an impact player" on the court, and not waste his big chance at sports success. His mother was acutely aware that her son was only ten years old and that many people wanted to "buy" him. She wanted people to know that her son was "not for sale," but the world of youth sports constructed by the Golden Triangle transforms talented athletes of any age into commodities.

When an athlete from a low-income family has exceptional talent and plays a highly commercialized sport, a family's limited resources may not pose an obstacle to participation in elite youth sports when the young athlete can attract sponsors. However, being affluent enables a family to subsidize the big-time sports aspirations of less-talented young athletes or their parents. For example, Alsever (2006) wrote about a young baseball player whose parents spent $30,000 between the time he was ten and the time he was sixteen for coaches, private trainers, performance tests, baseball camps, tournaments, and travel with elite teams to advance his career prospects. He was the starting catcher on his high school team, but he had no guarantee that his parents' investment would pay off. Children and adolescents from less-affluent families with equivalent but not exceptional talent do not have the same opportunities for access to elite sports development as their peers, and without expensive sports training and private sports club experience, they may even be at a disadvantage in competing for a place on their high school teams. Thus, social class is likely to be a significant filter in access to participation in certain high school sports as well as elite youth sports in general.

The sports network in which the Golden Triangle draws talented young prospects from various backgrounds into a big-time realm of youth sports is global, which we can see from a recent series of articles about young Nigerian boys with dreams of playing in the NBA. Saslow (2006a, 2006b, 2006c) showed how the path from a one-bedroom apartment in Enugu, Nigeria, to the United States could include stops in Lagos, Nigeria, Senegal, France, and Belgium, as young basketball hopefuls try to join the nearly fifty of their countrymen on NCAA men's basketball teams. As Saslow observed, young Nigerian prospects were treated as commodities by the various coaches, scouts, and middlemen who hoped to profit from these prospects if they became college and NBA stars. Even though it was a violation of NCAA rules, U.S. colleges paid Nigerian coaches about $5,000 for each talented player they identified and delivered. One coach alleged that approximately half of the colleges paid for this service because the international market for players had become so competitive. Some players tried to market themselves, even though they often needed help to deal with visa problems. A number of these players first play for U.S. high schools as a stepping-stone to playing in college, and they hope at least to be able to return home with a college degree if their professional basketball dream does not become a reality.

When promising young athletes, from Nigeria or the United States, learn that their "commodity value" no longer attracts interest, as many will ultimately learn, their adjustment to being more ordinary athletes or even nonathletes will depend on how much of themselves they have invested in their American Sports Dream. For all but a relatively few athletes, serious sports involvement ends in adolescence. Those who have thought of themselves only as athletes and have dreamed only of a future in sport are likely to have difficulty dealing with the transition from seeing themselves as star athletes with a promising future to also-rans and, ultimately, former athletes (Adler and Adler 1991). They are not likely to be as prepared for the future as their "non-jock" peers are, especially if they have sacrificed their studies and other opportunities to accumulate educational and cultural capital outside sport. In addition, they may have to deal with the lingering effects of having sacrificed their bodies to pursue their big-time sports dream.

Parental Influence in Youth Sports

Parents influence the vulnerability of their children to the costs of big-time youth sports. Even in extreme sports, which are sometimes characterized as countercultural, young stars and their parents face choices between the "normal" life of a teenager and competing at increasingly higher and more demanding levels of their sport. For example, Higgins (2006) reported on young stars in extreme sports, which he called "new sports," such as skateboarding, snowboarding, surfing, and motocross racing. These young athletes are choosing between being regular high school students and concentrating on their sport. Being serious athletes in these sports might involve home schooling, attending a sports academy, pursuing independent study, or dropping out of school entirely. In some cases, parents seemed more interested in their child's commercial success than in their chance to grow up more normally as teenagers. In one case, a young professional skateboarder dropped out of his sport for six months to be "a regular high school student" and do things such as hang around with friends, go to dances, and participate in school sports, but his mother, who was his manager, remarked, "He was out of circulation for six months, out of the magazines. It hurt his career" (Higgins 2006).

A number of studies cited by Hedstrom and Gould (2004) provide a general picture of parental influence in youth sports. For example, parents, and especially fathers, are the most important influence shaping the sports experiences of their children, and children's initial and continuing involvement in sport tends to reflect their parents' perceived interest in their involvement. Winning matters more to children when the outcome matters more to their significant others, such as parents, and children enjoy sports more when they perceive less pressure from their parents. Although in one survey cited by Hedstrom and Gould, coaches in a variety of high school sports frequently cited parents as a problem, other researchers they cited found both positive and negative influences of parents on their children's experiences in youth sports. The major problems parents pose for their children are putting too much emphasis on winning, having unrealistic expectations, coaching their own child, and either criticizing or pampering their child.

Parents whose children are truly talented athletes face the dilemma of all parents with gifted children. They must choose between exposing their talented child to the sacrifices, pressures, and rewards of pursuing their talent on the one hand and, on the other hand, trying to protect their child from these influences so that he or she can grow up as a more normal teenager. When they allow or encourage their child to pursue success in big-time youth sports, responsible parents have to figure out how to provide the guidance and emotional support needed for their child to cope successfully with both stardom and disappointment and with the multiple pressures in the highly competitive and corporate world of big-time youth sports. Parents who are less protective of their athletic children, want them to be stars, and are less concerned about their children's interests than their own may allow them to be exploited or may view their children as commodities to be used for their own or their family's benefit. The resistance to exploitation may be more difficult for lower-income families. However, the lure of the big time, especially when it involves the temptations of hype, fame, and material inducements from the Golden Triangle, can affect young athletes and their families across the social class spectrum.

Dropout and Access Issues in Youth Sports

It is easy to picture children and adolescents who crumble emotionally or physically in the face of pressure from parents, coaches, or the demands of the sport itself and leave sport disappointed, dispirited, or turned off by sport. In fact, research suggests that young people are more likely to quit sports because their interests have moved on to other things than because their sports experience was perceived as negative (Fullinwider 2006:9). Quitting sports is most common around the ages of eleven and twelve, and it continues throughout adolescence. By the age of thirteen, 75 percent of children who participated in sport in the United States have dropped out, and approximately 35 percent of youth participants drop out of their sport each year, although some drop out of one sport and pursue another (Fullinwider 2006:9; Hedstrom and Gould

2004:22). The main reasons researchers found to explain dropout rates in school and nonschool sports are, first, lost interest in the sport and, after that, lack of fun, perceptions of the coach as biased or a poor teacher, and the desire to participate in other activities. According to research (Hedstrom and Gould 2004:23–24), dropouts have tended to be critical of an excessive emphasis on winning, insufficient playing time, and limited opportunities to develop their skills, which were generally blamed on coaches. Females are more turned off than their male counterparts by a perceived overemphasis on winning and were more likely to experience physical and emotional traumas in sport. They tend to be interested in the social aspects of sport, such as relationships and comparisons with teammates, rather than in winning. Research also has shown that African-American and Latino dropouts from youth sports have been more likely than their Caucasian counterparts to cite an overemphasis on winning, needing time to study, and the perceived inadequacies of the coach as a teacher as reasons for leaving sport (Hedstrom and Gould 2004:24).

It is important to try to understand why children and adolescents drop out of sport, especially when it is related to how adults organize sports and the amount of pressure parents put on their children to succeed. However, we must remember that as sport becomes more elite, young people are increasingly likely to be cut rather than quit. Furthermore, the chance to participate varies a great deal between poorer and more affluent areas. For example, Ewing and her associates (2002:41) observed that compared with a 75 to 80 percent rate of childhood sports participation in the suburbs, only 10 percent of children in the inner city of Detroit participated in sport. Fullinwider (2006:14–15) pointed out that poor urban communities tend to have limited public funds to support community sports programs, and their high school sports programs tend to be underfunded and to rely on poor facilities and equipment. He also cited research showing how opportunities for physical activities outside of school are severely restricted in these poor communities by factors such as unsafe places to play, parents and other caregivers who do not have time to supervise or encourage these kinds of activities, cramped housing, and few examples of adults and older children who could serve as role models in these activities.

Thus, for many young people who live in poor communities or whose parents are poor, the questions of whether or not sport is fun and whether sport socialization is beneficial or detrimental to their development are irrelevant because sports participation is not an option. As Edwards has observed for young black males in the inner city, the chance to make it in sport is becoming less realistic as sports opportunities evaporate and as their lives become more detached from the culture and roles of the mainstream. This pattern of restricted access to sport for less-affluent youths is not confined to the United States, as a study in England showed. Collins and Buller (2003) found that opportunities for athletically talented young people to participate in an elite sports development program in cricket, table tennis, and squash were much less available to youths from less-affluent than from more-affluent households. Furthermore, those who participated in the program but were less successful tended to be largely ignored and felt abandoned or neglected. Thus, even though the program was successful in improving the skills and competitive success of the most talented young athletes, it also raised issues of access and elitism. As the corporate emphasis in youth sports increases, these issues are likely to become more widespread. The public policy issues are how to create, fund, and run enough sports programs to meet the needs of boys and girls of varying ages and levels of ability and from diverse social backgrounds.

For one often-neglected U.S. minority, American Indians, new youth sports opportunities are being created by an interesting recent development in the fortunes of this ethnic group. With substantial revenue from gambling operations on their reservations, upstate New York Indian tribes have been able to create a lacrosse league for one thousand American Indian players aged three to twenty (Hu 2007). They were able to hire coaches and referees, purchase equipment, and restore playing fields to provide high-quality sports opportunities to many children and youths who would otherwise not have had the chance to play this traditional Indian game in organized competition. Lacrosse was a sport of elite prep schools and a limited number of colleges and universities for many years, but in recent years it has become one of the fastest-growing sports in the United States (Hu 2007). The financial windfall from gambling enabled the New York Indian tribes to regain their cultural heritage as well as to provide chances for their young people to play this increasingly popular sport. Although the lacrosse program of the "North American Minor Lacrosse Association" was seen by its organizers more as a cultural investment than as an elite youth sports program, some lacrosse experts anticipated a stream of American Indian lacrosse players into four-year colleges in the coming years (Hu 2007). If so, it would reverse a well-entrenched pattern of ignoring American Indians in college athletic recruiting and of near invisibility of American Indians in college sports, which Simpson (1987) reported earlier and we noted in chapter four. In this case, Indians would be playing "their" game.

Conclusion: Socialization and Youth Sports in a Changing World

What can we conclude about the socialization of children and adolescents in and through sports? First, even though participation is not evenly distributed across social groups in countries such as the United States, a large number of young people participate in sport every year. Second, participation drops off substantially beginning with the onset of adolescence. Third, the nature, pressures, and rewards of sports participation vary considerably, depending on how good boys and girls are at their sport and how successful they are in competition. Fourth, youths are exposed to a number of possible types of socializing lessons in sport, about gender and social class; gender and race; class, race, and ethnicity in high school athletics; sexual orientation; disability; character and adult expectations; and citizenship and nationalism. In most cases, the lessons that are internalized from sport tend to reproduce the culture and social structure of sport and the larger society, but young sports participants also find that they have to learn to adjust to frustrations and disappointments and adapt to challenges and opportunities. When their sports roles and experiences become especially meaningful for them and they are expected to view them seriously, young people may find that their self-concept and view of the social world are influenced by sport. Fifth, young people may derive a number of academic and social benefits from high school sports participation, but the nature of their sports experience and its outcomes are likely to be filtered by their social status and backgrounds. Sixth, youth sports are becoming increasingly professionalized and commercialized, with the influence of the Golden Triangle becoming increasingly prevalent with the expansion of big-time youth sports in high school and nonschool settings. Whether or not athletically talented young people enjoy big-time sports and continue to participate depends on a variety of factors, including their level of success and the influence of adults, such as their parents. As sports become more elite, corporate, and commercialized in high schools, the issue of the relationship of athletics to the school is becoming more salient. Seventh, there are various reasons why increasing numbers of young people leave sport as they get older, but in addition to dropouts, young people who have no access or limited access to adequately supported sports programs pose an important challenge for public policymakers.

As youth sports become more corporate and commercialized and more tied to the Golden Triangle, their relationship to the forces of social change in society becomes more important to explore. An important question in this context is how youth sports are accommodating the increasing diversity of society as they become more influenced by powerful corporate and commercial forces of change in the larger society. Another important question is whether young people will lose interest in sport, drop out of sport, or find fewer opportunities for traditional sports involvement at younger ages as youth sports become more corporate and commercial. A stronger emphasis on high-pressure and highly organized private club sports and high school sports limited to the most talented and most committed could increase interest in alternative recreational activities that young people organize and control. Of course, as in the case of a number of "extreme sports," if these activities become very popular, they may attract the Golden Triangle and be transformed into the types of activities a number of participants sought to escape. The pressures of competing and the importance of winning in sports realms dominated by the Golden Triangle can lead to social deviance among athletes and other sports participants and social problems for sport. Social deviance and social problems are the main focus of the next chapter.

Note

1. The total number of participants here (i.e., over 46 million) is higher than the previously cited estimate of 40 million because the numbers in these various sports categories very likely include boys and girls who are counted more than once because they play more than one type of sport, for example, club sports and high school sports. Fullinwider proposed that the estimated total of 40 million was probably conservative (p. 37).

8

Sport, Social Deviance, and Social Problems

People who subscribe to the Dominant American Sports Creed and accept the idea that sport builds character are likely to believe that athletes and coaches generally do what is expected, right, and good. Furthermore, those who make sports figures their heroes see these people as paragons of virtue to be honored and emulated. We have learned from past chapters, however, that real athletes and coaches frequently fail to meet these ideals of character, conformity, and virtue. Heroic ideals of character are abstractions that would be difficult for any real person to embody, but we will see in this chapter that sport creates temptations, pressures, conflicts, and perhaps even a sense of arrogance that may lead both stars and more ordinary athletes and coaches to break the rules of sport and sometimes even the laws of society and to act in less than noble ways on and off the field. A major focus of this chapter is *social deviance*, which refers to behavior that is perceived to violate the rules or norms of society. Although classical social theorists such as Durkheim have argued that deviance occurs in all societies, it is also true that people in authority generally try to control deviance or give the impression of controlling deviance to maintain order. Furthermore, we tend to look down on people who engage in deviance. In looking at various forms of deviance in this chapter, we will see that perceptions of deviance and reactions to it can be varied or complicated, depending on the nature of the deviance and who is engaging in it.

This chapter is also about social problems created by the impact of recurrent and serious social deviance. *Social problems* are conditions in society that are widely viewed as sources of social disruption, tension, or difficulty for society (Nixon and Frey 1996:99). These conditions are defined by powerful people or organizations, the mass media, and many members of the public as *highly undesirable* because they are perceived as cases of deviance or disruption that challenge the social order *or* because they are conditions of society that cause difficulties or deprivations for broad or less-advantaged segments of the population in a society. Thus, social problems may range from forms of deviance such as violence, drug abuse, and criminal behavior to other undesirable conditions of society mainly affecting less-advantaged people or minorities, such as poverty, illiteracy, racism, sexism, and various environmental problems.

We will be primarily interested in this chapter in *social deviance–related social problems* involving sports participants that are perceived as threats to the social order. We have already considered a range of social problems of prejudice, discrimination, and segregation related to class elitism, sexism, racism, homophobia, and ableism, and we will continue to examine these problems throughout this book as *problems of social inequality*. It is important to recognize that problems of social inequality in society and sport may contribute to various types of deviance-related social problems, including violence, illegal drug use, sexual abuse, and other criminal behavior by athletes, coaches, and sports administrators and spectators. Furthermore, even though sports officials and coaches have a vested interest in maintaining conformity to the rules and social order in their sports, they may implicitly or explicitly contribute to conditions that encourage deviant behavior, such as hazing and drug use by athletes or violence by spectators.

In the last chapter, we considered the conditions of commercialization, professionalization, and the heavy emphasis on specialization and winning in youth sports that largely result from the influence of the Golden Triangle. We also saw how these conditions could contribute to the development of problems of excessive stress, pathogenic dietary practices, physical pain, and disabling injuries among young athletes. Research has suggested that young people are likely to engage in poor sportsmanship, cheating, and other deviant practices when parents and coaches fail to live up to the public messages about good character that they assert. Of course, problems resulting from emphases on commercialization and professionalization and on winning as the sole measure of success in sport are not confined to youth sports. We will see in this and future chapters how these forces of the Golden Triangle and related influences have produced problems in other realms of sport as well, from college athletics to professional sports and the Olympics. In this chapter, we will concentrate on five major types of *deviance-related social problems of sport* concerning: (1) aggression and violence by players and spectators or fans related to sports competition, (2) sexual violence and other crimes by players and coaches outside the sports arena, (3) the use of illegal performance-enhancing drugs (called "doping"), (4) gambling and fixing the outcomes of sports contests, and (5) hazing. In future chapters, we will examine problems such as illegal payments and cheating in the recruitment, subsidization, and academic support of college athletes and political violence and terrorism in the sports arena.

Studying Social Deviance and Social Problems in Sport Sociology

Since social deviance and social problems can undermine social norms, disrupt the social order, and cause harm to people and organizations, understanding deviance and problems in sport is obviously important. However, as Coakley (2007:152–154) has suggested, gaining a clear grasp and accurate understanding of deviance and problems in sport can be challenging. One reason is that the forms and causes of social deviance and social problems in sport vary. This implies that we cannot explain all types of deviance and problems by focusing on a single cultural or social structural factor or by using a single explanatory framework, such as structural functionalism or conflict theory. Furthermore, the same type of deviance, such as doping, could occur for different reasons in different sports settings and could be explained by different theories. Another reason is that a number of types of acceptable or expected behavior in sport are deviant or problematic elsewhere in society. Consider the example of boxing. You would be arrested on the street for doing what boxers do to each other in the ring. In some sports, such as National Hockey League (NHL) hockey, players and officials are discovering that the boundary between the ice and the laws of society may be breaking down, with a few cases of players being criminally charged for assaulting other players with their sticks during the course of a game. Sometimes behavior that is permitted in the broader society is considered deviant in sport. For example, a student-athlete might be benched for missing classes because a coach or athletic department has rules requiring class attendance, while his or her classmates suffer no penalty for their absences because their professor does not have attendance requirements.

It may seem odd, but people could be considered deviant or their behavior could be problematic because they conform too much rather than not enough. Coakley (2007:157–160) distinguished between *deviant overconformity*, which involves conforming too much, and *deviant underconformity*, which involves not conforming enough. Deviant underconformity is what we usually view, and will view in this book, as social deviance. We have given many examples of it, such as crime, sexual assault, and illegal drug use. Deviant overconformity is not usually viewed as deviance because people are generally doing what they are expected to do, but this conformity becomes overconformity when it exceeds the boundary for normal or acceptable behavior and becomes risky or dangerous. For example, an athlete who is expected by coaches to "train hard" in the off-season may overconform and hurt herself by training too many hours a day and pushing her body too hard. Or, coaches may devote so many hours to their sport that they sacrifice personal relationships with family and friends, and high school or college athletes may devote so much time to sport that they hurt their performance in school.

In some cases, an intense desire to do what is expected or needed to succeed could lead to deviant behavior. Intense coaches frequently implicitly or explicitly exhort their teams to "go the extra mile" and "do whatever it takes" to win. Less-talented athletes may be frustrated that they are not doing enough when even their extreme physical sacrifices are not making them successful, and as a result, "doing whatever it takes" may be interpreted as implying that they must be willing to cross the line into the realm of dubious or illegal practices, including cheating and doping, to help them succeed. Coaches who are highly committed to winning because they know it is necessary to keep their job may be similarly influenced to engage in deviant recruiting practices to bring in the athletes needed to win when legal recruiting is not successful enough.

The increasing influence of science, technology, and medicine in sports training and performance has pushed athletes and sport into new and uncharted territory. In the second chapter, we noted Hoberman's (1992) critique of these developments in sport as elements of the rationalization of sport, which has turned athletes into "mortal engines." The new "robots" of sport use new medications, new therapeutic strategies, and new equipment and other technologies to heal, rehabilitate, and strengthen their bodies and to improve their training and performance. Sports officials are constantly faced with the challenge of determining what makes competition "fair."

With a steady stream of experimentation and innovations, it can be difficult to know whether particular practices are acceptable or fair and should be permitted by the rules. For example, the question of whether or not it is fair to allow athletes with disabilities to compete in the mainstream with wheelchairs or prosthetic limbs is especially perplexing. These athletes have historically been excluded from the mainstream of sport, but the technology that allows them to compete in the mainstream may give them an advantage over able-bodied competitors. Thus, the effort to use technology to overcome the problem of exclusion of athletes with disabilities from sport may create new legal and practical issues and problems concerning access, the rules of competition, and fairness. As athletes and coaches continually push the norms or boundaries of what is acceptable, fair, or permitted in sport, they create new challenges for sports officials who must decide what is allowed and what is not in sport. For sport sociologists, this means that the study of social deviance and social problems is not always straightforward.

Sport sociologists have used various perspectives to try to understand social deviance and social problems in sport. We will consider *four different perspectives*: structural functionalism, social conflict theory, critical theory, and symbolic interactionism (see Coakley 2007:155–157; Nixon and Frey 1996: 100–103). For *structural functionalists*, social deviance occurs when people fail to conform enough and threaten the social order. Merton (1938, 1957) proposed a *social strain* approach, which conceptualized social conformity and deviance in terms of the compatibility of people's beliefs and actions with widely accepted cultural goals and values and institutionalized social norms and roles in society. In this framework, conformity exists when beliefs are compatible with established cultural goals or values, and actions are compatible with institutionalized norms and roles. For example, people in the United States conform when they embrace the values of the American Dream and work hard in school and their job to become an occupational and financial success. Social deviance can take a number of different forms, when people fail to accept cultural goals or values or fail to act according to institutionalized norms and roles. For example, people engage in the form of deviance called *innovation* by Merton when they embrace established cultural goals and values, such as winning in sport, but engage in behavior, such as cheating, that violates institutionalized norms and roles. *Ritualism* is a type of deviance in which people follow the rules but do not care about the prevailing goals or values in their group, organization, or society. Scholarship athletes may become ritualists in their senior year when they faithfully do what their coach expects of them so that they can keep their scholarship and graduate but do not care whether their team wins or loses, perhaps because they no longer see much playing time or because they have become bored or burned out by too many years of practices and games.

Structural functionalists usually see the causes of deviance in flawed or inadequate socialization in which people do not learn, understand, or accept what they are expected to do, or in structural factors such as strong role expectations or conflicting role demands that lead to the types of social strain that were identified by Merton. Since structural functionalists tend to emphasize the importance of social order, they also focus on *social control*, which involves efforts to reduce or eliminate social deviance and social problems in order to reinforce the importance of conformity and preserve the existing social order. From this perspective, social control strategies in sport could involve creating new policies or rules to deal with a type of deviance, such as steroid use, that has escalated to the point of becoming a serious social problem in a sport. Social control in sport also could involve making the enforcement of certain norms stricter or more consistent, as when basketball referees are told to call more fouls when there is contact under the basket. Or, officials in a sport may develop ways of detecting and punishing more norm violators, as in the case of implementing new drug testing procedures in a sport. Sports officials also may try to create more awareness of the norms and the consequences of not conforming to them. For example, they may warn players that first-time violators of a league's new and tougher drug policies will be punished.

Instead of focusing on the importance of social conformity to maintain social order and to avoid the disruptiveness of social deviance, *social conflict theorists* tend to look at social conformity and deviance in terms of their relationship to the interests of different social classes. From a social conflict perspective, the dominant normative structure of society, including the legal system, is seen as a biased reflection of dominant class interests, and social deviance is essentially violating the rules, regulations, and laws of the dominant class. Thus, social deviance is behavior that threatens or disrupts the dominant classes, and more privileged and powerful people are likely to favor the tough prosecution of laws and other established norms to protect their own interests. While structural functionalists tend to see social control as a means to maintain social order for the good of the sport in general and everyone involved in it, social conflict theorists would be more likely to see social control as a means to protect the narrower interests of the power structure of sport, which we have called the Golden Triangle. Thus, according to a social conflict theorist, maintaining social conformity and social order in a sport keeps players and coaches in their place and unruly fans under control. For example, players who speak out about the unfairness, oppressiveness, or incompetence of coaches or coaches who complain about lack of support from general managers or owners may be branded as "troublemakers" who are not "team players" and find themselves demoted, waived, traded, or fired. A sport under control preserves the prestige and profitability of the sport for the owners, investors, officials, and sponsors who constitute the Golden Triangle, and being "under control" means that control of the sport remains firmly in the hands of those at the top of the power structure.

From a social conflict perspective, the norms of sport reflect the interests of those with the most power, and some of these norms pose risks or dangers for athletes. For example, the hegemonic sports culture in the United States makes risk, pain, and injury seem normal or even heroic (Nixon 1993). In this kind of cultural context, players may be pushed to overconform by training harder and harder and hitting their opponents with more and more force, which ultimately will lead to injuries for many of them. Although most coaches and officials in pro football, for example, would acknowledge, in principle, that high injury rates are a problem in their sport and argue that they try to limit the number of injuries, the popularity of their sport benefits from a high intensity of training and physical contact, which leads to injuries. High injury rates are a problem for them in terms of the public image of the sport. Although they do not want to see their top players hurt and out of action, they have replacement players to keep fans watching. A social conflict theorist might argue that high injury rates are a more serious problem for players than for coaches and management in their sport because serious injuries or the accumulation of injuries over a career can reduce a player's effectiveness, end his or her career, and lead to chronic disabilities. Putting aside the issue of how much football players and other athletes are rewarded for their physical sacrifices, what is relevant to consider from a social conflict perspective is that players have little choice about taking physical risks and making sacrifices if they want to play. Whether or not they play and how they play the game are decisions made by others who use their power to exploit players.

The differences between structural functionalists and social conflict theorists regarding social deviance and social problems should be apparent. Structural functionalists define deviance as the failure to conform to established norms and typically view rule violators as disruptive and even immoral, while social conflict theorists define deviance as behavior that violates the interests of people with economic power and typically view rule violators as exploited victims of a biased normative and social control structure. We can see why structural functionalists are likely to focus on social problems as cases of extensive rule breaking that threaten the established social order, while social conflict theorists are likely to focus on social problems as matters of inequality that represent oppression or exploitation of people with lower status and less power. From a structural functional perspective, social control is necessary to prevent or minimize social deviance and social problems that disrupt social stability and order in sport and society, whereas from a social conflict perspective, social control is intended to prevent or minimize those forms of social deviance and social problems that threaten the interests of the dominant classes.

Critical theorists remind us that power struggles can result from inequalities in sport, and sometimes these struggles may be related to norms about acceptable and unacceptable behavior. Consider the clash between white owners and minority players in the National Basketball Association (NBA) in which the matter of how players dressed became contested terrain. Concerned about a deviant "hip-hop" or "gangsta" image that might be projected to mostly white fans and white corporate sponsors by the clothing and lifestyle of a number of young black players, NBA officials established a dress code before the 2005 season. The code stipulated that players were required to wear business-casual clothing when engaged in league or team business, sport coats and dress shoes and socks on the bench when not in uniform, and business-casual attire or "neat warm-up suits issued by their team" when leaving the arena. They were explicitly not permitted to wear chains, pendants, or medallions over their clothes; sleeveless shirts; shorts; unapproved T-shirts, jerseys, or sports apparel; sunglasses when indoors; or headphones except when in the locker room or on the team bus or plane (NBA 2007). Some players complained that the dress code was "racist," focusing on young black players whose jewelry, clothing, and lifestyle might be offensive or hostile to the white business class that the NBA targets in its promotions and advertising. They argued that how players dressed did not necessarily reflect their character, and pointed to well-dressed businesspeople, such as Enron executives, who had committed serious crimes (Associated Press 2005). In an instructive statement about the nature of power and social control in the NBA, in other sports, and in the larger society, a player who opposed the dress code and believed it was racist nevertheless said, "You have to listen to the people who employ you. . . . The people who are paying us make the rules. You need to abide by the rules or don't work. I want to work" (Associated Press 2005). Despite the acknowledged power of the owners to control their behavior off the court as well as on, some players sought loopholes and ways to get around the code and a few flaunted or publicly challenged the dress code, but even the dissenters were not willing to jeopardize their careers by carrying their protests too far in regard to a dress code.

The case of the NBA dress code illustrates how powerful people such as league officials, wealthy fans, and corporate sponsors can construct or manipulate conceptions of what is deviant and what is acceptable or normal. *Symbolic interactionists* pay special attention to conformity, deviance, and social problems as social constructions. They focus on how particular types of behavior are *labeled* as acceptable or deviant in different social and cultural contexts and different types of social interaction. From a symbolic interactionist *labeling theory* perspective, the key to understanding the nature and dynamics of social deviance is not the rule breaking itself but how people react to particular behavior and label it as rule breaking or deviance. These are matters with fuzzy boundaries that are negotiated in social interaction.

Labeling theory assumes that social deviance is socially constructed by people or organizations who label certain behavior or people as deviant because they are perceived as wrong, immoral, or breaking the rules. The deviant labeling process is often affected by the status and power of the labelers over those who are labeled. For example, coaches have the status and power to make labels such as "troublemaker," "disruptive influence," or "disappointment" stick for athletes who play for them, but unless players are stars, it is difficult for them to make a label such as "incompetent," "unfair," or "abusive" stick for their coach. If players are labeled as a failure because they are cut or waived from a team or if they are labeled as drug users following a drug test, that label may stigmatize them as well as change their career opportunities and change their relationship to teammates, other players, the media, and other members of the Golden Triangle. Initial labels may stick, too, after suspensions are served, jail terms are completed, and even after the athlete, coach, referee, or other alleged deviant is cleared of charges. The mass media and the Golden Triangle in general are powerful influences in labeling sports figures as deviants as well as heroes. For example, they can make owners or players the "good guys" or "bad guys" in a strike or lockout by applying labels such as "greedy," "unappreciative," or "unreasonable" to one side or the other, and these labels may affect fan perceptions and reactions.

A symbolic interactionist perspective can help us understand why a particular action, such as an apparent trip in front of the goal in soccer, results in a foul and penalty kick on some occasions but not others; why violations of the rules in a game or even alleged crimes such as sexual assault by star players are overlooked while similar actions by lesser players are not; why hitting an opponent is expected in sports such as boxing or football but can result in arrest and imprisonment if it occurs in the home, in a bar, or on the street; or why it is more difficult for players to label coaches as deviant than it is for coaches to put deviant labels on players. The social construction or social labeling of deviance in all these cases involves a process of identifying, defining, and responding to behavior as social deviance.

Deviant labels matter when people, such as parents, teachers, judges, league officials, sportswriters and commentators, and coaches, have the status and power to make labels stick. When a person or group is labeled by these types of people as a deviant, others may treat them as deviant and, eventually, they may even begin to think of themselves as deviant, develop a deviant identity, and act in ways that confirm that identity. That is, deviant labels can produce a "self-fulfilling prophecy" in which people believe the labels applied to them and change their behavior accordingly. For example, tennis players who double fault on match point in a big match and go on to lose the match may be labeled by the press, other players, and fans as "chokers," especially if it happens more than once. These players may begin to believe their label, become increasingly nervous on big points in big matches, and ultimately become their label. Thus, labels do not merely describe perceived behavior. They have the potential to shape it.

Social Deviance and Contemporary Social Problems of Sport

Equipped with a general understanding of what social deviance and social problems are and how various sociological theories could explain deviance and problems in sport, we will use these kinds of conceptual and theoretical tools to examine the five major types of deviance-related social problems identified earlier in the chapter. All of these social problems represent unethical practices and ethical dilemmas, which Eitzen (1996) called "the dark side" of sport. "Dark side" also applies to behavior that diminishes the reputation of athletes and coaches, threatens the integrity of sport, and is broadly seen as undesirable by people in and out of sport. The problems addressed in this chapter are not a comprehensive list of all the deviance-related problems that could be found in sport today, but they help us see that the realities of sport are messier and more complex than idealized images often constructed by the Golden Triangle. The first problem we will consider is sports violence.

Violence in Sport

Revelations about the "blood sport" of dogfighting that arose in the case of National Football League (NFL) star quarterback Michael Vick provoked the ire of animal-rights activists and appalled much of the U.S. public and many sports fans. This case drew attention to a popular but illegal sport, and Vick's indictment, which ultimately led to his guilty plea and incarceration, provided many gruesome details about the breeding and training of pit bulls for brutal and deadly competitions and about the inhumane killing of dogs that were not vicious enough to compete successfully (Duggan 2007). This kind of blood sport is not new in the history of sport, however. In ancient Rome, blood sports of animal versus animal and animals versus men and women were staged with the encouragement of political leaders as public spectacles to entertain or distract the idle masses and dispose of "undesirable" members of the population such as criminals and Christians (Nixon and Frey 1996:19–20). Although the more "civilized" societies of modern times generally officially prohibit more extreme forms of blood sport, vestiges of the history of these kinds of sport can still be found today in "legitimate" or legal sports such as boxing and other violent sports. Societies that permit these sports expect them to be regulated in ways that minimize extreme and deadly forms of physical confrontation. Yet the most seriously disabling consequences of these sports often become apparent after the athletes have left the arena and the spectators have stopped watching.

We may be accustomed to seeing hard hits in many popular sports today, and contact and collisions may be key elements in media coverage and promotion of these sports. For at least some of the fans of these sports, the contact and collisions may be exciting and part of their appeal. However, other types of physical confrontations in sport, such as fights among players, spectators hurling projectiles at players or referees, and players going into the stands to assault spectators who have taunted them, tend to create negative publicity, turn off fans and sponsors, and cause problems for sports officials and sometimes legal authorities in the larger society. Even though these latter kinds of incidents tend to be relatively infrequent in contemporary sports, they can have serious implications for a sport's integrity and public image, the sanctity of the sports arena, and the physical well-being of players and fans. That is, they can be a serious social problem for a sport. The perception of physical aggression, confrontations, or collisions as "violence" and as a problem in sport may have less to do with whether people are hurt or how much they are hurt than with who is hurt, how many are hurt, and whether the aggression is outside the rules. In this section, we will consider problems of violence in sport involving both players and spectators or fans.

Player violence occurs when athletes use physical force in a sports contest in a way that is outside the rules of the sport and may be intended to harm an opponent. Since sport frequently involves physical force, contact, or aggression and since physical and verbal threats and intimidation are often viewed as "part of the game" in many sports, it can be difficult to distinguish between ordinary or accepted physical confrontations, which we will refer to as *aggression*, and violence. With this blurry distinction, it can be difficult to know whether we are cheering legitimate aggression or violence after seeing an especially forceful tackle or block. In addition, we may overlook the deviant nature of certain violent acts when they serve our purposes, such as knocking the opposing team's star out of the game for a couple of plays or stopping the opponent's drive to the basket, the goal line, or the goal. In society, we usually give praise and awards for bravery to police officers who kill dangerous suspects and soldiers who kill enemy combatants. In sport, however, we have some ambivalence about intense aggression and violence when the physical contact that provokes our excitement and applause leads to a serious injury. Both intense aggression and violence are major concerns in sport because they may lead to injuries, but violence is usually a greater concern because it is outside the rules.

Sport sociologists continue to rely on Michael Smith's (1986) conception of four major types of player aggression and violence, which he formulated over twenty years ago. He distinguished among brutal body contact, borderline violence, quasi-criminal violence, and criminal violence (Nixon and Frey 1996:

106–108). These different types of aggression and violence differ in legality and acceptance, and each type may differ in intensity, intent to harm the opponent, and severity of outcomes. *Brutal body contact* is physical contact that occurs within the rules of a sport. Examples are "legal" collisions, punches, hits, tackles, and body checks. Since these types of contact could result in serious injuries, disabilities, and even death, they have prompted criticism from some sports observers. However, since they occur within the rules of a sport, criticism of these kinds of contact are, in effect, an indictment of the sport itself because it permits intense physical aggression. Thus, for these critics, the social problem is allowing aggression as a normative or accepted part of the sport because it inevitably hurts the competitors and can severely injure them in some cases.

Borderline violence involves physical assaults that routinely occur in a sport but violate the rules of the game. Coaches and players often accept or tolerate them as part of the game, and referees, umpires, and judges may overlook them at times because they are so widely accepted. Borderline violence is "ordinary deviance," and its punishment, such as a foul or penalty call or, in more serious cases, ejection from the game, is usually in the context of the specific competition where the infraction occurred. Official sanctions from a league or sports body, such as suspensions and fines, have generally been limited for borderline violence, but public pressure has sometimes been applied to try to increase the severity of sanctions. Examples are "brush-back" pitches in baseball, the violent use of elbows in soccer and basketball, fistfights in hockey, intentional bumping of cars in "no bump zones" to gain an advantage in NASCAR racing, and holding in football to prevent harm to the quarterback. Although expected, such practices often cause retaliation.

Quasi-criminal violence involves physical assaults that violate the informal norms accepted by players and coaches as well as the formal rules of the sport and public laws. It typically generates more anger or outrage than borderline violence because most people in the sport do not accept it. Informal and formal reactions are likely to be more severe when the action is perceived as intentional and leads to very serious injuries. In addition to official, media, and public condemnation, this type of violence may result in large fines and lengthy suspensions. Examples of quasi-criminal violence are flagrant, intense, and debilitating late hits and fouls, "sucker punches" during player brawls, and the use of a bat, club, or stick to assault an opponent.

Criminal violence is violence that is perceived as a crime by the criminal justice system because prosecutors and the courts see it as a violation of the laws of society as well as a serious violation of the norms of sport. Certain kinds of highly aggressive and violent sports behavior occur relatively frequently, are perceived as exciting by fans, and may be featured in media promotions of a sport, even though they are outside the formal rules of sport and are violations of the law or crimes outside the sports arena. Examples include high-speed collisions in auto races; tackling in football; the highly aggressive types of assault that occur in boxing, kickboxing, and ultimate fighting; and a range of other types of physical contact, which might include the use of sticks, in a range of other sports. Sports officials generally prefer to police themselves to avoid external legal intervention because they realize that the prosecution of certain sports-related acts by athletes, coaches, or others in their sport could lead to wider and closer external scrutiny and control of their sport. They also tend to be quite harsh in their treatment of quasi-criminal violence. The vigilance of sports officials and the prospect of harsh punishment within the sport, public condemnation, and possible external prosecution have made cases of criminal violence in sport relatively rare. However, a rapid, substantial, and highly publicized increase in the number of quasi-criminal incidents producing serious, life-threatening, or debilitating injuries or a change in the culture of public tolerance of aggression and violence in sport could alter this pattern.

Violence on the field may result from a variety of factors. For example, individual athletes may learn to be aggressive and violent as a result of socialization into sport that teaches them from an early age, especially if they are males, to be as "tough" and aggressive as possible. This kind of socialization seems to occur among male athletes with disabilities as well as able-bodied male athletes. An example is "murderball," which is an intensely competitive, highly aggressive, and sometimes violent form of quadriplegic wheelchair rugby. The athletes who play this sport seem to be trying to gain respect for themselves as men and for their sport by playing with an intensity and level of aggression that critics have found objectionable in highly aggressive mainstream sports (Coakley 2007:204–205).

A number of researchers have tied aggression and violence in sport to the construction or affirmation of masculinity (Coakley 2007:203–206; Young 2000:392). However, although violence is more common in men's sports than in women's sports, it is not restricted to men. For example, Theberge's (1999, 2000b) study of women on an elite Canadian ice hockey team, which was discussed in chapter four, showed that even though body checking was not allowed, the women still enjoyed the physical aspects of their sport. Nevertheless, women may differ from men in the meanings they ascribe to physical contact and violence. For men, being physical in sport is often a way of demonstrating masculinity, while women are not as likely to use physicality to define their female identity. This might explain why women's sports tend to be less aggressive and violent than men's sports are and why women in sports such as World Wrestling Entertainment (WWE) wrestling or boxing seem to prompt ambivalent or negative popular reactions, especially among those with more traditional values (Coakley 2007:200–202).

Unlike players, people who watch or follow sports in their roles as spectators and fans are not permitted to engage in physical aggression. Sports-related spectator or fan aggression is almost always against the law and characterized as violence. Thus, *spectator and fan violence* involves any type of physical aggression related to a sports contest that is initiated by spectators or fans. It can occur in a variety of contexts, including the sports arena, a bar while watching a game, the street after a game, or at home as a reaction to the action or outcome of a game. Although the most serious cases of player violence have led to condemnation inside and outside sport as well as civil lawsuits or criminal prosecution in the worst incidents, some types of spectator and fan violence have been viewed as a major social problem by authorities in society. A prominent example is "soccer hooliganism."

Passionate sports fans in a number of countries around the world have engaged in various types of violence, including riots, fighting, and assaults of referees, to express their dissatisfaction with the effort of their team, hostility toward opposing fans, or displeasure with decisions by referees (Young 2000:

Greek fans clash with each other during a Euro 2008 Group C qualifying soccer match be-tween Greece and Turkey at the Karaiskaki stadium in the port of Piraeus, near Athens, on Saturday, March 24, 2007. Soccer hooliganism, often associated with British soccer fans, has become a problem in many countries. (AP Photo/Thanassis Stavrakis, File)

384, 390). In recent years, fans of various sports have also engaged in celebra-tory violence, such as fighting, vandalism, and looting, following their team's *victory* in a big game. The term *soccer hooliganism* has frequently been applied to the violent behavior by British soccer fans, and British authorities have in-vested in research to try to understand this violence (Young 2000) and develop policy and security measures to try to control it.

British soccer hooliganism began before World War I and reached a peak in 1985 in Brussels, Belgium, prior to the final game of the European Cup Cham-pionship between the British Liverpool club and the Italian Juventus club (BBC 2000; Haley and Johnston 1998). The match attracted approximately sixty thousand spectators. A pack of belligerent British fans, many of whom had been drinking heavily, put pressure on a retaining wall of the aging Heysel Stadium to get at opposing Italian fans, and this pressure caused the barrier to collapse. The collapse and ensuing panic crushed or trampled spectators, resulting in the deaths of thirty-nine mostly Italian spectators and injuries to hundreds of oth-ers. Following this tragedy, all British soccer clubs were banned from European Cup competition until 1991. Although the magnitude of the Heysel tragedy was unusual, it was not the most deadly incident, and very violent and lethal soccer hooliganism has been and continues to be a serious problem in soccer in coun-tries around the world (Doukas 2006). In 2007, spectator violence in Italy that resulted in the death of a policeman along with numerous injuries and arrests led to a policy of barring spectators from stadiums with inadequate safety and security (News Services 2007; Sanminiatelli 2007). At about the same time, the German soccer federation threatened to bar fans from the stadium if teams could not control spectators. In addition, the coach and players of one of the German clubs threatened not to play if fans previously involved in hooligan violence were present at their matches (Kammerer 2007).

Unlike elsewhere in the world, soccer hooliganism generally has not been seen as a serious social problem in North America. Fewer people watch and attend soccer matches in the United States and Canada, and North American soccer fans have displayed less passion about the soccer teams in their countries. Young (2000) compiled a list of significant riots following sports events in North America between 1968 and 1994 (p. 384) and a list of major incidents of crowd violence at sports events on other continents between 1985 and 1996 (p. 390). He found that all twelve North American riots involved fans of the "Big Four" professional sports leagues in the United States and Canada—ice hockey, football, basketball, and baseball. Seven of the nine cases of crowd violence in other countries involved soccer, one involved basketball, and the other involved cricket. It is noteworthy that rugby is not on Young's list, since it is tremendously popular in many parts of the world. However, one can find evidence of individual violent incidents and ongoing violence in this sport and others. For example, supporters of a team in the National Rugby League of Australia, where rugby is a major sport, were recently criticized as "hooligans" for their ongoing violence (SportsAustralia 2006), and violence at a girls' rugby club tournament in California involved the vicious beatings of two coaches and a referee and fighting among adults and teenagers, which resulted in police seeking criminal charges against ten people (Schevitz 2005).

There have been a number of attempts to identify the reasons for fan or spectator violence. For example, adolescent subculture explanations have focused on patterns of increasingly aggressive behavior after World War II in the more deviant segments of working-class adolescent subcultures, such as skinheads, that have led to the escalation of profanity, pushing, and shoving into more serious forms of violence at soccer matches. The explanations proposed by Dunning and his colleagues of the "Leicester School" have been grounded in the most extensive and systematic research conducted so far. They have emphasized the deprived social and economic status of hooligan groups, the importance of aggressive displays of masculinity in their culture, and historical traditions of strong family and neighborhood ties that have resulted in violent actions to defend their home turf against the "invasion" of opposing fans (Dunning 1993:59–64; Young 2000:387–388). Thus, soccer matches may provide opportunities for rival gangs to play out masculinity rituals and fight with each other to gain control over turf and assert their physical dominance. These confrontations have been difficult for the police and civil authorities to control because tough police tactics have seemed to increase the solidarity of the gangs and make them more prone to violence (Nixon and Frey 1996:109–110).

It is difficult to predict specific instances of spectator or fan violence, and the presence of fifteen thousand or more highly charged spectators seated close to one another in an indoor event or from twenty-five thousand to one hundred thousand or more excited spectators at an outdoor event could make outbreaks of violence very difficult to control for arena or stadium staff members. Semyonov and Farbstein's (1989) study of soccer violence in Israel indicated that player violence affected spectator violence, but spectator violence had no effect on player violence. Thus, one approach to controlling violence among spectators and fans could be to control the intensity of aggression and violent displays among players. Beyond these factors, it appears that controlling spectator and fan violence involves controlling the kinds of factors, from ethnic, racial, and class frustrations to the excessive use of alcohol and drugs, that make people more prone to violence in society in general. Furthermore, the fact that spectator and fan violence, as well as player violence, nearly always involves men tells us that factors related to the socialization and experiences of certain types of men need to be better understood to learn more about what causes their participation in sports violence. What we know about masculinity, aggression, and socialization into sport suggests that the ways males learn to play certain types of sports may contribute to their violent behavior as athletes and later as spectators or fans.

It could be argued that if sports did not provide opportunities to display aggression and even violence in relatively controlled settings, we would have more violence elsewhere in society. This is a structural functional argument about the value to society of aggression and violence in sport as a safety valve or alternative to violent crime. Although there are no definitive conclusions to be drawn from past research, there is some evidence to contradict this argument. For example, studies (e.g., Keefer, Goldstein, and Kasiarz 1983; Sipes 1973) have found that contact sports such as boxing, ice hockey, and football are more popular in more militaristic societies and during wartime. Others have shown that displays of aggression or violence on the field may intensify rather than defuse hostile feelings among spectators, especially when these displays are very dramatic or intense (see Nixon 1984:222–223). Thus, according to these studies, aggressive and violent sports may be part of the cultural fabric of societies that are more generally violent.

Crime, Sexual Violence, and the Criminal Justice System

Even for sports with a culture of aggression that appeals to fans, sports officials are not likely to want their sport to have a reputation for violence or their players to be viewed as "criminals" for their displays of borderline violence or intensely brutal body contact on the field. The perception that a sport is intensely competitive but under control preserves its respectability and helps insulate it from intervention by external authorities. On the other hand, acts of violence in the sports arena occasionally lead to external intervention by the criminal justice system and criticism from the press, legislators, and the public. Athletes and coaches also face criticism, penalties within their sport, and criminal prosecution for various types of crimes off the field. For example, the arrests of nine players on the Cincinnati Bengals NFL team in a nine-month period in 2006 and 2007 drew the attention of the NFL commissioner and caused the Bengals coach to announce plans to deal more strictly with player misconduct (Baltimore Sun 2007a). Furthermore, in the spring of 2007, after seeing more than fifty arrests of NFL players between early 2006 and early 2007, the commissioner announced a tougher personal-conduct policy and imposed two of the strictest suspensions of players for off-field behavior. A player facing felony charges in two states was suspended for the entire upcoming season and was expected to meet strict standards for reinstatement. A second player, who was arrested four times in three states since being drafted in 2005, was suspended for the first half of the upcoming season and also was expected to meet specific conditions before returning to the field (Bell 2007). Efforts by the NFL commissioner to clean up the image of the league were made more complicated by the case of Michael Vick, which resulted in substantial media coverage, public revulsion, and the suspension of one of the league's stars.

Relatively high actual or perceived rates of crime by athletes complicate the careful efforts by the Golden Triangle to create and promote images of athletes and their sports that make them worthy of public attention, admiration, and support. Athletes may become popular because they are fierce competitors on the field, but the public will be less impressed if they learn that their favorite athletes are criminals in their personal lives. In this section, we will consider the types of crime by athletes and coaches that have been reported in the media and also examine facts, issues, and controversies in recent research about crime, sexual violence, and the criminal justice system.

Arrests for involvement in activities such as dogfighting are unusual. However, a search of the Internet and indexes of major newspapers, sports magazines, and newsmagazines will generate a lengthy list of stories about athletes accused of or arrested for various illegal acts, including possession or use of recreational drugs such as marijuana and cocaine, breaking and entering, aggravated robbery, arson, domestic violence, rape, fighting, assault, disorderly conduct, attempted murder, and murder. In addition, we have read about coaches charged with acts ranging from driving under the influence to inappropriate or illegal sexual conduct and child sexual abuse (e.g., see Starr and Samuels 2000). These stories have tainted the reputations of major and minor sports, sports teams, and their stars.

A special investigative report in *Sports Illustrated* magazine focused on child molestation by coaches in youth sports (Nack and Yaeger 1999). Although there was no systematic research documenting the prevalence of this kind of sexual abuse, the authors used a computer database to find newspaper stories about more than thirty cases in an eighteen-month period in the late 1990s. Most of the victims were boys. There have also been reports of college coaches who have sexually abused their players or engaged in inappropriate sexual conduct with them (e.g., Wolverton 2006c). These cases of sexual deviance in youth and college sports have typically involved troubled individuals who found opportunities in sport to display their deviant tendencies. Gang rape by athletes has also been the subject of a number of stories in the media, and the recent case of alleged rape by members of the Duke University lacrosse team generated headlines and extensive news coverage. Since this story was so highly scrutinized and is relatively complex, we will examine its complexities as a social problem in a "Sport in the News" feature.

Research has generally shown that high school athletes have lower rates of delinquency than students from similar backgrounds who do not play sports. Although there is no evidence that playing sports *causes* a reduction in delinquency rates (Coakley 2007:172), a study of Maryland high schools in a county near Washington, D.C., suggested that having more students involved in varsity and junior varsity sports may reduce the number of in-school "disturbances" (Langbein and Bess 2002). Disturbances included suspensions for

Sport in the News Feature 8.1:
The Duke Lacrosse Scandal

Much has been written about the story known as "the Duke lacrosse sex scandal." In fact, one sports news source alone, ESPN.com, posted over seventy reports about this scandal between March 2006 and January 2007. The purpose of this feature is not to provide an expert legal analysis or to give a complete history of this incident or the people involved in it. We are instead approaching this incident from a sociological perspective. We will consider the most basic facts of the case, major allegations about it from those involved, and how the media have constructed it as a social problem. Even our relatively brief consideration of this case should reveal a number of sociological aspects that have made it both complex and of enduring interest to the public and various expert observers. I have drawn from a varied sample of reports and analyses from major news sources, including *Time* (Gregory 2006), *Sports Illustrated* (Price and Evans 2006), *Newsweek* (Meadows and Thomas 2006), and *The New Yorker* (Boyer 2006) magazines; ESPN.com (ESPN 2006); ABC News (Setrakian and Francescani 2007); insidehighered.com (Johnson 2006); *USA Today* (Brady and Marklein 2006); the *New York Times* (Arenson 2006; Wilson and Glater 2006); and *The Chronicle of Higher Education* (e.g., Lipka 2006a, 2006b, 2006c, 2007a; Wolverton 2006a).

With so many facts in dispute about this case, it is difficult to determine exactly what happened. However, a few facts seem undisputed. On the night of March 13, 2006, members of the second-ranked Duke lacrosse team attended a party at an off-campus house rented by team captains. Their entertainment involved alcohol and two African-American exotic dancers who were hired from a local escort service to perform a striptease. One was a single mother of two who attended a local historically black college and earned money as a self-described "stripper." The other was an escort service worker who was wanted by the police for violating probation in a 2001 case involving embezzlement. The two women danced for a brief time and then abruptly left after one of the men made a vulgar sexual remark, another made a racial slur, and the women and men engaged in an argument. After leaving, one of the dancers alleged that she had been choked, sodomized, and raped. The local district attorney (DA) subsequently charged three of the lacrosse players with forcible rape, a first-degree sexual offense, and kidnapping. Duke cancelled the 2006 lacrosse season, the coach resigned, and a new coach was eventually hired. One player graduated, but the other two were continuing students and were suspended from school, pending legal developments in their case.

The prosecutor pursued the case to enhance his chances of reelection, but he eventually had to drop the rape charges, and then the sexual offense and kidnapping charges, due to lack of evidence. After the rape charges were dropped, the lacrosse team was reinstated and the two suspended players who were still students were offered a chance to return to school. Ethics charges were filed against the DA for his handling of the case, including his suppression of DNA evidence that failed to link any of the forty-six players who had given DNA samples to the alleged rape. Parenthetically, the forty-seventh member of the team, its only African American, was not tested because the accuser alleged that her attackers were white. The North Carolina attorney general's office took over the case and initiated a thorough review, which resulted in disbarment for the prosecutor, who was found guilty of multiple ethics violations by a North Carolina Bar disciplinary committee. The players' attorneys planned legal action against the disgraced former prosecutor, while the players themselves went on with their lives. The one who graduated found a new job in finance after having lost his first job offer when he was indicted, and the two others made plans to continue their educations and lacrosse careers at Brown University and Loyola College in Maryland. It is unlikely that all the facts about this case will be fully known, except to those directly involved in it. Members of the team remained united in their silence about the details of the incident, except to profess their innocence.

The Duke case is not the first involving allegations of gang rape against college athletes, but it drew national headlines and extensive coverage because, according to communications professor Robert Thompson of Syracuse University, it represented a "journalistic perfect storm" of the "national flash points of race, class, gender, (sexual) violence, money, and privilege" (Brady and Marklein 2006). The *sexual violence* charges raise the persisting concerns among feminist scholars, women's rights advocates, and critics of sport about close-knit men's sports teams, especially in contact sports, as breeding grounds for learning sexist ideas about *gender* relations and proving masculinity by dominating and using women. The *racial* dimension of the case is that the strippers were black and the team was almost exclusively white. In addition, while 11 percent of the Duke University students were black, 44 percent of the residents of Durham, the town where it is located, were black. The additional fact that only one of the forty-seven lacrosse players was black suggests a racial divide between the town and the team and perhaps even the university, which might have encouraged racist remarks known to have been made by players during and after the incident. The elements of *class*, *money*, and *privilege* are reflected in the affluent backgrounds of the players, the much less advantaged status of the dancers they hired to entertain them, and the elite status of Duke University in a blue-collar town with a substantial minority population. Although there appeared to be some justification for questioning the validity of at least the rape charges against the athletes, it is evident that their privileged backgrounds and the substantial financial resources of their families made it easier for them to hire prestigious lawyers and to try to influence the media accounts of this event than it was for the accuser to manage her case in the public's eye.

The many media reports and analyses of this case presented a constantly evolving picture of a complex social problem that could be viewed from multiple, shifting, and sometimes contradictory perspectives. For example, Duke's prestigious national reputation was besmirched by the allegations of rowdy behavior and rape, which raised broader questions about the nature of student culture at Duke and similar campuses. In addition, this case raised questions about the amount of money invested in athletics at Duke and the fragile relationship between athletics and academics and between athletes and the rest of the student body on this campus. Duke officials found themselves criticized both for acting precipitously before the facts were in to discipline the lacrosse players *and* for dragging their feet in responding to the situation. Some observers believed that the Duke case would prompt officials on other campuses to consider stricter punishment for athletes who violated campus and athletic codes of behavior or at least to look more closely at what was going on among athletes on their campuses. With the specter of a Duke-like scandal in mind, college officials might pay attention to off-field behavior as well as to athletic and academic performance in determining whether to renew athletes' financial aid each year (Wolverton 2006a).

The picture of privileged white athletes sexually exploiting and assaulting lower-status black women in the Duke case flips around the stereotype that rape is a crime of black athletes from lower-class backgrounds (Leonard 2007), but it also reinforces notions about the problematic implications of male bonding and hypermasculine socialization in certain men's team sports for all male athletes in these sports. At the same time, initial judgments of athletes "gone wild" were mitigated by facts that weakened the accuser's case and that raised questions about preconceptions of guilt and innocence and about the meaning of justice for both accusers and accused. One commentator (Johnson 2006) referred to a kind of "groupthink" that had occurred soon after news of the story became public, encouraging many faculty members and students to jump on a bandwagon of critics assailing the athletes for their alleged misdeeds before the facts of the case and the guilt or innocence of the alleged attackers had been determined. This commentator also suggested that the allegations were consistent with the preconceptions of a number of critics of sports at Duke and elsewhere and that a type of reverse prejudice based on class and race and reflecting "political correctness" was at work early in this "non-rape" case,

continues

as he called it. The idea of a "rush to judgment" was reinforced when the North Carolina attorney general ultimately announced that all charges would be dropped in April 2007 (Lipka
2007a).

In fact, initial opinions seemed to change when more became known about the case and
when the rape charges were dropped. Sometimes overlooked by the media and other observers of this case was a pattern of crimes and misdemeanors involving Duke lacrosse players.
For example, between 1996 and 2006, forty-one players were charged with misdemeanors in
the local area, and in 2004–2005, fifteen of the forty-seven team members were charged with
misdemeanor crimes that included disturbing the peace, public urination, and public drunken-
ness. Although they were less than 1 percent of Duke's undergraduates, lacrosse players were
implicated in 33 percent of the arrests for open container violations, with one-quarter involving disorderly conduct and almost a third involving alcohol-related unsafe behavior (Leonard
2007). Thus, their behavior was disproportionately deviant, which may have been why some
critics quickly jumped to the erroneous conclusion that the accused players were guilty in the
alleged sex scandal.

The complexity of this case should discourage premature conclusions about who is responsible for problematic behavior and whether the problem is what we think it is. It also shows
how people in the Golden Triangle as well as people outside it, including critics of sport, use
the mass media to try to construct their version of incidents of problematic behavior (see
Leonard 2007). While I generally focused on "responsible" media accounts and analyses, I was
able to find very different interpretations of the "facts" of this case over time and at any given
time. The existence of these different interpretations emphasizes the importance of reserving
judgment until essential facts have been uncovered, especially when ostensibly problematic behavior has the kind of complexity and explosive implications characterizing the Duke lacrosse
"sex scandal." We also need to remember about this case that the absence of evidence of actual rape does not erase the clear evidence of elitism, sexual exploitation of women, and racial
tension and racism that was found.

misconduct such as truancy, cutting classes, and serious disrespect of teachers and serious incidents involving weapons, drugs, thefts, vandalism, fighting,
and sex offenses. Larger schools generally had more disturbances, but having
more students involved in interscholastic athletics in bigger schools tended to
reduce the number of disturbances. Higher participation rates in the most elite
sports such as football and basketball also tended to have a greater effect on reducing disturbances in bigger schools. Since the data were gathered about
schools and not about individual students, the researchers could not draw conclusions about whether sports participants or nonparticipants were relatively
more involved in the disturbances. However, their results suggest that schools
with higher athletic participation rates may have higher levels of student commitment to the school and its standards, which could minimize misconduct.

A recent study of high athletic participation and self-reported involvement in
serious physical fighting in the previous twelve months among males indicated
that the relationship between athletic participation and delinquent behavior
may be influenced by the type of sport males play. Kreager (2007) used data
from the National Longitudinal Study of Adolescent Health and found that approximately 40 percent of male respondents said that they had been in a serious fight. He also found, as other researchers generally did, that age, an intact
family, socioeconomic status, attachment to parents, and commitment to the
school reduced the likelihood of engaging in violence and that black males were

relatively more likely than other male students to get involved in violence. Furthermore, involvement in nonathletic extracurricular activities reduced the chance of being involved in fighting by more than 25 percent.

Regarding the effects of athletic participation, Kreager discovered that only football players and wrestlers among the male athletes had a higher risk of getting into a serious fight when compared with male nonathletes. There was no relationship between athletic participation and fighting for basketball, baseball, tennis players, and other male athletes. In fact, playing tennis significantly *reduced* the likelihood of getting involved in fights. Being part of peer networks associated with football appeared to play an important role in determining whether high school males got involved in fights. Kreager's research showed that males with a high percentage of friends who played football were more likely to fight than were those without friends on the football team. One of Kreager's general conclusions was that for high school males, being involved in peer networks tied to highly masculinized contact sports increased the risk of violence. Thus, along with the type of sport, peer networks seem to have a significant effect on whether high school males get involved in deviant activities such as fighting.

A national survey of 5,275 high school athletes in the United States in 2005 and 2006 by the Josephson Institute (Geer, Arizmendez, and Jarc 2007) revealed both "good news" and "bad news" about athletes and deviance. On the one hand, most of the athletes in the survey trusted and admired their coaches, learned useful life skills and positive values from them, and were less cynical about ethical issues and less inclined to steal than their nonathlete peers were. On the other hand, both male and female athletes were more likely than their classmates to cheat in school, and many admitted that they were willing to cheat or engage in unethical behavior such as using the other team's playbook or faking an injury. Over 6 percent of the male athletes and 2 percent of the female athletes admitted using performance-enhancing drugs in the previous year, with gymnasts and baseball players the most likely male athletes to use these drugs and softball players the most likely drug users among female athletes. Athletes in major sports had higher rates of deviance. For example, among the boys, baseball, football, and basketball players were most likely to cheat on the field and in school and do things that involved deliberate injuries, intimidation, and conscious violation of the rules. Among the girls, basketball and softball players were most likely to do things that were illegal or unsportsmanlike. Thus, athletes with the most at stake, including public attention and college scholarships, seemed to be most willing to bend or break the rules, both on and off the field, to get what they wanted.

While deviant behavior and attitudes among high school athletes may cause public concern, deviance and social problems among older athletes tend to generate more widespread publicity and public reaction. For example, highly publicized arrests of college athletes and superstar professional athletes such as former heavyweight boxing champion Mike Tyson, Hall of Fame baseball player Kirby Puckett, and basketball star Kobe Bryant of the Los Angeles Lakers on charges of sexual assault have put the problem of sexual assault among athletes in the national spotlight and have raised questions about its prevalence in college and professional sports. This kind of publicity has raised other questions as well. For example, two ABC News journalists asked: "Is jock culture a training ground for crime?" (Tapper and Taylor 2006).

The ABC journalists cited research findings showing higher sexual assault rates for college athletes than for students who did not play sports, and suggested explanations that focused on the star status of athletes, the special treatment they received, and the sense of entitlement this status and attention encouraged. If male athletes believe they are less accountable for their actions than other people are because they are stars, if they are socialized to believe that being a man means that they can and should dominate women, and if their relations with females are affected by drugs or alcohol, we can understand why some male athletes might try to exploit, batter, or sexually assault girls and women, including their wives. When sexist and sexually exploitative ideas about women are reinforced in a culture of close-knit men who value physical displays of their masculinity, we can also understand why men in team sports might be more likely to commit sexual assault than are men in individual sports or men who do not participate in sports. Traditional male socialization in general may teach boys lessons about sexual domination, but participating in a hypermasculine sports culture could intensify the influence of these lessons for some males.

The extent to which we can generalize about the relationship between male athletic participation and sexual assault and other crimes has been debated in the research literature and on editorial pages. Benedict and his colleagues have done extensive research on rape and other crimes by athletes (e.g., Benedict 1997, 2004; Benedict and Yaeger 1998; Crosset, Benedict, and McDonald 1995; Crosset, Ptacek, McDonald, and Benedict 1996). In his book about "public heroes (and) private felons," Benedict (1997) reported evidence from his study of news stories between 1986 and 1996 showing that more than 425 male college and professional athletes had been accused of violent crimes against women during this period. In just two years, 1995 and 1996, 199 athletes were charged with physical or sexual attacks of women. Benedict noted that these cases were especially significant because sexual assaults typically were not reported to the police or the press. These kinds of findings seem to suggest that sexual assault by athletes occurs frequently enough to constitute a significant social problem for the sports these athletes play as well as for society. We may get the impression that athletes in these sports are "out of control." Critics of these studies have cautioned against overgeneralizing about the criminal tendencies of athletes, though, especially since some of these generalizations may perpetuate racist stereotypes of black males and might reflect racial biases among social control agencies (Berry and Smith 2000).

Despite evidence of crimes or alleged crimes by male athletes in major sports, the celebrity status of high-profile athletes and coaches, which is created and reinforced by their sports, the media, and corporate sponsors, may somewhat insulate these sports stars from negative publicity, and even from prosecution and conviction in some cases, when they are accused of crimes. A study by *USA Today* of 168 sexual assault allegations against athletes over a 12-year period between 1991 and 2003 showed how much athletes were insulated from prosecution and conviction in such cases (Weir and Brady 2003). The 168 allegations involved 164 athletes, and only 22 cases went to trial and convictions were obtained in six. Forty-six of the cases resulted in a plea agreement, and in one case, the defendant pleaded guilty as charged. Overall, more than two-thirds of the athletes accused of sexual assault in the *USA Today* study were not charged, had the charges dropped, or were acquitted. The three cases of Mike Tyson, Kirby Puckett, and Kobe Bryant are consistent with this pattern. Tyson went to prison after being convicted of rape, while Puckett and Bryant were acquitted in their sexual assault trials.

Even when star athletes are exonerated, we may be left with a memory of earlier accusations, criminal charges, and personal doubts and with questions about how or whether to root for the tainted heroes. In his analysis of the Kobe Bryant rape case, Markovitz (2006) noted newspaper stories that raised these kinds of questions and reported the conflicted feelings of Los Angeles Lakers fans and parents who were disillusioned about the criminal charges against one of their favorite players. He proposed that efforts by the media to explain these contradictory feelings about sports stars as hero or felon—to use Benedict's words—were superficial because they typically focused on ideas of celebrity, the price of fame, and the difficulty of getting beyond the mediated images to the real person.

Markovitz suggested that the Kobe Bryant case and, by implication, similar types of cases involving heroes who have apparently fallen off their pedestal, were about deeper problems of race, gender, and violence in U.S. popular culture and how they were handled by the mass media. How should we view the case of a prominent black athlete accused of raping a white woman? How do we disentangle concerns about racist stereotypes from concerns about sexual assault in the context of what Markovitz and others saw as the sexist treatment of the rape victim by the legal system and segments of the media? Although the races of the accuser and the accused were reversed, the Duke lacrosse sex case also raised difficult and complex questions about race, gender, status, and sexual violence among sports figures. We can expect that unbiased help with sorting through the deeper and more troubling aspects of these kinds of cases will be least likely to come from the elements of the media most intimately tied to the interests of the Golden Triangle, since raising these kinds of sociological questions may cast doubt on the carefully constructed images of sports stars as celebrities and heroes by the Golden Triangle. In addition, the popular media are more oriented to dramatic headlines and stories about fans' conflicted feelings that resonate with readers and viewers than to lengthy and probing analyses of race, gender, status, and deviance in sport and society that could be more upsetting to the public and have more complex explanations and answers.

Additional evidence from Benedict's research shows why we have to be careful not to jump to sweeping conclusions from individual studies or limited data (Coakley 2007:173–174). In one study (Benedict and Yeager 1998), he found that over 21 percent of a sample of NFL players had been arrested at least once for serious crimes since starting college, but in later research (Blumstein and Benedict 1999), he found that arrest rates for NFL players for domestic violence and other types of assault were less than half the arrest rates for males with similar backgrounds in the general population. Since NFL players earn salaries that are much more than the average, we should not be surprised that Blumstein and Benedict also found that NFL players had lower-than-average arrest rates for property crimes. Benedict's (2004) study of the criminal histories of 177 NBA players in the 2001–2002 season revealed that 40 percent had a police record for a serious crime, but this crime rate was lower than the crime rates of age and racial peers of these players.

Lapchick (2000) observed that a five-year pattern in the 1990s of approximately 70 to 100 sexual assaults by athletes and coaches per year, which may seem alarmingly high, was actually a tiny fraction of the number of sexual assaults, rapes, and attempted rapes in the United States each year, which was nearly 205,000 in 2004 (Giddens, Duneier, and Appelbaum 2007:311). Without minimizing its significance, any case in which an athlete or coach is accused of sexual assault or another serious crime is likely to generate much more publicity than similar cases involving less-prominent people. In a curious twist, we see that the celebrity that the Golden Triangle creates for these athletes and coaches increases their star status and makes their sports popular and commercial successes, but being cast as celebrities also makes sports stars more vulnerable to criticism when they are accused of crimes. This is another complicating factor in the dilemma for fans noted by Markovitz (2006). Image making by the Golden Triangle may insulate these sports figures more than the average person from prosecution and conviction for alleged crimes, but reading about even relatively few cases of such allegations may seem disappointing or alarming to a sports public led to expect more heroic, more virtuous, or at least better-than-average behavior from their sports stars. When we put athletes and coaches on a pedestal, we do not expect them to fall to the level of more ordinary people, which may be why we exaggerate the deviant tendencies of athletes and coaches when they are compared with the rest of the population. Of course, some might argue that the substantial fame, money, and other rewards that major sports stars earn justify holding them to a higher-than-average standard of behavior.

Doping

Whatever the actual crime rates of athletes and coaches, we know that under certain conditions, some of them commit crimes and that things they learn and experience in sport may increase rather than decrease their chances of being involved in this deviant behavior. In the case of the illegal use of performance-enhancing drugs by athletes, called "doping," the deviance is intimately tied to pressures from their sports role. Doping has become a serious global problem in sports. Prompted by the doping scandal in bicycling at the 1998 Tour de France, the International Olympic Committee (IOC) led an effort to establish the World Anti-Doping Agency, or WADA, in 1999, with a mandate "to promote and coordinate the fight against doping in sport internationally" (WADA website, http://www.wada-ama.org/en/). WADA is an independent foundation governed by representatives from governments and the IOC. It provides rules, regulations, and drug testing for international competitions, and it typically makes the news when one or more prominent athletes fail a drug test before or during a major international sports event.

The overall picture of illegal performance-related drug use (e.g., see Yesalis and Bahrke 2005) is a little complicated. For example, the use of some substances is banned all the time, while other types of substances are banned only during competition. In addition, drug policies have been stricter and drug testing has been more frequent and systematic in some sports than in others. Anabolic steroid use is widely banned but relatively frequent and has received a lot of attention. The use of hormones and blood and oxygen transfer agents,

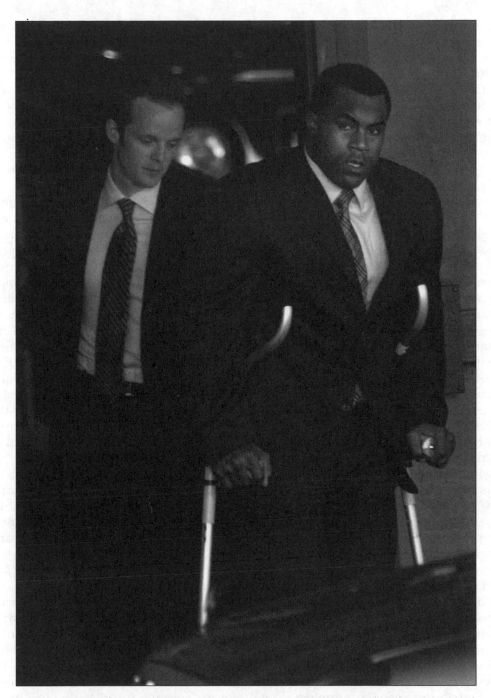

Baltimore Ravens running back Jamal Lewis, on crutches, leaves the federal courthouse in Atlanta Wednesday, January 26, 2005, after he was sentenced to four months in prison for using a cell phone to try to set up a drug deal about four years earlier. The sentence issued in federal court was what Lewis expected under an agreement reached with prosecutors in October. This case illustrates what some critics have viewed as a growing problem of crime among NFL players and athletes in some other major sports. (AP Photo/John Amis)

chemical and physical manipulation, and gene doping are prohibited at all times by WADA, while WADA prohibits other types of drug use, including the use of alcohol, narcotics, stimulants, and medications such as beta-blockers, during competition (see WADA "Prohibited List" on its website).

CBC Sports Online (CBC 2003) proposed a list of the ten most influential and strange drug cases over the past few decades: (1) extensive government-sponsored drug use by East German athletes, which resulted in serious adverse health effects for a number of them, ranging from liver cancer and organ damage to infertility and psychological problems; (2) the initiation of drug testing at the 1983 Pan Am Games, which caught many athletes by surprise and led to the sudden withdrawal of over two dozen athletes and nineteen failed drug tests; (3) the U.S. track-and-field cover-ups of drug use, which permitted many U.S. medalists to compete in the Olympics between 1988 and 2000 despite their use of banned drugs; (4) the case of Canadian sprinter Ben Johnson, who lost his Olympic gold medal and world record and was banned from his sport for two years following a positive drug test for steroids; (5) the case of Irish swimmer Michelle Smith, who catapulted from mediocre to Olympic champion in a relatively brief period and was suspended for four years following a manipulated drug sample despite her efforts to avoid out-of-competition testing; (6) the use of various banned substances by the Chinese swim team over a fifteen-year period, which elevated them into the top rank of swimming until their swimmers began to fail drug tests, with over forty testing positive in the 1990s; (7) the ongoing saga of the drug scandals associated with bicycling and the Tour de France, including allegations against Lance Armstrong, and Floyd Landis's failed drug test following his spectacular rise to the top and victory in the 2006 Tour; (8) the association of Major League Baseball's home run records with allegations of doping, which cost Mark McGwire election into the Hall of Fame in 2006 despite seventy home runs in a season and nearly six hundred in his career and which have stained Barry Bonds's career home run record; (9) blood transfusions and other forms of doping by top cross-country skiers; and (10) the status of the steroid nandrolone as the most popular drug intentionally or unintentionally used by athletes, including those who tested positive for its use after ingesting improperly labeled nutritional supplements, vitamins, and energy drinks that contained this substance.

We can add to this list the "BALCO (Bay Area Laboratory Co-Operative) scandal." BALCO was founded by Victor Conte as a "sports nutrition center," and it had a number of very prominent clients, including U.S. Olympian Marion Jones, who admitted to illegal drug use, and San Francisco Giants star Barry Bonds, who publicly claimed only to have gotten "nutritional supplements" from BALCO. However, the U.S. Anti-Doping Agency identified BALCO as the source of the banned steroid THG. Conte and three other associates were indicted on federal charges for conspiracy to distribute and possess with intent to distribute anabolic steroids, conspiracy to commit fraud with mislabeled drugs, and money laundering. The names of more than twenty-five prominent athletes in track and field, baseball, and football have been tied to this scandal, and a number of track-and-field athletes were stripped of titles and received suspensions for using THG. Conte and one of his indicted coconspirators served time in jail for their crimes, while the two others who were indicted received probation. Claims of innocence by those not yet found guilty of steroid use in this case have been challenged in the press and have received a dubious reception from fans (Dure 2007). While still claiming innocence, Barry Bonds was indicted 100 days after breaking the career home run record on felony charges for lying about his use of performance-enhancing drugs and for obstruction of justice in the four-year investigation leading to these charges (Wilson and Schmidt 2007).

The *CBC Sports Online* list and the BALCO scandal suggest how widespread doping is at the highest levels of sport. The repeated doping cases in the Tour de France indicate how entrenched in the structure and culture of some sports doping has become. Brewer's (2002) study of professional cycling between 1950 and 2001 shows how the institutionalization of deviant practices such as doping in a sport is tied to the kinds of commercial influences we have associated with the Golden Triangle. According to Sokolove (2007), after the fall of the Berlin Wall and Communist East Germany at the end of the 1980s, government sponsorship of doping for nationalistic purposes gave way to doping practices increasingly driven by commercial influences and organized on the "BALCO model" of a loose network of athletes and coaches. In professional cycling, as doping practices have become more extensive and more highly organized in recent years, these practices have become widely recognized as a major problem in the sport, which has created major public relations and internal control problems.

Prior to the 2006 Tour de France and before Floyd Landis claimed victory in this race and then failed a drug test to put his win in doubt, the second-, third-, and fourth-place finishers in the 2005 race and a number of other prospective competitors were withdrawn from the race because they were implicated in a blood doping scandal. Some observers called the race the "Tour de Farce," and fans were divided between those who continued to support their heroes and others who openly criticized or mocked the cyclists as "convicts of the road" (Fotheringham 2006). The fact that doctors and team managers were under investigation for their role in the alleged blood doping scandal is consistent with Brewer's idea that professional cycling has become organized to facilitate such practices. Wieting (2000) found evidence of cheating at various times in the history of the Tour de France, but the apparent difference now is that doping is institutionalized as part of the social and cultural fabric of the sport. Doping has increased and become more entrenched in the sport as teams have become bigger, better organized, and better financed and have developed more technically sophisticated means of enhancing performance. Similarly, sponsors have extracted more prestige from being associated with the winners. The informal but influential "rules of the game" about winning now increasingly condone illegal or ethically questionable performance-enhancing measures, such as doping. Thus, despite the adverse publicity for riders and their teams and their sport when they get caught for doping, it has become so deeply entrenched in the organization and culture of the sport that we continue to read about top stars who engage in these practices.

Brewer saw the relationship between commercialization and the rise of doping as one of "unintended consequences." Rather than viewing doping as an inevitable and direct consequence of increasing commercialization, he thought that the rationale for increased doping has largely been the performance pressures on riders who compete in a physically grueling sport. Since there is more at stake in a more commercialized sport, commercialization can intensify the already existing pressures to improve performance and to win that come from influences such as the Sport Ethic. A culture in which sports heroes are expected to do everything they can to win, find an edge, take risks, make sacrifices of their bodies, and even play hurt encourages the risky behavior of doping (Lipsyte 2005). This is the kind of culture associated with the Sport Ethic, and it is encouraged by the images and messages of the Golden Triangle, which push athletes to "Just Do It" and accept no limits. Furthermore, in the United States, athletes live in a society where consumers are routinely exposed to ads for prescription and nonprescription drugs and alcohol and where there is widespread recreational drug use. In this kind of society, it can be especially difficult to convince athletes that drug use to make them better athletes is wrong or unwise, especially if they assume that their opponents are getting a performance boost from doping. With a peculiar kind of logic, athletes have continued to use banned substances despite the adverse publicity and threats to their career and health.

Persisting drug scandals and suspicions of widespread illegal drug use can undermine the commercial base of a sport and the financial opportunities for athletes in the sport by scaring away commercial sponsors. This has happened in the Tour de France. For example, in 2007, the Discovery Channel team, which had arguably been the most successful team in the Tour over the past decade with eight winners in the previous nine races, decided to disband. They made this decision despite their success and despite a "clean" doping report card. Some team members, including Lance Armstrong, had been accused of doping, but none had ever failed a test for banned substances. The owners of the team nevertheless decided to disband after winning the 2007 Tour because the Discovery Channel had decided to end its involvement in cycling and the sport's persisting drug scandals had made it difficult to find new sponsors. The team's general manager commented, "It's just not an environment conducive to a big investment" (Kennedy, Bechtel, and Cannella 2007). Thus, the Golden Triangle will be drawn to a sport because of the commercial opportunities it promises, but the sport will lose its appeal when its reputation is tainted by major scandals related to problems such as doping. In recent years, the willingness of the Golden Triangle to invest and its desire to disinvest in a sport or in individual athletes have been closely tied to their reputation for controlling doping and avoiding drug scandals.

Carstairs (2003) suggested that efforts to discourage and control doping in sport were complicated by societal acceptance of the use of "performance-enhancing" drugs such as Prozac and Ritalin as legitimate outside sport. She proposed that the issues of what was and what was not doping and whether particular substances should or should not be banned were contested terrain. For example, she observed that some athletes have been widely condemned for doping, others have received a lot of public sympathy and support in the face of doping allegations or positive drug tests, and many have contested doping accusations and positive test results. Carstairs presented cases from various sports contexts showing that public perceptions of doping and the athletes who have actually or allegedly used drugs have been affected by the nature of the substance, how it was used, and the athlete's age, race, nationality, and gender. The cases of Barry Bonds and Lance Armstrong illustrate how public image, popularity, and perhaps race may influence public reactions to allegations of doping. The often surly Bonds was presumed guilty of doping by many baseball fans outside of San Francisco, which is the home of his Giants team, while allegations of doping by popular hero and cancer survivor Lance Armstrong have generally been challenged or ignored by his U.S. fans. Of course, in Europe, where Armstrong's image is much less stellar and fans are often nationalistic, cycling fans have been more critical and the cycling establishment has been more inclined to question his claims of innocence.

Doping is perceived as a significant social problem in sport because it can make competition unfair by giving drug users an advantage, because it can pose serious health risks, and because it casts doubt on the idea of athletes as heroes and role models (Carstairs 2003). Furthermore, a public perception of extensive doping or doping among major stars in a sport can be problematic for sports officials, even if it is not true. This kind of perception raises basic questions about the integrity of the sport and its stars and can create the impression that sports officials have lost control of their sport. Sports officials may want to appear tough on doping to retain media and corporate support from the Golden Triangle and to ward off government intervention. In some cases, sports anti-doping agencies also might collaborate with law enforcement officials to control illegal drug use in sport (e.g., Shipley 2007a). Doping practices can be deeply entrenched in the fabric of a sport and highly resistant to control efforts, though, as the Tour de France has shown. With evidence of the inadequacy of drug tests as a means to identify drug users—Marion Jones never tested positive despite her acknowledged drug use—and to prevent illegal drug use, WADA began pushing governments to make their laws tougher and invest more in criminal investigations. However, most nations were lagging in their implementation of this law enforcement, versus drug testing, approach to uncovering doping (Shipley 2007b).

A *USA Today*/Gallup poll of self-described sports fans conducted in 2007 showed that approximately two-thirds of the 563 respondents did not think that professional baseball or football was doing enough to address the doping problem among athletes in their sport (Ruibal 2007). Sixty-seven percent said professional baseball was not doing enough, 63 percent said professional football was not doing enough, and these results compared to "not doing enough" responses of 48 percent for professional basketball, 43 percent for track and field, 42 percent for professional cycling, and 31 percent for cycling. When asked to estimate how pervasive they thought the use of performance-enhancing drugs in these sports was, the percentages of those saying "all or almost all" players were involved in doping were 33 percent for football, 27 percent for baseball, 21 percent for track and field, 20 percent for cycling, 16 percent for basketball, and 9 percent for swimming. Thus, with the exception of basketball, there was a moderate correlation between opinions about doping control efforts and perceptions of the amount of doping in these sports.

It is not clear how much these poll results were correlated with actual anti-doping efforts or patterns of doping in these sports. However, as Ruibal (2007) pointed out, opinions about the adequacy of doping control measures may have reflected how these various sports approached doping and they may also have somewhat reflected how important these sports were to fans. For example, the perceptions of doping control and doping in cycling may reflect the more limited exposure to this sport and its lesser importance among the fans who responded to the poll. Anti-doping programs in football, baseball, and basketball were negotiated in collective bargaining between management and players' unions, while track and field, cycling, and swimming adhered to the World Anti-Doping Code promulgated and administered by WADA. Ruibal quoted a senior U.S. Anti-Doping Agency official as saying, "History has revealed that when sports try to handle anti-doping internally, the result is a conflict between profit motive and clean sport, and clean sport usually loses." Although Major League Baseball (MLB) and the NFL used WADA-accredited labs for drug testing, fans' opinions seemed to suggest that they believed that these sports did not have enough independent or external monitoring of their drug testing and were not as tough as necessary.

The perception among a number of members of the U.S. Congress of a recent steep escalation in doping among athletes resulted in public hearings and legislative proposals for stricter penalties and more federal power over drug policies and enforcement in six major sports leagues operating in the United States—Major League Baseball, Arena Football, the NFL, the NHL, the NBA, and Major League Soccer (Epstein 2005). League officials and the players' unions of these sports have resisted these proposals because they threatened to impose externally administered and standardized drug policies on all these sports, which would limit their own control of their sports. Sports officials want to control the image of their sport as well as the competition to ensure their sport's popularity and financial success. Players' unions want to protect athletes from unreasonable threats to their privacy rights and from the possibility of inaccurate or manipulated test results. Thus, we can see that beyond the possible effects of actual doping on the fairness of competition or the health of the athletes, the problem of doping is one of power, autonomy, perception, image making, and marketability for sports and the Golden Triangle. The *USA Today*/Gallup poll results suggest that fans' opinions may reflect some sense of this more complex picture of doping controls in major sports.

The establishment of WADA by the IOC offers interesting insights into the intertwining of drug control efforts with the commercial interests of the Golden Triangle. Part of the public rationale for WADA was concern about the spreading influence of doping at the highest levels of sport, including the 1998 drug scandal in cycling. However, the journalists Begley and Brant (1999) suggested that the IOC may have created WADA in response to a more specific criticism that the IOC itself had not been tough enough in dealing with doping among Olympic athletes. Since the IOC president selected the chair of the IOC television and marketing division to head WADA, the IOC faced further criticism that it was more concerned about "preserving the Olympic brand" than about ridding sport of doping (Sokolove 2007).

When he was with the IOC, WADA head Dick Pound was primarily responsible for negotiating the big-money contracts with commercial sponsors and television that transformed the financial value and revenue potential of the Olympics. Although Pound has waged a relentless public campaign to rid sport of doping and preserve the integrity of sport, skeptics have pointed to the irony that his success in his prior IOC position had contributed to the creation of a highly commercialized global sports environment in which cheating and doping have become more tempting and common among athletes (Sokolove 2007).

Revelations by a *Sports Illustrated* investigative team have demonstrated the intricate web of connections linking athletes to drug distribution networks, which involve the Internet, doctors, pharmacies, and ostensible anti-aging clinics or "wellness centers" (Llosa and Wertheim 2007). Thus the problem of controlling doping is made more challenging because it is tied to complex drug networks as well as to the Sport Ethic and the commercial interests and success of the Golden Triangle.

Other Problems in Sport: Gambling, Fixing, and Hazing

We will briefly consider two additional social problems in sport. The first is gambling and fixing, and the second is hazing. Although there are publications such as the *Journal of Gambling Studies* and numerous books and articles about legal and policy aspects of gambling, sports gambling has received relatively little attention from sport sociologists. The paucity of sport sociology research and writing in this area is curious because sports betting is highly institutionalized and very popular in the United States and in other countries, even though many forms of sports gambling are illegal throughout most of the states in the United States. Legal and illegal sports gambling also generates a great deal of revenue, conservatively estimated to be $300 billion per year, which was about equal to the total gross domestic product of nations such as Poland, Austria, and Saudi Arabia in 2005 (Horrow 2006; Weinberg 2003). Compulsive gambling or gambling addiction is a recognized social problem (Lesieur 1987). Compulsive sports gamblers include fans, coaches, athletes, and others inside and outside sport, and this addiction can result in suicide attempts and substance abuse and can disrupt jobs, families, and social relationships (Nixon and Frey 1996:116).

In the United States, sports gamblers legally bet on horse races, go to one of the licensed sports books or locations, or play Sports Action in the Oregon state lottery to place legal bets on a variety of sports events. While sports books are restricted to Nevada casinos in the United States, legal sports gambling locations and opportunities are widely available in a number of other countries, such as Great Britain. Of course, many people in the United States informally participate in office betting pools for major events such as the National Collegiate Athletic Association (NCAA) men's basketball championships (called "March Madness") and the Super Bowl or place illegal bets with bookies. Legal betting on professional and college basketball alone produced over $540 million in revenue in Las Vegas in 2005 (Horrow 2006). A recent University of Delaware study showed that about 21 percent of eleventh graders bet on sports over the course of the year (cited in Horrow 2006), and a study of approximately 21,000 male and female college athletes in the United States (Petr, Paskus, and Dunkle 2004) conducted by the NCAA in 2003 showed that about 69 percent of male athletes and 47 percent of female athletes reported having engaged in some type of gambling behavior in the previous year. Although betting on sports was against NCAA rules, 35 percent of the males in the study and 10 percent of the females reported betting on sports and 20 percent of males and 5 percent of females said they gambled on collegiate sports events in the previous year. Less than 50 percent of these athletes indicated that they were aware of the NCAA rules on sports gambling. The researchers labeled less

Patrons watch television as they wait in the Caesars Palace sports book for the 2006 Men's College Basketball Tournament bidding sheets in Las Vegas, Nevada, on Monday, March 13, 2006. Although legal sports gambling is limited in the United States, it is a huge industry, with much money bet illegally in this country. The possible connection among gambling, organized crime, and fixing is perceived as a serious threat to the integrity of sport by sports officials. (AP Photo/Jane Kalinowsky)

than 5 percent (about 640 of nearly 12,800) of the male respondents and one-half of 1 percent (about 39 of over 7,700) of the females as compulsive or pathological gamblers based on their self-reported behavior. In a three-part investigative report on what he termed the "epidemic" of gambling among college students in general, Layden (1995a, 1995b, 1995c) found that for many of the college students who gambled, their interest in sports was largely motivated by their interest in gambling (also see Layden 2004).

Legalization of sports betting in the United States has been a subject of ongoing debate, involving a variety of political, economic, moral, and practical arguments (e.g., Weinberg 2003). However, with a few exceptions, the sports establishment in the United States has been publicly opposed to sports gambling. In particular, the NCAA and major professional sports have prohibited gambling by athletes and coaches and have generally treated those involved in gambling very harshly. Major League Baseball's ban of one of its legends, Pete Rose, for gambling activities is an example. This ban has prevented him from being eligible for election into the Hall of Fame in his sport and has been a subject of much debate since it was imposed. As with doping, sports officials fear that the integrity of their sport could be compromised by gambling, since athletes, coaches, teams, or referees could be influenced by gambling interests to manipulate the outcomes of games. For this reason, the NBA commissioner reacted very strongly to the scandal in 2007 involving a referee who pleaded guilty in federal court to betting on games he officiated. The commissioner called him a "rogue, isolated criminal" (Milton 2007), but league officials were worried that the betting could involve other referees and might be linked to organized crime figures who pressured the "rogue referee" and perhaps others into fixing games.

"Fixing" is a form of bribery or extortion and refers to the manipulation of the outcome of sports contests for money from gamblers or those representing gambling interests, such as organized crime syndicates. Evidence of actual fixing scandals indicates that the sports establishment's concerns about adverse effects of gamblers and gambling interests on sport may be warranted. Fixing cases have characterized a number of sports, ranging from the notorious "Black Sox Scandal" in the 1919 World Series that involved eight members of the Chicago White Sox who were banned from the league, including the great "Shoeless" Joe Jackson, to "bagged" horse races, dubious knockouts in boxing, fixed outcomes of jai alai and soccer matches, and point shaving in college basketball (Nixon and Frey 1996:115).

With the substantial salaries, prize money, and pensions earned by professional athletes in many major sports today, we would not expect athletes in these sports to be tempted by fixers. However, recent evidence (David 2006) revealed that just before the 2006 World Cup, teams were pressuring referees to fix matches in the top two Italian soccer leagues. In this scandal, four teams were penalized, with three teams, including the renowned Juventus, demoted to the second division. Thus, we see that prominent and lucrative professional sports remain vulnerable to fixing, even when gamblers are not directly implicated. Prompted by this case, Italian prosecutors were investigating separate cases involving possible sports fraud, illegal betting, and false bookkeeping. In addition, a former top-division Belgian soccer coach was banned for life in 2007 and his team was relegated to a lower division as a result of their involvement in match fixing (Baltimore Sun 2007e).

Large sums of money bet on sports contests could intensify fixing pressures, for example, with fixers trying to bribe athletes, coaches, managers, referees, or teams to beat the point spread set by oddsmakers and win by fewer points than predicted. A sport seems especially vulnerable to the deviant influences of gamblers and fixers when gambling is not strictly regulated; when the gambling activities of athletes, coaches, and others in the sport are not monitored; and when stars or key participants in the sport feel undercompensated or are tied to criminals through their gambling debts. An article about possible recent efforts to fix matches in men's professional tennis (Drape 2007) quoted the captain of the U.S. Davis Cup team as saying that detecting fixing was difficult and that he would not be shocked to learn that lower-ranked players had thrown matches. The article also pointed out that the global growth of Internet gambling had significantly increased sports gambling and implied that with more money at stake, there might be more attempts to influence the outcomes of events in sports such as horse racing, soccer, and tennis, which were especially attractive to bettors.

College sports officials worry that bookmakers, including students who have easy access to athletes on their campus, can use athletes' gambling debts to induce them to fix games, for example, by missing a key foul shot, dropping a touchdown pass, playing poor defense, or letting a shot go into the net (Naughton and Selingo 1998). Gamblers also may seek inside information about the injury status of key players to give them an advantage in placing bets. The 2003 NCAA sports gambling study found that 2.3 percent of the Division I-A football players and 2.1 percent of male basketball players who were surveyed reported that they had been asked to rig the outcome of a game due to a gambling debt, and 1.1 percent of the football players and 0.5 percent of the basketball players said they accepted money for playing poorly in a game (Petr, Paskus, and Dunkle 2004). A number of highly publicized fixing scandals have occurred in college basketball in the United States since the early 1950s, and scandals at Tulane and the University of San Francisco led their presidents to drop the sports for a number of years (Nixon and Frey 1996:115). The NCAA data suggest that another similar scandal is possible.

As with the unintended connection between commercialization and doping, the Golden Triangle has unintentionally and intentionally encouraged gambling and even deviant gambling-related practices such as fixing by popularizing sports, publishing point spreads, and giving airtime or column inches to ads or presentations by "betting services." On the one hand, sports officials are generally committed to avoiding the taint of gambling-related connections to organized crime and publicity about rigged outcomes. On the other hand, by making sports more appealing to gamblers, they also create conditions conducive to illegal betting and fixing.

Coontz (2001:261) found that the forty-seven sports bookmakers she studied did not fit the popular stereotype of being "slick operators looking for the 'fast buck, the quick fix, or the desire to get something for nothing' (who were) tied to organized crime." Instead, she found no connection to organized crime among the bookies she studied. She also found that they worked hard, were honest with their customers, and saw themselves as independent business entrepreneurs providing a service in great demand rather than as criminals. Whether or not organized crime and fixing concerns are exaggerated, the fear of gambling influences on sport remains strong among sports officials, and the reality is that gambling has led to some prominent fixing scandals and may be related to other cases of fixing that have been unnoticed. The dilemma of gambling and fixing is like the dilemma of doping because both types of social problems are fed by the popularity and commercial success of sport. As the article on tennis suggested, the growing popularity of Internet gambling is likely to complicate efforts to address the problems associated with sports gambling.

Hazing has received a lot of publicity in recent years, but it is not a recent phenomenon. It is a form of initiation that has been a long-standing tradition in many types of groups and organizations (Trota and Johnson 2004). Hazing may be relatively innocuous, but the term often has a negative connotation because it can involve intense experiences of degradation, humiliation, and physical abuse for new or probationary members at the hands of more established members of a group or organization (Wahl and Wertheim 2003). In some extreme cases, hazing has resulted in death. Groups using hazing and other initiation rites have ranged from the military, police and fire departments, religious orders, and community service organizations to fraternities, sororities, and sports teams. There are very different estimates of the pervasiveness of hazing in contemporary sports in the United States. For example, according to a 1999 survey by Alfred (N.Y.) University, 80 percent of NCAA athletes indicated that they had experienced some type of hazing in college, and 42 percent of the respondents said they also had experienced hazing in high school (Wahl and Wertheim 2003). In contrast, survey data reported by the NCAA in 2005 indicated that less than 10 percent of student-athletes said they had been hazed as college athletes and about the same percentage said they had hazed their college teammates (Hosick 2005). Despite these varying estimates, researchers generally believe that many hazing incidents are not reported because victims fear retaliation or isolation from teammates for revealing this behavior (Wahl and Wertheim 2003).

In conjunction with its television series *Outside the Lines,* ESPN published a five-part online series about *Rites and Wrongs: Hazing in Sports* (Farrey 2002a, 2002b, 2002c, 2002d, 2002f). In addition, with the help of hazing expert Hank Nuwer, ESPN (Farrey 2002e) compiled a list of sixty-eight alleged and confirmed hazing incidents in high school, college, and professional sports in the United States that received media attention between 1980 and 2000, with one case involving hazing of athletes on one team by teammates and members of two other teams. Since many hazing cases are unreported and unpublicized, these sixty-eight cases are probably only a fraction of the actual hazing cases that occurred during this time period. They nevertheless are suggestive of certain patterns among the most publicized and serious cases over this time span.

Forty-five of these incidents, or over 66 percent, were reported between 1996 and 2000, indicating either an escalation in this type of behavior or closer media scrutiny in recent years. The incidents involved twelve different sports, but football (twenty-nine incidents), baseball (ten), soccer (nine), wrestling (eight), and hockey (six) were the only ones with more than two reported incidents. Fifty-one of the incidents involved high school athletes, sixteen involved college athletes, and one involved NFL players. Although this evidence suggests that hazing is predominantly associated with men's team sports, there were four incidents in the ESPN list involving women's sports—with one each in softball and gymnastics and two in soccer. In the worst incident, an athlete died as a result of a drinking ritual, but there were many other incidents in which "initiates" were forced to drink large quantities of alcohol, run around nude, or simulate sexual acts. In addition, there were a number of incidents involving physical or sexual assault. NCAA data showed that over 50 percent of those involved in hazing said that alcohol was a factor and that alcohol was involved in relatively more of the women's than of the men's hazing cases (Hosick 2005).

In a highly publicized recent hazing case not included in the ESPN list, three high school football players sodomized three of their younger teammates with broom handles, pinecones, and golf balls during a preseason camp, while teammates watched (Wahl and Wertheim 2003). Over the four days of this camp, which took place in an isolated rural setting several hours away from where the boys lived and went to school, the victims experienced up to ten different attacks. This case provides valuable insights into the conditions under which more problematic cases of hazing are likely to happen in sport, why hazing is extreme or violent at times, and why it often is unreported.

First, there was a tradition of hazing in which younger team members expected to go through an initiation and assumed that they would have their

chance to initiate younger teammates in future years. *Second*, the hazing occurred at a remote site in cabins out of sight of the coaches who were supposed
to be their chaperones. *Third*, the culture of the football team was conducive to
hazing, since it was about proving masculinity by displaying aggression and
demonstrating the capacity to "take it" from others. Sexual humiliation is an
especially degrading form of hazing in this context because sexual prowess is
a mark of masculinity and pride. *Fourth*, this case involved a number of young
athletes who lacked fully mature judgment. In addition to being impaired by a
lack of maturity, the judgment and behavior of these boys seem to have been
affected by a process of *groupthink*. In groupthink, powerful norms of group
loyalty and cohesion create pressures to conform or go along with the group
(Janis 1972). Among these young football players, strong expectations of displays of team loyalty and solidarity might have discouraged them from questioning dubious practices by teammates or coaches and encouraged them to go
along with the hazing. *Fifth*, a strong code of silence to protect the hazing traditions as well as the assailants led to a lack of disclosure about the hazing
among both witnesses and victims. The witnesses honored the code of silence,
and the victims apparently were too humiliated and fearful of their attackers
to talk about what was done to them. It was not until the pain, injuries, and
bleeding resulting from their hazing were noticed by parents and doctors that
the boys disclosed some of the details of their hazing.

Additional aspects of this case reveal how the status of coaches and the
value of athletics in the school and in the community may influence how school
authorities, members of the community, and students respond to hazing allegations. School officials and supporters of athletics in the school and community initially tried to minimize or "bury" the incident and rally behind the athletes accused of the attacks. When family friends of the victims called on the
school board to fire the school principal and coaches, they received anonymous
death threats. At a school board meeting following disclosure of the alleged incident, an estimated two-thirds of those in the audience, including parents,
current and former athletes, graduates of the school, and faculty members,
were there to support the coaches. Reporters trying to interview people in the
community about the case generally received a very unfriendly reception. Perhaps most significant for the victims was that when their identities became
known to other students, they were made victims a second time, experiencing
insults and derisive name-calling from many of their classmates.

Despite substantial support for the accused assailants in their own community, police in the town where the attacks took place prosecuted the case. The
three older players responsible for the attacks admitted their roles in the hazing and were sentenced in juvenile court. They were suspended from school a
few months after the incident. The five coaches who supervised the preseason
training camp were rebuked by the grand jury convened for this case, which
said that the coaches were "more concerned with being coaches of a football
team than interested in the well-being of the players as students" (Healy 2004),
and two of the coaches were removed from the classroom and reassigned to administrative jobs away from direct contact with students. Administrators in the
school district, who had tried to obtain information about the incident and received no cooperation from players or their parents, voted unanimously to can-
cel the school's football season. They claimed to be unaware of the hazing tra-

dition at the camp and accepted no responsibility for this incident, but they asserted their intention to do more to prevent future attacks.

Prevention of hazing seems to involve avoiding a potentially explosive mix of elements. These elements include: (1) an isolated setting; (2) a repeated and intense emphasis from coaches on team bonding, which may promote groupthink and a code of silence; (3) a tradition of hazing or initiation rituals; (4) a culture of hypermasculinity or bravado; and (5) slack or negligent supervision. As one expert on hazing law said, "You get a *Lord of the Flies* mentality. The environment is about bonding and power, and it's easy for things to get out of control" (quoted in Wahl and Wertheim 2003:75). The elements of team bonding, displays of power or dominance, and aggression are deeply entrenched in many sports realms, especially in male team sports. This culture also may include sexist, racist, or homophobic elements that become part of the hazing rituals. Holman (2004) suggested that athletic leaders who were socialized in this type of culture and who were participants in hazing themselves as athletes often seem more interested in defending the image of their sport than in bringing about real change in hazing practices. As long as coaches and sports officials do not recognize or accept the need for a change in the culture of their sports, hazing is likely to remain a problem.

Conclusion: Controlling Sports-Related Social Deviance and Problems in a Changing World

Public awareness of hazing and the other kinds of social problems we have considered in this chapter could be an important step in controlling these problems, but it is not sufficient to reduce or eliminate them. Prevention and social control efforts are likely to have limited effectiveness unless the underlying social structural and cultural factors that contribute to these problems are addressed. Authorities have turned to extreme measures to try to prevent future problems such as spectator violence, as in the case of barring spectators from soccer stadiums in Italy that fail to meet minimum safety and security standards. In addition, to maintain order and in some cases to avoid outside intervention, sports authorities have imposed severe penalties to punish serious deviants, including suspending players for quasi-criminal violence during a game; banishing players from their sport for misdeeds such as chronic or serious gambling, fixing, and doping; and canceling a team's season after its players have been accused or found guilty of sexual assault, violent hazing, or other crimes. Fear of drug use or publicity about this problem seems to be a strong motivator of cooperation in social control among sports bodies in different sports. In the spring of 2007, representatives of the NFL, NBA, MLB, NHL, and the U.S. Olympic Committee met with the Drug Enforcement Administration and other U.S. federal agencies to try to address the doping issue in their sports (Shipley 2007a). This kind of meeting may reflect a concern shared by all these sports bodies that if they do not show a serious commitment to dealing with this issue, they will find that control and enforcement will be handled by these external agencies.

Despite their professed commitment to controlling deviance and problems in their sports, sports authorities seem to be reluctant to impose severe penalties to deter misconduct by athletes in their sport. For example, in a study of punishment of athletes in the four major North American professional sports leagues, the NFL, NBA, NHL, and Major League Baseball, between 1995 and 1999, the researchers concluded that punishments such as fines and suspensions were not severe enough to serve as effective deterrents (Nagel, Southall, and O'Toole 2004). They concluded that the patterns of punishment that they found were not primarily aimed at deterring deviance among the players, but instead were a "well orchestrated and highly effective public relations campaign by the leagues and player associations to insure profit maximization" (Nagel, Southall, and O'Toole 2004:26). That is, punitive actions by league officials were intended to make the leagues appear to the media and fans as tough on certain kinds of player misconduct, but were not really taken seriously by players. Athletes are actually being rational in disregarding league policies if they think that their behavior serves their career or personal interests, that they probably will not be caught, or that they will not be punished seriously if they are caught. Consider the punishments imposed by Major League Baseball and the NFL, for example. Eighty-one percent of MLB punishments for fighting and intimidation involved penalties such as suspensions but not fines—which meant that players could take a rest for a while and did not lose any money as a result of their misbehavior. The NFL punishments would seem to reinforce a reputation as "tough on drug use," since it had twenty-nine of the thirty-two drug punishments identified in this research. However, it was the only league during the period of the study to have a comprehensive drug testing policy, and only six of the twenty-nine drug punishments were for using performance-enhancing drugs and the other twenty-three were for recreational drug use. This explains the substantial skepticism about NFL doping control efforts among sports fans interviewed for the *USA Today*/Gallup poll cited earlier.

Social control in some sports frequently seems to focus more on damage control and keeping a sport popular and profitable through skillful public relations and marketing than on actually eliminating deviance and social problems or making athletes responsible for their misbehavior. This kind of social control *as image control* may impress or serve the interests of the sports media and corporate sponsors who are the partners of sport in the Golden Triangle, even if it often makes more knowledgeable fans skeptical. The NFL has seemed better at this kind of "social control" than other sports such as baseball and cycling. *Sports Illustrated* columnist Jack McCallum (2006) observed that despite the arrests of numerous NFL players for an assortment of crimes in recent years and numerous cases of drug policy violations (albeit for recreational use and not doping) by NFL players, the league itself had generally avoided the kind of searing criticism faced by other sports. For example, the press has launched a barrage of criticism at MLB for alleged and actual steroid use, professional cycling for doping, and the NBA and the NHL for fighting. He called the NFL the "No Fault League" for its ability to escape this criticism, but continuing publicity about arrests of NFL players and the resulting strict personal-conduct policy implemented by the NFL commissioner may reflect fault lines and cracks in the facade of the No Fault League (Jarrett Bell 2007). As in other major sports seen as having social problems, realities seem to have overtaken public relations and image making in the NFL, forcing the NFL to become tougher in its social control efforts.

If we use a social conflict perspective, which focuses on the influence of economic interests and commercial incentives, we can understand why sports authorities often seem to move very slowly and meekly in resolving allegations of deviance or actual social problems involving big stars or popular teams. When they drag their feet, however, they invite growing criticism and outside intervention, which compound their dilemma of social control. Thus, to understand the causes and complex dynamics of patterns of social deviance, social problems, and social control in many sports contexts, we may have to look beyond economic or commercial factors within sport to examine relations of power and control between sport and structures of power and authority in the larger society, such as relations involving government agencies, public opinion, and serious journalists. In addition, the occurrence of particular types of social deviance and social problems and the ways sports authorities try to control them may be influenced by the major forces of social change we have considered throughout this book.

For example, sociodemographic changes, such as the increasing social class, racial, and ethnic diversity of players and fans, have created divisions and tensions among fans, among players, and between fans and players that have sometimes erupted into violence. Furthermore, the organizational, economic, and political forces at work in major sports today make it difficult to keep deviance and social problems, or at least media and public perceptions of deviance and problems, under control. The increasing organizational control and commercialization of sport by the Golden Triangle have turned the social control of deviance and social problems into "damage control" to minimize media criticism and adverse public reactions. In addition, increasing access to new scientific applications and new technologies to enhance performance has pushed athletes, coaches, and teams to experiment more and, in an increasing number of cases, it appears, to go beyond the legitimate boundaries of their sports.

We might conclude from the research on punishments in professional sports leagues that sports authorities often seem to want to appear tough without actually being tough. However, there are problems that tarnish the image of a sport and its stars, and there are problems that disrupt the competition and lead to serious injuries and even deaths. Thus, social deviance and social problems pose a challenge to sports authorities to figure out whether they need more punishment or basic changes in the culture or structure of their sport. Whenever deviance and problems become a focus of media attention, the people who control sports have the compelling challenge of how to address these issues in ways that maintain their control and do not risk the loss of fan loyalty, lost support from the Golden Triangle, or intervention from public authorities. Social deviance, social problems, and social control issues reveal the complexity of sport and its relationship to the larger society. In the next chapter, about sport and higher education, we will see that some problems may be fostered by the growing influence of the Golden Triangle and become embedded in the basic structure of sport, despite recurring reform efforts to uproot them.

9

Sport and
Higher Education

Historical Background

The opponents in the first intercollegiate sports contest in the United States and the sport at which they competed might surprise you. In the context of contemporary big-time college athletics, the commercial sponsorship of this inaugural event may not seem so surprising, but other aspects of its organization were very different from major college sports today. According to sports historians (e.g., Betts 1974), college athletics began with an eight-oared barge or crew race between Harvard and Yale on Lake Winnipesaukee in New Hampshire in 1852. While there were no paying spectators and no mass media coverage, this event could be characterized as professional as well as commercial. It was the idea of a railroad owner and real estate developer. His railroad went from Boston to Lake Winnipesaukee. His idea was to market vacation lots he wanted to sell in the southern New Hampshire lake area through a sports event. Crew was a popular sport at that time, and he hoped to get wealthy friends and families of the Harvard and Yale rowers to ride his railroad to the race and invest in his vacation lots (Deford 2005). The athletes were induced to compete with offers to pay all their expenses and provide "lavish prizes" and "unlimited alcohol" (Bok 2003:35).

Although we generally do not think of "Ivy League" institutions as athletic powerhouses today, their role was pivotal in the growth, popularization, and commercialization of college athletics in the United States. By 1850, Harvard had organized intramural and interclass competitions and a sports day for its students. The sports day was called "Bloody Monday," and it was quickly copied by other institutions and became a model for sports competition among colleges and universities (Nixon 1984:106–110; Nixon and Frey 1996: 142–144). Intercollegiate sports in the United States did not begin with the organizational trappings that we typically associate with college athletics today. For example, in their earliest days, students controlled their sports, faculty members were involved if students wanted them to be, and colleges and universities did not officially sanction or authorize them (Nixon 1984:106–107). These sports were more similar to the student-run "club" model on many campuses today than to university-run sports programs, and this model had its roots in the student governance of athletics in private secondary schools of England in the nineteenth century. The model persists today in secondary schools and universities in Great Britain (Sage 1998:229).

During the second half of the nineteenth century, college sports—including both intramural and intercollegiate programs—grew slowly and steadily and eventually evolved into activities that were bureaucratically organized and controlled by higher education institutions and alumni. Students lost control of their sports as administrators, faculty members, and alumni sought increasingly bigger roles in athletics. Many faculty members and administrators were dubious about the purposes of athletics in academic institutions; they saw athletics growing beyond the capacity of students to run them responsibly or effectively; and they had concerns about issues such as professionalism, financial mismanagement, and poor sportsmanship. At the same time, alumni wanted to see better-run athletic programs to generate both greater success on the field and more revenue. These concerns and desires led to the formation of faculty athletic committees, which either gave institutions regulatory control over student athletics or delegated authority over athletics to faculty, students, and alumni.

By the early 1900s, students had completely lost control over athletics and, as athletics became more bureaucratized and commercialized, the faculty role in college sports diminished and the role of administrators and alumni grew. As college athletics expanded throughout the late nineteenth century and into the twentieth century, colleges and universities hired professional coaches, marketed to paying spectators, and recruited athletes to compete for their teams, as athletics came to be seen as a vehicle to serve institutional ends. The basic structure of college athletics as we know it today was largely in place by the 1920s, with smaller colleges broadly emphasizing physical recreation and intercollegiate athletics as a part of student life and many bigger institutions organizing intercollegiate athletics as a form of entertainment with elite athletes. The commercialized entertainment-oriented form of college sport was justified by college officials as a means to market the institution to prospective students, increase student morale and institutional loyalty, build alumni support, enhance the institution's visibility and reputation, and make money (Sage 1998:230–231).

As intercollegiate athletics became more popular in the late nineteenth century, colleges and universities tried to create more uniform standards for competition, academic eligibility, and other matters. This standardization usually occurred within newly formed conferences of similar types of institutions. Football, which began with a game between Princeton and Rutgers in 1869 and developed into a uniquely U.S. form (see Riesman and Denney 1951), became a very popular college sport. In 1876, the popularity of football resulted in the formation of the Intercollegiate Football Association by Harvard, Yale, and Princeton. Despite regulatory efforts, a number of problems arose in college football concerning issues such as academic integrity, professionalism, institutional control, and injuries and even deaths of players (Betts 1974; Nixon and Frey 1996:145).

By 1905, concerns among faculty members, college administrators, and prominent officials had risen to a level where there were calls for abolishing the sport. The Intercollegiate Athletic Association of the United States (IAAUS) was formed in 1905 to address these concerns and establish regulatory control that emphasized responsible and effective institutional control, academic integrity, ethical behavior, and the welfare of student-athletes. The IAAUS became the National Collegiate Athletic Association (NCAA) in 1910, and it remains the dominant organizational and regulatory body in college athletics in the United States. The NCAA has been able to preserve college football and has overseen the organizational, popular, and commercial growth of college athletics in general. It remains formally committed to its organizing principles, but it has had to contend throughout its existence with many of the same issues and problems that faced the IAAUS at its inception.

Although sports are an important part of the culture of many nations and foreign athletes come to the United States to compete in college sports, college sports in other countries are not the highly organized corporate and commercial activities that they are in the United States. In the United States, "big-time" college sports have become very popular among alumni and fans and are a major commodity for the Golden Triangle. Prominent sportswriter Frank Deford (2005) referred to the mix of higher education and big-time athletics as "America's Modern Peculiar Institution," and we can add that big-time intercollegiate athletics, with its extensive and lucrative ties to the Golden Triangle, has been a uniquely U.S. phenomenon. We will see that this peculiar institution has generated intense passions as well as strong criticisms, that the conception of college athletics as amateur sport is highly dubious at its big-time levels, and that the connection between athletics and education on college campuses is often tenuous.

Assessing the Justifications for College Athletics

One of the earliest and most enduring justifications for college athletics in the United States is the idea that sport builds character (Bok 2003:47; NCAA 2006). We are familiar with this kind of belief as a basic tenet of the Dominant American Sports Creed and as a major justification for sports for young people and in schools. We can trace the origins of this justification for sports in colleges and universities in the United States to the "muscular Christian" idea that took root in the British private secondary schools in the first half of the eighteenth century. Throughout the twentieth century, advocates of college sports extolled their capacity to make athletes courageous, manly (since sports were supposed to be for males, according to the prevailing gender ideology), and disciplined, and sports competition was supposed to teach the values of displaying skill and achieving excellence, which were tied to the dominant U.S. ideology of the American Dream. Thus, playing sports in college was tied to deeply held perceived virtues and cultural values in the United States. We saw in the discussion of social deviance and social problems in sport in the last chapter and we will see in this chapter that playing sports does not immunize college students from questionable, undesirable, or deviant behavior. Nevertheless, the ideological power of beliefs in character building and in the broader Dominant American Sports Creed has seemed to fend off many of the criticisms related to actual misbehavior and social problems in college sports. In fact, many of the justifications have persisted, despite seemingly compelling contradictory evidence.

People often believe the justifications because even though they are not generally true, they see a number of prominent examples that seem to validate them. For example, consider the argument that *college sports provide access to a college education and a chance for a college degree for minority and poor youths* (Bok 2003:47–48). It is true that very talented athletes from minority and lower-class backgrounds have been able to attend college with the support of an athletic scholarship, earn a college degree, and go on to a successful career in sports and a number of other occupations. It is also true that college graduation rates are generally higher for black male athletes than for their black male counterparts in college who do not play sports (Coakley 2007:500). On the other hand, with the more stringent NCAA initial and continuing eligibility rules today, many young athletes from disadvantaged backgrounds lack the academic qualifications to be eligible to play college sports. Furthermore, many of those who receive athletic scholarships or grants-in-aid lack the academic preparation, commitment, and time to succeed in the college classroom and earn their college degrees. Later in this chapter, we will consider the academic experiences and success of student-athletes in more detail.

Two other justifications are that *sports success will generate more alumni donations and that publicity about college athletic success will attract more and better applicants* (Bok 2003:48, 49–51). According to Frederick Rudolph (1962) in his book *The American College and University*, "By 1900 the relationship between [college] football and public relations had been firmly established and almost everywhere acknowledged as one of the sport's major justifications" (385). A more recent variation of this justification of big-time football and commercialized college sports in general was offered by the chancellor of the University of Kansas, Robert Hemenway, who was also the chair of the NCAA's Division I board of directors (quoted in Suggs 2004b). He asserted that successful football and basketball teams produced a sense of community and a kind of "social capital" that justified their expense. He said, "Social networks have value," adding, "that's what we create with 50,000 or 60,000 in the football stadium. . . . When I go to meet our alumni, the first thing they ask about is how we're doing on the field." In a related comment, University of Maryland president Dan Mote said, "A very visible, very successful athletic program gives you lots of entrées. It changes the understanding of state government, the state legislature, and of the business community and alumni" (quoted in Bok 2003:50).

The effects of winning on external financial support or donations, public and legislative support, and student applications may be more restricted than advocates of big-time athletics generally assume or assert. Those who have looked at the relevant research literature have concluded that winning teams in football and men's basketball may not lead to increases in donations (Staurowsky 2002) *or* applications from *better* students, even though they may lead to an increase in the *number* of student applications (Suggs 2004b). When winning produces more donations, those donations tend to be earmarked for athletics rather than for educational purposes of the university (Suggs 2004b). A report by economist Robert H. Frank, called "Challenging the Myth: A Review of the Links among College Athletic Success, Student Quality, and Donations," which was released in September 2004 by the Knight Foundation–sponsored Commission on Intercollegiate Athletics (KCIA), cast further doubt on the conclusion that winning college athletic teams lead to bigger gifts from alumni and better students in the applicant pool (Jacobson 2004). Frank argued that if successful big-time athletic programs generated the indirect benefits that advocates of these programs

256 ❖ Chapter 9

claimed, the effects tended to be small. In his report to the KCIA, Frank recognized that alumni giving and applications for admission sometimes increase after highly successful seasons at a small number of institutions, but he also pointed out that these increases tend to be small and short-lived. Furthermore, research has indicated that while donations to the 119 largest athletics departments have substantially increased in recent years, overall giving to those colleges and universities has remained fairly stable over that same time period (Wolverton 2007c). Thus, we might conclude that when athletics generates more giving, the donations are often targeted exclusively for athletics and this athletic giving might be adversely affecting giving to the university for other purposes, since donors may place limits on the overall amount they are willing to donate to the institution. In addition, Frank observed that there was "not a shred of evidence to suggest that an across-the-board *cutback in spending* [emphasis added] on athletics would reduce either donations by alumni or applications by prospective students" (quoted in Jacobson 2004). Institutions in the Ivy League, prestigious small colleges, and major private research institutions such as the University of Chicago, MIT, and New York University have successfully raised billions of dollars without the benefit of "big-time" athletic programs.

Another type of justification for college athletics is that winning teams increase school spirit and student morale. Over 26,000 respondents to an unscientific *SI On Campus* online poll provided some interesting insights into how sports-minded students may think about college athletics and athletes (Wertheim 2007). The poll results tended to show that their college's sports reputation was not the primary factor affecting their college choice, they saw sports as more popular on their campus than studying and sex but less popular than drinking, they thought athletes were seen as celebrities who got special academic treatment, and they did not think that basketball and football players were well integrated into the general student body at their school. Respondents were nearly evenly divided (48 percent agreed; 52 percent disagreed) about whether they would be bothered if academically less-qualified athletes were allowed to attend their school. Unlike a more representative cross section of the U.S. public that responded to a more scientific poll about college athletics (KCIA 2006), a large majority (85 percent) of the respondents to the *SI On Campus* poll were not bothered by football or basketball coaches' being paid more than professors.

We will consider the other poll results later in the chapter. However, we can say at this point that the *SI* poll respondents probably represent the students who cared the most about sports on their campus, since they visited the *SI* website and took the time to respond to the poll. It appears that these sports-minded people viewed big-time athletics as entertainment with celebrity athletes and well-paid coaches. However, it is not clear from these results how much the spirit or morale of these campus sports fans or their campuses in general was affected by athletic success or how much colleges and universities *as institutions of higher education* benefited from the amount or kind of interest that sports-minded students express about athletics on their campus. There is little scientific evidence at this time that would answer these questions.

The case of Ohio State University reveals how complicated assessing the arguments for and against big-time college sports can be. In terms of the number of athletes and varsity teams, the size of its operating budget, and the amount of athletic revenue it generates, it has the biggest intercollegiate athletics program in the United States. It attracts many of the nation's top high school athletes to play for its athletic teams, wins national championships, and takes pride in the academic accomplishments of over nine hundred student-athletes whose average GPA is higher than 3.0 (Ohio State University 2007). At the same time, it has been embarrassed by recruiting violations, relatively low graduation rates for male basketball and football players, allegations from a prominent former football star of inappropriate academic help and improper gifts from boosters, and a lawsuit from a former men's basketball coach who was fired for giving recruits illegal cash inducements (Lapchick 2006, 2007; Wertheim 2007). Despite these kinds of embarrassments and a continuing series of troubling questions about the overall justification for athletics on college campuses, college sports and especially the big-time programs wed to the Golden Triangle remain well entrenched in the United States. We will examine the problems and cycles of reform efforts in college athletics, but first we will consider the dominant features of the peculiar institution of college athletics in the United States.

Organization and Stratification of College Athletics in the United States

The organization of college athletics is hierarchical in various ways. The NCAA dominates college sports with over 1,000 member institutions and over 360,000 student-athletes in 2006–2007 (Jones and Levine 2006), dwarfing the competing National Association of Intercollegiate Athletics (NAIA) in size and visibility. The NAIA had 282 members and 45,000 student-athletes in 2007. Furthermore, the NAIA lost over one-third of its members between 1993 and 2007 and has had difficulty getting sponsors. It faced a steep uphill climb in its renewed efforts to improve its image and regain lost members (Wolverton 2007b). Since the most corporate and commercialized college sports programs fall under the organizational umbrella of the NCAA, it will be the primary focus of this chapter.

The NCAA is internally stratified, with a hierarchy of three major divisions, from the highest or "big-time" Division I to the lower-level Divisions II and III, and five divisions overall. Division I-A (recently renamed the "Football Bowl Subdivision") has over 100 members, and they have big-time football programs. Football teams from eleven conferences and a few independents such as Notre Dame, Army, and Navy in the Football Bowl Subdivision compete in the Bowl Championship Series (BCS) for the right to participate in one of five major bowl games, including one each year designated as the national championship bowl game. Football Bowl Subdivision teams that do not qualify for one of the five BCS bowl games may qualify to play in another bowl game. The BCS bowl games are the most prestigious, most widely publicized, and most lucrative bowls, and they generate the most television revenue. However, there has been a proliferation of less-elite postseason football bowl games, reflecting their perceived potential to generate revenue for the sports entrepreneurs, advertisers, and media who constitute "local Golden Triangles" associated with these games. They are also perceived as important sources of revenue and publicity for football programs, their institutions, and their conferences once the regular season has ended.

Below the Division I-A Football Bowl Subdivision in the NCAA hierarchy is Division I-AA, which is now called the "NCAA Football Championship Subdivision." It also has over 100 members, but its football programs are smaller-scale with smaller stadiums and fewer paying spectators. The remaining 100 members in Division I have big-time basketball programs but do not have football. In 2007, the NCAA Division I board of directors approved a four-year moratorium on accepting additional members because its membership had been swollen in recent years with a steady stream of new members wanting to play basketball at the top level (Powers 2007b). With 330 members overall and nearly 25 other prospective members in the pipeline that would not be affected by the moratorium, directors were worried that Division I had grown too big.

In general, within Division I, there is a stratification of conferences, with the top six conferences—which I will call the "Elite 6"—generating considerably more revenue from sources such as television contracts, bowl games, and gate receipts than the other conferences. The Elite 6 include the Southeastern Conference (SEC), Big Ten, Atlantic Coast Conference (ACC), Big 12 Conference, Pacific-10 Conference, and Big East Conference, and in 2002–2003, they produced revenue ranging from over $68 million in the Big East to over $122 million in the SEC (Suggs 2004a). The near-elite Conference USA generated over $30 million that year, which was nearly four times more than the next-richest conference. At the bottom of this list was the Northeast Conference with $1.2 million. The Elite 6 conferences include the institutions with the most visible and successful big-time programs in football and men's basketball, which are the major revenue generators in college athletics. With much more conference revenue, football and men's basketball programs in the Elite 6 conferences generally have a competitive advantage over programs in less-affluent conferences, since individual institutions in Elite 6 conferences have more money than programs in non-elite conferences to spend on coaches, recruiting, facilities, financial and academic support for athletes, and operating expenses (Wertheim 2007:59). In addition, elite conferences have had more seats than less-elite conferences on the NCAA Management Council, and thus have been able to exercise more power over the rules that govern college athletics (Suggs 2004a).

The kinds of inequalities in athletics money, status, and power within Division I are magnified when we look at differences between Division I in general and the other NCAA divisions. Division II, with nearly three hundred members, and Division III, with over four hundred members, typically include smaller universities and colleges with less-lofty athletic ambitions and much less corporate and commercial organization. However, athletic programs at the Division II and Division III levels may have more varsity sports and more participants than many of their counterparts in Division I. In general, the different NCAA divisions reflect the structured inequalities or stratification of college athletics in the United States, with "higher" levels having more athletic talent, more financial support for programs, more financial and academic support specifically for athletes, more commercialization, more visibility, and more economic and political power in the NCAA. The biggest of the big-time programs in Division I draw the most interest, coverage, and investment from the Golden Triangle.

The "big-time" programs in Division I in general generate the most revenue but also are the most expensive and often require university subsidies to operate. In our discussion of the business of college sports later in this chapter, we will see that big-time football has the potential to generate the most revenue but also has the most financial risk when investment in it does not "pay off" with wins, gate receipts, television revenue, and corporate sponsorships. Within athletic departments of individual institutions, football and men's basketball generally sit at the top of a hierarchy, which separates big-time men's sports from both women's sports and men's lower-tier sports, which are less funded or are designated as "non-revenue." That is, athletic departments are stratified into what we can call "Tier I" and "Tier II" sports. Tier I includes the "big-time" programs at the top, and Tier II includes the other programs, which are generally not expected to produce any or much revenue and receive less funding than the Tier I programs. Title IX has reduced a substantial amount of the inequality between men's and women's programs in general, but women's programs are typically more similar to Tier II men's nonrevenue programs than to Tier I men's programs in their funding, commercialization, and corporate sponsorship. Although it typically is

Rutgers' Epiphanny Prince (10) goes up for a shot against the defense of Tennessee's Nicky Anosike (55) during the first half of the NCAA Women's National Championship game Tuesday, April 3, 2007, in Cleveland. Women's basketball reflects the popular growth and commercialization of women's sports in the NCAA. However, basketball is the only women's sport in the top tier of the NCAA's Golden Triangle, and it is still much less commercialized and supported than the men's game. (AP Photo/Amy Sancetta)

not funded or publicized to the same extent as men's basketball, women's college basketball has achieved Tier I or "big-time" status at a few institutions, such as the University of Tennessee and the University of Connecticut.

In chapter four, data were presented showing racial and gender inequalities in the opportunity structure of college sports for athletes, coaches, and administrators. For example, although black athletes had numerous opportunities to participate in a few sports, such as basketball and football for males and basketball and track and field for females, they were relatively invisible in most other sports. American Indians are even more underrepresented than African Americans and Latinos in college sports. According to 2002 data (cited by Boeck 2007), 0.8 percent of students at four-year colleges were American Indians, but only 0.3 percent of male athletes and 0.3 percent of female athletes were American Indians. In comparison, 7 percent of college students were Latino and 3.5 percent of male athletes and 2.8 percent of female athletes were Latino. African Americans were 11.1 percent of all students and 17.7 percent of male athletes and 10.4 percent of female athletes.

We are more familiar with the prejudice and discrimination faced by African-American and Latino athletes, but as we observed in chapter four, American Indians have faced a number of factors reducing their chances of being recruited and of participating in college sports (Simpson 1987). The issue of Indian mascots helps us understand why American Indians often feel that they are demeaned and devalued in college athletics on predominantly white campuses. For many fans of a number of college sports teams, Indian nicknames and mascots have long engendered pride and affection as part of their institutional tradition (Infante 2007). However, as Davis (2002) observed, for many American Indians, the Indian mascots have reflected racist stereotypes that misrepresented and demeaned them as Indians, just as the playing of "Dixie" and the waving of the Confederate flag demeaned blacks and sexist team names demeaned female athletes. By fostering racist stereotypes, mascots may undermine efforts to improve relations between Indians and other ethnic and racial groups on campus and in the community. Opponents have also protested the use of Indian nicknames and mascots because Indians did not control these symbols of their culture.

The NCAA viewed this matter as serious enough to warrant a policy prohibiting schools with "hostile and abusive" American Indian nicknames, logos, and mascots from hosting postseason tournaments. Nearly twenty institutions faced restrictions from the NCAA. Some were removed from the list after winning appeals with support from local Indian tribes, others changed their Indian nicknames or other Indian symbols, and some continued to fight the policy. On some campuses, the NCAA policy caused substantial controversy and strong institutional opposition to the NCAA. Florida State University (Seminoles) and the University of Utah (Utes) were two of the most prominent cases of institutions with big-time programs to win their appeals and be removed from the restricted list, while the University of Illinois (Fighting Illini) and William and Mary (The Tribe) are two well-known institutions that made changes, albeit reluctantly. William and Mary retained its nickname but discontinued using a logo with Indian feathers. The University of Illinois was permitted to retain its nickname but was compelled to drop its mascot, the fictional "Chief Illiniwek." However, by dropping the ban of the Chief during the 2007 Homecoming fes-

James (Jim) Francis Thorpe, (1882–1953), a Sauk and Fox Indian from Oklahoma, was one of the most outstanding athletes of the twentieth century, even though, as an Indian, he generally received much less media and popular attention than other star athletes of his era. In this photo, he wears the football uniform of the Carlisle Indian School, Pennsylvania, ca. 1909. (Corbis)

tivities, citing the constitutional right of free expression, the Illinois chancellor was signaling his institution's willingness to continue its struggle with the NCAA (Zirin 2007) and was also demonstrating the complexities of trying to resolve this issue on resistant campuses. An irony of the demeaning and discriminatory treatment of Indians in college sports is that one of the greatest U.S. and college athletes was an Indian, Jim Thorpe, and one of the greatest U.S. college football teams consisted of Thorpe and his Indian teammates. A "Sport in the News" feature focuses on the interesting and infrequently told story of

Sport in the News Feature 9.1: American Indians, Jim Thorpe, and Their Unrecognized Imprint on College Football

Although many sports fans may recognize the name of "Jim Thorpe," perhaps as the only prominent American Indian athlete they can name, few know the story of how his Carlisle Indian Industrial School team transformed college football in the United States in the early 1900s. It is a reflection of the low status of Indians in U.S. society and sport that this Carlisle Indian team has received little credit for its accomplishments in historical accounts or records of college football. Sportswriter Sally Jenkins (2007b) has rectified this historical oversight with her carefully researched story about the accomplishments of this great team. Thus, this is a "Sport in the News" feature that combines elements of a systematic research study. It is different from other news features because it is based on historical journalism and relates historical events about the Carlisle Indian Industrial School football team and Jim Thorpe to contemporary issues concerning the status of Indians in college sports today as reflected in the Indian mascot controversy.

The success of Thorpe's Carlisle Indian team against the top U.S. college football teams in the early part of the twentieth century is a little-known story today, which Sally Jenkins (2007b) recently brought to public attention in her book *The Real Americans: The Team That Changed a Game, a People, a Nation*. Her book tells how American Indians transformed college football—and got little or no credit for it. With a track star new to football, Jim Thorpe, and with the coaching of the legendary Pop Warner, the Carlisle Indians became the most exciting team in college football in 1907. Jenkins observed that most histories of the sport attributed the first use of the forward pass to Gus Dorais and Knute Rockne of Notre Dame in 1913. In fact, her research showed that the Indians were the first team to throw deeply and regularly downfield six years earlier in 1907. This historical inaccuracy is important because it deprived the Indians of recognition for an innovation that changed the sport and also may have saved it by curtailing the violence and deaths that almost caused football's abolition at that time.

The glory days of the Carlisle Indian School football team ended when Thorpe quit, after the revelation that he had taken money to play semipro baseball, which also cost him his Olympic medals. Thorpe's medals were restored in 1982, long after his death about thirty years earlier, but his case revealed both the complexity and hypocrisy in college (and Olympic) sports regarding amateurism. College athletic officials have long maintained that their sports were played by amateurs, but the reality is that play for pay has been part of college sports since the first college sports event, and allegations of professionalism and under-the-table or illegal subsidies for athletes have long been a part of the history of college sports. Thorpe knew that a number of other college athletes at the time he played had done exactly what he did and were not punished for it. This is why he did not think he was doing anything wrong returning to Carlisle to play college football after taking $15 a week to play baseball for two summers in 1909 and 1910.

In the NCAA today, athletes may legally compete in a college sport as long as they were not previously compensated for playing that sport, which means that they could have been paid to play another sport. The NCAA has also granted exemptions from their amateur rule to foreign athletes in non-elite sports such as tennis who have accepted some prize money beyond their expenses in the sport. In fact, a number of foreign athletes who previously received much more than compensation for their expenses for playing a sport have played that sport for their college without an exemption (Drape 2006). Jim Thorpe's transgression of playing baseball for pay would not be a violation of NCAA rules today in relation to his participation in football. He had not disguised his identity by using an assumed name when he played baseball as a number of others had. When a reporter publicized his semipro experience and news leaked to his coach, Pop Warner urged him to admit what he had done to the Amateur Athletic Union in a letter of confession that Warner wrote and Thorpe was advised to sign. The admission cost him both his amateur status as a college athlete and the Olympic medals he had earned in 1912. He said to his coach, "I don't understand, Pop. What's that two months of baseball got to do with all the jumping and running and field-work I did in Stockholm [the site of the Olympics]? I never got paid for any of that, did I?" (Jenkins 2007b:288).

The story of Jim Thorpe and the Carlisle Indians football team highlights the important contribution of American Indians to the history of the big-time college sport of football. This story also shows how Jim Thorpe became a victim of the inconsistent enforcement of amateur standards in college, and it draws attention to the ongoing challenge of maintaining at least the appearance of amateurism in a context of increasing commercialism in college sports. The Olympics ultimately gave up the charade of amateurism, and NCAA now permits the kind of professionalism that cost Jim Thorpe his amateur status. Most importantly, Jenkins's historical account reveals the significant contradiction between the important athletic accomplishments of Indian athletes and the demeaning use of Indian mascots by college sports teams that rarely have given Indian student-athletes a chance to participate on them.

this team and its impact on college football. The feature also raises interesting questions about amateurism and professionalism in college athletics in terms of Thorpe's experience.

The Indian mascot controversy demonstrates the disenchantment of at least some institutions with the NCAA on some issues as well as the power of the NCAA to exercise control over its member institutions. The authority of the NCAA has been challenged both by its own institutions and by outside critics on a number of occasions in its history, but it remains the dominant organization in college athletics today. As the Indian mascot issue reveals, the NCAA has even been able to compel powerful and highly prominent institutions to comply with its policies. Thus, the NCAA remains the most powerful force in college athletics as its governing authority. We have seen that within the NCAA, member institutions are organized into a highly stratified hierarchy of status, money, and power and that within member institutions, especially at the highest NCAA levels, sports programs tend to be stratified into two main tiers based on revenue-producing expectations and performance. Furthermore, among participants, opportunities to participate at the Tier I level in particular sports may vary according to gender, race, or ethnicity.

From the AIAW to NCAA Women's Sports

The NCAA faced a serious challenge to its power and financial status in the 1970s following the passage of Title IX. As women's college sports exploded during this period, a new organization arose to foster this growth and provide major competitive opportunities for women in college athletics. The Association for Intercollegiate Athletics for Women (AIAW) was established by an organization of women physical educators in 1971 as the first major governing body for women's intercollegiate athletics (Morrison 1993; Nixon and Frey 1996: 147–148). The AIAW grew out of an earlier organization, the Commission on Intercollegiate Athletics for Women (CIAW), which was formed in 1966 to sponsor national championships for women. However, it soon became clear that a much larger institutional membership organization with wider institutional representation was needed for this purpose, and thus the AIAW replaced the CIAW.

The AIAW began with lofty principles and goals. Its organizers embraced an amateur model of athletics and tried to establish policies that respected the rights of student-athletes. Its founding principles emphasized striving for and rewarding excellence in sport but also using sport as a chance for education and development for those who do not win; women governing and leading women; women serving as role models to empower other women; providing numerous, inclusive, and diverse sports opportunities for women and opportunities for women with different skill levels; and accommodating athletes who wished to transfer, return to school after dropping out, or try out for the Olympics (Morrison 1993:61–62). Many AIAW members wanted to create an organization that differed from the NCAA and men's athletics in being less bureaucratic and less commercialized and more responsive to the needs of student-athletes. At first, there were no athletic scholarships, no transfer limitations, and no limits on the number of sports a college or university could offer. The AIAW also depended on self-policing and the integrity of individual institutions rather than a formal enforcement unit to maintain control over possible excesses or deviance in athletic programs.

As an indication of the lack of "big-time" or large-school dominance in the early years of the AIAW, a tiny eight-hundred-woman college in Pennsylvania, Immaculata College, was able to win the first three AIAW national basketball championships from 1972 to 1974 (Byrne 2005). However, even during these early years, conflicts arose about the direction of the organization, and the AIAW began to drift toward a more competitive, professionalized, and commercialized sports model that favored bigger institutions. For example, in 1973, AIAW institutions began offering athletic grants-in-aid or scholarships rather than strictly need-based scholarships to athletes, and in 1975, television covered a regular-season women's college basketball game for the first time (Jenkins 2007a). Immaculata defeated the University of Maryland in that game and then went on to play in front of twelve thousand spectators in the first women's college game at Madison Square Garden in New York City later that season. Immaculata was AIAW runner-up in 1975 and 1976, but it lacked the money and desire to continue competing at the top level of the evolving women's basketball game. The first nationally televised broadcast of the AIAW basketball championship, which was tape delayed, was in 1978, and by then, the larger universities had begun to take over the sport, with UCLA defeating Maryland (Jenkins 2007a). Title IX, which had created the interest in women's sports that was needed to justify the investment of television and the Golden Triangle, ironically may have created an environment in which it was increasingly difficult for smaller institutions to compete successfully against much bigger ones, as Immaculata once did (Byrne 2005). Pushed by Title IX to create more opportunities and better funding for women's sports, the bigger universities became increasingly difficult competitors for much smaller institutions with much smaller athletic budgets and recruiting capabilities.

The AIAW was able to grow during the 1970s despite some organizational problems related to administrative inexperience and internal disagreements among member institutions. Its growth was made easier by the absence of organizational competition or interference from the NCAA, which had no interest at the time in sponsoring championships in women's sports. The AIAW grew from 278 charter member institutions in 1971 to 950 members in 1981, and in 1980–1981, it sponsored 39 championships. Thus, the AIAW was able to take advantage of the surge in popularity of sports among girls and women that was made possible by Title IX. The AIAW estimated that at the beginning of the 1980s, 120,000 women were competing in college sports, in comparison to 180,000 men in college athletics (Eitzen and Sage 1997:293; Nixon 1984:122). Along with providing regular and high-level competitive opportunities for female athletes in college, it gave women the chance for leadership roles as coaches and athletic administrators. However, the growing success of the AIAW ultimately led to its demise, as it tempted the NCAA to get involved in women's sports.

In the context of the growing popularity of women's college sports and the uncertainties associated with the future influence of Title IX on NCAA men's sports, NCAA member institutions voted at the association's 1981 convention to sponsor women's championships and govern women's sports without any additional cost to member institutions (Nixon and Frey 1996:148). In addition, the NCAA offered a television package for both men's and women's championships that guaranteed a national audience for the women, and it scheduled its national championships for women at the same time the AIAW scheduled its championships. Although the women received less support than the men to travel to championships and less championship revenue, the assorted inducements offered by the NCAA to the women led to a rapid decline in AIAW membership as institutions switched from the AIAW to the NCAA. Within months of the NCAA vote, there was a 20 percent drop in AIAW membership and a 48 percent decline in Division I AIAW championship participation. Perhaps the final blow was notification by the NBC television network that it would not televise future AIAW championships and that it would not pay the approximately $500,000 it had agreed to pay the AIAW from 1981 to 1983. Faced with these new realities, the AIAW executive board concluded that it could no longer operate effectively on behalf of female college athletes and decided to dissolve the association in 1982 (Morrison 1993:64).

Beyond the AIAW: Gender Equity and the Financial Arms Race in College Athletics

Since the NCAA seized control of women's college sports from the AIAW in the early 1980s, female participation has continued to expand. As noted in chapter four, it grew exponentially at a rate of 500 percent between 1971, the year before Title IX was passed, and 2004 (Coakley 2007:241). Furthermore, the average number of women's intercollegiate sports teams per institution steadily increased from 2.50 in 1970 (pre–Title IX), to 5.61 in 1978 (the Title IX compliance date mandated by the federal government), to 8.45 in 2006 (Carpenter and Acosta 2006). With women's and men's sports teams being added and cut between 1988–1989 and 2003–2004, NCAA member institutions had a net gain of 2,102 women's sports teams and a net gain of 70 men's sports teams during this time period (Women's Sports Foundation 2007). Additional data from a study sponsored by the Women's Sports Foundation (Cheslock 2007) revealed that female participation increased by 11,000 between 2001–2002 and 2004–2005 and that male participation grew by 10,000 during this four-year period at 1,895 institutions of higher education. Despite the impressive pattern of increases in college sports participation opportunities for females, however, women still lagged behind men in participation in the 2004–2005 academic year, with females representing 41.3 percent of college athletes despite being 55 percent of students enrolled in college in the fall of 2004 (Cheslock 2007). Furthermore, from 2003–2004 to 2004–2005, female participants in NCAA college sports programs increased by nearly 4,000, while male participation increased in that year by over 5,500 (Women's Sports Foundation 2007).

Although joining the NCAA has resulted in benefits for women's sports programs in participation opportunities, funding, media attention, and commercial support, it also has had costs. Under the AIAW, women's college sports were administered and coached by women, but under the NCAA, many female directors of women's athletics became associate directors of athletics for women's sports and many women coaches lost their jobs to male coaches, who saw new opportunities in a more professionalized and commercialized world of women's college athletics. According to the annual Racial and Gender Report Card compiled for 2005–2006 by the Institute of Diversity and Ethics in Sport of the University of Central Florida (Lapchick, Martin, Kushner, and Brenden 2006), approximately 60 percent of the head coaches of Division I women's sports teams were women, while 3.5 percent of the head coaches of Division I men's teams were women. Coaching opportunities for women in women's sports were best in Division III, where over 43 percent of head coaches were women, while they were worst in Division II, where 33.5 percent of head coaches were women. In the most commercialized women's sport, basketball, 64.3 percent of the head coaches were women, but for cross-country and track and field, which are very popular among women athletes, less than 21 percent of the coaches were women in 2005–2006. None of the commissioners of Football Bowl Subdivision conferences were women; all were white men. Women were 7.8 percent of the athletic directors in Division I. Opportunities for women to be directors of athletics were significantly better in the lower divisions, with women representing nearly 19 percent of the athletic directors in Division II and over 27 percent in Division III.

According to the 2002–2003 NCAA Gender Equity Report, the status of women's college sports programs had substantially improved in some areas over the previous decade, but women still lagged behind the men in a number of key areas, especially at the highest Division I Bowl Subdivision level. For example: (1) there was an average of 253 female and 325 male participants at each institution; (2) the average total expenditures at these institutions were $5.4 million for women's sports and $12.6 million for men's sports; (3) the average institutional athletic recruiting expenditures were $164,800 for women's sports and $382,000 for men's sports; (4) the average scholarship expenditures at each institution were $1.9 million for women's sports and $2.6 million for men's sports; and (5) the average amounts of money spent by institutions on head coaches' salaries were $620,000 for women's sports and $1.2 million for men's sports. The female athletic participation rate of 41.3 percent in 2004–2005 was nearly 14 percent lower than the 55 percent female representation among four-year college students enrolled in fall 2004 (Cheslock 2007).

These statistics about gender differences raise questions about the meaning of gender equity and how it can be achieved. Although "gender equity" in college athletics does not necessarily imply equality, Title IX, as a civil rights law, requires an effort to eliminate discrimination and achieve fairness in the distribution of opportunities and rewards. The "teeth" of Title IX is the fact that failure to comply can result in a withdrawal of federal funds from an institution. The U.S. federal government, the NCAA, and individual colleges and universities have wrestled with the challenge of constructing reasonable and practical legal guidelines for complying with Title IX and achieving gender equity. Compliance with Title IX in athletics requires meeting standards in three areas: athletic participation, athletic financial assistance, and other program areas involving the treatment of athletes (Cheslock 2007). Among these "other areas" are the quality, maintenance, and availability of locker rooms and other facilities; academic support; publicity; recruitment; and the quality and compensation of coaches. Perhaps the best-known standards for Title IX compliance concern participation. Institutions can meet Title IX requirements and demonstrate gender equity in participation by meeting one of three tests, showing *proportionality, history of progress*, or *accommodation of interest*.

Meeting the proportionality test means showing that the percentages of females and males in athletics are approximately equal (within a few percentage points) to the percentages of female and male undergraduates at an institution. The continuing gender gap in participation rates helps explain why rowing has become the fastest-growing female college sport in recent years. Its roster size is comparable to football's, with some women's crew teams having over one hundred members (Miller 2007). Of course, having a women's crew team is not feasible on many campuses and, with an increasingly unequal gender ratio in student enrollment, many institutions have tried to comply with Title IX by using a different strategy. They have cut Tier II men's sports to improve the ratio of female-to-male athletes, they have tried to show that they have had a recent history of expanding women's athletic programs, or they have tried to demonstrate that they have fully accommodated the athletic interests and abilities of the traditionally underrepresented sex on their campus. Although methods such as email surveys to show accommodation of interest have been widely criticized, the cuts in men's sports have aroused the most controversy.

Cuts of Tier II men's sports have understandably angered coaches, athletes, and fans of these sports, and many of these people have blamed Title IX for the cuts (Suggs 2005). Some prominent advocates of women's sports and gender equity (e.g., Lopiano 2002/2005) as well as critics of the substantial and growing financial investment in big-time men's sports (e.g., Zimbalist 2006:247–250, 266–268) have argued, however, that the blame has been misguidedly aimed at Title IX. Research has shown, as we have observed, that although the quantity of women's sports teams has increased by a large number since 1988–1989, men have also had a net gain, albeit a modest one, in sports teams during that period (Women's Sports Foundation 2007). Decreases in the number of male athletes have been heavily concentrated in a few sports, such as tennis and wrestling. However, a study of 738 NCAA institutions showed that between 1995–1996 and 2004–2005, the number of football players increased by more than 4,000, the number of baseball players increased by over 1,500, the number of male lacrosse players increased by over 1,000, and the number of male soccer players increased by over 750 (Cheslock 2007). When focusing on a four-year sample of 1,895 institutions of higher education from 2001–2002 to 2004–2005, this study also showed that only two men's sports, tennis and volleyball, had reductions of more than 60 athletes, while 12 men's sports increased by at least that number in that period. Football, baseball, lacrosse, and soccer had the biggest gains, as in the 10-year survey. Perhaps most interesting among the results of this research is that the only NCAA level with net losses in men's participation levels in the 10-year survey was the I-A Football Bowl Subdivision.

These statistics provide a factual context for considering the debates about Title IX and program cuts. The author of the Women's Sports Foundation study acknowledged that other studies have had different results and different conclusions about whether there was a net gain or loss in men's teams or participation (Cheslock 2007). Without getting into complicated arguments about methodological differences among these studies, the most compelling points made by the Women's Sports Foundation study may be that net reductions in opportunities for male athletes were only at the highest NCAA level and that Title IX was not the cause of substantial cuts in men's sports. In the latter regard, the study's author pointed to the net gain of seventy men's sports from 1988–1989 to 2003–2004. He also observed that another study showed the biggest decline in men's participation from 1984 to 1987, which was a period when college athletics was exempt from Title IX due to a Supreme Court ruling, implying that Title IX could not have been the cause of the reductions.

A number of college sports experts and commentators have proposed that policy debates and research should be redirected from program cuts and Title IX to the effects of the "financial arms race" of unrestrained spending in the big-time sports programs (Weistart 1998; Nixon 2005, 2007b). The pattern of substantial and increasing spending by big-time football and men's basketball, and by some women's basketball programs, has been stretching athletic department budgets tighter and tighter and may explain why the reductions in men's participation opportunities have been concentrated at the highest level of college sports. Lower-tier women's and men's sports all must compete with the elite Tier I men's sports for limited athletic resources, as the Tier I sports caught up in the arms race constantly seek more resources. In this environment, it is very difficult to meet the self-perceived financial needs of the biggest of the big-time programs *and* try to rectify gender inequities. Institutions with big-time sports programs or aspirations face a continuing dilemma of how to deal with both challenges.

One recent case of an Elite 6 institution shows how Title IX and the arms race may combine to influence program and resource allocation decisions. In this case, Syracuse University announced that it would cut its men's and women's swimming and diving teams after the 2007–2008 season and add a women's ice hockey team for the 2008–2009 season (Lipka 2007b). It had added three other women's teams since 1996 and expected to meet the proportionality requirement of Title IX by 2008–2009. The athletic scholarships that had been awarded to male swimmers would be used for women ice hockey players. On the surface, this case seems to be a clear-cut demonstration of the influence of Title IX over athletic decisions. However, it also should be noted that it was easier and less expensive to recruit ice hockey players than swimmers to this northern New York institution, that a needed pool replacement would cost $25 million while the ice rink used by men's and women's club hockey teams needed only minor renovations, and that the university opened a multimillion-dollar football training facility in 2005 and planned to open a similar facility for men's and women's basketball in 2008 (Lipka 2007b). Furthermore, the men's basketball team, a past national champion accustomed to big-time success, did not qualify for the men's tournament in 2007, losing out on a chance to earn the financial rewards of success in this lucrative event. Thus, both Title IX and financial pressures seem to influence major decisions by athletic directors with big-time athletic programs, and they may also have a significant influence over athletic decisions at institutions with aspirations to move up to big-time status.

College presidents and the president of the NCAA have expressed concerns about the risks of a continuing arms race for the long-term financial integrity or viability of college athletics (Brand 2006; NCAA 2006; Sloan 2007). They also have understood the need to figure out how to reduce gender inequities in college sports. Despite this recognition, university leaders and the NCAA have not been able, or have not tried, to harness the escalating spending patterns in big-time men's sports, and many presidents have been reluctant or unwilling to redirect resources to lower-tier and women's programs. Coaches' compensation is a significant aspect of the arms race in big-time college sports, and one expert on the economics of college sports has argued that paying big-time coaches less money would leave more resources to achieve gender equity, without having to cut Tier II men's sports (Zimbalist 2006:248–249). The steeply escalating compensation packages paid to coaches in big-time college football and men's basketball and to some coaches of the most successful or ambitious women's basketball teams have become a source of considerable controversy in recent years.

The Business of College Athletics

The existence of an arms race in college athletics implies the existence of a marketplace in which different athletic programs or "firms" try to outbid each other for the services of the most talented coaches, try to create an appealing and classy image of their program with big-name coaches and superior equipment and facilities, try to use that image to brand their program as superior to the brands of their rivals, and try to use their superior brand to market and "sell" their program more effectively to recruits, boosters, donors, sponsors, and media outlets. This is the *business* of big-time college sports. Although colleges and universities and the NCAA may be serious about the idea of the student-athlete and the academic integrity of college athletics, the NCAA and its member institutions that compete at the Division I level are also quite serious about the business of college sports. They are committed to success on the field and in the athletic marketplace I just described. This dual commitment to academic integrity and commercial success in college athletics may be difficult to sustain, though.

One former president of a very prominent Elite 6 university acknowledged the intrinsic value of athletics for student-athletes but also pointed to a number of serious shortcomings of big-time athletic programs. James Duderstadt (2000), a former president of the University of Michigan, sharply criticized big-time football and men's basketball as commercial entertainment businesses, noting their corruption of academic values, their lack of relevance to the academic mission of the university, and the deviance of athletes and coaches. Despite such harsh criticisms from a former "insider" and rhetoric about reform in the NCAA (NCAA 2006), there is little evidence of the NCAA or its big-time members' moving away from their commercial ties to the Golden Triangle. Indeed, once an institution's leadership has bought into the rationale for Tier I success—to enhance institutional visibility, prestige, and external support—it may have fallen into an "athletic trap" from which it is very difficult to escape. That is, the "institutional enhancement rationale" that leads institutions into the financial arms race of ever-increasing spending on Tier I athletics may result in ceding institutional control over athletics to big-name coaches, athletic directors, powerful athletic boosters (alumni, trustees, and wealthy athletic donors), television executives, and corporate sponsors, who believe most strongly in the need for increased investment in elite—almost always men's—athletic programs.

The biggest of the big-time programs, such as Ohio State University, may reap major rewards from consistent success on their athletic fields and filled seats in their football stadiums and basketball arenas (Suggs 2002). However, even though Ohio State generated $104.7 million in revenue in athletics in the 2006 fiscal year, which was the most revenue earned by any athletic department that year, it spent over $100 million—which does not include capital expenditures for new and renovated facilities—to produce a surplus of less than $3 million (Wertheim 2007). Some of the other institutions at the top of the NCAA's top tier spent less and earned more, such as Ohio's archrival Michigan, which produced a surplus of $17.5 million from its $85.5 million in revenue, but others earned little or no surplus despite spending almost as much as Ohio State. For example, the University of Virginia earned no surplus despite spending $92.7 million. Among the major women's basketball programs, only seven generated a surplus, led by the University of Connecticut with almost $1 million. The biggest deficit produced by any individual sports program was $3.9 million for the University of Houston football program (Wertheim 2007). Of course, the financial world of the biggest of the big-time athletic programs in the Elite 6 conferences is very different from that of those at the bottom of the highly stratified Division I. For example, the smallest programs, such as VMI, Louisiana-Monroe, and Louisiana-Lafayette, earned between $5.5 million and $8 million in revenue, and none of these athletic programs enjoys the visibility, prestige, or athletic success of the highly commercialized big-time programs in Division I.

University officials, trustees, and athletic boosters often seem to justify the escalating expenditures in terms of the "realities" of the marketplace and a "more investment equals more wins" rationale (Nixon 2007b). Those who defend rising compensation for coaches argue that it is legitimate because these payments are supported by athletic revenues and donations rather than state taxes. How much money do big-time coaches earn in college sports? The average compensation for head football coaches in the Division I Bowl Subdivision was over $900,000, according to the 2005–2006 AAUP faculty compensation survey (AAUP 2007), which was nearly 2.5 times more than the average compensation for presidents of these institutions and nearly 9.5 times more than the average compensation for full professors at these universities. The highest-paid football coach earned nearly $3.5 million, while the lowest-paid coach in the Bowl Subdivision earned $130,000. According to a *USA Today* survey in 2007, at least 42 Bowl Subdivision football coaches earned $1 million or more (Upton and Wieberg 2007). Although the best-paid head coaches of Division I men's basketball teams did not earn as much as their counterparts in football, coaching compensation in men's basketball reached almost $2.2 million in 2006–2007, and 20 of the 65 head coaches in the NCAA men's basketball tournament in 2007 earned at least $1 million in compensation. I have called the escalating competition to hire star coaches a "star wars arms race" (Nixon 2007b), and as long as it continues, big-time coaches' compensation packages will continue to rise. Coaches at the lower-level "mid-major" institutions will also continue to benefit from this arms race, although to a lesser extent than those hired by Elite 6 institutions. For example, men's basketball coaches outside the Elite 6 "power conferences" that generate the most revenue earned an average of $400,000 in 2006–2007 (Brady and Upton 2007).

My research (Nixon 2007b) has shown that paying top dollar for star coaches in football and men's basketball does not guarantee the high national rankings in these sports that presidents, athletic directors, and athletic boosters seek. I looked at whether twenty-five of the best-compensated football coaches and twenty-five of the best-paid men's basketball coaches in 2006–2007 had teams in the top twenty-five season-end rankings in three seasons, 2002–2003, 2005–2006, and 2006–2007. I found a 40 percent to 60 percent chance that these coaches had a top-twenty-five team. Thus, playing in the star wars arms race is risky. However, the desire to hire star coaches in these sports is understandable because successful big-name coaches tend to have the most success in recruiting and research has indicated that, at least in I-A Bowl Subdivision football, there tends to be a mutually reinforcing relationship between recruiting and winning (Langelett 2003). These results imply that a top recruiting class increases the chances of a high team ranking and that having a high ranking increases the chances of continued success in recruiting the best talent. Successful big-name coaches are most likely to attract these top recruiting classes. These self-reinforcing patterns mean that an effective way to move up into the top rankings is to hire a coach with recruiting success and a successful record at another institution, which helps explain the star wars arms race in coaches' compensation.

The star wars arms race also affects women's college basketball, which is the most lucrative sport for coaches of women's teams, and two women's basketball coaches earned $1 million in 2007. One was a male. The longtime and now-legendary female coach at the University of Tennessee Pat Summitt started her career at Tennessee earning $8,900 in 1974. She signed a six-year, $7.8 million contract in 2006, and she supplemented her base compensation in 2007 by several hundred thousand dollars by winning her conference title and her seventh national championship (Patrick 2007). As women enjoy the increasing rewards of success as their sports become more prominent and commercialized, they may face more competition from men for these lucrative jobs

(Wilson 2007). In addition, like their big-name male counterparts, they are likely to feel more of the pressure of having to win in big-time programs, and they are more likely than in the past to be fired for not meeting the raised expectations of their institutions and boosters (Patrick 2007).

Lucrative contracts with television and apparel makers have brought in large sums of money for a number of institutions, which has seemed to add fuel to the star wars arms race (Upton and Wieberg 2006). The most money is available to the best of the big-time programs, and thus many institutions seem to be driven to spend more to achieve this status. However, the more universities embrace the marketplace and a business model for athletics and the more they spend, the more they tempt legislators to treat them as for-profit businesses with associated tax obligations. One prominent member of Congress, the chair of the House Ways and Means Committee, wrote to the NCAA president that "excessive compensation . . . makes less revenue available for other sports, causes many athletic departments to operate at a net loss, and may call into question the priorities of educational institutions." He went on to ask: "What actions has the NCAA taken to encourage its member institutions to curb excessive compensation for college coaches?" (quoted in Upton and Wieberg 2006).

Despite its financial and political risks, the arms race has become widespread in Division I of the NCAA. At a rank below the most commercialized big-name programs, many "mid-majors" have joined the arms race and are feeling its pressures. As the Wichita State athletics director said, "I think it's a challenge at any level to keep coaches who are having success. . . . I think that if you are at a program that may not be perceived as being at the very top of the food chain . . . the challenge is greater" (quoted in Brady and Upton 2007). Thus, escalating salaries are the price of admission to the big-time college sports world for those with upwardly mobile ambitions, just as they are the cost of doing business at the top level. Similarly, these institutions, like their more elite counterparts, are likely to feel the pressure to upgrade their equipment and facilities and make themselves more attractive to athletic recruits, boosters, donors, fans, and the Golden Triangle.

According to NCAA data for 2004–2005 presented to the Knight Commission (Fitzpatrick 2007), more than 90 percent of Division I athletic programs had deficits averaging $7.1 million and only 7 percent (22/313) of Division I athletic departments were self-supporting. The departments with surpluses tended to have the most elite football programs, such as Ohio State. Although athletic spending was only 4 to 5 percent of all university expenditures, athletic spending increases, driven by the arms race, were four or five times higher than the rate of increase of spending in other areas of university budgets. The star wars arms race and the athletic facilities arms race were major reasons for the escalation in athletic spending. The biggest individual expense item in most athletic operating budgets was athletic scholarships, which cost a total of $1.2 billion nationwide, and $150 million was spent on academic support staff and programs for athletes. Athletic departments with deficits typically relied on direct subsidies from their institution's general funds or student fees to balance their budgets. Institutional contributions in the Football Bowl Subdivision were 21.6 percent of revenue, or an average of $7.8 million. Subsidies for other Division I institutions with football were 71.1 percent of athletic budgets, which was an average of $7.6 million. Non-football Division I institutions received subsidies that were 73.6 percent of their athletic budgets and averaged $6.7 million.

Television contracts and football bowl money explain the substantial revenue differences among programs in Division I (Suggs 2004a). For example, the Elite 6 conferences have received almost half of the revenue from the 11-year NCAA $6.1 billion contract with CBS sports for the NCAA men's basketball tournament, while the other half of the revenue is divided among the 24 remaining Division I conferences. Programs in the most elite conferences can depend on large and increasing amounts of revenue from major sources such as television and the lucrative football bowl games that are part of the Bowl Championship Series, while programs in the lesser conferences earn much less revenue. Although they generate the most revenue, the Elite 6 programs also spend the most, but their actual financial bottom line sometimes may be difficult to figure out. Financial reports for athletics may underestimate deficits because they

From left, George Mason's Lamar Butler, Jai Lewis, and Tony Skinn appear on a live television feed during the team's press conference following their practice for the Final Four basketball championship in Indianapolis, Friday, March 31, 2006. The television monitor is below a promotional poster for the NCAA. George Mason was the Cinderella team in the NCAA Men's Final Four, and lost to eventual winner Florida. George Mason experienced the media boost from the Golden Triangle that a team and school receive when they participate in a Golden Triangle "mega event" in college sports. This is an unusual case of a "mid-major" outside the Elite Six conferences and top echelon of college sports making it to the Final Four. (AP Photos/Darron Cummings)

count institutional subsidies as revenue or they may fail to count capital expenditures as expenses. Capital investments for new or renovated facilities can cost hundreds of millions of dollars and result in millions of dollars of annual debt service (Nixon 2007b). Furthermore, according to one estimate, athletic departments at tax-supported universities in the United States are given more than $1 billion in student fees and general institutional funds and services (Alesia 2006a).

Using more conservative financial figures that defined revenue only in terms of money from external sources, the NCAA president reported in his State of the Association Address in January 2007 that a tiny fraction of NCAA member institutions, six, had consistently had a surplus in athletic revenues during the previous decade and that 52 percent of I-A Football Bowl Subdivision programs needed subsidies of greater than 5 percent per year (Michel, Sopp, and Stafford 2007). The arms race and other financial demands seem to have strained nearly all athletic budgets in the big-time world of Division I athletics. A possible implication of current revenue and spending patterns and the athletic arms race is that it will be more and more difficult in the future for institutions outside the Elite 6 conferences or with less athletic success in these conferences to generate the athletic revenue needed to pay for star coaches, recruitment, and financial and academic support for athletes to attract the star athletes required to win and achieve the top-ranked status that presidents, athletics directors, boosters, and fans desire. As the stratification at the Tier I level increases, the gap between the top and bottom is likely to become more entrenched, with the elite potentially becoming smaller over time.

According to some critics of the NCAA as a business, one of its most significant peculiarities is that it has been allowed to ignore antitrust laws and operate as a cartel. For example, Zimbalist (1999) argued that the NCAA was a cooperative economic network of firms in a market (i.e., member institutions in the athletic marketplace) that restricts the economic freedom (and legal rights) of labor (i.e., athletes) in college sports in many ways. This is the definition of a labor cartel, and it is typically illegal for businesses to operate this way in the United States, since the capitalist marketplace is supposed to be competitive and it is not supposed to restrict the economic rights of workers to sell their services to the highest bidder and maximize their economic opportunities. The existence of the star wars arms race indicates that coaches have been taking advantage of the athletic marketplace, even breaking contracts at times to move on to more lucrative opportunities, but the core "workers" in the business of college sports have not enjoyed the same economic rights as their coaches. You might point out that college athletes are students and are not really "workers" in a conventional sense and that many big-time athletes are compensated with scholarships, which allow them to attend and graduate from higher education institutions that may be very prestigious and may cost up to nearly $50,000 per year. Yet, star athletes do not have a chance to earn the rewards of the highly commercialized world of college sports that are available to star coaches, and their economic rights as athletes are far more restricted than are the economic rights of coaches. In fact, the economic structure of the NCAA as a cartel is not set up to benefit workers, per se, whether athletes or coaches.

Economic cooperation among member institutions of the NCAA—and with other elements of the intercollegiate Golden Triangle—is intended to maximize financial gain for big-time athletic departments, the major sports media, and corporate sponsors. As we can see in the case of the star wars arms race in coaches' compensation, the operation of a free market, which is how capitalism is supposed to operate, can make the financial viability of athletic programs very precarious. Colleges and universities have found it easier to cooperate as a cartel in the case of athletes, and as a result athletes have faced a number of restrictions. Zimbalist (1999) noted a number of examples of structural factors that have restricted athletes but also have contributed to the success of this cartel: (1) athletes are treated as amateurs—or student-athletes—and are not allowed to receive direct compensation for their play; (2) until the rule was modified in the 1998–1999 academic year, athletes could not have a job during the school year; (3) the number of athletic scholarships in each sport and the maximum financial value of individual scholarships are limited; (4) athletes are not allowed to employ an agent to represent or counsel them; (5) athletes who sign a letter of intent to attend a college must attend that institution or they will have to wait a year before competing for another institution; and (6) athletes who transfer from one college to another must sit out a year.

Some rules, such as the NBA's requirement that basketball players wait a year after high school graduation and until age nineteen to enter the professional draft, show the cooperative relationship between the NCAA and other members of the Golden Triangle to serve their mutual economic interests. The minimum-age rule assures the NCAA of access to outstanding athletes—albeit perhaps only for one year—who otherwise might have skipped college and gone directly to the professional level, while it also provides another year of seasoning for top prospects and gives the NBA a clearer sense of their readiness for the professional game. There are also rules that reflect the stated educational purposes of the NCAA, such as the rule that athletes must meet NCAA-prescribed initial and continuing academic eligibility standards to be permitted to compete. However, the kinds of NCAA rules cited by Zimbalist help institutions limit their costs, they give them some assurance that the athletes in whom they have invested a great deal in recruiting will play for them, and they enable coaches to maximize their control over athletes as they try to maximize their own chances of success.

Some college sports observers, and even a member of Congress (Barker 2007a), have proposed making big-time college athletes professionals, like their coaches, allowing them to share more fully in the revenue their "work" generates. This is called the "pay-to-play" argument. An economist at Cal State–San Marcos, Robert Brown, proposed an example of what this idea might mean in reality (Alesia 2006b). He calculated that a star college basketball player on a big-time team who was drafted by the NBA was worth about $900,000 to $1.2 million per year to his athletic department each year he played in college. Players in the NCAA men's basketball championship game presumably would have the most relative value to their institutions and thus would be entitled to the most pay. Using the 2005 NCAA championship teams as examples, Brown proposed a model for paying these players. He specifically proposed giving the players a "conservative" 50 percent share of the revenue, since 57 percent of the team revenue in the NBA and 59 percent in the NFL were spent on player salaries. By this formula, players on the champion North Carolina team would have received $7.6 million of the total men's basketball revenue of $15.2 million. With individual player shares based on minutes played, their individual shares would have ranged from $147,196 to $1.18 million. The University of North Carolina spent a total of $318,097 on scholarships for these student-athletes in 2004–2005. Players on the runner-up University of Illinois team would have earned $5.8 million of the total team revenue of $11.6 million, and individual shares would have ranged from $71,739 to $972,539. Illinois spent a total of $317,484 that year for their basketball players.

In view of the financial, as well as political and philosophical, implications, it is difficult to imagine the NCAA embracing play-for-pay ideas. Furthermore, there is little evidence of big-time NCAA athletes organizing to achieve this goal. It appears that college athletes do not care much in general about changing or eliminating the many rules or restrictions imposed by the NCAA. Most seem to enjoy their sports and many take advantage of their educational opportunities, and some big-time student-athletes each year use their college sports experience as a springboard to a professional sports career. However, at the most commercialized levels of college sports, the various restrictions faced by athletes reflect the contradictions of a cartel-like multibillion-dollar business and the principles of amateurism and education that the NCAA invokes to describe the purposes of college athletics. These principles are invoked when NCAA officials try to burnish the image of college athletics for the media, the public, and boosters or when they try to convince members of Congress that college athletics should not be treated as a business or lose its nonprofit, tax-exempt status despite the billions of dollars it generates as part of the Golden Triangle. The NCAA president has defended his organization's federal tax-exempt status, arguing that despite rapidly escalating expenses, college athletics still has a predominantly educational mission (Wolverton 2006b). He has also defended commercialism as necessary for the financial survival of college athletics and of higher education in general (Brand 2006). How much commercialism is necessary and how much is too much are difficult to know, but the ongoing arms race suggests that many presidents and athletic directors believe that more spending and more commercial activity to support that spending are needed to remain or become successful at the highest levels of college sport.

Athletics and Education: The Student-Athlete

In chapter three, we considered how difficult it was to move from college sports to a professional sports career. We recall that the estimated percentages of athletes moving from college to professional sport (or at least of being drafted by the professional league) were 1.3 percent in men's basketball, 1 percent in women's basketball, 2 percent in football, 10.5 percent in baseball, 4.1 percent in men's ice hockey, and 1.9 percent in men's soccer (Coakley 2007:344). Even though the chances are higher for athletes on big-time sports teams in Elite 6 conferences, the overwhelming majority of elite student-athletes will never have the chance to pursue a professional sports career. In view of this reality and the public relations benefits of marketing the educational benefits of college sports, the NCAA has focused its advertising on the educational accomplishments and occupational successes of the many athletes who have used their experience as student-athletes and college degrees to pursue careers outside sports and have become leaders in society. The image of this kind of student-athlete is in direct contrast to the image of stars in a highly commercialized entertainment business. In this section, we will address what it is like to be a student-athlete in a big-time athletic program, and how athletics affects the student role for big-time student-athletes.

A number of college athletes have received illegitimate and legitimate special academic treatment. The illegitimate treatment has included arrangements by assistant coaches for surrogates to complete quizzes and tests in correspondence courses taken by athletic prospects who were trying to improve their academic qualifications and meet initial NCAA academic eligibility standards, academic fraud by assistant coaches who have awarded a grade of "A" on dubious academic grounds to athletes in their class and who encouraged these athletes to provide misleading information to university and NCAA investigators, athletic department staff members and tutors for athletes who have completed assignments for athletes, coaches and athletic administrators who have pressured professors to change grades of athletes, and professors who have given inflated grades to athletes, requiring little work and no attendance (Suggs 1999; Hawes 2004; Osburn 2007; Wasley 2007). These cases have involved both highly prestigious athletic programs and institutions and lesser ones. The NCAA has also had to address the issue of "diploma mills." These private secondary "schools" provide student-athletes with the grades needed to be eligible for college athletics without requiring appropriate, or even any, schoolwork. Although the NCAA has been criticized for problems in its efforts to control diploma mills and ensure the integrity of academic credentials (Saslow 2007), the existence of actual diploma mills as well as the various cases of academic fraud at the college level demonstrate the challenge of ensuring that highly sought-after athletes are also academically capable of being college students. Problems seem to arise when coaches and athletic administrators whose status, compensation, and jobs depend on winning believe that student-athletes who are highly valued for their athletic talents cannot legitimately meet academic eligibility standards as students. Like other students, student-athletes are capable of cheating on their own, but the cases of academic cheating cited here reflect the active complicity of these coaches, administrators, or others who can gain personally from helping student-athletes become or remain eligible to compete or feel pressure to help ensure the eligibility of student-athletes.

Student-athletes also receive special treatment that is considered legitimate by the NCAA and is openly supported by member institutions. For example, institutions may admit athletic prospects who meet NCAA academic requirements but do not meet the customary academic standards the institutions use to make admissions decisions. At my university, we have used the term "special admit" to refer to student-athletes, as well as band members, dancers, and others with special and desirable talents, admitted under these conditions. We established a quota of approximately thirty for the number admitted on this basis. In order to ensure the academic success or continuing eligibility of student-athletes and especially those with special admit status, institutions with big-time or high-level athletic programs typically have a special academic support structure in place for student-athletes, which provides advising, tutoring, and other academic services. Student-athletes are also permitted to register for courses before other students on many campuses so that they can avoid conflicts between their classes and their athletic activities. These practices are generally accepted by college officials as normal and reasonable academic accommodations to athletics. However, they also set student-athletes apart from other students, which is contrary to the NCAA philosophy and also may not serve student-athletes well as students.

Some scholars have questioned the appropriateness of preferential treatment of athletes in the admissions process in higher education (e.g., Fried 2007). It might seem unlikely that this preferential treatment would occur at elite and highly selective colleges and universities. However, in a study of thirty-three academically selective colleges and universities that did not offer athletic scholarships, Bowen and Levin (2003) found that recruited athletes at these institutions were as much as four times more likely to be admitted than were other applicants with similar academic qualifications (also see Shulman and Bowen 2001). They also found that the typical recruit was much more likely to finish college in the bottom third of the class than was either the typical walk-on or the student who did not participate in college athletics. In addition, their evidence showed that recruited athletes "underperformed," which means that they did worse academically than predicted by their test scores and high school grades. The authors argued that over the previous four decades, the division between athletics and academics had gotten much worse. Before jumping to the conclusion that all student-athletes are "dumb jocks" or uninterested in the classroom, it should be pointed out that one of the researchers, Sarah Levin, was a Harvard doctoral student at the time of the research and was an All-American collegiate athlete. This reminds us that despite the various illegitimate and legitimate accommodations to the perceived or actual academic shortcomings of student-athletes, there are also serious and outstanding scholar-athletes in college athletics. Thus, we must be careful not to make sweeping generalizations about the academic abilities or deficiencies or the academic accomplishments or failures of student-athletes. We will see in this section that although the athletic role can make it difficult to be serious students in some cases, student-athletes approach their student role in a variety of ways with differing levels of success.

How well do student-athletes perform as students? Because they can be compared more easily and systematically than grades, graduation rates are used as an indicator of academic success of athletes by the federal government, the NCAA, and colleges and universities. Higher education institutions are required by the federal government to publish their graduation rates. For a long time, the NCAA relied on a federally defined measure of six-year graduation rates, but became unhappy with it because it did not account for incoming transfer students (e.g., from community colleges) and penalized institutions for students who transferred to other institutions in good standing and graduated from those institutions. Believing that this rate was not a valid indicator of actual graduation rates and that it generally underestimated actual graduation rates, the NCAA devised its own graduation success rate (GSR) for Division I to replace the federal graduation rate (FGR) in 2005. The GSR modified the FGR by accounting for incoming transfers and excluding outgoing transfers, as long as they left in good academic standing. The NCAA also devised an academic progress rate (APR) in 2004 to measure the academic success of athletic programs. Institutions that fail to achieve a satisfactory APR are penalized by the NCAA. We will look at recent data using these measures of academic performance of athletic programs.

The GSR data show a much rosier picture of academic success than do the FGR and APR statistics. Graduation rates are based on a six-year period following initial matriculation. Thus, the graduation rate of a class starting in 1999 would be based on the percentage of graduates in 2005. According to NCAA data, the overall NCAA GSR four-year average for student-athlete cohorts starting between 1996 and 1999 was 77 percent, one percentage point higher than the four-year average for cohorts beginning a year earlier. This was much higher than the overall FGR rate for the student-athlete cohort that started in 1999, which was 63 percent. This was 2 percent higher than the all-student FGR for the same six-year period, which indicates that student-athletes in general tend to graduate at a slightly higher rate than students in general.

At the Division I level, the women's GSR of 86 percent was substantially higher than the men's rate of 70 percent. For both women and men, there were significant variations by sports and institutions in both the FGR and GSR four-year averages for the cohorts between 1996 and 1999. For Division I women, the FGRs ranged from 65 percent in basketball and bowling to 86 percent in gymnastics, and the GSRs ranged from 70 percent in bowling to 94 percent in fencing, field hockey, gymnastics, and skiing. The GSR for women's basketball was 82 percent. The FGRs for men's Division I sports varied from 45 percent in basketball to 76 percent in lacrosse, with the FGR in I-A football 55 percent and in I-AA football 54 percent. The Division I men's GSRs varied from 59 percent in basketball to 89 percent in skiing, with the I-A football rate 66 percent and the I-AA football rate 64 percent. The two big-time men's sports, football and basketball, were significantly lower than the overall GSR four-year average of 77 percent, but both Division I men's basketball and football at the I-A Football Bowl Subdivision level had GSR gains of nearly 5 percent for cohorts starting between 1995 and 1999. The big-time Division I women's sport of basketball improved a little more than 2 percent during this period, but still had a lower four-year average GSR (82 percent) for cohorts starting between 1996 and 1999 than any other women's Division I sport except bowling and riflery.

According to the "Defining Academic Reform" document on the NCAA website, the APR is the "fulcrum upon which the entire academic-reform structure rests." Seen as a better measure of a team's academic performance than the six-year graduation rate because it shows how many athletes on a team are on track to earn their degree, the APR gives two points overall each term to student-athletes who meet academic-eligibility standards (one point) and remain at an institution (another point). A team's APR is the total points awarded a team divided by the total points possible. An APR score of 925 (out of 1,000), which is comparable to a 60 percent GSR, is a criterion score decided by the Division I board of directors. Teams failing to meet this standard are subject to immediate penalties, and teams that do not reach the 900 APR standard—equivalent to an approximately 45 percent GSR—will receive historical penalties. Immediate penalties involve financial aid restrictions and can be reversed by corrective actions. Historical penalties, resulting from chronically low academic performance, are more severe and are less easily corrected than immediate penalties.

They might involve warnings, team practice and financial aid restrictions, post-season bans, and ultimately restricted membership status. Squad-size adjustments for teams with small sample sizes were used until the 2007–2008 report, at which point the four-year period for calculating the APR could be used for the first time.

Three years after implementing the APR in the 2003–2004 academic year, NCAA data showed that 112 teams at 75 Division I institutions received a warning or faced at least partial scholarship losses (Powers 2007a). The previous year, 99 teams at 65 Division I institutions were told they could have their scholarships cut. In the spring of 2007, the overall APR average for Division I athletes was 960, with the men's average 950 and the women's average 970. There was no more than a 2 percent difference in the rates for the Football Bowl Subdivision, Football Championship Subdivision, and Division I without football for men or women. The NCAA reported in 2007 that 44 percent of men's basketball teams, 40 percent of football teams, and 35 percent of baseball teams would not have met the 925 standard and would have lost scholarships if a squad-size adjustment was not used. It was the last year they could benefit from this adjustment. The three-year average for men's basketball was 927, which was the lowest APR, and it was 931 for football and 934 for baseball. The three-year average was 960 for women's basketball. Although it was only ahead of bowling (942) and skiing (959)—riflery was not included in this report—women's basketball was between 26 and 33 points above the lowest-rated men's sports and was at the level of the overall average for all male athletes.

Whatever the specific implications of the full implementation of APR penalties beginning in 2008, it is apparent that the NCAA is serious about trying to improve the academic performance of student-athletes and punish coaches who recruit athletes who are academically underprepared or uncommitted. Five-year trends in GSRs for the 1995–1999 cohorts in men's basketball and football have been up, but APR numbers raise the specter of trouble on the horizon for some big-time programs in these sports. Big-time basketball coaches face an especially big challenge because their best players are often able to leave before graduating to begin their professional careers. It appears that football (and baseball) coaches face similar challenges.

In addition to publishing an annual Racial and Gender Report Card, Richard Lapchick and the Institute for Diversity and Ethics in Sport publish academic performance data each year for football bowl–bound and men's basketball tournament teams (Bartter 2006, 2007), which shed further light on this issue. The researchers used the most recent NCAA GSR data, for the cohort starting in 1999–2000 and the four-class average of cohorts starting 1996–1999, and they used APR data for 2004–2005 and 2005–2006. In football, 38 percent (24) of the 64 teams competing in bowl games after the 2006 regular season had an APR of 925 or less, including one of the two teams, Ohio State (925), playing in the BCS national championship game. Thirteen of these bowl-bound teams (54.2 percent) with low APRs were members of the BCS conferences, which competed in the most prestigious and lucrative bowls. Four teams had scores below 900, with the lowest 851. In basketball, 40 percent (26) of the 65 teams competing in the 2007 NCAA men's basketball tournament had an APR of 925 or less, and they included the national champion Florida (903) and runner-up Ohio State (911). Nine of these 65 teams (14 percent) had an APR of 900 or less, with the lowest 756.

In addition to suggesting possible future resource cuts and other restrictions for a number of the top teams in the two most highly commercialized or big-time college sports, the academic performance and graduation figures point to another issue, a racial gap. We can examine this racial gap with relatively conservative figures showing the percentage of teams graduating half of their black players and the percentage graduating half of their white players. In football, 57.8 percent of the bowl-bound teams, which were arguably the best in the nation in the 2006 season, graduated 50 percent or more of their African-American players, while 95.3 percent graduated half or more of their white players, which reflects a nearly 38 percent racial gap. The researchers also reported that overall, at the 119 Football Bowl Subdivision institutions, black football players had a 49 percent graduation rate, while the rate for their white counterparts was 62 percent, a 13 percent overall gap among football players. In basketball, 54 percent of the tournament teams graduated 50 percent or more of their black players and 95 percent graduated 50 percent or more of their white players, resulting in a slightly higher 41 percent racial gap among top basketball teams. In Division I in general, the GSR for black basketball players was 51 percent and for white players was 76 percent, a 25 percent overall gap.

Lapchick found this gap "startling" because it represented the first time in their annual studies that the racial gap in graduation rates between athletes in a particular men's sport was greater than the racial gap in graduation rates for male students in general on college campuses, which was 24 percent. The higher graduation rate of black male student-athletes than black male students who did not play sports and a modest trend of improving graduation rates for black male athletes have provided little consolation for those concerned about the racial gap issue, especially because black and white student-athletes in big-time programs are supposed to receive substantial academic support to help them make academic progress and graduate and because student-athletes have pressures from the NCAA to stay on track academically that do not apply to other students. The persistence of the racial gap is a major issue because the biggest of the big-time men's sports are so heavily reliant on black student-athletes, with 58 percent of Division I male basketball players and over 45 percent of football players African American. This racial gap issue is not raised for big-time women's college basketball because women's Division I teams have a much higher GSR—over 20 points—than the men and because women's sports generally do not get as much attention as men's sports. Before drawing conclusions about the meaning of the racial gap or relatively low graduation rates for black males in college sports, however, you should read the "Focus on Research" feature. It shows how statistics about graduation rates can be interpreted in different ways, especially when race is taken into account in the analysis, and it suggests caution when pointing an accusatory finger at athletics or athletes in interpreting the causes and implications of graduation rates.

Although they offer a standardized way of comparing academic success across groups, institutions, and time, FGRs, GSRs, and APRs tell us little about the meaning of the experiences of student-athletes as athletes or students. A comprehensive picture of the perspectives of student-athletes was recently provided by the preliminary findings of NCAA studies presented at the NCAA Convention in 2007 (NCAA 2007). The researchers analyzed how student-athlete perspectives and experiences varied in terms of factors such as sport, gender,

Focus on Research Feature 9.2:
Graduation Rates, Race, and Simpson's Paradox

In a paper that has been cited on the Internet but has not been published, economist Victor Matheson (2005) examined the relationship between the graduation rates for male athletes in general and for football and men's basketball players and the rates for male nonathletes at Division I colleges and universities. Matheson noted anecdotal reports in the media about specific men's basketball teams with glaringly low graduation rates. He questioned the sweeping criticism of big-time men's basketball and other men's sports prompted by these reports. In looking at past research, he saw a mixed picture, with some studies showing higher graduation rates for student-athletes than for students in general and others showing that increased athletic success was associated with lower graduation rates among student-athletes. His modest study suggests the need for a more sophisticated analysis. He used National Collegiate Athletic Association (NCAA) data showing the six-year graduation rates for scholarship athletes who began in 1997–1998. He focused on the 2004 NCAA Graduation-Rates Report for Division I, which relied on the Federal Graduation Rate measure. The NCAA had not begun using the Graduation Success Rate (GSR) in 2004, and its use would not have been appropriate in this study because the GSR has not been used to calculate graduation rates for students in general. He focused on Division I because it is where the big-time programs demanding the most commitment and getting the most money and publicity are.

Matheson proposed that a cursory look at the data seemed to support *and contradict* critics of men's sports. For example, the graduation rate for female athletes with athletic scholarships in Division I was 69 percent, which was 7 percent higher than the 62 percent rate for their non-athlete peers. However, male athletes in Division I graduated at a lower rate than nonathlete male students in general at this level—that is, 55 percent for all male athletes versus 57 percent for all male students. The graduation rate for football players was also 55 percent, while male basketball players graduated at a 44 percent rate. These numbers clearly reinforce criticisms of male student-athletes as students, especially in basketball. However, Matheson's reanalysis took into account race and ethnicity and showed different patterns.

Black male athletes in general graduated at a much higher rate than black male students in general (48 percent vs. 36 percent). Both black and white football players graduated at higher rates than nonathletes of their respective races. That is, for whites the graduation rate was 5 percent higher for the football players (65 percent vs. 60 percent), and for blacks the graduation rate was 12 percent higher for the football players (48 percent vs. 36 percent). The reason the overall football graduation rate was lower than the rate for all male students (55 percent vs. 57 percent) is that scholarship players were predominantly black and black students generally graduated at lower rates than other students. However, imagine that football players of different racial and ethnic groups graduated at the rates found for each of these groups in this NCAA data set but that football scholarships were allocated according to the percentage of each ethnic or racial group in the general student population. For example, Asian-American males would get 7.3 percent of the football scholarships because they were 7.3 percent of the general male student population, African-American males would get 9.3 percent of the football scholarships because they were 9.3 percent of all male students, and white males would get 72 percent of the football scholarships because they were 72 percent of all male students. Matheson calculated that if this were true, then the graduation rate for scholarship football players would be 60 percent and not 55 percent. The 60 percent rate was 3 percent *higher* than the overall rate for male students at Division I institutions in that year.

Matheson proposed that this was a classic case of *Simpson's Paradox*, which is a reversal of results when data from two or more dissimilar groups are combined. Controlling for racial differences produced the paradox. He did a similar recalculation for all male athletes and, although he did not find the same reversal as in football, he found that the graduation rates rose to nearly

57 percent, which was about the same as the graduation rate of male students in general. When he focused on male basketball players, the graduation rate was also higher, rising from 44 percent to 48 percent, but still much lower than the overall male graduation rate. Although the disproportionate number of black males receiving basketball scholarships largely accounts for the lower graduation rate for basketball, Matheson reminds us that the black male basketball players graduated at a much higher rate than other black male students. He concluded that the low graduation rates for basketball players in general and black basketball players in particular compared with students in general were not a failure of the big-time athletic system. Instead, they could be viewed as a result of the failure of Division I universities as educational institutions to remediate the educational deficiencies of black male students who come from poorer families and poorer schools than other male students. In fact, the academic support structures in athletics may do more to help black male student-athletes than academic support systems in the larger university do to help black male students in general.

Even if you did not follow all the technical details of Matheson's analysis, it should be evident that the same raw data—such as the NCAA's reported graduation rates—can be interpreted in different ways to justify very different conclusions. Accounting for racial differences among scholarship athletes and finding Simpson's Paradox for football players and different results for male scholarship athletes in general and for male basketball players led Matheson to emphasize the need to be careful in using graduation rates as an indicator of the academic success of scholarship athletes. Thus, we need to be careful not to jump to conclusions about the adverse effects of athletics on academic performance when relatively low graduation rates are reported for athletic teams.

and NCAA division. The results represent responses to two surveys. One got its responses from 8,500 former student-athletes who graduated from high school and started their college athletic careers in 1994 and were about 29 years old at the time of the survey. Although the 30 percent response suggests some caution in generalizing from these results, they seem to represent a wide cross section of former NCAA student-athletes. In the second study, more than 20,000 current student-athletes at 61 percent (627) of NCAA member institutions responded. While the *NCAA News* concluded that these studies validated the value of athletics (Brown 2007), others interpreted some of the results somewhat more critically (e.g., Knobler 2007; Wolverton 2007a). I will cite some key findings from the original data to show the positive and negative aspects of student-athletes' perceived and actual experiences and how they vary.

Sixty-nine percent of Division I male athletes in football and basketball said that their professors viewed them more as an athlete than as a student. Fewer athletes in these sports in Divisions II and III felt this way. Among male athletes in other Division I sports, 57 percent felt this way, and among Division I female athletes, 52 percent had this opinion. Again, the percentages declined for those at the Division II and III levels. However, more than 75 percent of the student-athletes within each of the divisions who had this view of professors nevertheless said they had generally positive feelings about their relationships with professors. Another question asked whether athletic participation prevented the student-athletes from majoring in what they really wanted. There were 23 percent in Division I football and men's basketball who answered yes but with no regret, and 9 percent in these sports responded yes with regret. The findings for the other Division I men's sports were 17 percent yes with no regret and 5 percent yes with regret, and among female athletes in Division I, 18 percent responded affirmatively with no regret and 6 percent said yes with regret. The percentages were significantly lower at the Division II and III levels for male and female athletes. While there were obviously exceptions, these results generally show a positive view of relationships with professors and of their choice of major.

Since a similar pattern of differences existed across the divisions and since we can assume that pressures and demands of the athletic role are greatest at the Division I level, I will focus on Division I for the remainder of the reported results. Student-athletes were asked whether they thought that athletic participation affected their overall GPA. Responses among Division I athletes varied by sport and gender. For example, 71 percent of baseball players, 68 percent of football players, 67 percent of male basketball players, 62 percent of males in other sports, 62 percent of female basketball players, and 60 percent of females in other sports said they believed their GPA would be higher if they did not play sports. This result is not surprising, since any serious extracurricular activity, from the marching band and theater to student clubs and student government, takes time away from studying and course work. However, it is not clear how much time spent in sport actually would be spent on academic work if student-athletes did not play sports. For student-athletes, the need to conform to NCAA progress-to-degree requirements to remain eligible for athletics compels them to spend at least enough time on academics to do the course work and get the grades needed to keep them on track to graduate. In fact, many of the male student-athletes responded that they wanted to spend more time on sports than they currently did.

The data from the former Division I athletes, who became college athletes in 1994, showed that 88 percent had graduated from college. This was higher than the overall six-year GSR of 77 percent for student-athletes recently reported by the NCAA and implied that many student-athletes who had not earned their degree in six years continued their education to complete their baccalaureate studies. Twenty-seven percent of these former athletes earned a postbaccalaureate degree (e.g., MBA, PhD, MD, JD) within twelve years after starting their undergraduate studies. Compared with the 12 percent of former athletes who had not yet earned their degree, the degree holders were more likely to have a positive view of their overall education, their choice of major, their coach's influence on their athletic experience, their coach's influence on their academic experience, and their academic advisers. In regard to negative aspects of their experience, those with degrees were more likely than those without degrees to say that athletics had a negative impact on their GPA but less likely to say they had regrets about being prevented from majoring in something else. The former athletes overwhelmingly (89 percent) believed that the skills and values derived from their college athletic experience helped them secure their current job, and 91 percent of the former student-athletes said they had a full-time job, which was 11 percent higher than a sample of fellow students who did not participate in college athletics.

Overall, the NCAA data about the perspectives of current and former student-athletes and their graduation rates reflect a *generally* positive conception of the student-athlete experience in college sports. A case study of a big-time men's basketball team presented by the Adlers (Adler and Adler 1991) suggests that the student-athletes most likely to have negative academic experiences and not graduate are those who become detached from their academic role due to the perceived or actual demands of being an athlete, who develop a narrow sense of self built around being an athlete, who have an inflated sense of their importance because they are athletes, and who spend little time thinking about a future without sports. Big-time sports tend to encourage these tendencies, especially among male athletes. Thus, males who play big-time college sports and do not pursue a professional sports career after college, which is the overwhelming majority of them, are poorly prepared for life after college if their "role engulfment" in the athlete role distracted them from their studies and resulted in a failure to graduate. Those who are most engulfed in the athlete role seem to pursue what I would call an "eligibility education" approach, which focuses disproportionately on sport and only enough on academics to remain eligible to play sports. In the Adlers' study, this orientation was encouraged by the subculture of players' basketball teammates because their team was so highly ranked, they received so much attention from the media and boosters, and they had deluded themselves into thinking they would play pro basketball. They chose less-demanding majors, chose courses on the basis of when they were scheduled, and tried to find shortcuts in their classes so that they could meet the demands of their coach on the basketball court. As a result, players developed unrealistic expectations of their postcollege opportunities in sport and were not well prepared for lives not based on basketball after their careers ended.

Public Perceptions of U.S. College Athletics

We earlier considered various justifications for big-time college sports, and many represent an institutional enhancement rationale of some sort. For many college students who do not participate in athletics at their school and for many millions of other spectators and fans, big-time college sports events are popular entertainment. In a December 2005 Knight Commission–sponsored systematic survey of 502 U.S. adults aged 18 and older, the respondents were asked what they thought about various aspects of this commercialized world of big-time U.S. college sports (KCIA 2006). This study showed that 83 percent had an overall positive opinion of college athletics. It also found that a majority or near-majority accepted beliefs about the benefits of big-time college sports, which the researchers called "myths" because research they cited showed that they were *generally* not true. The results showed that 78 percent believed that athletic departments with big-time athletic programs were profitable; 84 percent believed that successful teams typically increased alumni donations to a university; 55 percent believed that successful big-time programs tended to enhance the quality of student applicants; and 42 percent of all respondents and 57 percent of those who identified themselves as sports fans thought that more spending on salaries and operating expenses tended to produce more victories on the field. These myths are major components of common institutional enhancement rationales used to justify big-time college sports. We examined these types of beliefs at the beginning of this chapter and came to a conclusion similar to the poll's authors' about their dubious validity.

Despite having positive views of big-time college athletics and its claimed benefits, the U.S. public nevertheless seems to have reservations about the amount of investment, to question the influence of the Golden Triangle, and to reject the idea of big-time athletics as amateur sport. For example, 60 percent believed that college sports were more like professional sports than amateur sports; 61 percent said college sports had become too commercialized; 74 percent thought that commercial interests often prevailed over academic values and traditions; 74 percent believed that there was a conflict between commercialization and academic values; and 73 percent agreed with the statement that college sports as a big business conflicted with the values of higher education. Over half of the self-identified sports fans and 66 percent of the respondents who were college graduates agreed with this last statement. In addition, 59 percent of respondents in general and of sports fans thought that college athletes were exploited by corporate advertisers.

There were other findings indicating that nearly three-quarters of the respondents believed that coaches were paid too much, and 82 percent said they were concerned about assistant football coaches being paid much more than senior professors. Furthermore, 77 percent were concerned about the influence of TV networks on the timing of college football and basketball games, since this scheduling causes athletes to miss classes and travel at inconvenient times in many cases. Large majorities of respondents also expressed the beliefs that athletic revenue should be shared with the rest of the institution and with men's and women's sports beyond the big-time football and basketball programs and that expenditures on these big-time sports should be reduced. Most respondents had concerns about the athletes, with 93 percent saying they were concerned, and 73 percent saying they were very concerned, about the use of steroids and other forms of doping in college sports, and with 83 percent worried and 49 percent very worried that the pressure to compete caused college athletes to play hurt.

Despite the overall positive opinion of college sports held by 83 percent of the respondents, 44 percent believed college sports were "out of control" and 47 percent said they were not. If "out of control" is interpreted as unconstrained commercialization, corruption, and other forms of deviance, it appears that for nearly half of the U.S. public, their enthusiasm for college sports is tempered by concerns about how it is organized and what is happening in the highly commercialized realms, in terms of money, misplaced priorities, outside influence, and the impact on student-athletes. Yet a poll conducted for the Knight Commission in 1990 showed that 75 percent of respondents thought college sports were out of control, and another poll in 1993 showed that 52 percent of respondents held this belief. These past results indicate that the 44 percent in the 2005 survey subscribing to this belief are part of a trend of *declining* concern about the direction or culture of college sports. The success of the intercollegiate Golden Triangle and individual higher education institutions in "selling" the myths supporting big-time sports and the enjoyment of college sports as entertainment may explain how big-time college sports remain popular despite widespread questions and concerns.

Conclusion: Cycles of Reform and Change in College Sports

Although it seems that the enthusiasm of the U.S. public for big-time college sports has not been substantially diminished by questions, concerns, or ambivalence, there still are people whose concerns animate a strong desire for change or reform. The continued existence of the Knight Commission on Intercollegiate Athletics (KCIA) since the 1990s reflects the persistence of reform efforts in the recent history of college sports. This persistence and the continuing publicity the KCIA and other reform-minded groups, such as the faculty-driven Drake Group, have received suggest a different environment of contemporary big-time athletics than in the past.

Critics and reformers have tried to change or even abolish college athletics since its early years (Nixon and Frey 1996:160–162). For example, around the beginning of the twentieth century, a number of prominent faculty members and journalists raised concerns about how commercialized and professionalized college sports damaged the academic integrity and reputation of institutions of higher education. A number of critics were especially concerned about violence and deaths in college football, and demands for its abolition led to more regulation of college football and athletics in general and the formation of the NCAA. These early reform efforts were followed by a number of other calls for reform as big-time college sports evolved and became more popular (Nixon and Frey 1996:160–162). A Carnegie Foundation for the Advancement of Teaching study supervised by Howard Savage resulted in reports in 1929 and 1931 that drew attention to problems of professionalism and the lack of control over college sports by students. An investigation by the American Council on Education (ACE) in 1951–1952 was also concerned about professionalism, especially in football, but it brought special attention to the scandals involving gambling and fixing in college basketball. It recommended greater involvement in the governance of college athletics by college presidents, along with dropping spring football and discontinuing postseason bowls. Another ACE probe, in the 1970s, raised serious questions about governance, academic integrity, and financial and ethical issues in college athletics, but like the prior Carnegie and ACE studies, it drew little attention and had little effect on the continuing commercial and popular development of U.S. college sports.

Around 1990, when a Knight Commission survey found that 75 percent of Americans thought that college sports were out of control, Congress was conducting probes of NCAA regulatory and enforcement practices and ongoing corruption and issues of academic integrity in college sports (Nixon and Frey 1996: 161). This was the environment that inspired the formation of the Knight Commission on Intercollegiate Athletics. It was formed in 1989 with money from the Knight Foundation to examine and deal with a history of more than ten years of ongoing and highly publicized scandals in college sports. Its aim was to achieve reforms that got commercialism under control and that emphasized the need for presidential control over college athletics and the need for academic and financial integrity in college sports. Although its assessments and recommendations have not dramatically differed from the types of recommendations produced by earlier inquiries, the KCIA has had more influence because it has had more funding to sustain its oversight of college sports, because it has included a number of prominent people on its study panel with connections to the Golden Triangle, and because it has effectively used the mass media to publicize its work. Panel members have included many current and former college presidents; the president of the American Council on Education; policy experts; a former member of the U.S. Congress; current and former corporate executives, including the former NBC CEO; and the former executive director and president emeritus of U.S. Olympic Committee.

The KCIA has published a series of reports and policy papers and has supported various surveys, as we have seen. Two of its most important publications were in 1991 and 2001 (KCIA 1991, 2001). A review of the major analysis, findings, and recommendations of these reports is an appropriate way to end this chapter, since it enables us to see where college athletics has been and where it could go. The 1991 report described an environment in which coaches were hired and fired as a result of win-loss records and received substantial financial rewards if their programs achieved national stature. This environment encouraged recruiting violations; the abuse of athletes, who were encouraged to sacrifice their bodies to win; and corrupt practices to attract and retain top athletes and keep them academically eligible. The factors shaping this environment were identified as profit-driven television interests and corporate sponsors at the national level and local media and business sponsors, whose money and publicity exerted influence over how and when college sports were played; overzealous boosters who provided illegal under-the-table payments and gifts to athletes; and academic and athletic administrators, including presidents and athletic directors, and professors who failed to exercise sufficient oversight and control over athletics. The 1991 report characterized the problems in college athletics as deeply rooted, long-standing, and systemic, and it pointed to commercialism as the common underlying factor linking all the other factors contributing to the corruption of college athletics. In effect, this analysis pointed to the Golden Triangle as the root of the problems in college athletics. The intercollegiate Golden Triangle includes ambitious presidents, athletic directors, coaches, and boosters and profit-oriented media corporations, corporate sponsors, and local businesses. The KCIA implied that this Golden Triangle had created and sustained a commercial culture in college sports that pushed aside or replaced academic or educational values.

The 1991 KCIA report identified three possible futures in college athletics: (1) self-corrective action by higher education institutions; (2) government intervention and regulation to clean up academic and financial problems in college athletics; or (3) a continuing pattern of corruption, misplaced priorities, and abuses that would ultimately destroy the intrinsic value of college athletics and the credibility of claims about its legitimate place in higher education. The report favored institutions taking control to correct the problems in college athletics, and it called for basic structural changes in the administration of athletic programs, with presidents exercising appropriate oversight and leadership. In order to achieve a shift in priorities and direction, mechanisms ensuring academic and financial integrity would have to be put in place. To provide accountability, athletic programs needed to be certified as meeting academic, administrative, and financial standards. The NCAA established a certification process, and, as we have seen, it has made efforts to increase academic performance of student-athletes. Furthermore, the NCAA president has tried to encourage institutions to get spending under control.

By 2001, KCIA panel members saw some progress in addressing the corruption they had found ten years earlier, but they also had continuing concerns about threats to academic values in college sports. They argued that the entire higher education community needed to work together to "reassert the primacy of the educational mission of the academy" (KCIA 2001). The major persisting problems they specifically identified were the academic challenges and deficiencies of student-athletes, the financial arms race, and unrestrained external commercial influence—which we have viewed as the influence of the Golden Triangle. It appears that the colleges and universities and the NCAA have been listening. We have considered how the NCAA has been tightening academic requirements with tougher initial and continuing academic eligibility standards for student-athletes, more accountability of athletic programs for the progress toward degree and graduation of their student-athletes, and calls from the NCAA president and various past and current institutional presidents to bring the arms race under control. At the same time, the NCAA has reasserted the need for external commercial ties; the NCAA and big-time programs are seeking increasing amounts of money, publicity, and media coverage from the Golden Triangle; and the arms race has continued. The emerging arms race in women's basketball indicates that the desire for a different, less commercial kind of sport for women probably died with the death of the AIAW nearly three decades ago. Given the opportunity, women, too, seem to be getting caught up in the type of environment the Knight Commission has criticized and tried to reform.

Reformers may not see much change—or change of the kind they would like—in the history of college athletics. The problems identified by the earliest reformers and critics persist, with many rooted in the commercialism, professionalism, and compelling need to win that have long characterized college sports. However, if we look at the last three decades, we can see a number of significant changes in college athletics, and some are in the direction urged by reformers, as we just observed. It is true that big-time college athletics is still very much about money, and the amount of money available to the biggest winners has continued to increase as the influence of the intercollegiate Golden Triangle has continued to grow. Part of this growth has included the increasing recruitment of foreign players, reflecting the globalization of U.S. college athletics. As we saw in chapter seven, a number of these young foreign prospects are manipulated by entrepreneurial coaches, scouts, and brokers in a largely unregulated international market for athletes, which brings a number of these athletes to the United States with unrealistic expectations about college and professional sports opportunities and leaves others behind in their homeland with unfulfilled promises (Saslow 2006a, 2006b, 2006c).

In the current world of college athletics, student-athletes must meet higher academic standards than in the past if they want to compete, and their institutions must meet higher academic standards if they want to avoid severe restrictions on resources and their opportunities to compete for the status and money earned by the most successful programs. In addition, women have become a fixture after being invisible in college sports for most of their history. Title IX has transformed the face of college sports, and institutions have made a number of changes, including adding women's sports and cutting nonrevenue men's sports over the past few decades. In this context, debates have raged, sometimes in court, about whether cuts in men's sports have been due more to Title IX or the resource needs of the biggest of the big-time programs, usually football and men's basketball and now women's basketball as well. Despite significant gains in female participation, gender equity has remained elusive. Women have not done as well as men in getting top administrative and coaching jobs since the demise of the AIAW and the NCAA taking control of women's sports. Female coaches in big-time women's college basketball often have to compete with male candidates for their jobs. Although compensation for coaches in women's basketball has reached the $1 million level, top-paid coaches in this sport include men as well as women, and the extent of future commercial growth and increases in compensation in women's sports will depend on the interest and revenue women's sports generate as popular entertainment. At this point, with the exception of a few women's programs, they are lagging well behind the big-time men's programs.

Homophobia remains an unspoken issue in men's sports, but it has gotten more publicity in women's sports. Yet even in some realms of women's college sports, homosexuality remains a "dirty little secret" (Redden 2007). Lesbian coaches and teams having or allegedly having lesbian athletes sometimes find themselves victims of negative recruiting, in which opponents use negative stereotypes about sexual orientation as a scare tactic to discourage recruits from playing for a particular coach or on a particular team. Although black male athletes are well established and fairly widely accepted in college football and basketball, black men have found it difficult to be hired as athletics directors and football coaches and some successful black female athletes have had their achievements and themselves deflated by demeaning racist comments on talk radio because they were strong and aggressive (Kinkhabwala 2007).

A task force established by the NCAA concluded in 2006 that there was no crisis in college sports (NCAA 2006). However, it recognized the need for reform in four main areas: (1) fiscal responsibility to moderate the growth of athletic budgets, (2) fuller integration of athletics into the educational mission of the university, (3) strengthening presidential leadership in the face of possible interference from internal board members or external supporters uncommitted to the academic and financial integrity of college athletics, and (4) ensuring the overall well-being of student-athletes. These issues overlap with concerns raised by the Knight Commission, but the tone of the presidential task force report is not as dire and is more confident. Whether reforms occur in the ways the presidents said they should will depend on the extent to which their reform agenda aligns with the most powerful forces of change in the college sports environment.

These forces of change are the ones on which we have been focusing throughout this book, and these are not easily controlled by college presidents. The sociodemographic influences of the gender imbalance in college student enrollment, the increasing diversity of college students, and the amount of influx of foreign students all will shape who plays college sports and how gender equity is approached. The Golden Triangle will continue to push the organizational and commercial growth of big-time college sports and encourage the use of the latest technologies. These technologies might include illegal drugs and dubious training and competitive practices among a number of ambitious programs, coaches, and athletes highly committed to winning. As the capitalistic marketplace of big-time athletics continues to expand, publicity and money from the Golden Triangle are likely to continue to fuel the ambitions of institutions to be at the top of the college sports status hierarchy and to participate in an arms race to ensure their success. Despite their stated intentions to the contrary, college and university presidents and the NCAA will yield more control over college athletics to the sports media and corporate sponsors if big-time athletic success remains as important as it is now. The nature of their relationship to the other, more powerful elements in the intercollegiate Golden Triangle may be the major factor shaping how college athletics changes in the future. The structure of the Golden Triangle will be explored in more detail in the next chapter, which will focus on the professional sports industry and professional sports careers.

10

The Professional Sports Industry and Sports Careers

Golden Triangle is a colorful and evocative term suggested by Smart (2005: 144), which incorporates important ideas about the dominant power structure in sport from Aris's (1990) conception of the "Sportsbiz," Maguire's (1999) conception of the "global media-sport complex," and Messner, Dunbar, and Hunt's (2000) conception of the "sports/media/commercial complex." Social network analysis helps us see the linkages in Golden Triangles connecting the prominent and influential "players" or "actors" from the sport, media, and corporate sectors. These linkages are based on common economic interests and are relations of economic power. The dominant people and organizations in Golden Triangles act in mutually supportive and even relatively coordinated ways within and sometimes across networks related to specific sports to maximize their shared economic interests. In this book, I have stretched Smart's original use of the term "Golden Triangle" beyond his conception of an "indivisible trinity" of *professional* sport, *television*, and corporate sponsorship to apply to all highly commercialized sports and to include other media along with television. However, in this chapter, we will focus on Golden Triangles related to professional sports.

A major theory of this book is that the growing influence of the generic Golden Triangle on a global scale and of specific Golden Triangles in their particular domains has made commercialization and the capitalistic pursuit of profit increasingly important in various big-time sports realms. I have tried to show how processes such as organizational rationalization, commercial partnerships, the pursuit of profits, and capitalist expansion in the global cultural economy have linked the major actors in the generic Golden Triangle and affected the nature of the influence of the Golden Triangle over big-time sports. In the last chapter, we considered the powerful influence of commercial interests related to the Golden Triangle in big-time college athletics. In this chapter about professional sports, we will see that the interests of "the game," the integrity of sport, and the welfare of athletes and fans often seem to be less significant than the business interests of the Golden Triangle. Whether in highly commercialized amateur sport or professional sport, an enduring issue is the relative balance between the value of the sport as a game and the economic demands on sport as a business enterprise. The Golden Triangle may construct playful images of sport and athletes, but it ultimately is most concerned about its business interests. In the next section, I will present a picture of the Golden Triangle of professional sports that provides a more comprehensive and detailed conception of Golden Triangles in general than we have considered thus far. This conception will show who the major actors in a particular sports-related Golden Triangle are, how these dominant individuals and organizations are connected, and how they act in ways that benefit each other.

The Golden Triangle and the Global Power Network in Professional Sports

Professional sports depend on money and exposure from television and other major sports media and on corporate sponsors for their economic success as entertainment businesses. The sports media and corporate sponsors of sport derive financial revenue and prestige from their association with professional and big-time quasi-professional sports and their stars. In its most inclusive "generic" form, "the" Golden Triangle of professional sports is a major element in the contemporary global cultural economy. All the Golden Triangles that dominate the various big-time professional sports and those aspiring to become "big-time" are part of this generic Golden Triangle of professional sports. The most ambitious of these Golden Triangles of specific professional sports operate transnationally and seek profitability and prominence in the global markets of the global cultural economy of sport. In pursuit of these ambitions or to cement their stature, the Golden Triangles of professional sports organize large-scale "mega-events" (Horne and Manzenreiter 2006) that reach the widest and most affluent possible media audiences.

I do not want to overstate the extent of integration, cooperation, or coordination among sports, media, and corporate commercial interests within the generic Golden Triangle, within the generic Golden Triangle of professional sports, or within sport-specific Golden Triangles, but I will argue that the Golden Triangles associated with specific professional sports tend to operate in similar ways with similar capitalistic goals. Despite these similarities, the structures of the generic Golden Triangle of professional sports and the generic Golden Triangle of all commercialized sports are complex, and relations among actors within these generic Golden Triangles are dynamic. For example, the actors representing different sports, media, and corporate sponsors within the generic Golden Triangle of professional sports may disagree, compete, or cooperate; have unequal status; and engage in relationships with each other that change over time or in different contexts. Since sports media organizations and corporate sponsors may invest in several big-time sports and have a reach that stretches nationally or globally, their economic resources and power tend to be greater than the resources and power of specific sports. This is why a sport often may seem to bend to the influence of its media and corporate partners when staging or marketing sports events and why sports interests may seem to be less important than business interests in various realms of professional sport—and other commercialized sports.

Sometimes newer sports enterprises seriously compete with more established sports businesses for a share of the sports marketplace controlled by the more established elements of the Golden Triangle of a sport. This is one of the ways that Golden Triangles change. For example, fantasy leagues have fought legal battles with established professional sports organizations such as Major League Baseball, the NFL Players Association, NBA Properties, WNBA Enterprises, NASCAR, and the PGA Tour over the right to use athletes' names and statistics without paying a licensing fee (McCarthy 2007a). This is a significant battle as fantasy leagues try to achieve a more prominent place in the Golden Triangles of these professional sports since there are an estimated 17 million fantasy sports players, fantasy sports are a $1.5 billion business, and the established professional sports and star athletes make substantial amounts of money from controlling the commodification and sale of athletes' images and achievements.

Research by Harvey, Law, and Cantelon (2001) revealed the prominence of media and entertainment corporations in the Golden Triangle for the four major North American professional sports leagues—that is, the National Football League (NFL), National Basketball Association (NBA), National Hockey League (NHL), and Major League Baseball (MLB). Their findings are consistent with annual lists of the most powerful people in sport proposed by publications such as the *Sporting News* and the *SportsBusiness Journal.* For example, the Top 25 on the *Sporting News* "Power 100" in January 2006—which was actually twenty-eight people due to ties in rank—included twelve executives in the media business, along with league commissioners, the National Association for Stock Car Auto Racing (NASCAR) CEO, the chairman of Nike, the executive director of the NFL Players Association, and two U.S. senators and a congressman involved in investigating steroids in sport. The Top 25 on the *SportsBusiness Journal* list of its fifty most influential people in the sports business in 2006 included ten media executives, as well as league commissioners, the NASCAR CEO, the chairman of Nike and CEO of adidas, sports team owners, the NCAA president, and the executive director of the MLB Players Association. There were no athletes or coaches on either list, and there was only one black male on each list and one woman on one of the lists.

Although unscientific, these lists reflect the opinions of people with substantial sports business expertise about who makes the most influential decisions shaping sports today. The Harvey, Law, and Cantelon study is a more systematic and scientific analysis of where power resides in the major professional sports leagues in North America and of how the most powerful actors in the Golden Triangle for these sports are connected. Their description of the structure of the dominant power network in this sector of sport should provide a general indication of what Golden Triangles look like and how they operate in other sectors of the big-time global sports marketplace.

The prominence of the media in the various Golden Triangles in the sports world should not be surprising, since the communication enterprises that construct, market, and sell cultural products are at the heart of the contemporary global cultural economy and have powerful effects on popular culture, which includes the sports entertainment business. The more traditional media of television and radio combine with the Internet, e-commerce, satellite communications, and cable operations to form the core of this economy. In professional sports, media and entertainment businesses are highly represented among franchise owners. Harvey, Law, and Cantelon revealed a substantial number of ties between professional sports franchises in North America and the media and entertainment industry, with almost one-third (31 percent) of the owners of these franchises from this sector of the economy. This was nearly two and a half times more than the industry with the next-highest owner affiliation, which was real estate (13 percent). Nine percent of owners were sole investors, and 12 percent of these franchises had no majority owner. Media conglomerates have intentionally tried to expand their businesses by investing in sport. The one exception to this pattern among the major North American professional sports leagues is the NFL, which has prohibited corporate ownership since 1970.

Harvey, Law, and Cantelon identified five general patterns of media/entertainment ownership in North American sports leagues, and they offered a case study of each type. The first type, *global media conglomerates*, was illustrated by News Corp, which was founded by Rupert Murdoch. Twenty-seven percent (ten) of the thirty-seven media/entertainment owners were this type, and they were the largest media/entertainment enterprises in the Golden Triangle, with the most valued assets, ownership or control over the most corporations, and the broadest geographical scope of operations. Beginning with two inherited Australian newspapers, Murdoch expanded his holdings to include more newspapers in his native country and others, film and television studios, Fox Broadcasting, the British Sky satellite television network, Sky radio, and various other media and entertainment businesses. He has bought and sold many businesses, but the acquisitions and investments linking him most directly to sport have included partial or full ownership of the Fox Sports Network, the Los Angeles Dodgers in MLB, and several major sports arenas where teams in the NBA and NHL play. He has 9.9 percent ownership of several top teams in English Premier League soccer, which is the limit for crossover ownership in the league. He was blocked from purchasing the most profitable club in the league, Manchester United, because it was feared that his company would have too much control over European soccer. News Corp also started new rugby leagues in Australia and the United Kingdom to rival existing leagues (Denham 2004). In addition, he owned local cable rights for over 93 percent of the NHL, NBA, and MLB; the Fox Sports Networks spent $4.4 billion for an eight-year contract to broadcast National Football Conference games in the NFL; and Fox has interests in The Golf Channel and various other sports broadcasting outlets. The wide scope of News Corp's power in producing, marketing, staging, and distributing sports "products" in the global Golden Triangle is evident from this list of holdings.

A second type of media/entertainment ownership pattern, *national media conglomerates*, included businesses that were also very diverse enterprises but tended to have a more limited geographical scope of operations than global media corporations such as News Corp. Sixteen percent (six) of the media/entertainment owners were this type. Comcast is an example. It has mostly limited its operations to North America. However, it has had joint ventures with other enterprises in the global Golden Triangle operating more broadly or in other geographical areas. Comcast started as a small cable operator in Tupelo, Mississippi, and was acquired by new owners who expanded its influence across the state and then renamed the company Comcast and relocated to Philadelphia. It began purchasing local cable companies and then entered the bigger and more profitable business of cellular telecommunications. It eventually created Sprint

PCS with other investors. Computer software giant Microsoft bought a large number of shares in Comcast, and Comcast used its growing financial resources to enter into joint ventures with major entertainment companies such as Disney. It became a major player in sports in the Philadelphia area by investing in the company that owned the local NHL and NBA teams and sports arenas in the city. It started Comcast SportsNet as a joint venture with the owners of the Philadelphia Phillies MLB team. As one of the three biggest and richest cable operators in the United States and with its connections in various Golden Triangle power networks across the United States, Comcast has been able to become a major player in the North American Golden Triangle.

The third pattern identified by Harvey, Law, and Cantelon involves owners with *other entertainment businesses* that are not part of large conglomerates such as News Corp and Comcast. These businesses were 19 percent (seven) of the media/entertainment owners. Arison's Carnival Corporation is an example. Carnival is the largest cruise line in the world, and its owner, Micky Arison, is also the owner of the Miami Heat NBA team. He has been listed by *Forbes* magazine as among the one hundred wealthiest people in the world as well as by the *Sporting News* and the *SportsBusiness Journal* on their Top 100 sports power lists. In the tradition of beer manufacturers that bought MLB teams to use sport to cross-promote their original business, Arison has been able to use his ownership of a professional basketball team to cross-market his cruise line. This reflects an indirect link between his sports and leisure entertainment businesses. Arison used his wealth to purchase a place in professional sports, and he has used his status as an owner to gain power in the NBA by becoming chair of the league's board of governors.

The fourth media/entertainment ownership pattern involves owners with *information technology businesses*, and it represented 24 percent (nine) of the media/entertainment owners. This type is illustrated by the holdings of Paul Allen, who cofounded Microsoft with Bill Gates, was on its board of directors, and derived considerable wealth from being one of the largest shareholders in the company. The owners in this category do not have primary business holdings that link them as directly as other types of owners to a major media/entertainment conglomerate. However, franchise owners in this category, such as Paul Allen, are noteworthy because they are major figures in the new global cultural economy dominated by information or communication technologies. He has consistently been ranked among the five wealthiest individuals in the world. Like Arison, he has owned sports teams, in his case NBA and NFL teams, as private companies. The connection of his sports investments to the media/entertainment complex has been through Microsoft, which has had a number of media/entertainment ventures such as WebTV, and through Allen's controlling interest in a major U.S. cable operator, Charter Communications, which has also been involved in producing content for interactive TV. Having individual capitalists such as Micky Arison and Paul Allen in a Golden Triangle at the regional, national, or global level further extends the reach and power of the Golden Triangle through their personal assets and ties to media and entertainment businesses.

The fifth type of ownership pattern involves owners with *local/regional entertainment businesses*, and this type represented 14 percent (five) of the media/entertainment owners. Although their media and entertainment holdings and operations are not as extensive as those of the big global or national conglomerates, they are similarly structured as businesses but on a local or regional level. The cable service company Adelphia Communications, which started in Pennsylvania, is an example. Constantly facing possible competition in its area from the big conglomerates such as Comcast, it has tried to strengthen its market position by investing in other businesses such as digital television and Internet access to provide new services to its customers. It also formed partnerships with other cable operators and bought other communication companies to expand its cable customer base in its region. It even gave up customer service in the East and Midwest to rival Comcast in return for a chance to sell cable, digital television, and high-speed Internet services in more lucrative areas in California and Florida. Although not as big as Comcast, Adelphia gradually expanded its business in selected regions in the United States, and this expansion included professional sport, with investments in an NHL team, ownership of sports arenas, and purchase of naming rights to an NFL stadium.

The prominence of owners with media/entertainment business connections in the Golden Triangle of major North American professional sports leagues shows the intertwining of sports, media, and corporate sponsorship interests and the concentration of their economic power in this Golden Triangle. This pattern very likely represents the types of network connections in other Golden Triangles involving other sports and sports in other geographical areas. Harvey, Law, and Cantelon's research suggests how corporate capitalist interests, especially those in the media and entertainment sector, penetrate and control professional sports in general. With economic power in the generic Golden Triangle of professional sports highly concentrated in big corporations, Golden Triangles are able to impose their interests on the sports public, employees of sports businesses, and competing firms outside the boundaries of these networks of power.

We examined in the last chapter the implications for athletes of economic cooperation and a high concentration of power among "firms" in the cartel-like NCAA. These kinds of arrangements in professional sports tend to strengthen the market position and profitability of Golden Triangles in professional sports and reinforce their economic power. Those in dominant positions in Golden Triangles in professional sports can exercise their control over their sports and wider sports markets in various ways. For example, they can decide to produce, market, and broadcast certain sports and sports events and not others; they can decide how they want to package and deliver sports events and broadcasts; they can decide who is allowed to own a professional sports franchise or invest in a professional tournament or event, where franchises will be located, and where and when events will take place; they can demand public investment in arenas and stadiums as a condition for franchise location in a particular city; they can decide how much media coverage particular leagues, events, and athletes receive; they can decide how much it costs to attend sports events, who plays in them, and who gets to be a star; and they can decide whether or not to charge a fee for access to televised sports events.

A basic principle of supply and demand in market economics is that when there are fewer firms selling highly valued or demanded products, firms will have more power over consumers and their choices. Similarly, as we saw in college athletics, when firms in an industry such as sport work together to maximize their individual and collective economic interests, they can significantly restrict employment and compensation opportunities for workers. In the ensuing sections of this chapter, we will see how the major actors in the Golden Triangles of professional sports have taken advantage of their economic networks and power. I will examine major aspects of the economic and organizational structure of professional sports and how this structure affects owners, their relations with players and fans, and the evolution of the stadiums and the economies of the cities where pro sports are played. Then we will turn our attention to expansion of the global sports marketplace. After that discussion, our focus will shift to the careers of professional athletes and how they are affected by risk, pain, and injuries. The chapter will conclude with a consideration of professional athletes and sports in the context of a changing global cultural economy.

Relatively little of this chapter addresses women's professional sports because relatively few big-time professional sports opportunities have been available for women athletes. We have already considered in previous chapters the discrimination and stereotyping faced by black women in sports such as professional tennis and professional basketball, but women in professional sports and their sports generally have received little attention from researchers. In fact, women and women's sports have had relatively little influence in the Golden Triangle of professional sports. Even in relatively more popular and commercialized women's sports such as tennis and golf, the top female players have had to fight for compensation and media coverage equal to those of their male counterparts.

Monopoly Capitalism and the Economics of Professional Sports Leagues

In the last chapter, we considered how the NCAA operated as a labor cartel to restrict the rights and economic opportunities of athletes. This arrangement is meant to keep costs under control and ensure that college athletes are professionals only to the extent that they receive athletic grants-in-aid or scholarships to cover their expenses as students. Even though they pay their players more directly as professionals, professional sports leagues have also operated as cartels and restricted the rights and economic opportunities of their athletes. Furthermore, a structure of monopoly capitalism at the highest levels of professional team sports has served the financial interests of the league and individual owners and created league stability (Nixon and Frey 1996:172–182; Coakley 2007:382–384). The idea of monopoly capitalism implies the pursuit of profit by firms in a market, such as a sport, under restricted conditions of economic competition. A *cartel* is a self-regulating monopoly, and in *monopolies*, there is exclusive control of a good or service with only one seller providing that particular good or service. This makes it possible for the seller to manipulate the price of the good or service and maximize profits. A *monopsony* exists when there is only one buyer of a good or service in a market. This has meant that athletes wanting to play a professional sport have typically been limited to one league and have only been able to negotiate a contract with the team drafting them. We will take some liberties in the use of these economic terms in using "monopoly capitalism" to refer to monopolistic and monopsonistic practices by professional sports league cartels.

An economic structure of monopoly capitalism, which has allowed professional sports leagues to operate as cartels, to restrict economic competition, and to control their markets, has distinguished professional sports from other businesses in the United States. There is supposed to be a free and competitive market in the United States, and antitrust laws have generally made restraint of free trade illegal for U.S. businesses. The U.S. Supreme Court and Congress permitted monopolistic practices in professional sports for a long time because they were reluctant to treat professional sports as conventional businesses. They have also accepted arguments about how unrestrained economic competition and a lack of internal regulation within a sports league could harm the competitive balance on the playing field, cause many teams to fail financially, and undermine the appeal of the sport. Thus, although teams in a professional sports league compete on the field, their *economic* competition has been restricted for their mutual benefit by monopoly capitalism. As Karl Marx would have predicted, monopoly capitalism is an economic system that benefits owners and their business partners in the Golden Triangle, but puts players and other employees of these owners, consumers such as sports fans, and the cities where professional sports teams play in a disadvantaged bargaining position in their relations with professional sports owners and leagues.

Monopoly capitalism in professional sports has been increasingly limited over the last few decades by legal challenges, pressure from Congress, and the power of players with agents and as organized collective bargaining units or unions. However, monopoly capitalism has had an enduring impact on the organization and operation of professional team sports and the nature of players' relationships with owners and management. Operating under monopoly capitalism, major North American professional sports leagues have used monopsonistic devices such as a player reservation system or "reserve clause," which bound a drafted player to a particular team for the duration of his career or until the player's owner decided to trade or release him. This meant that players had little bargaining power in salary negotiations because owners knew players could not play for anyone else if they wanted to play in the league. Thus, owners did not have to worry about salary wars with other owners for the services of top players. This arrangement ended with the establishment of relatively unrestricted "free agency" between the late 1970s and early 1990s in the major North American professional sports leagues. With free agency, under specified conditions, players could try to sell their services to the highest bidder among teams in a league at the end of their contract period. The beginning of free agency was associated with the beginning of the trend in escalating player salaries in professional sports leagues.

Owners in North American professional sports leagues have benefited from acting together as a single seller of the national broadcasting rights to their games, and they have agreed to share the revenues from national media contracts. Negotiating pooled media contracts has enabled team owners to have predictable revenues, given them power in relations with television, and allowed them to influence television sports announcers and commentators. This is why announcers and commentators are unlikely to be too critical of the teams or sports they cover. In addition to strengthening a sport's bargaining position with the media, economic cooperation has enabled sports officials to control the number of games available to viewers and sometimes even prevented fans from seeing their home team play on television under certain conditions when games were not sold out.

The NFL has maintained the strictest control over television rights contracts and television exposure, which has made its television rights fees the highest in North American professional sports and made it the richest North American league. For example, in 2006, estimated annual media rights fees in the North American sports industry varied from $3.7 billion for the NFL to $767 million for the NBA, $560 million for MLB and the stock car racing circuit NASCAR, and $70 million for the NHL, which was hurt by the effects of a lost season due to a management-player conflict (Coakley 2007:414). We can see the different implications of monopoly and the free marketplace if we compare how the NFL and MLB handle local broadcast rights. Individual NFL teams are not permitted by the league to negotiate their own television contracts for local broadcasts of their games, and television revenue has been split evenly among the teams (Lowry 2003).

In an effort to increase its power and profits in the media segment of the Golden Triangle of its sport, the NFL created a league-owned network, the NFL Network. It does not yet rival the number of viewers of the NFL's network broadcast partners NBC, Fox, or CBS or its cable partner ESPN, and its attempt to expand viewers by pressing major cable operators such as Time Warner, Comcast, and Charter Communications to carry the network as part of their basic or digital cable packages has met resistance from these carriers (McCarthy 2007b). This "media war" within the NFL's Golden Triangle has resulted in restricted access for fans to some prime NFL games that were only available on the NFL Network, as the NFL has tried to get customers of resistant cable companies to switch to a company offering the NFL Network as part of its standard package. This example, along with the fantasy league challenge, shows how major players within Golden Triangles are continually driven by the capitalist imperative to protect or expand their markets and profits. While such examples demonstrate economic competition within Golden Triangles, they also reveal how Golden Triangles grow overall in power and wealth.

In contrast to the NFL, MLB permits teams to negotiate local television contracts, and as a result, there have been large differences in local television revenue earned by MLB teams in more- and less-lucrative local markets. For example, the disparity between the big-market New York Yankees and small-market Pittsburgh Pirates has been 10 to 1 or more (Mondello 2006:286). A more extreme discrepancy was between the Yankees and the failing Montreal Expos in 2002, when the Yankees earned $60 million from local broadcast fees and the Expos earned $500,000, which was a 120 to 1 ratio (Coakley 2007:384). The bargaining position of the Expos was severely compromised by their impending demise as an MLB franchise.

Women's professional sports leagues such as the Women's United Soccer Association (WUSA) and the Women's National Basketball Association (WNBA) have historically been unsuccessful in taking advantage of a monopoly position in their sport. They have been hampered by their limited popular appeal and live gate attendance, which have prevented them from negotiating lucrative national television contracts. As a result, the WUSA suspended operations in 2003 after three seasons. Although the WNBA knocked out a competing league, the American Basketball League, in 1999 and has survived for more than ten seasons, in part due to subsidies from the NBA, it has continued to struggle financially and lagged far behind the NBA in attendance, revenue, and media coverage. It shifted from a centrally run league to individual franchises owned and operated by NBA owners in 2002. Some teams were sold to owners outside the NBA, but most were still owned by NBA teams in 2006. Dual ownership presented possible conflicts of interest for owners more committed to their NBA than to their WNBA teams (Heath 2006b).

Established professional sports leagues have used the collective power of the cartel and monopolistic practices to deflect or control competition from new or prospective leagues or teams. For example, exclusive use clauses in arena or stadium contracts have substantially restricted the options for potential rival teams in a new or competing league looking for a place to play. In addition, long-term and lucrative television and radio contracts and established relationships with the local press have given older leagues advantages over new leagues in terms of media revenue and exposure. With a less-established "brand name" or reputation, less media exposure, and less revenue, new leagues have found it difficult to attract the star players needed to build a fan base and the interest of national media and corporate sponsors. Furthermore, new teams have had difficulty attracting fans in the face of competition not only from the established league in their sport but also from other established sports and leagues in the professional sports marketplace. These reasons explain why new leagues in established sports have typically failed in recent decades. They also explain why women's sports leagues and leagues in sports outside or on the fringes of the hegemonic or dominant sports culture in North America, such as Major League Soccer (MLS) and its indoor soccer counterpart the Major Indoor Soccer League (MISL) and the Major League Lacrosse (MLL) outdoor lacrosse league, have struggled to attract enough fans to become financially successful. However, while new leagues may struggle for financial survival against the established league in their sport, their existence benefits players in the established league, who can leverage a possible contract offer from a new league to improve their bargaining position with owners.

Established leagues have protected existing franchises and inflated their financial value by limiting the number of teams in the league and controlling the location and relocation of franchises. According to sports economists (e.g., Alexander and Kern 2004), the estimated market value of professional sports franchises varies by sport and within sports depending on factors such as the size of the market in which a club plays, how much it wins, and the presence of a new facility. Regional identity seems to affect franchise values in MLB but not in other North American professional sports leagues because MLB does less than the other leagues to minimize revenue differences among teams. We can also assume that average franchise values of different sports vary according to the revenue potential in the sport and its prestige or popularity. We will look more closely at the estimated value of professional sports franchises in the next section on "the numbers" in professional sports.

The Numbers: Franchise Values, Money, and Professional Sports

Although I do not want to dwell on numbers, numbers give us a fuller and more concrete sense of the economics of professional sports. Golden Triangles in professional sports and the sports world in general are driven mainly by a profit motive, and professional sports and professional athletes are the most open and least equivocal in the sports world about their desire to make money. Thus, in this section, we will consider figures for franchise values, revenues, profits and losses, and salaries. They will help us see the economic hierarchy in the commercialized sports world and the hierarchies within different sports.

Each year, *Forbes* magazine[1] collects information from team executives, sports bankers, public documents, and other sources to estimate the franchise values in major North American sports leagues and in European soccer (Blum 2007a). Although the officials of some teams have disputed these estimates, they represent the best available data from a relatively authoritative source about how much franchises are worth. The factors used to calculate these franchise values include the amount of revenue sharing a team gets from its league, the size of the city and media market where it plays, the value of its stadium, and how well its market brand is managed. Thus, the most valued franchises are in leagues that generate and share the most revenue, play in the biggest cities with the biggest media markets, have the most valuable and usually newest stadiums, and have the most recognizable and respected brands among sports merchandisers, advertisers, consumers, and potential investors.

The franchise values of top teams in the major North American professional sports leagues indicate the relative status of these leagues in the Golden Triangle of North American professional sports as well as their place in the hegemonic sports culture of the United States and Canada. We can compare franchise values for 2006–2007. The NFL had the most valuable franchises that year, with 5 of 32 teams (16 percent) valued at more than $1 billion and 13 teams (41 percent) valued at more than $900 million. The most highly valued franchise was the Washington Redskins at $1.4 billion, and the least valued was the Minnesota Vikings at $720 million. Although the New York Yankees were the second-most-valuable franchise in North America at $1.2 billion, MLB franchises were generally valued at much less than NFL franchises, with the second-most-valued MLB franchise, the New York Mets, estimated to be worth $736 million. The least valued MLB franchise was the Florida Marlins at $244 million. NBA franchise values ranged from $592 million for the New York Knicks to $230 million for the Portland Trailblazers. In the NHL, franchise values ranged from $332 million for the Toronto Maple Leafs to $127 million for the Washington Capitals. Although there was a substantial range in these franchise values in the major North American professional sports leagues, it was much lower than the range for European soccer clubs, which was over $1.3 billion for the 25 most valued clubs. According to *Forbes* estimates in 2007, the range for these teams was from $1.5 billion for Manchester United (England) and $1 billion for Real Madrid (Spain) to $140 million for Aston Villa (England).

Along with franchise values, team revenue, profits and losses, payrolls, and the money athletes earn from salaries, endorsements, and prize winnings are frequent subjects of sports news stories. The most valued franchises tended to generate the most revenue, but they were not necessarily the most profitable. Using *Forbes* estimates, we can see approximately how much revenue and profit (before taxes and interest payments) were earned by the top revenue producer and profit maker in each of the major North American leagues and in European soccer. The Washington Redskins generated the most revenue in the

NFL ($303 million), and they were also the most profitable team (over $108 million). In MLB, the New York Yankees produced the most revenue ($302 million), but with its big payroll, it was the only team with an operating deficit ($25 million). Surprisingly, the most profitable team, the Florida Marlins ($43 million), was the least valued MLB franchise and produced the least revenue ($122 million). In the NBA, the most valued franchise, the New York Knicks, produced the most revenue ($185 million), but it also had the biggest operating deficit ($39 million). The most profitable team was the fourth-most-valued franchise, the Chicago Bulls, and it earned $48.5 million. The NHL team that produced the most revenue ($119 million) was the most valued franchise, the Toronto Maple Leafs, and it also was the most profitable ($41.5 million). In soccer, the second-most-valued club was Real Madrid, and it generated the most revenue ($374 million). The most profitable European soccer club ($92 million) was the most valued franchise in the sport, Manchester United. These numbers show that in some cases, team owners may be more motivated to win than to make money in sport. Of course, this is a luxury that can only be afforded by owners who are wealthy enough to sustain losses in sport and who do not have stockholders or investment partners demanding profits. The desire to win is not likely to be a higher priority than making money for corporations that own sports teams, broadcast sports, or make investments as sponsors.

The *wealth gap* between the biggest and smallest revenue producers in a sport is an indication of the difference in the money teams are able to spend on things such as player salaries to try to win. The wealth gap can be measured by comparing as a percentage the revenue generated by the poorest team (i.e., the team that produced the least revenue and had the least to spend) with the revenue earned by the richest team (i.e., the biggest revenue producer) in a sport. Lower percentages reflect bigger wealth gaps. Wealth gap percentages ranged from 24 percent in European soccer, which was not organized into a single league or cartel, to 40 percent in MLB, 42 percent in the NBA, 47 percent in the NHL, and 53 percent in the NFL.[2] In general, the leagues or sports with higher percentages and smaller wealth gaps put more restrictions on economic competition among teams in their league or sport. The European soccer teams in this data set were not part of a single league or cartel and, without monopolistic restrictions, had the most economic competition and the most inequality. In contrast, monopolistic practices by the NFL cartel enabled it to be very successful in generating revenue as a league. Acting as a cartel, the NFL created revenue-sharing arrangements that resulted in the smallest wealth gap or least league inequality among these sports. However, even in the NFL, small-market teams such as the Jacksonville Jaguars have worried about profitability and their ability to compete financially and athletically with richer teams in bigger and more affluent cities that were able to generate more revenue from luxury suites and sponsorships. The Jaguars dropped in eleven years from first in revenue to twenty-fourth of thirty-two in 2005 (Carpenter 2006).

A major expense for teams is their players, and player payrolls have significantly escalated for professional sports teams in the era of free agency. For example, the total cost of player salaries for the Seattle Seahawks in 2005 was nearly $101 million, the highest in the NFL that year, and this was 53 percent of its revenue.[3] The MLB team with the biggest payroll in 2007, the New York

Yankees, spent almost $190 million on player salaries, which was 62 percent of its revenue. In the NBA in 2006–2007, the Phoenix Suns spent the most on player salaries, over $82 million, which was 62 percent of its revenue. The NHL team with the biggest payroll that year, the New Jersey Devils, spent nearly $50 million on player salaries, which was 81 percent of its revenue. The team with the lowest player payroll in these four sports in these reporting years was the Tampa Bay Devil Rays in MLB. Its payroll was $24 million, which was only 18 percent of its revenue. This explains why the team was able to generate a profit of over $20 million. Even more striking is the case of the Florida Marlins in MLB, which had a payroll of only $31 million, which was 25 percent of its league-low revenue of $122 million. However, with low player costs, it was able to generate a profit of over $43 million, which was the highest in the league.

Along with team payrolls, median compensation for players varied among the leagues and within leagues. For example, according to *USA Today* reports, the median player salary[4] for NFL teams in 2005 ranged from a high of $821,000 to a low of $385,000. The team median salary in MLB in 2007 ranged from $3.6 million to $380,000; in the NBA in 2006–2007, it ranged from $5.2 million to $1.4 million; and in the NHL in 2006–2007, it ranged from $1.9 million to $625,000. In an effort to control escalating salaries in a free agency marketplace, leagues have established some form of a cap on player salaries, with the rigidity of the cap varying among leagues. For example, the NFL cap in 2006 was a team limit of approximately $102 million in player salaries.[5] Major League Baseball established a team salary threshold, which was $148 million in 2006. Teams that exceeded the threshold were penalized with a "luxury tax," which was officially called a "competitive balance tax bill" by the league. The New York Yankees paid the highest luxury taxes from 2003 to 2006, totaling nearly $100 million. The NBA calculated its cap in terms of a percentage of league revenues, and the cap averaged approximately $46 million per team in 2004–2005. The league allowed a number of exceptions. The NHL had an upper limit to its "team payroll range," which was about $44 million per team in 2006–2007.

Professional sports differ in their economic structure and how athletes get paid. For example, unlike salary-based sports such as the NFL, NBA, NHL, MLB, and soccer, sports such as tennis and golf are winnings based, with athletes earning prize money in tournaments. Furthermore, unlike the professional sports organized as leagues, sports such as tennis and golf have tours that operate under the auspices of a coordinating or governing body in the sport. The organization of these latter sports may be complex and varies from sport to sport. For example, the governing body for golf in the United States is the U.S. Golf Association (USGA), and the Professional Golfers' Association (PGA) Tour organization runs elite golf tournaments, including its elite PGA Tour, the Champions Tour for golfers fifty and older, and the Nationwide Tour for second-tier professional golfers.[6] Women are permitted to compete in PGA Tour events, but relatively few have qualified or been invited. U.S. golf tournaments for top women professionals are run by the Ladies Professional Golf Association (LPGA). These organizations certify eligibility for tournament participation, establish the rules for sponsoring tournaments that are part of their tours and for distributing prize money to tournament participants, and work with local tournament committees to organize tournaments.

The PGA Tour describes itself on its website as a tax-exempt membership organization of professional golfers with the aims of expanding golf domestically and internationally, increasing financial benefits for professional golfers, ensuring the integrity of the game, and working with local tournament organizers to raise money for charitable causes in their communities as well as for tournament prize money. With some historic exceptions, local tournament committees are required by the PGA Tour to be nonprofit organizations, and local events rely on a corps of volunteers. The elite professional golfers who compete in PGA Tour events have earned over $10 million in a season, and winners of individual events frequently earn over $1 million for their victory. In 2007, the PGA Tour generated $950 million in revenue, elite golfers on the PGA Tour competed for $270 million in prize money, and tour events raised more than $100 million for charities (Doyle 2007). The major sources of prize money are television revenue and sponsors of local tournaments. The PGA Tour subsidizes over half of the cost of local tournaments, and its television contract covering 2003–2006 was for $850 million (Sports Biz 2005). The LPGA Tour Champions tournament in 2006 was the first LPGA event to offer a $1 million prize to the winner.

Other major professional tournament sports such as tennis are generally organized in the way golf is, but there are individual-competitor sports such as boxing that are organized very differently, with competing governing bodies, highly influential promoters, and boxers whose careers are heavily influenced by managers and trainers. A single major boxing event can generate more revenue than most big-league professional sports teams outside the NFL earn in a season. For example, Floyd Mayweather defeated Oscar De La Hoya in a junior middleweight title fight in 2007 that generated the most revenue ever produced in the sport (Rafael 2007). It earned over $150 million, with $120 million in pay-per-view revenue, $19 million at the gate, and over $10 million more from foreign TV and merchandise sales and sponsorships. Over 2.1 million people paid to watch the fight. De La Hoya and Mayweather were guaranteed $23.3 million and $10 million, respectively, and with the fight's big financial success could have earned as much as $50 million and $20 million. These numbers are in stark contrast to the financial fortunes of most boxers, who typically make only modest amounts from their dangerous sport (Newfield 2001).

NASCAR differs from other major sports in North America in large part because it has been dominated by a single family. Under the monopolistic control of the France family, NASCAR has ascended rapidly to elite status in the Golden Triangle of North American professional sports. It sanctions various stock car and truck race series and events in North America, with the Nextel Cup series its elite property. Seventeen of the twenty most attended sports events in North America in 2005 were NASCAR races, with an average attendance at these events of 125,000 (Oliver Ryan 2005). The France family has used a complex network of companies, subsidiaries, and affiliates to control NASCAR, dictating sanctioning fees, the scheduling of races, and the distribution of television revenue (Newberry 2002/2005). It also controlled a publicly traded company that owned or had investments in a majority of the tracks used on the NASCAR circuit. NASCAR signed an eight-year, $4.5 billion television contract with Fox, Speed, TNT, and ABC/ESPN, beginning in 2007 (Edmonds 2005).

Jimmie Johnson celebrates in victory lane after winning the NASCAR Nextel Cup series Checker Auto Parts 500 auto race at Phoenix International Raceway Sunday, November 11, 2007, in Avondale, Arizona. Jimmie Johnson is a rising star in NASCAR, and NASCAR is a rising star in the Golden Triangle of North American sports. (AP Photo/Jason Babyak)

Car owners finance race teams that employ drivers and large support crews, and they generate revenue from sponsors, the NASCAR television contract, and the success of their drivers. In an effort to reduce costs as well as to improve safety and competitive performance, NASCAR introduced a universal car design, the "Car of Tomorrow," for its Nextel Cup Series in 2007. The France family distributes approximately 25 percent of the money from its NASCAR television contract to race teams as prize money (Gage 2007). The average NASCAR Nextel Cup team generated $12.3 million in profit in the 2006 season. In comparison, it was estimated that MLB teams averaged $16.5 million in profit at that time. NASCAR revenue for the fifteen richest team owners in 2007 ranged from $189 million for Roush Fenway Racing with lead driver Matt Kenseth and $163 million for Hendrik Motorsports with lead driver Jeff Gordon to fifteenth-ranked Haas CNC Racing, which produced $37 million in revenue with lead driver Jeff Green. Auto racing is an expensive sport, with the high cost of personnel, cars, travel, and research and development. While the top two NASCAR teams each earned about $39 million in profit, four of the top fifteen teams produced a deficit. Because the sport is organized essentially as a partnership between NASCAR and independent race teams rather than as a league cartel in the way the NFL, the NBA, the NHL, and MLB are, drivers have not had unions or collective bargaining agreements with the NASCAR organization. NASCAR drivers work for the owner of their car and race team. They have not had the benefits unions have negotiated in a number of other professional sports, but the drivers have been gaining power in their relationship with team owners with the help of agents, who have handled their financial affairs and negotiated their contracts with owners. The top forty NASCAR drivers each earn several million dollars per year.

The growth in NASCAR licensing fees and sponsorship rates flattened somewhat around 2007, but the average value of NASCAR race teams was estimated to be $120 million, an increase of 67 percent from the previous year. The increase reflected a 21 percent increase in the number of cars competing in the elite Nextel Cup series from 2006 to 2007, which substantially increased opportunities for attracting more sponsorship money. Each team had a primary sponsor and numerous other sponsors, which was a major source of revenue. Primary sponsors included auto, oil, industrial power tool, farm equipment, chemical, retail, beer, food, shipping, and telecommunications corporations and the U.S. Army. These sponsors represented both the older manufacturing and newer high-tech and service economies, reflecting both the diverse audience the sport has tried to build and the desire of major corporate sponsors to diversify their sports investments.

Unlike NASCAR, in the NFL, MLB, the NBA, and the NHL, free agency, the amount of the salary cap, and the portion of league revenue distributed to players have been major issues in collective bargaining negotiations between player unions and management. Disagreements have sometimes resulted in work stoppages or strikes by players or lockouts by owners. For example, MLB had three strikes between 1972 and 1994–1995 that resulted in significant numbers of lost games; the NFL had strikes in 1982 and 1987; the NBA had a lockout in 1998–1999; and the NHL had a lockout in 1995 and another that cancelled the 2004–2005 season.[7]

Although market value and dollars define the commercial character of professional sports and the Golden Triangle of professional sports, we must ask what the relationship is between money and success on the field for sports franchises. What we find is that highly valued and very profitable franchises such as the Washington Redskins may be losers on the field, that franchises such as the New York Yankees are consistent winners but do not necessarily win the championship in their sport despite spending the most and even paying "luxury taxes" and incurring debts to get the best talent, and that less-prestigious and smaller-market franchises with relatively small player payrolls can achieve financial and competitive success. Furthermore, the Pittsburgh Steelers won the NFL Super Bowl in 2006 with the tenth-highest payroll, the St. Louis Cardinals won the MLB World Series in 2006 with the eleventh-highest payroll, the San Antonio Spurs won their fourth NBA Championship in nine years in 2007 with the sixth-highest payroll, and the Anaheim Ducks won the NHL Stanley Cup with the sixteenth-highest payroll in 2007. These results also show that teams in mid-sized or small cities and media markets can become the top team in their sport.

The case of Billy Beane, the general manager of the Oakland Athletics MLB franchise, shows how an objective and innovative rational management strategy can offset a small budget to help a team achieve financial and competitive success (Lewis 2003). Beane's case was used to illustrate rational choice theory in chapter two, which was contrasted with the more common approach to decision making in his sport that relied on traditional knowledge and subjective judgments of experienced "baseball people." Because his approach was unconventional, a highly publicized book about it (Lewis 2003) provoked considerable controversy (also see Lewis 2004). Beane's statistically based strategy for evaluating talent and drafting underrated and less-expensive talent enabled him to create a division champion team with more than one hundred wins in 2002 with the third-smallest payroll in MLB that year. Although the development and success of his players, the continually escalating cost of competition for players, and his desire to retain top players inflated his payroll, it was still seventeenth in MLB in 2007, $110 million lower than the Yankees, and many million lower than the payrolls of teams with which his team competed very successfully on the field. However, the escalation in his payroll demonstrates the need for even the most efficient executives to spend more money to keep up with the competition, and it shows the strain of the wealth gap for poorer smaller-market teams trying to keep up. Oakland had the seventeenth-ranked payroll but was tied for twenty-third in revenue in 2007, and it had $156 million less revenue than the Yankees and was $9 million to $41 million poorer in revenue than the other three teams in its division that year.

Sports Monopolies, Fans, and the Evolution of Sports Stadiums

We have seen that despite a wealth gap between leagues and between teams in leagues, cartel-like arrangements and monopolistic practices have enabled many professional sports and sports franchises to be financially successful. We have also seen that when the grip of monopoly capitalism is loosened in a sport, the wealth gap in that sport tends to increase and athletes tend to make more money. In large part, the financial success of professional sports has been tied to the appeal of these sports, of their stars, and of their merchandise to sports consumers and fans. Bigger live and media audiences have attracted more interest and investment from the Golden Triangle, which makes sports big-time commercial ventures. When a professional sport has its reputation tarnished by a scandal, such as doping in cycling and MLB, gambling by an NBA referee, criminal behavior in the personal lives of NFL players, or match fixing in soccer, it puts its status in the Golden Triangle at risk because of the possibility it will lose the respect of fans.

Despite being essential for the commercial success of sports, fans have not always been accorded special status by professional sports, unless they could pay for it. Like players, they have been affected by the monopolistic economic structure of professional sports. Fans have especially felt the effects of sports monopolies in access to games on television and in ticket prices. When a local professional team is the only one in an area playing in its sport's major league, owners can significantly inflate ticket prices. For example, in the four major North American team sports, ticket prices increased between 1991 and 2004 from 99 percent in the NHL to 142 percent in the NBA (Coakley 2007:341). By 2005, the average ticket prices for a game were $58.95 in the NFL, $45.92 in the NBA, $41.19 in the NHL, and $21.27 in MLB. The average "Fan Cost Index"

(FCI) for each of these sports that year was $329.82 for the NFL, $267.37 for the NBA, $247.84 for the NHL, and $164.43 for MLB (McCarthy 2006). The FCI is an estimate of the cost of attending a sports event for a family of four (including four game tickets, parking, two beers, four soft drinks, four hot dogs, two programs, and two hats). The FCI for NASCAR race fans has been even higher. The average ticket price for NASCAR Nextel Cup races in 2005 was $88 (Oliver Ryan 2005).

Average ticket prices and FCI estimates for the major professional sports in North America show that the people who control these sports have exploited their monopolistic control of their sport and sports markets to inflate the price of being a spectator. They have raised ticket prices to a level where lower-income and middle-income fans of these sports either cannot afford to attend live events or must use a substantial portion of their discretionary income to attend, especially if they want to take their family. Professional sports owners and marketers also seem to understand Veblen's concept of conspicuous consumption, which we discussed in chapter three. This idea implies that making live attendance more expensive and more exclusive increases the status value of attendance at live sports events. As a result, owners have been able to raise ticket prices even more for championships and other special events, and sports marketers have been able to charge very high prices for special seating, access to the action, and VIP treatment at sports events. For example, celebrities have paid $1,750 to sit courtside in a "Hollywood seat" at a New Jersey Nets NBA game and $110,000 or more to sit in these seats for the season. Season ticket prices include the cost of "personal seat licenses" (PSLs), which are fees that must be paid for the right to purchase season tickets. PSLs cost $37,500 per ticket for front-row seats at Nets games in the 2006 season. The team also sold twelve-person courtside suites at $250,000 per season, and suite holders were allowed to shake hands with players and get their autographs.

The challenge for NASCAR has been to maintain its traditional rural southern U.S. fan base as it expands to a wider audience to satisfy the media and advertisers (Brown and Bryant 2006). Some executives have seemed to be sensitive to the implications of making their sport appear too exclusive. For example, the Dover International Speedway built a glass-enclosed structure over the center of the track. However, it does not sell seats in this structure. It gives them away as promotional prizes to regular fans of the sport. As the Dover Motorsports executive vice president said, "Half the seats are always filled with real fans. We don't want to make it for the elite" (USA Today 2006). At the same time, the speedway hosts celebrities in this area, and ticket prices for its Nextel Cup races could be expensive, for example, ranging from $43 to over $260 for a race in 2007, according to the speedway's website. For the premier race on the NASCAR circuit, the Daytona 500, fans could pay $5,000 each to sit in one of the eighty seats in President's Row, a section on top of the Daytona International Speedway with a view of victory lane, the finish line, and the pits for the race cars and crews. These eighty fans also got to sit above the nearly 170,000 spectators in the other seats at the speedway for this race.

Huge sports facilities serve the interests of owners, who can increase their revenue from gate receipts with a bigger stadium, since along with media, concessions, and parking revenue, ticket sales are a major source of income in professional sports (Lowry 2003). Ritzer and Stillman (2001) have argued that

as sports facilities have grown in size, they have become increasingly rationalized or McDonaldized, risking their appeal to fans. Based on rational economic
logic that more seats equaled more money, arenas and stadiums got bigger and
bigger. In addition, they staged increasingly spectacular displays to attract
spectators, with an assortment of types of entertainment along with the sports
event itself, including music; fireworks; exploding scoreboards; concession
stands selling food, beer, and ice cream; distinctive architecture; and flags to
commemorate past successes and to honor the nation. This has long been part
of the history of professional sports.

Ritzer and Stillman observed that there has been an evolution of the ballpark
from those built in the early modern era in the early part of the twentieth century to ballparks constructed in the late modern era from the 1960s through the
1980s to those built in the current postmodern period, which began in the
1990s. In MLB, ballparks of the earliest era included Boston's Fenway Park,
Brooklyn's Ebbetts Field, Pittsburgh's Forbes Field, and Chicago's Wrigley Field,
which had a charm typically associated with their relatively small size, distinctive architectural features, and the intimacy possible among spectators. These
stadiums were made for baseball and were not suited for anything else. The new
stadiums of the next, late modern era in cities such as Houston, Pittsburgh,
Philadelphia, and Toronto lacked the enchanting qualities of the older ones,
since they were built as large multiuse facilities with artificial turf and domes
for protection from weather. Ritzer and Stillman proposed that the ballpark was
among the reasons for a significant drop in MLB attendance in the late 1980s
and early 1990s. Fans had become disenchanted with the big salaries of players who left their local fans to take advantage of free agency and get a bigger
salary. They were also unhappy with owners who demanded that taxpayers
fund new stadiums, and they found little appeal in the sterile environment of
the "late modern ballpark."

The construction of a new Baltimore Orioles stadium at Camden Yards in
1992 began the postmodern period for ballparks. The ballparks of this period
were "postmodern" because they seemed to represent a rejection of the sterile,
standardized, nondescript, and dull stadium of the late modern period. They
were meant to capture the nostalgia of the past through architecture that called
to mind the charm of the earlier ballparks, while also making a day or night at
the ballpark thoroughly entertaining. Other ballparks, in Cleveland; Arlington,
Texas; Denver; Atlanta; Phoenix; San Francisco; Houston; Detroit; and Seattle,
followed the lead of Baltimore. However, Ritzer and Stillman argued that these
new ballparks only simulated the charming environment of the early modern
ballparks and that beneath the appearance of a return to the past, there was
clear evidence of "postmodern" rationalization and McDonaldization in the
newest ballparks. Owners charged more for tickets and offered special seating,
such as luxury boxes, for very high prices. They also developed new ways for
spectators and other consumers to spend money in and around the ballpark,
such as food courts, video arcades, amusement park play areas, and ATMs,
turning the ballpark into a virtual shopping mall. Furthermore, merchandise
giveaways, scoreboard displays, fireworks, sideline antics by mascots, and cas-
cades of water marking various parts of the game as well as entertainment between innings distract from the game and seem to be intended to make attending a ball game entertaining for those not really interested in baseball.

Ritzer and Stillman argued that MLB teams gave the appearance of making ballparks less modern and less McDonaldized by adding a few nostalgic elements, such as the façade of old ballparks, and by trying to make attending ballgames more comfortable and fun. At the same time, though, these teams remained highly rational, calculating, McDonaldized, and "modern" in their basic approach as they raised ticket prices, provided elite and very expensive seating and consumption opportunities for spectators, and emphasized forms of entertainment to broaden their fan base and increase attendance. By making the ballpark a "theme park" and its setting like a shopping mall, teams in MLB ironically may have diluted the appeal of the live event to more serious baseball fans. Ritzer and Stillman were concerned that the new ballparks ultimately replaced a leisure escape experience for fans with a "mass-produced, manipulated, rationalized, simulated, and commodified" consumption experience (111). In his analysis of McDonaldization, Ritzer (2004b:7) called these mall-like postmodern ballparks "cathedrals of consumption."

Thus, the ballpark experience has become an important commodity in the contemporary cultural economy of sport constructed by the sports club owners and promoters and their media and corporate partners. Nostalgic ideas of authenticity are part of the construction of this experience, but Ritzer and Stillman contend that this is actually very calculated. Earlier in this book, we discussed Smart's argument that authenticity is a primary reason for the appeal of sport in an era when so much seems calculated, planned, predictable, or McDonaldized. Recognizing this, the Golden Triangle has blended an appearance of nostalgic authenticity with rationally calculated commercial strategies to expand their markets and be more profitable. This kind of commercial and capitalistic motivation seems ultimately more important to the Golden Triangle than preserving or restoring authenticity in sport.

Cities and states have felt pressured to build or renovate arenas and stadiums for professional sports franchises in an effort to keep an existing franchise in town or to attract a team that a league has decided will be allowed to relocate. The key here is that professional sports leagues operate as cartels to limit the number and location of franchises to make them more valuable. When local fans or politicians want a team in a major professional league in their area, they often must pay the price to get their wish, with public subsidies of their stadium or arena. Proponents and opponents have debated these subsidies, and the controversy and debates are addressed further in a "Focus on Research" feature.

Global Expansion in the Global Sports Marketplace

The capitalist growth imperative of the Golden Triangle has pushed professional sports to try to cross new borders to expand their visibility, markets, consumers, and profits. This has meant at least two things. Professional sports that have been part of the hegemonic culture of sports in North America have tried to expand to a wider world market, and major professional sports overseas have sought to enhance their status in the global sports marketplace and global cultural economy (Nixon and Frey 1996:182–186). Maguire (1990) provided a case study of how professional sports, media, and corporate sponsors

Focus on Research Feature 10.1:
Building Professional Sports Facilities with Public Funds

Debates about public subsidies of professional sports facilities are not new (see Nixon and Frey 1996:178–182). On one side, proponents have made several arguments to justify the subsidies, which are supposed to attract or retain a professional sports franchise. They include various economic development arguments, such as job creation, increased spending in the local economy, improvement of the city's reputation or brand in the business world to attract new businesses, and attraction of tourists to the city. Proponents also argue that the new sports facilities pay for themselves with revenues from ticket sales, sales taxes from purchases made in the stadium or arena and in the local community, and increased property taxes resulting from the boost in the local economy caused by the new facility. In addition, there are claims of less-tangible benefits such as increased community pride from living in a city that has a local professional team to follow and that receives national attention for being part of the world of major league professional sports.

Economists Roger Noll and Andrew Zimbalist (1997) used economic analysis to assess arguments and data that were supposed to show the benefits of stadium or arena construction, and they concluded that the arguments were overstated because they were based on faulty economic reasoning. They stated that economic growth occurs when a community's human or capital investment or its natural resources, such as land, become more productive. Construction of a new professional sports facility contributes to economic growth in a community only when the facility is the most productive way to make capital investments and use local land and workers. After looking at relevant evidence about the economic effects of these kinds of facilities, Noll and Zimbalist concluded that new sports facilities had a very small or even negative impact on overall economic activity and employment. These facilities typically failed to attract significant numbers of tourists or new businesses.

Research about investment by small towns and small cities in minor league baseball facilities shows that their economic payoff depended on how well the public and private sectors cooperated with each other in the planning and use of the stadium for local economic and community development (Johnson 1995). In a small town in Maryland, town officials with big sports ambitions negotiated an unwise agreement with private investors to build a minor league facility and sports complex. As a result, the town suffered operating losses and a growing public debt they had difficulty paying off, while the private investors enjoyed a steady stream of healthy profits from their part of the investment (Fenton and Garland 2007).

Baltimore's Oriole Park at Camden Yards, which was a primary example of Ritzer and Stillman's (2001) concept of a "postmodern ballpark," seemed to be a counterexample to the idea of unrealized expectations from stadium investment. Unlike cities whose new stadiums failed to generate new revenue from a significant number of out-of-town tourists, about one-third of those attending most games in the early years of Oriole Park at Camden Yards were from out of town. However, Noll and Zimbalist calculated that the net economic gain for Baltimore in new jobs and tax revenue was $3 million per year, which was a tiny percentage of the $200 million public investment in the stadium for Maryland taxpayers. In addition, Oriole attendance has dropped in recent years, with the ballpark no longer new, the team struggling on the field, and a new MLB team in nearby Washington, D.C.

Noll and Zimbalist observed that the local professional sports teams that play in these new stadiums or arenas generate substantial revenue from national merchandise licensing and media contracts. However, they also pointed out that these economic gains were offset by highly paid athletes making their homes and spending much of their income elsewhere, by the sharing of ticket and other forms of team revenue with other teams in other cities in a league, and by stadium or arena employees largely being seasonal, part-time, and poorly paid. In addition, when consumers spend their discretionary income on sports attendance, they may be spending less on other types of local recreation or entertainment, such as movies, restaurants, or other attractions. This is called substitute spending, and it does not infuse new money into a local economy.

According to Noll and Zimbalist, the reason why the public and public officials are willing to spend large sums of public money on major league professional sports facilities is that the monopolistic structure of professional sports leagues has enabled them to restrict the number of franchises, thereby making cities with teams in a major professional sports league part of an exclusive club. Thus, leagues and teams can pressure a city or state to invest in a new stadium or major renovations. They can either promise the placement or relocation of a team in a city or they can threaten relocation out of the city if it fails to meet the league's or team's demands. As a result, politicians and voters typically yield to a sport's influence and agree to use public funds to construct or renovate stadiums and arenas for private or corporate franchise owners. Owners pay very little to lease these facilities and still are permitted to receive substantial revenue from stadium and arena concessions and merchandise sales. Despite these very favorable arrangements, some teams have relocated when they were unable in later years to secure a better facility in their current location and were able to find more favorable financial arrangements in another city. When they have departed, they have left behind an albatross for taxpayers and politicians, who typically have had no tenant or revenue source to replace the departing team.

Having spent many years studying this much-debated issue, Zimbalist (2006:162–163) proposed a synthesis of what had been learned, which he suspected would not satisfy either side. In considering his observations, it should be apparent at this point that the arguments about public subsidies of sports facilities are ultimately about the value of a professional sports franchise to a community. Communities that value professional sports often must pay the cost of facilities to secure and retain a professional team. Facilities—along with the local media market—are a major reason why teams locate to, remain in, or move from a particular city.

Zimbalist's first point was that there was a consensus among econometric studies that a professional sports team or a facility by itself could not ensure a boost in the local economy. There may be some boost in major economic indicators such as per capita income or employment in certain cities, but when the evidence from all cases in a league is examined together in a statistical analysis, the data have shown no economic impact. Thus, it would be overly optimistic for a particular city to expect that their new stadium, arena, or sports franchise would produce an economic impact, since none was found when the league was looked at as a whole. Zimbalist added that if the construction of a sports facility was accompanied by other commercial or residential investment in the area, the overall project could have a positive impact on a city. The problem is that sports facilities tend to be used relatively few times in a year, which is why Zimbalist suggested that politicians and city planners needed to do a careful cost-benefit analysis comparing the use of public land and resources for a sports facility with other uses, such as another business, housing, or schools.

Zimbalist's second major conclusion in his synthesis was that a sports stadium or arena could cause a shift in local economic activity within a metropolitan area. This could be productive even if it does not increase income or employment if it gives new life to a center city or a depressed neighborhood. Although a sports team and its new facility could cause local substitute spending, it could also generate new spending in the area around the sports facility from people who would not typically spend their money in this area for other purposes. Of course, viewed more broadly, this kind of spending still could be a form of substitute spending, since people who live outside the city where a sports team plays and attend sports events in this city are transferring their recreational dollars from their own locality to a sports team and nearby restaurants, hotels, and recreational venues in another city.

Zimbalist's third point was that professional sports teams provide noneconomic and intangible benefits to a city and consumers that are difficult to measure. Area residents may feel

continues

some ownership of a team, which makes it a kind of public good. While they literally could be considered part owners of a facility if their taxes subsidized its construction, the type of ownership implied here is more social or cultural. It refers to feeling a part of a local professional sports team, sharing in its victories and defeats, and connecting to other people with common sentiments and attachments. This sense of community ownership, pride, and commitment is undermined when an owner threatens to move a team, but Zimbalist suggested that the chance for a community to gain these types of benefits might justify some amount of public subsidy of a team's facility in the same sense that there is a justification for public investment in a community park or concert hall. Thus, while the economic justifications for public subsidies of sports stadium or arena construction may be relatively weak, especially when owners pay little for leases and earn substantial income from the use of the stadium, there may be a stronger justification on social or cultural grounds.

This social or cultural justification is qualified by cases such as Baltimore that are supposed to represent the good things that can happen to a city in decline when it invests in its sports teams. New baseball and football stadiums helped to solidify and expand the development of a glistening "Inner Harbor" area to replace a sagging industrial and commercial area of this city, and many in the city reveled in a Super Bowl championship in 2001. However, memories fade and this sports success did nothing to change life only a short distance away from the Inner Harbor and the sports complex. Baltimore continued to struggle with serious problems of crime, poverty, racial segregation, and public education, and it continued to lose major businesses and population. This is why researchers who studied sport and redevelopment in postindustrial Baltimore referred to the city's sports "renaissance" as a "façade of redevelopment" (Friedman, Andrews, and Silk 2004), calling into question the extent to which a professional sports team or its stadium can fundamentally affect the social, cultural, or economic life of a city.

Shea Stadium, left, will be replaced by a new stadium under construction, right, shown in this aerial photo on Wednesday, August 29, 2007, in the Queens borough of New York. Shea Stadium, home of the New York Mets, was built in 1964. The new stadium, to be called Citi Field, is scheduled to open for the 2009 season. Stadium construction is often a source of controversy when public funds are used to build stadiums for professional sports teams. (AP Photo/Mark Lennihan)

combined their efforts between 1982 and 1990 to try to expand the NFL's reach to England. He studied how a Golden Triangle of the NFL, Budweiser manufacturer Anheuser-Busch, and British television worked together in this effort to promote U.S.-style football in a culture where soccer, rugby, and cricket were well established. He showed that this venture was motivated at least as much by the desire to expand merchandising, sponsorship, and endorsement opportunities as it was by the desire to see NFL football take root in this foreign culture. Thus, this was a case of attempted economic globalization reflecting cultural globalization or Americanization as well.

The attempt by the NFL to expand its markets to England is not unique for North American professional sports leagues. Although it has struggled to gain a foothold in Europe, the NFL has continued its efforts overseas. For example, it had plans to stage a preseason "China Bowl" game between NFL teams on Chinese soil before 2010 in an effort to catch up with the NBA and move ahead of MLB in China (MacLeod 2007). In chapter five, we considered how Major League Baseball has tried to use its recently created World Baseball Classic to expand its overseas markets, and in chapter six, we considered how the NBA has used "the China Global" Yao Ming to extend its reach to Chinese and other Asian markets at home and abroad. Yao Ming represents both the more international appeal of the NBA and the increasing reliance on foreign players by North American professional sports. With its huge market and expanding economy, China has been a primary target of global expansion initiatives in professional sports.

The NBA has been the most aggressive and most successful among the North American professional sports leagues over the past two decades in the pursuit of globalization (Larmer 2005). In 1989, the NBA commissioner made his first trip to China to try to arrange a television deal with China's state-run television monopoly for free programming to try to expose the Chinese people to the NBA. Although he met some initial official resistance, he learned that the Chinese people were already watching pirated videotapes of Michael Jordan and the Chicago Bulls. The commissioner was more successful in his forays in other countries. Before going to China, he had already extended the reach of the NBA into Europe, played regular-season games in Japan, and signed the first NBA player from the former Soviet Union (Larmer 2005). These NBA globalization initiatives and parallel efforts and plans by other North American sports have made the global sports marketplace quite crowded and competitive.

In the global sports marketplace, different sports have hegemonic influences in different sectors of varying geographic scope. North American sports have had difficulty nudging aside or sharing space with sports such as soccer, rugby, and cricket in a number of geographical areas. In chapter five, we considered these global expansion problems for U.S. and North American sports. Some sports scholars have argued, however, that the major North American professional sports leagues have become dependent on an expanding global market to offset the saturation of the domestic sports market (Miller, Rowe, McKay, and Lawrence 2003). They have also argued that these sports leagues have become increasingly dependent on a foreign labor pool to offset the escalating cost of domestic athletes in a free-agent marketplace.

According to Miller, Rowe, McKay, and Lawrence, professional sports in North America, Germany, and Great Britain inundated their domestic media markets in the 1990s and the early part of the new century. For example, Rupert

Murdoch's desire to dominate the sports media business on a global scale drove a trend in overbidding for TV rights into the new century. However, a viewer surge that prompted rising television rights fees was followed by fluctuations or declines in viewers, which made the media more circumspect in making decisions about further investments in sport. In the United States, NFL TV ratings remained strong, but, as I noted earlier, growth of the TV audience for NASCAR flattened after its huge gains in popularity and media exposure. MLB has seen its ratings go up and down, and after a lockout cancelled the 2004–2005 season, the NHL suffered a huge drop in its TV audience and revenue and was only able to secure a contract with a second-tier cable channel for the season and most of the playoffs.

Following the 2007 NBA Championship series, which had the lowest TV ratings since the event was first telecast in prime time, sportswriter Christine Brennan observed that many people in the United States who watched major North American sports events in the past, when there were only three major networks, were no longer watching. She added that this change in viewer habits might be permanent (Brennan 2007). She quoted a sports business expert who said that "there's so much sport on TV now, it's not special anymore." He suggested that this generation was used to channel surfing between sportscasts and to other kinds of programs and was often content to watch a portion of a sports event and then get the final score and highlights on ESPN's *Sports-Center* or a cell phone. This oversaturation was a major point made by Miller, Rowe, McKay, and Lawrence, and they thought it was the reason that professional sports in North America focused on overseas markets to compensate for their domestic overproduction of sports.

Professional sports in the United States, Canada, and other high-income countries seek affluent foreign consumers of their broadcasts and licensed merchandise. At the same time, they utilize labor from low-income countries to supplement their increasingly expensive local labor pool and control their labor costs. For example, MLB established baseball academies in the Dominican Republic and other poor Latin American countries to cultivate talented baseball players who could be signed for cheaper contracts than those of current players in the MLB pool. The migration of these players to MLB has transformed the face of this league, as we noted earlier in the book. Miller and his colleagues pointed to the globalization efforts of the NBA in Europe, Australia, Asia, and Mexico in the 1990s, which were meant to extend both their talent pool and their fan base. In 1992, the NBA had twenty-one foreign players from eighteen countries, but by 2007 these numbers had increased to eighty-three foreign players from thirty-seven countries (Walker and Thomson 2007). The WNBA began with a globalization strategy by bringing in talented foreign players from countries such as Brazil and Australia to give the league instant credibility and enable it to attract foreign fans. In its 2002 season, 25 percent of WNBA players were born outside the United States (Miller, Rowe, McKay, and Lawrence 2003). For fans, having athletes from their country playing in other countries meant that they could follow players both at home and abroad. The challenge for professional sports executives was to make the link between foreign athletes and fans in their country of origin and give foreign fans chances to see their homegrown athletes play abroad.

Although Miller and his colleagues emphasized the exploitative nature of employing foreign athletes as "cheap labor" or at least as labor cheaper than that available in the existing domestic talent pool, the recruitment of a "foreign legion" (Walker and Thomson 2007) of athletes by professional sports leagues serves other purposes for the Golden Triangle in each of these sports. In MLB, for example, Asian baseball players have signed increasingly lucrative contracts in recent years. When the Boston Red Sox signed Japanese star pitcher Daisuke Matsuzaka for over $103 million in 2007, they were building on a trend of Japanese and other Asian imports to MLB. However, unlike the Latin American talent market, the Asian talent market is in more affluent countries or in countries, such as China, with growing economies and sports markets. Thus, there were chances for lucrative media, sponsorship, and marketing deals and merchandise sales.

When the MLS signed English soccer star David Beckham to a $250 million compensation package, the league obviously was not seeking "cheap" foreign labor. Beckham had global iconic status, which was comparable to the status and appeal of Michael Jordan and was the reason the MLS was willing to pay him so much money, despite his fading skills. His compensation contrasted sharply with typical compensation in the league, in which many players earned less than $100,000 per year. However, the first game he started for the LA Galaxy drew a record MLS crowd of over 66,000 in New Jersey, which far exceeded the average crowd of less than 12,000 that had watched the opponent Red Bulls play during ten previous home games that season (Blum 2007b). The MLS was hoping Beckham would give the league and soccer in the United States a major boost, attracting significantly more coverage, fans, and sponsors than it had in the past and creating a foundation for future growth and financial success. A boost from a global icon was the same thing North American Soccer League (NASL) officials had hoped Pelé would inject into U.S. soccer and their league over thirty years earlier. Because of the economic structure of the MLS, all teams would benefit from any increased league revenue Beckham produced (Walker and Thomson 2007).

The relative lack of interest in U.S. football in most of the world has prevented the NFL from utilizing a cheap foreign talent pool to reduce its player costs or from using foreign players to increase its global popularity. However, it has continued its efforts to globalize its appeal. Recognizing the worldwide popularity of soccer, the league has signed cross-promotional deals with soccer clubs, such as FC Barcelona in 2002, which also was meant to gain more visibility for the soccer club in the U.S. market. This is similar to the deal involving Manchester United and the New York Yankees, which was the only U.S. sports team with global brand recognition after Michael Jordan ended his career with the Chicago Bulls. The capitalist growth imperative of the generic Golden Triangle means that professional sports will continually try to expand their global talent pools, fan bases, and consumer markets, and that the Golden Triangles of competing sports may overlap at times to pursue their mutual economic interests. Thus, for economic reasons, sports, as well as politics, may create "strange bedfellows."

Professional Sports Careers

I have already said a great deal in this book about the stardom and careers of professional athletes in the global cultural economy of sport; about how race, ethnicity, and gender affect their opportunities; about the deviant behavior of some of them; about their relations with owners and management; and about how much money and fame they can earn from their sports stardom. I can add that the NBA has generally provided the best playing, coaching, and executive opportunities for people of color among men's professional sports in the United States, and that opportunities for minorities in the NFL and MLB were improving (Lapchick, Martin, Kushner, and Brenden 2006). As we have observed, however, black major leaguers have become fewer as Latino and Asian players have increased in the past decade. In addition, black owners in the NBA and other professional sports were rare, as were female top executives. The first and only female president of an NBA franchise left the Washington Wizards in 2007 after over fifteen years in the position. For several years, she also simultaneously managed business operations of the Washington NHL franchise, which had the same owner as the Wizards. For women, the best source of playing, coaching, and executive opportunities in a professional sports league has been the WNBA.

Although lower social class can make success in sport more elusive, some sports in some nations seem to be dominated at the highest levels by athletes from lower-class backgrounds. For example, in the United States, many NBA stars not only are black but are from lower-income families. This pattern also exists in soccer in many countries. Brazil has one of the proudest soccer histories in the world, and the vast majority of its national team members have typically been from lower-income backgrounds. The "Sport in the News" feature about Brazilian soccer players provides some insight into how the social structure and culture of a sport and a society can influence the path to success in the world's most popular sport. We also see in this feature that soccer players in Brazil often seem to have succeeded despite the organization of professional soccer in their country rather than because of it and that for the vast majority of those who become professional soccer players in Brazil, the dream of international stardom and wealth is an illusion, just as the American Dream is typically an illusion in U.S. sports.

The careers of professional athletes in the elite sports are filled with many rewards but also have a variety of stresses as these athletes pursue what former NBA star and U.S. senator Bill Bradley called a "life on the run" (Bradley 1976). We have read about what it means to be a sports star, with widespread fame and the chance to make a lot of money, but this status has also meant being treated as a commodity. Professional athletes make a living by using their bodies, and they routinely deal with pain, injuries, and the possibility that their career could end in an instant from one of those injuries. They also have to perform in a public setting where both successes and failures are witnessed and analyzed and where being judged unsuccessful or not successful enough can lead to fewer opportunities to play or, ultimately, the end of a career. Bradley wrote about the stresses and sense of impermanence from constant travel and the loneliness from being on the road so much. In addition, as public figures, professional athletes often have to deal with invasions of their privacy and, as famous public figures, they need to try to hold in check a "gloried self" (Adler and Adler 1991) that exaggerates their sense of self-importance and may lead to irresponsible personal behavior.

Professional athletes in different sports share a lot of common career experiences, but there are also significant differences between the careers of athletes

Brazilian Soccer and the Path to Success for Brazilian Soccer Players

This feature is primarily based on news articles by *New York Times* reporter Larry Rohter (2001, 2006) about corruption in Brazilian soccer and the "unpaved path to soccer excellence" the sport provides for promising young Brazilian players. Brazil is well-known for its consistent excellence in global soccer competition and for the superb talents of its greatest players. Its victory in the 2002 World Cup made it the only five-time winner of this event, and it has more professional teams than any other country in the world (Muller 2004). Officials of the North American Soccer League (NASL) brought Brazil's legendary Pelé to North America in 1975 to boost the league's popularity after seven years of play and uneven success. Importing Pelé was similar to the signing of David Beckham by NASL's successor, MLS, three decades later to enhance that league's and the sport's popularity and commercial success. Pelé had retired from Santos F.C. of Brazil in 1974, and his signing by the New York Cosmos of the NASL a year later brought the league and the sport unprecedented media coverage in the United States (Hammons 2003). He later became Brazil's sports minister in the mid-1990s.

In the soccer world outside the United States, news of Pelé's migration to North America was greeted by a cool reception (Hammons 2003), since Europe was considered the appropriate destination for the elite soccer players in the world. In fact, many top Brazilian players since Pelé have ascended to play at the highest levels of European soccer. Most of these soccer stars have managed to overcome disadvantaged backgrounds and achieve success despite disorganization and corruption in the soccer business in their country. Brazilian soccer and the development of players have been influenced by an often-uncoordinated mix of the national sports ministry, a national confederation that has partnered with transnational corporate sponsors such as Nike, domestic professional clubs, domestic and foreign player agents, independent private soccer schools, and foreign clubs and their scouts. Sports officials and agents engaged in corrupt practices that have involved often-unsuspecting players, blemished the reputation of the sport, and reduced attendance for a while several years ago (Rohter 2001).

Despite a lack of coordination and perhaps partially because of a lack of regulation, the Golden Triangle of soccer in Brazil has produced more than $15 billion each year in gate receipts, television revenue, player salaries and contract transfer fees, advertising, and apparel sales. This commercial success, coupled with a relative absence of regulation, has bred corruption, tempting officials of the sport to engage in illegal activities to pocket some of this money and attracting unscrupulous agents focused more on their own interests than on the interests of players they are supposed to represent. A government inquiry in 2001 led to allegations of various kinds of wrongdoing, including collusion between some Brazilian team managers and European player agents to buy and sell the rights of players illegally for their personal gain and to accept payments for naming marginal players to the national team to increase their resale value to foreign teams. In addition, after signing a $400 million sponsorship agreement with Nike in 1996, the Brazilian Soccer Federation was embroiled in a scandal in which officials allegedly underreported income and received kickbacks from intermediaries in the Nike deal. The lack of profitability of many professional clubs in Brazil also led to a tripling of the sale of Brazilian players to foreign teams, from seven hundred to two thousand, between 1997 and the year 2000 (Rohter 2001). In 2005, a Brazilian businessman was arrested along with a referee for allegedly acting as an intermediary between an Internet gambling syndicate and two soccer referees in a scheme to fix matches in the Brazilian national soccer championships (Astor 2005).

Brazilian soccer players have succeeded in this disorganized and corrupt environment because sandlot soccer is well entrenched in Brazilian culture, providing many opportunities to play at the grassroots level, and because young players are motivated by Brazilian soccer stars who serve as powerful role models. Just as Michael Jordan and other black basketball superstars inspired many young black males to pursue their American Dream through basketball,

continues

Pelé and the stars who followed him have been an inspiration for poor young Brazilians who have pursued their Brazilian version of the American Dream through soccer. They see contemporary stars such as Ronaldinho earn as much as $35 million in a year and gain worldwide fame in the world's most popular sport. As in the United States, though, the dream is an illusion for most who play the game. According to figures from 1998, only 4.3 percent of Brazilian professional soccer players earned more than $1,350 per month, and 83.4 percent earned less than the equivalent of U.S. $120 per month (Muller 2004). Nevertheless, the unusual passion of Brazilians for the game and young players' desire to emulate their heroes help explain the exceptional success of Brazilian players at the global level. Rohter (2006) suggested, however, that there was more to the explanation of Brazilian soccer success, which reflected the distinctive character of Brazilian society for poor people.

Rohter cited experts on Brazilian society and soccer who attributed the unusual creativity, smoothness, and grace that have distinguished Brazilian players to the confusion and unpredictability of daily life. They suggested that these aspects of Brazilian society, which were also found in the chaotically organized professional soccer world, have encouraged improvisation and "dribbling around the rules and barriers." In the traditional path to soccer success that Rohter described, rising young stars were often identified by amateur scouts and referred to local teams, who signed them as teenagers. The best local players were then sold to regional teams, and the best players at the regional level were sold to one of approximately twenty national-level clubs. The best players at the national level played for the Brazilian national team and were likely to be signed by European teams, which typically paid much more than teams in Brazil and were at the top of the global professional soccer hierarchy. As long as Brazilian soccer players stayed in their country and were part of the business of Brazilian soccer, they were treated as commodities for their teams to sell; had few contractual rights, much like professional athletes in North America before the advent of free agency; and were always vulnerable to replacement by a rising star from the plentiful soccer pipeline in the country.

As national sports minister, Pelé was able to get the legislature to reduce the power of clubs and increase the rights of players. The unanticipated outcome of the "Pelé Law" was increased power for agents, which accompanied the reduced power of clubs. With clubs having fewer scouts, the impresarios often used their own scouts to identify talented players and then signed them to personal management contracts and guided their careers until they became good enough to be sold to a European team. Players often were bought and sold as teenagers. European clubs have also invested in Brazilian teams or negotiated development contracts with them to give them better access to the top talent in Brazil. In addition, instead of relying on Brazilian clubs and their scouts or independent Brazilian agents, they have used their own agents to find promising young players and have signed them to contracts early in their soccer careers. Thus, the Brazilian soccer pipeline that has supplied Europe with great Brazilian players is similar to the Dominican baseball pipeline to Major League Baseball that Klein (1991a, 1991b) described. This kind of globalization, which has deprived poorer countries of great indigenous talent to serve the interests of richer and more powerful foreign sports leagues, is seen as exploitation by critics of globalization and is a reason for the international antiglobalization movement, which we will discuss in the next chapter. However, criticism of globalization is tempered somewhat in this case by a picture of a disorganized and corrupt professional soccer environment that many Brazilian players have had to navigate if they remained at home.

in different professional sports and even within the same sport. For example, athletes in the most commercialized sports earn more money and are more famous than athletes in less-prominent sports in the generic Golden Triangle of professional sports, and the star athletes in the most elite professional sports earn more money and fame than do other athletes in their sport. The discussion of sports stars in chapter six showed that some sports stars are elevated above all others in the generic Golden Triangle as major cultural celebrities and even achieve iconic status. David Beckham, Michael Jordan, Tiger Woods, and now perhaps Yao Ming occupy a special status as global stars and heroes. A number of sports stars are regularly in the pantheons of popular celebrities such as the *Forbes* "Celebrity 100." The *Forbes* list is meant to be a collection of the "world's most powerful and best-paid celebrities," and in 2007, it included rock stars, actors and actresses, models, popular authors, and TV personalities as well as eighteen sports stars. The sports celebrities were pro golfers; soccer, tennis, NBA, and MLB players; Formula One auto racers; and a boxer. Two-thirds were Americans, all thirteen males were in the top fifty, and the five women were ranked fifty-first or lower. The top athlete on the list was Tiger Woods at #2 (behind Oprah Winfrey), and Michael Jordan still made the list at #35, despite being retired from the NBA for several years. Tiger Woods's status as the top sports celebrity in 2007 is explained by both his dominant status in his sport and the fact that he reportedly earned nearly $111.9 million in the previous year from tournaments and endorsements (Freedman 2007).

Athletes in winnings-based sports can compete for very large financial prizes in tournaments, races, or other competitions and translate their prominence or popularity in their sport into large endorsement contracts, but they are not salaried, as their counterparts in team sports are, and they cannot sign the long-term employment contracts that exist in major professional sports leagues. The 2007 "Fortunate Fifty" list of the top fifty U.S. money earners in sport, compiled by *Sports Illustrated* (Freedman 2007), was dominated by NBA players (led by Shaquille O'Neal at #4 with $35 million), who made up half the list. There were also twelve MLB players (led by Derek Jeter at #8 with $29 million); five NFL players (led by Peyton Manning at #12 with $23 million); three NASCAR drivers (led by Dale Earnhardt, Jr., at #10 with $20 million); three golfers (led by #1 Tiger Woods with $111.9 million); two boxers (with Oscar De La Hoya #2 on the list with $55 million); and one woman, golfer Michelle Wie (whose $20.2 million in income placed her twenty-second on the list).

The *Sports Illustrated* "International 20" list was dominated by nine soccer players and was led by Formula One racer Fernando Alonso of Spain, who earned $35 million. There were two other athletes in motor sports on the list (including at #4 motorcycle racer Valentino Rossi, who earned $30 million), three MLB players (led by Ichiro Suzuki at #7 with $24 million), two NBA players (led by Yao Ming at #6 with $27.5 million), one male tennis player (Roger Federer at #3 with $31.3 million), one female tennis player (Maria Sharapova at #8 with $23.8 million), and one golfer (Vijay Singh at #17 with $16.4 million). The international and U.S. lists are made up predominantly of male athletes in team sports. We do not see a lot of sports on these lists because only those most commercialized and highly placed in the generic Golden Triangle of professional sports generate the revenue and have the endorsement opportunities that result in these large income amounts. For example, compared with the millions earned on average by players in the major North American professional sports leagues, the average salary in 2004–2005 in the WNBA was under $52,000 and in MLS was less than $65,000. The WNBA and MLS average salaries seemed reasonable in view of the median U.S. family income of $53,500 that year, but these salaries were a fraction of the salaries earned in the "big money" sports leagues (Coakley 2007:391).

Tiger Woods, other golfers, and tennis players demonstrate how rich, famous, and influential athletes in winnings-based individual-competitor sports can be. However, their sports are structurally different in a way that makes the careers and lives of these kinds of professional athletes different from the careers and lives of salaried professional athletes in team sports. Unlike athletes in salaried sports, those in the winnings-based sports face "*structured uncertainty*" (Theberge, cited in Nixon and Frey 1996:199). Although they may have their own sponsors, athletes in winnings-based sports depend on the paycheck they get from competing, and the amount they earn in competition depends on how well they do. In this sense, these sports are structured to be "meritocratic." That is, the most successful competitors generally make the most money as athletes. Some athletes in winnings-based sports who have had modest success in competition, such Anna Kournikova and Michelle Wie, have been able to parlay their physical attractiveness or promise of future success into substantial endorsement income. Salaried athletes in team sports get paid whether they play or not, and their pay is related to their salary contract and generally not to how well they do in a particular competition.

The relationship between an athlete's record in competition and his or her pay varies according to the structure of the sport, and it can be very different for athletes in salaried, winnings-based, and other types of sports. One of those "other types" is boxing. Boxers must deal with trainers, managers, and promoters, who share their boxing revenue, control boxers' careers, and strongly influence their lives. Athletes in sports such as auto, motorcycle, and bicycle racing experience both the financial uncertainties of solely winnings-based sports and the financial assurances of team sports. These athletes are salaried by team owners and also derive income from a portion of the prize money awarded for their racing success and from merchandise sales and endorsements. In these complex *mixed-structure* sports, they represent teams as they race against other individuals, including their own teammates, and team members at least indirectly benefit from the success of teammates who earn money for their team. In European professional bicycle racing, teams are financed by major sponsors, riders are paid salaries and earn money from their success in races as well as from merchandise sales and endorsement contracts, and team members have designated roles in races, with their major job in big races being to follow the instructions of the team manager to support the team's star rider. The reliance on agents by athletes in some mixed-structure sports has improved their financial status. In NASCAR, for example, salaries of drivers have escalated in recent years, and their guaranteed base salary now is typically the major source of their income. A new salary standard for top NASCAR drivers was set in 2003 when Tony Stewart signed a contract with Joe Gibbs Racing guaranteeing him an annual base salary of at least $5 million (Jenkins 2005).

As in salaried sports, the amount of money earned in winnings-based sports varies significantly across and within these sports and between men and women. We can compare professional golf and tennis as examples, using data from 2006.[8] In golf, the PGA money leader earned $9.9 million, and the LPGA money leader earned $2.6 million. Ninety-three male and eleven female golfers earned $1 million or more, and the #50 money earner among the men earned $1.6 million while the #50 female golfer earned $274,304. The golfer at the bottom of the male list, at #263, earned $6,000, and the lowest-ranked female golfer, at #197, earned $2,000. In tennis, the ATP (men's) money leader earned $8.3 million in tournament prize money, and the WTA (women's) money leader earned $4.2 million. Fourteen male and eight female tennis players earned $1 million or more, and the #50 male earned $456,005 and the #50 female earned $251,563. Thus, we can see that top golfers and tennis players can make a lot of money, that the PGA offers the most opportunities for substantial ($1 million or more) tournament income, and that the top man earns two to four times more than the top woman in these sports.

There is a wide spread in earnings in these sports because money is distributed very unequally in each tournament. Consider two major golf tournaments. In the 2007 Master's, the winner received $1.3 million, the three second-place finishers each received $541,333, and the three tenth-place finishers each earned $181,250. The golfer who finished sixtieth earned $15,950, but thirty-six golfers failed to "make the cut" because of their low scores after two of the four rounds and earned nothing. One withdrew. Thus, nearly 40 percent of the golfers who qualified for and competed in the Master's did not earn any money in this tournament. In the 2007 LPGA championship, the winner was awarded $300,000, the second-place finisher received $179,038, and the four women who tied for tenth place each received $35,730. Eighty-four golfers made the cut, and the one who finished last among them earned $3,273. Over 44 percent of the female golfers who qualified for this major championship did not earn any money in it, with sixty-one not making the cut, five withdrawing, and one not competing. The approximately six hundred golfers who compete in one of the three PGA Tour divisions and the approximately five hundred female touring professionals with active or inactive status in the LPGA represent a tiny fraction of the twenty-eight thousand men and women who are members of the PGA of America and make their living as teaching or club pros.[9] However, as we have seen, being a member of the touring elite does not guarantee big paychecks or even any paycheck for those who do not play well enough to make the cut and share in the tournament purse.

Many professional sports exist on the fringe or outside the generic Golden Triangle, and athletes in these sports often have difficulty making enough money to live comfortably. Even those in the most lucrative winnings-based sports face financial uncertainty if they do not win, rarely finish "in the big money" among the tournament or race leaders, and do not play consistently well enough to qualify regularly for tournaments or races. They may find themselves struggling to support themselves financially and meet all their expenses if they do not have a sponsor. Less-successful professional athletes in these winnings-based sports and athletes competing on a lower-tier or satellite tour, in a less lucrative sport, or in a minor league or developmental league must manage their finances carefully to afford their "life on the run." In winnings-based sports in which athletes must pay all their expenses, transportation, hotels, food, training, coaches, agents, managers, and various support people can be quite costly.

Being under contract in a league such as the WNBA or MLS may only provide a relatively modest salary. Being a developmental player means you must make a financial sacrifice to pursue your professional sports dream. For example, the ninety young (twenty-five years old or less) developmental players in the MLS each earned less than $20,000 in 2007, with fifty-seven earning the starting salary of $12,900 (Bell 2007). Making the senior roster of their MLS team might not result in a huge boost in pay, since the minimum salary was $33,000 in 2008. Although players in minor leagues of more commercially successful professional leagues in North America may make more money than developmental players in the MLS, their pay is also likely to be fairly modest if they did not receive a more than modest signing bonus as a draftee in one of the early rounds of their league's draft. For example, minor leaguers in the Oakland Athletics MLB organization could earn salaries from $850 to $2,150 per month in their first year, depending on the level of the minor league team, and they could negotiate higher salaries after the first year.[10]

Athletes today can earn money playing many different types of sports and at various levels of competition. When a sport exists on the fringe or outside of the generic Golden Triangle, it generates much less media attention, corporate investment, and revenue than do sports more centrally located and highly placed in the Golden Triangle. As a result, relatively few of the top athletes in these "peripheral sports" earn more than a modest living, and the stars of these sports attract attention in relatively narrower sports subcultures, such as rodeo, skiing, and marathon running, or in certain countries, as is the case with cricket, curling, and field hockey. Some, such as the alternative sports on the Dew Sports Tour or in the X Games, which we examined in chapter six, may move up the sports hierarchy in the generic Golden Triangle in the future. The same may be said someday about women's professional sports such as the WNBA, softball, and soccer. However, others such as boxing and horse racing only periodically capture our attention and have seemed to slide down the sports hierarchy in recent decades. In addition, there are many relatively old and new professional sports such as bowling, billiards, lacrosse, and track and field that seem destined to remain on the periphery in the professional sports world.

If athletes are given a chance to pursue a professional sports career at some level in one of the many professional sports, they will find that the financial sacrifices they must make are associated with the level of commercial development of the sport and its centrality in the generic Golden Triangle. They will also find that their financial security and legal rights are associated with the structure of their sport as a winnings-based, salary-based, or mixed-structure sport. Their financial security and legal rights are also related to the extent to which athletes in their sport have effectively organized as an association or collective bargaining unit or have powerful agents to deal with the owners and officials who control how, when, and where their sport is played and how its revenue is distributed.

Risk, Pain, and Injuries in the Lives of Professional Athletes

The Golden Triangle and professional sports are organized to make money, and, perhaps surprisingly, the welfare of individual athletes often is not their primary concern. Owners, coaches, and league officials do not like to see stars get hurt, lose their effectiveness, or retire, but injuries are a common experience for professional athletes and they become "old" and retire significantly earlier than do people in most other types of occupations. Although athletes are able to compete as professionals in their fifties and sixties in some sports such as golf, and may remain stars at the age of forty or older in sports such as baseball, older athletes are unusual in the sports world in general. The physically demanding nature of most professional sports, especially if they are contact and high-intensity sports, generally makes it difficult for stars to retain their status past their thirtieth or thirty-fifth birthday and makes it difficult to sustain a professional sports career for that long for most other professional athletes. Debilitating pain and injuries are part of the life of professional athletes, and we will see in this section how the structure of many sports contributes to the aging and disablement of professional athletes. We will also see how the physical effects of professional sports careers leave an enduring imprint on the lives of many athletes after their playing days are over.

Howe (2004) studied the effects of commercialization and professionalization in Welsh rugby union football on its players. He found that these athletes constantly struggled with the idea that they were merely physical objects or "mortal engines" being manipulated by training regimens meant to make their bodies as competitive as possible. The pressures on athletes to take risks with their bodies increased as their sports were transformed from amateur to professional. Howe found that along with a risk culture there was a cost culture in the professional version of the sport, where decision making about risk was influenced by financial considerations. Before money was openly available, elite participants were likely to try to take care of themselves physically, but with money to be made, athletes became more likely to take significant physical risks, especially toward the end of their careers (188–189).

As the sport became more professionalized, it invested in more professionalized sports medicine to ensure that players would be able to compete, despite the risk and occurrence of injuries. Howe cited the medical officer of the Welsh Rugby Union, who acknowledged that there was a great deal of injury in the sport but claimed that the game was becoming safer with rule changes and stricter enforcement of the rules. Howe noted, however, that 50 percent of all injuries still occurred as a result of legitimate tackling, which was called "brutal body contact" in chapter eight and was within the rules. Despite instruction in appropriate ways to tackle and the use of soft shoulder padding, tackling has become more severe as the sport has become more professionalized, and there have been more instances of violent tackling intended to inflict pain (Howe 2004:133).

Howe argued that in addition to professionalization, the influence of U.S. football on rugby in Great Britain contributed to its increased contact, violence, and injuries. In U.S. football, every play involves intense physical contact, which was different than the traditional pattern in rugby where this kind of behavior occurred mainly during set pieces such as scrums and line-outs. The highly aggressive tackling found in U.S. football could make rugby much more dangerous than it had been because the game is more continuous than is U.S. football, which stops when the ball carrier is tackled. Wearing more protective clothing or equipment may provide a false sense of security, too, since this protection often does not prevent injuries from violent or highly aggressive tackles. Despite stated efforts to make the sport safer with rules and rule enforcement, sports medicine, and protective clothing and equipment, playing for money seems to have contributed to more risk taking in the rugby league Howe studied. This generalization would seem to apply more broadly across sports.

After three weeks of the 2004 NFL season, the number of players on the injured reserve (IR) list was 39 percent higher than the average for the same span between 1998 and 2003. The average for 1998–2004 was 105 players by the third week, but in 2004 the number was 146, and 33 of these players were starters (King 2004). Since the official roster limit per team was 53, less than 20 percent into the 2004 season, nearly 9 percent of all rostered players and approximately 4.5 percent of starting offensive and defensive players were unable to play for the rest of the season. IR is the most serious disability status in the NFL for those who might be able to play again, since players placed on the IR list cannot play or practice with the team during the remainder of the season. In a *Sports Illustrated* article prompted by these injury statistics, King (2004) wrote that the various theories proposed by team officials, coaches, players, and trainers all pointed to a common explanation of the rising injury rates: the increasing size, strength, and speed of the players, which led to harder and more damaging collisions. He also suggested that the limited time for recovery from physical wear and tear and injuries in the off-season and during the season could be making players more susceptible to serious injuries.

Even though NFL officials, executives, coaches, and players would like to avoid serious injuries and minimize injuries in general, they face a basic dilemma related to the nature of their sport. This dilemma exists in all sports to varying extents. That is, by their very nature, training, practicing, and competing in sport stress the body, and at the highest levels of sport and in the most aggressive sports, the stresses are greatest. In professional sports, athletes are expected by coaches and fans to play hard. In doing so, athletes put themselves at risk of pain, injury, and disablement. We can understand why athletes who have the chance to earn fame and money playing a sport they love might take risks with their body to be able to play professional football or any other professional sport. Beyond these social and economic incentives, there are structural and cultural factors explaining why professional athletes accept risk, pain, and injury and ignore the possibility that many will experience chronic pain and serious disabilities after their playing days end.

In chapter two, I briefly referred to my research revealing a culture of risk, pain, and injury in sport (e.g., Nixon 1993, 2004). This culture overlaps with the "Sport Ethic" first described in chapter six (see Coakley 2007:161–164), which emphasizes putting sport above everything else; constantly striving to be the best; accepting risk, pain, and injuries as part of the game; and not letting anything get in the way of sports success. In this context, injuries become "normal." For athletes who tie sport to their masculinity, getting hurt and playing with pain and injuries can be a source of pride, which gains them admiration for their toughness. Numerous studies in recent years have focused on the influence of these kinds of social and cultural factors on athletes' vulnerability to injury (e.g., see Young 2004), and they also show the frequency of injuries in sport and their economic and human costs for society and athletes (White 2004). Along with competition each year from younger players, injuries are a major reason why the average length of careers in major professional sports leagues is approximately five years and why the average in the NFL is about three and a half years (Eitzen 2006:183).

The sports media, sports executives, coaches, and players reinforce physical risk taking by emphasizing the Sport Ethic and glorifying as "heroic" those who

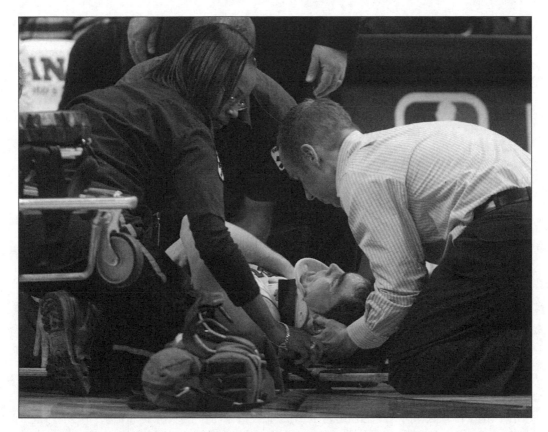

Toronto Raptors medical staff and paramedics help Jose Calderon, center, after he was injured on a play during NBA action against the Golden State Warriors in Toronto, Canada, Sunday, December 17, 2006. Calderon was removed from the court by medical staff on a stretcher. Injuries are an ever-present risk of a career in professional sports, and they can have long-term consequences for retired athletes. (AP Photo/Adrian Wyld, CP)

endure pain and injuries to continue playing. Sports officials may introduce rules, tighten enforcement, or impose suspensions and fines as means to control injury rates and the aggression and violence affecting them. However, it is not necessarily in the financial interests of sports officials and executives to transform the structure or culture of their sports to ensure safety. Furthermore, sport as physical competition is inherently risky whether or not contact is involved, and risk is part of its attraction for athletes. Athletes pushing themselves to peak and sometimes violent performances also make sports more exciting and more appealing to fans. However, especially for those in the most physical sports, the aftermath of their usually relatively brief professional sports careers involves adjusting to the lingering effects of injuries as well as to less-prestigious and less-remunerative occupations. Those who were not stars and did not earn the big money and financial security of stars face a bigger drop in their economic status. Those who retired before the major escalation in salaries and prize money from free agency and increased media and corporate investment, who played sports with weak unions, or who had poor financial advice have faced major economic and social adjustment issues in their retirement years.

A significant issue for retirees from professional sports, especially sports as dangerous as the NFL, is severe chronic disability. In chapter four, when I discussed people with impairments and disabilities and the various ways they might participate in or excel at sports, I was not referring to the kinds of debilitating disabilities that end athletes' careers or become chronically disabling conditions after they retire. All sports wear down athletes' bodies, but more combative and violent sports are more disabling. Very little systematic research has tracked the effects of professional sports injuries on the lives of athletes after their careers are over (Nixon 2000). An exception was a study commissioned by the NFL Players Association (NFLPA) in 1990, which surveyed 645 players whose careers ranged from the early 1940s to 1986. In a five-part series reporting major findings from the survey, the *Chicago Sun-Times* also interviewed former players (see summary of series in Nixon and Frey 1996:201-202). The study showed that one-third of the former players retired because of a disabling injury, and almost two-thirds reported living with the effects of a football injury. Despite the lingering effects of their football-related injuries, most who were interviewed said they would play football if they had a chance to do it over again. However, the survey provided evidence of a number of players who questioned the value of damaging their bodies in the sport. It also showed a pattern of increasingly damaging long-term effects of playing in the NFL between the end of the 1950s and the end of the 1970s. Thirty-eight percent of players retiring before 1959 reported having a permanent football injury; by the late 1970s this percentage had increased to 66 percent, and it seemed to stabilize at this level in the 1980s. A follow-up NFLPA-sponsored study showed that in 1993, 61 percent said they retired with a permanent injury, suggesting that the sport had become slightly less dangerous compared with the previous two decades, but it also showed that from 1990 to 1993, the percentage of players reporting a disabling injury as the main reason for retiring increased from 37 percent to over 41 percent (Nixon and Frey 1996:202).

We can understand why former professional football players and other retired professional athletes might try to minimize the significance of their sports-related injuries and even disabilities if they internalized the beliefs of the Sport Ethic and treated pain and injuries as a normal part of their sports career. Furthermore, having been a professional athlete still might define their identity even decades after the end of their sports career, and their sports memories might help in their adjustment to a life that is not as exciting or otherwise as rewarding as sport was. Eventually, though, former professional athletes with serious disabilities that develop shortly or long after their playing days have to find ways to cope financially, emotionally, and physically with these disabilities. In less-commercialized sports, pensions and health and disability insurance tend to be modest, if they are available at all. Even in the richest sports, such as the NFL, which have generous retirement and disability benefits for recently retired players, older retired players with disabilities have had relatively meager disability benefits and they and their families have struggled to find ways to pay for the rehabilitation, accommodations, and care their disabilities have required.

An official of the NFL testified to a congressional panel investigating the NFL's disability benefits system that the NFLPA and the league had constructed "the most generous disability benefits in professional sports, and possibly the entire business world" (Barker 2007b). The NFL fund provided pension, disability, and death benefits and was valued at $1.1 billion. It awarded up to $110,000 per year to ex-players deemed "totally and permanently disabled" within 15 years of their NFL retirement. However, a member of Congress, whose husband was a former NFL player, expressed her concern about the relatively small number of retired players—approximately 300—who qualified for disability benefits out of the approximately 10,000 who had played in the NFL. A number of former NFL players, including Hall of Famers, appeared before the panel and spoke of their disabilities and their difficulties gaining benefits. Between 1993 and 2007, 675 of 1,052 (64 percent of) initial claims were denied at the first stage of review, and players complained that having to qualify within 15 years of retirement for disability benefits left out players whose effects of their injuries began to manifest themselves later in life. Furthermore, the causal connection between sports and chronic disability is likely to blur when the effects of sports injuries remain latent for many years. Public pressure from retired players led the NFL and the NFLPA to set up a $7 million fund to provide free surgery for joint replacement for uninsured retired players. A number of former players welcomed this fund, but others noted that the money would be stretched thin among the more than 9,100 retired players and was approximately equal to the annual salary of the union's executive director (Murray 2007).

The controversy and debate about the long-term effects of sports concussions on former NFL players illustrate the problem of proving damage from sports injuries later in life. Some research has shown that football concussions can cause permanent brain damage, mental deterioration, and clinical depression (Schwarz 2007). The NFL has contradicted this research with studies it has funded. However, despite denying these effects of playing football, the league and the NFLPA set up the "88 Plan" to pay $88,000 per year for nursing home care and up to $50,000 per year for adult day care for retired players with dementia and Alzheimer's disease who lacked the financial means to care for themselves. The plan bears the jersey number of Hall of Fame tight end John Mackey, one of the first former players to qualify. Thirty-five retired players were approved in the first four months the plan was in effect, and nineteen other applications were under consideration (NFL News 2007). While denying certain long-term effects, the NFL recognizes the damage that can result from concussions in the short term, especially if players are pushed back into action too soon after a concussion. As a result, the league has taken steps to improve equipment and to penalize contact such as helmet-to-helmet hits that could cause concussions.

Athletes in all professional sports risk pain and injuries because physical risks are built into the structure of sport in general. Even in the elite sports in the Golden Triangle, rational business decisions are made about which athletes deserve compensation for their physical sacrifices and how much they deserve. In the NFL, older veterans have been pressuring the league and the NFLPA to increase their relatively modest retirement and disability benefits, while current players who play at least three years and three games in those three years have a wide range of retirement benefits to ease their adjustment in retirement and to help them cope with the mental health, physical disability, and financial problems older players have experienced (Murray 2006). These benefits become more generous with more years of play. More recent NFL veterans with enough years of play to qualify for the most generous of these benefits are in the elite of retired professional athletes. The many other professional athletes who sustain serious and disabling sports injuries and are not in this elite have fewer resources from their sport than their elite counterparts have to cope with the effects of these injuries. For the wealthiest and most popular sports such as the NFL, disgruntled veterans have been able to attract attention from the media and the U.S. Congress to help them wage their campaign to get more assistance from their sport to help them deal with their disabilities. Other sports outside the public eye and lower down the commercial hierarchy of professional sports have much less to offer those who were damaged by their sport. This helps explain the title of Young's (2004) collection of sociological studies of sports-related injuries, "Sporting Bodies, Damaged Selves."

Conclusion: Professional Athletes, Professional Sports, and Change in the Global Cultural Economy

Although professional sports share the stage in the big-time sports world with many college and high school sports, Olympic sports, and even some youth sports, they usually occupy center stage in sport and in the Golden Triangle. Professional sports stars are the biggest stars of sport, and they are the most valued commodities in the Golden Triangle and are among the most valued commodities in the global cultural economy. Like other stars in the entertainment world or politics, their careers may be relatively brief, and in sport, careers might end abruptly after one hard hit or one sudden twist of an ankle, knee, or shoulder. Accustomed to the money and attention and seeing no better alternatives, aging professional athletes also might try to hang on and stretch out their careers long after their peak and for as long as someone will pay them to play. Professional athletes are the stars of sport, and in a number of sports they have organized themselves and used agents to gain substantially more leverage in their relations with owners and corporations seeking their endorsement. However, the most powerful actors in professional sports today are the owners, executives, and investors in the dominant power networks of the generic Golden Triangle. Their financial investments, revenue-generating activities, and decisions shape the games we see and the sports professional athletes play.

Professional athletes have had their own impact on society and fans. Their play and their status as stars, celebrities, or heroes bring viewers and listeners to broadcasts, spectators into stadiums, and potential consumers to sports-related ads and sports merchandise. When we see professional athletes continuing to excel at physically demanding sports in their late thirties or forties and when we see professional athletes extend their careers even further on senior or champions tours, we are reminded of how athletes have been able to redefine the meaning of aging and *old* in their sport and for society. However, the body eventually breaks down for even the most fit athletes, and voluntary or involuntary sports retirement happens usually long before the customary retirement age in society. We know that in the most competitive and physically demanding professional sports leagues, careers of athletes rarely last longer than five or six years. In other sports, careers may last longer, but retirement is still likely to come no later than the middle age of life, at a time when their counterparts in other occupations are generally reaching their prime. Even memories of stardom and money in the constant glow of the Golden Triangle are ultimately sullied by the realities of chronic pain and disability when often-injured or seriously injured *former* sports stars age. These realities are harsher when damaged retired professional athletes were never stars, played sports on the fringe or outside the commercial core of the Golden Triangle, or lacked the education, occupational skills, contacts, or wise investments to translate their sports success into career or financial success following their careers as professional athletes.

The increase in the number of professional sports has created more opportunities to be a professional athlete, and the growing commercial success of a number of professional sports has made it possible to live comfortably or perhaps extravagantly as a professional athlete and, in a few sports, to live well after retiring from sport. However, even for those whose careers are very brief and who never achieve much recognition or success, being a professional athlete means doing something that is a dream for many and a reality for a tiny fraction of those dreamers. The less-glamorous facts about professional sport for athletes and the slim likelihood of becoming a professional athlete do not seem to diminish the dream or the number of dreamers.

The less-glamorous facts are part of a life on the run, and some elements of this life may be more common in more elite sports or for bigger stars. Along with the physical risks and the possibility of serious chronic disability that could happen to any professional athlete, the downside of professional sports careers may include constant travel; the frequent glare of the media and regular public scrutiny of private as well as sports lives; the temptations of doping; the competitive stresses and high expectations from owners, promoters, sponsors, coaches, managers, and fans; difficult negotiations with management and owners; having to win to get paid in certain sports; having to deal with a major career transition after sport for which they may be unprepared; and coping with possible postcareer mental and physical health problems and disabilities with limited resources. Popular conceptions of professional sports careers as exciting, glamorous, and very well compensated make the transition to life after being a professional athlete more difficult, even when athletes realize that the popular idealizations of their career are partially or largely untrue for them.

Professional sport is part of the popular imagination in countries around the world because sport has authentically dramatic and exciting qualities, as Smart pointed out. However, the generic Golden Triangle of professional sport also continually invents and manipulates images of sports and sports stars to appeal to the popular imagination and contemporary consumers' tastes. As part of the Golden Triangle, professional sport is essentially an entertainment *business*. Wealthy people and corporations invest in it in part because they are attracted by its popular cultural appeal but ultimately, for the major investors, because they see it as a way to advance their financial interests through the Golden Triangle. Professional sport is an important "player" in the global cultural economy, and it can be manufactured, marketed, and sold in ways that respond to the shifting demographics of many regions and nations. When it is overexposed in one market, a professional sport may be manufactured, marketed, and sold in new markets. It can be McDonaldized, as the evolution of sports stadiums has demonstrated, to reflect changing social and cultural currents in a society. It can utilize new technologies to make it more popular and to make athletes and teams more successful. It can increase its profitability by planning and making decisions by eschewing conventional wisdom in a sport and using the modern rational statistical "Moneyball" approach of a Billy Beane. It can also take advantage of popular interest to manipulate public policy decisions, such as decisions about investing public tax dollars in sports facilities for private enterprises, to serve sports business interests.

Retaining the popular appeal of professional sports is the foundation of their commercial success because popular interest makes sports attractive investments for the media and corporate interests in the Golden Triangle. The sports, media, and corporate actors in the Golden Triangle have to do a balancing act to align the mediation and commercialization of the business of sport with the elements of the game that are most appealing to spectators and fans. In trying to expand sports audiences with more entertaining spectacles, they need to be careful not to alienate the more serious fans who are the most reliable customers in the sport. Findings from an unscientific reader survey conducted in 2006 for the *SportsBusiness Journal* and its affiliated *SportsBusiness Daily* publication are suggestive in this regard (SportsBusiness Journal 2006). Its readers ranged from students to a diverse range of other people and organizations interested in the sports business. Asked what they thought was the biggest threat to sports, 28.3 percent said "disconnect with fan base" and 21.6 percent said "use of drugs/integrity of the game." Other specific responses were "rising ticket prices" (15.4 percent), "inflated salaries" (14 percent), "overcommercialization" (12.1 percent), and "losing competitive balance" (5.3 percent).

Thus, it is evident that among those who are interested in the business of sport, a number of economic issues, along with competitiveness on the field, are perceived as significant threats to sport or to sport as a business. However, relatively more of these respondents perceived unresponsiveness to fans' interests and insufficient honesty or authenticity as the biggest threat. These results imply that the people who run sports through the Golden Triangle must strike a balance between their economic interests and the desire of sports fans to see games and stars that interest them and appear authentic or unmanipulated. How well these powerful people maintain this kind of balance in the context of the forces of change in society and the global cultural economy may be the key to understanding the future popularity and commercial success of specific professional sports and professional sports in general. The future of sport will be an explicit focus of the next chapter, which will be about the politics of sport and the social, economic, and political influences likely to shape the future of sport.

Notes

1. See the franchise value databases compiled by the magazine at www.forbes.com.

2. The NFL percentage would have been higher except that the New Orleans Saints, the team generating $7 million less revenue than the next-lowest revenue producer, and

the city of New Orleans were still recovering from the economic and social effects of Hurricane Katrina.

  3. Estimates are based on revenue figures from www.forbes.com in 2006–2007 and payroll figures from www.usatoday.com in 2005 for the NFL and in 2006–2007 for the other leagues.

  4. The median is a statistical measure that is the midpoint in a set of numbers, with half greater and half lower than the median.

  5. This information about salary caps was found on official league or players' association websites.

  6. Major sources of information about golf were official PGA Tour and related websites for golf publications.

  7. Information about strikes and lockouts was obtained from the websites of these sports leagues as well as news organizations.

  8. Data were derived from official PGA and LPGA websites for golf and from an Associated Press World Stream source in LexisNexis and a tennisessentials.com website for tennis.

  9. Figures were calculated from statistics on PGA Tour, LPGA, and PGA of America websites.

  10. Figures are from the Vancouver Canadians website. The Canadians were a Single-A minor league team in the Oakland Athletics organization.

11

Sport, Politics, and the Future

Concepts of Power and the Politics of Sport

This last chapter is about sport, politics, and the future. Throughout this book, we have been considering the effects of powerful and pervasive sociodemographic, organizational, economic, political, and technological processes that have expanded the reach and influence of corporate and commercialized sports around the world. We have seen how the power of the Golden Triangle has combined with these social processes to influence what sports we see, how they are organized and run, who the stars of sport are, and how sports are played, seen, and consumed. In this chapter, we will emphasize politics and power, and consider how people have used power in the political arena to make and shape decisions that have influenced sport in the past and will influence its future.

Politics refers to the political realms of society where power is exercised by governments or governing bodies. These political realms also include the actions of citizens and others outside official government who try to influence how they are governed, the rules and policies of governments or governing bodies, and the enforcement or effects of these rules and policies. Power is used when the officials of a sport try to protect their sport's integrity and its established rules by imposing stiff fines and suspensions for violent actions on the field by players or for violations of a league's drug policy. Power is also used when fans write letters or complain to reporters about the competence of a coach, the commitment of a team owner to getting the best players, or the price of tickets. The U.S. Congress exercised power when it investigated doping in professional sports and clearly conveyed the message that if the leagues did not develop stronger drug policies and enforcement procedures, it would intervene. When league officials create new rules to make their sport more exciting or to increase the pace of games, they are exercising their rule-making power, and they usually do these kinds of things to increase the appeal of their sports to the sports public. These are all cases of *political power*, which is the primary focus of this chapter.

Power has been a pervasive theme of this book, and we have considered various forms of power exercised by governments, regulatory bodies in sport, individuals, and of course, the Golden Triangle, which I have characterized as the dominant network of power in the corporate and commercialized sports world. Following the lead of Max Weber, sociologists generally use the term *power* to refer to the capacity of people acting individually or collectively to get what they want from others in the face of their perceived or actual resistance. Power is a kind of social interaction in which people try to get what they want from others by effectively using resources, ranging from persuasion to material inducements and threats to coercion. This book has devoted a lot of attention to the *economic power* of Golden Triangles, which involves the power wielded by organizations and individuals in the economic arena, where goods and services are manufactured, distributed, and consumed. We have seen that Golden Triangles also exercise *cultural power*, which is about the power of organizations or individuals to create or disseminate influential cultural ideas and products such as the Sport Ethic, sports events, and images of sports stars. In a cultural economy, economic and cultural power overlap as economic enterprises try to beat their competitors at the production, marketing, and sales of cultural goods and services. Golden Triangles compete and sometimes cooperate with each other in this global cultural economy, and sport itself is a major cultural product of these Golden Triangles.

As I suggested earlier, when officials of a governing body in sport, such as the National Collegiate Athletic Association (NCAA), a professional sports league, the Fédération Internationale de Football Association (FIFA), or the International Olympic Committee (IOC), establish or enforce rules and policies in a sport or decide to penalize a team or suspend an athlete, they are exercising their political power. Sociologists usually refer to the legitimate political power wielded by formal organizations or agencies of government as *authority*. The legitimacy of authority may be based on tradition or the special persuasive powers of charismatic individuals, but in modern societies, authority is usually legitimized as the rule of law. Max Weber conceptualized this rational-legal kind of authority as a characteristic of modern bureaucracies, and it is linked to a position in an organization. Holding a position of authority means that you have a right to expect people to accept your decisions and policies as binding, as long as they are within formally defined boundaries. The authority of a professional sports league commissioner is illustrated when players pay fines or serve suspensions without question or turn to a formal appeals process to try to modify a league decision. The players recognize that the league commissioner has the authority to make these kinds of decisions and that questioning them requires following formal procedures. Authority systems are hierarchical, which means that when policies or rules conflict, the relevant policies and rules of the superior authority have precedence. For example, when the U.S. Congress passed Title IX, it meant that public educational institutions at the primary, secondary, and postsecondary levels were compelled to create gender-related opportunities and practices consistent with the principle of gender equity embedded in the new federal law.

When people in positions of authority want others to do things they have no right to expect them to do or when their authority is weak, they may turn to *interpersonal, group,* or *organizational power*, which involves mobilizing individual or collective resources to get their way. For example, owners of sports franchises have no right to expect taxpayers to fund a new stadium, so they may believe they have to threaten to move their team to another city to get local politicians and voters to approve new stadium construction. The NCAA has authority to govern its member institutions, but it has no authority over the U.S. government. Thus, the NCAA has used its organizational power to try to influence the U.S. Congress not to regulate its commercial activities and not to remove the tax-exempt status of its members. Similarly, Major League Baseball (MLB) and other professional sports leagues have implemented drug policies to try to avoid congressional intervention in their sport. One of the resources that the NCAA and professional sports can use to try to sway legislators, government officials, and the public is the prominent place of their sports in the popular culture. Sports officials, coaches, and athletes can use the popularity of their sport as a political resource when the people they want to influence are passionate about sports, admire sports stars, or recognize the value of sport in society or the sports business in the economy. People may be deferential and more easily influenced under these conditions. Thus, sports officials try to boost or protect the image of sports for political purposes as well as for economic reasons.

When people have no formal authority but want to influence the public, governing officials, or governing bodies to change beliefs, attitudes, behavior, rules, or policies, they rely on interpersonal, group, or organizational power. In past chapters, we considered this type of power in cases of a high school athlete who was disabled and went to court to get school athletic officials to allow her to compete in mainstream track events, of women who have used Title IX to try to reduce gender discrimination in high school and college athletics, of reform efforts to make college athletics more consistent with its purported educational mission, and of professional athletes who have used agents or organized as unions to negotiate with owners and management in their sport. We will pay special attention later in this chapter to other cases of individuals and organized social movements that have indirectly and directly challenged sports officials and the power structure of sport from within and outside sport. These cases of *oppositional power* have focused on issues ranging from the revival of a sports franchise to globalization, the environment, and human rights. Oppositional politics of these types reminds us of the concept of sport as contested terrain. These cases suggest that the use of power is often prompted by inequalities and involves struggles to make sport and society fairer for people with lower status and fewer resources.

Theoretical Perspectives and the Politics of Sport

We can try to understand the politics of sport from various sociological perspectives. For example, *structural functionalists* would see the compatibility between the values of sport as a societal institution and the dominant values of U.S. society, such as the American Dream. From this perspective, we can understand how U.S. sport reinforces a belief in the American Dream, and how this belief contributes to stability in society. Belief in the American Dream contributes to social stability because people are likely to accept the dominant structure of society when they think it provides widespread opportunities for mobility and success. It contributes to political stability because people are likely to accept the authority of those in the elite because they believe they have earned their status. The enduring appeal of the American Dream is a powerful source of support for members of the elite. A recent survey of 2,200 largely middle-class Americans showed that a large majority continued to believe that the American Dream was possible and that they were responsible for their own financial success or failure even though most said that they lived from paycheck to paycheck, that their children would have a harder time doing better than their parents than they had, and that the middle class seemed to be shrinking (Wallechinsky 2006). Thus, in the United States, the ideology of the American Dream is emphasized in sport, and from a structural functional perspective, it functions to reinforce the stability of the dominant culture and social structure of the society. However, it also at least implicitly legitimizes the status and power of those in dominant positions in sport and elsewhere in society. This roughly parallels the case of the Soviet Union, where ideology in sport was meant to contribute to political stability. In the case of the Soviet Union, though, political leaders tried to bolster support for their regime by *intentionally and systematically* incorporating instruction in communist and nationalistic ideology into state-run sports training programs and by associating its sports success with the virtues of communism and socialist society.

The idea that the sports accomplishments of national sports teams can overcome divisions, fuel nationalistic pride, and unify nations also reflects a structural functionalist perspective. This was the theme of a number of news stories when the Iraqi soccer team upset the Saudi Arabians 1–0 to win their first Asian Cup Championship (e.g., Farrell and Gelling 2007; Wahl 2007). Across Iraq, this victory produced celebrations, flag waving and other expressions of national pride, and a chance to forget the ravages of war, sectarian violence, and suicide bombings. The fact that the winning goal was scored by an Iraqi Sunni Muslim, the goal scorer was assisted by a pass from an Iraqi Kurd, and the lead was protected by an Iraqi Shiite Muslim goalkeeper would seem to have powerful symbolic significance, since these three ethnic groups were fighting with each other in the war raging in their country. The respite from war was only temporary, though. Despite the excitement and pride felt by many Iraqis after the championship victory, the fragile Iraqi government was unable to use the residue of these feelings to stop the war, internal ethnic conflicts, or suicide bombings and create political stability and peace.

Although sports contests may not have the capacity to overcome ethnic divisions and political conflicts that governments cannot resolve or to produce enduring political changes in a country or the world, a structural functionalist perspective at least enables us to see that sport may provide brief respites from political turmoil. Symbolic interactionists offer another way to look at politics and sport. Through the eyes of a symbolic interactionist, we are able, for example, to gain a deeper understanding of how the Golden Triangle creates political images and meanings in sport. Patriotic anthems and displays, flags, and other political symbols are frequently part of sport, and symbolic interactionists draw our attention to the meanings and implications of these patriotic symbols and displays in sport. We can see how their orchestrated presence in the sports arena publicly ties sport to dominant cultural values and established institutions in the larger society and nation. We recall that a major theme of the Dominant American Sports Creed expressed this connection in the idea that sport promotes patriotism.

U.S. sports fans are encouraged to demonstrate their patriotism "to honor America" publicly by singing the national anthem, standing reverently facing the flag, or watching military jets fly overhead during sports events. These symbolic displays of patriotism in sport reinforce an idea that being a sports fan *means* that you steadfastly believe in your country and perhaps also its political leadership. Even in the Olympics, where the competition is technically between individuals from around the world and not between nations, athletes wear national uniforms, carry national flags during opening and closing ceremonies, and stand on a victory platform to listen to the national anthem of the gold medal winners.

A symbolic interactionist perspective can also help us understand why political struggles have arisen between sports traditionalists and Indian and feminist activists who have tried to rid sport of widely recognized symbols they have perceived as offensive and degrading, such as Indian mascots, team names, and logos and gendered team names such as "Lady Tigers" or the oxymoronic "Lady Rams." Symbols can be powerful means of defining a group's status or identity in society. They may be perceived as demeaning, racist, or sexist or they may be seen as a source of pride or allegiance. These power struggles over ethnic and gender symbols have involved people with very strong views on both sides of these issues, who have constructed very different meanings of these symbols (Eitzen 2006:33–48).

Conflict and critical theorists also are interested in these types of struggles over symbols and their meaning, and they would point to inequalities that give some people and groups more power than others to institutionalize the symbols and meanings they prefer. With the issue of Indian mascots, team names, and logos, Indian advocates were able to pressure the NCAA to implement a ban in cases where it perceived these symbols as "hostile or abusive" (ESPN 2005). Their political success could be at least partially attributed to the fact that ethnic diversity and the rights of ethnic minorities had become very sensitive issues on many college campuses. The NCAA did not want to project an image of racial or ethnic insensitivity. This case demonstrates the complex nature of many political struggles. Indian advocates were not able to get bans against all institutions they saw as targets for change, and the NCAA faced some prominent but very unhappy NCAA member institutions affected by the ban. They also had to deal with opposition from unhappy fans and even some Indian tribes who disagreed with the policy. Since the NCAA had the right to formulate this kind of policy and enforce sanctions against those who failed to accept it, unhappy parties realized they could not ignore it and instead threatened legal action. Thus, political struggles often have "messy" or unsatisfying outcomes for all parties, and may become prolonged as aggrieved parties continue their struggle as long as they have the desire and resources to do so. Longer political struggles put lower-status parties at an increasing disadvantage unless they can get a quick legal victory in the courts or can gain popular support, because their lower status implies that they have relatively fewer resources to sustain their opposition.

The *political economy* perspective is a critical perspective for understanding how political power and capitalism combine in sport and shape how sports are organized and used by powerful people and organizations (Nixon and Frey 1996:32–33). Political economy particularly emphasizes network ties linking sports, media, and corporate elites to government elites, which involve Golden Triangles using governments for their economic purposes and governments using sports for their political purposes. For example, legislative, judicial, and administrative decisions by governments influenced by neoliberal economic beliefs have often created a favorable economic environment for sports investors and sports bodies to make money. Similarly, even in the United States, where the federal government has had relatively little direct control over sports, government officials and elected politicians have used sports and athletes to try to increase their popularity among voters and as a means to conduct foreign policy.

Although there are many possible ways to approach the politics of sport, Houlihan (2000) offers a useful distinction between politics *and* sport and politics *in* sport. *Politics and sport* mainly refers to how governments exercise power over or through sports in the public domain for their political ends. For example, governments may decide to use public funds to host an Olympics or build a stadium. *Politics in sport* concerns how various individuals and organizations outside government and inside and outside sport use power to pursue their own political, economic, or social interests in ways that affect sport. Examples of this perspective include efforts to pressure sports officials to increase access to sport for women or minorities, movements to get Nike customers to stop using Nike products until the company addressed the sweatshop issue, or advocacy to try to get sports to be more environmentally responsible or to get nations to treat access to sports for people with disabilities as a human rights issue. We will use Houlihan's conception of politics and sport and politics in sport as a basic framework for the remainder of the chapter, and we will address the kinds of issues I have used to illustrate these perspectives. "Politics of the Olympics" will be a bridge topic between these two themes because the Olympic Games have been a site and target of politics for much of their modern history since the end of the nineteenth century. Politics has also been anathema to Olympic officials because they have typically tried to steer away from politics, asserting that the Olympics was above politics or apolitical. We will see that such assertions have not reflected the reality of the Olympics.

Politics and Sport: Government Power and the Political Uses of Sport

Governments have tried to control, use, or otherwise intervene in sports for political purposes in a number of different ways (e.g., see Houlihan 2000: 215–220; Nixon and Frey 1996:273–288). One type of intervention has involved the regulatory role of government. For example, the Swedish government banned boxing due to its extreme violence as a "blood sport." In Italy, government officials barred spectators from soccer stadiums that could not meet safety and security standards following the death of a policeman during an episode of spectator violence. In the United States, a stronger internal regulatory body for college athletics, new rules, and innovations in the game curtailed violence in college football and averted a government ban of the sport in the early twentieth century. At the state level in the United States, legislatures have occasionally played a controversial regulatory role in sports, as when Texas legislators approved the "no pass, no play" law, which prohibited high school athletes and band members with failing grades from participating in these extracurricular activities.

The regulatory effects of legislation on sport may not be fully anticipated when laws are passed. An example is Title IX, which has profoundly affected high school and college sports in the United States, but which was not initially seen as a means to achieve gender equity in sports. The politics of Title IX also shows that the perceived failure of government agencies to enforce a law can prompt public criticism and direct public pressure toward government. Thirty-five years after the passage of Title IX, a report released by the National Women's Law Center complained that the U.S. Department of Education's Office of Civil Rights was lax in fulfilling its responsibility to enforce Title IX (Lipka and Wolverton 2007). The report was intended to focus public debate and pressure on issues such as inequitable facilities and access to female coaches for female college athletes and the adverse effects on women's programs of disproportionate spending on football and men's basketball in college athletics.

National Governments and the Governance of Sport

Although sports officials in the United States are often reluctant to encourage government intervention in their sports because it reduces their own control, there are times when sports bodies cooperate with governments to deal with difficult and intractable problems. For example, Houlihan (2000) noted that the success of IOC and World Anti-Doping Agency (WADA) efforts to fight doping in Olympic sports depended on the cooperation of governments. In North America, officials of professional sports leagues have typically tried to fend off government involvement in their efforts to control doping, but congressional pressure and its threatened intervention spurred the leagues to establish tougher anti-doping policies and drug enforcement procedures.

Sometimes, governments affect sports by their decisions to apply the law differently to sports than to other kinds of activities or organizations in a society. For example, as we saw in the last chapter, the U.S. Supreme Court and Congress have not made big-time college athletics and professional sports leagues subject to antitrust laws that usually apply to U.S. business and commercial activities. As a result, various commercialized sports have engaged in monopolistic practices that have increased their power, profitability, and commercial growth. At various times, the courts have recommended that Congress address these practices in sport, and some members of Congress have raised questions about the unusual business of professional sports and the commercialization of college athletics. However, the U.S. government has generally been reluctant to get involved in sport, and in this way, the United States has been different than many other countries.

The United States has been relatively unusual among nations participating in the Olympics in its lack of a centralized federal sports authority to regulate and sponsor Olympic sports. This reflects a political ideology of limited government and a belief in private individual initiative as well as a tradition of strong and independent national sports organizations (NSOs) for Olympic sports in the United States (Coakley 2007:388–389). However, federal involvement in Olympic sports increased in the United States in the late 1970s after a period of declining U.S. performance in international competition and conflicts among major amateur sports organizations, including the NCAA, the U.S. Olympic Committee (USOC), and the Amateur Athletic Union (AAU). In 1978, the U.S. Congress, with the backing of the president, passed the Amateur Sports Act. It made USOC the major coordinating body for U.S. amateur sports, which are now usually called Olympic sports because of the growing element of professionalism in these sports. The government also authorized a onetime appropriation to fund three Olympic training centers (Nixon and Frey 1996:275).

Despite its designated central role in amateur and Olympic sports in the United States, the USOC has existed in the shadow of the NCAA. The USOC was supposed to coordinate the NSOs of sports not under the auspices of the NCAA, but it has been much weaker than the NCAA in its regulatory role because the NSOs it is supposed to coordinate have fought hard to maintain their autonomy. These individual governing bodies have been unwilling to yield much control over either the athletes or the flow of resources in their sports. In the U.S. tradition of commercialism in the sports marketplace, these bodies have raised their own money to support athletes, training, and events, and have not wanted to share the revenue their sports have generated. Thus, limited government intervention and limited subsidies in the United States have opened the door for these Olympic sports, as well as the NCAA, to pursue their sports and economic interests through ties with the Golden Triangle.

A combination of political expediency, political values, and the traditional power of the sports establishment probably explains much of the autonomy given to U.S. sports by the U.S. government. Many other nations take a more active role in sports, with federal sports ministries or agencies overseeing all national sports bodies, formulating policies for them, and providing government subsidies. Having control over sport has enabled government leaders to manipulate or exploit sports and athletes for their political purposes. For example, government-sponsored sports academies and training programs have been used to socialize athletes to embrace a national political ideology or culture, as in the political education of athletes in the Soviet Union (Riordan 1980) and other communist nations. The role of government leaders in this kind of political socialization is more subtle in democratic nations such as the United States, where the rhetoric of the American Dream in politics and sport asserts the superiority of the U.S. way of life. In her study of ideology, politics, and market forces in Cuban baseball, Baird (2005) showed how baseball in Cuba differed from Major League Baseball as a result of being in a state-run, rather than a market-driven, system. A detailed examination of her study gives us a fuller and deeper understanding of the imprint of government and ideology on sport in different kinds of political systems, which is why her study is a "Focus on Research" feature.

On a continuum of nations distinguished by the amount of control their national government exercises over sport and the extent to which that control over sport is centralized, nations such as Cuba, in which the central government runs sport, would be at one end and nations such as the United States, with its minimal official involvement in a highly decentralized sports system, would be at the other end. Of course, these distinctions are not quite as sharp as implied here, since Cuba sometimes responds to the demands of the marketplace and particularly the desire for more compensation and freedom

Focus on Research Feature 11.1:
Ideology, Politics, and Market Forces in Cuban Baseball

Baird (2005) did a case study of Cuban baseball in which she studied the influence of ideology, politics, and market forces. She noted that some baseball analysts attributed the consistent excellence of Cubans in international competition to the superiority of Cuban socialist organizing principles. She also quoted some Major League Baseball (MLB) fans as saying that the lack of commercialization in the Cuban game made it more attuned to genuine fans, since there were no promotional distractions at the ballparks and players were more accessible to fans. Compared with MLB, the Cuban game seemed more authentic and Cuban players seemed more enthusiastic about their sport. Baird evaluated these kinds of perceptions by studying the organization and outcomes of Cuban baseball during Castro's regime in contrast to those of Major League Baseball in the United States.

Baird's description of the contemporary business of Major League Baseball resonates with our description in chapter ten of MLB after the emergence of free agency, although she gives little attention to the persisting monopolistic elements. She observed that MLB today operates according to the ideology of the free market, with teams privately owned and purchased in a financially competitive marketplace. Teams hire players in a competitive labor market, with the players who can generate the most revenue for their team owner getting the biggest contracts. The decisions that teams and the league make about issues such as ticket prices, promotional giveaways, overseas marketing, player development, and the number and location of teams in a league are all profit-motivated business decisions. Competitive imbalances resulted from differences in the market sizes and revenue potential of the locations where teams played, since teams in more lucrative markets could earn more and pay more for players.

Sports have been important in Castro's Cuba, as they were in the Soviet Union and other communist countries, because they symbolized for its leaders the values and virtues of socialism. Castro reorganized baseball in Cuba after the 1959 revolution according to socialist principles. He and other Cuban government officials have frequently used the performance of their nation's athletes as a marker of the success of their socialist revolution. Following the Soviet communist model, athletes were educated in socialist and nationalistic ideology during their athletic training and were expected to be advocates of their government and sports system. U.S. athletes also learn about values and ideologies in their sports culture, and we often hear U.S. athletes give thanks to God or affirm the American Dream or the Sport Ethic in interviews following big victories. However, as Baird suggests, the difference in Cuba is that the mobility of Cuban athletes in their sports system is more directly and explicitly tied to their public support of the government.

Cuban government officials have characterized U.S. professional sports as a "capitalist perversion of athletics" (Jamail 2000:49), and Castro has equated professional sports in the United States under capitalism with a form of slavery in which I would suppose that profit-motivated owners were the slavemasters (Jamail 2000:29). Being good at baseball was especially appealing to Castro because Americans invented the game and he loathed the U.S. government and the global capitalist system in which the United States was so heavily invested. Major League Baseball represented the things he despised about the United States and capitalism. In his socialist model, baseball teams were "owned" by the government, which paid players minimal salaries. According to official policy, all players earned about the same amount, which was about $10 to $15 per month in 2003 and was equivalent to what most of the Cuban workforce earned. Players played for the team in their region and did not move between teams. There were no wealthy teams to buy the best players, since there was no market to make some teams wealthier than others. The government placed players on teams in the regions where they lived. Advertising did not exist in the stadium or in media coverage, and games cost nothing to attend before 1994. When financial hard times occurred in Cuba, it became necessary to charge a small price for admission to games, but the aim was to keep game tickets inexpensive to allow ordinary people to attend games.

Thus, as Baird pointed out, Cuban baseball and the Cuban sports system in general were managed to serve the interests of the Cuban people as a whole and not as individuals. This emphasis on the public good is a basic socialist principle derived from Karl Marx, and it contrasts with the preeminence of private interests in a capitalist marketplace. Under socialism, the government articulated and represented the public interest. In this model of sport, there was no place for market forces or the Golden Triangle. There was no market to create economic inequalities among teams or players, since the government controlled the economics of the sport.

We can ask whether the Cuban baseball system has served the public interest as well as, or has been accepted by the players as much as, Cuban officials have claimed. Was it a socialist sports "utopia"? Baird evaluated the effects of government control over Cuban baseball, and her analysis revealed a mixed picture that was clearly not of a utopia. On the one hand, there was a successful government-run baseball talent development system, with a number of regional sports academies, instructional schools, schools for the refinement of the most talented athletes, and high-performance centers that produced many excellent baseball players and outstanding Cuban national teams. On the other hand, there have been many players who have been disgruntled about the restrictions on their careers and economic opportunities imposed by the government. In addition, teams in more populous regions had a demographically based competitive advantage because they had more potential players in their labor pools.

Cuban players were paid a paltry amount compared with players with equivalent talent in the United States, Japan, Italy, and Latin America, and they were prohibited from playing overseas, were compelled to finish their careers with their assigned teams, and then were reassigned to other employment by the government after their sports careers ended. Although they were officially viewed as traitors, more than eighty Cuban players defected between 1991 and 2000 and continued to attract the interest of Cuban fans when they played overseas. Faced with the disgruntlement of players, the political embarrassment from defections of star players, and a chronically distressed economy and need for hard currency after the demise of the Soviet Union and its financial aid, Cuban leaders compromised their egalitarian socialist principles. They yielded somewhat to the marketplace and in 1995 began an experiment that loosened restrictions on player movement and compensation. They allowed players to retire early and play overseas in certain countries. They created a marketing department in the sports ministry to sell their players to foreign leagues and took 80 percent of the players' foreign earnings.

About eighty-five baseball players and one thousand athletes and coaches overall left Cuba under this early retirement plan. However, fans became unhappy with this plan and with the government's management of baseball because many of their favorite players retired early to play overseas and their depleted national teams were no longer dominant in international competition. With attendance dropping off during the national championship series and with many fans expressing their disapproval of the early retirement experiment, the government ended the experiment in 1998 after three years. This resulted in a new surge in player defections, which prompted a resurrection of negotiations with foreign baseball clubs to sign Cuba's top baseball players.

Baird revealed a number of significant cracks in the Cuban socialist model of baseball. Cuban leaders kept a tight rein on the sport and players to project a socialist example, but then faced various problems that pushed them to resort to capitalistic practices. They could not simultaneously keep players and fans happy, maintain a competitive balance among regionally based teams in the Cuban League, deal with their economic problems, and uphold their socialist principles. Their political compromises and strategic "flipflops" highlighted the dilemma posed by baseball for Cuban officials. Socialist principles and a managed economy were difficult to sustain in the management of sport when the country faced severe economic problems caused in part by its political ideology. As Baird observed, trying to regulate baseball to demonstrate the superiority of a political ideology was ultimately very costly for those from whom the Cuban regime most wanted support, the stars of their athletic system and the people who loved their sports stars.

among athletes, and the U.S. government has gotten directly involved in sports at times to clean up organizational feuds, improve the performance of U.S. sports teams, or make a political point through sports. Located between Cuba and the United States on the continuum are nations such as Canada, the United Kingdom, and Australia, where there has traditionally been less government involvement in sports than in Cuba but much more than in the United States. In Canada, the United Kingdom, and Australia, the national government has funded NSOs, shaped their policies, and regulated their organizational practices. In these countries, government funding, policy, and regulation have increasingly emphasized elite sports development and performance (Green 2004; Green and Houlihan 2006).

According to a study by Green and Houlihan (2006), the national governments in the United Kingdom and Australia have promised national sports organizations (NSOs) more autonomy in recent years, but these organizations were required to adhere more closely to government standards for organizational performance to justify more independence and government funding. Green and Houlihan focused their research, which included examining documents and conducting interviews, on the NSOs in the United Kingdom and Australia that governed "athletics," which included track and field, cross-country, road running, and related kinds of sports. UK Athletics and Athletics Australia were recipients of large amounts of government funding but had histories of financial problems, limited success in getting more people involved in their sports at the grassroots level, disintegrating club structures, and poor results at the international level. In general, they had fallen short of government expectations of organizational efficiency and success. As a result, both national governments have increased their influence over these NSOs in recent years and put pressure on them to "modernize" to become more efficient and produce more success in elite events in their sports.

UK Athletics and Athletics Australia were promised more opportunities for self-regulation as long as they adopted modern business technologies and practices such as regular performance reviews, strategic planning, and annual government audits and reviews. Thus, according to Green and Houlihan, the promise of more autonomy was an illusion since these NSOs actually had to accept more centralized control over how the organizations were run to meet government expectations and receive government support. By making the NSOs accountable for compliance to this kind of business model, political leaders in the United Kingdom and Australia were subjecting sport to the same business-oriented neoliberal policies that were being applied to other sectors of government in these countries. By achieving success in the sports realm, the political leaders were able to enhance the credibility and appeal of their political approaches in general. Green and Houlihan suggested, however, that a consequence of this approach in sport was that accountability for sports performance was shifted away from the traditional stakeholders of sports clubs, volunteers, athletes, and coaches to the central government and commercial sponsors. According to Green and Houlihan, the neoliberal modernization approach pushed by political leaders in the United Kingdom and Australia reflected their instrumental approach to sports and their desire to increase commercialism and the influence of the media and other sports-related industries over sports. Thus, increased government influence over the NSOs meant the imposition of neoliberal policies that gave more power in sport to the Golden Triangle as well as to government itself.

Sport, International Relations, and Wars without (and with) Weapons

Although government leaders in the United States have generally been reluctant to become directly involved in sport, they have been like leaders of other nations in their desire to see their national teams perform well in international competition. Indeed, perceptions of declining performance led U.S. leaders to get more involved in sports in the 1970s than they had in the past. Government efforts to regulate, subsidize, or assist Olympic sports reflect the importance government leaders attribute to their nation's stature in the global sports hierarchy. These government leaders like to win in international competition because it is a means of showing the superiority of their sports, athletes, and way of life over those of other nations. They may use victories in international competitions to bolster their popular support; to build national solidarity, identity, or loyalty; or, more generally, to promote their nation's political ideology or culture among other nations. As we saw in the case of the Iraqi soccer victory, sport may be limited in its capacity to help political leaders achieve enduring outcomes of these kinds. Governments have been more successful under some circumstances in using sporting contacts as a way to open up diplomatic channels and improve relations with other nations. For example, the U.S. and Chinese governments used "ping-pong diplomacy," which involved exhibition ping-pong matches between U.S. and Chinese teams in the early 1970s, as a first step in establishing broader relations between the nations. A more recent case involves the "baseball diplomacy" of the Baltimore Orioles in their exhibition games with a Cuban all-star team in 1999, and this series is the subject of a "Sport in the News" feature. This feature and the prior research feature are companion pieces using Cuba to elucidate important insights about politics and sport.

Hostile nations may choose to confront each other in sport, with sport serving as a surrogate for military conflict in a "war without weapons" (Goodhart and Chataway 1968). In this sense, athletic competition is a symbolic substitute for the bloodier and more costly conflict of a war, and a nation trumpets its wins on the athletic field instead of its conquests on the battlefield as an indication of its national superiority. Government officials have used sports boycotts to protest the actions of another country. The boycott of South Africa and of nations having sporting contacts with South Africa to try to end South Africa's racist apartheid system is a prominent example of how this kind of organized political action through sport has helped bring about social change. The international sports boycott was followed by an international economic boycott, which ultimately led to the end of apartheid in 1993 (Nixon and Frey 1996:288–289). The antiapartheid movement is also an example of a case of effective political pressure on Olympic sports officials, who banned apartheid South Africa from the Olympic Movement for nearly three decades. We will consider a number of other examples of Olympic boycotts in our examination of the politics of the Olympics in the next section.

⬜   **Sport in the News Feature 11.2: "Beisbol Diplomacy"**

What may be most distinctive about the "beisbol diplomacy" undertaken by Peter Angelos, owner of the Baltimore Orioles, in his two games with the Cuban national team in 1999 is that it represented the initiative of a private citizen. Since there was a long-standing embargo against Cuba from the early days of Fidel Castro's regime, formal diplomatic ties did not exist and other kinds of ties were severely restricted. Thus, Angelos had to obtain approval from his own and the Cuban government as well as from Major League Baseball to play the games he planned, and he and his Major League Baseball team served as a surrogate for the U.S. State Department and government in broaching relations with Cuba. The games were possible because U.S. president Bill Clinton had begun to relax restrictions on communications and travel between the two countries (Knowlton 1999). On the surface, the two games between the Orioles and a Cuban all-star team in 1999 might appear simply to be a gesture of goodwill aimed at thawing relations between two hostile countries. However, a closer look at the political context and implications of these games reveals a much more complex picture.

Political scientist Wayne Smith, an expert on Cuba, accompanied a college baseball team from The Johns Hopkins University that played in Cuba in 1986 and also attended the Orioles games with the Cubans in Havana and Baltimore in 1999 (JHU 1999). He found that the Cuban crowd in both cases cheered for the good plays of the U.S. ballplayers and stood respectfully during the U.S. national anthem. During the Orioles game in Havana, Cuban president Fidel Castro greeted both teams and sat next to Orioles owner Peter Angelos. Castro very likely took pride in the performance of the Cuban team, which lost by one run in eleven innings in Havana but soundly defeated the Orioles 12–6 in Baltimore two months later. He was less pleased by news of the defection of a Cuban coach after the game in Baltimore (Matthews, Matthews, and Hermann 1999).

Defections can be a sensitive issue and a political risk for both sides in efforts at sports diplomacy. In her study of Cuban baseball, which I highlighted in a "Focus on Research" feature in this chapter, Baird (2005) showed that the Cuban government treated defections of star players seriously. Since ballplayers were instruments of ideology for Castro, their defection was seen as a political embarrassment and a defeat for his regime and caused harsh reactions. For example, one of the stars of the games with the Orioles and one of the best pitchers in Cuba, Jose Contreras, defected three years later while playing in Mexico and signed a Major League Baseball contract with the New York Yankees (Baxter 2002). His defection was surprising and particularly embarrassing for Castro, who trusted his loyalty, considered him one of his favorites, and rewarded him with an expensive car and apartment. Castro denounced Contreras as a traitor who had traded his country for money, and he made life very difficult for the wife and two daughters Contreras left behind when he defected. His family was eventually smuggled into the United States to rejoin him (De Valle, Baxter, and Figueras 2004).

Defections were an issue for the United States and Major League Baseball as well, since they undermined the spirit of the diplomacy of sporting contacts. For the Orioles, defecting players were an issue because their management publicly stated that the club had no interest in actively pursuing Cuban defectors. However, this statement provoked criticism from anti-Castro politicians and activists in the United States, and one U.S. senator called for an investigation to determine whether the Orioles were actually violating civil rights or immigration laws by not hiring Cuban defectors (Bash and Todd 2000). The Orioles had spent a great deal of money scouting prospects in the Caribbean, but had not signed any defecting players at that point. They were ultimately cleared of "anti-defector" discrimination charges (Fisher 2001), but a thirteen-month Justice Department investigation showed the complex political implications of a sports diplomacy initiative launched by people in sport rather than by government officials. Clinton wanted to use the games as a humanitarian means to gain the sympathy of the Cuban people, but he was not interested in bolstering Castro's regime (Knowlton 1999), which may be why the Justice Department responded to political pressure to investigate the Orioles after the games were over. Mutual antagonism between the governments and hostility toward Castro in the United States were part of the political landscape of this experiment in baseball diplomacy and help explain why political controversy swirled around the games in the United States. Castro had long been an enemy of anticommunist politicians and Cuban exiles as well as the U.S. government. Some of Castro's opponents were MLB players who had escaped from Cuba with their families when they were children. The intensity of feelings against Castro among Cuban expatriates raised serious security concerns prior to the series, which threatened to jeopardize the proposal for the games (Chass 1999). The game in Baltimore was not disrupted by protest, but it caused bitter feelings among those virulently opposed to Castro and spawned conflicts with those seeking rapprochement with Cuba and other U.S. enemies in the interests of international cooperation and world peace.

Peter Angelos's "beisbol diplomacy" may have ignited some political fires, but it ultimately had little effect on U.S.-Cuba relations, which in 2008 remained hostile. In addition, political attitudes remained complex and divided. An Associated Press scientific poll of one thousand U.S. adults in 2007 showed that while more Republicans (82 percent) than Democrats (59 percent) had an unfavorable opinion of Castro, the majority of people identifying with both parties had negative opinions (Fox News 2007). Furthermore, 62 percent of Republicans and 50 percent of Democrats did not expect to see a democracy in Cuba after the death of Fidel Castro. At the same time, 72 percent of Democrats and 51 percent of Republicans said they were in favor of diplomatic relations with Cuba, even though 48 percent of all respondents said the United States should maintain its trade embargo against Cuba. Results differed along ethnic lines, with much higher percentages of Latinos than non-Latinos saying that they expected a democratic government to follow Castro's regime and that Cuba would be better off after his death.

Even when a sport is a major part of the cultures of nations engaging in sports diplomacy, it appears that a sports exchange is unlikely to transform animosities among people and resolve tensions between governments unless sport is part of an intentionally designed broader strategy of rapprochement involving informal government-to-government contacts, as in the case of ping-pong diplomacy between the United States and China. The U.S. government may have approved the Havana and Baltimore baseball games because it saw them as a way to appeal to two different constituencies with little political cost to itself. For those seeking improved relations with Cuba, the games could represent a preliminary step in rapprochement with Cuba. For those adamantly opposed to relations with Castro's Cuba, they could represent a politically meaningless gesture of goodwill undertaken by a baseball owner (DeLay 1999). Seeing no political gains from this exchange, the Clinton administration did not build on it, and the ensuing Bush presidency had even less interest in closer ties with Cuba while Castro was still alive. Thus, sports diplomacy is ultimately constrained by the political landscape and by governments, over which even the economically and culturally powerful Golden Triangle may have limited political power.

Sometimes sports competition between hostile nations escalates from a war without weapons to violence and a war *with* weapons. For example, in 1969 during a World Cup qualifying competition, a long-standing border dispute between El Salvador and Honduras erupted into violence between spectators in a San Salvador soccer stadium. El Salvador won the game and their strong nationalistic sentiments led to the burning of Honduran flags on the field and attacks on Honduran spectators as they fled the stadium. This violence precipitated a protest from the Honduran government, a counterprotest by the government of El Salvador about mistreatment of Salvadoran immigrants and refugees by Honduras,

---

the severing of diplomatic relations by El Salvador, and, a month later, a five-day armed conflict, which has been called the "Soccer War" (Morello 1997). Although historical tension between the nations was the underlying cause of this international conflict, a soccer match provided a trigger for the conflict.

Another example of sport, politics, and political violence involved the disintegrating Yugoslav Federation. Sack and Suster's (2000) study of two soccer matches in 1990, one resulting in the worst riot in Yugoslavian soccer history and the other used by Croatians to celebrate their nationalism, showed how soccer played a role in Croatia's efforts to gain international legitimacy and achieve political independence. The soccer riot occurred two weeks after the election of Franco Tudjman as president of Croatia, presaging the bloody, nearly decade-long war in the Balkans. The riot occurred in Maksimir Stadium in the Croatian capital of Zagreb, where the Croatian Dinamo Zagreb team was to face the Serbian Belgrade Red Star team. Unlike the soccer hooliganism in Britain and other countries that we considered in chapter eight, this soccer violence in Croatia was political violence.

According to Sack and Suster, the soccer clubs representing these two teams, the Bad Boy Blues from Croatia and the Serbian Delije club, were paramilitary organizations rather than just fan clubs. In the hours preceding the match, the Dinamo and Red Star fans had clashed in the streets. After they entered the stadium and prior to the match, Red Star fans sang nationalistic songs, shouted verbal abuse at Croatian fans (including "we will kill Tudjman"), and then tore down commercial signage and began to attack the Croatian fans. Red Star fans claimed that they had used the signs to ward off the stones thrown at them by Dinamo fans. These exchanges set off a wider and more violent conflict in the stadium between the Bad Boy Blues and the Delije Red Star supporters. The Bad Boy Blues, who had been enraged by the Serbian fans' verbal tirade, tried to retaliate by storming the field. When the Serb-dominated police tried to repulse and control them, the violence escalated. The ensuing riot resulted in scores of injuries and the cancellation of the soccer match, but it also reflected the strong ethnoreligious and political differences between these fans. Sack and Suster concluded that the confrontation at the Maksimir soccer stadium was part of the political agendas of the Bad Boy Blues and Delije.

Following the Maksimir soccer riot, Tudjman's Croatian government created a divisive new constitution that declared Croatia the homeland of the Croatians and reduced the status of their former partners, the Serbians, to a national minority, made Croatian the national language, and purged Serbians from the civil service, the court system, and the police. These actions were part of a pattern of spiraling tension between the Croatians and Serbs in Croatia, which resulted in a war that lasted for a number of years and was part of the larger Balkan conflict. Tudjman used an exhibition soccer match in Maksimir Stadium with the United States in 1990 as a part of his nationalistic strategy. Although still a republic in the Yugoslav Federation at the time, Croatia filled the stadium with a number of Croatian patriotic symbols, from flags to the design of players' uniforms. The boldest of these symbols was the label "Croatian National Team," which the Croatians used to describe their all-star team that played the United States. This was the clearest statement of Tudjman's ultimate political intentions, which culminated in his declaration of the independence of Croatia in 1991. He wanted to give his political regime and his political agenda international legitimacy, and playing the United States was a very visible way of doing this. Although the U.S. players and coaches may not have been aware of the political significance of the match, the fact that it was cleared by the U.S. State Department suggests at least implicit U.S. government approval of Tudjman's regime and perhaps also his desire for independence.

Politics of the Olympics: Ideals and Realities

The soccer riots in El Salvador and in Zagreb contained elements of both *sport and politics* and *sport in politics*. That is, political leaders stoked the nationalistic feelings that led to these violent episodes on the one hand, and on the other hand, sports fans from different nations and ethnic groups used these sports venues to express their political differences as well as their fervor for their teams. The Olympic Games have provided many examples of these two types of relationships between politics and sport. The politics of the Olympics includes the uses of sport by national governments for their political purposes—or, politics *and* sport—as well as examples of political economy and politics *in* sport, in which individuals and nongovernmental organizations have used sport for their political purposes. The Olympic Games have frequently been the site of political displays and actions because they are arguably the most prestigious venue where the nations of the world gather to compete in sport and because they attract worldwide attention. The meeting of nations in a highly publicized global sports "mega-event" (Horne and Manzenreiter 2006) creates conditions highly conducive to politics. In this section, we will explore the often-political nature of the Olympics and the role of political economy in the Olympic Games.

The Olympic Games were reborn as the Modern Olympics in 1896[1] and their history has been marked by a pattern of politics, even though the rhetoric of the Olympics and the Olympic ideals disavow political purposes for the Games. We will consider the inconsistencies between Olympic ideals and political realities after briefly summarizing the ideals that inspired the rebirth of the Olympics at the end of the nineteenth century. The original goals and ideals of the Modern Olympics were espoused by a French nobleman, Baron Pierre de Coubertin, who is generally considered the founder of the Modern Games (Nixon 1988a; Nixon and Frey 1996:289–294). The original Olympic ideals were amateurism, the preeminence of athletes as individuals unaffiliated with government or commercial sponsors or professional clubs, sportsmanship, and international understanding. Olympic athletes were supposed to compete in friendly competition and build ties across national borders and cultures in competition and in the Olympic Village. According to the Olympic charter, Olympic competitions were also supposed to be hosted and funded by cities and not by national governments or private corporations. All of these ideals and organizing principles have been violated at various times in the history of the Modern Olympics.

Olympic officials eventually gave up the rhetoric and pretense of amateurism after trying to suppress, penalize, or ignore cases of "shamateurism" for many years. Olympic shamateurism included under-the-table payments by corporate sponsors to athletes and government subsidies of athletes. The amateur ideal was supposed to glorify the idea of sport for its own sake, but it actually officially restricted Olympic sport to those wealthy enough to participate on an international level without financial subsidies. Athletes and others had decried the hypocrisy of shamateurism because so much money was being made from sponsors and the media in capitalistic sports systems and by Olympic organizations and because so many athletes and teams were being subsidized by their governments. The commercialization and global media attention that contributed to the global growth of sport and the Olympics made it inevitable that professionalism would intrude into the Olympic arena, first illegally and then openly. The Golden Triangle became the financial backbone of the Olympics, and its desire to expand markets and commercial opportunities by showcasing the world's best athletic talent ultimately overcame the anachronistic, elitist, and frequently abused ideal of amateurism. Thus, the economic power of the Golden Triangle reshaped the official culture of the Olympic Games, and Olympic officials then promulgated a policy that permitted NSOs and national Olympic committees to embrace professionalism openly and select professional athletes to compete in the Olympics.

The ideals of the Olympics have been violated for political purposes in sometimes subtle and sometimes very public ways. In fact, some historians have proposed that the founding of the Modern Olympics by Baron de Coubertin was colored by his political motives. He wanted to use international sports competition to inspire French men to higher levels of physical fitness and military preparedness after the disappointing performance of French soldiers during the Franco-Prussian War in 1870–1871 (Nixon and Frey 1996:289). At the same time, he seemed genuinely committed to establishing a relatively informal sports competition among amateur athletes at the international level that embodied the principles of international understanding and world peace. Yet from the beginning of the Olympic Games in 1896, national affiliations of athletes and teams were emphasized, as athletes displayed flags and wore clothing representing their nation. A parade of nations became a highlight of the opening ceremony, the playing of the national anthem of victorious athletes became a hallowed ritual of the Games, and the media have routinely published unofficial medal rankings of the nations. Athletes realized that they were not competing for themselves. They represented the pride of their nation.

The Olympics as a Stage for Politics

As the Modern Olympic Games have evolved, national governments, protest groups, and terrorists have used the Olympic stage for their political purposes (Senn 1999). In 1936, Hitler used his "Nazi Olympics" in Berlin as a propaganda vehicle. He wanted the Olympics to help him build popular support in Germany for his extremely nationalistic and fascist Nazi ideology and regime and to demonstrate the superiority of the Aryan race. According to historian Richard Mandell (1971), he also used the Olympics to distract the world from his aggressive militaristic plans to conquer neighboring countries and extend his international influence. IOC officials disregarded international concerns about Hitler and Germany's exploitation of the Games for their political ends because the Germans assured them that the Games would adhere to Olympic standards. They adopted a position of ignoring internal politics of members and host nations as long as the Games met their sporting expectations. This became a consistent pattern in the actions of Olympic officials.

Politics again visited the Olympics in Germany in the 1972 Munich Games, but this time, the politics came from different sources than the German government. A victory stand demonstration by African-American runners Vincent Matthews and Wayne Collett, in which they protested racism in the United States by turning their back on the flag and casually talking during their national anthem, caused a disapproving reaction from spectators and "disgust" among IOC officials, who banned them from subsequent Olympic competition in Munich and in the future (Time 1972a). Although their behavior provoked negative reactions, the political significance of the runners' behavior and its aftermath paled in comparison to the invasion of the 1972 Munich Games by terrorists.

The Black September Movement was a little-known militant Palestinian rights organization. In an Olympic setting where security was relatively lax and in a world in which there was a history of ongoing political tension in the Middle East, eight members of Black September scaled a fence and invaded the Olympic Village in a carefully planned early-morning guerrilla operation (Time 1972b). They took nine of their hostages, who were all members of the Israeli Olympic team, from the Olympic Village, killed two others, and captured world attention as their siege continued over the next twenty hours. Their political aims were to gain freedom for two hundred Arab prisoners in Israeli jails and, more broadly, to get international attention for their Palestinian cause. However, their actions caused outrage in many parts of the world and provoked Israeli retaliatory military strikes against suspected guerrilla bases in neighboring Arab countries. This violent invasion of the Games embarrassed the German Olympic hosts, who were trying to use this event to create a positive national image that would put the memory of the 1936 Olympics and Nazism out of people's minds. The tragic episode ended with the deaths of the Israeli hostages and five of the terrorists and the surrender of the remaining terrorists in a gun battle as the terrorists were en route to a plane that was supposed to be their means of escape. The response of Olympic officials was consistent with a past history of trying to sustain an image of the Games as apolitical. With many years of Olympic experience that went back to the 1936 Games, the IOC president in 1972, Avery Brundage, had to acknowledge the tragedy of the massacre but still asserted that "the Games must go on," leaving virtually no time for the Israelis to mourn their dead team members.

The political significance and impact of the behavior on the victory stand by the U.S. runners in 1972 did not match the political importance or implications of the massacre at the Munich Games, but this protest is noteworthy because it is reminiscent of a similar but much more highly publicized protest by two black U.S. runners at the 1968 Olympics in Mexico City (Lewis 2006). In fact, Matthews and Collett claimed that they were not staging a protest in 1972, even though Collett responded to the negative reaction of fans by raising his fist in a black power salute. The photo of a similar salute by gold medal winner Tommie Smith and bronze medal winner John Carlos on the victory stand in 1968 (see Nixon and Frey 1996:274) has become a prominent visual reminder of politics in the Olympics.

Smith had broken the world record in the two-hundred-meter race, and he and Carlos stood on the victory stand with their heads bowed, shoeless and

An Arab terrorist extends his hand as he talks with another terrorist, leaning from an upper window, during discussions with Munich chief of police Manfred Schreiber, far left, and West German Interior Minister Hans-Dietrich Genscher on September 5, 1972. They were outside the building of the Munich Olympic Village where thirteen Israeli team members were being held hostage by the Arab terrorists of the Black September movement. Nine of the Israeli hostages, five terrorists, and a German police officer died in a shoot-out at the airport when the terrorists tried to escape by plane. Two other members of the Israeli team died before the hostages were taken from the Olympic Village. This incident is known as the "Munich massacre." (AP Photo)

Extending gloved hands skyward in racial protest, U.S. athletes Tommie Smith, center, and John Carlos stare downward during the playing of the "Star Spangled Banner" after Smith received the gold and Carlos the bronze for the 200-meter run at the Summer Olympic Games in Mexico City on October 16, 1968. Smith and Carlos presented a powerful image of protest, which angered U.S. Olympic officials and caused their being banned from further Olympic competition. Australian silver medalist Peter Norman is at left. He supported Smith and Carlos, and as a result, was criticized by Australian Olympic officials and many of his countrymen. (AP Photo)

wearing black socks, and each with a black-gloved fist thrust upward. They also wore civil rights medals that reflected the influence of Harry Edwards and his Olympic Project for Human Rights (Leonard 1998). Edwards encouraged an African-American boycott of the 1968 Olympics and inspired the quiet but powerfully symbolic actions of Smith and Carlos to protest racism in U.S. sports and society. Their political statement was broadcast around the world, and predictably it outraged IOC officials, who interpreted it as an inappropriate injection of domestic politics into the Olympic arena. Smith and Carlos were sent home and lost their Olympic medals. An interesting but lesser-known aspect of this protest was that the silver medal winner in the two-hundred-meter race, Australian Peter Norman, also wore a civil rights badge during the medal ceremony and publicly expressed his sympathy for the cause Smith and Carlos represented. His gesture of solidarity resulted in a reprimand from Australian Olympic authorities, ostracism by the Australian media upon his return home, and exclusion from the 1972 Olympics, for which his performance during Olympic trials in his country seemed to qualify him (Lewis 2006). Thus, the mainstream media, as a key element of the Golden Triangle, appeared to share the same aversion to politics in the Olympics that was expressed by Olympic officials. This is predictable because the interests of the Golden Triangle are not served by political disruptions and challenges to authorities in sport or society.

Perhaps not as cleverly or well orchestrated for propaganda purposes as the Nazi Olympics in 1936 and certainly not as dramatic or deadly as the terrorism in 1972, Olympic boycotts have been more organized and more numerous than the kinds of individual protests occurring in 1968 and 1972. They have been matters of international politics carried out by national governments. Threatened and actual boycotts have spanned several decades of Olympic history. For example, in 1956, the boycott issues were the Soviet suppression of Hungarian resistance to Soviet occupation and military attacks of Egypt after its nationalization of the Suez Canal. In 1968, 1972, and 1976, the issue was sporting contacts with South Africa. In 1980, the United States boycotted the Moscow Games to punish the Soviets for their occupation of Afghanistan. In 1984, the Soviets and their allies boycotted the Los Angeles Olympics, ostensibly because of concerns about the safety of their athletes and anti-Soviet feelings in the United States but perhaps more importantly as retaliation against the U.S. boycott in 1980 and because the Soviets perceived the 1984 Games as the "Capitalist Olympics." The 1984 Los Angeles Games were organized for the first time by a private corporation instead of a city as Olympic rules stipulated (Nixon 1988a). The Soviet Union had stayed out of the Olympics until 1952 because it saw the Games as a tool of capitalist nations, but when they entered the Olympics, they tried to win to demonstrate the superiority of their ideology and way of life. North Korea boycotted in 1988, because it was not selected as cohost with South Korea for the Olympics that year.

The "Two Chinas" issue created a dilemma for IOC officials about whether to recognize the People's Republic of China or Taiwan or both. A civil war overthrew Nationalist Party control of China in 1949 and established the People's Republic of China (PRC), known simply as "China" today, with the Chinese Communist Party as the single ruling party of the nation. The Nationalists fled to the island of Taiwan, where they established a rival government called the "Republic of China." Vacillating decisions by the IOC, inviting the PRC in 1952 and recognizing Taiwan as the Chinese representative in 1956, led to a boycott by Taiwan in 1952 and by the PRC from 1956 until 1980 (Xiao 2004). China participated in the 1980 Winter Games in Lake Placid, New York, but boycotted the 1980 Moscow Olympics to protest the Soviet invasion of Afghanistan. The 1984 Summer Olympics was the first time since 1948 that a Chinese delegation representing opposing factions in the country had competed in the Games. The IOC awarded China the right to host the 2008 Games in Beijing, which reflected China's desire for greater global recognition of its emerging status as a world power. However, the prospect of a Chinese Olympics led Chinese intellectuals and dissidents to call on the government to honor a commitment to human rights that was consistent with the "Olympic spirit" and raised the specter of possible protests from people sympathetic to the Tibetan independence movement and possible boycotts by nations with human rights concerns in China (Cody 2007).

In a modified boycott, the Islamic Republic of Iran has prohibited its athletes from competing against Israelis in sports events because the Iranian govern-

Fans at the Los Angeles Memorial Coliseum display a banner proclaiming "To Russia with Love! Having a Great Time/Wish You Were Here/From All of Us" on Sunday, August 5, 1984. Following the American-led boycott of the 1980 Summer Olympics in Moscow, the Soviet-led boycott of the 1984 Summer Olympics caused Eastern Bloc countries and allies including the Soviet Union, Cuba, and East Germany to boycott these Olympics. These boycotts and the U.S. fans' displays are an example of politics and sport in the Olympics. (AP Photo/Rusty Kennedy)

ment has refused since its inception in 1979 to recognize the legitimacy of Israel's existence. This policy may have caused the Iranian world judo champion to report overweight and be disqualified from his first-round match against an Israeli in the 2004 Olympics in Greece. The Iranian news agency quoted him as saying he would not compete because he sympathized with the Palestinians in their conflict with the Israelis and did not recognize Israel as a nation (Kaufman 2004). Unlike the cases of the black U.S. runners, whose protests opposed their government and represented politics *in* the Olympics, this protest is an example of an athlete being used by his government to express its political ideology and thus represents politics *and* the Olympics.

Despite many instances of governmental and political "intrusions," the Olympics has had a consistent pattern of commercial growth, indicated by the increasing number and financial value of commercial sponsorships and the steady increases in media rights fees. For example, broadcast rights fees for the Summer Games increased from $400,000 in 1960, to $87 million in 1980, to $705 million in 2000, to $894 million in 2008. Rights fees for Winter Games increased from $50,000 in 1960, to $15.5 million in 1980, to $375 million in 1998, to $613 million in 2006 (Coakley 2007:415). The commercial growth of the Olympics reflects the growing partnership of sport, media, and corporate sponsors in the Olympic Golden Triangle. China's embrace of capitalism meant that this partnership would continue. Unlike the Soviet communists who organized the 1980 Moscow Games and were dedicated to a government-controlled socialist economy, Chinese political leaders welcomed and actively sought commercial investment by the Golden Triangle to support its 2008 Beijing Games. The ongoing global expansion of capitalism created sharply contrasting ideological climates and a very different political economy of the Olympic Games in communist-led China in 2008 than in the communist Soviet Union in 1980.

The most explicit example of political economy merging *democratic* politics and capitalist free enterprise economics in Olympic organizing was the 1984 "Capitalist Olympics" in Los Angeles (Nixon 1988a; Nixon and Frey 1996: 291–294). The LA Games were organized by the private Los Angeles Olympic Organizing Committee (LAOOC) with a relatively modest $500 million budget and with the intention of generating a surplus to be shared with USOC and amateur sports organizations in Southern California and elsewhere in the United States. The IOC had to accept this unprecedented organizational structure because Los Angeles voters had opposed public funding of the Games by a three-to-one margin and no other city was prepared to host the 1984 Summer Games. In contrast to a series of large deficits generated by prior Olympic Organizing Committees, the LAOOC produced a $250 million surplus. The surplus was made possible by a then-record $225 million media contract, over $125 million in commercial sponsorship money, and, despite the LA voters' sentiments to the contrary, a public contribution worth an estimated $100 million for security. Thus, part of the unique political economy of the LA Olympics was that democratic politics, in which local citizens rejected public financial responsibility for the Olympics, made it possible for the private LAOOC to employ a new businesslike and entrepreneurial approach as organizers of the Games. In the end, though, taxpayers still made a large contribution in police and security services. This is comparable to professional sports franchise owners' relying on public subsidies to offset their own costs and boost profits, but in the case of the LA Games, the voters formally opposed public financial investment.

The LA Games established a new standard for selling commercial rights to use the Olympic brand and they institutionalized corporate sponsorships as a major means of financing the Games. Since LA voters had voted against their city's Olympic proposal, the IOC was compelled to break its own rules about hosts and accept the LAOOC bid. It had no other bids from cities willing and able to host the 1984 Summer Games. The cost overruns and deficits incurred by previous Olympic hosts, especially in Montreal in 1976, scared away many other potential hosts. The expanded role of commercialism and the Golden Triangle made the 1984 LA "Capitalist Games" financially successful but was a source of controversy among Olympic purists and among those whose political ideology clashed with capitalism. The Soviet Union was particularly unhappy. The clashing ideologies of the United States and other democratic nations with their free enterprise capitalist economies and the Soviet bloc communist nations with their state-run socialist economies were often a source of political tension in Olympic history during the existence of the Soviet Union.

In 1984, the Soviet Union was not willing to see the Olympics used as an advertisement for capitalism, which was the antithesis of its own system. This kind of ideological opposition also kept the Soviet Union from participating in the Olympics until 1952. Early Soviet leaders were influenced by Marxist-Leninist ideology and viewed the Olympics as an instrument of capitalism. They believed that popular culture and spectator sports based on the commercialized and professional model in capitalist countries were a distraction from the serious matters of class struggle in their country (Edelman 1993). Through their ideological lens, spectator sports such as the Olympics were intended to make people in capitalist nations forget the exploitation and oppression of working people under capitalism, and in this way they strengthened the hold of capitalists over their workers and of political leaders over their citizens. Thus, in this sense, commercialized spectator sports were comparable to religion in Marxist thinking. Marx had referred to religion as an "opiate of the masses," which meant that it clouded people's vision and made them lose sight of their true class interest of class struggle against their capitalist oppressors. Political leaders in the early years of the Soviet Union were interested in sports and physical exercise for different reasons than spectator enjoyment or commercial profit. They promoted mass participation in physical activity to increase the health, fitness, productivity, and military readiness of Soviet citizens.

The Soviet leadership changed its view of sport under Stalin, and began to develop elite sports programs. It joined the Olympic Movement and first competed in the Olympics in 1952 with the clear political intention of showing the world the supremacy of its communist system. Soviet leaders promoted Olympic medal winners and other successful elite athletes as heroes and role models comparable to the heroes of industrial production in the factories, and they were used to educate people about the communist values of discipline, integrity, patriotism, military fitness, and acceptance of Soviet authority. According to Edelman (1993), the elite model of Soviet sport and the insistence on winning in international competition that began with Stalin did not satisfy Soviet citizens or accomplish its ideological purposes with them (Monaghan 1993). Soviet sports fans were generally unimpressed by the dominant Olympic performances of many of the Soviet athletes because they competed in sports that were relatively less popular in the Soviet Union. Government support of these sports diverted resources from the spectator sports, such as soccer, ice hockey, and basketball, that most interested them. Furthermore, fights on the field and among fans were common in Soviet sports, which political leaders attributed to "poor education" (Monaghan 1993). Thus, the response of Soviet citizens to elite spectator sports in their country helps us see that the common conception of a powerful totalitarian state and a passive citizenry in the Soviet Union was not completely accurate (Edelman 1993).

The contrast between political ideology and reality in the Soviet Union and in many other countries parallels the contradictions between Olympic ideals and realities that we have been examining. The Modern Olympic Games were envisioned as a gathering of athletes from around the world to compete for the joy of sport in an environment that fostered sportsmanship and international cooperation and peace. We have seen, though, that the Games allowed nationalistic displays from the outset and have frequently been exploited for political purposes by individuals, groups, and nations. The Games have also developed into large-scale and highly commercialized spectacles featuring now openly professional athletes that serve the interests of the Golden Triangle of

Olympic officials, the media, and corporate sponsors as well as host and participating nations.

Sustaining the Olympic Myth for Inspiration and Profit

I have argued elsewhere (Nixon 1988a) that although it has been largely untrue in Olympic history, the idealized conception of the Olympics—or the "Olympic myth"—that Olympic officials continue to espouse helps Olympic promoters maintain the popularity of the Games and further inflates the value of the Olympic brand. In addition, the people who host and organize an Olympics seem to believe that there is something special about the Olympics that will ensure social and economic benefits for their city and nation. Olympic media investors and corporate sponsors also seem to think that the mythical appeal of the Olympics will translate into prestige and profits, with large audiences of viewers and potential consumers. Some critics of the Olympics (e.g., Lenskyj 2000) have emphasized the self-serving behavior of Olympic organizers and officials, their excessive and extravagant spending, their unresponsiveness to local community needs, the financial and political scandals, and the instances of racism, sexism, and class elitism that have diluted or distorted the Olympic ideals. While recognizing these problems, other critical analysts have pointed to the capacity of these Games *as games* to capture our attention and have special significance for those who compete in them. For example, Cantelon (2002) wrote that a reason why the media are especially interested in the Olympics is "the authentic sense of enchantment embedded in Olympic competition" (104).

We are reminded again of Smart's argument about the power of sport's perceived authenticity, which is conveyed by the Olympic ideals and which Olympic promoters and investors have exploited for popular and commercial success. We seem to want the Olympic Games to be different from reality, that is, authentically pure sport played for noble reasons. This mythical conception is more uplifting, inspiring, and appealing than the political and economic realities. Yet paradoxically, we also seem to be drawn to the Olympics because of its nationalistic displays and the medals our nation wins, and we like the spectacle, with the opening and closing ceremonies often among the most popular parts of the Games for spectators and television viewers. In fact, the media have tailored their broadcast "feeds" for different audiences, and they have been criticized for being politically biased in their coverage and for catering to the patriotic feelings of their audiences (Nixon 1988a).

We should not be surprised that the media, as part of the Golden Triangle, might manipulate their portrayal and coverage of the Olympics in ways that they think will most appeal to their audience. As Cantelon (2002) suggested, understanding the Olympics requires an understanding of political economy and capitalist influence, and we have associated these patterns with the Golden Triangle. He also suggested that some critics missed the important distinction between Olympism as a sports movement and the Olympics as a capitalist business enterprise embedded in politics. The essential paradox of the Olympics is that both the mythical ideals and the crasser realities of politics, commerce, and the Golden Triangle coexist in the Games and contribute to their success. The Golden Triangle uses the myths to market the Olympics and compete for its share of the increasingly crowded and competitive global sports marketplace. In doing so, it sells its products, including its telecasts of the Olympics, official Olympic merchandise, and products advertised by "official Olympic sponsors," and it also sells the ideology of consumer capitalism.

In the contemporary political economy of the Olympics, the communist nation of China has turned toward capitalism and joined the Olympic Golden Triangle. The pressures of trying to compete internationally in sport and in the global marketplace of capitalism are likely to pose significant challenges for Chinese communist leaders. As suggested earlier, their restrictions of political freedom and civil rights are likely to be an increasing target for internal dissenters and external protest groups as China increases its visibility on the world stage in events such as the Olympics. Olympic officials and hosts have had relatively little success keeping politics out of the Olympics over its history.

The Olympics has been an especially prominent site for politics and economics to mix in sport because government leaders often use Olympic medals as the ultimate measure of the success of their nation's Olympic sports programs. Government sports officials and officials of governing bodies in sport have increasingly turned to corporate sponsors and corporate partners in the Golden Triangle to increase the funding of their Olympic sports programs. The Los Angeles Olympics provided a model for this kind of relationship. The expanded role of the Golden Triangle in the Olympics in 1984 prompted strong government criticism from the Soviet bloc nations, but in more recent years, the strongest criticisms of the relationship of sports to its capitalist partners in the Golden Triangle have come from nongovernmental organizations and protest groups. This contested terrain of sports has expanded beyond the boundaries of the Olympics, and the political challenges confronting the leaders of sport and their Golden Triangle partners have focused on a variety of issues and have come from a variety of sources. We will examine the contested terrain of sport from a sport *in* politics perspective in the next section.

Sport as Contested Terrain: Politics of Access in Sport

The people who run sports have faced challenges from critics and reformers who have seen racism and sexism in decisions and policies about who gets to play, how much it costs to play, who gets the most opportunities and resources, who gets covered by the media, who gets paid the most, and the names and mascots teams use. In previous chapters, we considered how sport has become contested terrain around these kinds of issues. They are issues involving allegations and practices of prejudice, discrimination, unfairness, and inequality. In recent years, we have read more about struggles over sports access for people with disabilities as their political voice has become louder. These struggles demonstrate the complexity of decisions and policies addressing matters of fairness. We recall from chapter seven that disabled athletes such as Tatyana McFadden have used the courts to try to compete against able-bodied opponents in mainstream high school track meets. On the international level, officials of the world governing body of track relied on researchers to tell them whether prosthetic legs unfairly advantaged a South

African runner who aspired to compete in the Olympics (Longman 2007). Both legs had been amputated below the knees in his infancy.

Past efforts by a Sport for the Disabled Movement to integrate athletes with disabilities into medal events in the Olympics have largely been unsuccessful (Nixon 2000:427). The International Paralympic Committee (IPC), which is the global governing body of the Paralympic Movement and the counterpart of the IOC in disability sports, has had more success in its negotiations with the IOC than disability activists have had. In 2001, the IPC signed an agreement with the IOC ensuring that its premier event, the Paralympic Games, would take place after the Olympics at the same venue as the Olympics and obligating the host Olympic city to host the Paralympics as well.[2] This cooperation between the two international sports governing bodies makes sense because the IPC was not trying to threaten the IOC or compete for its turf. Furthermore, the IPC has modeled its organization after the IOC as it has become more commercialized, sought more media coverage of the Paralympic Games, and made the Paralympics more elite.

The more elite IPC classification system, which has reduced the number of athletes eligible to compete in order to meet the organizational and media demands of a more commercialized Paralympics, has prompted criticism from those who favored wider participation opportunities for people with all levels of disability and ability in sport. Howe and Jones (2006) argued that increased IPC control over classification systems in disability sports has reduced the power of individual governing bodies in disability sport and of athletes. They also argued that the IPC's more elite approach to classification and the related disempowerment of disability sport organizations and athletes posed a serious threat to the IPC's own ideology of Paralympism. This ideology is characterized by the IPC motto "empower, inspire, achieve" (Howe and Jones 2006:31), and it emphasizes empowerment of a wide cross section of athletes with disabilities to serve as role models of achievement for other people with disabilities and to educate people in general about athletes with disabilities. However, the more elite classification system limited Paralympic participation to a smaller number of more elite athletes, which could be seen as a result of the IPC's desire to forge closer ties with the IOC and the Golden Triangle so that it could achieve more status for itself and more recognition for elite athletes with disabilities.

Sport as Contested Terrain: Challenging Sport and the Golden Triangle

Access for people with disabilities, members of other minority groups, and women is a major example of an issue in the contested terrain of sport that has pitted advocates for change against sports officials and governing bodies. Many other kinds of issues have spawned political tensions and direct confrontations between protesters or advocates of change and sports authorities. For example, Major League Baseball player Curt Flood went to the U.S. Supreme Court to challenge his sport's player reservation system, which allowed him to be traded without his approval (Nixon 1984:171). He failed, but in subsequent years, players in his sport and others organized in unions to challenge the power of the owners over players. In English soccer, fans have organized into

Independent Supporters Associations and have challenged the rapidly changing and increasingly commercialized culture of the sport (Nash 2000). For example, these fan groups have protested the rising prices of tickets and have
tried to influence the design of new stadiums to make them more attuned to
the needs of fans and the community. It was found that these groups tended
to have more influence over lower-status clubs than over wealthier and more
successful clubs (Nash 2000). Grassroots movements have also opposed public spending for stadiums and for the Olympics, and in a few cases, grassroots
movements of fans have tried to "save" a sports franchise that intended to move
or cease operations. For example, in Canada, fans organized to try to revive a
Canadian Football League franchise that had folded (Wilson and White 2002).
The Knight Commission is a prominent recent example of attempts to reform
college athletics in the United States that have spanned the past century and
tried to make college sports less violent, less commercialized, less corrupt, and
more consistent with educational objectives.

Title IX has often been a flash point for controversy and conflict in U.S. college sports, and a Title IX case involving a Supreme Court ruling revealed how
costly it can be for colleges and universities to retaliate against those who challenge them on this issue (Lipka 2007c). In 2005, the Supreme Court decided
that individuals who claim sex discrimination can sue for damages if their institution retaliates against them for confronting it with Title IX issues as a
"whistle-blower." This Supreme Court ruling was the legal basis for a jury decision that ordered California State University at Fresno to pay its former
women's volleyball coach $5.85 million. The university alleged that the coach
did not schedule enough tough matches, did not perform well enough in postseason play, and failed to attract enough spectators to matches, but the coach
convinced the jury that her firing was punishment for her long history of advocating for gender equity on her campus and that she was a victim of discrimination based on her gender and perceived sexual orientation. Although a university appeal could reduce the award, this case demonstrates that the law can
be a powerful tool to offset the imbalance in resources in political battles between individuals and large and powerful institutions in the Golden Triangle.
This particular case involved the use of legal power to try to get people in authority to change their behavior and follow the existing law. Other cases of politics in sport are about changing the law or other aspects of the structure of
sport, and they have involved collective action by groups and organizations.

Activists and advocates of change in sport have frequently construed issues
such as gender equity as moral or ethical matters of fairness related to civil
rights or basic human rights. Human rights activists have focused on people in
sport and have used sport to address a wide array of human rights issues. Along
with gender equity and women's rights, these issues have included apartheid in
South Africa, athletes' rights, children's rights, and workers' rights (Kidd and
Donnelly 2000). Some of these activists and advocates for change have taken a
relatively moderate approach and have worked "within the system" to bring
about change. Others have had more radical aims and have been more confrontational. An example of a more moderate approach to human rights and social change in sport is the work of Eli Wolff at Northeastern University's Sport
in Society Center.[3] Initially focused on rights and opportunities for people with
disabilities in sport, his work expanded to encompass human rights in and

through sport and the role of athletes and sport in bringing about local, national, and global social change. In his disability work, he has worked with the media to increase the visibility of athletes with disabilities, advised the NCAA on student-athlete disability issues, drafted a section of the United Nations (UN) Disability Treaty regarding the universal right of people with disabilities to participate in sport, and helped prepare a legal brief for the Supreme Court regarding golfer Casey Martin's effort to use a cart to participate in PGA events with his physical disability.

Working within the circles of power on behalf of a reputable organization such as the Sport in Society Center helped give Wolff political leverage in many of his actions. When the work of change agents resonates with established or widely accepted values *and* bolsters the status, image, popularity, or commercial success of sport, it understandably tends to be applauded by the power structure of sport and society. These kinds of change agents often move easily among powerful members of the Golden Triangle, and in some cases may even become part of it, as when the director of the Sport in Society Center at Northeastern became the institution's athletic director. Sometimes, however, efforts to bring about change split the Golden Triangle, as when advocates for American Indians worked with the NCAA leadership against certain NCAA member institutions to rid them of mascots, team names, logos, and merchandise that demeaned Indians. The antiapartheid movement also offers an example of a powerful sports organization acting against a member as a result of outside political influence. Activists influenced the IOC to ban South Africa from the Olympic Movement in 1964 as a result of its apartheid policies. In their effort to isolate apartheid South Africa from the rest of the sporting world, activists also inspired boycotts of events such as the Olympics where nations that continued to have sporting contacts with South Africa were competing. As I noted earlier in this chapter, the sports boycott was followed by a global economic boycott. The boycotts ended in the early 1990s with the end of apartheid and the approval of a new constitution giving all races equal rights, and South Africa was readmitted to the Olympic Movement in 1992.

Some cases of political activism in sport have targeted major corporations in the Golden Triangle doing business with sports organizations, athletes, and the sports public. Nike became a target of a global anti-sweatshop movement that opposed both the practices of specific transnational corporations and the broader processes of economic globalization or global capitalist expansion. Nike has been a major player in the Golden Triangle for several decades. In previous chapters, we considered its role in creating sports icons to sell its footwear, apparel, and equipment products; corporate philosophy; and marketing taglines. It has had a significant influence on the global culture and cultural economy of sport. It has also become very wealthy as a result of its sports business. There are over 6,500 sporting goods manufacturers, and Nike has been the richest and most powerful (Sage 2005). In 2007, for example, it set a new record with sales of $16 billion and profits of $1.5 billion (Associated Press 2007). Nike became a target of activists because of the way it generated its profits.

Nike and other transnational corporations have been criticized for operations in low-income countries. Like many major corporations today, Nike moved its factories from a wealthy capitalist nation, the United States, with its relatively expensive labor force and cost of operations, to parts of the world where wages were low and the political climate was favorable to its manufacturing, export, and profit-making aims. By 1998, approximately 450,000 workers at over 450 factories were making sporting goods for Nike in Southeast Asia in countries such as Indonesia, Vietnam, and China. When evidence began to surface that Nike paid its workers in these countries less than $1 per day, which was less than was needed for basic subsistence; that it employed children; and that it subjected workers to oppressive management and working conditions and long hours, it became the focus of the emerging antiglobalization and "anti-sweatshop" movements (Sage 2005).

Sage (1999) constructed a case study of the "Nike Transactional Advocacy Network" that was organized to protest Nike's behavior and try to get it to change its manufacturing practices in low-income nations. The network was spearheaded by activists who specifically opposed Nike for its labor practices but also opposed the general patterns of economic globalization in which workers in poor nations were exploited in the manufacturing of products for sale in richer nations. Their protests were aimed at global expansion of capitalism for profit and the neoliberal policies that allowed transnational corporations to operate virtually without constraint in many parts of the world. The Nike social movement was strengthened by its ties to labor organizations, religious organizations, human rights organizations, individual activists, and students. Students organized United Students Against Sweatshops (USAS) in 1998. The movement against Nike was the first global social movement to make extensive use of the Internet, and its political tactics included demonstrations, protests, editorial columns in newspapers, TV advertisements, sit-ins, and marches. It also urged consumers and sports organizations buying Nike products to boycott the company. Activists wanted Nike to pay workers a subsistence wage, provide safe working conditions, allow workers to organize, and respect the human rights of their workers. They hoped that their efforts would damage Nike's brand name and reputation enough to compel it to change its practices (Sage 1999, 2005).

According to Sage, the Nike movement became so effective that the Nike logo was associated with sweatshops and unfair labor practices for many consumers. The protests seemed to contribute to a sharp decline in Nike's earnings, which were also hurt by a dip in several Asian economies in the late 1990s, which reduced the earnings of many transnational corporations doing business in Asia at that time. As a result of the combination of the ongoing protests and declining profits, Nike executives began to change conditions in the production facilities. They increased the minimum age of factory workers, adopted U.S. Occupational Safety and Health Administration (OSHA) standards, expanded educational programs for workers, and increased monitoring of factory conditions. As a result of the protests, Nike also found that negotiations with some of its high-visibility customers had changed. USAS organized chapters at over two hundred universities by 2003, and student activists were able to persuade administrators at their schools and corporations to provide full disclosure of locations and labor practices of factories manufacturing products used by their university's sports teams and sold with its institutional logo. They also got commitments that manufacturers would adhere to a code of conduct for their workers and that universities would expect manufacturers to honor this commitment (Giddens, Duneier, and Appelbaum 2007:424–425).

The Nike case shows the far-reaching effects on the global economy of powerful corporate players in the Golden Triangle that derive their profits from our interest in sports-related products and the sports stars who help sell them. It also shows the amount of resources and the size and type of oppositional network needed to influence large and wealthy transnational corporations in the Golden Triangle and in the global economy. Recent record-breaking sales and earnings demonstrate the capacity of powerful transnational corporations to survive relentless pressure and recover from temporary downturns in their prestige and profits. Sage (2005) observed that "the Nike social movement showed that popular struggles can improve the plight of workers who labor under oppressive and unjust conditions in the global economy" (p. 373). However, he added that it was not clear whether Nike was more interested in improved public relations or in fundamental change, including increasing workers' wages and working conditions. Throughout the battle with its antagonists, Nike was able to spend huge sums of money for public relations to deflect criticism, protect its brand, and project an image of corporate social responsibility. It appeared to make concessions to protesters, but, as Sage observed, reports of wages and factory conditions revealed mixed results and the persistence of problems at many factories a few years after the Nike CEO announced changes in a "New Initiatives" speech.

The major corporate sponsors in the Golden Triangle tend to retain the loyalty of the athletes who endorse their products, despite political protests against these companies. For example, the Nike movement could not enlist the public support of famous athletes such as Michael Jordan who endorsed Nike products. Star athletes have been loyal to the companies whose products they endorse because these companies have helped make them rich and famous, and they have not wanted to risk losing the support of their sports-consuming fans by taking a controversial political stand. These athletes have generally tried to remain "apolitical," even though their failure to take a position on social issues or political candidates clearly reflects their political values. Michael Jordan took a political position when he failed to speak out against Nike sweatshops. Rising NBA star LeBron James, who was also a "Nike star," took a political position when he did not sign a petition that was signed by nearly all his teammates calling for China to support United Nations action to defuse the genocidal violence in Darfur (Leitch 2007). Both Jordan and James chose to make commercial values and their business interests a higher priority than human rights. Star athletes may be more likely to take political stands on issues involving the *politics of brands* than on social issues.

Branding is a big issue in the commercial world of Golden Triangle sports, and star athletes sometimes choose to defy the sponsor of their sport by displaying a brand they personally endorse. For example, the press considered it to be a powerful political statement when NASCAR driver Jamie McMurray drank a Coke, the product of one of his sponsors, after winning the Pepsi 400, and when NFL star Brian Urlacher wore a hat with a brand name that competed with the Super Bowl sponsor Gatorade during Super Bowl Week (Leitch 2007). Even Michael Jordan, who steered away from the sweatshop issue, engaged in the politics of brands as a member of the 1992 Olympic "Dream Team" when he refused to appear on the victory stand wearing the red, white, and blue U.S. warm-up suit with the logo of official Olympic sponsor Reebok. He compromised by wearing the team clothing but covering its logo with the U.S. flag. He drew some harsh criticism from the press for being more concerned about representing Nike than about representing his country, but he asserted, "I do not believe in endorsing my competition. . . . I feel strongly about loyalty to my own company" (quoted in LaFeber 2002:100).

The world in which Nike, star athletes, and others in the Golden Triangle operate and prosper is described by Barber's (2006) term *McWorld*. He coined the term to refer to the globalization of politics through forces such as the McDonaldization of organizations and culture and the influence of the market imperatives of capitalism. This world is focused on profits and expanding markets, and according to Barber, "Human rights are needed to a degree [in McWorld], but not citizenship or participation—and no more social justice and equality than are necessary to promote efficient economic production and consumption" (456). The rationalistic, capitalistic, and antidemocratic imperatives of McWorld explain the suspicions and concerns of antiglobalization activists about the ultimate motives of Nike and other powerful transnational corporations (e.g., see Giddens, Duneier, and Appelbaum 2007:424–425, 678–681). These suspicions and concerns are consistent with the analysis of capitalism and globalization by sport sociologists with critical Marxist and neo-Marxist perspectives (Beamish 2002).

As capitalist enterprises, Nike and the other dominant actors in the Golden Triangle are obligated to respond to the interests and wishes of owners or stockholders, which usually involve maximizing stock values, profits, and dividends. The star athletes they hire to endorse their products are generally loyal to them and the commercial values of McWorld, while being reluctant to question their sponsors' political actions. By pursuing their own economic and political interests, the most powerful and famous actors in the Golden Triangle McWorld may ignore or blatantly disregard values of social responsibility. Governments can constrain corporations and compel them to comply with laws and regulations that make them act more socially responsible. However, in a climate of neoliberalism, which gives capitalists and corporations considerable freedom, governments are not inclined to do much to constrain them. In addition, since they operate across national borders, transnational enterprises are difficult for governments to monitor or control, which is why global social movements and global nongovernmental organizations may be more likely than governments to monitor these transnational corporations and hold them responsible for their actions.

Sport, Green Politics, and the Future

Nongovernmental organizations (NGOs) exist outside government as private organizations. Many are focused on social issues, are international in scope (INGOs), and have a mission of social justice or social change (Giddens, Duneier, and Appelbaum 2007:170–171, 678–681). Change-oriented NGOs and INGOs are often part of networks with local grassroots organizations and voluntary associations. INGOs include world health organizations such as Doctors Without Borders, human rights organizations such as Amnesty International and Human Rights Watch, and various environmental organizations associated with the "green movement" such as Greenpeace and Friends of the Earth. Although they lack the legal power of national governments, some have been able to attract global interest in their causes, influence world opinion, and effectively pressure governments and corporations to change. The Nike social movement illustrates the range of strategies and tactics these kinds of organizations use to accomplish their aims. In a world where transactions among people are increasingly crossing national borders, organizations structured to operate across borders are especially well suited to pursue the global politics needed to achieve their missions and goals. We will explore in this section how the global green movement may be connected to sport and how it might shape the future of sport, including how, where, and by whom it is played in the future.

The global green movement is an example of a "new social movement," which is distinguished by a broad agenda for change, including extensive cultural changes as well as changes in the distribution of resources or power (Giddens, Duneier, and Appelbaum 2007:422–423). The Global Greens is an international network of green political parties and social movements around the world (Global Greens 2001). The well-known slogan "think globally, act locally" captures its activist approach. According to the charter of the Global Greens (2001), the basic mission of this movement challenges the "dogma of economic growth" and the patterns of production and consumption it creates, which are central aims of McWorld. Members of the green movement identify a long list of problems associated with the pursuit of short-term profits by McWorld and the pursuit of national interests by national governments, including environmental degradation, the extinction of species, human exploitation, social injustice, racism, poverty, corruption, crime, and violence. They have tried to protect the natural environment and various endangered species, conserve the world's natural resources, and create policies such as biodiversity and sustainable development. The green movement and Green Party politicians have pursued their aims through electoral politics within nations and confrontational but nonviolent global political strategies. It should be evident that their conception of the world conflicts with the basic ideology, interests, and behavior of McWorld and the Golden Triangle.

A major issue of the green movement in recent years has been global warming and climate change. Although many politicians, corporate leaders, and even scientists initially rejected the idea of global warming, it is now much more widely accepted. U.S. climate policy is now explicitly focused on reducing the ratio of greenhouse gas emissions to economic output, funding a variety of initiatives to support the science and technology of climate change, and encouraging public-private partnerships to reduce the release of greenhouse gas into the atmosphere (EPA 2007). Greenhouse gases such as carbon dioxide are produced when we burn coal, oil, and gas, and global warming occurs because the accumulation of these gases in our atmosphere acts like the glass of a greenhouse, which allows the sun's rays to enter but not escape the atmosphere. As a result, the earth has been getting warmer, which threatens to produce a number of detrimental consequences for life on earth. National and global efforts to address this issue have been complicated by political conflicts in legislatures and among governments about how much new regulations controlling greenhouse gas emissions would cost businesses (e.g., see Lieberman and McCain 2003).

Olympic organizers and the IOC have addressed environmental issues in the Olympics for a number of years (e.g., see Cantelon and Letters 2000; Lesjø 2000), and in 2007, *Sports Illustrated* published a cover story about global warming (Wolff 2007). It is likely that many of its readers had not previously given much thought to how this issue related to sport. This story identified a number of ways sport has already been affected by global warming and by other kinds of change in the natural environment and suggested how sport may be affected by environmental change in the future. Some of the effects of environmental change are limited to specific sports, while others have much broader implications that stretch beyond sport. For example, melting ice caps and warmer oceans are major effects of global warming, which could endanger coastal areas where many sports teams play and sports fans live, as these coastal areas are flooded. We got a glimpse of this kind of effect from a different weather-related cause, when Hurricane Katrina flooded New Orleans in 2005, causing the relocation of the local population and local sports teams. Relocations caused by global warming would be permanent.

Warmer temperatures have led to the migration of certain species to new habitats, which has led to environmental damage in some cases. For example, beetles attracted by somewhat warmer temperatures have found new homes in ash forests in the Northeast and destroyed many of the ash trees used to make high-quality Major League Baseball bats. Warmer temperatures and less snow have threatened the financial survival of many ski slopes and resorts at lower elevations. With their heavy reliance on energy sources that produce greenhouse gases, sports arenas and stadiums will be compelled to use new designs that are more energy efficient in the future. We can look at NASCAR's "Car of Tomorrow" in part as a reflection of concerns about energy costs and efficiency in motor sports. Influenced by changing attitudes about the environment and pressure from a global antigolf movement (Maguire, Jarvie, Mansfield, and Bradley 2002:92–95), golf course architects, developers, and owners have taken steps to be more environmentally responsible. They have used new biofuels for energy, adopted conservation measures, avoided pesticides, recycled, and created natural environments that contribute to biodiversity by supporting various kinds of plants and animals.

The environment is a major issue for China in its preparations for the 2008 Beijing Olympics. China's rapid economic development in the late twentieth and early twenty-first centuries was accompanied by a significant and dangerous increase in air pollution caused by more cars and more factories. Concerned that air pollution would endanger the health of athletes, IOC officials made acceptance of China's bid to host the Olympics contingent on a commitment to improve air quality. There was a genuine basis for this concern, as the air during the 2006 Hong Kong Marathon was thick with smog, which caused twenty-two runners to be hospitalized with pollution-related symptoms. To address this issue, the Chinese government had many local businesses replace coal with natural gas as their source of energy, and it relocated a number of factories that relied on fossil fuels many miles away from the Olympic site. The London hosts of the 2012 Games are already making plans for a greener Olympics, with buses powered by alternative fuels and rules keeping private automobiles away from Olympic venues (Wolff 2007).

The environmental politics of the Olympics demonstrates how powerful sports organizations can influence governments to bring about social changes, at least for a particular event in a particular location at a particular time. According to Cantelon and Letters (2000), the increasing importance of environmental issues in the global political arena in the early 1990s made IOC officials more receptive to concerns about the environmental effects of their mega-events. However, the IOC had little experience dealing with global environmental issues and could offer little practical guidance in environmental planning to local organizers. As a result, the 1992 Winter Games in Albertville, France, had a number of adverse environmental effects, which were strongly criticized by environmentalists. For example, the large-scale construction projects at the various Olympic venues in the Albertville region permanently carved up the landscape, transformed the natural environment, and damaged the ecosystem in the area. A global network of environmentalists used media interest in the Albertville Games to draw attention to the environmental damage caused by construction for these Games and to reinforce their general message about the environmental problems caused by such mega-events.

IOC officials were concerned that Albertville had blemished the Olympic reputation and brand. They knew that future Olympics had to be more environmentally friendly than Albertville was, but they lacked the knowledge and experience to ensure that this would happen. Cantelon and Letters argued that without the fortuitous choice of Lillehammer, Norway, to host the Winter Games two years after Albertville, the IOC would have continued to flounder in providing environmental direction to local Olympic organizers. The Norwegians organized a "Green Olympics," which provided the organizing model Olympic officials needed to guide future hosts. I will use a case study of the Lillehammer Games to demonstrate how planning and staging sports mega-events (Horne and Manzenreiter 2006) can be shaped by the contemporary politics of the environment and the power relations in the social network of individuals, groups, and organizations involved in event organizing.

According to Lesjø (2000), a commitment to being the "Green Games" was not part of Lillehammer's official Olympic bid. The Lillehammer Olympic bid proposed the "Compact Games," with all venues located in a small city as opposed to a wide geographical region, which had been the case in Albertville. The idea of the "Green Games" emerged after the bid was approved, and it emerged over a number of years from the interplay of various parties in a complex network of power relations. This network included the Norwegian prime minister, who had been chairperson of a UN environmental commission that had issued a major report on sustainable development and the environment while she was chair. She brought attention to the environmental issue when she presented the IOC with Lillehammer's bid to host the 1992 Winter Games. The network also included the Norwegian environmental ministry, which pushed for an environmental emphasis in the Games. However, according to Lesjø, the most influential environmental actors in this network were local grassroots activists representing the Norwegian Environmental Organization. The environment did not become a formal or public priority in the Games until the local activists pushed for this emphasis. They put pressure on the Lillehammer Olympic Organizing Committee (LOOC), its business clients, and IOC officials, and they pushed for protective environmental measures in the location of venues and in construction projects.

Lesjø used the term *co-optation* to describe the relationship between the environmental activists and the Olympic organizers. Co-optation implies that organizations accept potentially troubling or dangerous outsiders into their midst in order to control them and protect the organization from destabilizing disruption or change. In this case, the local activists were given access to some aspects of the agenda-setting process and were able to make recommendations, but they had no formal authority over final decisions. Even without formal authority, though, the activists were able to exercise power within the planning network. The LOOC was pressured into working with environmental activists after years of resistance because it was facing pressure from the IOC and the government ministry of the environment as well. The possibility of favorable media publicity also influenced their shift to an emphasis on the "Green Games." Environmentalists manipulated these aspects of the political context to their advantage, and the IOC and LOOC officials ultimately embraced the Green Games and environmentalism to show how environmentally responsible they were. Thus, in cases of co-optation, the original intentions and goals of outsiders may be blunted to some extent, but the co-opted outsiders also are given a chance to exercise influence that they may not have had if they had remained entirely outside the organization and its structure of decision making.

The IOC supported the environmentalists because it was sensitive to possible environmental criticism after the Albertville Games, and it saw an opportunity to enhance the Olympic image. Lesjø noted, however, that the IOC's approach to the environment was a moderate "light green." Their marketing strategy was "corporate environmentalism," which was compatible with the basic dependence of the Olympics and Olympic organizers on corporate support and the Golden Triangle. The IOC was not likely to develop an environmental ethic that reflected the radical critique of corporate and consumer capitalism advanced by the Global Greens, for example. The concept of "corporate environmentalism" implies awareness among IOC officials that their environmental commitment was restrained by their dependence on corporate investment. IOC officials' light green embrace of this green issue may have been motivated primarily to deflect public criticism and create an *image* of social responsibility, and it is unlikely that it was meant to pose any kind of serious challenge or threat to the basic policies or behavior of their corporate investors or their relationship to them.

The local activists involved in the Lillehammer planning network may not have satisfied the demands of the most radical environmental critics of the Olympics as a mega-event or fundamentally changed the structure of the Olympic Golden Triangle. However, they were successful in getting the LOOC to shift its primary planning focus from the Compact Games to the Green Games. Furthermore, IOC officials were so impressed by the media and public reaction to the Green Games that they added the environment as one of the core tenets of the Olympic Movement. Although their strategy of corporate environmentalism may not imply a deep commitment to fundamental social change, the formal adoption of an environmental ethic now places the IOC in a position of having to demonstrate that this commitment is real, which could pose problems when environmental concerns conflict with the corporate policies and practices of sponsors and investors (Lesjø 2000). The Beijing Games of 2008 are a test of this commitment.

There may have been some unique aspects of the Lillehammer Games related to their timing and location, but Lesjø's study of these Games casts light on more general patterns linking sport, politics, economics, and society. It shows how networks of power relations among people in government, sport, business, the media, and the community can shape the plans and decisions for mega-events in sport. In the case of Lillehammer, the initial rational planning process was significantly altered by the politics of the environment. The politics of the environment can be problematic for the Golden Triangle because its mega-events are large-scale national or international events that are televised around the world and depend on global media and corporate promotion and substantial corporate investment (Horne and Manzenreiter 2006). The scale of these events, the large construction projects they may require, and the large crowds they attract could result in significant environmental damage.

Lillehammer showed that political activists can transform the planning and staging of sports mega-events when they build political ties with other political actors from more established realms of power such as government and the Golden Triangle and take advantage of a political climate favoring their cause. The politics of the Lillehammer Games occurred in a context where there were an environmentally conscious host city and nation, a recent history of environmental disaster in the Olympics, and increasing global concern about environmental issues. The prominence of the air pollution issue in planning the 2008 Beijing Olympics shows that green politics is likely to remain a major planning issue in the future for organizers of sports mega-events such as the Olympics. Sports officials in the future may routinely face difficult decisions that force them to balance environmental demands against the desire for fans to have accessible and attractive places to view sports and the interests of corporate sponsors and investors only willing to make voluntary concessions to the environment if it helps their bottom line (Maguire, Jarvie, Mansfield, and Bradley 2002:85–92).

Conclusion: Contemporary Forces of Change and the Future of Sport

This final chapter has addressed the most pervasive and important themes that have been threaded throughout the book and given it coherence. We have considered inequality, power, globalization, and the dominant influence of the Golden Triangle in the global cultural economy of sport. We have seen that powerful forces of sociodemographic, organizational, economic, political, and technological change have spread across the world and transformed how sport is organized, who gets a chance to play, who can afford to watch, and how sport, sports stars, and other sports products are constructed, marketed, and sold to sports consumers. In some ways, these change processes have facilitated capitalist commercial expansion and pursuit of profits by the generic Golden Triangle. In other cases, they have pressed the Golden Triangle to alter its actions, policies, or image to increase or avoid losing its hold over the sports public and consumers. These forces of change have also created a variety of new social issues for the Golden Triangle to address, from ethnic diversity to biodiversity, from McDonaldization to alternative sports, and from new media to new technologies for cheating.

In the changing world of sport, children and youths have had increasing opportunities to play sports at a "high level" and fans have had a variety of new ways to access sports, but the opportunities and access have been affected by the economic status of families and fans. High school sports have increasingly moved in the direction of corporate and commercialized college sports. College sports have continued along their commercial path, but the NCAA and individual institutions have had to pay more attention to women, minorities, and academic achievement of athletes. The major professional sports have gotten richer, and their stars have also gotten richer as they have cashed in on their fame to sign lucrative endorsement contracts. A variety of professional sports now crowd the sports landscape and vie for media coverage and sponsor and consumer dollars. The political economy of financing sports facilities has brought professional sports into the political arena as leagues and owners have sought public financing to help them make more profit for themselves. The dependence of sports stars on the Golden Triangle for their wealth and fame has made most of these stars reluctant to step into politics, unless it involves their personal career or earning potential. Some professional, big-time college, and Olympic athletes have broken rules to get more of the rewards of the Golden Triangle, and some have broken the law, causing embarrassment for themselves and their sport and problems for the sports officials, coaches, and society that must deal with their deviance. The Olympics has grown along with the rest of the Golden Triangle, and the politics of the Olympics has gotten more complicated in recent years. Having bowed to professionalism and still faced with the politics of nationalism and protest, Olympic officials and organizers now have to deal with new social movements such as the green movement that have pressured them to become more socially responsible.

The generic Golden Triangle has seemed to adapt fairly well to the changing world, if we use increasing media coverage, expanding markets, and bigger profits as major indicators of its success. Certainly, these are the measuring sticks the dominant players in the Golden Triangle use, since they are driven by capitalist, market-oriented, McWorld goals. However, in the political environment of contemporary sports, there are dangerous and militant new forces to address along with the contested terrain created by more moderate old and new social movements. In his analysis of contemporary world politics, Barber (2006) contrasted McWorld with "Jihad." The term *jihad* literally means holy war or hostile acts against an enemy, and it has been used in recent years to refer to the militant actions by radical Muslims in defense of a fundamentalist form of Islam. Barber used the term to represent the forces in the contemporary world that are diametrically opposed to the forces of globalization represented by McWorld. McWorld seeks to make the world a single commercially and culturally unified global marketplace tied together by modern markets, communication, and technology. In McWorld, national borders and identities are meaningless.

Of course, nations and nationalism still matter in the world today. For example, although it inhabits McWorld and seeks to expand its business as widely as possible in the global sports marketplace, the Golden Triangle still exploits national governments, identities, and differences for its political and commercial purposes. While the Golden Triangle might use national or ethnic pride to sell its products, it has no interest in deepening cleavages or causing hostility among nations or ethnic or religious groups in nations or the world. It needs a more peaceful setting in which to do business. In contrast, Jihadists have no interest in promoting a peaceful world, international cooperation, or coexistence among warring factions within nations. According to Barber, the forces of Jihad are aimed at dividing or "retribalizing" large parts of the world by nationality, ethnicity, or religion, and they have used war and terrorism to accomplish their divisive aims. The Black September terrorism at the 1972 Olympics illustrates this kind of politics in sport. The attack of the United States on September 11, 2001 (or "9/11"), and subsequent terrorist attacks by Islamic extremists in Spain, England, and other countries symbolize the contemporary level of hostility of Jihad toward the countries where McWorld is dominant.

Terrorist tactics have been used by various groups and even nations for political ends, but the terrorism and other kinds of hostile actions in the battle of Jihad versus McWorld described by Barber are especially relevant to the sports world we have been examining in this book. The ideological hostility and violence of Jihad against McWorld is also a threat to the Golden Triangle, since the Golden Triangle is a highly visible symbol of McWorld. The ideology and actions of Jihad are a threat to the power, cultural legitimacy, and economic and organizational rationale of the Golden Triangle and, more generally, are a threat to the legitimacy of modern sport as a rational, corporate, and highly commercialized enterprise. As in the case of the 1972 Olympics, sports megaevents may be convenient venues for playing out Jihadist politics or the broader politics of Jihad versus McWorld. These kinds of acts may not be so narrowly focused on a specific nation, such as Israel, in the future, since many nations are the enemies of Jihad.

One of the concrete indicators of the growing concern about this kind of threat in modern sport is the increasing cost of security for major sports events. This is not the kind of world envisioned by Baron de Coubertin when he founded the Modern Olympics in 1896. It is important to remember, though, that while people in nations dominated by McWorld may fear and despise Jihad as reactionary, fanatical, morally reprehensible, and dangerous, people in the nations and regions dominated by Jihad have similar attitudes toward McWorld. Part of the attraction of militant Islamic Jihadist movements such as Hezbollah, which operates in a very divided Lebanon and contributes to its divisions, is that they inspire ethnic pride and a strong sense of community among their followers, who receive education, social welfare, and other services from the movement. For these followers of a Jihadist movement, terrorists are not seen in negative terms, but instead are lionized as courageous freedom fighters and defenders of their cause.

Jihad and McWorld are pushing the world in opposite directions, much as glocalization and grobalization represent opposing forces of change. There are no bridges across diversity in a world dominated by Jihad, as particular nations and ethnic and religious groups seek ideological and political dominance over others and their way of life. Their ideology directly clashes with the McWorld ideology of modernism and capitalist development. The cultural and economic globalization driven by McWorld spreads market economics and popular consumer culture around the world, which Jihadists see as a direct threat to their traditional cultural ideals.

According to Barber, McWorld is like Jihad in one noteworthy respect. It is not focused on making the world more democratic. Neither Jihad nor McWorld needs democracy and neither seeks it. Jihad has little interest in cooperation or compromise with its enemies, and McWorld operates according to a corporate bureaucratic and capitalist model oriented to rational decision making and the pursuit of profit, which leaves little room for democratic values or participatory decision making. In fact, transnational corporations often find it more expedient and profitable to do business with autocratic than with democratic political leaders because they do not have to worry about building popular consensus for their business activities (Barber 2006:456).

Thus, in the post-9/11 political climate of McWorld versus Jihad, the Golden Triangle is not likely to spread democracy, but it will be responsive to politics and political movements to the extent that they threaten its image, popularity, profitability, power, or stability. The case study of Lillehammer, the politics of pollution and the Beijing Olympics, increased attention to security at sports mega-events, and tougher anti-doping policies and enforcement in response to congressional scrutiny are different kinds of examples that illustrate this point. Just as Olympic leaders failed in their efforts to "keep politics out of the Olympics," the powerful people and organizations that dominate the Golden Triangle cannot keep global, national, or local politics or the other major social forces of change out of their sports world because sport is interwoven with society. Similarly, government leaders are likely to find that it may be difficult to stifle the appeal of modern sport, prevent the sometimes-violent behavior of some of its most ardent supporters, or keep sport from influencing their politics. At times, political leaders impose their ideology on sport, despite possible sanctions from sports officials and other nations, as in the continuing support for apartheid by South Africa in the face of a global sports boycott and then a global economic boycott or in the Iranian prohibition of competition against Israel. In South Africa, global political pressure forced the leaders to change. Sometimes political leaders who place a high value on sport and use it to advance their political ideology find that the conflicting realities of sport force them to compromise their ideological principles, as when Cuban leaders bent their commitment to socialism in baseball to rescue the sport from threats to its viability or success. The case of Iranian women in the soccer stadium, which we considered in a "Sport in the News" feature in chapter five, showed that ideology, politics, and sport can mix in complicated ways for political leaders trying to uphold very traditional ideologies in the face of modern influences in sport.

My analysis of the power of the Golden Triangle showed its influence over popular culture and its capacity to create compelling and seemingly authentic images of sport that make it an oasis, field of dreams, or fantasyland for sports fans and consumers. We have seen that sport is both image and reality. In this and previous chapters, we have seen that the Golden Triangle and the sports world it constructs are very real and have real effects. The major social issues, problems, and conflicts of the larger world penetrate the sports arena, and the major social forces that transform societies around the globe also transform sport. Specific predictions of the future by sociologists and other social scientists are notoriously unreliable, and I have no crystal ball for predicting exactly how sport will change. People stop doing things they have done in the past, they reverse course, and new and totally unexpected events happen and innovations are invented that transform historical trends. Nevertheless, I still feel confident in predicting that the Golden Triangle will continue to dominate the world of big-time sports on a global level and even to influence sports that are played at the international level in the Jihad-dominated parts of the world. Nationalism will coexist with globalization to make sports both relevant to national identity and useful for political purposes, and, especially, important for economic reasons.

The Golden Triangle will find that its commercial purposes, capitalist imperative of growth, and economic and political actions will be increasingly challenged by an assortment of antiglobalization, human rights, equal rights, and environmental activists. A more threatening challenge could come indirectly or directly from the forces of Jihad, which could disrupt the stability of world financial markets, free trade, the free flow of communication, and democratic institutions that allow the Golden Triangle to pursue growth and profits without interference. Jihad could also make it increasingly unsafe to stage the mega-events that are the premier showcase of the Golden Triangle. Since the sports and events of the Golden Triangle are such prominent symbols of McWorld and the global cultural economy, the complex and dynamic interplay of sport, politics, and economics on the global level should provide useful clues about how society will change in the future. Thus, sport in a changing world is ultimately about how the world is changing.

Notes

1. The Summer Games have been held every four years since 1896, except during the world wars in 1916 and in 1940 and 1944. The Winter Games were held every four years between 1924 and 1992, with the exception of 1940 and 1944. They have been held every four years since 1994, since Olympic officials wanted to stagger the schedules of the Winter and Summer Games. For the sake of brevity, instead of referring to Winter or Summer Games, I will refer to the host city and year in most cases.

2. Factual information about the IPC and the Paralympic Games was derived from the IPC website.

3. Information about the center's work can be found at its website, http://www.sportinsociety.org.

References

AAUP. 2007. *Financial Inequality in Higher Education: The Annual Report on the Economic Status of the Profession, 2006–2007*, March–April. Retrieved April 27, 2007 (http://www.aaup.org).

Adler, Patricia A., and Peter Adler. 1991. *Backboards and Blackboards: College Athletes and Role Engulfment.* New York: Columbia University Press.

Adler, Patricia A., and Peter Adler. 1998. *Peer Power: Preadolescent Culture and Identity.* New Brunswick, NJ: Rutgers University Press.

Alesia, Mark. 2006a. "Colleges Play, Public Pays." *Indianapolis Star*, March 30. Retrieved April 2, 2006 (http://www.indystar.com).

Alesia, Mark. 2006b. "Tourney Money Fuels Pay-to-Play Debate." *Indianapolis Star*, April 1. Retrieved April 2, 2006 (http://www.indystar.com).

Alexander, Donald L., and William Kern. 2004. "The Economic Determinants of Professional Sports Franchise Values." *Journal of Sports Economics* 5:51–66.

Alsever, Jennifer. 2006. "A New Competitive Sport: Grooming the Child Athlete." *New York Times*, June 25. Retrieved October 1, 2006 (http://www.hyper-parenting.com/nytimes16.htm).

Amdur, Neil. 1971. *The Fifth Down: Democracy and the Football Revolution.* New York: Delta.

Anderson, Elijah. 1999. *The Code of the Street: Decency, Violence, and the Moral Life of the Inner City.* New York: W.W. Norton.

Anderson, Kristin L. 1999. "Snowboarding: The Construction of Gender in an Emerging Sport." *Journal of Sport & Social Issues* 23:55–79.

Andrews, David L. 1996. "The Fact(s) of Michael Jordan's Blackness: Excavating a Floating Racial Signifier." *Sociology of Sport Journal* 13:125–158.

Andrews, David L. 2000. "Posting Up: French Post-Structuralism and the Critical Analysis of Contemporary Sporting Culture." Pp. 106–137 in *Handbook of Sports Studies*, edited by J. Coakley and E. Dunning. London: Sage Publications.

Andrews, David L., Ben Carrington, Steven L. Jackson, and Zbigniew Mazur. 1996. "Jordanscapes: A Preliminary Analysis of the Global Popular." *Sociology of Sport Journal* 13:428–457.

Arenson, Karen W. 2006. "Duke Grappling with Impact of Scandal on Its Reputation." *New York Times*, April 7, p. A14.

Aris, Stephen. 1990. *Sportsbiz: Inside the Sports Business.* London: Hutchinson.

Arms, Robert L., Gordon W. Russell, and Mark L. Sandilands. 1987. "Effects on Hostility of Spectators of Viewing Aggressive Sports." Pp. 259–263 in *Sport Sociology:*

Contemporary Themes, 3rd ed., edited by A. Yiannakis, T.D. McIntyre, M. Melnick, and D.P. Hart. Dubuque, IA: Kendall/Hunt.

Associated Press. 2004. "Gay Athletes Keep Orientation to Themselves." *Chicago Sun Times*, August 17. Retrieved July 10, 2006 (http://www.suntimes.com).

Associated Press. 2005. "Pacers' Jackson: Dress Code Is 'Racist.'" *MSNBC.com*, October 20. Retrieved January 16, 2007 (http://www.msnbc.msn.com).

Associated Press. 2006. "Iran Bars Women from Attending Soccer Matches." Retrieved June 12, 2006 (http://soccernet.espn.go.com).

Associated Press. 2007. "Nike Profits Jump in Latest Quarter." *kgw.com*, June 27. Retrieved July 11, 2007 (http://www.kgw.com).

Astor, Michael. 2005. "Arrest Made in Brazil Soccer Scandal." *USA Today*, September 30. Retrieved June 23, 2007 (http://www.usatoday.com).

Atkinson, Michael, and Brian Wilson. 2002. "Bodies, Subcultures and Sport." Pp. 375–395 in *Theory, Sport & Society*, edited by J. Maguire and K. Young. Amsterdam: JAI/Elsevier Science Imprint.

Babbie, Earl R. 2007. *The Practice of Social Research*, 11th ed. Belmont, CA: Wadsworth.

Bahramitash, Roksana. 2004. "Myths and Realities of the Impact of Political Islam on Women: Female Employment in Indonesia and Iran." *Development in Practice* 14:508–520.

Baird, Katherine E. 2005. "Cuban Baseball: Ideology, Politics, and Market Forces." *Journal of Sport & Social Issues* 29:164–183.

Ball, Donald. 1976. "Failure in Sport." *American Sociological Review* 41:726–739.

Baltimore Sun. 2007a. "NFL Notes." *Baltimore Sun*, January 23, p. 4C.

Baltimore Sun. 2007b. "Former NBA Player Comes Out." *Baltimore Sun*, February 8. Retrieved February 8, 2007 (http://www.baltimoresun.com).

Baltimore Sun. 2007c. "Off the Court: Amaechi." *Baltimore Sun*, May 6, p. 3D.

Baltimore Sun. 2007d. "Materazzi Reveals Insult to Zidane." *Baltimore Sun*, August 19, p. 4D.

Baltimore Sun. 2007e. "Et Cetera: Soccer." *Baltimore Sun*, August 22, p. 4E.

Barber, Bernard. 2006. "Jihad vs. McWorld." Pp. 449–459 in *Readings for Sociology*, 5th ed., edited by G. Massey. New York: W.W. Norton.

Barker, Jeff. 2007a. "Congressman Thinks Colleges Should Pay Athletes." *Baltimore Sun*, May 2. Retrieved May 9, 2007 (http://www.baltimoresun.com).

Barker, Jeff. 2007b. "Ex-NFL Players Tell It to Congress." *Baltimore Sun*, June 27. Retrieved June 27, 2007 (http://www.baltimoresun.com).

Bartter, Jessica. 2006. *Keeping Score When It Counts: Assessing the 2006–2007 Bowl-Bound College Football Teams*. The Institute for Diversity and Ethics in Sport. Orlando: University of Central Florida.

Bartter, Jessica. 2007. *Academic Progress/Graduation Success Rate Study of Division I NCAA Men's Basketball Tournament Teams*. The Institute for Diversity and Ethics in Sport. Orlando: University of Central Florida.

Baseball Almanac. 2006. "Record Books: Baseball Milestones." Retrieved June 2, 2006 (http://www.baseball-almanac.com).

Bash, Dana, and Brian Todd. 2000. "Helms Calls for Probe of Baltimore Orioles Hiring Practices." *CNN.com*, May 26. Retrieved July 5, 2007 (http://archives.cnn.com/2000).

Baudrillard, Jean. 1988. *Jean Baudrillard: Selected Writings*. Stanford, CA: Stanford University Press.

Baxter, Kevin. 2002. "Cuban Pitcher Contreras Defects." *Baseball America.com*, October 5. Retrieved July 15, 2007 (http://www.baseballamerica.com).

BBC. 2000. "The Heysel Disaster." *BBC News*, May 29. Retrieved January 19, 2007 (http://news.bbc.co.uk).

Beamish, Rob. 2002. "Karl Marx's Enduring Legacy for the Sociology of Sport." Pp. 25–39 in *Theory, Sport & Society*, edited by J. Maguire and K. Young. Amsterdam: JAI/Elsevier Science Imprint.

Begley, Sharon, and Martha Brant. 1999. "The Real Scandal in International Sport: Doping." *Newsweek*, February 15, pp. 48–54.

Bell, Jack. 2007. "Positions Available: $12,900 to Start, Advancement Possible." *New York Times*, May 9. Retrieved May 9, 2007 (http://www.nytimes.com).

Bell, Jarrett. 2007. "Conduct Unbecoming: NFL Sets New Standard with Suspensions." *USA Today*, April 10. Retrieved April 11, 2007 (http://www.usatoday.com).

Bellah, Robert, Richard Madsen, William M. Sullivan, Ann Swidler, and Steven M. Tipton. 1985. *Habits of the Heart: Individualism and Commitment in American Life.* Berkeley: University of California Press.

Benedict, Jeff. 1997. *Public Heroes, Private Felons: Athletes and Crimes against Women.* Boston, MA: Northeastern University Press.

Benedict, Jeff. 2004. *Out of Bounds: Inside the NBA's Culture of Rape, Violence, and Crime.* New York: HarperCollins.

Benedict, Jeff, and Don Yaeger. 1998. *Pros and Cons: The Criminals Who Play in the NFL.* New York: Warner Books.

Berger, Peter. 1963. *Invitation to Sociology: A Humanistic Perspective.* New York: Random House/Doubleday.

Berger, Peter. 1986. *The Capitalist Revolution: Fifty Propositions about Prosperity, Equality, and Liberty.* New York: Basic Books.

Berlin, Peter. 2006. "A Contrite Zidane Apologizes, but Says His Family Was Slurred." *New York Times*, July 13. Retrieved July 13, 2006 (http://www.nytimes).

Berry, Bonnie, and Earl Smith. 2000. "Race, Sport, and Crime: The Misrepresentation of African Americans in Team Sports and Crime." *Sociology of Sport Journal* 17: 171–197.

Betts, John Rickards. 1974. *America's Sporting Heritage: 1850–1950.* Reading, MA: Addison-Wesley.

Billings, Andrew C. 2000. "In Search of Women Athletes: ESPN's List of the Top 100 Athletes of the Century." *Journal of Sport & Social Issues* 24:415–421.

Birrell, Susan. 1988. "Discourses on the Gender/Sport Relationship: From Women in Sport to Gender Relations." *Exercise and Sport Sciences Review* 16:459–502.

Birrell, Susan. 2000. "Feminist Theories for Sport." Pp. 61–76 in *Handbook of Sports Studies*, edited by J. Coakley and E. Dunning. London: Sage Publications.

Bissinger, H.G. 1990. *Friday Night Lights: A Town, a Team, and a Dream.* New York: HarperCollins.

Blum, Ronald. 2007a. "Yankees Valued at $1.2 Billion by Forbes." *Associated Press*, April 19. Retrieved May 10, 2007 (http://www.forbes.com).

Blum, Ronald. 2007b. "Record Crowd Sees Red Bulls Top Galaxy 5–4." *Associated Press*, August 19. Retrieved August 24, 2007 (http://www.usatoday.com).

Blumstein, Alfred, and Jeff Benedict. 1999. "Criminal Violence of NFL Players Compared to the General Population." *Chance* 12(3):12–15.

Boeck, Greg. 2007. "Native American Athletes Face Imposing Hurdles." *USA Today*, February 23. Retrieved March 21, 2007 (http://www.usatoday.com).

Bok, Derek. 2003. *Universities in the Marketplace: The Commercialization of Higher Education.* Princeton, NJ: Princeton University Press.

Boorstin, Daniel J. 1962. *The Image, Or What Happened to the American Dream.* New York: Atheneum.

Boorstin, Daniel J. 1964. *The Image: A Guide to Pseudo-Events in America.* New York: Harper and Row. Republication of *The Image, Or What Happened to the American Dream.*

Boston Globe. 2006. "Kids in a Money Machine." *Boston Globe* Editorial, July 29. Retrieved August 11, 2006 (http://www.boston.com/sports).

Bowen, William G., and Sarah A. Levin. 2003. *Reclaiming the Game: College Sports and Educational Values.* Princeton, NJ: Princeton University Press.

Boyer, Peter J. 2006. "Big Men on Campus." *The New Yorker*, September 4, pp. 44–61.

Bradley, Bill. 1976. *Life on the Run.* New York: Quadrangle.

Brady, Erik, and Mary Beth Marklein. 2006. "A Perfect Storm: Explosive Convergence Helps Lacrosse Scandal Resonate." *USA Today*, April 26. Retrieved January 25, 2007 (http://www.usatoday.com).

Brady, Erik, and Jodi Upton. 2007. "Mid-Majors Squeezed to Pay Up." *USATODAY.com*, March 3. Retrieved March 16, 2007 (http://www.usatoday.com).

Brand, Myles. 2006. "Commercialism Controlled When Activity Aligns with Mission." *NCAA News*, April 24. Republished as "Clips Guest Commentary." *College Athletics Clips*, May 1, 2006. Retrieved May 1, 2006 (http://www.collegeathleticsclips.com).

Brandmeyer, Gerard A., and G. Fred McBee. 1986. "Social Status and Athletic Competition for the Disabled Athlete: The Case of Wheelchair Road-Racing." Pp. 181–187 in *Sport and Disabled Athletes*, edited by C. Sherrill. Champaign, IL: Human Kinetics.

Brayton, Sean. 2005. "'Black-Lash': Revisiting the 'White Negro' through Skateboarding." *Sociology of Sport Journal* 22:356–372.

Brennan, Christine. 2007. "Fans Becoming More Casual about Championship Viewing." *USA Today*, June 13. Retrieved June 14, 2007 (http://www.usatoday.com).

Bresnahan, Mike. 2005. "Swoosh Comes to Shove." Pp. 156–162 in *Sport in Contemporary Society: An Anthology*, 7th ed., edited by D.S. Eitzen. Boulder, CO: Paradigm Publishers.

Brewer, Benjamin. 2002. "Commercialization in Professional Cycling 1950–2001: Institutional Transformations and the Rationalizations of 'Doping.'" *Sociology of Sport Journal* 19:276–301.

Broad, K.L. 2001. "The Gendered Unapologetic: Queer Resistance in Women's Sport." *Sociology of Sport Journal* 18:181–204.

Brown, Dan, and Jennings Bryant. 2006. "Sports Content on U.S. Television." Pp. 77–104 in *Handbook of Sports and Media*, edited by A.A. Raney and J. Bryant. Mahwah, NJ: Lawrence Erlbaum Associates.

Brown, Gary T. 2007. "Research Validates Value, and Values, of Athletics." *NCAA News*, February 12. Retrieved February 20, 2007 (http://www.ncaa.org).

Buffington, Daniel. 2005. "Contesting Race on Sundays: Making Meaning out of the Rise in the Number of Black Quarterbacks." *Sociology of Sport Journal* 21:19–37.

Byrne, Julie. 2005. "Remembering Immaculata during This Year's NCAA Women's Basketball Tournament." *Duke University News & Communications*, March 18. Retrieved April 20, 2007 (http://dukenews.duke.edu).

Cantelon, Hart. 2002. "Book Review: Helen Jefferson Lenskyj's *Inside the Olympic Industry: Power, Politics, Activism.*" *International Review for the Sociology of Sport* 37:103–106.

Cantelon, Hart, and Michael Letters. 2000. "The Making of the IOC Environmental Policy as the Third Dimension of the Olympic Movement." *International Review for the Sociology of Sport* 35:294–308.

Carlson, Deven, Leslie Scott, Michael Planty, and Jennifer Thompson. 2005. "Statistics in Brief: What Is the Status of High School Athletes 8 Years after Their Senior Year?" National Center for Education Statistics, September. Washington, DC: U.S. Department of Education Institute of Education Sciences.

Carpenter, Les. 2006. "A Solution, or Merely a Cover?" *Washingtonpost.com*, September 27. Retrieved June 27, 2007 (http://www.washingtonpost.com).

Carpenter, Linda Jean, and R. Vivian Acosta. 2006. *Women in Intercollegiate Sport: A Longitudinal Study Twenty Nine Year Update 1977–2006.* Project Supported by Smith

College Project on Women & Social Change and Brooklyn College. Retrieved June 4, 2007 (http://webpages.charter.net/womeninsport).

Carrington, Ben. 1998. "Sport, Masculinity, and Black Cultural Resistance." *Journal of Sport & Social Issues* 22:275–298.

Carstairs, Catherine. 2003. "The Wide World of Doping: Drug Scandals, Natural Bodies, and the Business of Sports Entertainment." *Addiction Research & Theory* 11:263–281.

Castañeda, Lupe, and Claudine Sherrill. 1999. "Family Participation in Challenger Baseball: Critical Theory Perspective." *Adapted Physical Activity Quarterly* 16(4): 372–388.

Castells, Manuel. 1996. *The Rise of the Network Society*, Vol. 1 of *The Information Age: Economy, Society and Culture*. Oxford: Blackwell.

Caudwell, Jayne. 2003. "Sporting Gender: Women's Footballing Bodies as Sites/Sights for the (Re)Articulation of Sex, Gender, and Desire." *Sociology of Sport Journal* 20: 371–386.

CBC. 2003. "10 Drug Scandals." *CBC Sports Online*, January 19. Pp. 406–413 in *Sport and Contemporary Society: An Anthology*, 7th ed., edited by D. S. Eitzen. Boulder, CO: Paradigm Publishers.

Chadiha, Jeffri. 2007. "The Right to Roll." *SI.com*, February 20. Retrieved November 27, 2007 (http://sportsillustrated.cnn.com).

Chass, Murray. 1999. "Orioles-Cuba Series Raises Security Concerns." *New York Times*, January 5. Retrieved July 15, 2007 (http://www.cubanet.org).

Cheslock, John. 2007. *Who's Playing College Sports? Trends in Participation*. East Meadow, NY: Women's Sports Foundation, June 5.

Chicago Sun-Times. 2004. "About the Games." *Chicago Sun-Times*, August 17. Retrieved July 10, 2006 (link from page http://www.suntimes.com).

CNNMoney. 1999. "CBS Renews NCAA B'Ball." *CNNMoney.com*, November 18. Retrieved June 4, 2007 (http://money.cnn.com).

Coakley, Jay. 2007. *Sports in Society: Issues and Controversies*, 9th ed. Boston: McGraw-Hill Higher Education.

Cody, Edward. 2007. "Before Olympics, a Call for Change." *Washington Post*, August 8. Retrieved August 14, 2007 (http://www.washingtonpost.com).

Cole, Cheryl L. 2000. "Body Studies in the Sociology of Sport: A Review of the Field." Pp. 439–460 in *Handbook of Sports Studies*, edited by J. Coakley and E. Dunning. London: Sage Publications.

Coleman, James S. 1990. *Foundations of Social Theory*. Cambridge, MA: Harvard University Press.

Collins, Michael F., and James R. Buller. 2003. "Social Exclusion from High-Performance Sport." *Journal of Sport and Social Issues* 27:420–442.

Cooley, Charles Horton. 1961. "The Social Self." Pp. 822–828 in *Theories of Society: Foundations of Modern Sociological Theory*, edited by T. Parsons, E. Shils, K.D. Naegele, and J.R. Pitts. New York: Free Press.

Coontz, Phyllis. 2001. "Managing the Action: Sports Bookmakers as Entrepreneurs." *Deviant Behavior* 22:239–266.

Crosset, Todd. 1995. *Outsiders in the Clubhouse: The World of Women's Professional Golf*. Albany: State University of New York Press.

Crosset, Todd, and Becky Beal. 1997. "The Use of 'Subculture' and 'Subworld' in Ethnographic Works on Sport: A Discussion of Definitional Distinctions." *Sociology of Sport Journal* 14:73–85.

Crosset, Todd W., Jeffrey R. Benedict, and Mark A. McDonald. 1995. "Male Student-Athletes Reported for Sexual Assault: A Survey of Campus Police Departments and Judicial Affairs Offices." *Journal of Sport & Social Issues* 19:126–140.

Crosset, Todd W., James Ptacek, Mark A. McDonald, and Jeffrey R. Benedict. 1996. "Male Student-Athletes and Violence against Women: A Survey of Campus Judicial Affairs Offices." *Violence against Women* 2:163–179.

Curry, Timothy. 1991. "Fraternal Bonding in the Locker Room: A Profeminist Analysis of Talk about Competition and Women." *Sociology of Sport Journal* 8:119–135.

Daniels, Donna. 2000. "Gazing at the New Black Woman Athlete." *ColorLines* 3:25–26.

David, Ariel. 2006. "Sports Tribunal Demotes Juventus, Lazio, and Fiorentina for Match-Fixing." *USA Today*, July 14. Retrieved February 2, 2007 (http://www.usatoday.com).

Davis, Kingsley, and Wilbert E. Moore. 1945. "Some Principles of Stratification." *American Sociological Review* 10:242–249.

Davis, Laurel. 1997. *The Swimsuit Issue and Sport: Hegemonic Masculinity in* Sports Illustrated. Albany: State University of New York Press.

Davis, Laurel. 2002. "The Problems with Native American Mascots." *Multicultural Education* 9 (Summer):11–15.

Dawley, Heidi. 2006. "Early Word: World Cup Viewing Soars." *Media Life: Sports TV*, June 15. Retrieved June 19, 2006 (http://www.medialifemagazine.com).

Deford, Frank. 2005. "America's Modern Peculiar Institution." Pp. 145–154 in *Declining by Degrees: Higher Education at Risk*, edited by R.H. Hersh and J. Merrow. New York: Palgrave Macmillan.

DeLay, Jeanine A. 1999. "The Curveball and the Pitch: Sport Diplomacy in the Age of Global Media." *The Journal of the International Institute* 7 (Fall). Retrieved July 15, 2007 (http://www.umich.edu/~iinet/journal).

Denham, Bryan E., Andrew C. Billings, and Kelby C. Halone. 2002. "Differential Accounts of Race in Broadcast Commentary of the 2000 NCAA Men's and Women's Final Four Basketball Tournaments." *Sociology of Sport Journal* 19:315–332.

Denham, David. 2004. "Global and Local Influences on English Rugby League." *Sociology of Sport Journal* 21:206–219.

Dent, Gail (NCAA Contact). 2005. "NCAA 2002–2003 Gender Equity Report Indicates Slight Gains for Women Participating in Intercollegiate Athletics." *NCAA*, February 7. Retrieved April 27, 2007 (http://www.ncaa.org).

De Valle, Elaine, Kevin Baxter, and Tere Figueras. 2004. "Yankee Pitcher, Cuban Family Reunite." *Miami Herald*, June 23. Retrieved July 15, 2007 (http://www.miamiherald.com).

Dolan, Matthew. 2007. "Student Fights for Ability to Score." *Baltimore Sun*, May 10, p. 3B.

Donnelly, Michele. 2006. "Studying Extreme Sports: Beyond the Core Participants." *Journal of Sport & Social Issues* 30:219–224.

Donnelly, Peter. 1996. "The Local and the Global: Globalization in the Sociology of Sport." *Journal of Sport & Social Issues* 20:239–257.

Donnelly, Peter. 2002. "George Herbert Mead and an Interpretive Sociology of Sport." Pp. 83–102 in *Theory, Sport & Society*, edited by J. Maguire and K. Young. Amsterdam: JAI/Elsevier Science Imprint.

Douglas, Delia. 2005. "Venus, Serena, and the Women's Tennis Association: When and Where 'Race' Enters." *Sociology of Sport Journal* 22:256–282.

Douglas, Delia, and Katherine M. Jamieson. 2006. "A Farewell to Remember: Interrogating the Nancy Lopez Farewell Tour." *Sociology of Sport Journal* 23:117–141.

Doukas, Spiro G. 2006. "Crowd Management: Past and Contemporary Issues." *The Sport Journal* 9(2). Retrieved January 20, 2007 (http://thesportjournal.org).

Doyle, Matt. 2007. "An Oklahoma Tour Stop Not Feasible Yet." *Tulsa World*, April 25. Retrieved June 20, 2007 (http://www.tulsaworld.com).

Drape, Joe. 2006. "Foreign Pros in College Tennis: On Top and under Scrutiny." *New York Times*, April 11. Retrieved June 11, 2007 (http://www.nytimes.com).

Drape, Joe. 2007. "Talk of Efforts to Fix Matches Rattles Pro Tennis." *New York Times*, November 25. Retrieved November 25, 2007 (http://www.nytimes.com).

Duderstadt, James J. 2000. *Intercollegiate Athletics and the American University: A University President's Perspective.* Ann Arbor: University of Michigan Press.

Duggan, Paul. 2007. "A Blood Sport Exposed." *Washington Post*, August 22. Retrieved August 22, 2007 (http://www.washingtonpost.com).

Duncan, Margaret Carlisle, and Michael A. Messner. 2005. "Gender in Televised Sports: News and Highlights Shows, 1989–2004." Report commissioned by the Amateur Athletic Foundation of Los Angeles (AAF). Retrieved December 2, 2007 (http://www.aafla.org/9arr/ResearchReports/tv2004.pdf).

Dunning, Eric. 1993. "Sport in the Civilising Process: Aspects of the Development of Modern Sport." Pp. 39–70 in *The Sports Process: A Comparative and Developmental Approach*, edited by E.G. Dunning, J.A. Maguire, and R.E. Pearton. Champaign, IL: Human Kinetics.

Dure, Beau. 2007. "BALCO Investigation Timeline." *USA Today*, January 25. Retrieved January 30, 2007 (http://www.usatoday.com).

Eckholm, Erik. 2006. "Plight Deepens for Black Men, Studies Warn." *New York Times*, March 20. Retrieved March 20, 2006 (http://www.nytimes.com).

Edelman, Robert. 1993. *Serious Fun: A History of Spectator Sports in the USSR*. New York: Oxford University Press.

Edmonds. 2005. "NASCAR Announces Lucrative New Television Contracts, but without NBC." *Edmonds INSIDELINE*, December 8. Retrieved June 18, 2007 (http://www.edmonds.com/insideline).

Edwards, Harry. 1969. *The Revolt of the Black Athlete*. New York: Free Press.

Edwards, Harry. 1973. *Sociology of Sport*. Homewood, IL: Dorsey Press.

Edwards, Harry. 1998. "An End to the Golden Age of Black Participation in Sport?" *Civil Rights Digest* 3 (Fall):19–24.

Eichelberger, Curtis. 2005. "High School Football Goes Luxe with Skyboxes, Video Scoreboards." *Bloomberg.com*, November 16. Retrieved October 15, 2006 (http://www.bloomberg.com).

Eichelberger, Curtis. 2006. "U.S. Soccer, a World Cup Dud, Sustains Pro League with TV Deals." *Bloomberg.com*, July 7. Retrieved July 13, 2006 (http://www.bloomberg.com/).

Eitle, Tamela McNulty, and David J. Eitle. 2002. "Race, Cultural Capital, and the Educational Effects of Participation in Sports." *Sociology of Education* 75:123–146.

Eitzen, D. Stanley. 1996. "Ethical Dilemmas in American Sport: The Dark Side of Competition." *Vital Speeches of the Day* (January 1):182–185.

Eitzen, D. Stanley. 2003. *Fair and Foul: Beyond the Myths and Paradoxes of Sport*, 2nd ed. Lanham, MD: Rowman and Littlefield Publishers.

Eitzen, D. Stanley. 2006. *Fair and Foul: Beyond the Myths and Paradoxes of Sport*, 3rd ed. Lanham, MD: Rowman and Littlefield Publishers.

Eitzen, D. Stanley, and George H. Sage. 1997. *Sociology of North American Sport*, 9th ed. Madison, WI: Brown and Benchmark.

EPA. 2007. "U.S. Climate Policy and Actions." United States Environmental Protection Agency. Retrieved July 12, 2007 (http://www.epa.gov/climatechange/policy).

Epstein, Edward. 2005. "Congress at Work on 3 Steroids Measures: Proposals Focus on Banning Athletes, More Federal Power." *San Francisco Chronicle*, May 24. Retrieved January 28, 2007 (http://www.sfgate.com).

ESPN. 2005. "NCAA American Indian Mascot Ban Will Begin February 1." *ESPN.com*, August 12. Retrieved July 4, 2007 (http://sports.espn.go.com).

ESPN. 2006. "Legal Experts Question Remaining Duke Charges." *Associated Press*, December 23. Retrieved January 25, 2007 (http://sports.espn.go.com).

ESPN. 2007. "McNabb Says Black QBs under More Pressure." *ESPN.com*, September 19. Retrieved December 1, 2007 (http://sports.espn.go.com).

Esposito, John L. 1986. "Islam in the Politics of the Middle East." *Current History* (February):53–57, 81.

Esposito, John L. 1992. *The Islamic Threat: Myth or Reality?* New York: Oxford University Press.

Ewing, Martha E., Lori A. Gano-Overway, Crystal F. Branta, and Vern D. Seefeldt. 2002. "The Role of Sports in Youth Development." Pp. 31–47 in *Paradoxes of Youth and Sport*, edited by M. Gatz, M.A. Messner, and S.J. Ball-Rokeach. Albany: State University of New York Press.

FARE (Football Against Racism in Europe). 2006. "New System of 'Fan Embassies' in All Host Cities." *Football Unites*, June 9. Retrieved July 18, 2006 (http://www.farenet.org).

Farrell, Stephen, and Peter Gelling. 2007. "With Eyes Fixed on a Distant Soccer Field, Iraqis Leap at a Reason to Celebrate." *New York Times*, July 30. Retrieved July 30, 2007 (http://www.nytimes.com).

Farrey, Tom. 2002a. "Athletes Abusing Athletes." *ESPN.com*, June 3. Retrieved February 8, 2007 (http://espn.go.com/otl).

Farrey, Tom. 2002b. "It's Not All Fun and Games." *ESPN.com*, June 3. Retrieved February 8, 2007 (http://espn.go.com/otl).

Farrey, Tom. 2002c. "Laws Get a Workout." *ESPN.com*, June 3. Retrieved February 8, 2007 (http://espn.go.com/otl).

Farrey, Tom. 2002d. "Like Fighting, Part of Game." *ESPN.com*, June 3. Retrieved February 8, 2007 (http://espn.go.com/otl).

Farrey, Tom. 2002e. "Sports Hazing Incidents." *ESPN.com*, June 3. Retrieved February 8, 2007 (http://espn.go.com/otl).

Farrey, Tom. 2002f. "They Call It Leadership." *ESPN.com*, June 3. Retrieved February 8, 2007 (http://espn.go.com/otl).

Fatsis, Stefan. 2006. "Fans Say ESPN's World Cup Coverage Deserves Penalty." *Wall Street Journal*, July 5. Retrieved July 13, 2006 (http://online.wsj.com/public).

Fenton, Justin, and Greg Garland. 2007. "Minor League, Major Troubles." *Baltimore Sun*, July 14. Retrieved July 14, 2007 (http://www.baltimoresun.com).

Fine, Gary Alan. 1987. *With the Boys: Little League Baseball and Preadolescent Culture*. Chicago: University of Chicago Press.

Fisher, Eric. 2001. "Probe of Orioles Finds No Violations." *Washington Times*, August 17, p. B1.

Fitzpatrick, Frank. 2007. "Most Division I Colleges Have to Subsidize Sports, NCAA Finds." *Philadelphia Inquirer*, May 15. Retrieved June 12, 2007 (www.philly.com/inquirer/business).

Foley, Douglas E. 1990. "The Great American Football Ritual: Reproducing Race, Class, and Gender Inequality." *Sociology of Sport Journal* 7:111–135.

Fotheringham, William. 2006. "Tour de France in Chaos after Doping Claims." *The Guardian*, July 1. Retrieved January 28, 2007 (http://www.guardian.co.uk).

Fox News. 2007. "Poll: Americans Want Ties with Cuba after Castro Dies." *Associated Press*, February 7. Retrieved July 5, 2007 (http://www.foxnews.com).

Frank, Andre Gundar. 1979. *Dependent Accumulation and Underdevelopment*. London: Macmillan.

Freedman, Jonah. 2007. "The 2007 Fortunate 50." *SI.com*, no date. Retrieved June 23, 2007 (http://sportsillustrated.cnn.com).

Fried, Barbara H. 2007. "Punting Our Future: College Athletics and Admissions." *Change*, May/June, pp. 8–15.

Friedman, Michael T., David L. Andrews, and Michael L. Silk. 2004. "Sport and the Façade of Redevelopment in the Postindustrial City." *Sociology of Sport Journal* 21:119–139.

Fullinwider, Robert K. 2006. *Sports, Youth and Character: A Critical Survey.* Circle Working Paper 44. The Center for Information & Research on Civic Learning & Engagement. February. Retrieved September 2, 2006 (http://www.civicyouth.org).

Gage, Jack. 2007. "The Most Valuable NASCAR Teams." *Forbes.com,* June 15. Retrieved June 20, 2007 (http://www.forbes.com/business).

Gans, Herbert J. 1972. "The Positive Functions of the Undeserving Poor." *American Journal of Sociology* 78:275–288.

Geer, Jay, Al Arizmendez, and Rich Jarc. 2007. *Survey of High School Athletes: What Are Your Children Learning? The Impact of High School Sports on the Values and Ethics of High School Athletes.* Josephson Institute of Ethics. Released February. Retrieved March 9, 2007 (http://www.josephsoninstitute.org/sports_survey/2006/).

Giddens, Anthony. 1990. *The Consequences of Modernity.* Stanford, CA: Stanford University Press.

Giddens, Anthony, Mitchell Duneier, and Richard Appelbaum. 2007. *Introduction to Sociology,* 6th ed. New York: W.W. Norton.

Glanville, Jennifer. 1999. "Political Socialization or Selection? Adolescent Extracurricular Participation and Political Activity in Early Adulthood." *Social Science Quarterly* 80:279–290.

Glick, Daniel, Sherry Keene-Osborn, T. Trent Gegax, Matt Bai, Lynette Clementson, Devin Gordon, and Daniel Klaidman. 1999. "Anatomy of a Massacre." *Newsweek,* May 3, pp. 24–30.

Global Greens. 2001. *Charter of the Global Greens, Canberra 2001.* Retrieved July 12, 2007 (http://www.global.greens.org.au/Charter2001.pdf).

Goffman, Erving. 1959. *The Presentation of Self in Everyday Life.* Garden City, NY: Doubleday/Anchor.

Goffman, Erving. 1967. *Interaction Ritual: Essays on Face-to-Face Behavior.* Garden City, NY: Doubleday/Anchor.

Goldsmith, Pat António. 2003. "Race Relations and Racial Patterns in School Sports Participation." *Sociology of Sport Journal* 20:147–171.

Goodhart, Philip, and Christopher John Chataway. 1968. *War without Weapons.* London: W.H. Allen.

Gordon, Devin. 2006a. "You Don't Know Bode." *MSNBC/Newsweek,* January 23. Retrieved June 29, 2006 (http://www.msnbc.msn.com).

Gordon, Devin. 2006b. "Why Bode's Been a Nobody." *MSNBC/Newsweek,* February 23. Retrieved June 29, 2006 (http://www.msnbc.msn.com).

Grasmuck, Sherri. 2003. "Something about Baseball: Gentrification, 'Race Sponsorship,' and Neighborhood Boys' Baseball." *Sociology of Sport Journal* 20:307–330.

Green, Mick. 2004. "Power, Policy, and Political Priorities: Elite Sport Development in Canada and the United Kingdom." *Sociology of Sport Journal* 21:376–396.

Green, Mick, and Barrie Houlihan. 2006. "Governmentality, Modernization, and the 'Disciplining' of National Sporting Organizations: Athletics in Australia and the United Kingdom." *Sociology of Sport Journal* 23:47–71.

Gregory, Sean. 2006. "Fraternity of Silence." *Time,* April 10, p. 65.

Grey, Mark A. 1992. "Sports and Immigrant, Minority and Anglo Relations in Garden City (Kansas) High School." *Sociology of Sport Journal* 9:255–270.

Griffin, Pat. 1992. "Changing the Game: Homophobia, Sexism, and Lesbians in Sport." *Quest* 44:251–265.

Guttmann, Allen. 1978. *From Ritual to Record: The Nature of Modern Sports.* New York: Columbia University Press.

Guttmann, Allen. 1993. "The Diffusion of Sports and the Problem of Cultural Imperialism." Pp. 125–137 in *The Sports Process: A Comparative and Developmental Approach,* edited by E.G. Dunning, J.A. Maguire, and R.E. Pearton. Champaign, IL: Human Kinetics.

Guttmann, Allen. 2000. "The Development of Modern Sports." Pp. 248–259 in *Handbook of Sports Studies*, edited by J. Coakley and E. Dunning. London: Sage Publications.

Halberstam, David. 1991. "A Hero for the Wired World." *Sports Illustrated*, December 23, pp. 76–81.

Haley, A.J., and Brian S. Johnston. 1998. "Menaces to Management: A Developmental View of British Soccer Hooligans, 1961–1986." *The Sport Journal* 1(1). Retrieved January 19, 2007 (http://www.thesportjournal.org).

Hall, M. Ann. 1978. *Sport and Gender: A Feminist Perspective on the Sociology of Sport.* CAHPER Sociology of Sport Monograph Series. Ottawa: Canadian Association for Health, Physical Education and Recreation.

Hammons, David. 2003. "North American Soccer League Remembered." *National Soccer Hall of Fame*, May. Retrieved June 22, 2007 (http://www.soccerhall.org).

Hanson, Sandra L. 2005. "Hidden Dragons: Asian American Women and Sport." *Journal of Sport & Social Issues* 29:279–312.

Hardin, Marie Myers, and Brent Hardin. 2004. "The 'Supercrip' in Sport Media: Wheelchair Athletes Discuss Hegemony's Disabled Hero." *Sociology of Sport Online (sosol)* 7 (June). Retrieved July 3, 2006 (http://physed.otago.ac.nz).

Hargreaves, Jennifer. 1994. *Sporting Females: Critical Issues in the History and Sociology of Women's Sports.* London: Routledge.

Hargreaves, Jennifer, and Ian McDonald. 2000. "Cultural Studies and the Sociology of Sport." Pp. 48–60 in *Handbook of Sports Studies*, edited by J. Coakley and E. Dunning. London: Sage Publications.

Harris, Art. 1999. "From Little League to Madness: Portraits of the Littleton Shooters." *CNN.com*, April 30. Retrieved November 26, 2006 (http://www.cnn.com).

Hartmann, Douglas. 2000. "Rethinking the Relationship between Sport and Race in Amateur Culture: Golden Ghettos and Contested Terrain." *Sociology of Sport Journal* 17:229–253.

Harvey, Jean, Alan Law, and Michael Cantelon. 2001. "North American Professional Team Sport Franchise Ownership Patterns and Global Entertainment Conglomerations." *Sociology of Sport Journal* 18:435–457.

Harvey, Jean, Geneviève Rail, and Lucie Thibault. 1996. "Globalization and Sport: Sketching a Theoretical Model for Empirical Analyses." *Journal of Sport & Social Issues* 20:258–277.

Hawes, Kay. 2004. "University of Georgia Placed on Probation for Violations in Men's Basketball." *NCAA News Release*, August 5. Retrieved June 7, 2007 (http://www.ncaa.org).

Healy, Patrick. 2004. "2 L.I. Coaches in Hazing Case Are Removed from Teaching." *New York Times*, March 25. Retrieved April 22, 2005 (http://www.nytimes.com).

Heath, Thomas. 2006a. "Looking for High-Flying Rewards." *Washingtonpost.com*, June 21. Retrieved June 27, 2006 (http://www.washingtonpost.com).

Heath, Thomas. 2006b. "A Matter of Value Instead of Profit." *Washingtonpost.com*, July 12. Retrieved June 20, 2007 (http://www.washingtonpost.com).

Hedstrom, Ryan, and Daniel Gould. 2004. "Research in Youth Sports: Critical Issues Status." *White Paper Summaries of Existing Literature*. A Project Conducted for the Citizenship through Sports Alliance. Kansas City, MO: Institute for the Study of Youth Sports; East Lansing: Michigan State University.

Heino, Rebecca. 2000. "New Sports: What Is So Punk about Snowboarding?" *Journal of Sport & Social Issues* 24:176–191.

Henderson, Amy. 1999. "From Barnum to 'Bling Bling': The Changing Face of Celebrity Culture." *Hedgehog Review*, Fall. Retrieved August 12, 2005 (http://www.virginia.edu).

Hiaasen, Rob. 2006. "Head Games." *Baltimore Sun*, July 11, pp. 1E, 6E.

Higgins, Matt. 2006. "For New-Sport Athletes, High School Finishes 2nd." *New York Times*, September 20. Retrieved September 20, 2006 (http://www.nytimes.com).

Hoberman, John M. 1992. *Mortal Engines: The Science of Performance and the Dehumanization of Sport*. New York: Free Press.

Hoch, Paul. 1972. *Rip Off the Big Game: The Exploitation of Sports by the Power Elite*. New York: Doubleday.

Hohler, Bob. 2006a. "Sneaker War: Ethical Questions Raised as Amateur Basketball Recruiters Engage in a High-Stakes Battle for Blue-Chip Recruits." *Boston Globe*, July 23. Retrieved August 11, 2006 (http://www.boston.com).

Hohler, Bob. 2006b. "Sneaker War: Wading in Cesspool." *Boston Globe*, July 24. Retrieved August 11, 2006 (http://www.boston.com).

Hohler, Bob. 2006c. "Sneaker War: Are You Kidding?" *Boston Globe*, July 25. Retrieved August 11, 2006 (http://www.boston.com).

Holman, Margery. 2004. "A Search for Theoretical Understanding of Hazing Practices in Athletics." Pp. 50–60 in *Making the Team: Inside the World of Sport Initiations and Hazing*, edited by J. Johnson and M. Holman. Toronto: Canadian Scholars' Press.

Homans, George C. 1961, 1974. *Social Behavior: Its Elementary Forms*. New York: Harcourt Brace Jovanovich.

Horne, John, and Wolfram Manzenreiter, eds. 2006. *Sports Mega-Events: Social Scientific Analyses of a Global Phenomenon*. Malden, MA: Blackwell Publishing.

Horrow, Rick. 2006. "You Can Still Bet on It: Gambling and March Madness." *CBS SportsLine.com*, March 17. Retrieved February 2, 2007 (http://cbs.sportsline.com).

Hosick, Michelle Brutlag. 2005. "The Hidden Hazards of Hazing." *NCAA News Online*, September 26. Retrieved October 5, 2005 (http://www.ncaa.org). Archives.

Houlihan, Barrie. 2000. "Politics and Sport." Pp. 213–227 in *Handbook of Sports Studies*, edited by J. Coakley and E. Dunning. London: Sage Publications.

Howe, P. David. 2004. *Sport, Professionalism and Pain: Ethnographies of Injury and Risk*. London: Routledge.

Howe, P. David, and Carwyn Jones. 2006. "Classification of Disabled Athletes: (Dis)Empowering the Paralympic Practice Community." *Sociology of Sport Journal* 23:29–46.

Howell, Jeremy W., David L. Andrews, and Steven J. Jackson. 2002. "Cultural and Sport Studies: An Interventionist Practice." Pp. 151–177 in *Theory, Sport & Society*, edited by J. Maguire and K. Young. Amsterdam: JAI/Elsevier Science Imprint.

Hu, Winnie. 2007. "Indian Tribes Rediscovering Lacrosse." *New York Times*, July 13. Retrieved July 13, 2007 (http://www.nytimes.com).

Hughes, Rob. 2006. "Soccer: The Delicate Overlap between Sports and Politics." *International Herald Tribune*, April 26. Retrieved June 12, 2006 (http://www.iht.com).

Hughson, John. 2000. "The Boys Are Back in Town: Soccer Support and the Social Reproduction of Masculinity." *Journal of Sport & Social Issues* 24:8–23.

Infante, Nick. 2006. "Fans Behaving Badly." *College Athletics Clips*, June 6. Retrieved June 27, 2006 (http://www.collegeathleticsclips.com).

Infante, Nick. 2007. "The Chief's Last Dance." *CollegeAthleticsClips.com*, February 16. Retrieved March 30, 2007 (http://www.collegeathleticsclips.com).

Ingham, Alan, and Alison Dewar. 1999. "Through the Eyes of Youth: 'Deep Play' in Peewee Ice Hockey." Pp. 7–16 in *Inside Sports*, edited by J. Coakley and P. Donnelly. London: Routledge.

Isidore, Chris. 2006. "It's Still Miller Time for Advertisers." *CNNMoney.com*, February 9. Retrieved June 29, 2006 (http://money.cnn.com).

Israel, Maya. 2006. "BMW ORACLE Racing Re-Christens America's Cup Yacht." *MCADCafe*. Retrieved July 10, 2006 (http://www10.mcadcafe.com).

Jackson, Steven J., and David L. Andrews. 1999. "Between and Beyond the Global and the Local." *International Review for the Sociology of Sport* 34:31–42.

Jacobson, Jennifer. 2004. "Winning Sports Teams Have Little Effect on Colleges, Report Says." *Chronicle of Higher Education*, September 17, p. A35.

Jamail, Milton H. 2000. *Full Count: Inside Cuban Baseball.* Carbondale: Southern Illinois University Press.

Janis, Irving L. 1972. *Victims of Groupthink.* Boston: Houghton Mifflin.

JBHE (Journal of Blacks in Higher Education). 2006. "News & Views: Black Women Students Far Outnumber Black Men at the Nation's Highest-Ranked Universities." *Journal of Blacks in Higher Education,* July 17. Retrieved July 17, 2006 (http://www.jbhe.com).

Jenkins, Chris. 2005. "Agent Steers NASCAR toward Other Sports' Ways." *USA Today,* August 18. Retrieved June 24, 2007 (http://www.usatoday.com).

Jenkins, Sally. 2006. "Only Medal for Bode Is Fool's Gold." *Washingtonpost.com,* February 26. Retrieved June 29, 2006 (http://www.washingtonpost.com).

Jenkins, Sally. 2007a. "History of Women's Basketball." *WNBA.com.* Retrieved April 20, 2007 (http://www.wnba.com).

Jenkins, Sally. 2007b. *The Real Americans: The Team That Changed a Game, a People, a Nation.* New York: Doubleday.

JHU. 1999. "Interview with Wayne Smith." *The Gazette Online: The Newspaper of the Johns Hopkins University,* April 19. Retrieved July 5, 2007 (http://www.jhu.edu/~gazette).

Johnson, Arthur T. 1995. *Minor League Baseball and Local Economic Development.* Champaign: University of Illinois Press.

Johnson, K.C. 2006. "The Academy and the Duke Case." *Insidehighered.com,* December 28. Retrieved December 28, 2006 (http://insidehighered.com).

Jones, Shaka, and Shana Levine. 2006. *2006–2007 Guide for the College-Bound Student-Athlete.* Indianapolis, IN: NCAA. Retrieved June 12, 2007 (http://www.ncaa.org).

Judd, Ron. 2006. "Ode to Bode: Join Team or Get off It." *Seattle Times,* February 9. Retrieved June 29, 2006 (http://seattletimes.nwsource.com).

Kammerer, Roy. 2007. "German Soccer Team May Walk off Field." *Baltimore Sun,* February 13. Retrieved February 13, 2007 (http://www.baltimoresun.com).

Karp, David A., and William C. Yoels. 1979. *Symbols, Selves and Society: Understanding Interaction.* New York: J.B. Lippincott.

Kaufman, Jason, and Orlando Patterson. 2005. "Cross-National Cultural Diffusion: The Global Spread of Cricket." *American Sociological Review* 70:82–110.

Kaufman, Michelle. 2004. "Politics, Not Sport, Come First for Iranian Athlete." *Washington Post,* August 16. Retrieved July 8, 2007 (http://www.washingtonpost.com).

KCIA. 1991. *Keeping Faith with the Student-Athlete.* Knight Commission on Intercollegiate Athletics. Retrieved June 10, 2007 (http://www.knightcommission.org).

KCIA. 2001. *A Call to Action.* Knight Commission on Intercollegiate Athletics. Retrieved June 10, 2007 (http://www.knightcommission.org).

KCIA. 2006. "Poll: Americans Are Concerned about College Sports." *Executive Summary,* January. Knight Commission on Intercollegiate Athletics. Retrieved May 26, 2007 (http://www.knightcommission.org).

Keefer, Robert, Jeffrey H. Goldstein, and David Kasiarz. 1983. "Olympic Games Participation and Warfare." Pp. 183–193 in *Sports Violence,* edited by J.H. Goldstein. New York: Springer-Verlag.

Kennedy, Kostya, Mark Bechtel, and Stephen Cannella. 2007. "Goodbye to All That." *Sports Illustrated,* August 20, p. 28.

Kidd, Bruce. 1991. "How Do We Find Our Own Voices in the 'New World Order'?" A Commentary on Americanization." *Sociology of Sport Journal* 8:178–184.

Kidd, Bruce, and Peter Donnelly. 2000. "Human Rights in Sports." *International Review for the Sociology of Sport* 35:131–148.

Kiefer, Peter. 2006. "Racial Incidents Mar Italy's Celebration." *New York Times,* July 11. Retrieved July 18, 2006 (http://www.nytimes.com).

King, Peter. 2004. "Painful Reality." *Sports Illustrated,* October 11, pp. 60–63.

Kinkhabwala, Aditi. 2007. "The Righteous Scarlet Knights." *Sports Illustrated*, April 23, pp. 16–18.

Kivisto, Peter. 2004. *Key Ideas in Sociology*, 2nd ed. Thousand Oaks, CA: Pine Forge Press.

Klein, Alan. 1991a. "Sport and Culture as Contested Terrain: Americanization in the Caribbean." *Sociology of Sport Journal* 8:79–85.

Klein, Alan. 1991b. *Sugarball: The American Game, the Dominican Dream.* New Haven, CT: Yale University Press.

Klein, Alan. 2000a. "The Anthropology of Sport: Escaping the Past and Building a Future." Pp. 129–149 in *Handbook of Sports Studies*, edited by J. Coakley and E. Dunning. London: Sage Publications.

Klein, Alan. 2000b. "Latinizing Fenway Park: A Cultural Critique of the Boston Red Sox, Their Fans, and the Media." *Sociology of Sport Journal* 17:403–422.

Klis, Mike. 2003. "Fewer Blacks Step up to the Plate in Pro Baseball." *Denver Post*, May 11, pp. 1A, 14A–15A.

Knobler, Mike. 2007. "Athletes Choose Majors to Accommodate Sports." *Atlanta Journal-Constitution*, January 7, p. IA.

Knoppers, Annelies, and Anton Anthonissen. 2003. "Women's Soccer in the United States and the Netherlands: Differences and Similarities in Regimes of Inequalities." *Sociology of Sport Journal* 20:351–370.

Knowlton, Brian. 1999. "Expanding Ties, Clinton Extends a Hand to Cuba." *International Herald Tribune*, January 6. Retrieved July 15, 2007 (http://www.iht.com).

Kowinski, William Severini. 1985. *The Malling of America: An Inside Look at the Great Consumer Paradise.* New York: William Morrow.

Kreager, Derek A. 2007. "Unnecessary Roughness? School Sports, Peer Networks, and Male Adolescent Violence." *American Sociological Review* 72:705–724.

LaFeber, Walter. 2002. *Michael Jordan and the New Global Capitalism.* New York: W.W. Norton.

Landers, Melissa A., and Gary Alan Fine. 1996. "Learning Life's Lessons in Tee Ball: The Reinforcement of Gender and Status in Kindergarten Sport." *Sociology of Sport Journal* 13:87–93.

Langbein, Laura, and Roseana Bess. 2002. "Sports in School: Sources of Amity or Antipathy." *Social Science Quarterly* 83:436–454.

Langelett, George. 2003. "The Relationship between Recruiting and Team Performance in Division IA College Football." *Journal of Sports Economics* 4:240–245.

Lapchick, Richard E. 2000. "Crime and Athletes: New Racial Stereotypes." *Society* 37 (March/April):14–20.

Lapchick, Richard. 2006. "Keeping Score When It Counts." Institute for Diversity and Ethics in Sport, December 4. Orlando: University of Central Florida.

Lapchick, Richard. 2007. "Academic Progress/Graduation Success Rate Study of Division I NCAA Men's Basketball Tournament Teams." Institute for Diversity and Ethics in Sport, March 12. Orlando: University of Central Florida.

Lapchick, Richard, Stacy Martin, Danielle Kushner, and Jenny Brenden. 2006. *The 2005 Racial and Gender Report Card.* Report of the DeVos Sport Business Management Program. Orlando: University of Central Florida. Retrieved December 1, 2006 (http://www.bus.ucf.edu/sport).

Larmer, Brook. 2005. "The Center of the World." *Foreign Policy*, September/October, pp. 66–74.

Lasch, Christopher. 1979. *The Culture of Narcissism: American Life in an Age of Diminishing Expectations.* New York: Warner Books.

Layden, Tim. 1995a. "Bettor Education." *Sports Illustrated*, April 3, pp. 68–74.

Layden, Tim. 1995b. "Book Smart." *Sports Illustrated*, April 10, pp. 68–70.

Layden, Tim. 1995c. "You Bet Your Life." *Sports Illustrated*, April 17, pp. 46–48.

Layden, Tim. 2004. "Book 'Em." *SI.com*, May 14. Retrieved February 2, 2007 (http://sportsillustrated.cnn.com).

Lealand, Geoff. 1994. "American Popular Culture and Emerging Nationalism in New Zealand." *National Forum: The Phi Kappa Phi Journal* 74(4):34–37.

Lederman, Doug. 2006. "Gender Gap Grows." *Inside Higher Ed*, July 12. Retrieved July 12, 2006 (http://insidehighered.com).

Leitch, Will. 2007. "In Brand We Trust." *New York Times Play*, July 12. Retrieved December 1, 2007 (http://www.nytimes.com/2007/07/12/sports/playemail).

Lenskyj, Helen Jefferson. 2000. *Inside the Olympic Industry: Power, Politics, and Activism.* Albany: State University of New York Press.

Leonard, David. 1998. "What Happened to the Revolt of the Black Athlete?" *ColorLines*, Summer. Retrieved July 8, 2007 (http://www.colorlines.com).

Leonard, David J. 2007. "Innocent until Proven Innocent: In Defense of Duke Lacrosse and White Power (and against Menacing Black Student-Athletes, a Black Stripper, Activists, and the Jewish Media)." *Journal of Sport & Social Issues* 31:25–44.

Lesieur, Henry R. 1987. "Deviance in Sport: The Case of Pathological Gambling." *Arena Review* 11:5–14.

Lesjø, Jon Helge. 2000. "Lillehammer 1994." *International Review for the Sociology of Sport* 35:282–293.

Lewin, Tamar. 2006. "At Colleges, Women Are Leaving Men in the Dust." *New York Times*, July 9. Retrieved July 11, 2006 (http://www.nytimes.com).

Lewis, Michael. 2003. *Moneyball: The Art of Winning an Unfair Game.* New York: W.W. Norton.

Lewis, Michael. 2004. "Out of Their Tree." *Sports Illustrated*, March 1, pp. 66–74.

Lewis, Richard. 2006. "Caught in Time: Black Power Salute, Mexico, 1968." *The Sunday Times*, October 8. Retrieved July 8, 2007 (http://www.timesonline.co.uk).

Lieberman, Joe, and John McCain. 2003. "Climate Change and Federal Policy: A Response to Inaction on Global Warming." *San Francisco Chronicle*, August 1. Retrieved July 12, 2007 (http://sfgate.com).

Lipka, Sara. 2006a. "DNA Tests Return No Match for Duke Lacrosse Players Accused of Rape." *Chronicle of Higher Education*, April 11. Retrieved April 11, 2006 (http://chronicle.com/daily).

Lipka, Sara. 2006b. "Duke Incident Raises Issues about Culture of the Campus." *Chronicle of Higher Education*, April 21. Retrieved May 22, 2006 (http://chronicle.com/weekly).

Lipka, Sara. 2006c. "Duke U. Reinstates Men's Lacrosse Team for Next Season." *Chronicle of Higher Education*, June 16, p. A40.

Lipka, Sara. 2007a. "North Carolina Attorney General Exonerates Duke Lacrosse Players." *Chronicle of Higher Education*, April 12. Retrieved April 12, 2007 (http://chronicle.com/daily).

Lipka, Sara. 2007b. "Syracuse Becomes Latest University to Cut Athletic Teams, Citing Finances and Title IX." *Chronicle of Higher Education*, June 5. Retrieved June 5, 2007 (http://chronicle.com/daily).

Lipka, Sara. 2007c. "Jury Orders Fresno State U. to Pay Ex-Coach $5.85 Million in Discrimination Case." *Chronicle of Higher Education*, July 11. Retrieved July 11, 2007 (http://chronicle.com).

Lipka, Sara, and Brad Wolverton. 2007. "Title IX Enforcement Called 'Deeply Troubling.'" *Chronicle of Higher Education*, June 29, pp. A1, A33–A34.

Lipsyte, Robert. 1996. "Little Girls in a Staged Spectacle for Big Bucks? That's Sportainment!" *New York Times*, August 4, p. 28.

Lipsyte, Robert. 2005. "Outraged over the Steroids Outrage." *USA Today*, March 21. Retrieved January 28, 2007 (http://www.usatoday.com).

Litke, Jim. 2006. "Bode on His Performance: 'I Did It My Way.'" *MSNBC.com*, February 26. Retrieved June 29, 2006 (http://www.msnbc.msn.com).

Llosa, Luis Fernando, and L. Jon Wertheim. 2007. "Inside the Steroid Sting." *Sports Illustrated*, March 6, updated March 12. Retrieved March 12, 2007 (http://sportsillustrated .cnn.com).

Longman, Jeré. 2007. "An Amputee Sprinter: Is He Disabled or Too-Abled?" *New York Times*, May 15. Retrieved May 17, 2007 (http://www.nytimes.com).

Lopez, Mark Hugo, and Kimberlee Moore. 2006. "Participation in Sports and Civic Engagement." *Fact Sheet.* The Center for Information & Research on Civic Learning & Engagement, February. Retrieved September 24, 2006 (http://www.civicyouth.org).

Lopiano, Donna. [2002] 2005. "The Real Culprit in the Cutting of Men's Olympic Sports." *Women's Sports Foundation*, March 26. Pp. 294–296 in *Sport and Contemporary Society: An Anthology*, 7th ed., edited by D. S. Eitzen. Boulder, CO: Paradigm Publishers.

Lowry, Tom. 2003. "The NFL Machine." *Business Week*, January 27, pp. 86–91, 94.

Loy, John W., and Douglas Booth. 2000. "Functionalism, Sport and Society." Pp. 8–27 in *Handbook of Sports Studies*, edited by J. Coakley and E. Dunning. London: Sage Publications.

Loy, John W., and Douglas Booth. 2002. "Emile Durkheim, Structural Functionalism and the Sociology of Sport." Pp. 41–62 in *Theory, Sport and Society*, edited by J. Maguire and K. Young. Amsterdam: JAI/Elsevier Science Imprint.

Loy, John W., Jr., and Gerald S. Kenyon, eds. 1969. *Sport, Culture and Society: A Reader on the Sociology of Sport*. New York: Macmillan.

Lucas, Shelley. 2000. "Nike's Commercial Solution." *International Review for the Sociology of Sport* 35:149–164.

MacLeod, Calum. 2007. "China Bowl a Misstep for NFL in Sport's Race to China." *USA Today*, April 4. Retrieved April 5, 2007 (http://www.usatoday.com).

Maguire, Joe A. 1990. "More Than a Sporting Touchdown: The Making of American Football in England 1982–1990." *Sociology of Sport Journal* 7:213–237.

Maguire, Joseph. 1999. *Global Sport*. Cambridge, UK: Polity Press.

Maguire, Joseph, Grant Jarvie, Louise Mansfield, and Joe Bradley. 2002. *Sport Worlds: A Sociological Perspective*. Champaign, IL: Human Kinetics.

Maguire, Joseph, and Kevin Young. 2002. *Theory, Sport and Society*. Amsterdam: JAI/ Elsevier Science Imprint.

Mandell, Richard D. 1971. *The Nazi Olympics*. New York: Macmillan.

Markovits, Andrei S., and Steven L. Hellerman. 2001. *Offside: Soccer and American Exceptionalism*. Princeton, NJ: Princeton University Press.

Markovitz, Jonathan. 2006. "Anatomy of a Spectacle: Race, Gender, and Memory in Kobe Bryant Rape Case." *Sociology of Sport Journal* 23:396–418.

Martens, Rainer, and James A. Peterson. 1971. "Group Cohesiveness as a Determinant of Success and Member Satisfaction in Team Performance." *International Review of Sport Sociology* 6:49–59.

Martin, Thomas W., and Kenneth J. Berry. 1987. "Competitive Sport in Post-Industrial Society: The Case of the Motocross Racer." Pp. 269–284 in *Sport Sociology: Contemporary Themes*, 3rd ed., edited by A. Yiannakis, T.D. McIntyre, M.J. Melnick, and D.P. Hart. Dubuque, IA: Kendall/Hunt.

Martinez, Andres. 2006. "Goooooal-obalization!" *Latimes.com*, June 4. Retrieved June 19, 2006 (http://www.latimes.com).

Marx, Karl, and Friedrich Engels. 1978. "Manifesto of the Communist Party." Pp. 473–478 in *The Marx-Engels Reader*, 2nd ed., translated by R.C. Tucker. New York: W.W. Norton.

Matheson, Victor A. 2005. "Research Note: Athletic Graduation Rates and Simpson's Paradox." Faculty Research Series, Working Paper No. 05-06. Department of Economics, College of Holy Cross, Worcester, MA. Unpublished manuscript.

Matthews, Mark, Joe Matthews, and Peter Hermann. 1999. "Cuba Coach Defects as Team Leaves." *Baltimore Sun*, May 5. Retrieved July 15, 2007 (http://www.baltimoresun .com).

May, Reuben A. Buford. 2001. "The Sticky Situation of Sportsmanship: Contexts and Contradictions in Sportsmanship among High School Boys Basketball Players." *Journal of Sport & Social Issues* 25:372–389.

Mayeda, David Tokiharu. 1999. "From Model Minority to Economic Threat: Media Portrayals of Major League Baseball Pitchers Hideo Nomo and Hideki Irabu." *Journal of Sport & Social Issues* 23:203–217.

McCallum, Jack. 2006. "See No Evil, Hear No Evil." *Sports Illustrated*, October 9, pp. 18–19.

McCarthy, Michael. 2006. "Front-Row Tickets Take Back Seat to Once-in-Lifetime Thrills." *USA Today*, February 28. Retrieved June 18, 2007 (http://www.usatoday .com).

McCarthy, Michael. 2007a. "Fantasy Sports Ruling Could Have Wide Impact." *USA Today*, October 16. Retrieved October 17, 2007 (http://www.usatoday.com).

McCarthy, Michael. 2007b. "Packers-Cowboys: The Big Game Few Will See." *USA Today*, November 28. Retrieved November 30, 2007 (http://www.usatoday.com).

McChesney, Robert W. 1989. "Media Made Sport: A History of Sports Coverage in the United States." Pp. 49–69 in *Media, Sports & Society*, edited by L. Wenner. Newbury Park, CA: Sage Publications.

McKindra, Leilana. 2006. "Hidden Barriers: Sociological Factors, Other Issues Limit Non-Caucasian Access to Certain Sports." *NCAA News*, April 10. Retrieved July 18, 2006 (http://www.ncaa.org).

Mead, George Herbert. 1934. *Mind, Self and Society*. Chicago: University of Chicago Press.

Meadows, Susannah, and Evan Thomas. 2006. "Duke Rape Case: What Really Happened?" *Newsweek*, April 10. Retrieved January 23, 2007 (http://www.msnbc.msn .com).

Media Info Center. 2004. "Average Circulation of Top 100 ABC Magazines, 2004." *Media Management News & Data*. Northwestern University Media Management Center. Retrieved July 21, 2006 (http://www.mediainfocenter.org).

Meier, Kenneth J., Warren S. Eller, Miner P. Marchbanks III, Scott Robinson, J.L. Polinard, and Robert D. Wrinkle. 2004. "A Lingering Question of Priorities: Athletic Budgets and Academic Performance Revisited." *Review of Policy Research* 21:799–807.

Mellgren, Doug. 2006. "America's Cup a Lesson in Team Diversity." *Chicago Sun Times*, July 2. Retrieved July 10, 2006 (http://www.suntimes.com) [in Archive].

Mennesson, Christine. 2000. "'Hard' Women and 'Soft' Women: The Social Construction of Identities among Women Boxers." *International Review for the Sociology of Sport* 35:21–33.

Merton, Robert K. 1938. "Social Structure and Anomie." *American Sociological Review* 3:672–682.

Merton, Robert K. 1957. *Social Theory and Social Structure*. Glencoe, IL: Free Press.

Messner, Michael A. 1990a. "Boyhood, Organized Sports, and the Construction of Masculinities." *Journal of Contemporary Ethnography* 18:416–444.

Messner, Michael A. 1990b. "When Bodies Are Weapons: Masculinity and Violence in Sport." *International Review for the Sociology of Sport* 25:197–211.

Messner, Michael A. 1992. *Power at Play: Sports and the Problem of Masculinity*. Boston, MA: Beacon Press.

Messner, Michael A. 2005. "Center of Attention: The Gender of Sports Media." Pp. 87–97 in *Sport in Contemporary Society: An Anthology*, 7th ed., edited by D.S. Eitzen. Boulder, CO: Paradigm Publishers.

Messner, Michael A., Michele Dunbar, and Darnell Hunt. 2000. "The Televised Sports Manhood Formula." *Journal of Sport & Social Issues* 24:380–394.

Michel, Lindsay, Brian Sopp, and Michaele Stafford. 2007. "Athletics Costs Outpace Returns." *Daily Tar Heel*, April 26. Retrieved May 2, 2007 (http://www.dailytarheel.com).

Miller, Ed. 2007. "IX Reasons for College Crew." *Roanoke Times*, May 26. Retrieved June 4, 2007 (http://www.roanoke.com/sports/college).

Miller, Kathleen E., Merrill J. Melnick, Grace M. Barnes, Michael P. Farrell, and Don Sabo. 2005. "Untangling the Links among Athletic Involvement, Gender, Race, and Adolescent Academic Outcomes." *Sociology of Sport Journal* 22:178–193.

Miller, Toby, David Rowe, Jim McKay, and Geoffrey Lawrence. 2003. "The Over-Production of U.S. Sports and the New International Division of Cultural Labor." *International Review for the Sociology of Sport* 38:427–440.

Mills, C. Wright. 1956. *The Power Elite*. New York: Oxford University Press.

Mills, C. Wright. 1959, 2000. *The Sociological Imagination*. New York: Oxford University Press.

Milton, Pat. 2007. "Donaghy Set to Plead Guilty in Gambling Case." *Baltimore Sun*, August 15. Retrieved August 15, 2007 (http://www.baltimoresun.com).

Miracle, Andrew W., Jr., and C. Roger Rees. 1994. *Lessons of the Locker Room: The Myth of School Sports*. Amherst, NY: Prometheus Books.

Monaghan, Peter. 1993. "Sports in the Soviet Union." *Chronicle of Higher Education*, July 7. Retrieved July 9, 2007 (http://chronicle.com).

Mondello, Michael. 2006. "Sports Economics and the Media." Pp. 277–294 in *Handbook of Sports and Media*, edited by A.A. Raney and J. Bryant. Mahwah, NJ: Lawrence Erlbaum Associates.

Moore, Molly. 2006a. "France Reacts to Zidane's Red Card: Star's Final Act Stuns the Nation." *Washingtonpost.com*, July 11. Retrieved July 11, 2006 (http://www.washingtonpost.com).

Moore, Molly. 2006b. "Zidane Says 'Harsh' Insults by Italian Led to Head Butt." *Washingtonpost.com*, July 13. Retrieved July 13, 2006 (http://www.washingtonpost.com).

Morello, Danielle. 1997. "Soccer War." *Inventory of Conflict and Environment (ICE) Case Studies*, Case Study #32/35. Retrieved July 7, 2007 (http://www.american.edu/ted/ice).

Morrison, L. Leotus. 1993. "The AIAW: Governance by Women for Women." Pp. 59–66 in *Women in Sport: Issues and Controversies*, edited by G.L. Cohen. Newbury Park, CA: Sage Publications.

MSNBC. 2007. "Tim Hardaway Says He Wants 'Second Chance.'" *MSNBC News Service*, March 14. Retrieved May 13, 2007 (http://www.msnbc.msn.com).

Muller, Antonio J. 2004. "Soccer Culture in Brazil." *The Sport Journal* 7 (Winter). Retrieved June 23, 2007 (http://www.thesportjournal.org).

Murray, Ken. 2006. "The NFL's Forgotten Players." *Baltimore Sun*, July 2. Retrieved July 2, 2006 (http://www.baltimoresun.com).

Murray, Ken. 2007. "NFL, Union Unveil Plan for Needy Retirees." *Baltimore Sun*, July 27. Retrieved July 27, 2007 (http://www.baltimoresun.com).

Myers, Jim. 2006. "{Talking Béisbol}." *Baltimore Magazine*, June, pp. 146–151.

Nack, William, and Don Yaeger. 1999. "Every Parent's Nightmare." *Sports Illustrated*, September 13, pp. 40–53.

Nagel, Mark S., Richard M. Southall, and Terrence O'Toole. 2004. "Punishment in the Four Major North American Professional Sports Leagues." *International Sports Journal* 8:15–27.

NASBE. 2004. *Athletics and Achievement: The Report of the NASBE Commission on High School Athletics in an Era of Reform.* Alexandria, VA: National Association of State Boards of Education.

Nash, Rex. 2000. "Contestation in Modern English Professional Football." *International Review for the Sociology of Sport* 35:465–486.

National Geographic. 2006. "Soccer Unites the World Map." *National Geographic*, June, Special Insert.

Naughton, Jim, and Jeffrey Selingo. 1998. "A Point-Shaving Scandal Rattles Northwestern U." *Chronicle of Higher Education*, April 10. Retrieved February 19, 2007 (http://chronicle.com).

NBA. 2007. "NBA Player Dress Code." *NBA Website.* Retrieved January 16, 2007 (http://www.nba.com).

NCAA. 2006. *The Second-Century Imperatives: Presidential Leadership—Institutional Accountability.* A Report from the Presidential Task Force on Division I Intercollegiate Athletics. Retrieved October 31, 2006 (http://www2.ncaa.org).

NCAA. 2007. "Student-Athlete Perspectives on Their College Experience: Preliminary Findings from the NCAA GOALS and SCORE Studies." Presented at the Annual NCAA Convention, January 6, Orlando, FL.

NCES (National Center for Education Statistics). 2004. "Postsecondary Education." *Digest of Education Statistics, 2004*, ch. 3, table 206. Retrieved July 17, 2006 (http://nces.ed.gov/programs/digest).

NCWGE (National Coalition for Women and Girls in Education). 2002. *Title IX Athletics Policies: Issues and Data for Education Decision Makers.* Report from the National Coalition for Women and Girls in Education, August 27. Retrieved March 21, 2005 (http://www.ncwge.org).

New York Times. 2001. "College Basketball: Women Get More Coverage." *New York Times*, July 6. Retrieved June 4, 2007 (http://query.nytimes.com).

Newberry, Paul. 2002/2005. "NASCAR: A Big Money Machine." Pp. 227–233 in *Sport in Contemporary Society: An Anthology*, 7th ed., edited by D.S. Eitzen. Boulder, CO: Paradigm Publishers.

Newfield, Jack. 2001. "The Shame of Boxing." *The Nation*, October 25. Retrieved June 21, 2007 (http://www.thenation.com).

News Services. 2007. "After Riot, Italian Officials Demand Tougher Security." *Washingtonpost.com*, February 5. Retrieved February 5, 2007 (http://www.washingtonpost.com).

News24. 2006. "'Sick Taunt' Riled Zidane." *NEWS24.com*, July 11. Retrieved July 11, 2006 (http://www.news24.com/News24/Soccer/News).

NFHS. 2006. "Participation in High School Sports Increases Again; Confirms NFHS Commitment to Stronger Leadership." Press Release of National Federation of State High School Associations, September 18. Retrieved September 30, 2006 (http://www.nfhs.org).

NFL News. 2007. "Thirty-Five Ex-NFL Players Qualify for Dementia-Alzheimer's Assistance." *NFL.com*, May 30. Retrieved June 28, 2007 (http://www.nfl.com).

Nixon, Howard L. II. 1976. "Team Orientations, Interpersonal Relations, and Team Success." *Research Quarterly* 47:429–435.

Nixon, Howard L. II. 1977. "Reinforcement Effects of Sports Team Success on Cohesiveness-Related Factors." *International Review of Sport Sociology* 4(12):17–38.

Nixon, Howard L. II. 1979. *The Small Group.* Englewood Cliffs, NJ: Prentice-Hall.

Nixon, Howard L. II. 1984. *Sport and the American Dream.* Champaign, IL: Leisure Press Imprint/Human Kinetics.

Nixon, Howard L. II. 1986. "Social Order in a Leisure Setting: The Case of Recreational Swimmers in a Pool." *Sociology of Sport Journal* 3:320–332.

Nixon, Howard L. II. 1988a. "The Background, Nature, and Implications of the Organization of the 'Capitalist Olympics.'" Pp. 237–251 in *The Olympic Games in Transition*, edited by J.O. Segrave and D. Chu. Champaign, IL: Human Kinetics.

Nixon, Howard L. II. 1988b. "Getting over the Worry Hurdle: Parental Encouragement and the Sports Involvement of Visually Impaired Children and Youths." *Adapted Physical Activity Quarterly* 5:29–43.

Nixon, Howard L. II. 1990. "Rethinking Socialization and Sport." *Journal of Sport & Social Issues* 14:33–47.

Nixon, Howard L. II. 1993. "Accepting the Risks of Pain and Injury in Sport: Mediated Cultural Influences on Playing Hurt." *Sociology of Sport Journal* 10:183–196.

Nixon, Howard L. II. 1994a. "Coaches' Views of Risk, Pain and Injury in Sport, with Special Reference to Gender Differences." *Sociology of Sport Journal* 11:79–87.

Nixon, Howard L. II. 1994b. "Social Pressure, Social Support, and Help Seeking for Pain and Injuries in College Sports Networks." *Journal of Sport & Social Issues* 18:340–356.

Nixon, Howard L. II. 1996. "Explaining Pain and Injury Attitudes and Experiences in Sport in Terms of Gender, Race, and Sports Status Factors." *Journal of Sport & Social Issues* 20:33–44.

Nixon, Howard L. II. 2000. "Sport and Disability." Pp. 422–438 in *Handbook of Sports Studies*, edited by J. Coakley and E. Dunning. London: Sage Publications.

Nixon, Howard L. II. 2002. "Studying Sport from a Social Network Approach." Pp. 267–291 in *Theory, Sport and Society*, edited by J. Maguire and K. Young. Amsterdam: JAI/Elsevier Science Imprint.

Nixon, Howard L. II. 2004. "Cultural, Structural and Status Dimensions of Pain and Injury Experiences in Sport." Pp. 81–97 in *Sporting Bodies, Damaged Selves: Sociological Studies of Sports-Related Injury*, edited by K. Young. Amsterdam: Elsevier.

Nixon, Howard L. II. 2005. "Resolving the Dilemma of Title IX versus Men's Nonrevenue Sports." Presented at the annual meeting of the North American Society for the Sociology of Sport, October 27, Winston-Salem, NC.

Nixon, Howard L. II. 2007a. "Constructing Diverse Sport Opportunities for People with Disabilities." *Journal of Sport & Social Issues* 31:417–433.

Nixon, Howard L. II. 2007b. "Star Wars Arms Races in College Athletics: Coaches' Pay and Indicators of Athletic and Institutional Status." Presented at the annual meeting of the North American Society for the Sociology of Sport, November, Pittsburgh, PA.

Nixon, Howard L. II, and James H. Frey. 1996. *A Sociology of Sport*. Belmont, CA: Wadsworth.

Nixon, Howard L. II, Philip J. Maresca, and Marcy A. Silverman. 1979. "Sex Differences in College Students' Acceptance of Females in Sport." *Adolescence* 56:755–764.

Nogawa, Haruo. 2003. "Institutionalized Discrimination against Japan-Born Korean Athletes: From Overt to Covert Discrimination." *Culture, Sport, Society* 6 (Summer/Autumn):219–238.

Noll, Roger G., and Andrew Zimbalist. 1997. "Sports, Jobs, and Taxes: Are New Stadiums Worth the Cost?" *Brookings Review* 15 (Summer):35–39.

Novak, Michael. 1976. *The Joy of Sport*. New York: Basic Books.

Ohio State University. 2007. "Points of Pride." Retrieved March 20, 2007 (http://www.cstv.com).

Olian, Cathy. 2006. "Golden Boy Bode Miller." *CBS News*, January 8. Retrieved June 29, 2006 (http://www.cbsnews.com).

Olson, Bradley, and Jeff Seidel. 2006. "Wheelchair Athlete, Teammate Disqualified: McFadden Accused of 'Pacing' Runner at Championship." *Baltimoresun.com* (*Baltimore Sun*), May 28. Retrieved May 31, 2006 (http://www.baltimoresun.com).

Oriard, Michael. 1993. *Reading Football: How the Popular Press Created an American Spectacle.* Chapel Hill: University of North Carolina Press.

Osburn, Stacey. 2007. "NCAA Division I Committee on Infractions Penalizes McNeese State University for Violations in Basketball, Track and Field." *NCAA News Release*, February 8. Retrieved June 7, 2007 (http://www.ncaa.org).

Parsons, Talcott. 1951. *The Social System.* New York: Free Press.

Patrick, Dick. 2007. "Rising Salaries Increase Pressure on Top Women's Coaches." *USA Today*, March 7. Retrieved April 27, 2007 (http://www.usatoday.com).

Patton, Cindy. 2001. "'Rock Hard': Judging the Female Physique." *Journal of Sport & Social Issues* 25:118–140.

Pearson, Demetrius W., and C. Allen Haney. 1999. "The Rodeo Cowboy: Cultural Icon, Athlete, or Entrepreneur." *Journal of Sport & Social Issues* 23:308–327.

Penner, Mike. 2006. "PRO: A Pitch from Two Sides." *Latimes.com* (*Los Angeles Times*), June 5. Retrieved June 19, 2006 (http://www.latimes.com).

Pennington. Bill. 2006. "On Slippery Slope, Bode Miller Apologizes." *International Herald Tribune*, January 13. Retrieved June 29, 2006 (http://www.iht.com).

Petr, Todd, Thomas S. Paskus, and Jason B. Dunkle. 2004. *NCAA National Study on Collegiate Sports Wagering and Associated Behaviors.* Indianapolis, IN: NCAA.

Phillips, Angus. 2006. "The Best Boats Money Can Buy Are Ready for America's Cup." *Washingtonpost.com.* Retrieved July 10, 2006 (http://www.washingtonpost.com).

Plummer, David. 2006. "Sportophobia: Why Do Some Men Avoid Sport?" *Journal of Sport & Social Issues* 30:122–137.

Powers, Elia. 2007a. "NCAA's Evolving Academic Picture." *Inside Higher Ed*, May 3. Retrieved May 3, 2007 (http://www.insidehighered.com).

Powers, Elia. 2007b. "What's Next for Division I?" *Inside Higher Ed*, August 15. Retrieved August 15, 2007 (http://www.insidehighered.com).

Price, Michael, and Andrew Parker. 2003. "Sport, Sexuality, and the Gender Order: Amateur Rugby Union, Gay Men, and Social Exclusion." *Sociology of Sport Journal* 20:108–126.

Price, S.L., and Farrell Evans. 2006. "The Damage Done." *Sports Illustrated*, June 26, pp. 75–84.

Prisbell, Eric. 2006. "An Endless Summer League: 16 Year-Old Star Eschews Prep Team for AAU." *Washington Post*, July 6. Retrieved July 6, 2006 (http://www.washingonpost.com).

Pronger, Brian. 2005. "Sport and Masculinity: The Estrangement of Gay Men." Pp. 332–345 in *Sport in Contemporary Society: An Anthology*, 7th ed., edited by D.S. Eitzen. Boulder, CO: Paradigm Publishers.

Pugmire, Jerome. 2006. "Zidane Ends World Cup Career with Head Butt, Red Card." *USA Today*, July 9. Retrieved July 9, 2006 (http://www.usatoday.com).

Putnam, Robert D. 2000. *Bowling Alone: The Collapse and Revival of American Community.* New York: Simon and Schuster.

Radio Free Europe. 2006. "Iran Reverses 27-Year Ban of Women at Sports Matches." *Radio Free Europe/Radio Liberty*, April 24. Retrieved June 12, 2006 (http://www.rferl.org).

Rafael, Dan. 2007. "De La Hoya 'Ecstatic' That Fight Was Richest Ever." *ESPN.com*, May 9. Retrieved June 20, 2007 (http://sports.espn.go.com/espn).

Raney, Arthur A. 2006. "Why We Watch and Enjoy Mediated Sports." Pp. 313–329 in *Handbook of Sports and Media*, edited by A.A. Raney and J. Bryant. Mahwah, NJ: Lawrence Erlbaum Associates.

Raney, Arthur A., and Jennings Bryant, eds. 2006. *Handbook of Sports and Media.* Mahwah, NJ: Lawrence Erlbaum Associates.

Redden, Elizabeth. 2007. "'Dirty Little Secrets' in Women's Sports." *Inside Higher Ed*, April 30. Retrieved April 30, 2007 (http://insidehighered.com).

Rees, C. Roger, Wolf-Dietrich Brettschneider, and Hans Peter Brandl-Bredenbeck. 1998. "Globalization of Sports Activities and Sport Perceptions among Adolescents from Berlin and Suburban New York." *Sociology of Sport Journal* 15:216–230.

Renfro, Wallace I. 2001. "NCAA Reaches Agreement with ESPN, Inc. for Television Rights to 21 Championships." *NCAA News Release*, July 5. Retrieved June 4, 2007 (http://www.ncaa.org).

Reuters. 2006. "No-Show World Cup Nations Still Tuning in to Watch." *YAHOO!NEWS*, June 16. Retrieved June 16, 2006 (http://news.yahoo.com).

Rhoden, William C. 2006. *Forty Million Dollar Slaves: The Rise, Fall, and Redemption of the Black Athlete.* New York: Random House.

Riesman, David, and Reuel Denney. 1951. "Football in America: A Study in Cultural Diffusion." *American Quarterly* 3:309–319.

Rigauer, Bero. 1981. *Sport and Work,* translated by A. Guttmann. New York: Columbia University Press.

Rigauer, Bero. 2000. "Marxist Theories." Pp. 28–47 in *Handbook of Sports Studies,* edited by J. Coakley and E. Dunning. London: Sage Publications.

Rinehart, Robert. 2005. "'Babes' & Boards: Opportunities in New Millennium Sport?" *Journal of Sport & Social Issues* 29:232–255.

Rinehart, Robert, and Chris Grenfell. 2002. "BMX Spaces: Children's Grass Roots' Courses and Corporate-Sponsored Tracks." *Sociology of Sport Journal* 19:302–314.

Riordan, James. 1980. *Soviet Sport.* New York: New York University Press.

Ritzer, George. 1993. *The McDonaldization of Society.* Newbury Park, CA: Pine Forge Press.

Ritzer, George. 2003. *Contemporary Sociological Theory and Its Classical Roots: The Basics.* Boston: McGraw-Hill.

Ritzer, George. 2004a. *The Globalization of Nothing.* Thousand Oaks, CA: Pine Forge Press.

Ritzer, George. 2004b. *The McDonaldization of Society: Revised New Century Edition.* Thousand Oaks, CA: Pine Forge Press.

Ritzer, George, and Todd Stillman. 2001. "The Postmodern Ballpark as a Leisure Setting: Enchantment and Simulated De-McDonaldization." *Leisure Sciences* 23:99–113.

Robertson, Roland. 1992. *Globalization: Social Theory and Global Culture.* New York: Russell Sage.

Robertson, Roland. 2001. "Globalization Theory 2000+: Major Problematics." Pp. 458–471 in *Handbook of Social Theory,* edited by G. Ritzer and B. Smart. London: Sage.

Rohter, Larry. 2001. "Huge Soccer Scandal Taints National Obsession of Brazil." *New York Times*, March 23. Retrieved June 22, 2007 (http://www.nytimes.com).

Rohter, Larry. 2006. "In Brazil, Unpaved Path to Soccer Excellence." *New York Times*, June 25. Retrieved June 25, 2006 (http://www.nytimes.com).

Rojek, Chris. 2001. *Celebrity.* London: Reaktion Books.

Rostow, W.W. 1960. *The Stages of Economic Growth: A Non-Communist Manifesto.* Cambridge, UK: Cambridge University Press.

Rudolph, Frederick. 1962. *The American College and University.* New York: Random House Vintage Books.

Ruibal, Sal. 2001. "X Games, No Longer Bad, Go Suburban." *USA Today*, August 17. Retrieved June 27, 2006 (http://www.usatoday.com).

Ruibal, Sal. 2007. "Poll: Fans Want Action on Doping." *USA Today*, June 22. Retrieved June 27, 2007 (http://www.usatoday.com).

Rushin, Steve. 2006. "Air and Space: A Billion People *Can* Be Wrong." *Sports Illustrated*, February 6, p. 19.

Ryan, Joan. 2005. "Female Gymnasts and Figure Skaters: The Dark Side." Pp. 149–155 in *Sport in Contemporary Society: An Anthology*, 7th ed., edited by D.S. Eitzen. Boulder, CO: Paradigm Publishers.

Ryan, Oliver. 2005. "What Fuels the Racing Business." *CNNMoney*, September 5. Retrieved June 17, 2007 (http://money.cnn.com/magazines/fortune).

Sack, Allen L., and Zeljan Suster. 2000. "Soccer and Croatian Nationalism: A Prelude to War." *Journal of Sport & Social Issues* 24:305–320.

Sage, George H. 1998. *Power and Ideology in American Sport*, 2nd ed. Champaign, IL: Human Kinetics.

Sage, George H. 1999. "Justice Do It! The Nike Transnational Advocacy Network: Organizations, Collective Actions, and Outcomes." *Sociology of Sport Journal* 16:206–235.

Sage, George H. 2005. "Corporate Globalization and Sporting Goods Manufacturing: The Case of Nike." Pp. 362–382 in *Sport in Contemporary Society: An Anthology*, 7th ed., edited by D.S. Eitzen. Boulder, CO: Paradigm Publishers.

Sandomir, Richard. 2006. "Cup Ratings Are Up, but Fans Deserve Better." *New York Times*, July 11, 2006. Retrieved July 13, 2006 (http://www.nytimes.com).

Sanminiatelli, Maria. 2007. "Italians to Play with No Fans." *Washingtonpost.com*, February 8. Retrieved February 8, 2007 (http://www.washingtonpost.com).

Saraceno, Jon. 2006. "Apathetic Attitude Adds up to This: Bode Miller Has Blown It, Badly." *USA Today*, February 19. Retrieved July 1, 2006 (http://www.usatoday.com).

Saslow, Eli. 2006a. "Turning Promise into a Commodity." *Washington Post*, January 29. Retrieved January 31, 2006 (http://www.washingtonpost.com).

Saslow, Eli. 2006b. "Opportunity Realized a World Away." *Washington Post*, January 30. Retrieved January 31, 2006 (http://www.washingtonpost.com).

Saslow, Eli. 2006c. "Trading Diamonds for Blue Chips." *Washington Post*, January 31. Retrieved January 31, 2006 (http://www.washingtonpost.com).

Saslow, Eli. 2006d. "Is There Such a Thing as a Perfect 10?" *Washingtonpost.com*, July 4. Retrieved July 4, 2006 (http://www.washingtonpost.com).

Saslow, Eli. 2007. "School Administrators Say NCAA Crackdown on 'Diploma Mills' Is Flawed." *Washington Post*, March 7. Retrieved June 7, 2007 (http://www.washingtonpost.com).

Schantz, Otto J., and Keith Gilbert. 2001. "An Ideal Misconstrued: Newspaper Coverage of the Atlanta Paralympic Games in France and Germany." *Sociology of Sport Journal* 18:69–94.

Schell, Lea Ann "Beez," and Margaret Carlisle Duncan. 1999. "A Content Analysis of CBS's Coverage of the 1996 Paralympic Games." *Adapted Physical Activity Quarterly* 16:27–47.

Schevitz, Tanya. 2005. "Girls Rugby Game Turns Violent, 2 Coaches and Referee Beaten in Brawl Police Say." *San Francisco Chronicle*, May 16. Retrieved January 26, 2007 (http://sfgate.com).

Schulz, Brad, and Mary Lou Sheffer. 2004. "The Changing Role of Local Television Sports." *The Sport Journal* 7(1). Retrieved June 19, 2006 (http://www.thesportjournal.org).

Schwarz, Alan. 2007. "Concussion Tied to Depression in Ex-NFL Players." *New York Times*, May 31. Retrieved May 31, 2007 (http://www.nytimes.com).

Segrave, Jeffrey O. 2000. "Sport as Escape." *Journal of Sport & Social Issues* 24:61–77.

Seidel, Jeff. 2007. "Role of Disabled Athletes Expanded." *Baltimore Sun*, February 11, p. 12D.

Semyonov, Moshe, and Mira Farbstein. 1989. "Ecology of Sports Violence: The Case of Israeli Soccer." *Sociology of Sport Journal* 6:50–59.

Senn, Albert Eric. 1999. *Power, Politics, and the Olympic Games*. Champaign, IL: Human Kinetics Publishers.

Setrakian, Lara, and Chris Francescani. 2007. "Former Duke Prosecutor Nifong Disbarred." *ABC News*, June 16. Retrieved August 22, 2007 (http://abcnews.go.com/TheLaw).

Sheringham, Sam. 2006. "Baseball: A Hit Heard around the World." *International Herald Tribune*, March 21. Retrieved June 19, 2006 (http://www.iht.com).

Sherrill, Claudine. 1986. "Social and Psychological Dimensions of Sports for Disabled Athletes." Pp. 21–33 in *Sport and Disabled Athletes*, edited by C. Sherrill. Champaign, IL: Human Kinetics.

Shipley, Amy. 2007a. "A Wider Front in Doping Battle: Law Enforcement Takes the Lead in Sports Probes." *Washingtonpost.com*, March 2. Retrieved March 9, 2007 (http://www.washingtonpost.com).

Shipley, Amy. 2007b. "Doping Divide May Taint Olympics." *Washingtonpost.com*, November 14. Retrieved November 14, 2007 (http://www.washingtonpost.com).

Shulman, James L., and William G. Bowen. 2001. *The Game of Life: College Sports and Educational Values*. Princeton, NJ: Princeton University Press.

SI.com. 2005. "Homosexuality and Sports." *SI.com* (*Sports Illustrated*), April 12. Retrieved July 12, 2006 (http://sportsillustrated.cnn.com).

Silk, David. 1999. "Local/Global Flows and Altered Production Practices: Narrative Constructions at the 1995 Canada Cup of Soccer." *International Review for the Sociology of Sport* 34:113–123.

Silk, Michael, and David L. Andrews. 2001. "Beyond a Boundary? Sport, Transnational Advertising, and the Reimagining of National Culture." *Journal of Sport & Social Issues* 25:180–201.

Simpson, Kevin. 1987. "Sporting Dreams Die on the 'Rez.'" *Denver Post*, September 6, pp. 1C, 19C.

Sipes, Richard G. 1973. "War, Sports and Aggression: An Empirical Test of Two Rival Theories." *American Anthropologist* 75:64–86.

Sloan, Scott. 2007. "Cost of College Coaching Explodes." *Lexington Herald-Leader*, April 8. Retrieved May 24, 2007 (http://www.kentucky.com).

Smart, Barry. 2005. *The Sport Star: Modern Sport and the Cultural Economy of Sporting Celebrity*. London: Sage Publications.

Smith, Michael D. 1986. "Sports Violence: A Definition." Pp. 221–227 in *Fractured Focus: Sport as a Reflection of Society*, edited by R.E. Lapchick. Lexington, MA: Lexington Books.

Snider, Mike. 1996. "Michael Jordan's Bigger Than Basketball; He's a Pop Icon." *USA Today*, July 19, p. 3D.

Sokolove, Michael. 2007. "The Scold." *New York Times Magazine*, January 7. Retrieved January 28, 2007 (http://www.nytimes.com).

Spencer, Nancy. 1997. "Once upon a Subculture: Professional Women's Tennis and the Meaning of Style, 1970–1974." *Journal of Sport & Social Issues* 21:363–378.

Sports Biz. 2005. "The PGA Tour: Sand Trap Ahead." *BusinessWeek*, October 31. Retrieved June 20, 2007 (http://www.businessweek.com).

SportsAustralia. 2006. "Time for Authorities to Step In." *SportsAustralia.com*, March 22. Retrieved January 26, 2007 (http://www.sportsaustralia.com).

SportsBusiness Journal. 2006. "2006 SBJ/SBD Reader Survey." *SportsBusiness Journal*, December 3. Retrieved December 5, 2006 (http://www.collegeathleticsclips.com). Original source (http://www.sportsbusinessjournal.com).

Starr, Mark, and Allison Samuels. 2000. "A Season of Shame." *Newsweek*, May 29, pp. 56–60.

Staurowsky, Ellen J. 2002. "Appendix C: The Relationship between Athletics and Higher Education Fund Raising: The Myths Far Outweigh the Facts." Pp. 48–56 in *Title IX Athletics Policies: Issues and Data for Education Decision Makers*, edited by the National Coalition for Women and Girls in Education (NCWGE). Retrieved March 21, 2005 (http://www.ncwge.org).

Steele, David. 2007. "Gay Players Shouldn't Wait to Come Out." *Baltimore Sun*, February 8. Retrieved February 8, 2007 (http://www.baltimoresun.com).

Stoddart, Brian. 1988. "Sport, Cultural Imperialism, and Colonial Response in the British Empire." *Comparative Studies in Society and History* 30:649–673.

Stone, Gregory. 1955. "American Sports: Play and Display." *Chicago Review* 9:83–100.

Sugden, John, and Alan Tomlinson. 1996. "What's Left When the Circus Leaves Town? An Evaluation of World Cup USA 1994." *Sociology of Sport Journal* 13:238–258.

Sugden, John, and Alan Tomlinson. 2000. "Theorizing Sport, Social Class and Status." Pp. 309–321 in *Handbook of Sports Studies*, edited by J. Coakley and E. Dunning. London: Sage Publications.

Suggs, Welch. 1999. "Scandals Force Colleges to Reassess Roles of Academic Advisers for Athletes." *Chronicle of Higher Education*, December 3. Retrieved June 7, 2007 (http://chronicle.com/weekly).

Suggs, Welch. 2002. "How Gears Turn at a Sports Factory." *Chronicle of Higher Education*, November 29, pp. A32–A37.

Suggs, Welch. 2004a. "Big Money in College Sports Flows to the Few." *Chronicle of Higher Education*, October 29, pp. A46–A47.

Suggs, Welch. 2004b. "Colleges' Expenditures on Athletics Can't Be Calculated, Panelists Tell Knight Commission." *Chronicle of Higher Education*, November 5. Retrieved March 21, 2005 (http://chronicle.com/weekly).

Suggs, Welch. 2005. *A Place on the Team: The Triumph and Tragedy of Title IX*. Princeton, NJ: Princeton University Press.

Sullivan, David B. 2006. "Broadcast Television and the Game of Packaging Sports." Pp. 131–145 in *Handbook of Sports and Media*, edited by A.A. Raney and J. Bryant. Mahwah, NJ: Lawrence Erlbaum Associates.

Szymanski, Stefan, and Andrew Zimbalist. 2005. *National Pastime: How Americans Play Baseball and the Rest of the World Plays Soccer*. Washington, DC: Brookings Institution Press.

Tapper, Jake, and Audrey Taylor. 2006. "Is Jock Culture a Training Ground for Crime?" *ABC News*, April 18. Retrieved January 22, 2007 (http://abcnews.go.com).

Taub, Diane E., and Kimberly R. Greer. 2000. "Physical Activity as a Normalizing Experience for School-Age Children with Physical Disabilities." *Journal of Sport & Social Issues* 24:395–414.

Theberge, Nancy. 1999. "Being Physical: Sources of Pleasure and Satisfaction in Women's Ice Hockey." Pp. 146–155 in *Inside Sports*, edited by J. Coakley and P. Donnelly. London: Routledge.

Theberge, Nancy. 2000a. "Gender and Sport." Pp. 322–333 in *Handbook of Sports Studies*, edited by J. Coakley and E. Dunning. London: Sage Publications.

Theberge, Nancy. 2000b. *Higher Goals: Women's Ice Hockey and the Politics of Gender*. Albany: State University of New York Press.

Thiboutot, A., R.W. Smith, and S. Labanowich. 1992. "Examining the Concept of Reverse Integration: A Response to Brasile's 'New Perspective' on Integration." *Adapted Physical Activity Quarterly* 9:283–292.

Thompson, Shona M. 2002. "Sport, Gender, Feminism." Pp. 105–127 in *Theory, Sport and Society*, edited by J. Maguire and K. Young. Amsterdam: JAI/Elsevier Science Imprint.

Tierney, John. 2006. "Let the Guys Win One." *New York Times*, July 11, p. A19.

Time. 1972a. "Dampening the Olympic Torch." *Time*, September 18. Retrieved July 8, 2007 (http://www.time.com).

Time. 1972b. "Horror and Death at the Olympics." *Time*, September 18. Retrieved July 8, 2007 (http://www.time.com).

Tocqueville, Alexis de. 1853/1969. *Democracy in America*, edited by J.P. Mayer. Garden City, NY: Doubleday.

Trota, Brian, and Jay Johnson. 2004. "A Brief History of Hazing." Pp. x–xvi in *Making the Team: Inside the World of Sport Initiations and Hazing*, edited by J. Johnson and M. Holman. Toronto: Canadian Scholars' Press.

Tucker, Tim. 2006. "Woods' Popularity Passes Jordan." *Atlanta Journal-Constitution*, June 11. Retrieved June 19, 2006 (http://www.ajc.com).

Tye, Larry. 2005. "Kids and Sports: Injured at an Early Age." Pp. 143–148 in *Sport in Contemporary Society: An Anthology*, 7th ed., edited by D.S. Eitzen. Boulder, CO: Paradigm Publishers.

Upton, Jodi, and Steve Wieberg. 2006. "Contracts for College Coaches Cover More Than Salaries." *USATODAY.com*, November 16. Retrieved May 23, 2007 (http://www.usatoday.com).

USA Basketball. 2004. "Games of the XXVth Olympiad—1992." Retrieved July 6, 2006 (http://www.usabasketball.com).

USA Today. 2006. "Taking Sporting Event Seats to the Next Level." *USA Today*, February 28. Retrieved June 18, 2007 (http://www.usatoday.com).

Veblen, Thorstein. 1899. *Theory of the Leisure Class*. New York: Macmillan.

Verba, Sidney, Kay Lehman Scholzman, and Henry E. Brady. 1995. *Voice and Equality: Civic Volunteerism in American Politics*. Cambridge, MA: Harvard University Press.

Vinton, Nathaniel. 2006. "Bode Miller Switches from Atomic Skis to Head." *Ski Racing*, April 22. Retrieved July 1, 2006 (http://www.skiracing.com).

Wahl, Grant. 2007. "What a Ball Can Do." *Sports Illustrated*, August 6, p. 25.

Wahl, Grant, and L. Jon Wertheim. 2003. "A Rite Gone Terribly Wrong." *Sports Illustrated*, December 22, pp. 68–75.

Walker, Childs, and Candus Thomson. 2007. "Foreign Legion." *Baltimore Sun*, May 11. Retrieved May 11, 2007 (http://www.baltimoresun.com).

Walker, J. 1988. *Louts and Legends: Male Youth Culture in an Inner-City School*. Sydney, Australia: Allen and Unwin.

Wallechinsky, David. 2006. "Is the American Dream Still Possible?" *Parade.com*, April 23. Retrieved April 2, 2007 (http://www.parade.com).

Wallerstein, Immanuel. 1974. *The Modern World-System*. New York: Academic Press.

Walton, Theresa A. 2004. "Steve Prefontaine: From Rebel with a Cause to Hero with a Swoosh." *Sociology of Sport Journal* 21:61–83.

Wang, Chih-ming. 2004. "Capitalizing the Big Man: Yao Ming, Asian America, and the China Global." *Inter-Asia Cultural Studies* 5:263–278.

Wasley, Paula. 2007. "Auburn U. Settles with Professor Who Handed out Easy Grades to Athletes." *Chronicle of Higher Education*, August 10. Retrieved August 14, 2007 (http://chronicle.com/weekly).

Waters, Mary C. 2006. "Optional Ethnicities: For Whites Only?" Pp. 136–145 in *Readings for Sociology*, 5th ed., edited by G. Massey. New York: W. W. Norton.

Weber, Max. 1978. "Class, Status, and Party." Pp. 926–939 in *Economy and Society*, edited by G. Roth and C. Wittich, vol. 2. Berkeley: University of California Press.

Webster, Nick. 2006. "Why Is the World Cup Bigger Than Any American Sporting Event?" *FoxSoccer.com*, June 8. Retrieved June 16, 2006 (http://msn.foxsports.com).

Weiberg, Steve, and Jodi Upton. 2007. "Success on the Court Translates to Big Money for Coaches." *USA Today*, March 8. Retrieved April 27, 2007 (http://www.usatoday.com).

Weinberg, Ari. 2003. "The Case for Legal Sports Gambling." *Forbes.com*, January 27. Retrieved February 2, 2007 (http://www.forbes.com).

Weir, Tom, and Erik Brady. 2003. "In Sexual Assault Cases, Athletes Usually Walk." *USA Today*, December 22. Retrieved February 24, 2006 (http://www.usatoday.com).

Weistart, John. 1998. "Title IX and Intercollegiate Sport: Equal Opportunity?" *Brookings Review* 16 (Fall):39–43.

Wertheim, L. Jon. 2005. "Gays in Sport: A Poll." *SI.com* (*Sports Illustrated*), April 12. Retrieved July 12, 2006 (http://sportsillustrated.cnn.com).

Wertheim, L. Jon. 2007. "Ohio State the Program: Big Wins, Big Money, Big Spirit." *Sports Illustrated*, March 5, pp. 55–69.

Wertheim, L. Jon, and George Dohrmann. 2006. "Going Big-Time." *Sports Illustrated*, March 13. Retrieved March 13, 2006 (http://premium.si.cnn.com).

Whannel, Garry. 2000. "Sport and the Media." Pp. 291–308 in *Handbook of Sports Studies*, edited by J. Coakley and E. Dunning. London: Sage Publications.

Wheaton, Belinda, and Alan Tomlinson. 1998. "The Changing Gender Order in Sport?" *Journal of Sport & Social Issues* 22:252–274.

Whitaker, Brian. 2006. "President Lifts Ban on Women Watching Football in Iran." *The Guardian*, April 25. Retrieved June 12, 2006 (http://www.guardian.co.uk).

White, Philip. 2004. "The Costs of Injury from Sport, Exercise and Physical Activity: A Review of the Evidence." Pp. 309–331 in *Sporting Bodies, Damaged Selves: Sociological.Studies of Sports-Related Injury*, edited by K. Young. Amsterdam: Elsevier.

Whiteside, Kelly. 2006. "Concerns Raised over Racism during Cup." *USA Today*, June 2. Retrieved July 18, 2006 (http://www.usatoday.com).

Wieting, Stephen G. 2000. "Twilight of the Hero in the Tour de France." *International Review for the Sociology of Sport* 35:348–363.

Wile, Jon, and Sonny Amato. 2006. "'Adrenaline': Extreme Sports." *Washingtonpost.com*, June 21. Retrieved June 27, 2006 (http://www.washingtonpost.com).

Williams, Trevor, and Tarja Kolkka. 1998. "Socialization into Wheelchair Basketball in the United Kingdom: A Structural Functionalist Perspective." *Adapted Physical Activity Quarterly* 15:357–369.

Wilson, Brian. 2002. "The 'Anti-Jock' Movement: Reconsidering Youth Resistance, Masculinity, and Sport Culture in the Age of the Internet." *Sociology of Sport Journal* 19:206–233.

Wilson, Brian, and Robert Sparks. 1996. "'It's Gotta Be the Shoes': Youth, Race, and Sneaker Commercials." *Sociology of Sport Journal* 13:398–427.

Wilson, Brian, and Philip White. 2002. "Revive the Pride: Social Process, Political Economy, and a Fan-Based Grassroots Movement." *Sociology of Sport Journal* 19:119–148.

Wilson, Brian, Philip White, and Karen Fisher. 2001. "Multiple Identities in a Marginalized Culture: Female Youth in an 'Inner-City' Recreation/Drop-In Center." *Journal of Sport & Social Issues* 25:301–323.

Wilson, Duff, and Jonathan D. Glater. 2006. "Files from Duke Rape Case Give Details but No Answers." *New York Times*, August 25. Retrieved August 25, 2006 (http://www.nytimes.com).

Wilson, Duff, and Michael S. Schmidt. 2007. "Bonds Charged with Perjury in Steroids Case." *New York Times*, November 16. Retrieved November 16, 2007 (http://www.nytimes.com).

Wilson, Robin. 2007. "Where Have All the Women Gone?" *Chronicle of Higher Education*, May 4. Retrieved June 4, 2007 (http://chronicle.com/weekly).

Wilson, William Julius. 1996. *When Work Disappears: The World of the New Urban Poor*. New York: Alfred A. Knopf.

Wolff, Alexander. 2002. "Special Report: The High School Athlete: Part I." *Sports Illustrated*, November 18, pp. 74–92.

Wolff, Alexander. 2007. "Going, Going Green." *Sports Illustrated*, March 12, pp. 36–45.

Wolff, Eli A., and Mary A. Hums. 2003. "Sport without Disability: Understanding the Exclusion of Athletes with a Disability." Presented at the annual meeting of the North American Society for the Sociology of Sport, November, Montreal, Canada.

Wolverton, Brad. 2006a. "Duke Crisis Ripples through College Sports." *Chronicle of Higher Education*, April 21. Retrieved May 22, 2006 (http://chronicle.com/weekly).

Wolverton, Brad. 2006b. "NCAA Defends Tax-Exempt Status as Congressional Scrutiny of Colleges Increases." *Chronicle of Higher Education*, November 24, p. A42.

Wolverton, Brad. 2006c. "A Coach's Secrets." *Chronicle of Higher Education*, December 8. Retrieved December 8, 2006 (http://chronicle.com/weekly).

Wolverton, Brad. 2007a. "Athletics Participation Prevents Many Players from Choosing Majors They Want." *Chronicle of Higher Education*, January 8. Retrieved January 9, 2007 (http://www.chronicle.com/daily).

Wolverton, Brad. 2007b. "A Small Athletics Association Tries to Revamp Its Image." *Chronicle of Higher Education*, March 23, pp. A33–A35.

Wolverton, Brad. 2007c. "Growth in Sports Gifts May Mean Fewer Academic Donations." *Chronicle of Higher Education*, October 5, pp. A1, A34–A35.

Women's Sports Foundation. 2007. "2007 Statistics—Gender Equity in High School and College Athletics: Most Recent Participation & Budget Statistics." *Womenssportsfoundation.org*. Retrieved June 4, 2007 (http://www.womenssportsfoundation.org).

Wood, Chris, and Vince Benigni. 2006. "The Coverage of Sports on Cable TV." Pp. 147–169 in *Handbook of Sports and Media*, edited by A.A. Raney and J. Bryant. Mahwah, NJ: Lawrence Erlbaum Associates.

Woodward, J.R. 2004. "Professional Football Scouts: An Investigation of Racial Stacking." *Sociology of Sport Journal* 21:356–375.

Xiao, Li. 2004. "China and the Olympic Movement." *Getting Ready for the Games: Beijing 2008*. Retrieved July 9, 2007 (http://www.china.org.cn/english).

Yesalis, Charles E., and Michael S. Bahrke. 2005. "Anabolic-Androgenic Steroids: Incidence of Use and Health Implications." *President's Council on Physical Fitness and Sports Research Digest*, March, series 5, no. 5.

Young, Kevin. 2000. "Sport and Violence." Pp. 382–407 in *Handbook of Sports Studies*, edited by J. Coakley and E. Dunning. London: Sage.

Young, Kevin, ed. 2004. *Sporting Bodies, Damaged Selves: Sociological Studies of Sports-Related Injury*. Amsterdam: Elsevier.

Zimbalist, Andrew. 1999. *Unpaid Professionals: Commercialism and Big-Time College Sports*. Princeton, NJ: Princeton University Press.

Zimbalist, Andrew. 2006. *The Bottom Line: Observations and Arguments on the Sports Business*. Philadelphia: Temple University Press.

Zirin, Dave. 2007. "Chief Concern." *SI.com*, October 30. Retrieved October 30, 2007 (http://sportsillustrated.cnn.com).

Index

cut from teams, 36–37. *See also*
African Americans; American Indians;
Asian athletes in U.S.; Athletes with
disabilities; Gay athletes; Latinos;
Lesbian athletes; Professional
athletes; Racial and ethnic minorities;
Sports stars; Women athletes
Athletes with disabilities, 115–116; and
culture's idealization of the body, 117;
and Mainstream model, 118t., 121;
and Marathon model, 118t., 120–121;
media portrayal of, 78–79; and
Minimally Adapted Mainstream
model, 118t., 121; and Mixed-
Paralympics model, 118t., 119–120;
models of opportunity, 117–121,
118t.; and Olympics, 359–360; and
Paralympics, 79, 118t., 119; rights
and resources, 117; and Special
Olympics, 118t., 119; "supercrips,"
116; wheelchair racers, 120–121; and
wheelchair rugby, 116–117, 120; and
youth socialization, 196–197
Athletics Australia, 344–345
Authority, 335; versus interpersonal,
group, or organizational power,
335–336
Auto racing. *See* NASCAR

BALCO scandal, 238–239
Ballparks. *See* Facilities
Baltimore Orioles; and beisbol
diplomacy, 345, 346–347; stadium,
310, 312
Baseball: and African American players,
104–105, 107, 111; and Asian
players, 104, 317; and athletes with
disabilities, 121; beisbol diplomacy
(Cuba versus Baltimore), 345,
346–347; Cuban system, 341–344;
and Latinos, 104, 111–113, 129–130,
148, 317; video game, 139. *See also*
Major League Baseball; World
Baseball Classic; World Series
Basketball: and African Americans, 103,
107; caste structure of NBA, 103,
104; collegiate women's, 259; and
global migration, 45; German and
U.S. youth participation, 188;
Olympic "Dream Team" (1992), 57.
See also National Basketball
Association
Beane, Billy, 16, 38–39, 40, 307–308

Beckham, David, 132, 134, 138,
180–181, 317, 321; statue in Bangkok
temple, 175
Biking: BMX biking, 189–190; and youth
participation, 188
Bissinger, H. G., 193–194
Black athletes. *See* African Americans
Black September Movement, 351, 352
Blair, Bonnie, 80
Blood transfusions. *See* Doping
Bodybuilding, and women athletes, 95
Bonds, Barry: allegations of doping, 238,
239, 241; record-tying homerun, 17
Boston Red Sox: long-awaited success
of, 175; mixed reactions of Latino
fans, 111–113, 112
Bowerman, Bill, 166
Boxing: and African Americans, 107;
payment structure, 322; revenues,
305; Swedish ban on, 339; and
women athletes, 94–95, 96, 225
Bradley, Bill, 318
Bradman, Donald, 150
Brazilian soccer and players, 319–320
Brooks-Moon, Renel, 46
Brown, Jim, 81
Bryant, Kobe, 235

Calderon, Jose, 327
Camp, Walter, 38
Canada: and Americanization, 130; and
cricket, 145–146
Canadian Football League (CFL), 130;
and fan organizations, 361
Carlos, John, 351–354, 353
Cartels, 298
Carter, Jimmy, 18
Caste systems, 59
CFL. *See* Canadian Football League
Character: and college sports, 254; and
socialization in youth sports,
197–201
Chastain, Brandi, 81, 82, 162
Chicago White Sox, 175
China: embrace of Olympic
commercialization, 359; and
environmental concerns about 2008
Olympics, 367; and Olympic boycotts,
354; and Ping-Pong diplomacy, 19,
345; and U.S. sports leagues, 315
Class stratified societies, 59
Clemente, Roberto, 81
Coleman, James, 38–39

example, 50–51. *See also* Association
for Intercollegiate Athletics for Women;
Gender equity; Women athletes
Tour de France doping scandals,
151–152, 236, 238, 239, 240
Turner, Ted, 158–160
Tyson, Mike, 235; as "bad guy," 78

UK Athletics, 344–345
United States: and cricket, 145–146;
government reluctance to regulate
sport, 340–341; and Olympic
boycotts, 354, *355*; and Ping-Pong
diplomacy, 19, 345
U.S. exceptionalism: and choice of
sports, 142; and global sports culture,
139–147; and soccer, 75, 140–142
U.S. Olympic Committee (USOC),
340–341
U.S. Youth Soccer, 205–207

Violence in sport, 216, 223; and
affirmation of masculinity, 225; blood
sports, 222–223; borderline, 224;
brutal body contact, 224; criminal,
224–225; distinguished from
aggression, 223–225; by fans,
225–228; by players, 223–225; quasi-
criminal, 224–225; views on social
value of, 228; by women, 225

Waddell, Tom, 100
Weber, Max, 37–38, *37*; on authority,
335; on power, 335; and social
inequalities, 58–59, 84
Wie, Michelle, 91, 162, 321
William and Mary, College of, 260
Williams, Serena, 81, 109–110
Williams, Venus, 109–110
Windsurfing, 89
Wolff, Eli, 117, 361–362
Women athletes: African American, 105,
107–109; and bodybuilding, 95; and
boxing, 94–95, *96*, 225; in college
basketball, *259*; and competitions with
men, 91–94; contesting homophobia,
101–103; and Dutch soccer, 92–94;
and "female masculinity," 101–102;
and gender socialization in youth
sports, 191–192; and golf, 90–91, 100;
and Heraean Games, 69, 87; and ice
hockey, 90; male reactions to, 91;

media coverage of, 77, 80–81; more
limited economic opportunities for,
298, 300–301; NCAA and gender
equity, 265–269; and reluctance to be
perceived as lesbian, 80, 99–100; and
rugby, 101–102; and snowboarding,
89–90; and *Sports Illustrated* swimsuit
issue, 81; stars and media coverage,
151, 161–162; successful black
women athletes, 109–110; and team
sports, 90; and television, 134; and
U.S. soccer, 92–94; and windsurfing,
89; and women as majority on college
campuses, 88; and wrestling, 225. *See
also* Association for Intercollegiate
Athletics for Women; Gender equity;
Title IX
Woods, Tiger: and ethnic labels, 110; as
global star, 134, 138, 321; as "good
guy," 78; media image of, 77, 162
World Anti-Doping Agency (WADA), 236,
241, 242
World Baseball Classic, 140, 315
World Cup: English champion team
(1966), 150; fixing scandals, 245; U.S.
and global TV audiences compared,
140–141. *See also* Zidane, Zinedine
World Outgames, 101
World Series, 139–140

Yao Ming, 138, *163*, 180–181;
globalization of, 162–163, 164–165,
315, 321
Youth sports, 187, 213–214; alternative
or extreme, 189, 190; and athletic
shoe companies, 206, 208, 209; big-
time approach, 205–210, 214; club
sports, 187, 190; comparison of
German and U.S. teenagers, 188–189;
corporate, 187–189, 190; dropout and
access issues, 211–213; nonschool
sports, 187; and parental influence,
207–209, 210–211; and pressure,
198, 211; recreational sports
programs, 187–189, 190; school
sports, 187, 190; team versus
individual sports, 188–189. *See also*
Amateur Athletic Union (AAU); High
school sports; Socialization

Zidane, Zinedine, 111, 155–156

About the Author

Howard Nixon is Professor of Sociology at Towson University near Baltimore. Having studied and taught sport for thirty-five years, he is the author of several books and book chapters and many articles in sport sociology.